ASHGATE
RESEARCH
COMPANION

THE ASHGATE RESEARCH COMPANION TO THE THIRTY YEARS' WAR

ASHGATE
RESEARCH
COMPANION

The *Ashgate Research Companions* are designed to offer scholars and graduate students a comprehensive and authoritative state-of-the-art review of current research in a particular area. The companions' editors bring together a team of respected and experienced experts to write chapters on the key issues in their speciality, providing a comprehensive reference to the field.

The Ashgate Research Companion to the Thirty Years' War

Edited by

OLAF ASBACH

University of Hamburg, Germany

and

PETER SCHRÖDER

University College London, UK

ASHGATE

© Olaf Asbach, Peter Schröder and the contributors 2014

All rights reserved. No part of this publication may be reproduced, stored in a retrieval system or transmitted in any form or by any means, electronic, mechanical, photocopying, recording or otherwise without the prior permission of the publisher.

Olaf Asbach and Peter Schröder have asserted their right under the Copyright, Designs and Patents Act, 1988, to be identified as the editors of this work.

Published by
Ashgate Publishing Limited
Wey Court East
Union Road
Farnham
Surrey, GU9 7PT
England

Ashgate Publishing Company
110 Cherry Street
Suite 3-1
Burlington, VT 05401-3818
USA

www.ashgate.com

British Library Cataloguing in Publication Data
A catalogue record for this book is available from the British Library.

Library of Congress Cataloging-in-Publication Data
The Ashgate research companion to the Thirty Years' War / edited by Olas Asbach and Peter Schröder.
    pages cm
  Includes bibliographical references and index.
  ISBN 978-1-4094-0629-7 (hardcover) -- ISBN 978-1-4094-0630-3 (ebook) -- ISBN 978-1-4724-0343-8 (epub) 1. Thirty Years' War, 1618-1648. I. Asbach, Olaf, 1960- , editor of compilation. II. Schröder, Peter, 1965- , editor of compilation III. Title: Research companion to the Thirty Years' War.
  D258.A85 2014
  940.2'4--dc23
                                                                            2013033210

ISBN 978-1-4094-0629-7 (hbk)
ISBN 978-1-4094-0630-3 (ebk – PDF)
ISBN 978-1-4724-0343-8 (ebk – ePUB)

Printed in the United Kingdom by Henry Ling Limited,
at the Dorset Press, Dorchester, DT1 1HD

Contents

Notes on Contributors　　　　　　　　　　　　　　　　　　　　　　　　ix

The Thirty Years' War – An Introduction　　　　　　　　　　　　　　　1
Olaf Asbach and Peter Schröder

PART I: THE HOLY ROMAN EMPIRE OF THE GERMAN NATION

1　Imperial Politics 1555–1618　　　　　　　　　　　　　　　　　　　13
　　Joachim Whaley

2　The Palatinate and its Networks in the Empire and in Europe　　　25
　　Brennan Pursell

PART II: THE GREAT POWERS, COALITIONS AND CONFLICTING INTERESTS

3　The Emperor　　　　　　　　　　　　　　　　　　　　　　　　　39
　　Christoph Kampmann

4　The Spanish Monarchy and the Challenges of the Thirty Years' War　　53
　　Gabriel Guarino

5　Denmark　　　　　　　　　　　　　　　　　　　　　　　　　　　65
　　Paul Douglas Lockhart

6　Sweden　　　　　　　　　　　　　　　　　　　　　　　　　　　77
　　Pärtel Piirimäe

7　France and the Thirty Years' War　　　　　　　　　　　　　　　　87
　　Lucien Bély

8　The Papacy　　　　　　　　　　　　　　　　　　　　　　　　　101
　　Guido Braun

9　Non-splendid Isolation: The Ottoman Empire and the Thirty Years' War　　115
　　Maria Baramova

PART III: DIFFERENT STAGES AND THEATRES OF THE WAR

10	1618–1629 Ronald G. Asch	127
11	1629–1635 Toby Osborne	139
12	The Long War (1635–1648) Tryntje Helfferich	151
13	The Dutch–Spanish War in the Low Countries 1621–1648 Olaf van Nimwegen	163
14	The Thirty Years' War in Italy 1628–1659 Sven Externbrink	177

PART IV: RELIGION AND POLITICS

15	The Peace of 1555 – A Failed Settlement? Matthias Pohlig	193
16	The Edict of Restitution (1629) and the Failure of Catholic Restoration Marc R. Forster	205
17	Lutherans, Calvinists and the Road to a Normative Year Ralf-Peter Fuchs	217
18	The Thirty Years' War – A Religious War? Religion and Machiavellism at the Turning Point of 1635 Cornel Zwierlein	231
19	The Material Conditions of War John Theibault	245
20	The Experience of War Sigrun Haude	257
21	Strategy and the Conduct of War Peter H. Wilson	269

PART V: EXPERIENCE AND PRAXIS OF WAR

22	The Peace of Prague – A Failed Settlement? Martin Espenhorst (née Peters)	285
23	The Settlement of 1648 for the German Empire Axel Gotthard	297

| 24 | The Peace of Westphalia: A European Peace
Heinz Duchhardt | 309 |
| 25 | A Peace for the Whole World? Perceptions and Effects of the Peace Treaty of Münster (1648) on the World Outside Europe
Susan Richter | 319 |

Index 339

Notes on Contributors

Olaf Asbach is Professor for Political Science and Heisenberg Chair 'Europe and Modernity' at the University of Hamburg, Germany. Research areas: History of Political Ideas; State, Democracy and (Inter-) National Law in the Modern World System. His publications include *"Europa" – Vom Mythos zur "Imagined Community"?* (Hannover, 2011); 'Dynamics of Conflict and Illusions of Law: Making War and Thinking Peace in the Modern International System', in O. Asbach and P. Schröder (eds), *War, the State and International Law in Seventeenth Century Europe* (Farnham, 2010); *Vom Nutzen des Staates. Staatsverständnisse des Utilitarismus: Hume – Bentham – J. St. Mill* (Baden-Baden, 2009); *Die Zähmung der Leviathane. Die Begründung einer internationalen Rechts- und Friedensordnung bei Abbé de Saint-Pierre und Rousseau* (Berlin, 2002).

Ronald G. Asch is Professor at the University of Freiburg, Germany. He has held a research fellowship at the German Historical Institute London (1985–88) and a lectureship at the University of Münster in Germany (1988–1996). From autumn 1996 to spring 2003 he held the chair of Early Modern History at the University of Osnabrück. His publications include *Jakob I. von England und Schottland: König des Friedens im Zeitalter der Religionskriege* (Stuttgart, 2005); *Europäischer Adel in der frühen Neuzeit* (Cologne, 2008). He is the editor or co-editor of *Der Absolutismus – ein Mythos? Strukturwandel monarchischer Herrschaft ca. 1550–1700* (Cologne, 1996); *Frieden und Krieg in der Frühen Neuzeit. Die europäische Staatenordnung und die außereuropäische Welt* (Munich, 2001).

Maria Baramova is Assistant Professor in Early Modern History of South-Eastern Europe at the University of Sofia, Bulgaria. She holds Research Fellowships at the University of Vienna, Herzog August Bibliothek Wolfenbüttel, and the Leibniz Institute for European History, Mainz. Main research interests: History of Ottoman-Habsburg political relations, Geopolitics, History of Warfare, Peace Treaties. Her publications include *Empires and Peninsulas. Southeastern Europe between Karlowitz and the Peace of Adrianople, 1699–1829* (co-editor) (Berlin, 2010); *Power and Influence in Southeastern Europe, 16th–19th century* (co-editor) (Berlin, 2013); 'Pax Belgradensis – Pax Perpetua? Deutungen und Missdeutungen in den deutschen Medien der 1740er Jahre', in M. Espenhorst (ed.), *Unwissen und Missverständnisse im Europäischen Friedensprozess* (Göttingen, 2013); '"Die Übersetzung der Macht". Die Profile der habsburgisch-osmanischen Translationen im 16.–18. Jahrhundert', in H. Duchhardt et al. (eds), *Frieden übersetzen in der Vormoderne* (Göttingen, 2012).

Lucien Bély is Professor of Early Modern History at the University of Paris-Sorbonne Paris IV. His publications include: *Espions et ambassadeurs au temps de Louis XIV* (Paris, 1990); *Les Relations internationales en Europe XVIIe–XVIIIe siècles* (Paris, new edition, 2007); *L'Art de la paix en Europe. Naissance de la diplomatie moderne, XVIe–XVIIIe siècle* (Paris, 2007); *Les Secrets de Louis XIV. Mystères d'État et pouvoir absolu* (Paris, 2012).

Guido Braun is Lecturer at the University of Bonn. He has held research fellowships at the German Historical Institute, Paris (2004–2007) and at the German Historical Institute,

Rome (2001–2004). Main research interests: peace and security in early modern history. His publications include: *Von der politischen zur kulturellen Hegemonie Frankreichs, 1648–1789* (Darmstadt, 2008; French transl.: Villeneuve d'Ascq, 2012); *La connaissance du Saint-Empire en France du baroque aux Lumières (1643–1756)* (Munich, 2010); forthcoming: *Imagines imperii. Die Wahrnehmung des Reiches und der Deutschen durch die römische Kurie im Reformationsjahrhundert (1523–1585)* (Münster, 2014); *Assecuratio pacis. Französische Konzeptionen von Friedenssicherung und Friedensgarantie, 1648–1815* (Münster, 2011; French version 2010); *Frieden und Friedenssicherung in der Frühen Neuzeit. Das Heilige Römisch Reich und Europa* (co-editor) (Münster, 2013).

Heinz Duchhardt was Professor of Early Modern History and Director of the Institute of European History in Mainz, Germany (1994–2011) and previously professor at the universities of Bayreuth and Münster. His research interests include early modern history, the 'Sattelzeit' and modern history. His publications include: *Das Zeitalter des Absolutismus* (1989, 4th ed. under the title *Barock und Aufklärung*, 2008); *Balance of Power und Pentarchie. Internationale Beziehungen 1700–1785* (1997); *Europa am Vorabend der Moderne* (2003); *Stein. Eine Biographie* (2007).

Martin Espenhorst (née Peters) holds a research position at the Institute of European History, Mainz (Germany). He works on pre-modern peace studies, the Enlightenment and cooperatives' theories of the nineteenth century. His publications include: *Die Genossenschaftstheorie Otto v. Gierkes (1841–1921)* (Göttingen, 2000); *Altes Reich und Europa: Der Historiker, Statistiker und Publizist August Ludwig (v.) Schlözer (1735–1809)* (Münster, 2005); *Frieden übersetzen in der Vormoderne. Translationsleistungen in Diplomatie, Medien und Wissenschaft* (co-edited with H. Duchhardt) (Göttingen, 2012); *Unwissen und Missverständnisse im Europäischen Friedensprozess* (Göttingen, 2013).

Sven Externbrink is currently Lecturer at the Zentrum für Europäische Geschichts- und Kulturwissenschaften Heidelberg. He has been Assisting Professor and Lecturer at the universities of Marburg and Erlangen, research fellow at the German Historical Institute Rome and Visiting Professor at the universities of Heidelberg and Innsbruck. His research interests include the history of early modern international relations, the history of France, Italy and Savoy-Sardinia and Prussia. His publications include: *Le Cœur du monde – Frankreich und die norditalienischen Staaten (Mantua, Parma, Savoyen) im Zeitalter Richelieus 1624–1635* (Münster, 1999); *Friedrich der Große, Maria Theresia und das Alte Reich. Deutschlandbild und Diplomatie Frankreichs im Siebenjährigen Krieg* (Berlin, 2006); *Der Siebenjährige Krieg (1756–1763). Ein europäischer Weltkrieg im Zeitalter der Aufklärung* (Berlin, 2011); 'State-Building within the Holy Roman Empire: Brandenburg-Prussia and Savoy-Sardinia', in R.J.W. Evans, P. Wilson (eds), *The Holy Roman Empire 1495–1806* (Leiden, 2012).

Marc R. Forster is Professor of History at Connecticut College, New London, Connecticut, USA. His publications include: *Catholic Germany between the Reformation and the Enlightenment* (Houndmills, 2007); *Catholic Revival in the Age of the Baroque: Religious Identity in Southwest Germany, 1550–1750*. (Cambridge, 2001); *The Counter-Reformation in the Villages. Religion and Reform in the Bishopric of Speyer, 1560–1720* (Cornell, 1992); *Piety and Family in Early Modern Europe. Essays in Honour of Steven Ozment* (co-edited with B.J. Kaplan) (Farnham, 2005).

Ralf-Peter Fuchs is Associate Professor at the Institute of Modern History at Ludwig-Maximilians-Universität in Munich and has substituted the chair of Early Modern History in Bochum. His research interests include witchcraft, history of crime, history of honour and legal history. His publications include: *Ein Medium zum Frieden. Die Normaljahrsregel und die Beendigung des Dreißigjährigen Krieges* (Munich, 2010); *Hexerei und Zauberei vor dem Reichskammergericht* (Wetzlar, 1994); *Um die Ehre. Westfälische Beleidigungsprozesse vor dem Reichskammergericht (1525–1805)* (Paderborn, 1999). He is co-editor with Winfried Schulze of *Wahrheit, Wissen, Erinnerung. Zeugenverhörprotokolle als Quellen für soziale Wissensbestände der Frühen Neuzeit* (Münster, 2002).

Axel Gotthard is Professor of History at the University of Erlangen-Nürnberg. His publications include: *Säulen des Reiches. Die Kurfürsten im frühneuzeitlichen Reichsverband*, 2 vols (Husum, 1999); *Der Augsburger Religionsfrieden* (Münster, 2004; reprint 2006); *In der Ferne. Die Wahrnehmung des Raums in der Vormoderne* (Frankfurt/M. and New York, 2007); *Das Alte Reich 1495–1806*, 5th edn (Darmstadt, 2013).

Gabriel Guarino is Lecturer in Early Modern History at the University of Ulster. He is presently working on a comparative survey of the Viceregal courts of Spanish Italy. His publications include: *Representing the King's Splendour: Communication and Reception of Symbolic Forms of Power in Viceregal Naples* (New York, 2010); 'Here We Live Under Our Own Vine and Palm Tree: The Syncretism of African and Western Worldviews of Americo-Liberian Ex-Slaves', *Liberian Studies Journal* 27/1 (2002); 'Regulation of Appearances During the Catholic Reformation: Dress and Morality in Spain and Italy', in M. Yardeni and I. Zinguer (eds), *Les deux réformes chrétiennes: propagation et diffusion* (Leiden, 2004); 'Spanish Celebrations in Seventeenth-Century Naples', *The Sixteenth-Century Journal* 37/1 (2006).

Sigrun Haude is Associate Professor in the History Department at the University of Cincinnati. Her publications include: 'Social Control and Social Justice under Maximilian I of Bavaria (r. 1598–1651)', in C. Ocker et al. (eds), *Politics and Reformations: Communities, Polities, Nations, and Empires* (Leiden, 2007); 'War – A Fortuitous Occasion for Social Disciplining and Political Centralization? The Case of Bavaria under Maximilian I', in K. Mladek (ed.), *Police Forces. A Cultural History of an Institution* (New York, 2007); 'Religion während des Dreißigjährigen Krieges (1618–1648)', in G. Litz et al. (eds), *Frömmigkeit – Theologie – Frömmigkeitstheologie: Contributions to European History* (Leiden, 2005); 'Life, Death, and Religion During the Thirty Years' War', in R.J. Bast and A.C. Gow (eds), *Continuity and Change: The Harvest of Late-Medieval and Reformation History* (Leiden, 2000).

Tryntje Helfferich is Associate Professor of History at the Ohio State University, Lima. Her research interests include the intersection of religion and politics in the seventeenth century, early modern European military history, and early modern European gender history. Her publications include: *The Iron Princess: Amalia Elisabeth and the Thirty Years War* (Cambridge, Mass., 2013); *The Thirty Years War: A Documentary History* (Indianapolis, 2009); 'A Levy in Liège for Mazarin's Army: Practical and Strategic Difficulties in Raising and Supporting Troops in the Thirty Years War', *Journal of Early Modern History* 11 (2007); 'Civilians in the Thirty Years War' (with P. Sonnino), in L. Frey and M. Frey (eds), *Daily Lives of Civilians in Wartime Europe, 1618–1900* (Westport, Conn., 2007).

Christoph Kampmann is Professor of Early Modern History at the Philipps University of Marburg. His publications include: *Reichsrebellion und kaiserliche Acht. Politische Strafjustiz im Dreißigjährigen Krieg und das Verfahren gegen Wallenstein* (Münster, 1993); *Arbiter und Friedensstiftung. Die Auseinandersetzung um den politischen Schiedsrichter im Europa der Frühen Neuzeit* (Paderborn et al., 2001); 'Peace Impossible? The Holy Roman Empire and the European State System in the Seventeenth Century', in O. Asbach and P. Schröder (eds),

War, the State and International Law in Seventeenth Century Europe (Farnham, 2010); *Europa und das Reich im Dreißigjährigen Krieg* (2nd edn, Stuttgart, 2013); *Sicherheit in der Frühen Neuzeit. Norm – Praxis – Repräsentation* (as co-editor) (Cologne et al., 2013).

Paul Douglas Lockhart is Professor of History and Director of Graduate Programs in History, Wright State University, Dayton, Ohio, USA. His publications include: *Denmark, 1513–1660: The Rise and Decline of a Renaissance Monarchy* (Oxford, 2007); *Frederik II and the Protestant Cause: Denmark's Role in the Wars of Religion, 1559–1596* (Leiden, 2004); *Sweden in the Seventeenth Century* (Basingstoke, 2004).

Olaf van Nimwegen has held a number of research posts in the Netherlands. Since 2010 he has been Affiliated Researcher at the Research Institute for History and Culture at Utrecht University. His main research interest is New Military History from 1500 to 1900. His publications include four major books on Dutch military history: *De subsistentie van het leger* (Amsterdam, 1995); *De Republiek der Verenigde Nederlanden als grote mogendheid 1713–1756* (Amsterdam, 2002), for which he was awarded the Schouwenburg Prize for military history in 2004; *The Dutch Army and the Military Revolutions 1588–1688* (Woodbridge, 2010; originally published in Dutch in 2006); *De Tachtigjarige Oorlog. Van opstand naar geregelde oorlog 1568–1648* (co-authored with L. Sicking, R. Prud'homme van Reine and A. van Vliet) (Amsterdam, 2013).

Toby Osborne is a Senior Lecturer in History at the University of Durham, UK. He obtained a first class degree in history at Balliol College, Oxford (1990), where he also took his doctorate (1996). He came to Durham in 1996 after holding a lectureship at Christ Church, Oxford. His publications include: *Dynasty and Diplomacy in the Court of Savoy: Political Culture and the Thirty Years' War* (Cambridge, 2003); 'Abbot Scaglia, the duke of Buckingham and Anglo-Savoyard relations during the 1620s', *European Studies Review*, 30, I (2000); '"Chimeres, Monopoles and Strategemes": French exiles in the Spanish Netherlands during the Thirty Years' War', *The Seventeenth Century*, XV (2000); 'Van Dyck, Alessandro Scaglia and the Caroline Court: Friendship, Collecting and Diplomacy in the early seventeenth century', *The Seventeenth Century* 22 (2007).

Pärtel Piirimäe is Pro Futura Scientia Fellow at the Swedish Collegium for Advanced Study and Associate Professor of History at the University of Tartu, Estonia. He is currently completing a book on war and morality in early modern Europe. His publications include: 'Just War in Theory and Practice: the Legitimation of Swedish Intervention in the Thirty Years' War', *Historical Journal* 45 (2002); 'The Westphalian Myth and the Idea of External Sovereignty', in H. Kalmo and Q. Skinner (eds), *Sovereignty in Fragments: The Past, Present and Future of a Contested Concept* (Cambridge, 2010); 'War and Polemics in Early Modern Europe', in M. Calaresu et al. (eds), *Exploring Cultural History. Essays in Honour of Peter Burke* (Aldershot, 2010); 'Alberico Gentili's Doctrine of Defensive War and its Impact on Seventeenth-Century Normative Views', in B. Kingsbury and B. Straumann (eds), *The Roman Foundations of the Law of Nations: Alberico Gentili and the Justice of Empire* (Oxford, 2010).

Matthias Pohlig is Assistant Professor of Early Modern History at the University of Münster. His research interests include early modern historiography, humanism, religious history (sixteenth to seventeenth centuries) as well as questions of historical theory and the Ottoman Empire. His publications include: *Zwischen Gelehrsamkeit und konfessioneller Identitätsstiftung: Lutherische Kirchen- und Universalgeschichtsschreibung 1546–1617* (Tübingen, 2007),

Säkularisierungen im frühneuzeitlichen Europa. Methodische Probleme und empirische Fallstudien (with U. Lotz-Heumann, V. Isaiasz, R. Schilling, H. Bock, and S. Ehrenpreis) (Berlin, 2008).

Brennan Pursell is Associate Professor of History at DeSales University, Pennsylvania. His publications include: *The Winter King: Frederick V of the Palatinate and the Coming of the Thirty Years' War* (Farnham, 2003); 'Elector Palatine Friedrich V and the Question of Influence Revisited', *The Court Historian*, 6/2 (2001).

Susan Richter currently holds the Chair of Early Modern History at the University of Heidelberg. She is Co-Leader at the Project 'Discursive Practices of Political Legitimation' and Deputy of the Research Area A in the Cluster of Excellence 'Asia and Europe in a Global Context' in Heidelberg. She has been visiting professor in Munich and visiting fellow at the German Historical Institute, Washington. Her main research interest is History of Ideas and Political Thought. Her publications include: *Fürstentestamente der Frühen Neuzeit. Politische Programme und Medien intergenerationeller Kommunikation* (Göttingen, 2009) (awarded the Ruprecht-Karls-Prize). *Pflug und Steuerruder – Konstruktionen neuer Herrschafts- und Gesellschaftsmodelle nach agronomischen Vorstellungen in Frankreich und dem Alten Reich im 18. Jahrhundert anhand antiker und asiatischer Vorbilder* (forthcoming).

Peter Schröder is Senior Lecturer in Early Modern History at University College London. His main research interest is History of Political Thought. He has been visiting professor at universities in Paris, Rome and Seoul, and visiting research fellow at the *Royal Flemish Academy of Belgium*. His publications include: *Die Leitbegriffe der deutschen Jugendbewegung in der Weimarer Republik. Eine ideengeschichtliche Studie* (Münster, 1996); *Naturrecht und absolutistisches Staatsrecht. Eine vergleichende Studie zu Thomas Hobbes und Christian Thomasius* (Berlin, 2001); *Niccolò Machiavelli* (Frankfurt/Main, 2004) and *Hobbes* (Stuttgart, 2012).

John Theibault is Director of the South Jersey Center for Digital Humanities at Richard Stockton College of New Jersey. His publications include: *German Villages in Crisis: Rural Life in Hesse-Kassel and the Thirty Years War, 1580–1720* (New Jersey, 1995); *A Short History of Early Modern Europe 1600–1815: Contests for a Reasonable World* (co-authored with L. Rosner) (New York, 2000); 'The Rhetoric of Death and Destruction in the Thirty Years War', *Journal of Social History* 27 (1993); '"Da er denn mit traurmutigem hertzen gesehen wie jaemmerlich dass Dorf uber die helfft in die Asche gelegt...": Die Erfassung und Einordnung lokaler Kriegserfahrungen auf Amtsebene im Dreißigjährigen Krieg', in B. v. Krusenstjern and H. Medick (eds), *Zwischen Alltag und Katastrophe: Der Dreißigjährige Krieg aus der Nähe* (Göttingen, 1999).

Joachim Whaley is Professor of German History and Thought in the Faculty of Modern and Medieval Languages at the University of Cambridge and a Fellow of Gonville and Caius College. His publications include: *Religious Toleration and Social Change in Hamburg 1529–1819* (Cambridge, 1985; paperback edition 2002); *Germany and the Holy Roman Empire*, 2 vols (Oxford, 2012).

Peter H. Wilson is G.F. Grant Professor of History at the University of Hull, having previously worked at the universities of Sunderland and Newcastle. He works on German history and war in European history. His publications include: *War, State and Society in Württemberg, 1677–1798* (Cambridge, 1995); *German Armies: War and German Politics 1648–1806* (London, 1998); *From Reich to Revolution: German History 1558–1806* (Basingstoke, 2004); and *Europe's Tragedy. A History of the Thirty Years War* (London, 2009).

Cornel Zwierlein is Associate Professor at the University of Bochum, Germany; he is currently Visiting Fellow at the Department of History at Harvard University. He has taught Early Modern History at the University of Munich from 2001 to 2008. Research interests: social, cultural and environmental history of early modern Europe (especially Germany, Italy, France, England); 'European Africa': French-English-German political and scientific exchanges in the Early Modern Mediterranean. His publications include: *Die Entstehung neuer Denkrahmen im 16. Jahrhundert und die Wahrnehmung der französischen Religionskriege in Italien und Deutschland, 1559–1598* (Göttingen, 2006) (awarded the Max Weber Prize by the Bavarian Academy of Sciences); *Machiavellismus in Deutschland – Chiffre von Kontingenz, Herrschaft und Empirismus* (co-edited with A. Meyer) (Munich, 2010).

The Thirty Years' War – An Introduction

Olaf Asbach and Peter Schröder

The Thirty Years' War (1618–1648) remains a puzzling and complex subject for students and scholars alike. One might even ask whether the term 'Thirty Years' War' is justified in the first place, since the war seems to dissolve into a series of individual conflicts with different issues, often with no real common denominator, and different participants, without any clear beginning or end. One might thus think of the European conflicts as, for instance, the war between Sweden and Poland[1] or the struggle between France and the Spanish and Austrian Habsburgs for hegemony in Europe as being distinct episodes which cannot be conflated under a single label.

But there was one central issue which justifies the contemporary judgement that the 'Thirty Years' War' was a contest with a definite beginning and a definite end and with a structure giving coherence to the various military campaigns, rather than simply an amorphous series of individual wars: the struggle for the constitution of the Holy Roman Empire and – inseparable from this question – the balance of political and religious forces in Central Europe. The beginning of this conflict was clearly a German war: at stake were internal issues of the empire. This conflict was increasingly internationalised, especially from 1630 onwards, when Sweden invaded the empire. Thus several phases can and have to be distinguished. However, until 1629 the conflict was essentially centred on the imperial constitution and the relationship between the confessions. The war was fought by German Protestants (Lutherans and Calvinists) and Catholics alike in order to enforce their own 'authentic interpretation' of the Peace of Augsburg (1555). This happened notably when the Emperor issued the Edict of Restitution in 1629, where it was claimed that the Edict was the authentic interpretation of the Peace of Augsburg. The war was thus manifold: about the empire, about religion and about power politics in Europe. This was also reflected in the Peace of Westphalia, a treaty which, after all, had the twofold aim of both settling international relations and of introducing a settlement for the empire, and all this by simultaneously, and fundamentally, changing the relationship between politics and religion.

This research companion brings together leading scholars of the field to synthesise the existing knowledge, which remains somewhat fragmented along the dividing lines of linguistic, and hence 'national', historiography. Over the course of 25 chapters the complexities of the Thirty Years' War are explored in a comprehensive, comparative and, we believe, innovative approach. The chapters draw on recent research which is not always available in English. A selected bibliography at the end of each chapter provides suggestions for further reading in English. Where English literature is scarce we have also supplied the most pertinent scholarship which is available in foreign languages. The chapters of this volume aim to furnish a narrative of the historical events and a more analytical evaluation

---

[1] See R.I. Frost, *The Northern Wars 1558–1721* (Harlow, 2000).

of the existing historiography. Interpretations do necessarily vary, and as editors we were keen to present the existing differences in this volume. Where appropriate, cross-references are given to other chapters in this volume. Even the student who is new to this subject will realise that some chapters make bolder claims than others for a revisionist interpretation of the existing scholarship. We believe that the balance of historical information and analysis on the one hand, and interpretative re-evaluation on the other will allow the reader to reach his own judgement on these admittedly complicated and controversial issues, which we do not want to settle prematurely in this introduction. In recent years the focus on various aspects of the Thirty Years' War has been considerably sharpened. For instance, discussion of the conduct of the war, the experience of it for soldiers and the ordinary population has attracted new research. The same holds true for the role religion played in this conflict. For the first time this research companion attempts to present these various fields of research in one comprehensive volume. Given the complexities of this European war, a proper understanding of it must begin by looking closely at the preceding situation within the empire and the emerging European state system.

The two chapters in Part I pursue this task by firstly looking at the antecedent imperial politics of the Austrian Habsburgs and secondly by studying the Palatinate, which had triggered the conflict with the Emperor and eventually the empire. Joachim Whaley's analysis of imperial politics from 1555 to 1618 challenges the dominant nationalist narrative of German history. He provides a compelling alternative to the view that the period after 1555 was little more than a hopeless division and destabilisation of the empire, which eventually led to the Thirty Years' War. This chapter demonstrates that, in fact, the empire functioned with increasing effectiveness over this period There were confessional divisions and tensions, which were increasingly exacerbated from the 1570s onwards. The confessional divisions between Catholics and Protestants, as well as between the different Protestant creeds, posed a serious challenge to the stability of the imperial constitution. Despite existing antagonisms, Whaley demonstrates that all parties had a strong desire to resolve these differences peacefully. Whaley shows that the various newly founded institutions of the empire, such as the imperial court or the imperial circles, actually worked much better than has often been assumed. Throughout the period, the German princes as a whole were unwilling to be dragged into disputes outside the empire, while solidarity was reinforced by the repeated and growing Turkish threat. Even in the years immediately preceding 1618, which saw the emergence of a Protestant Union and a Catholic League, there was a marked reluctance to destabilise the empire by upsetting the delicate balance of powers, established during the Reformation years, in opposition to the monarchical ambitions of Charles V. The crises that precipitated the war were generated within the Habsburg territories rather than in the empire more generally.

Brennan Pursell's chapter examines *Kurpfalz*, the Electoral Palatinate – a prosperous and influential territory, and one of the seven estates which held the right to elect the Emperor of the Holy Roman Empire. The Palatinate played an important role, not only as part of the imperial constitution, but also in connection with some of Western Europe's greatest powers. Although it was only a small estate on a European scale, it was nevertheless well organised internally and displayed a glittering and sophisticated court. In 1618, the ambitious Elector Palatine Frederick V, leapt into the arena normally reserved for Europe's mightiest warlords. He was convinced that his many worthy connections would support him in the pursuit of his princely ambitions in Bohemia. As it transpired this was a catastrophic miscalculation and instead of obtaining new wealth and prominence for the Palatinate, he triggered a war which would last 30 years. Nevertheless, that the empire itself became embroiled in the conflict had more to do with Ferdinand II's response to the Bohemian crisis than with any particular issue or desire for confrontation within the empire itself. Although the war was precipitated by the actions of a German prince, the Elector of the Palatinate, these actions only became the catalyst for armed conflict when Ferdinand II pursued the would-be king of Bohemia into the empire and set about asserting royal powers that would have had implications for all princes, not just the Palatine outlaw. This turned the situation into another protracted struggle over the German constitution and for the preservation of 'German liberty', which was only resolved by the Peace of Westphalia in 1648.

After these two introductory chapters which provide the wider context for the intricate, constitutional and political framework of the empire, chapters 3–9 in part II consider the great powers and coalitions. A detailed analysis of the Emperor, who has to be regarded as the key political and military figure of the Thirty Years' War, begins this survey. Christoph Kampmann shows that the traditional picture of the two Emperors, Ferdinand II (1619–1637) and his son Ferdinand III (1637–1657), needs to be revised in many respects. Regarding the role of the Emperor, not only does the Austrian Habsburg branch need to be considered, but also the Spanish, especially since the variety of scholarly opinions concerning the effects of the Thirty Years' War on the Spanish Monarchy can be positioned between two extremes. On the one hand, there are those who judge Spain's involvement as a complete failure, further exacerbating its allegedly inevitable decline. On the other hand, those at the opposite end of the spectrum emphasise Spain's resilience vis-à-vis the immense challenges it had to face, all at once, from its numerous continental enemies as well as from its rebellious provinces. Gabriel Guarino traces the various related historiographical debates, and proposes a balanced view of thinking about this question.

Paul Douglas Lockhart investigates why the king of Denmark, Christian IV (1596–1648) became involved in the German war in 1625. Christian was also a German prince, and from the earliest days of the Reformation the kings of Denmark had been at the centre of nearly every attempt to fashion an international Protestant alliance. Fearing the extension of Habsburg (and therefore Catholic) influence into his German lands, and under great pressure from England and the Dutch Republic, Christian IV took up the banner of 'German liberties' in 1625 despite his own kingdom refusing to support him. Though the resulting four-year war ended in a crushing defeat for the Danish king, his intervention helped to keep the anti-Habsburg cause alive in the years between the defeat of the Elector Palatine and the open involvement of Sweden and France in the war.

Sweden's intervention in Germany, originally limited both in its aims and its scope, developed over time into a massive military engagement that lasted for 18 years. It was over this period that the German war was increasingly transformed into a European war. In his chapter Pärtel Piirimäe follows these developments from the Swedish point of view, reassessing the military, political, diplomatic and economic aspects of Sweden's 'German war' in the light of recent scholarship. He also studies more thoroughly than has previously been the case the ideological aspects of the war, both in terms of how legal and moral arguments affected Sweden's motivations and war aims, and of how these were put into use instrumentally for political purposes. This allows him to examine the different phases of the Swedish engagement, from Gustav Adolf's vision of the German constitution to Oxenstierna's demands for *assecuratio* and *satisfactio*. Sweden's collaboration with imperial estates in the context of the imperial constitution demonstrates how these aims were also pursued politically.

In his chapter Lucien Bély considers why and how France began a long war against Spain and the Habsburgs, and also how this war drastically changed the monarchy, political practices and ideas, the organisation of administration, and conceptions of diplomacy. An examination of diplomatic initiatives shows how these were aimed both at avoiding a direct struggle and at the maintenance of France's friendship with German and Italian princes, with the greater power protecting the smaller ones. France tried to prevent a general victory for the imperial cause in Germany by supporting the intervention of Sweden. This 'guerre couverte', combined large-scale diplomacy with local or regional military interventions. Richelieu gave new cohesion to the royal policy, trying to balance the Catholic traditions of the country with the necessity of offering help to Protestant princes. Furthermore this chapter considers how the declaration of war obliged France to make a substantial financial commitment which led to urban riots and rural unrest and which gave the State a new dimension and new ambitions. In the end, this policy led to a general crisis and civil war, the Fronde. The conduct of the war required new organisation of the army, as well as new strategic approaches. Collaboration with Swedish forces remained the preferred option of the French Court throughout the war. The military successes allowed for a new kind of diplomacy as Cardinal Mazarin became Prime Minister. Those new goals brought about a change in alliances and the United Provinces made peace with Spain. Although the Peace of Westphalia brought peace in Germany, the two main powers, Spain and France, went on confronting each other. Only the Peace of the Pyrenees in 1659 concluded the war between Spain and France.

Guido Braun explores how, during the Thirty Years' War, Papal diplomacy contributed to negotiations. The Papal room for manoeuvre was limited, especially as the Bourbon *most Christian king* of France had declared war on the Habsburg *Catholic king* of Spain and invaded the Holy Roman Empire ruled by a Habsburg Emperor (1635). Papal representatives at the negotiations in Cologne (1636/38) and the congress of Westphalia (1643–1649)[2] finally contributed to the peace treaty signed by Emperor Ferdinand III and the French king Louis XIV (1648), while the negotiations between France and Spain were failing (as just mentioned, in 1659 these powers concluded the peace treaty of the Pyrenees as a result of direct negotiations without Papal mediation). However, according to the Pope, the Franco-Spanish war was the main conflict in the Thirty Years' War. Furthermore, the Papal mediation in Westphalia was not mentioned in the peace treaty of 1648 because Innocent X (1644–1655) did not accept its religious implications and, in 1650, protested formally against its conclusion. In fact, despite the Holy See's quest for peace, the papacy acted like a war party during this conflict as far as Catholic interests were concerned. The original objective of the congregation 'de Propaganda Fide' (founded in 1622) was to limit the progressive expansion of Protestantism and to 'reconquer' lost territories for the Catholics, especially in the empire. Moreover, in order to support the Catholic armies, the papacy partly financed the Catholic League during the war's first period. However, under the pontificate of the francophile Pope, Urban VIII (1623–1644), they did not support the Habsburg princes against their Protestant enemies as they had done before. On the other hand, the Papal nuncio refused to meet Protestant representatives and intervened in the negotiations with the aim of conserving Catholic interests in Westphalia. For most historians, the papacy ceased to be a great European power after 1648, but in reality, Braun argues, Papal mediation continued to be an important instrument of the reestablishment of peace, at least between Catholic powers in the second part of the century.

The Ottoman Empire was not party to the conflicts of the Thirty Years' War, and the chapter by Maria Baramova examines the reasons behind the Ottomans' choice not to engage in it. This is done from the European perspective as it is mirrored in the writings by European diplomats and political actors. First of all, the internal instability of the Ottoman Empire, due to a succession of palace coup d'états, provincial rebellions, mutinies and a fluctuating economy obstructed the Ottoman war machine. But it was the external factors shaping the Ottoman foreign policy which played an even greater role. On the one hand, the Ottomans fought a long war in the east with the Safavids until 1639. In the West, on the

---

[2] Peace was officially concluded in 1648, but the congress lasted formally until 1649.

other hand, they mobilised what was left of their war-making capability against Poland, rather than against the Habsburgs, despite their overt encouragement to the Bohemian and Hungarian rebels and promises of military assistance to the Winter King (Frederick V). With the conclusion of the Long War in 1606, the focus of Ottoman strategy in Europe had shifted towards the north as a result of a series of factors: the appearance of the Zaporozhian Cossacks in the Black Sea; the often successful Polish interventions in the Ottoman sphere of influence, Moldavia and Wallachia; the weakening Ottoman control over the Crimean Khanate; and the appearance of the Romanovs as a major power. Furthermore, the Habsburg threat was of less significance for the Ottomans in the seventeenth century, evident from the fact that even after the conclusion of the war with the Safavids, the Ottomans declared war against Venice, at a time when the Habsburgs were losing in the Thirty Years' War. A further reason for Ottoman reluctance to fight the Habsburgs is that the Ottomans could not rely on their Transylvanian vassals. Bethlen Gábor was not a dependable ally as he signed several ceasefires and peace treaties with the Emperor. György Rákóczi, who succeeded Bethlen as the prince of Transylvania contrary to the wishes of the Ottomans, was negotiating with the Swedes, whose presence near their border put fear into the Ottomans' hearts. The failure of military operations undertaken by the provincial governors (e.g. that of Murtaza Pasha in 1626) further dissuaded the Ottomans who had memories of the Long War in their mind. Instead, to the dismay of many, both sides opted to cooperate for peace: they frequently renewed the treaty of Zitva Torok, tried to solve border problems with ad-hoc commissions, agreed to destroy fortifications that were erected contrary to the treaty, and deliberately ignored numerous reasons to go to war such as the conquest of Waitzen by the governor of Buda in 1619, or the Austrian military assistance to the Poles in 1621.

Part III explores the different stages and theatres of the war, as well as the conflicting interests of the parties and the resulting alliances and loyalties. Given the complex relations of the different powers involved in the war, this part will take up the narrative and analysis already pursued in part II from a different perspective. The reader can thus examine the war by analysing the key actors in part II, as well as through a chronological approach in part III. The existing overlap is intended to better allow the reader to disentangle the various threads of which this complex war is woven.

Ronald G. Asch discusses the first 10 years of the Thirty Years' War, which saw a continuous escalation of hostilities as more and more European powers were drawn into a conflict which had begun as a regional conflict in Bohemia. However, soon other powers, such as Spain and later Denmark, were to involve themselves, while at the same time the impact of the events in Central Europe deeply affected even those countries, such as England or the Dutch Republic, which had remained, at first glance, on the margins of the war. At the same time the religious element of the conflict, which was present right from the beginning, became more prominent in the 1620s with the eventual decision to reclaim all ecclesiastical property lost during the preceding 80 years for the Roman Church in the Edict of Restitution. As far as the various theatres of the war are concerned this chapter concentrates mainly on the Habsburg lands, southern Germany and the imperial Circle of Lower Saxony. But it also has to be noted that the eastern front of the Habsburg Empire saw repeated attempts by the ruler of Transylvania, Bethlen Gábor, to gain control over northern (Habsburg) Hungary.

Toby Osborne concentrates on the period 1629–35, which was bookended by important peace treaties and new conflicts. The period of 1629 to 1630 saw the end of England's wars with France and Spain, but the extension of conflict in northern Italy over the succession to Mantua and Monferrato, until its settlement in 1631 (see also chapter 14). With the treaty of 1635, agreed at Prague, a limited peace in the empire was achieved (see also chapter 22), but so was the initiation of a 'hot' war between France and Spain after years of surrogate conflict. The interval also saw the intervention of Sweden in the empire, marking what has often been seen as the 'Swedish period' of the Thirty Years' War. Over the course of this period, the aims of war, it has often been argued, were reoriented, with religion decreasing in importance as an underlying issue. This contribution examines these issues by viewing the war in terms of three inter-connected strategic 'theatres': the Atlantic theatre, encompassing Britain and the Low Countries; the Mediterranean theatre, encompassing Italy; and the Baltic theatre, encompassing Sweden and the empire.

The year 1635 has often been described as the point at which the Thirty Years' War finally threw off its local and religious character, and became a truly Europe-wide political phenomenon. This traditional interpretation has rested on two great events that occurred in that year: first, the Catholic Emperor came to terms with most Protestant imperial princes at the Peace of Prague, and second, the French openly joined the war, sending their armies against both the Holy Roman Emperor and the Spanish. Recent scholarship, however, suggests that historians have perhaps overestimated the extent to which 1635 marked a decisive break in the nature and meaning of the war. Instead, Tryntje Helfferich argues, the period from 1635 to 1648 saw the maturation and development of the same political, constitutional, religious, social, and economic concerns which had driven the first half of the war. This chapter thus both provides an overview of the great events of the last third of the war, and explains the ongoing struggle by the war's participants (both within and outside the empire) to impose their vision of the proper religious and political structure of Central Europe.

These three chronological chapters are supplemented by two chapters (13–14) which deal with conflicts which, while forming part of the Thirty Years' War, also had their own dynamics and time span. When the Spanish and Dutch ambassadors ratified their part of the cluster of related agreements in the Treaty of Westphalia, they ended a conflict that had originated more than 80 years earlier as the *Dutch Revolt* (1566–1648). By 1618, however, even the hawks in Madrid acknowledged that there was little or no hope of forcing the Dutch provinces back into the Spanish fold. Spain was an empire on the defence, drawn into the emerging cluster of military conflicts that would become the Thirty Years' War not so much by aggressive imperialism as by a number of distinct yet nonetheless closely related issues: firstly, dynastic loyalty to their Austrian Habsburg relatives, a motive inextricably linked to the political structure and confessional balance of the Holy Roman Empire; secondly, the perceived need to maintain the 'Spanish Road', the vital connection between the Spanish Netherlands and the military resources of northern Italy; thirdly, even the less militant factions at the Madrid court appreciated that a need to protect the monarchy's interests and territories by anticipating and averting possible damage to Spanish prestige or *reputación*. In many respects, the final Peace of Münster only confirmed the status quo ante bellum. Yet the decades of conflict had tested the Spanish monarchy to its limits, and its structures, means and identities were compelled to adjust to events and to the pressures of incessant global conflict. The Dutch Republic, in turn, not only asserted its sovereignty but adapted to the challenges of war by gradually establishing its own imperial identity and ideology in both theory and practice. Olaf van Nimwegen's chapter follows the watersheds of the final phase of this 'Eighty Years War' and traces its manifold impact on these two very different powers and their relations with their European neighbours and the Holy Roman Empire in particular. Sven Externbrink's chapter analyses the role played by Italy during the Thirty Years' War. Despite the fact that Italy has been widely neglected in histories of the War, events there not only had an impact on future developments in Italy itself, but they were also of considerable importance for the unfolding war north of the Alps.

The chapters in part IV are dedicated to the religious controversies and demonstrate how religious politics informed the various war aims. Matthias Pohlig looks at the Peace of Augsburg of 1555 which secured half a century of peace between the religious and political parties of the Holy Roman Empire, but in the end it failed due to construction errors that had served as agreements in the middle of the sixteenth century but could not guarantee the peace in a situation of growing religious radicalism and international linkages of the Catholic and the Calvinist (less the Lutheran) camps. This period is characterised by confessionalisation, i.e. the interdependence of religious, cultural and political formation in the territorial states of the empire, as well as by attempts to stabilise the political (not religious) solutions of 1555. Whereas the Peace of 1555 had tried to exclude religion from political decision-making, this increasingly proved to be impossible. Dispute about the interpretation of the Peace of Augsburg fuelled the conflict after the outbreak of the war in 1618. Nevertheless, one can ask if the 1555 Peace was a failed settlement – and if yes, in which way. Political compromise and attempts to establish peace were repeatedly undermined by the divisive power of confessional strife. Marc R. Forster discusses the Edict of Restitution, promulgated at the height of Catholic military success. This was the most ambitious attempt by Emperor Ferdinand II to restore Catholic institutions lost to the Protestants during the previous century. The Edict sought to enforce a strict interpretation of the Ecclesiastical Reservation of the Peace of Augsburg of 1555, returning to Catholic possession a large number of monasteries, convents, and other institutions that had been secularised between the Peace and the outbreak of the war. The Edict provoked strong Protestant resistance, since Protestants correctly suspected that some Catholics saw it as a first step towards the full restoration of Catholicism and the suppression of Protestantism. The Edict also caused considerable conflict among Catholics, particularly between the Jesuits, who wanted to use the resources of the restored institutions for pastoral and educational purposes, and the older orders (such as the Benedictines and the Cistercians) who hoped to restore old monasteries to their (imagined) medieval glory. These conflicts, and the ultimate failure of the Edict, exposed the importance of the legal and constitutional arrangements that regulated religious conditions in the Holy Roman Empire, while also demonstrating that the religious changes of the sixteenth century could not be easily reversed. By the later 1630s all parties in the war gave up hope of ending the religious division of Germany and grudgingly recognised the need to adjudicate religious disputes. Ralf-Peter Fuchs assesses in his chapter the different strategies before and during the war that the Protestants pursued in reaction to the Catholics. In particular he analyses the principle of autonomy ('Freistellung'). This principle was modified after the Edict of Restitution. Shocked and unsettled the Protestants reflected about new strategies to save their cause. Initial offers to freeze confessional properties by normative years were made from 1630. Chapter 17 explores the Protestants' discussions and gives a short outlook on settlements which were made in 1635 and 1648. The assessment of the importance and relevance of religion in the Thirty Years' War remains controversial,[3] and these chapters show the panorama of the major events of the Thirty Years' War as they testify to the relationship between religion and politics. In chapter 18 Cornel Zwierlein challenges the predominant opinion that after the battle of Nördlingen, the death of Gustav Adolph and of Wallenstein, the official entry of France as Sweden's ally into the war marked a rupture with the religious signature of the whole war. Theory and practice of 'Italian' reason of state and Machiavellianism had spread throughout all European courts at that time and had assumed complex amalgams with law and religion. However, recent research has stressed that on many levels of early modern society, religion and confession still played a crucial

---

[3] See among the many works in particular the meanwhile *classical* study by M. Heckel, 'Die Krise der Religionsverfassung des Reiches und die Anfänge des Dreißigjährigen Krieges', in *Gesammelte Schriften*, ed. K. Schlaich (Tübingen, 1989), vol. 2, pp. 970–98. For a succinct summary and discussion of the existing scholarship see R.-P. Fuchs, *Ein 'Medium zum Frieden'. Die Normaljahrsregel und die Beendigung des Dreißigjährigen Krieges* (Munich, 2010), pp. 11–56.

role in everyday life. Conversions, confessionally mixed marriages, simultaneous churches, rituals and processions were still and for a long time very important. This chapter aims not to pursue the old question of whether the Thirty Years' War *was* a war of religion or not after 1635. Instead it analyses the aspects of differentiation and re-amalgamation of religion, culture and politics on the three levels and realms of political decision-making, elite cultures of learned discourse and everyday life. Readers might be less familiar with this line of argument. What all four authors show from different perspectives, however, is not only the way in which religious strife fuelled conflict, but also how religious conflict was conceptionalised and how possibilities for compromise and solving it were explored.

Part V explores the experience and material conditions of the war.[4] Constant warfare placed unprecedented strains on the European economy and society, due to both the costs of directly supporting military activity, and the impact of adapting to the disruptions caused by occupation and troop movements. John Theibault's chapter provides an overview of the social and economic structures that supplied the necessary materiel of war – soldiers, weapons, and provisions – with particular emphasis on Central Europe. It then explores how that materiel was provided: recruitment from the perspective of the communities from which soldiers were raised, taxation to support armies, regional development of arms industries. The new war tax, called 'contributions', and the special case of Wallenstein, with his vertically integrated supply chain based in his home territory of Friedland, are given particular attention. The social and economic effects of continual warfare can thus be assessed. One of the focal points in Sigrun Haude's chapter is the experience of fear and its manifestations. She investigates practical approaches to surviving the war, especially given the fact that most subjects could not rely on their authorities for help. This argument feeds also into Johannes Burkhard's thesis that bellicosity ensued not because of the existence of early modern states, 'but rather from the state's imperfections, failings and shortcomings'.[5] We do not pursue this particular aspect further in this volume,[6] nor have we specifically engaged with the recent and well-researched area of the presentation of the Thirty Years' War in propaganda and early modern media.[7] However, Sigrun Haude's contribution in particular provides a range of important references to this material.

In his chapter on the strategies and conduct of war, Peter H. Wilson argues that throughout the conflict, war remained firmly subordinated as an instrument of policy. Rulers certainly encountered difficulties with their senior officers. Wallenstein's secret diplomacy, for instance, alarmed Emperor Ferdinand, while the Swedish commanders forced Chancellor Oxenstierna to incorporate their demands as war aims through two mutinies in 1633 and 1636. However, the officers remained within the same world as the heads of state, defining war as a demonstration of power by a properly constituted

---

[4] On this topic see now also the study by H. Medick and B. Marschke, *Experiencing the Thirty Years War: A Brief History with Documents* (Boston and New York, 2013).

[5] J. Burkhard, 'Wars of States or Wars of State-Formation?', in O. Asbach and P. Schröder (eds), *War, the State and International Law in Seventeenth-Century Europe* (Farnham, 2010), p. 34.

[6] For further discussion see also J. Burkhard, 'Der Dreißigjährige Krieg als frühmoderner Staatsbildungskrieg', in *Geschichte in Wissenschaft und Unterricht*, 45 (1994): pp. 487–99; J. Burkhard, 'Die Friedlosigkeit der Frühen Neuzeit. Grundlegung einer Theorie der Bellizität Europas', in *Zeitschrift für Historische Forschung*, 24 (1997): pp. 509–74 and critically B. Teschke, 'Revisiting the "War-Makes-States" Thesis: War, taxation and social Property Relations in Early Modern Europe', in O. Asbach and P. Schröder (eds), *War, the State and International Law in Seventeenth-Century Europe* (Farnham, 2010), pp. 35–59.

[7] A good general overview is provided by D. Bellingradt, 'Die vergessenen Quellen des alten Reiches. Ein Forschungsüberblick zu frühneuzeitlicher Flugpublizistik im Heiligen Römischen Reich deutscher Nation', in A. Blome and H. Böning (eds), *Presse und Geschichte. Leistungen und Perspektiven der historischen Presseforschung* (Bremen, 2008), pp. 76–95.

authority (*potestas*) rather than illegitimate *violentia*. The main focus of the chapter is on how commanders sought to translate the exercise of *potestas* into actual military practice. This allows us to address key questions associated with the Thirty Years' War: did it last so long because the generals were unable to break a stalemate? Did it simply end through mutual exhaustion, as is often supposed? Wilson also explores how the armies actually operated in the field, examining how the war was actually fought.

Part VI concludes with an evaluation of the eventual peace settlement, the long and cumbersome way it was reached, and the rise of European diplomacy and balance of power politics as a result of the treaties of Westphalia at Münster and Osnabruck. In May 1635, the Emperor and the Prince Elector of Saxony signed the Peace Treaty of Prague. While it is true that nearly all German estates of the empire joined the treaty, the Peace of Prague still appears to have failed. War between France and Spain had broken out not 10 days before the Peace was signed. The Emperor had only just seized back his power to speak and act. Was the Peace of Prague therefore of only passing importance? Martin Espenhorst analyses the many dimensions of 1635 in order to systematically assess and evaluate the significance of the peace accord. He explores which components were created under constitutional law, whether short-term or long-term. Was the aim of this peace to create an absolute monarchy in the empire? To answer these questions one has to understand what the political and religious goals of the negotiations actually consisted of.

The last three chapters in part VI deal with the actual peace treaty which terminated the Thirty Years' War. Axel Gotthard looks into the debates surrounding the Peace of Westphalia as a settlement for the empire, while Heinz Duchhardt studies the Peace in view of its implications for the emerging European state system. And indeed, the Peace of Westphalia is one of the most remarkable documents of international law and international politics in pre-revolutionary times. Whether one believes in the existence of a 'Westphalian system' or a 'Westphalian era' or not, its effects as far as international law is concerned were long-lasting. Quite a number of solutions found in Münster and Osnabruck shaped the inter-relations of states for generations: the admittance of all political subjects, even those of a minor legal status; the technique of a peace congress with the abstention from plenary conferences; the language and the formation of key terms; the role of mediators. It is also notable that the papacy's objections to the Westphalian instruments were utterly ignored by all parties. One can see this, as a sign of the fading of Papal influence. To what extent parties attempted to put religious politics aside can be seen by the fact that the treaty itself anticipated Papal objection and stated at the very end of its stipulations that the Peace should be valid even if any of the European powers – it was clear to contemporaries that this was aimed at the papacy – would not be prepared to endorse the Peace. However, it would be misleading to assume that with Westphalia, religion entirely lost its influence on international politics.[8] What is evident, however, is that reference to Westphalia became almost a rule for all following peace treaties up to the revolutionary era.[9] References to the Peace of Westphalia were also omnipresent in polemics against Louis XIV. This suggests that the Peace remained open to interpretation and was consequently hotly contested in the subsequent political and military conflicts.

One aspect of the conflict which has only recently attracted scholarly attention is the role played by the world beyond Europe. The Thirty Years' War can be seen within a broader

---

[8] See D. Onnekink (ed.), *War and Religion after Westphalia, 1648–1713* (Farnham, 2009).

[9] For the history and philosophy of political thought regarding the Peace of Westphalia see with further references, O. Asbach and P. Schröder (eds), *War, the State and International Law in Seventeenth-Century Europe* (Farnham, 2010). See also the overview by J. Elliott, 'Europe after the Peace of Westphalia', in J. Elliott, *Spain, Europe and the Wider World 1500–1800* (New Haven and London, 2009), pp. 92–106.

context of European conflict of state and empire building and the struggle for dominance in maritime world trade. The Dutch struggle for independence, the quarrels of the French kings with the Habsburg Monarchy and English conflicts with Spain, Portugal and the Dutch took place alongside attacks on colonial territories and trade connections, with the result that decisions about war and peace in Europe changed the pattern of Atlantic trade and relations between European traders or companies and Asian and African sovereigns. Susan Richter's chapter explores the impact of European politics on the development of the so-called second Atlantic system, the shape of power dynamics between Europeans and peoples in Asia and Africa as well as its role in the further development of international law.

The Peace of Westphalia ended the Thirty Years' War and provided a crucial part of the empire's constitutional framework, if not that of the whole of Europe.[10] Despite the fact that it failed to establish lasting peace in Europe it was a crucial part of the development which fostered the legal framework and explored a new political modus of how international politics were to be conducted.

---

[10] See, as a prominent example, Jean-Jacques Rousseau's remark in 1758, according to which 'the Treaty of Westphalia will perhaps always be the basis of the political system [of Europe]. Thus, public Right, which the Germans study with such care, is … in certain regards, that of the whole of Europe' (*The Plan for Perpetual Peace, On the Government of Poland, and Other Writings on History and Politics*, ed. Chr. Kelly, Dartmouth, 2005, p. 35).

PART I
The Holy Roman Empire of the German Nation

Imperial Politics 1555–1618

Joachim Whaley

Did Germany slide into war in 1618? Many historians have certainly thought so. The period 1555–1618 has rarely been studied in its own right but rather as an adjunct to two larger narratives. Some have viewed it as little more than an extended prelude to war. Others have described a dismal phase in the story of the decline of the Holy Roman Empire, characterised by the triumph of the princes and the establishment of narrow provincialist confessional regimes, the prelude to the dominance of foreign powers over Germany after the Peace of Westphalia.[1]

The old nationalist master narrative of German history typically characterised the period after the Peace of Augsburg in 1555 as one of hopeless division and of growing tension and conflict that finally erupted in the Thirty Years' War. In 1855 Johann Gustav Droysen wrote that the Reformation had concluded Germany's national history.[2] The triumph of princely liberty in 1555, he declared, created an 'impossible situation, a political chaos'. The price the Germans paid for religious peace was 'complete political bankruptcy'. Parity between Catholics and Protestants paralysed the empire; the 'thoughts [of the Germans] became base and [their] hearts narrow'. In 1869, Heinrich von Treitschke echoed the 'manly tone of anger and contempt' with which Droysen had denounced the 'unspeakable humiliation' that resulted from the 'voluntary self-mutilation of a great, rich, martial nation' in agreeing to the terms of the Peace of Augsburg. This, he wrote, was Germany's 'darkest era'. He later conceded that the Peace had at least secured the future of Protestantism and 'freedom of thought', the foundations for Germany's Protestant destiny. Yet Treitschke insisted nonetheless that these decades constituted the 'ugliest period of German history.'[3]

Subsequent scholars generally followed this line. Moriz Ritter's three-volume study of *German History in the Age of the Counter-Reformation and the Thirty Years War* – still the most detailed account of the period – presented the Peace of Augsburg as the prelude to the 'dissolution of the imperial constitution 1586–1608'.[4] The Catholic historian Johannes

---

[1] For a more detailed discussion of the topics treated in this chapter, see J. Whaley, *Germany and the Holy Roman Empire*, Volume I: *Maximilian I to the Peace of Westphalia 1493–1648* (Oxford, 2012). Other useful surveys are: G. Schmidt, *Geschichte des Alten Reiches: Staat und Nation in der Frühen Neuzeit 1495–1806* (Munich, 1999); H. Rabe, *Deutsche Geschichte 1500–1600: Das Jahrhundert der Glaubensspaltung* (Munich, 1991); H. Schilling, *Aufbruch und Krise: Deutschland 1517–1648* (Berlin, 1988); M. Lanzinner, 'Das konfessionelle Zeitalter 1555–1618', in W. Reinhard (ed), *Gebhardt: Handbuch der deutschen Geschichte*, vol. 10, 10th edn (Stuttgart, 2001), pp. 3–203; and T. Brady, *German Histories in the Age of Reformations, 1400–1650* (Cambridge, 2009).
[2] A. Gotthard, *Der Augsburger Religionsfrieden* (Münster, 2004), pp. 623–5.
[3] Ibid., pp. 626–7.
[4] M. Ritter, *Deutsche Geschichte im Zeitalter der Gegenreformation und des Dreißigjährigen Krieges (1555–1648)*, 3 vols (Stuttgart, 1889–1908), vol. 2, pp. 3–232.

Janssen concurred when he repeatedly used words such as 'decay' and 'ruin' to characterise the development of German politics in this period.[5]

The caesura of 1945 undermined the old Prussian-German narrative of German history. Yet its rudiments were translated into the new narratives formulated by historians after 1945. Ironically, the old narrative translated quite easily into the new Marxist historiography of the former GDR. The triumph of the princes was equated with the resurgence of feudalism in a period of national decline. The activities of the confessional agents of the princes, the Protestant clergy and the Jesuits, seemed also to fit into this view.[6] In the Federal Republic, by contrast, the triumph of the princes was viewed as the prelude to the formation of confessional churches, which Ernst Walter Zeeden saw as the key feature of this period.[7] Strongly influenced by contemporary political developments in the 1950s, Zeeden presented the history of the empire after 1555 as the history of a divided Germany torn apart by the European religious conflict which led to the establishment of the new confessional regimes in the German territories.

This view was further developed by Heinz Schilling and Wolfgang Reinhard as the confessionalisation thesis, which focused on the significance of the development of both Catholicism and Protestantism, on the establishment of new social norms and their internalisation in educational systems, and on the imposition of a new social discipline on German society. While Schilling emphasised the significance of confessionalisation for the formation of the territorial state and Reinhard was more concerned with its social impact, both scholars argued that confessionalisation was linked to a modernisation process in European society. Contemporaries did not intend this outcome. For Reinhard, modernisation was an incidental by-product of the growth of state power and of the imposition of social discipline. For Schilling, the growing tension that exploded in 1618 and its tragic and bloody aftermath was a historically necessary systemic crisis that was the prelude to progress and modernisation in the longer term: the sheer intensity of the disaster of the war led Europeans to eliminate religion from politics after 1648.[8]

Even some of the alternatives to the powerful confessionalisation narratives have failed to liberate themselves from the underlying master narrative. Winfried Schulze has criticised the exclusive emphasis on religion and sees evidence of secularisation in politics and thought in the later sixteenth century.[9] Yet his argument still focuses on the formation of the territorial state. Martin Heckel has focused on the fact that the settlement of 1555 left the empire without a generally accepted body of imperial law. He too therefore argues that these decades saw an escalating and inevitable conflict which naturally exploded in war after 1618 and led to the secularisation of German imperial law in 1648.[10]

The old narrative explained the failure of the empire in terms of culpability, weakness, moral failure and lack of conviction. The new narrative suggests that the empire's failure to solve its problems and to overcome the consequences of the religious division was simply

---

[5] Gotthard, *Religionsfrieden*, pp. 635–6.
[6] A. Dorpalen, *German History in Marxist Perspective: The East German Approach*, (London, 1985), pp. 123–37.
[7] S. Ehrenpreis and U. Lotz-Heumann, *Reformation und konfessionelles Zeitalter* (Darmstadt, 2002), pp. 62–79.
[8] H. Schilling, *Konfessionalisierung und Staatsinteressen: Internationale Beziehungen 1559–1660* (Paderborn, 2007), pp. 416–20.
[9] Ehrenpreis and Lotz-Heumann, *Reformation*, pp. 72–3.
[10] M. Heckel, 'Konfessionalisierung in Koexistenznöten: Zum Augsburger Religionsfrieden, Dreißigjährigen Krieg und Westfälischen Frieden in neuerer Sicht', *Historische Zeitschrift*, cclxxx (2005), pp. 647–90, see pp. 665–9.

the German equivalent of the kind of development that occurred elsewhere in Europe in the later sixteenth century.

The problem with all of the grand confessionalisation narratives is their foundation on theoretical models of secularisation or modernisation. These often fail to do justice to the openness and uncertainty of outcome that attended German political life at this time. An alternative to this approach is provided by more recent studies that focus on the way that the empire functioned increasingly effectively during this period. The publication of the papers relating to the Augsburg diet in 1566, for example, shed new light on politics after 1555 and contradicted older perceptions of an early breakdown caused by confessional differences.[11] Georg Schmidt's study of the early modern empire published in 1999 also encouraged a new preoccupation with the state-like qualities (*Staatlichkeit*) of the empire, with the relationship between empire and territories as complementary aspects of a single system, and with the patriotic values that united both Catholics and Protestants in a German nation.[12] Despite fierce criticism from the leading exponents of the confessionalisation thesis, Schmidt's arguments have contributed to the emergence of a new picture of the early modern empire as a functioning polity.

There were certainly divisions and tensions. The most important of these were religious in origin or generated by other issues that were exacerbated increasingly from the 1570s by the confessional divisions between Catholics and Protestants but also between Protestants themselves. Yet the approach of all parties to the problems that arose indicates a strong desire to resolve differences peacefully.

Fundamentally, the issues that arose after 1555 revolved around the constitutional and governance issues that had preoccupied the empire since the 1490s. At the Worms Diet in 1495 Maximilian I had requested finance to fund campaigns against the French, the Turks, and Venice. The German estates declined to provide money for any offensive wars and strictly resisted any attempt to impose imperial taxation. At the same time, the estates also asserted their own position as co-regents with the emperor. Above all they succeeded in focusing attention on the problems of the empire. This resulted in agreement on four major measures: a perpetual peace; the means of maintaining that peace (including regular meetings of the diet); the establishment of a high court, the *Reichskammergericht*, to settle disputes between estates, complaints against them by subjects, and appeals against judgments handed down by territorial courts; and, finally, the institution of an imperial tax, the *Gemeiner Pfennig*.

Neither the imperial tax nor the imperial administrative body subsequently agreed at Augsburg in 1500 survived. The tax was soon abandoned because it failed to raise the sums anticipated and because the princes insisted on retaining the right to levy their own taxes. The imperial administration (*Reichsregiment*) was initially envisaged by the estates as a mechanism for controlling the emperor but its first incarnation in 1500–02 achieved little and its second incarnation in 1521–30 soon ran up against the resistance of the princes, who suspected Charles V and his regent Ferdinand of attempting to use it as an instrument of imperial government.[13]

By contrast, the regional associations (*Reichskreise* or circles) that were envisaged as adjuncts of the central administrative body took root. This was because they were unambiguously under the control of the estates and because they came to play a vital role in the implementation of legislation agreed between emperor and estates and in the execution of the judgments of the Reichskammergericht. As a sign of the determination of the estates

---

[11] M. Lanzinner and D. Heil, 'Der Augsburger Reichstag 1566: Ergebnisse einer Edition', *Historische Zeitschrift*, cclxxiv (2002), pp. 603–32.

[12] Schmidt, *Geschichte*, pp. 9–149.

[13] Whaley, *Germany*, pp. 34–5, 162–3, 299–301.

to keep the crown within the bounds of what had been agreed in 1495–1500, the limitation of royal power was further reinforced in 1519 when it was resolved that Charles V should sign an electoral capitulation (*Wahlkapitulation*) before his coronation.

This equilibrium was challenged in various ways by the Reformation and by Charles V. The first crisis arose over Charles V's early attempt to stamp out the Lutheran heresy. The Edict of Worms 1521 aimed to deal with Luther swiftly. However, the refusal of the elector of Saxony followed by others to implement it rendered it ineffective. In the following years, the estates were unanimous in their desire to quell the unrest generated by the religious movement and they moved swiftly to deal with the Peasants War in 1525. Yet they insisted that, pending a general council of the Church or a German national Church council, they alone had the right to determine religious matters in their own territory. Their ability to assert this position was aided by Charles V's absence from the empire throughout the 1520s and between 1532 and 1540. By the time Charles V returned his attention to German affairs in 1543, it was too late. His attempt to impose his will on Germany rapidly led to war. While it seemed that by 1548 the Emperor had triumphed, the princes soon led to a successful reaction against him. The Treaty of Passau 1552 was the first step to the Peace of Augsburg. This both reaffirmed the constitutional balance established around 1500 and provided answers to the religious questions thrown up by the intervening decades.

The Augsburg settlement extended the perpetual peace to matters concerning religion.[14] Rulers, including the councils of imperial cities and even the imperial knights, were now empowered to impose their religion on their subjects. The only proviso was that they were obliged to allow anyone who dissented the right to emigrate. Some questions were left unclear: the status of those ecclesiastical territories that had already been secularised (further secularisations were explicitly prohibited by the *reservatum ecclesiasticum*, which was itself challenged from the early 1580s) and the rights of Protestant nobles and towns in the Catholic ecclesiastical territories. But these things became contentious much later.

More important, though often neglected by traditional scholarship, was the way that the Augsburg settlement made the agreements of 1495–1500 truly workable for the first time. Furthermore, after decades of uncertainty and the bitter experience of war in the 1540s, there was a general will to participate and to make the Peace work. This was evident at several levels: in the attitudes of the emperors who succeeded Charles V, in the response of the German princes, and in the way that the institutions of the empire now operated.

Unlike Charles V, Ferdinand I (r. 1558–64) and Maximilian II (r. 1564–76) were truly German emperors. The imperial title had enhanced Charles's authority but his political vision was always European rather than German. His two successors had a very different perspective.

After long years as his brother's regent in Germany, as king of Bohemia since 1526, and as designated heir to the imperial throne since 1531, Ferdinand I had more experience of the German Empire than Charles V. Having inherited the Austrian lands from his grandfather Maximilian, Ferdinand was actually a German prince and he developed a relationship with the empire similar to that of previous emperors who had owned lands on its south-eastern periphery.

Maximilian II had been born in Vienna and, while he had fought with Charles V in the Schmalkaldic War in 1546–48, those experiences together with his treatment by Charles over the inheritance question turned him against his Spanish relatives and made him sympathetic to the position of the German princes. Initially deprived of the hope of a substantial territorial inheritance from the emperor, obliged to become *stadtholder* in Spain, and very nearly relegated from the imperial succession by Charles's determination to favour his own son

---

[14] On the Augsburg settlement, see the chapter by Matthias Pohlig in this volume.

Philip, Maximilian was saved only by the emperor's defeat and humiliation. On his return from Spain in 1551, he forged close bonds with leading Catholic and Protestant princes, while in Vienna he took over the business of government during his father's absence. By the time of his succession, he was well acquainted with the leading German princes and well versed in the practices of German government and politics in the empire.

It was, however, more than just geography and experience that linked these emperors with the empire. Crucially, both had a deep understanding of the religious issues in German politics and sympathy with those who stood between the lines.[15] Ferdinand I was a loyal Catholic who resisted the spread of Protestantism in his own lands. In the empire, however, he saw the need to negotiate and compromise and, in doing so, he aimed to avoid questions of dogma and the involvement of controversial theologians. He also persistently urged the papacy to reform and hoped that the Council of Trent might consider measures such as the recognition of communion under both kinds and the relaxation of celibacy, which he believed might tempt the German Protestants to re-join a reformed Church. That almost certainly misunderstood the Protestants' position but it reflected Ferdinand's essentially Erasmian views and it provided the basis for on-going negotiations in the empire, which avoided conflict.

Maximilian II's religious views were so unorthodox that they almost became an obstacle to his succession.[16] In Vienna after his return from Spain in 1552, he relished the heterodox atmosphere created by the presence of Netherlands, Spanish, and Italian intellectuals of both Catholic and Protestant persuasions.[17] While Ferdinand encouraged these figures as part of his irenic Catholic reform programme, it seems that Maximilian effectively abandoned his Catholic faith. For the sake of his inheritance, he swore solemnly that he would not leave the Church of Rome, but suspicions about his true loyalties remained. The papacy distrusted him and his views fostered the growth of Protestantism in his own lands, which contributed to the crisis that later engulfed the Habsburg lands. Yet, in the empire, Maximilian's views were as conducive as his father's had been to the pursuit of a policy of conciliation and compromise. Above all, Maximilian was also absolutely committed to the Peace settlement of 1555 and to his own role as arbitrator in the empire and co-regent with the diet.

The religious attitudes of Ferdinand I and Maximilian II also helped accentuate another key feature of the German political system. Both emperors were able to reach out beyond the confessional divide. They maintained friendships and correspondence with a wide variety of princes. They thus helped adapt the traditional networks of the German higher nobility to the new circumstances created in 1555.[18] The sense of solidarity among the German princes had been a key feature of the political negotiations around 1500. It was expressed in the

---

[15] See A. Kohler, *Ferdinand I. 1503–1564: Fürst, König und Kaiser* (Munich, 2003), pp. 115–18, 185–26, 277–85; and E. Laubach, *Ferdinand I. als Kaiser: Politik und Herrschaftsauffassung des Nachfolgers Karls V.* (Münster, 2001), pp. 29–140, 196–205, 359–516.

[16] M. Rudersdorf, 'Maximilian I.', in A. Schindling and W. Ziegler, *Die Kaiser der Neuzeit 1519–1918: Heiliges Römisches Reich, Österreich, Deutsches Reich* (Munich, 1990), pp. 79–97, see pp. 83–5, 89–93; P.S. Fichtner, *Emperor Maximilian II* (New Haven, CT, 2001), pp. 32–49; I. Auerbach, 'Maximilian II. und Rudolf II. als böhmische Könige, die böhmischen Stände und das Problem von Reformation und Gegenreformation in Böhmen', in H.-B. Harder and H. Rothe (eds), *Studien zum Humanismus in den böhmischen Ländern* (Dresden, 1998), pp. 17–55, see: pp. 23–6.

[17] H. Louthan, *The Quest for Compromise: Peacemakers in Counter-Reformation Vienna* (Cambridge, 1997), pp. 1–120; N. Mout, '"Dieser einzige Wiener Hof von Dir hat mehr Gelehrte als ganze Reiche Anderer"': Späthumanismus am Kaiserhof in der Zeit Maximilians II. und Rudolfs II. (1564–1612)', in N. Hammerstein (ed.), *Späthumanismus: Studien über das Ende einer kulturhistorischen Epoche* (Göttingen, 2000), pp. 46–64.

[18] The significance of these networks is emphasised (with numerous further references) by F. Brendle, *Der Erzkanzler im Religionskrieg: Kurfürst Anselm Casimir von Mainz, die geistlichen Fürsten und das Reich 1629 bis 1647* (Münster, 2011), pp. 15–16.

adoption of the name *Reichstag* (diet) for what had formerly generally been known as the *Hoftag* (gathering of the court) and in the introduction of the style 'Holy Roman Empire of the German Nation' to denote this polity defined by the participation of German princes in the diet. The reform of the empire was built on family, neighbourly, and regional allegiances and alliances that created a complex mass of interlocking and overlapping networks among the German higher nobility. Many of these were translated into the circles; disputes between and within them were now resolved by the imperial courts of justice. The devolution of decisions concerning religion to the territorial level both maintained the central decision-making functions of the diet to provide framework legislation and ensured that the solidarity of the princes was maintained. Despite periodic frictions, that remained fundamentally the case in the bi-confessional system that emerged by 1555.

The main effects of the settlement of 1555 were to confirm the rights of the princes in matters concerning religion, and to give a new impetus to the empire's key institutions. The traditional loyalty of the princes to the emperor was complemented by a desire to ensure that these institutions now actually fulfilled the functions that had originally been envisaged for them. The diet met seven times between 1556–57 and 1582.[19] The emperor attended personally and the discussions and deliberations followed the procedure laid down around 1500 and codified by the imperial arch-chancellor, the elector of Mainz, in 1570. On each occasion, the diet debated current problems of internal peace, the organisation of the circles, the state of the currency, the operations of the Reichskammergericht, and imperial taxes, notably for the various Turkish campaigns. In addition, there were three meetings of the electors, a general assembly of the circles, several so-called *Reichsdeputationstage* (special gatherings of representatives of the estates convened to discuss a range of issues specified by the diet), as well as a number of gatherings convened to discuss specific issues such as the Reichskammergericht and the distribution of the burden of imperial taxes.

Crucially, the circles now for the first time developed regular assemblies and specialist committees to deal with particular problems, notably the regulation of the currency.[20] They also appointed officers to lead and represent them as well as officials to assist and to coordinate the business of the circle. Not all the circles developed the same level of activity: those which comprised numerous small territories and those in middle and upper Germany tended to be the most active; in those dominated by large territories, they tended to carry out peacekeeping duties and other activities engaged in by circles elsewhere. Overall, however, the circles contributed significantly to the renewed vigour of imperial institutions generally after 1555. The formal constitution of regional organisations of imperial counts and imperial knights bound these groups too into the empire's institutional structure, offering them greater protection and ensuring the stability of the regions they inhabited.[21]

The same was true of the Reichskammergericht, which was joined from 1559 by the emperor's parallel court at Vienna, the *Reichshofrat*, forming a pair of occasionally competing but generally complementary supreme courts in the Reich.[22] The staffing of the Reichskammergericht was enhanced, funding increased, and procedures were improved. An increase in the number of cases brought to the court created the inevitable complaints but

---

[19] Lanzinner, 'Konfessionelles Zeitalter', p. 69. See also the essays on the sixteenth-century diet in M. Lanzinner and A. Strohmeyer (eds), *Der Reichstag (1486–1613): Kommunikation – Wahrnehmung – Öffentlichkeiten* (Göttingen, 2006).

[20] Lanzinner, 'Konfessionelles Zeitalter', pp. 72–4. The most comprehensive survey of Kreis activity is contained in W. Dotzauer, *Die deutschen Reichskreise (1383–1806): Geschichte und Aktenedition* (Stuttgart, 1998).

[21] G. Schmidt, 'Die politische Bedeutung der kleineren Reichsstände im 16. Jahrhundert', *Jahrbuch für Geschichte des Feudalismus*, xii (1989), pp. 185–206.

[22] Whaley, *Germany*, pp. 363–5.

on the whole the court was enormously respected and there were only seven appeals against its judgments between 1559 and 1585. The reform of the Reichshofrat also contributed to the pacification and 'juridification' of the Reich. It seems that the Reichshofrat rapidly won respect and gained in authority. Some litigants preferred it since its procedures were more flexible and more rapid than those of the Reichskammergericht. In particular, the Vienna court's custom of sending commissions to gather evidence on the ground both involved local powers in the conflict resolution process and solved many problems by local arbitration. The old view that the Reichshofrat was favoured by Catholic litigants is confounded by the fact that Protestants used it just as frequently. Furthermore, despite later claims of confessional bias, its caseload doubled between 1580 and 1610.[23] Both courts attracted cases from western and northern areas, as well as from the old core lands of middle and upper Germany, which demonstrated the growing reach of imperial justice and the contribution made by the courts to the integration of the empire.

The diet made a number of key decisions which exemplified the new sense of solidarity and purpose after 1555. The way that it made decisions and the nature of those decisions often puzzled contemporaries and reinforced the view of traditional historians that the empire was dysfunctional and weak. Around 1600, French observers characterised the imperial estates as 'irresolute', 'weak', 'stupid' and 'insensible' and complained that they were really not interested in public affairs. The Germans, Henri IV complained in 1609, 'do nothing but sleep or drink'.[24] This reflected ignorance of the protracted nature of decision-making in the empire as well as frustration at not being able to enlist the Germans in a cause congenial to France.

Discussion of foreign policy issues was every bit as complex as the discussion of domestic matters, but that did not mean the diet was ineffective. Around 1500, the German estates had made it clear that they would defend themselves but not promote purely Habsburg interests. The emperor's constant requests for money to help defend the empire against the Turks met with ready compliance: the princes not only agreed in principle to pay but, in contrast to their previous practice, actually paid more money than ever before. Indeed, the sum granted in 1576 brought in some 3.7 million gulden, more than all of the Turkish levies granted under Charles V before 1555 combined.[25]

The Livonia question clearly demonstrated the continuing significance of the distinction between German and purely Habsburg interests.[26] Livonia did not belong to the Holy Roman Empire as such but the German estates broadly supported Ferdinand I's claim that it was part of his wider empire. During the Nordic Seven Years War (1563–70) it became caught up in the struggle for hegemony in the Baltic between Denmark and Sweden. Although Maximilian II was able to broker the Peace of Stettin in 1570, Livonia remained under Polish-Lithuanian overlordship and then fell victim to a protracted struggle between

---

[23] Lanzinner, 'Konfessionelles Zeitalter', p. 76; S. Ullmann, *Geschichte auf der langen Bank: Die Kommissionen des Reichshofrats unter Kaiser Maximilian II. (1564–1576)* (Mainz, 2006), pp. 194–7, 291–8; S. Ehrenpreis, *Kaiserliche Gerichtsbarkeit und Konfessionskonflikt: Der Reichshofrat unter Rudolf II. 1576–1612* (Göttingen, 2006).

[24] F. Beiderbeck, *Zwischen Religonskrieg, Reichskrise und europäischem Hegemoniekampf: Heinrich IV. von Frankreich und die protestantischen Reichsstände* (Berlin: Berliner Wissenschafts-Verlag, 2005), pp. 205–6.

[25] Lanzinner, 'Konfessionelles Zeitalter', p. 71. See also W. Schulze, *Reich und Türkengefahr im späten 16. Jahrhundert: Studien zu den politischen und gesellschaftlichen Auswirkungen einer äußeren Bedrohung* (Munich, 1978) and P. Schmid, 'Reichssteuern, Reichsfinanzen and Reichsgewalt in der ersten Hälfte des 16.Jahrhunderts', in H. Angermeier (ed.), *Säkulare Aspekte der Reformationszeit* (Munich, 1983), pp. 153–99.

[26] Whaley, *Germany*, pp. 378–80; J. Lavery, *Germany's Northern Challenge: The Holy Roman Empire and the Scandinavian Struggle for the Baltic, 1563–1576* (Leiden and Boston, 2002), pp. 1–18, 136–41, 145–6.

Poland-Lithuania and Muscovy, which was only resolved in favour of Poland-Lithuania in 1582. Throughout the whole process, the diet remained passive, which the old nationalist historiography took to be a sign of its weakness and lack of national spirit. In reality, however, the diet simply applied the same criteria as it had done in the case of Maximilian I's Italian plans around 1500. The 'recuperation' of Livonia and Maximilian's efforts to place Habsburg candidates on the Polish throne in 1573 and 1575 were Habsburg projects rather than issues that concerned the empire as such. Indeed, the prospect that the acquisition of Livonia and Poland would enhance the emperor's power in the north was a distinct disincentive to action for many princes.

The diet's reluctance to become involved in the Netherlands conflict was equally significant. In the face of requests from the Dutch rebels for assistance against the tyrannical imposition by Spain of uncompromising religious policies the diet declined to intervene. The princes supported Maximilian's efforts to mediate in the dispute but even when the Netherlands conflict spilled over into the territory of the empire the princes habitually referred the matter to the emperor.[27] Even the fact that many German counts were personally related to William of Orange and the house of Nassau and that many counts themselves converted to Calvinism did not cause the diet to abandon its determination to maintain the peace and stability of the empire rather than plunge into a potentially ruinous conflict.

A similar determination to maintain the peace and to avoid involvement in religious controversy is evident in the approach to domestic issues. An attempt to mediate between the two religious parties in 1566–67 failed and in 1559 the diet simply confirmed the agreements that had been reached in 1555. Both sessions maintained the dialogue between emperor and estates and reinforced the common interest in peace and in the effective functioning of the circles and other imperial bodies. The session of 1566 provided an impressive demonstration of this consensus. A record levy was agreed to support the emperor's defence of the empire against the Turks. It was resolved to take firm action against the instability caused since 1558 by Wilhelm von Grumbach's pursuit of his grievances against the bishops of Würzburg.[28] This had raised fears of a new uprising of imperial knights, particularly as Grumbach found an ally in Duke Johann Friedrich II of Saxony, still smarting from the loss of the Saxon electoral title to his Albertine kinsmen in 1547. What was perceived as a fundamental threat to the status quo was met by concerted action when the diet commissioned the elector of Saxony, under the ultimate command of the emperor, to destroy Grumbach's forces. The religious peace was reaffirmed without further discussion of the question of reunification. Debate over the question of whether the elector of the Palatinate's conversion to Calvinism placed him outside the religious peace in the empire was simply avoided when the other Protestant princes swore that they recognised him as an adherent of the (Lutheran) Augsburg Confession.

The diet session of 1567 was largely concerned with the aftermath of the Grumbach affair. In 1570 the princes reasserted their traditional reluctance to strengthen the emperor's hand by refusing to entertain a plan to create a standing army under the emperor's command as well as permanent armouries and war chests in the circles for the emperor to draw on at all. The princes' refusal to acquiesce in this was once interpreted as yet another sign of the diet's inability to stand up for the German nation. In reality, however, creating such an army would have subverted the constitution and might have resulted in its transformation into a centralised state.[29] The sessions of 1576 and 1582 also demonstrated a continuing commitment

---

[27] A. Kohler, *Das Reich im Kampf um die Hegemonie in Europa 1521–1648* (Munich, 1990), pp. 23–4, 81–3. For further references, see Whaley, *Germany*, pp. 374–8.
[28] Ibid., pp. 390–93.
[29] Lanzinner, 'Konfessionelles Zeitalter', p. 62.

to the settlement of 1555. In 1576, Saxony and Bavaria helped thwart a Palatine initiative to demand formal recognition of the rights of Protestant nobles and towns in ecclesiastical territories (the *Declaratio Ferdinandea*), which the Catholics would have found unacceptable. In 1582, Rudolf II was able to defuse the potentially explosive issues thrown up by the disputes over question of Protestant worship in the Catholic imperial city of Cologne, over the demand of the Protestant administrator of the archbishopric of Magdeburg to take the Magdeburg seat in the college of princes, and over the conversion of the elector archbishop of Cologne, Gebhard Truchsess von Waldburg, to Catholicism (which ended in Waldburg's forcible deposition in 1584 and the election of a Bavarian Wittelsbach successor).[30]

It is generally assumed that the situation in the empire deteriorated decisively in the 1580s but there is little agreement about why this occurred. Some emphasise the significance of the death in 1586 of Elector August I of Saxony (r. 1553–86), the last leading member of what one might term the generation of 1555.[31] Others suggest that the fundamental reason was the cumulative outcome of the growing number of disputes and controversies that resulted from what they regard as the flawed religious peace.[32] A variant of this idea is the notion that the successful imposition of confessional regimes in many leading Catholic and Protestant territories by the 1580s generated a new uncompromising approach to politics in the empire. Heinz Schilling has taken this kind of explanation further by arguing that developments in the empire fed into a phase of religious fundamentalism before the Thirty Years' War.[33] Some argue that Rudolf II himself was responsible for the intensification of religious conflict in the empire, that he allowed himself increasingly to be influenced by uncompromising supporters of the militant Counter-Reformation.[34] Others emphasise the escalating pressure that grew from the conflicts in the Netherlands and in France or to the impact of news of the beginnings of a decisive Counter-Reformation policy in some of the Austrian territories.[35] Others again have sought the explanation at the much deeper level of a climatic crisis: a 'mini Ice Age' that began in 1570 and whose various effects generated a 'general crisis' by the 1590s and destabilised German society well into the first decades of the seventeenth century.[36]

There is unlikely to be a monocausal explanation. The unfolding of conflicts outside the empire may have contributed something. The movement of Spanish troops up the Rhine on their route from Spain via Genoa to the Netherlands and their incursions in the northwest as well as the periodic involvement of the Palatinate and others in the Protestant cause in France certainly caused reverberations in German politics. Yet the princes continued to abstain from direct involvement. They refused to be dragged into external disputes, and their solidarity was reinforced by the Turkish threat, in respect of which the diet voted substantial levies in 1594, 1597–98, and 1603 (on that occasion the highest levy ever agreed). The climate crisis undoubtedly also had a destabilising effect and it would be surprising if this had not affected the politics of the empire. It certainly had a more easily measurable

---

[30] Whaley, *Germany*, pp. 398–403.
[31] Lanzinner, 'Konfessionelles Zeitalter', p. 173.
[32] Rabe, *Deutsche Geschichte*, p. 604; Gotthard, *Religionsfrieden*, pp. 386–461.
[33] See essays in H. Schilling, (ed.), *Konfessioneller Fundamentalismus: Religion als politischer Faktor im europäischen Mächtesystem um 1600* (Munich, 2007).
[34] Rabe, *Deutsche Geschichte*, p. 605.
[35] Whaley, *Germany*, pp. 428–37; T. Winkelbauer, *Ständefreiheit und Fürstenmacht: Länder und Untertanen des Hauses Habsburg im konfessionellen Zeitalter*, 2 vols (Vienna, 2003), vol. 2, pp. 43–51, 55–8; and essays on Inner Austria and on Lower and Upper Austria in A. Schindling and W. Ziegler (eds), *Die Territorien des Reichs im Zeitalter der Reformation und Konfessionalisierung: Land und Konfession 1500–1650*, 7 vols (Münster, 1989–97), i, pp. 102–33.
[36] See essays in W. Behringer, H. Lehmann and C. Pfister (eds), *Kulturelle Konsequenzen der 'Kleinen Eiszeit'* (Göttingen, 2005).

impact on the German territories in terms of the problems posed by poverty, social unrest and peasant rebellions, and the various witch crazes after about 1580.[37]

It is not easy to evaluate the role of Rudolf II's policies. Judgements about his negative influence have often been influenced by the views of contemporaries such as Georg Erasmus von Tschernembl, the leader of the Protestant Austrian estates. His claim that Rudolf was nothing but a puppet controlled by the Roman curia was informed by his own visceral hatred of the Habsburg Counter-Reformation, for which he held Rudolf responsible.[38] Yet it is difficult to argue that the emperor could be held responsible for the disintegration of the political scene by virtue of any dereliction of duty.

Although Rudolf came to the throne with the reputation of being a hard-line Catholic, largely on the grounds of his education in Spain, he did not deviate from the course set by Ferdinand I and Maximilian II. Indeed the papacy regarded him with as much anxiety and suspicion as his predecessors.[39] Neither in Bohemia nor in the empire was Rudolf any more committed than Maximilian had been to the idea that a single faith should be predominant.[40] His permanent withdrawal to Prague in fact brought him closer to the empire: after the partition of the Habsburg lands following the death of Ferdinand I, it was Vienna that became remote, deprived of the access to the empire that had been given by the Tyrol and the Vorlande (until 1665 in the hands of a subsidiary Habsburg line that consistently promoted the Counter-Reformation). Prague was infinitely better placed for communications with north, middle, and southern Germany than Vienna had ever been, and it was free of the perennial threat of attack by the Turks that haunted Vienna.[41]

Rudolf may have inclined generally towards Catholicism in his appointments in Prague, but that indicated nothing of his own complex and essentially unorthodox beliefs, nor did it mean that he excluded Protestants, even Calvinists, from his court.[42] The fact that he did not travel may well have loosened some of the lines of direct communication established with the German princes by Ferdinand I and Maximilian II.[43] Yet there is every indication that Rudolf II governed effectively and successfully until about 1599–1600.[44] The crisis that began then was complex: partly related to Rudolf's illness or at least to the changed state of mind that so many contemporaries commented on; partly prompted by a loss of faith in his previous advisers and the transfer of his allegiance to a new group of predominantly Catholic courtiers; partly caused by the growing tensions within his own family as his brother Matthias and others agitated for him to reach a decision on the succession, a problem that drove him to distraction in his last years. The effect was quite clear: by 1603 the imperial

---

[37] Whaley, *Germany*, pp. 540–59.

[38] K. Repgen, *Die Römische Kurie und der Westfälische Friede, I/1: Papst, Kaiser und Reich 1521–1644* (Tübingen, 1962), p. 289 (fn. 243).

[39] A. Koller, 'Der Kaiserhof am Beginn der Regierung Rudolfs II. in den Berichten der Nuntien', in R. Bösel et al. (eds), *Kaiserhof – Papsthof (16.–18. Jahrhundert)* (Vienna, 2006), pp. 13–24; idem, 'Der Konflikt um die Obödienz Rudolfs II. gegenüber dem Hl. Stuhl', in idem (ed.), *Kurie und Politik: Stand und Perspektiven der Nuntiaturberichtsforschung* (Tübingen, 1998), pp. 148–64; F. Rottstock, *Studien zu den Nuntiaturberichten aus dem Reich in der zweiten Hälfte des sechzehnten Jahrhunderts: Nuntien und Legaten in ihrem Verhältnis zu Kurie, Kaiser und Reichsfürsten* (Munich, 1980), pp. 206–12.

[40] Auerbach, 'Maximilian II.', p. 19.

[41] J. Pánek, 'Rudolf II. als König von Böhmen', in H.-B. Harder and H. Rothe (eds), *Studien zum Humanismus in den böhmischen Ländern* (Dresden, 1998), pp. 1–16, see pp. 5–7.

[42] Ibid., pp. 9–10; R.J.W. Evans, *Rudolf II and his World: A Study in Intellectual History 1576–1612*, 2nd edn (Oxford, 1983), pp. 84–115.

[43] H. Noflatscher, 'Regiment aus der Kammer? Einflußreiche Kleingruppen am Hof Rudolfs II.', in J. Hirschbiegel (ed.), *Der Fall des Günstlings: Hofparteien in Europa vom 13. bis zum 17. Jahrhundert* (Ostfildern, 2004), pp. 209–34, see pp. 212–13.

[44] Ibid., pp. 219–22; Evans, *Rudolf II*, pp. 5–42.

treasurer Zacharias Geizkofler commented on the unbelievable chaos that prevailed in Rudolf's administration.[45]

The resulting lack of leadership inevitably exacerbated the problems. The growing controversy between Catholic and Protestant interpretations of imperial law and the refusal of both sides to accept the judgments of the courts in disputes which arose over the interpretation of the Peace of 1555 impaired the operation of both the Reichskammergericht and the Reichshofrat. In 1608, it also paralysed the diet itself. Rudolf's request for a levy to finance a force of 24,000 men failed. His representative, Ferdinand of Styria, tried to force through a ban on the imperial city of Donauwörth, a city in which both Catholics and Protestants enjoyed legal parity but where Protestants were impeding the public processions that the Catholic minority organised spurred on by the Dillingen Jesuits. The Protestant estates could not accept any of Ferdinand's proposals and the diet was dissolved without concluding any business at all.

This impasse led directly to the formation of the Protestant Union (14 May 1608) and the Catholic League (10 July 1609).[46] When a struggle began between Brandenburg and Palatinate-Neuburg over the succession to Duke Johann Wilhelm in Jülich-Kleve-Berg in March 1609, it seemed that the empire might plunge into a major war.[47] The involvement of the French king and Rudolf's diversion of troops intended for the Lower Rhine to threaten his brother Matthias in Upper Austria made this seem even more likely, especially as the troops plundered Prague, prompting the Bohemian estates to depose Rudolf in favour of Matthias. Yet Rudolf's death in January 1612 defused the situation, allowing Matthias to secure election to the imperial throne as well.

Matthias behaved perfectly correctly as emperor and actively promoted Cardinal Khlesl's plans to bridge the political divide in the empire by means of a 'composition'. Yet the pursuit of rigorous anti-Protestant policies in his own lands inflamed the legacy of bitterness and distrust left by the disputes of recent years and thwarted his attempt to convene a diet in 1613. Even so, there was a marked reluctance to destabilise the empire by upsetting the delicate balance of powers established around 1500. The German estates stepped back from the brink of war over Jülich-Kleve in 1614. Most members of both the Union and the League shrank back from becoming embroiled either with an international Protestant alliance in the one case or with the grand designs of the Spanish crown in the other. Indeed, among Protestants, the rhetoric of these years was not the language of war but rather the language of patriotism. As a French observer had commented sometime earlier, the confessional issue and its handling by the courts and the imperial administration divided Germans into two groups: 'good imperialists and Austrians' on the one hand and 'good Germans and good patriots' on the other.[48]

The crises that actually precipitated the Thirty Years' War were generated within the Habsburg territories rather than in the empire more generally. That Germany became embroiled in the conflict had more to do with Ferdinand II's response to the Bohemian crisis than with any desire for confrontation in the empire itself. Although the war was precipitated by the actions of a German prince, the elector of the Palatinate, these actions only became the catalyst for armed conflict when Ferdinand II pursued the would-be king of Bohemia into Germany and set about asserting royal powers that would have had implications for

---

[45] Noflatscher, 'Regiment', pp. 215–16.
[46] See essays in A. Ernst and A. Schindling (eds), *Union und Liga 1608/09: Konfessionelle Bündnisse im Reich – Weichenstellung zum Religionskrieg?* (Stuttgart, 2010).
[47] A.D. Anderson, *On the Verge of War: International Relations and the Jülich-Kleve Succession Crises (1609–1614)* (Boston, 1999), pp. 18–66.
[48] R. Kohlndorfer-Fries, *Diplomatie und Gelehrtenrepublik: Die Kontakte des französischen Gesandten Jaques Bongars (1554–1612)* (Tübingen, 2009), p. 110.

all princes and not just the Palatine outlaw.[49] This turned the crisis into another protracted struggle over the German constitution and for the preservation of 'German liberty'. This was only resolved when the Peace of Westphalia rebalanced the constitutional status quo first negotiated in the reign of Maximilian I.

Selected Bibliography

Anderson, A.D., *On the Verge of War: International Relations and the Jülich-Kleve Succession Crises (1609–1614)* (Boston, 1999).
Brady, T.A., *German Histories in the Age of Reformations, 1400–1650* (Cambridge, 2009).
Dorpalen, A., *German History in Marxist Perspective: The East German Approach* (London, 1985).
Evans, R.J.W., *Rudolf II and his World: A Study in Intellectual History 1576–1612*, 2nd edn (Oxford, 1983).
Fichtner, P.S., *Emperor Maximilian II* (New Haven, CT, 2001).
Lavery, J., *Germany's Northern Challenge: The Holy Roman Empire and the Scandinavian Struggle for the Baltic, 1563–1576* (Leiden and Boston, 2002).
Louthan, H., *The Quest for Compromise: Peacemakers in Counter-Reformation Vienna* (Cambridge, 1997).
Whaley, J., *Germany and the Holy Roman Empire*, Volume 1: *Maximilian I to the Peace of Westphalia, 1493–1648* (Oxford, 2012).
Wilson, P.H., *From Reich to Revolution: German History, 1558–1806* (Houndmills, 2004).

---

[49] On this, see the chapter by Brennan Pursell in this volume.

2

ASHGATE
RESEARCH
COMPANION

The Palatinate and its Networks in the Empire and in Europe

Brennan Pursell

Kurpfalz, the Electoral Palatinate, was a prosperous, influential estate of the Holy Roman Empire in 1618.[1] Among the empire's ca. 500 other estates, the Palatinate was internally organised despite its extreme territorial fragmentation, integrated in the empire and connected to some of Western Europe's greatest powers. The Palatinate's glittering, sophisticated court could have helped to mediate and mollify a variety of conflicts festering among Europe's bellicose, ruling elite, but it did the opposite. The reigning prince, Frederick V, leaped into the arena normally reserved for Europe's mightiest warlords, hoping that his many worthy connections would provide support, and that others would follow, join the fray and help him attain his ambition.[2] Doing so opened the floodgates to three decades of war.

The Palatinate deserves special attention in any study of the Thirty Years' War because of its central role in the development of the crisis, a point that hardly needs scholarly argument. The earliest written accounts of the tragedy from 1618 to 1648, by simple people such as Christoph Raph, a town clerk, Hans Heberle, a shoemaker, and Gallus Zembroth, a village major and wine-grower, cite the Elector Palatine as one of the war's originators and the Palatinate as one of the chief victims. A Lutheran pastor in Hessen, Johann Minck, wrote of Frederick V's infamous attempt to take over the kingdom of Bohemia, 'This gave rise to a large-scale war and devastation, not only in the Palatinate, but in the whole Roman

---

[1] Leading scholarly periodicals that publish articles about Palatine history are *Zeitschrift für die Geschichte des Oberrheins* and *Mitteilungen des historischen Vereins der Pfalz*. The latter features studies in local history, primarily administrative and territorial, as well as some brief biographies of notable people. The best collections of publications are at the university libraries in Heidelberg and Munich and at the *Institut für pfälzische Geschichte und Volkskunde* and the *Pfalzbibliothek* in Kaiserslautern. For documentary research, the *Landesarchiv* in Speyer has records and papers for the electoral Palatinate, the duchy of Zweibrücken and several other principalities and ecclesiastical estates in the region. The *Bayerisches Hauptstaatsarchiv* in Munich has the largest repository of unpublished archival materials from the reign of Elector Palatine Frederick V, in the *Kasten Blau* and *Kasten Schwartz* collections.

[2] See B. Pursell, *The Winter King: Frederick V of the Palatinate and the Coming of the Thirty Years' War* (Aldershot, 2003) for a full analysis of the man and his regime until his death in 1632. For a factual biography, see P. Bilhöfer, *Nicht gegen Ehre und Gewissen: Friedrich V., Kurfürst von der Pfalzder 'Winterkönig' von Böhmen (1596–1632)* (Heidelberg, 2004). For illustrated exhibition catalogues, see P. Wolf, M. Henker, E. Brockhoff, B. Steinherr and S. Lippold (eds), *Der Winterkönig Friedrich V. Der letzte Kurfürst aus der oberen Pfalz. Amberg, Heidelberg, Prag, Den Haag* (Augsburg, 2003); J. Laschinger (ed.), *Der Winterkönig: Königlicher Glanz in Amberg* (Amberg, 2004); S. Groenveld, *De winterkoning:balling aan het Haagse hof* (The Hague, 2003).

and Bohemian Empire. This lasted thirty full years, and was foretold by the comet … which appeared in 1618'.[3]

People, Land and Government

The Palatinate in 1618 reminds us that early seventeenth-century imperial estates, especially the principalities, had little in common with the modern, territorial nation-state and its extensive bureaucratic apparatus. An imperial estate was a community, an ordering of people, with political, legal, social, religious, economic, cultural and other ramifications, supported by the fruits of the people labouring on the land. The estate was usually embodied in a person, the prince, who, with his court, occupied the centre of political, cultural, artistic, economic, military and administrative influence in his estate, regardless of the actual place of residence.[4] As the loci of authority, prestige and honour, princes were the founts of patronage and preferment, the key to advancement in state, society, scholarship and frequently the church as well.[5] Princes usually received their authority, titles and dignity by right of inheritance and were expected to hold on to them until death. They were not office holders or bureaucrats; office holders were the prince's servants, supposedly for the good of the community of his subjects. Of course theory differed from practice, given the interest and ability of each individual prince, but the expectations were clear enough. Still, no prince was as absolute as he probably would have liked. Without the consent and support of his family, dynasty, household, noblemen, servants and many other people, the prince would have been just one man among many. According to Jeremy Black, 'the essentially contractual nature of government inherited from the Middle Ages prevailed, whatever its constitutional or political form; and the conviction that rulers were answerable to God did not absolve them from the need to govern legally and to avoid arbitrary rule'.[6]

When it comes to the history of the Thirty Years' War, the Elector Palatine counted more than the Palatinate. In the preceding three centuries, these princes, all members of the Wittelsbach dynasty, had developed for themselves a unique position of power in the Holy Roman Empire. Although sovereign in his estate, like the other six imperial electors, only the Elector Palatine could sit in judgement of the emperor if he were prosecuted by the archbishop-electors. The Elector Palatine was also one of the two imperial vicars who were supposed to rule in the emperor's stead during a period of interregnum. The last Elector Palatine to be elected King of the Romans was Ruprecht (r. 1400–10).[7] Since 1437 the Habsburgs had occupied the topmost seat in the empire. The Elector Palatine in 1618 ruled over about 600,000 commoners, making the Palatine estate one of the more populous in the empire, exceeded by Bohemia and Saxony each with over one million and Bavaria with 800,000.

---

[3] G. Mortimer, 'Did Contemporaries Recognize a "Thirty Years War"?', *The English Historical Review*, 116/465 (2001): pp. 124–36.

[4] In imperial free cities, an oligarchic council of urban magnates usually occupied the centre.

[5] For an interdisciplinary analysis of early modern courts, see J. Adamson, 'Introduction. The Making of the Ancien-Régime Court 1500–1700', in J. Adamson (ed.), *The Princely Courts of Europe. Ritual, Politics and Culture under the Ancien Régime 1500–1750* (London, 1999), pp. 7–41.

[6] J. Black, 'States and Societies in Early Modern Europe: A Revisionist Approach', *Historically Speaking*, xii/2 (2011): pp. 40–41.

[7] Ruprecht did not receive the imperial title, but there was no prince in the empire with higher dignity.

The Elector Palatine's land-holdings were extensive but not as big as Bohemia, Bavaria or Saxony in terms of total area. Unlike these more condensed estates, however, the Palatinate was fragmented, first cut into two separate parts, the Lower and the Upper Palatinates, then both of these fissured and scattered by the presence of numerous neighbouring and interspersing estates under the lordship of other princes and municipalities of the empire.[8]

The many districts of the Lower Palatinate centred around the area where the Neckar River flows into the Rhine, south of the archbishoprics of Trier and Mainz. In this region the Lower Palatinate was dispersed into more than a dozen separate parcels of land, with centres of authority based in towns such as Simmern, Kreuznach, Alzey, Oppenheim, Frankenthal, Mannheim, Heidelberg, Neustadt, Kaiserslautern, Germersheim, Mosbach and Umstadt. The Lower Palatinate's main strongholds were the fortress towns of Heidelberg, Mannheim and Frankenthal, garrisoned by the elector's standing army of 15,000 men. None of the many old castles perched on hilltops was able to house an army of significance. Apart from the three centres of military power, the Lower Palatinate was basically indefensible, especially in the outlying districts. There were no distinct, cohesive borders and no systematic border controls. This complexity and fragmentation rendered them impossible to defend.

The Lower Palatinate boasted one of the most temperate climates in Germany and exceptionally fertile lands, especially in the valley of the Rhine, which sustained the vast majority of the principality's population. There the Palatinate's fields, hills and forests produced grains for beer and bread, corn, fruits, nuts and supported sheep and other livestock. The slopes of the low mountain ranges west and east of the Rhine provided grapes for the Palatinate's famous wines, and further west a dramatic landscape of hundreds of densely forested hills offered timber and game. The Lower Palatinate's agricultural wealth sustained its relatively dense population living in towns, villages and hamlets.[9] The towns, the largest and most important being Heidelberg, hosted wine merchants, cloth workers, artisans, metalworkers and goldsmiths. Revenues from land rents, fees, taxes, customs and tolls on the traffic on the Rhine sustained the elector's court.

The Palatine court had its seat in the beautiful Heidelberg *Schloss* (castle) with its famous gardens, the *Hortus Palatinus*, both icons of Renaissance art and architecture.[10] The *Schloss* also housed the famous *Großer Fass*, an enormous barrel, built in 1589–91, that held 130,000 litres of wine. Heidelberg also boasted Germany's oldest university, founded in 1381. The faculty was small in the early seventeenth century, with about 20 professors on average,

---

[8] The full complexity of the electorate is detailed in W. Dotzauer, *Der historische Raum des Bundeslandes Rheinland-Pfalz von 1500–1815: Die fürstliche Politik für Reich und Land, ihre Krisen und Zusammenbrüche* (Frankfurt am Main, 1993), and H. Probst, *Die Pfalz als historischer Begriff* (2 vols, Mannheim, 1984). Probst's second volume is a collection of 14 facsimile maps of the Palatinate from the sixteenth to the eighteenth centuries. Another useful overview is M. Schaab, *Geschichte der Kurpfalz* (2 vols, Stuttgart, 1988, 1992), vol. 2. The *Institut für Fränkisch-Pfälzische Geschichte und Landeskunde* at the Ruprecht-Karls-Universität at Heidelberg (http://www.fpi.uni-hd.de) offers a virtual library about the Palatine electorate, *Geschichte der Kurpfalz*, with a useful map, bibliography, sources and other valuable information.

[9] The neighbouring duchy of Pfalz-Zweibrücken, by contrast, in the forested region to the west, had only 10,000 males over the age of 18 in 1606.

[10] For a thorough analysis of the gardens, see R. Patterson, 'The "Hortus Palatinatus" at Heidelberg and the Reformation of the World. Part I: The Iconography of the Garden', *Journal of Garden History*, i/1 (1981): pp. 67–104, and 'The "Hortus Palatinatus" at Heidelberg and the Reformation of the World. Part II: Culture as Science', *Journal of Garden History*, i/2 (1981), pp. 179–202. Concerning recent attempts to produce a digital rendition of the garden, see R. Leiner and S. Schmickl, 'Eine virtuelle 3D-Rekonstruktion des einstigen Heidelberger Schlossgartens (Hortus Palatinatus)', *Zeitschrift für die Geschichte des Oberrheins*, 151 (2003): pp. 175–98. On the arts at Frederick V's court, see A. Frese, F. Hepp and R. Ludwig (eds), *Der Winterkönig. Heidelberg zwischen höfischer Pracht und Dreißigjährigem Krieg* (Remshalden, 2004).

teaching and researching in arts (philosophy, logic and humanities), medicine, law and theology.[11] Under Elector Palatine Frederick IV, new chairs were founded for universal history and the Arabic language. The medical faculty offered public anatomical instruction using human dissection in 1574 and perhaps earlier. In 1600, the university opened its own press and bookstore. A mark of the university's prestige is the fact that roughly one third of matriculated students were foreigners. In 1618–19, Elector Palatine Frederick V sent three Heidelberg theologians to the famous Synod of Dordrecht in order to promote the Heidelberg Catechism of 1563.[12] The prince's library in Heidelberg, the *Bibliotheca Palatina*, was perhaps the greatest collection north of the Alps at the outbreak of the Thirty Years' War. The ruling princes of the Palatinate used their patronage to shape and support the university for the sake of supplying their subjects with teachers, clergymen, lawyers, administrators and doctors.

More or less in the middle of the elector's territories, on both sides of the Rhine, were a host of other imperial estates, ostensibly independent of the Elector Palatine: the imperial free cities of Worms and Speyer, the archbishopric of Worms, the bishopric of Speyer, the landgraviate of Hessen-Darmstadt and 60 imperial knights with holdings in the Palatinate, about half residing there. Some of these knights, such as the Hirschhorn, had large landholdings as big as some of the counties in the empire, while others had a little castle to their name, or just a subdivision of one. Some of these knights owed fidelity to the Elector Palatine, others to the Holy Roman Emperor directly, making allegiance a complex issue. The members of the Upper Rhine Knighthood elected a committee to represent them at meetings in Mainz, where they were supposed to make common decisions about political matters.[13]

Over 150 miles to the east of Heidelberg, in a forested region at a higher elevation, the smaller, poorer Upper Palatinate sustained a population of approximately 180,000, with slightly less than 20 per cent living in towns surrounded by medieval walls, none larger than Amberg, which had only about 5,000 residents. For centuries the Upper Palatinate's main source of wealth had been its iron and tin mines and hundreds of forges, foundries and hard-working smiths, but these industries were in decline by the early seventeenth century. Brewing wheat-beer, however, was on the rise. The economy of the region was overwhelmingly agricultural, operating just above subsistence and generally less productive than in the Lower Palatinate.[14]

The Upper Palatinate, like the Lower, lacked territorial and jurisdictional cohesion, although the fragmentation was not as extreme. The duke of Pfalz-Neuburg ruled lands bordering the Upper Palatinate to the south, and the prince of Pfalz-Sulzbach controlled territories in the middle that nearly severed the Upper Palatinate in two. The county of

---

[11] P.F. Grendler, 'The Universities of the Renaissance and Reformation', *Renaissance Quarterly*, 57/1 (2004), pp. 1–42. The number of faculty does not include arts teachers with bachelor's or master's degrees.

[12] A.L. Thomas, *A House Divided: Wittelsbach Confessional Court Cultures in the Holy Roman Empire, C. 1550–1650* (Leiden, 2010), p. 141. Andreas Cser, *Kleine Geschichte der Stadt und Universität Heidelberg* (Karlsruhe, 2007), p. 96.

[13] F. Maier, 'Die Reichsritterschaft im Pfälzer Raum während des Dreißigjährigen Krieges', *Mitteilungen des historischen Vereins der Pfalz*, 108 (2010): pp. 491–506. When Frederick V invited the Protestant imperial knights in the Palatinate to attend a meeting of the Protestant Union held in Nürnberg in 1619, the group agreed to maintain their unity and neutrality with regard to the crisis in Bohemia.

[14] T. Johnson, *Magistrates, Madonnas and Miracles: The Counter Reformation in the Upper Palatinate* (Farnham, 2009), pp. 17–26. For a tantalising argument about iron and tin investments supplying a possible motive for Frederick V's bid for the Bohemian crown, see P. Wolf, 'Eisen aus der Oberpfalz, Zinn aus Böhmen und die goldene böhmische Krone', in P. Wolf et al. (eds), *Der Winterkönig Friedrich V*, pp. 65–74.

Cham was autonomous, and the bishops of Regensburg, Bamberg and Eichstätt each administered their own small territories in the region. The Landgrave of Leuchtenberg ruled his little dominion in the middle of the Upper Palatinate, and, further south, the Elector Palatine governed two parishes just outside the walls of the city of Regensburg, the seat of the bishopric. The Elector Palatine's appointed governor of the Upper Palatinate, who was based in Amberg or Neumarkt, tried to govern these districts and towns on behalf of his distant, usually absent prince. Two hundred families in the Upper Palatinate enjoyed the privilege of lordship, including the administration of justice for lesser crimes and sometimes the right to appoint local clergy as well. They lived in hilltop castles and more fashionable country houses, drawing their wealth from the work of peasants, miners and craftsmen alike. Simple people living in villages and hamlets had little choice but to obey their rule.[15]

What held it all together? Nothing was more important than personal loyalty to the reigning members of the Wittelsbach dynasty, namely, the prince, his relatives, their spouses and their collective associates. This is not to say Palatine government was not developing as in the rest of Western Europe. Since 1480 a law code was in place that regulated marital relations, inheritance, fief and lien, trespass and crimes of violence, including court procedure and the appeal process.[16] This legal system had been uniformly imposed on all residents of the elector's lands in 1582. The Elector Palatine's central government included three top officials (High Steward (*Großhofmeister*), Chancellor and Marshall) supported by councils for the prince, court and church, various courts of law, chancellery, exchequer, etc., such offices occupied by a mix of noblemen and qualified commoners.[17] But around 1500, the elector also held the at least nominal fidelity of 500 fief-holders along the Rhine and Neckar, in, among and beyond the range of his own estates. Many of these and other members of the lesser nobility in the region belonged to the Palatine order of knighthood.[18] The Wittelsbach family ruled by right of birth.

In 1618, the elector's brother, Count Palatine Ludwig Philipp (1602–1655) ruled a northwestern subdivision of the Palatinate including Simmern, Sponheim and Lautern, and another line of the Wittelsbach dynasty, descendents of Ruprecht, King of the Romans, ruled the duchy of Pfalz-Zweibrücken west of the Palatinate. The fact that Elector Palatine Frederick IV chose his relative, Duke Johann II of Pfalz-Zweibrücken, to govern the Palatine electorate as regent until Frederick V reached his majority shows the trust between the two Wittelsbach family lines. When Frederick V left for Bohemia in 1619, he also called on Duke Johann to rule the Palatinate during his absence.[19]

A close associate of the Wittelsbachs, Prince Christian of Anhalt, served as *Statthalter* of the Upper Palatinate for 25 years under Fredericks IV and V until 1621.[20] His loyalty to the elector in Heidelberg was unquestioned, but his distance from that court inevitably restricted

---

[15] See V. Press, 'Die Grundlagen der kurpfälzischen Herrschaft in der Oberpfalz 1499–1621', in *Verhandlungen des Historischen Vereins für Oberpfalz und Regensburg*, 117 (1977): pp. 31–67.

[16] S. Weinfurter, *Das Reich im Mittelalter: Kleine deutsche Geschichte von 500 bis 1500* (Munich, 2008), pp. 217–8. Also see H.J. Cohn, *The Government of the Rhine Palatinate in the Fifteenth Century* (Oxford, 1965) for a full description.

[17] For an exhaustive description of Palatine government, see V. Press, *Calvinismus und Territorialstaat. Regierung und Zentralbehörden der Kurpfalz 1559–1619* (Stuttgart, 1970).

[18] Probst, *Die Pfalz als historischer Begriff* (2 vols., Mannheim, 1984), i, p. 50.

[19] Still other Palatine Wittelsbach lines, such as Pfalz-Veldenz, Pfalz-Sulzbach and Pfalz-Birkenfeld, are detailed in Probst, *Die Pfalz als historischer Begriff*, pp. 32–40.

[20] There is no scholarly monograph about Christian von Anhalt, but a posthumously published article by V. Press provides a good overview. See V. Press, F. Brendle and A. Schindling (eds), 'Fürst Christian I. von Anhalt-Bernburg, Statthalter der Oberpfalz, Haupt der evangelischen Bewegungspartei vor dem dreißigjährigen Krieg (1568–1630)', in K. Ackermann and A. Schmid (eds), *Staat und Verwaltung in Bayern. Festschrift für Wilhelm Volkert zum 75. Geburtstag* (Munich, 2003), pp. 193–216.

his influence on its decisions. Mainly through correspondence, Anhalt enthusiastically encouraged war between Protestants and Catholics in the empire and beyond, especially in the years following 1608, but his plans usually came to nothing. Oddly, during his years as *Statthalter*, Anhalt did nothing to improve the Upper Palatinate's defence works, as if he considered the region militarily insignificant.

The Elector Palatine's government was financially precarious, despite the agricultural, mineral and mercantile wealth of the Palatinate. Deficit spending was the norm. In 1602, the elector could expect an annual income of approximately 285,000 Gulden, against annual expenses of 430,000, and the total debt was 1.5 million Gulden. When Frederick V assumed the reins of power, it reached 1.8 million. Frederick's estate lacked the means to finance a major war on its own.

Religion and Confessionalisation

By the mid-sixteenth century, the Palatinate had instituted the Reformation: the electors closed monasteries and convents, revised doctrine and liturgy and placed the regulation of religion in the principality under the direct control of the prince and his Church Council (*Kirchenrat*). Confessional shifting, however, from Lutheranism to Calvinism in the 1560s and 1570s, then back to Lutheranism in 1576–1583, and then again to Calvinism in the later 1580s guaranteed instability and confusion.[21] Each change involved replacing clergy, university professors and governing officials, distributing new books and catechisms, adjusting rites, some iconoclasm and, at times, involved popular resistance and violent protests. Success was mixed. In 1593–95, authorities in Heidelberg found that only one third of heads of households could recite the Ten Commandments, the Apostles' Creed and the Lord's Prayer, or could explain baptism, the eucharist, salvation and faith according to Calvin's teaching.[22] Beyond the electorate's capital city, the level of knowledge must have been considerably worse, despite the widely available resource of the Heidelberg Catechism.[23]

The Upper Palatinate was a case in point. Calvinism was largely unwelcome and imposed on the populace, common and elite alike. The Elector Palatine, Frederick IV, took up residence himself in Amberg in 1596–98 to oversee official establishment of Calvinism in those territories, but the project had to accept the limitations of reality. In 1598, when the authorities ordered weekly training in Calvinist doctrine, they directed teachers to avoid the controversies that divided Lutherans and Calvinists. By 1618, the Upper Palatinate was still largely Lutheran, focusing on reading scriptures, hearing sermons, and singing psalms in schools and churches. Visitations showed slow progress, if any, in terms of literacy, knowledge of the Lord's Prayer, the Decalogue, and the Creed. The situation was slightly better in the towns than in the rural villages. In some parishes, despite decades of imposed Protestantism, the religious culture of the general populace maintained customs and beliefs closer to those of the Catholic Church before the Council of Trent.[24]

---

[21] D. MacCulloch recommends the term 'Reformed Protestantism' over 'Calvinism'. See D. MacCulloch, M. Laven, E. Duffy, 'Recent Trends in the Study of Christianity in Sixteenth-Century Europe', *Renaissance Quarterly*, 59/3 (2006): pp. 697–731.

[22] H. J. Cohn, 'The Territorial Princes of Germany's Second Reformation, 1559–1622', in M. Prestwich (ed.), *International Calvinism* (Oxford, 1985), p. 161.

[23] B. Vogler, 'Die Entstehung der Protestantischen Volksfrömmigkeit in der Rheinischen Pfalz zwischen 1555 und 1619', *Archiv für Reformationsgeschichte*, 72 (1981), pp. 158–96, 161–2.

[24] Johnson, *Magistrates*, pp. 27–39.

Many historians have fought for and against the confessionalisation thesis. Did the elite regime of prince, court and church create and impose group identities based on Christian confession, using various methods of indoctrination and social discipline, and did this process contribute to the development of the modern state and modernity itself?[25] The debate goes on, but few can deny that princes certainly intended and endeavoured to bring their people's faith into line with their own, no matter how well or badly they managed to carry out such a project. With some ingenuity, the Palatinate can be used as an example either way.

In the first decades of the seventeenth century, the elector's church was of necessity as tolerant as it was Calvinist. Fully aware of the sizeable Lutheran minority in the Lower Palatinate and the majority in the Upper, the electors supported irenic dialogue between Calvinist and Lutheran divines. By 1608, the elector had issued toleration edicts for Lutherans, Catholics, and even sectarian Christians residing in the electorate, as long as they practised their religion privately and lived in an orderly, quiet manner.[26]

Throughout the Palatinate, as elsewhere in early seventeenth-century Europe, the parish was synonymous with the community. The parish church stood in the middle of the settled area, its bell measuring time and marking events of significance, whether markets, festivals or grave emergencies. Confessional fluctuations and diversity in the region, however, frayed parish unity and uniformity. Still, co-existence was the norm. The few Catholics that remained in the Lower Palatinate went to the neighbouring bishopric of Speyer to attend Mass, for example, and Speyer's Calvinists in the other direction for Sunday services in the bordering villages.[27] Reality on the ground often differed gravely from the plans and papers discussed in the elector's privy and church councils.

While Heidelberg's theologians did not refrain from anti-Catholic polemic, they did not share in the apocalyptical expectations of some of the members of the Palatine court such as Christian of Anhalt. The Palatine irenic tradition welcomed the grounding of the Protestant Union in 1608, but did not promote the idea that a conspiracy of the Pope, Spain and the Habsburgs would attempt to wipe out Protestantism in the empire.[28]

---

[25] The scholarship concerning confessionalisation is enormous and still growing. For contrasting examples, see W. Reinhard and H. Schilling (eds), *Die katholische Konfessionalisierung* (Münster, 1995) and M. Forster, *Catholic Revival in the Age of the Baroque: Religious Identity in Southwest Germany, 1550–1750* (Cambridge, 2001).

[26] See G. Brinkmann, *Die Irenik des David Pareus: Frieden und Einheit in ihrer Relevanz zur Wahrheitsfrage* (Hildesheim, 1972); G.A. Benrath, 'Abraham Scultetus (1566–1624)', in K. Baumann (ed.), *Pfälzer Lebensbilder* (Speyer, 1970), pp. 97–116. On confessional toleration in the Palatinate, see Press, *Calvinismus und Territorialstaat*, pp. 514–51.

[27] M. Forster, *The Counter-Reformation in the Villages: Religion and Reform in the Bishopric of Speyer, 1560–1720* (Ithaca, 1992), p. 132 n. 54, 134–5. For a wider study about this practice of *Auslauf* and the use of clandestine churches, see B.J. Kaplan, 'Fictions of Privacy: House Chapels and the Spatial Accommodation of Religious Dissent in Early Modern Europe', *The American Historical Review*, 107/4 (2002): pp. 1031–64.

[28] See T. Sarx, 'Heidelberger Irenik am Vorabend des Dreißigjährigen Krieges', in A. Ernst and A. Schindling (eds), *Union und Liga 1608/09. Konfessionelle Bündnisse im Reich – Weichenstellung zum Religionskrieg?* (Stuttgart, 2010), pp. 167–96.

Networks

In 1618 Elector Palatine Frederick V's contacts and connections, both within the Holy Roman Empire and beyond, came as much from his family as from his confession.[29] The most important, formal network was the Protestant Union, also known as the Union of Auhausen, founded by his father and his associates in 1608. Established by the Lutheran and Calvinist princes of the Palatinate, Württemberg, Baden-Durlach, Ansbach, Kulmbach and Pfalz-Neuburg, the Union did not move the empire toward inevitable religious war but attempted to retain influence for Protestants and equilibrium with Catholics. The Union expanded quickly at first, adding the princes of Zweibrücken, Anhalt, electoral Brandenburg, Hessen-Kassel and imperial free cities such as Ulm, Straßburg and Nürnberg within two years, but the new association remained limited in scope and aim. The members never sought to set up a Protestant shadow state in the empire but to maintain the balance between the emperor's authority and the freedom of the estates to maintain their cultural and confessional diversity.[30] Moreover, the necessarily divergent local concerns of the Union princes and cities prevented the group from becoming anything more than a defensive alliance of the last resort, if at all.

The Union's first military action showed its lack of cohesion. In June 1610, troops from four Union member estates (the Palatinate, Hessen-Kassel, Ansbach and Baden-Durlach), without consulting the others, crossed the Rhine and attacked towns in Alsace where the Hapsburg Archduke Leopold was supposedly gathering arms and building up a military force. They killed dozens, perhaps as many as a hundred people, in the act. Other Union members regarded the deed as offensive. The Union was unquestionably part of the Elector Palatine's network in the empire and beyond, but the association was never meant to supplant the members' loyalty to the emperor. Frederick V's acquisition of Bohemia forced the issue, and almost all Union members rapidly shrank from the conflict, declared their neutrality and dissolved the alliance.[31]

Palatine relations with Britain were strong but complicated.[32] Frederick V's greatest personal and political triumph was to win the hand of Elizabeth Stuart, daughter of James I and VI, king of England, Scotland and Ireland, in 1613.[33] The wedding festivities were notably extravagant, and the many entertainments and literary compositions have produced great interest among scholars.[34] King James spent £93,293 on the celebrations, supposedly

---

[29] With diplomatic history out of fashion, most of the published research in this area is decades old. C.-P. Clasen, *The Palatinate in European History* (Oxford, 1963), provides a basic overview, but the text completely politicises the Calvinist confession and consigns the Palatine electors and their supporters to the same 'aggressiveness' routinely ascribed to communists throughout the world in one of the most heated phases of the Cold War. Many factual errors mar the text as well. A superior study, despite its age, is M. Prestwich (ed.), *International Calvinism, 1541–1715* (Oxford, 1985).

[30] G. Schmidt, 'Die Union und das Heilige Römische Reich deutscher Nation', in A. Ernst and A. Schindling (eds), *Union und Liga 1608/09. Konfessionelle Bündnisse im Reich – Weichenstellung zum Religionskrieg?* (Stuttgart, 2010), pp. 9–28.

[31] A. Gotthard, 'Norm und Kalkül. Über Württemberg, Baden und die Union von Auhausen', in Ernst, *Union und Liga*, pp. 29–61.

[32] For a highly theoretical and eclectic treatise on these relations, see M. Rüde, *England und Kurpfalz im werdenden Mächteeuropa (1608–1632). Konfession – Dynastie – Kulturelle Ausdrucksformen* (Stuttgart, 2007).

[33] There is no recent scholarly monograph of Elizabeth Stuart, but her letters have been published. See N. Akkerman (ed.), *The Correspondence of Elizabeth Stuart, Queen of Bohemia* (3 vols, Oxford, 2011–12). Also see M. Lemberg, *Eine Königin ohne Reich. Das Leben der Winterkönigin Elisabeth Stuart und ihre Briefe nach Hessen* (Marburg, 1996).

[34] The most complete treatment is C. Ginzel, *Poetry, Politics and Promises of Empire: Prophetic Rhetoric in the English and Neo-Latin Epithalamia on the occasion of the Palatine Marriage in 1613* (Göttingen, 2009). Also see L. Piepho, 'Making the Impossible Dream: Latin, Print, and the Marriage of Frederick V and

more than on 10 years of building and maintaining all his palaces in England.[35] Despite rather bellicose wedding panegyrics that frequently invoked Protestantism's struggle with the papacy, King James preferred a pacific foreign policy.[36] Also in 1613–14, James pursued a marriage between his son, Charles, and the Spanish Hapsburg Infanta Maria, daughter of King Philip III, a tantalising prospect that lasted until 1623. Pursuing such diverse marriages sent mixed messages, but when Frederick accepted the proffered crown of Bohemia in 1619, James condemned the move in no uncertain terms.

As for James's other kingdoms, Scotland may be considered part of the Palatine network. Many Scots, officers and soldiers, went to war in the empire on behalf of Elizabeth Stuart. The Elector Palatine and his wife relied on the services of Scottish diplomats such as James Hay, Earl of Carlisle, Sir James Spens, Andrew Sinclair and Sir Robert Anstruther to try to extract money and military commitments from the leaders of Denmark, Sweden, and the Dutch Republic.[37] The Elector Palatine had no official connections with any notable figures from Ireland. Most of the Irish who came to fight in the empire did so on behalf of the Habsburgs, the Catholic League, and Poland, but 89 are known to have fought for the Palatinate and other Protestant powers.[38]

After the wedding was over, the pair travelled to Heidelberg, an eight-week, 1,200 km journey, from April to June 1613, considered 'one of the most spectacular and memorable royal progresses of the era'.[39] It also revealed the names and nature of Frederick V's connections on the Continent.

In the United Provinces of the Netherlands, which had joined the Protestant Union in 1613, Frederick and Elizabeth visited more than a dozen towns, costing the Estates General at least £20,000. Frederick's mother, Electress Dowager Louise Juliana, was the daughter of William of Orange and connected to the dynasty of Nassau, which had supplied leaders in the Netherlands and court advisors and military commanders for the Palatinate. While in the United Provinces, the pair visited a Jesuit church in Emmerich and spent a night at a nunnery in Rhenen, gestures demonstrating their tolerance.

Further up the Rhine in Bonn, they met Johann Sigismund von Hohenzollern, the margrave-elector of Brandenburg, a member of the Union and the only other Calvinist

---

the Princess Elizabeth', *Reformation*, 14 (2009), pp. 127–59; K. Curran, 'James I and Fictional Authority at the Palatine Wedding Celebrations', *Renaissance Studies*, 20 (2006): pp. 50–67; G. Gömöri, '"A Memorable Wedding": The Literary Reception of the Wedding of the Princess Elizabeth and Frederick of Pfalz', *Journal of European Studies*, 34/3 (2004): pp. 215–24; J. Miller, *Falcký Mýthus. Fridrich V. a obraz české války v raněstuartovské Anglii* (Prague, 2004); H. Werner, '*The Hector of Germanie, or The Palsgrave, Prime Elector* and Anglo-German relations of early Stuart England: the view from the popular stage', in R. Malcolm Smuts (ed.), *The Stuart court and Europe: Essays in politics and political culture* (Cambridge, 1996), pp. 113–32; G. Schmitz, 'Die Hochzeit von Themse und Rhein: Gelegenheitsschriften zur Brautfahrt des Kurfürsten Friedrich V. von der Pfalz', *Daphnis*, 22 (1993): pp. 265–309. The Herzog August Bibliothek at Wolfenbüttel has put some of the German literary sources online: http://www.hab.de/bibliothek/wdb/festkultur/index-e.htm. The British Library has done the same with texts in English and French: http://www.bl.uk/treasures/festivalbooks/homepage.html.

[35] Curran, 'James I and fictional authority at the Palatine wedding celebrations'. Adamson, 'Introduction. The Making of the Ancien-Régime Court 1500–1700', p. 35.

[36] See W. B. Patterson, *King James VI and I and the Reunion of Christendom* (Cambridge, 1997). James commissioned Thomas Campion to write *The Lord's Masque* for performance on the wedding night. See W. R. Davis, *The Works of Thomas Campion* (New York, 1970).

[37] S. Murdoch (ed.), *Scotland and the Thirty Years' War, 1618–1648* (Leiden, 2001).

[38] D. Worthington, 'Towards a Bibliography of the Irish in Central Europe, 1618–1648', *Archivium hibernicum; or Irish Historical Records*, 56 (2002): pp. 206–27.

[39] On the logistics and expenses, see M. Brayshay, 'The Choreography of Journeys of Magnificence: Arranging the Post-Nuptial Progress of Frederick, the Elector Palatine, and Princess Elizabeth of England from London to Heidelberg in 1613', *Journal of Early Modern History*, 12 (2008): pp. 383–408.

elector of the empire.⁴⁰ One year later, Johann Sigismund would marry his son, Georg Wilhelm, to Frederick's sister, Elisabeth, further strengthening the bond between the two princes and their principalities. Continuing on their progress, Frederick and Elizabeth dined with the Catholic archbishop-elector of Mainz, Johann Schweikard von Kronberg, the archchancellor of the empire, the most influential of the three archbishop-electors in the electoral college. Confessional differences did not prevent hospitality between neighbouring princes, but discretion kept the stay short, to one night. The elector of Mainz gave Elizabeth the apartments reserved for the Holy Roman Emperor and his own private suite for Frederick's use.⁴¹ On the same journey, the young couple also met the archbishop-electors of Cologne and Trier. Despite differences in Christian confession, the reality of proximity and status, the fact that the Elector Palatine and the archbishop-electors were neighbours and colleagues in the empire, did not preclude basic hospitality and courtesy.

Frederick and Elizabeth also stopped in Worms, the main town of a miniscule bishopric, all but encircled by Palatine lands. It posed no threat, but there were tensions appropriate to the time period. Frederick complained to the bishop in 1618 about the growing number of Jesuits and their activities in or near Palatine territory. Palatine tolerance pertained to the status quo; it did not include Catholic evangelisation. Relations with the town and bishopric of Speyer were similar: neighbourliness had been the norm for centuries, right through the Reformation. The Palatine electors did not try to annex the bishopric of Speyer and the bishops tried to avoid incurring the electors' ire. Problems about church and school attendance and processions flared up from time to time, but the elector only sent in troops in 1609, in order to free peasants imprisoned by the bishop in a local insurrection. A real crisis began in 1617, when Bishop Philipp von Sötern began to build up the fortifications around the town of Udenheim, later known as Philippsburg. Frederick V complained, with the full support of the imperial free city of Speyer and the duke of Württemberg, insisting on Palatine rights of self-defence, free passage and open access to the castle, rights inherited from the later Middle Ages.⁴² The bishop for his part pleaded self-defence, but a fortress at Udenheim could have been used by other military powers, such as those of Spain or the Catholic league. The bishop made assurances but kept on building. After more than a year of fruitless complaints, in June 1618 troops from the Palatinate, Württemberg and the city of Speyer occupied the town and tore down the fortress. The bishop riposted with lawsuits.

Georg Friedrich, the Calvinist Margrave of Baden-Durlach, and Johann Friedrich, the Lutheran duke of Württemberg, both Palatine neighbours and Union members, came to Heidelberg to greet Princess Elizabeth on her arrival in her new home. Frederick V's relations with nearby Lutheran princes were generally amiable, but shared confession did not guarantee identical interests.⁴³ Landgrave Moritz of Hessen-Kassel, a Calvinist, tried to push Frederick and the Union to be more open and responsive to Lutherans in other parts of the empire. Landgrave Moritz had close contact with the Lutheran princes of Hessen-Darmstadt and electoral Saxony, and, perhaps out of jealousy, Moritz did not want to see the Union become a military tool to serve Palatine interests alone.

---

⁴⁰ On the Elector of Brandenburg, see B. Nischan, *Prince, People and Confession. The Second Reformation in Brandenburg* (Philadelphia, 1994).
⁴¹ Brayshay, 'The Choreography of Journeys of Magnificence', pp. 389–90.
⁴² V. Schmidtchen (ed.), *Festung im Spiegel der Quellen* (Wesel, 1988), pp. 43–4.
⁴³ On the duke of Württemberg, see A. Gotthard, *Konfession und Staatsräson: Die Außenpolitik Württembergs unter Herzog Johann Friedrich (1608–1628)* (Stuttgart, 1992). Court officials of the Palatinate and Württemberg, however, did quarrel about proper terms of address for their respective reigning princes. See Gregor Richter, 'Stuttgarter Quellen zu kurpfälzisch-württembergischen Titulaturstreitigkeiten 1583–1618', *Zeitschrift für die Geschichte des Oberrheins*, 147 (1999): pp. 381–92.

The Upper Palatinate widened Frederick's network further. First and foremost was the kingdom of Bohemia, under the control of the Habsburg kings and Holy Roman Emperors. Since 1608, a Palatine agent resided in Prague to represent the elector's interests to the monarchy and the Estates of Bohemia. Leander Ruppel served in this capacity during the crisis in Bohemia that ushered in the Thirty Years' War. Other Catholic neighbours of the Upper Palatinate included the bishops of Eichstätt and Regensburg, and Wolfgang Wilhelm, duke of Pfalz-Neuburg, a Wittelsbach relative who had converted to Catholicism in 1613, acquired Jülich and Berg in the Rhineland, and married Magdalena, the sister of Duke Maximilian of Bavaria. Lutheran neighbours of the Upper Palatinate included Joachim Ernst, Margrave of Ansbach, Christian, Margrave of Kulmbach, both members of the Protestant Union, and, most important, Johann Georg, the duke of Saxony, who valued his close relations with the Habsburg emperors more than with Union members, Johann Georg's Lutheranism notwithstanding.[44]

To the south of the Upper Palatinate lay the duchy of Bavaria, ruled by another branch of the Wittelsbach family. Palatine relations with their Bavarian cousins were particularly fraught with dynastic and Calvinist–Catholic rivalry.[45] Duke Maximilian, in corresponding with his brother, the archbishop-elector of Cologne, mentioned the possibility of converting Frederick V to Catholicism, which was wildly unrealistic. But just as unlikely was Frederick's attempt to persuade his Bavarian cousin to support his acquisition of Bohemia, or, for that matter, to bring Duke Maximilian to stand for election to the throne of the Holy Roman Emperor against the Habsburg dynasty.[46]

Two more kingdoms lay on the periphery of the Palatine network: Denmark and France. That Elizabeth Stuart was a niece of the king of Denmark, Christian IV, helped to strengthen the ties between Frederick V and that prince, who as duke of Holstein also led the Lower Saxon Circle. King Christian would take up arms in the 1620s on behalf of the Palatines, but only after the war first came to his doorstep.[47] Regarding France, the francophone Palatine court had military and financial support to Henry of Navarre during the wars that ravaged France in the later sixteenth century, but when Henry became king, he quickly distanced himself from the Palatine elector. In 1619, King Louis XIII and Cardinal Richelieu did not acknowledge Frederick's claim to the throne of Bohemia and stayed out of the conflict until the 1630s.[48]

In 1614, at the age of 18, Frederick V signed his last testament, indicating his priorities for the Palatinate and the allies he thought he could trust most. In the event of his death, he named his eldest son the heir of the electorate and stipulated that it remain Calvinist. The guardians would be Frederick's brother, Ludwig Philipp, and if he were yet too young, then Duke Johann II of Zweibrücken, Frederick's Wittelsbach relative, who was also married to his sister, Louise Juliane. As executors Frederick named King James I and his son, Charles, the Protestant Union and the Estates General of the United Provinces.[49]

---

[44] See H.-J. Herold, *Markgraf Joachim Ernst von Brandenburg-Ansbach als Reichsfürst* (Göttingen, 1973), and A. Gotthard, '"Politice seint wir bäpstisch". Kursachsen und der deutsche Protestantismus im frühen 17. Jahrhundert', *Zeitschrift für Historische Forschung*, 20/3 (1993): pp. 275–319.

[45] For a superb study of this long-standing, complicated relationship, particularly with regard to court culture and patronage, Renaissance humanism and marital ties, see Thomas, *A House Divided*.

[46] Thomas, *A House Divided*, p. 186. Pursell, *The Winter King*, pp. 68–70.

[47] See P. D. Lockhart, *Denmark in the Thirty Years' War, 1618–1648: King Christian IV and the Decline of the Oldenburg State* (Selinsgrove, 1996).

[48] R. Bireley, *The Jesuits and the Thirty Years' War: Kings, Courts, and Confessors* (Cambridge, 2003), p. 47.

[49] Press, *Calvinismus and Territorialstaat*, pp. 507–8.

Frederick V's attempt to win Bohemia backfired, and the ensuing war devastated his lands. The people of the Palatinate suffered terribly for it, while the prince lived out his days as an expensive, undesirable guest in the Netherlands.[50] Perhaps he should have listened to Thomas More's Raphael, who advised the king of France to stay out of war lest he needlessly bring ruin on himself and his people. Instead, he should stay in his principality, which is quite large enough, rule well, make it prosperous, and keep it peaceful, letting go of all thoughts of acquiring new lands. One never knows, but chances are that in that case, history would have been rather different.

Selected Bibliography

Brayshay, M., 'The Choreography of Journeys of Magnificence: Arranging the Post-Nuptial Progress of Frederick, the Elector Palatine, and Princess Elizabeth of England from London to Heidelberg in 1613', *Journal of Early Modern History*, 12 (2008): pp. 383–408.

Forster, M., *The Counter-Reformation in the Villages: Religion and Reform in the Bishopric of Speyer, 1560–1720* (Ithaca, 1992).

Ginzel, C., *Poetry, Politics and Promises of Empire: Prophetic Rhetoric in the English and Neo-Latin Epithalamia on the occasion of the Palatine Marriage in 1613* (Göttingen, 2009).

Gömöri, G., '"A Memorable Wedding": The Literary Reception of the Wedding of the Princess Elizabeth and Frederick of Pfalz', *Journal of European Studies*, 34/3 (2004): pp. 215–24.

Johnson, T., *Magistrates, Madonnas and Miracles: The Counter Reformation in the Upper Palatinate* (Farnham, 2009).

Kaplan, B., 'Fictions of Privacy: House Chapels and the Spatial Accommodation of Religious Dissent in Early Modern Europe', *The American Historical Review*, 107/4 (2002): pp. 1031–64.

Patterson, R., 'The "Hortus Palatinatus" at Heidelberg and the Reformation of the World. Part I: The Iconography of the Garden', *Journal of Garden History*, i/1 (1981): pp. 67–104.

Patterson, R., 'The "Hortus Palatinatus" at Heidelberg and the Reformation of the World. Part II: Culture as Science', *Journal of Garden History*, i/2 (1981): pp. 179–202.

Pursell, B., *The Winter King: Frederick V of the Palatinate and the Coming of the Thirty Years' War* (Aldershot, 2003).

Thomas, A., *A House Divided: Wittelsbach Confessional Court Cultures in the Holy Roman Empire, C. 1550–1650* (Leiden, 2010).

Werner, H., '*The Hector of Germanie*, or *The Palsgrave, Prime Elector* and Anglo-German relations of early Stuart England: the view from the popular stage', in R. M. Smuts (ed.), *The Stuart court and Europe: Essays in politics and political culture* (Cambridge, 1996), pp. 113–32.

---

[50] For a concise overview of the military campaigns that ravaged the Palatinate during the Thirty Years' War, see K. Scherer, 'Die Pfalz im Dreißigjährigen Krieg: Historischer Überblick', in W. Alter (ed.), *Pfalzatlas* (4 vols, Speyer, 1964–94), vol. 3 (1981), pp. 1398–1413.

PART II
The Great Powers, Coalitions and Conflicting Interests

3 The Emperor

Christoph Kampmann

Historiography

The emperor is the political and military key figure of the Thirty Years' War. Historiography never had any doubt about this fact which becomes evident by viewing the common historiographical terminology. The war, for example, is normally subdivided into four different periods (Palatine-Bohemian War, Lower Saxon-Danish War, Swedish War, Franco-Swedish War), all named after the respective main enemies of the emperor, who is thereby implicitly recognised as the central party of the war.

During the war the Holy Roman Empire was ruled successively by three emperors: Matthias (who died in 1619, 10 months after the outbreak of the war), Ferdinand II (1619–1637) and Ferdinand III (1637–1657). The historiography has dealt with these three emperors quite unevenly. Neither Matthias nor Ferdinand III have attracted much attention from historians.[1] In contrast Ferdinand II became one of the most controversial figures of German historiography since the nineteenth century. The *kleindeutsch*-Protestant Prussian tradition regarded Ferdinand II as chief culprit in the German catastrophe of the seventeenth century, because in his dependence on Jesuitical advisors he had followed an extreme Catholic-confessional, pro-Spanish policy which had disastrous consequences for the German nation. The answer of the *großdeutsch*-Catholic, pro-Austrian historiography was no less resolute in its apology for the allegedly peace-loving, pious emperor.[2]

In recent years less passionate, moderate views of Emperor Ferdinand II have become predominant.[3] It has been stressed that the influence of clerical advisors at the imperial court should not be overstated, because it was not greater than in other courts of that time.[4] Moreover it has been emphasised that confession did not play an exclusive role for Ferdinand II. This was only one political objective next to dynasty, territory and the imperial position within the Holy Roman Empire.[5] It has also been stated that Ferdinand

---

[1] For the scholarly neglect of Matthias cf. V. Press, 'Matthias', in A. Schindling and W. Ziegler (eds), *Die Kaiser der Neuzeit 1519–1918* (Munich, 1990), pp. 112–23, pp. 477–8, here p. 478; the historiographical position of Ferdinand III was described as 'cinderella of scholarship' by G. Parker (ed.), *The Thirty Years' War* (London, 1984), p. 291; see the similar judgement of L. Höbelt in his recent biography: *Ferdinand III. Friedenskaiser wider Willen* (Graz, 2008), pp. 9–10.

[2] For the ideological historiographical controversies around Ferdinand II see T. Brockmann, *Dynastie, Kaiseramt und Konfession. Politik und Ordnungsvorstellungen Ferdinands II. im Dreißigjährigen Krieg* (Paderborn etc., 2011), pp. 17–21.

[3] P. Wilson, *Europe's Tragedy. A History of the Thirty Years War* (London, 2009), p. 71, who describes Ferdinand – without denying his Roman Catholic stand – as 'rather devout than a fanatic'.

[4] For a deep revision of the picture of Ferdinand as a weak ruler see Brockmann, *Dynastie*, pp. 29–30.

[5] Ibid., pp. 22–6.

was quite a power-conscious political ruler who attached great importance to the formal procedures of law in the empire.[6] Consequently the imperial law court, the *Reichshofrat*, has been called the most important council within the imperial government during that period.[7] Despite these new interpretations of the character and personality of Ferdinand II the vital importance of imperial policy in the development and the escalation of the Thirty Years' War remains unchallenged.

The Emperor On the Eve of the Thirty Years' War

The Threefold Role of the Holy Roman Emperor

At the time of the Thirty Years' War the emperor had to act in three different, closely related, but sometimes conflicting roles: as monarchical head of the Holy Roman Empire, as ruler of the hereditary lands of the Austrian Habsburgs and as a member of the universal House of Austria. At the beginning of the seventeenth century the emperor faced serious challenges in all three roles.

Monarchical head of the Holy Roman Empire

First and foremost the emperor acted as elective monarchical head of the Holy Roman Empire – a position which was gravely affected by the Reformation and Confessionalisation.

On the one hand it belonged to the traditional tasks of the emperor to protect the Church (and Church property) as *advocatus ecclesiae* (defender of the Church). For the last decades of the sixteenth century the emperors had felt obliged to take this task more seriously by postulating the restitution of secularised property of the Catholic Church. This call for restitution of Catholic Church property, allegedly 'alienated' by the Protestants since the Reformation and especially since the Religious Peace of Augsburg (*Augsburger Religionsfrieden*), was at the heart of the confessional conflicts in the empire at the end of the sixteenth and the beginning of the seventeenth century.[8]

On the other hand it belonged to the traditional conception of the imperial position to safeguard peace and unity within the empire. Thus the foundation of armed confessional associations (Protestant *Union* in 1608 and Catholic *Liga* in 1609) had an alarming effect on the imperial government. Obviously *Union* and *Liga* resulted from the collapse of the ordinary legal procedures, especially the functional incapacity of the imperial law court (*Reichskammergericht*) and the imperial diet (*Reichstag*). By joining armed confessional federations many estates demonstrated clearly that they mistrusted (for good reasons) the ability of the emperor to protect the peace in the empire in times of growing confessional

---

[6] C. Kampmann, *Reichsrebellion und kaiserliche Acht. Politische Strafjustiz im Dreißigjährigen Krieg und das Verfahren gegen Wallenstein 1634* (Münster, 1993).

[7] The *Reichshofrat* as most important council of the imperial government: H. Rabe, *Reich und Glaubensspaltung. Deutschland 1500–1600* (Munich, 1989), pp. 313–15.

[8] A.P. Luttenberger, 'Kirchenadvokatie und Religionsfriede. Kaiseridee und kaiserliche Reichsidee im 16. und 17. Jahrhundert', in R. Gundlach and H. Weber (eds), *Legitimation und Funktion des Herrschers. Vom ägyptischen Pharao zum neuzeitlichen Diktator* (Stuttgart, 1992), pp. 185–232.

confrontation. Thus the course of the confessional conflict began to undermine the reputation of the emperor.[9]

Ruler of the Habsburg hereditary lands

The same is true for the position of the emperor as dynastic territorial ruler in some parts of the empire. Since the fifteenth century the Holy Roman emperors had come exclusively from the Austrian branch of the Habsburg family (the *Casa d'Austria*) which possessed a vast conglomerate of different territories in south-east and south-west Germany. The traditional Habsburg heartland consisted of the Austrian archdukedoms and the Austrian Forelands (*Vorderösterreich*) in south-west Germany. During the sixteenth century the House of Austria inherited the princedoms of the St Wenceslas crown (Bohemia, Silesia, Moravia) as well as the small part of Hungary which had not been occupied by the Ottoman Empire. In the course of Reformation and Confessionalisation the position of the Roman Catholic Austrian family as territorial ruler became precarious, because the majority of the inhabitants and especially the nobility adhered to the new reformed faith.

This was especially true for Bohemia, which as kingdom and electorship of the Holy Roman Empire was regarded as an indispensable part of the Habsburg inheritance. In contrast to the Austrian archdukedoms, Bohemia was not a purely hereditary monarchy. The Bohemian nobility claimed to have the right to elect or at least to accept their future king. It could be doubted whether this quite uncommon and uneasy situation of a Catholic princely family in mainly Protestant territories could last very long.[10]

In the last decades of the sixteenth century the Austrian rulers began to react by introducing counter-reformation measures in their princedoms. This happened in different ways: very harshly and resolutely in Inner Austria by Archduke Ferdinand (the later Ferdinand II) on the basis of the Augsburg Peace, and more smoothly and indirectly in Upper and Lower Austria as well as in Bohemia. However, the beginning of the seventeenth century witnessed a situation of rising confessional tension and crisis in the Austrian hereditary lands.

The emperor as member of the universal Casa d'Austria

The third important role of the emperor was as a member of the universal *Casa d'Austria*. Since the division of that dynastic house in an older line (governing in Spain including its overseas colonies as well as in northern and southern Italy and in Burgundy) and a younger line governing the Central European territories in the middle of the sixteenth century, both branches often proclaimed the unbreakable unity of the house – a unity that was solemnly and repeatedly underlined by marriages between members of both family branches. In fact, for the emperor the close family relationship to the kings of Spain was a blessing and a burden at the same time. Of course it was an advantage for the emperor that in times of crisis he could – at least potentially – rely on the alliance with the Hispanic World Empire. On the other hand Spain expected imperial support in sensitive areas as well, which consequently

---

[9] See now A. Ernst and A. Schindling, *Union und Liga 1608/09 – Konfessionelle Bündnisse im Reich – Weichenstellung zum Religionskrieg?* (Stuttgart, 2010).

[10] J. Bahlcke, 'Calvinism and estate liberation in Bohemia and Hungary (1570–1620)', in K. Maag (ed.), *The Reformation in Eastern and Central Europe* (Aldershot, 1997), pp. 72–91; F. Machilek, 'Böhmen', in A. Schindling and W. Ziegler (eds), *Territorien des Reichs im Zeitalter der Reformation und der Konfessionalisierung* (Munich, 1989), pp. 134–52.

created the danger of involvement in far-reaching conflicts.[11] One was the long-lasting war between Spain and the 'rebellious' Dutch Republic between 1566 and 1648.[12] The other was the even more fundamental struggle between Spain and France over political hegemony in Christendom, which repeatedly caused serious trouble in western Germany and northern Italy.

The Imperial-Austrian Crisis at the Beginning of the Seventeenth Century

After the turn of the century the emperor of the Austrian branch of the dynasty was drawn into one of the deepest crises of its history. The reason for this was the bitter conflict between Emperor Rudolph II (1576–1612) and his younger brothers, especially Archduke Matthias. Serious doubts about the mental capability of the emperor to rule the hereditary lands had arisen within the Habsburg family. The emperor regarded this as an attempt of his younger brothers to usurp his power and he reacted with harsh military measures. The succeeding 'fratricidal struggle' between Rudolph and Matthias (1606–11) had disastrous consequences for the dynasty. In their respective attempts to win over the estates of the hereditary lands Rudolph and Matthias gave generous privileges to the Protestant nobility in the Austrian archdukedoms and Bohemia. The most generous was the Royal Privilege (*Majestätsbrief*) of Rudolph II (1609), which solemnly granted tolerance to the Bohemian aristocracy – a serious blow to all attempts of counter-reformation in Bohemia.[13]

The whole crisis was a traumatic experience for the Austrian Habsburg family. They recognised that such inner conflict could – in their difficult confessional situation – easily lead to a mortal crisis. After the death of Rudolph and the succession of Matthias in Austria, Bohemia (1611) and the empire (1612), the dynasty agreed to take steps to avoid a similar crisis in the future. Archduke Ferdinand from the Graz branch of the family, well known for his fiercely counter-reformation policy, was designated as common heir and future head of the whole Austrian family. In 1617 King Philip III of Spain (1598–1621) was won over for that common solution in the secret Oñate Treaty: Madrid recognised the succession of Ferdinand in Bohemia and the empire and in return claimed the inheritance of the Austrian possession in the Alsace.[14] That paved the way for the designation of Ferdinand as future king of Bohemia by the Bohemian estates against surprisingly small Protestant resistance in 1617 and his election as the king of Hungary in 1618. Meanwhile Emperor Matthias (or his nearly omnipotent councillor Cardinal Khlesl, Bishop of Vienna) tried to resume the interrupted counter-reformation policy in the Austrian hereditary lands.[15]

---

[11] For the frequent political differences between Madrid and Vienna see R. G. Asch, *The Thirty Years' War. The Holy Roman Empire and Europe, 1618–1648* (London, 1997), p. 75; J.H. Elliott, 'Foreign Policy and Domestic Crisis: Spain 1598–1659', in K. Repgen (ed.), *Krieg und Politik 1618–1648. Europäische Probleme und Perspektiven* (Munich, 1988), pp. 185–202, here p. 185, and H. Ernst, *Madrid und Wien 1632–1637. Politik und Finanzen in den Beziehungen zwischen Philipp IV. und Ferdinand II.* (Münster, 1991).

[12] G. Parker, *The Dutch Revolt* (London, 1977).

[13] J. Bahlcke, *Regionalismus und Staatsintegration im Widerstreit. Die Länder der Böhmischen Krone im ersten Jahrhundert der Habsburgerherrschaft (1526–1619)* (Munich, 1994).

[14] O. Gliss, *Der Oñatevertrag*, Diss. phil. (Frankfurt/Main, 1930).

[15] W. Ziegler, 'Nieder- und Oberösterreich', in Schindling, Ziegler (eds), *Territorien*, pp. 118–33, here pp. 128–30.

Self-Preservation I: Imperial Policy After the Bohemian Rebellion of 1618

This process of slow improvement of the Austrian position was brought to a sudden halt by the outbreak of the Bohemian Revolution in May 1618. The action of radical representatives of the Protestant Bohemian nobility against Matthias's governors in the Hradschin took the imperial government completely by surprise.[16] Without troops and money Vienna could not react militarily against the establishment of a Protestant directorial government and against the efforts of the new government in Prague to bring the whole kingdom under its control. But the imperial government was determined not to give in and strictly avoided any acknowledgment of the new government in Prague. Instead Vienna followed a twofold strategy. On the one hand the imperial government tried to slow or to stop the rebellion by an ostentatiously moderate confessional and territorial policy. On the other hand Vienna began to look for foreign assistance to suppress the rebellion militarily. Pleas for help were directed to Roman Catholic princes in the empire, to Spain and to the Pope. In autumn 1618 the Spanish government decided after a dramatic internal discussion that Spain could not risk abandoning the Austrian branch, because that would mean the loss of the emperorship.[17] But at that moment the Spanish decision was not more than a glimmer of hope for Vienna: it was clear that it took considerable time until Spanish support would actually arrive.

Meanwhile the immediate danger for the Vienna government was growing steadily. It reached a new peak in the spring of 1619, when Emperor Matthias died in March. In the last months of his reign Matthias had not possessed real political influence anymore: in July 1618 already, the designated successor Ferdinand, unsatisfied with the conduct of affairs, had ordered the arrest of Cardinal Khlesl, seized power and had brushed Matthias aside. Together with the newly empowered Ferdinand, some of his closest advisors from Styria had taken on political duties in Vienna, e.g. the Count Johann von Eggenberg (1568–1634) and Maximilian von Trauttmansdorff (1584–1650), the latter remaining a key figure in the imperial government until the very end of the war.[18]

Despite the fact that in the end Matthias had been a purely nominal ruler, his death marked the beginning of the most dramatic stage of the uprising in the hereditary lands. After Matthias's death the rebellion of the Protestant estates spread over from Bohemia and Silesia to Moravia, Upper and Lower Austria and Hungary.[19]

In the light of this dramatic development Ferdinand and his advisors were convinced that the maintenance of Ferdinand's claim to be Matthias's rightful successor had to take political priority. That would be a necessary precondition to win over allies. In pursuing this aim in August 1619 Ferdinand achieved his first major victory: he was elected Roman emperor by the electors in Frankfurt, who in addition recognised him as lawful king of Bohemia. The results of the Frankfurt election turned out to be of great importance, because at the same time the Bohemian Estates carried out the final break by the deposition of Ferdinand. In his place they elected the leader of the *Union*, the Count Palatine Frederick V, as new king of Bohemia.

---

[16] A detailed account of the imperial policy in the face of the Bohemian Revolution, Brockmann, *Dynastie*, pp. 66–192.

[17] P.J. Brightwell, 'Spain and Bohemia: the Decision to Intervene', *European Studies Review*, 12 (1982): pp. 117–41.

[18] Cf. D. Croxton and A. Tischer, 'Trauttmansdorff and Weinsberg, Count Maximilian of', in D. Croxton and A. Tischer (eds), *The Peace of Westphalia. A Historical Dictionary* (Westport, 2002), pp. 297–9.

[19] A. Strohmeyer, *Konfessionskonflikt und Herrschaftsordnung. Widerstandsrecht bei den österreichischen Ständen (1550–1650)* (Stuttgart, 2006), pp. 240–54.

Bestowed with his new imperial dignity Ferdinand could continue his efforts to win over new allies for the coming showdown with the 'rebels' in the different hereditary lands. On his return from Frankfurt to Vienna he reached an agreement with the then most powerful Catholic prince of the Holy Roman Empire, Duke Maximilian of Bavaria, the leader of the Catholic *Liga*. In the Treaty of Munich Maximilian declared his willingness to support the emperor in the coming war with the Protestant 'rebels'. But in return the emperor had to pay a high price that highlighted his desperate situation. Ferdinand had to agree that the duke would lead the campaign personally with Ferdinand standing aside. Moreover Ferdinand had to pay all expenses and in an additional secret deal the emperor promised that he would bestow the Palatine electorship and the Upper Palatine on the duke once the new 'rebel's leader' Frederick V had been put under the imperial ban. Maximilian would retain Upper Austria as a sort of security until the fulfilment of the imperial promises. The Treaty of Munich between the emperor and the duke of Bavaria had the features of an imperial capitulation and contributed much to the prolongation and escalation of the war.[20]

In the short run the new treaty with Bavaria had positive effects for the emperor. Backed up by the new Bavarian alliance Ferdinand could win other allies against the Bohemian rebels in spring 1620, especially the (Lutheran) elector of Saxony – a success with a high symbolic value.[21] Meanwhile, in the face of a powerful pro-imperial alliance the efforts of the Bohemian government to get new allies failed almost completely. The Protestant *Union* declared its neutrality, and the king of England, father-in-law of the unfortunate Count Palatine, refused any help to the (in his eyes) contemptible Bohemian 'rebels'.[22]

In summer and autumn 1620 the Bavarian-led Catholic campaign in the hereditary lands took place. Maximilian and his competent general Tilly occupied Upper Austria first, attacked Bohemia and finally defeated the Bohemian army in the famous battle of the White Mountain. It was an easy victory with far-reaching effects: King Frederick fled the country and the directorial government collapsed.

According to the Treaty of Munich Emperor Ferdinand had remained in Vienna as a passive observer of military events, which restored his position in his hitherto rebellious princedoms. It was an imperial victory, not by his own power, but by that of his allies.[23]

The Consequences of the Bohemian Victory: New Possibilities – New Dangers (1621–1625)

The 'borrowed' victory proved to be a double-edged sword for Emperor Ferdinand. Advantages in the hereditary lands were countered by new dangers in the empire.

---

[20] D. Albrecht, *Maximilian I. von Bayern 1573–1651* (Munich, 1998), pp. 503–9.
[21] F. Müller, *Kursachsen und der Böhmische Aufstand 1618–1622* (Münster, 1996). In return Ferdinand promised the cession of Lusatia to Saxony, which was realised after the war.
[22] S. Adams, 'England und die protestantischen Reichsfürsten 1599–1621', in F. Beiderbeck et al. (eds), *Dimensionen der europäischen Außenpolitik zur Zeit der Wende vom 16. zum 17. Jahrhundert* (Berlin, 2003), pp. 61–84.
[23] For the term 'borrowed victory' (*geborgter Sieg*) see V. Press, *Kriege und Krisen. Deutschland 1600–1715* (Munich, 1991), p. 199.

New Possibilities: The Transformation of the Habsburg Territories

On the one hand the emperor gained new opportunities in the hereditary lands – opportunities which none of his predecessors had enjoyed since the middle of the sixteenth century, because the hitherto powerful Protestant opposition in the Habsburg territories was in complete tatters. And the imperial government was determined to use these new opportunities for a long-lasting transformation. All Protestant nobles who missed the opportunity of a last-minute reconciliation before the military defeat were punished severely whereby their land was confiscated and transferred to loyal noble (of course Roman Catholic) followers of the emperor. This had far-reaching consequences in all Habsburg territories, especially in Bohemia: The Bohemian Protestant nobility was almost completely replaced by a (quite international) Roman Catholic aristocratic elite, not only of Czech and German, but also of Italian and Spanish origin. However, the expectation that the imperial government could improve its difficult financial situation with the confiscation and transfer of property did not get fulfilled. To the detriment of the imperial treasury, a small circle of noblemen around Ferdinand's governor in Bohemia, Karl von Liechtenstein, (among them the later famous or rather notorious Albrecht von Wallenstein) used the opportunity to get extremely wealthy by confiscating, selling and buying 'rebel' property at the same time.[24] The losses were even greater because Liechtenstein had the right to mint coins and used that right to buy land with arbitrarily downgraded money thereby causing a veritable inflation in Central Europe (the *Kipper und Wipper* era).[25] The whole story reveals a very characteristic feature of the imperial government in the whole war: its remarkable economic and financial incompetence. In this respect the Vienna government differed considerably from other governments, e.g. the Bavarian government.

By contrast the measures of the imperial government to transform the hereditary territories with respect to constitution and confession were more effective. From the emperor's point of view all confessional and constitutional privileges had to be regarded as invalid after the rebellion. A transformation of the Habsburg territories in the Holy Roman Empire into hereditary, centralised, exclusively Roman Catholic territories began, thereby causing a major migration of Protestant inhabitants from Bohemia to the neighbouring adjacent Protestant territories. Small exceptions were made in Lower Austria and Silesia (due to some last-minute concessions by Ferdinand that were a sign of Ferdinand's 'deep legalism'[26]). The whole process came to a provisional end by the Bohemian *Verneuerte Landesordnung* (Renewed Constitution) of 1627, which turned Bohemia into a centralised, Roman Catholic, hereditary princedom. The republican, Protestant experiment in Central Europe was definitely at its end.[27]

New Dangers: The Ongoing War in the Empire

On the other hand Ferdinand had to pay a high price for his borrowed victory. His ally, Maximilian of Bavaria, was persisting in upholding the provisions of the Treaty of Munich, especially the translation of the Palatine electorship and the territory of the Upper Palatinate.[28] A first step was made by the emperor in January 1621: Frederick V, who after the occupation

---

[24] G. Mortimer, *Wallenstein. The Enigma of the Thirty Years War* (New York, 2010), pp. 37–51.
[25] U. Rosseaux, *Die Kipper und Wipper als publizistisches Ereignis (1620–1626). Eine Studie zu den Strukturen öffentlicher Kommunikation im Zeitalter des Dreißigjährigen Kriegs* (Berlin, 2001).
[26] For the 'deep legalism' of Ferdinand II see Wilson, *Europe's Tragedy*, p. 71.
[27] For the radicality of the measures in Bohemia see Machilek, 'Böhmen', pp. 149–50.
[28] Albrecht, *Maximilian I.*, pp. 583–4.

of the Upper and Lower Palatinate (*Oberpfalz/Unterpfalz*) by Bavarian and Spanish troops had to live in Dutch exile, was proscribed as a 'notorious rebel' whose dignities and territories could be regarded as completed fiefs.[29]

In Vienna there was no doubt that the translation of the Palatinate to Bavaria would make a peaceful compromise quite impossible, all the more so as Spain had occupied strategically important Palatine territories in the Rhine Valley. Such a radical and intimidating shift of power in Central Europe in favour of the Roman Catholic and Austrian cause would not be neither acceptable for Frederick, nor for many Protestant princes in the empire and European powers. France, the Netherlands, Denmark and Britain made that quite clear. But the emperor had no choice. In his financially desperate situation he was totally relying on his Bavarian ally and the army of the Bavarian-led *Liga*. Moreover Maximilian still had Upper Austria (*Oberösterreich*) in his hands, leaving no doubt that its restitution would depend on the completion of the Munich Treaty. At the Regensburg Electoral Assembly in 1623 Ferdinand solemnly invested Maximilian of Bavaria with the Palatine electorship *ad personam*, promising secretly to give it to Bavaria as hereditary fief in the long term.

So the war went on. The exiled Palatine government, which obtained subsidies from different European powers, recruited new mercenary armies in the Lower Saxon Circle (*Niedersächsischer Kreis*), which fought fierce battles with the army of the *Liga* under Tilly.[30] The defeat of Protestant armies could not halt the war. The Protestant princes in Lower Saxony – intimidated by the presence of powerful Catholic armies in their territories – accepted the offer of King Christian of Denmark to protect them and elected the Danish king, who had territorial interests in northern Germany, to the new commander of the imperial circle. This in fact meant war with the emperor and the *Liga*. The 'borrowed' victory of the emperor over Bohemia and Palatinate had led to a new stage of European military escalation.

The Structural Change of the Imperial Position After 1625. A New Monarchy? (1625–1630)

The imperial government was convinced that the Danish intervention demanded a clear military response. In recent years the offer of the wealthy Bohemian nobleman Albrecht of Wallenstein to build up an imperial army at his own expense had been rejected repeatedly. Now, in the face of the new danger, Ferdinand changed his mind: Wallenstein was given the task to recruit an imperial army.[31] It was quite typical for the imperial government that obviously no one had considered how to maintain the army: after a short time the new imperial army got into a deep financial crisis. But Wallenstein could overcome the crisis by his organisational talent and his lack of scruples: with implicit or even explicit imperial permission all territories of the Holy Roman Empire in which the imperial army was deployed had to pay for it – regardless of whether they were hostile to the emperor or neutral or even his allies.[32]

The permanent presence of an imperial army changed the position of the emperor and had far-reaching consequences in many respects. Firstly it changed the relationship between

---

[29] For a detailed account of the proscription of Frederick see Kampmann, *Reichsrebellion*, pp. 47–70.
[30] N. Mout, 'Der Winterkönig im Exil. Friedrich V. von der Pfalz und die Niederländischen Generalstaaten 1621–32', *Zeitschrift für Historische Forschung*, 15 (1988): pp. 169–94.
[31] Mortimer, *Wallenstein*, pp. 75–81.
[32] F. Redlich, *The German Military Enterpriser and His Work Force. A Study in European Economic and Social History* 1 (2 vols, Wiesbaden, 1964), vol. 1, pp. 359–65.

the emperor and his allies Bavaria and Spain. Thanks to the rise of Wallenstein's army, which at the end of the 1620s was the strongest military factor in Central Europe,[33] the emperor became a militarily independent power on his own.

Secondly the new imperial army contributed considerably to the shifting balance between the imperial-Catholic party and its Danish-Protestant enemies. Due to the military successes of Wallenstein and Tilly in 1626–27 the whole north of Germany and the Danish peninsula of Jutland were occupied. That meant that even those parts of the empire which traditionally, since the later Middle Ages had been out of imperial reach, now came under direct imperial control. Actually Emperor Ferdinand was more powerful in the empire now than any of his predecessors including Charles V in the first half of the sixteenth century.[34]

Thirdly the emperor had to face growing opposition from the estates of the empire. The exactions of the imperial army and the heavy financial burdens outraged the Protestant as well as the Catholic princes of the empire. Furthermore they feared that Ferdinand II and Wallenstein could use their new options to transform the empire into a centralised monarchy at the expense of the princely liberty (*Libertät*). Accordingly, some actions like the confiscation of 'rebel' property in the empire for the good of the army (including the dukedoms of Mecklenburg, which were transferred quite arbitrarily to Wallenstein in 1628) were seen with great suspicion.[35]

In fact there has been discussion in the historiography as to whether Ferdinand II had plans to transform the Holy Roman Empire constitutionally, with some historians denoting these alleged or real plans as 'absolutist' (speaking of Ferdinand's *Reichsabsolutismus*).[36] Recent research has convincingly shown that there is no evidence for such far-reaching imperial intentions. An important proof is Ferdinand's attitude towards the elective character of the Holy Roman monarchy – probably the most important obstacle for any absolutist plans. There is no indication at all that the imperial government even considered a modification of the elective monarchy.[37] It seems that the legalist and form-based approach of imperial policy always prevailed, even at the zenith of imperial power.[38]

This is even true for the area of most radical change in 1628–29, the confessional policy: Ferdinand's notorious 'Edict of Restitution' of the 'alienated', now Protestant Church property was based on a strictly Catholic interpretation of the Augsburg Religious peace, not on the open or silent abolition of this peace.[39]

---

[33] D. Albrecht, 'Ferdinand II. 1619–1637', in Schindling, Ziegler (eds), *Kaiser*, pp. 124–41 and 478–9, here p. 133.

[34] K. Repgen, 'Dreißigjähriger Krieg', in K. Repgen, *Dreißigjähriger Krieg und Westfälischer Friede. Studien und Quellen*, 2nd edn (Paderborn etc., 1999), pp. 291–318, here p. 296.

[35] The best account of the *Liga*-policy towards the emperor and Wallenstein is M. Kaiser, *Politik und Kriegführung. Maximilian von Bayern, Tilly und die Katholische Liga im Dreißigjährigen Krieg*, (Münster, 1999). For the confiscations see Kampmann, *Reichsrebellion*, pp. 71–104.

[36] A. Gotthard, 'Der deutsche Konfessionskrieg. Ein Resultat gestörter politischer Kommunikation', in *Historisches Jahrbuch*, 122 (2002): pp. 141–72, here p. 146.

[37] Brockmann, *Dynastie*, p. 459.

[38] This was already brought forward very convincingly by H.F. Schwarz, *The Imperial Privy Council in the Seventeenth Century* (Cambridge etc., 1943), p. 95.

[39] M. Heckel's view of the strict legalism of the *Restitutionsedikt* (*Deutschland im konfessionellen Zeitalter* [Göttingen, 1983], p. 146) has been confirmed by the results of Brockmann, *Dynastie*, p. 459.

The Crisis of Imperial Politics: From the Peace of Lübeck to the Peace of Prague (1629–1635)

The Edict of Restitution marked a first turning point in imperial policy. Despite the emperor's military strength the political and confessional limits of the imperial position became visible. The Protestant opposition in the empire hardened, and even pro-imperial, loyal Lutheran princes like the elector of Saxony abandoned the imperial cause now. Moreover the international situation deteriorated and the danger of a Swedish or French intervention was steadily increasing. This forced the emperor, and indeed Wallenstein, to conclude the remarkably moderate Peace of Lübeck with the king of Denmark, who promised his withdrawal from the empire in return for the territorial integrity of his Danish possessions (May 1629). Even more revealing for the constitutional limits of imperial power is the course of the electoral assembly in Regensburg 1630. The (Protestant *and* Catholic) electors showed the elderly emperor clearly that he would not have the slightest chance of having his son elected as his successor at any time in the future without the dismissal of the extremely unpopular General Wallenstein. In the end Ferdinand gave in and dismissed Wallenstein – a symbolic defeat of prime importance and a further indication of imperial weakness.[40]

The following years finally made clear that the imperial power rested on very shaky foundations and that Ferdinand again had had to 'borrow' his military strength: in the face of Swedish intervention and Swedish triumphs the emperor was only saved from total ruin by the organisational talents and wealth of the reappointed *Generalissimus* Wallenstein, who – after Gustav Adolf's death in 1632 – humiliated the emperor by a growing obstinacy and barely concealed threat of mutiny.[41] After Wallenstein's second dismissal, proscription and killing (February 1634) the imperial army got into a deep crisis: it was the Spanish army that fought the decisive imperial victory over Sweden at Nördlingen (September 1634) and liberated southern Germany from Swedish occupation.[42]

Due to the traumatic experiences of the years 1631 to 1634 the imperial government decided to change its political strategy. After 1634 a more conciliatory line in religious and military matters becomes obvious. It was of particular importance for Ferdinand to find an agreement with those Protestant estates which had been normally loyal to the emperor and were alienated by the rigid religious and military politics of the late 1620s, especially with the elector of Saxony. In fact such an agreement is included in the Peace of Prague between the emperor and Saxony in 1635. In contrast to the Edict of Restitution which was silently withdrawn by the emperor this peace provided that the confessional status quo of 1627 should be preserved for at least 40 years (*annus normalis* [normal date]). Moreover the imperial army, hitherto a scourge of all estates, should be totally restructured: as the sole regular army in the empire it should be divided under nominal high command of the emperor into an imperial, a Saxon and a Bavarian part, operating in different regions of the empire with one single intention: To end the war and to expel all other foreign armies.[43]

Within the empire the new, more conciliatory imperial strategy seemed to work. Almost all estates of the empire who were invited to accede joined the peace settlement. Apart from this, on the basis of the Peace of Prague the emperor was able to achieve another great

---

[40] Kaiser, *Politik*, pp. 279–302; Mortimer, *Wallenstein*, pp. 125–31, about the remarkably composed reaction of Wallenstein.

[41] For Wallenstein's fall and end see Kampmann, *Reichsrebellion*, pp. 101–72.

[42] For the decisive role of the Spanish army of Flanders at Nördlingen see Geoffrey Parker, *The Army of Flanders and the Spanish Road, 1567–1659* (Cambridge, 1972), p. 259.

[43] There is still no monograph about the Peace of Prague and the imperial policy, but an outstanding edition of the papers by K. Bierther, *Der Prager Frieden von 1635* (4 vols, Munich and Vienna, 1997), see Bierther's introduction, vol. 1, pp. *11–*241.

success at the end of his reign: his eldest son Ferdinand was elected as king of the Romans and followed his father as Emperor Ferdinand III in 1637.[44]

The acceptance of the Peace of Prague was increased by a 'patriotic' pro-imperial public propaganda that stressed the German, national character of the peace.[45] In one important respect this was misleading: the Peace of Prague and its enforcement only became possible because of the Spanish substantial military and financial support for the emperor before and after 1635.[46] In return Ferdinand II and – obviously even much stronger – Ferdinand III[47] provided assistance to Spain, directly (in northern Italy, the Alsace or the Picardie against France) or indirectly against the Netherlands. This renewed alliance of the House of Austria proved to be one important factor for the ultimate failure of the Peace.

The Failed Containment: Imperial Policy in the European War (1636–1645)

The Peace of Prague was based on one crucial precondition: that Sweden and France would accept the Prague agreement in the short or long term. But this proved to be an illusion. Sweden was not prepared to abandon its crucial objectives (satisfaction, recompense, amnesty); and for France it was completely unacceptable to be politically and militarily cut off from the Holy Roman Empire, all the more so as the emperor was obviously closely linked with the French arch-enemy Spain. Imperial diplomacy did what it could to come to a peaceful agreement with France that had never declared war on the emperor (but only on Spain in 1635). But this was fruitless, because Vienna obviously underestimated Richelieu's determination to prevent the Prague settlement.[48]

So in the end the use of military force against France and Sweden seemed to be the only means for the emperor to force through the Peace of Prague. But this proved to be an illusion, too. In 1636–37 the emperor was able to achieve some military successes against France and Sweden, but after 1638–40 the military balance shifted in favour of France and Sweden. As Spain was not able to help the emperor anymore in the early 1640s his military situation became dramatic. As a consequence an increasing number of princes and estates left the emperor and adhered to France and Sweden.

In the light of these dramatic developments it is remarkable for how long Emperor Ferdinand III and his closest advisors refused to give up their original political strategy of a separate 'German' peace and tried to avoid the universal peace congress that was favoured by France. Even after two disastrous military campaigns against Sweden and France in 1643–44 the emperor tried to uphold the illusion that the Peace of Prague could be the foundation of a peace for the empire.[49] And that it would be enough to come to separate

---

[44] H. Haan, *Der Regensburger Kurfürstentag 1636/37* (Münster, 1967).

[45] A. Wandruszka, *Reichspatriotismus und Reichspolitik zur Zeit des Prager Friedens von 1635* (Vienna, 1955).

[46] Cf. Haan, *Kurfürstentag*, pp. 230–31; very valuable for the massive Spanish support of the emperor, see Ernst, *Madrid*, pp. 236–7.

[47] The consistently pro-Spanish attitude of Ferdinand III, who had been more Spanish-oriented than any predecessor, is stressed by Höbelt, *Ferdinand*, p. 117 and p. 410.

[48] A detailed account of the imperial-French relation is in A.V. Hartmann, *Von Regensburg nach Hamburg. Die diplomatischen Beziehungen zwischen dem französischen König und dem Kaiser vom Regensburger Vertrag (13. Oktober 1630) bis zum Hamburger Präliminarfrieden (25. Dezember 1641)* (Münster, 1998).

[49] Concerning the disastrous military situation of the emperor and his remarkable obstinacy against the universal peace congress see C. Kampmann, *Europa und das Reich im Dreißigjährigen Krieg. Geschichte eines europäischen Konflikts* (Stuttgart, 2008), pp. 142–51.

settlements with France and Sweden. Obviously the imperial government regarded it as deeply dishonourable to negotiate with the foreign powers *and* the estates of the empire at the same time at one congress, because the latter were not seen as partners, but as subjects. Because of this tenacious obstinacy against a universal peace the emperor began to alienate more and more estates, which – in the face of the steadily spreading devastation of the ongoing war – doubted that the imperial strategy would some day lead to peace. From 1643 on a rising number of estates (and not only the traditionally anti-imperial outlawed princes like the Palatinate and Hesse-Cassel) began to withdraw from the Prague Peace settlement and to send emissaries to the Westphalian Peace Congress without imperial permission.

Only the military and political catastrophes of the year 1645 (the destruction of the imperial army at Jankov in March 1645, the successive Swedish campaign in Lower Austria, the simultaneous attack of Georg I Prince of Transsylvania on the hereditary lands from the south-east and the loss of the hitherto most loyal allies in the empire, especially the elector of Saxony) led to a rethinking at the imperial court. In the face of threatening military ruin and total political isolation in the Holy Roman Empire the emperor declared his willingness to enter serious negotiations at the universal peace congress in Westphalia.[50] This was revealed with the appointment of the closest and most influential advisor of Emperor Ferdinand III, Count Trauttmansdorff, as imperial ambassador at the Westphalian Peace Congress.

Self-Preservation II: The Emperor and the Peace of Westphalia

Soon after his arrival Count Trauttmansdorff became the key figure of the whole peace congress – a remarkable success considering the reluctance of the emperor to negotiate at all in Westphalia. Due to the disastrous military and political imperial situation in the last years of the war it was clear that the emperor had to make considerable concessions – and Ferdinand III and Trautmansdorff were prepared to do so. But with respect to the above mentioned multiple roles of the emperor as monarchical head of the empire, as ruler of the hereditary lands and as a member of the *Casa d'Austria* the willingness to make such concessions varied significantly.[51]

In his position as monarch of the Holy Roman Empire Ferdinand III conducted a remarkably conciliatory policy.[52] Ferdinand III abandoned the Peace of Prague and gave up some important imperial prerogatives: the estates of the empire received the *Ius Foederis*, i.e. the right to make treaties among each other and with foreign powers – an astonishing freedom for vassals. The empire was able to declare war and make peace only with permission of the estates. Painful concessions of similar importance were to be made with respect to confession. In this respect the emperor showed striking flexibility by granting a general amnesty from 1618 on, an 'annus normalis' in 1624 (more favourable to the Protestants then the 1627 of the Peace of Prague) with the recognition of the lawful equality of the confessions and of the reformed (Calvinist faith) as the third official confession in the

---

[50] For the crucial importance of Jankov see D. Croxton and A. Tischer, 'Jankov, Battle of', in Croxton, Tischer (eds), *Peace of Westphalia*, pp. 144–5.

[51] Cf. K. Ruppert, *Die kaiserliche Politik auf dem Westfälischen Friedenskongreß (1643–1648)* (Münster, 1979). The edition of the imperial correspondence from and to the congress within the framework of the *Acta Pacis Westphalicae* (*APW*) is almost completed and therefore extremely important; *APW*, series II, section A: *Die kaiserlichen Korrespondenzen* [1643–1648] (8 vols, Münster, 1969–2008).

[52] For a valuable account of the regulations of the Westphalian Peace Treaty concerning the emperor see K. Repgen, 'Die Hauptprobleme der Westfälischen Friedensverhandlungen von 1648 und ihre Lösungen', in *Zeitschrift für bayerische Landesgeschichte*, 62 (1999): pp. 399–438.

empire, and finally the unlimited validity of all these regulations. The same was true with regard to the territorial borders of the empire. It belonged to the traditional honour of the emperor to act as *semper Augustus* (expander of the empire at all times). But Ferdinand III had to concede the independence of the Dutch States General and the Swiss Confederation as well as that of some strategically important territories in the Alsace, which were placed under the sovereignty of France.[53] The territorial gains of Sweden were much less critical, because the Queen of Sweden took them as imperial fief.

More radical propositions of Sweden and some Protestant estates for a general transformation of the empire at the expense of the emperor (and the electors), which would have converted the emperorship into a sort of honorary presidency in the empire, were avoided.[54] The discussion about these ideas, which were quite popular among some Protestant estates after the experiences of the war, was postponed to the first diet after the war. In the end this discussion would not be brought to an end until the dissolution of the empire in 1806.

With respect to his position as ruler of the hereditary lands the emperor took a much firmer line than with the empire – and with great success. In general the transformation of his territories into centralised, almost exclusively Roman Catholic and hereditary princedoms was recognised in the Westphalian Peace Treaty. In this respect the position of the emperor and the House of Austria was much stronger after 1648 than before 1618.

As a member of the universal House of Austria, in turn, the emperor had to suffer severe political defeat. He had to cede the Austrian territories in the Alsace, which had been promised to the Spanish branch. Moreover the emperor was not allowed to help Spain in its ongoing military confrontation with France – a considerable blow to the emperor's reputation. Ferdinand III did what he could to avoid this sanction but in the end he had to give in.[55]

In general the imperial strategy at the Congress of Westphalia proved to be quite successful. Indeed, the concessions were painful, but in the long run they were not destructive for the imperial position.

In other respects the results of the Thirty Years' War were much more damaging for the position of the emperor. The imperial policy in the 1620s and the extreme reluctance to accept the congress in the 1640s had generated considerable mistrust against the emperor among Protestant and Catholic estates. A clear indication of this is the willingness to accept France and Sweden as foreign guarantors of peace (in fact as guarantors *against* the emperor).[56]

It took two decades to overcome this mistrust – a success which became possible due to the imperial policy and the aggressive military strategy of Louis XIV. So the Peace of Westphalia and its acceptance by the emperor created the basis of the breathtaking imperial comeback in the last third of the seventeenth century.[57]

---

[53] About the respective imperial-Franco negotiations see A. Tischer, *Französische Diplomatie und Diplomaten auf dem Westfälischen Friedenskongreß. Außenpolitik unter Richelieu und Mazarin* (Münster, 1999), pp. 239–93.

[54] One important and widely read advocate of such radical anti-imperial ideas was the lawyer Bogislaw P. Chemnitz in his *Dissertatio de ratione status in Imperio nostro*; see D. Croxton and A. Tischer, 'Chemnitz, Bogislaus Philipp von', in Croxton, Tischer (eds), *Peace of Westphalia*, pp. 55–6.

[55] Höbelt has pointed out that ironically Ferdinand III – the most 'pro-Spanish' of all emperors – had to make such concessions. Höbelt, *Ferdinand*, p. 410.

[56] Kampmann, *Europa*, pp. 167–70.

[57] A. Schindling, 'Leopold I.', in: Schindling, Ziegler, *Kaiser*, pp. 169–85.

Selected Bibliography

Asch, R.G., *The Thirty Years' War. The Holy Roman Empire and Europe, 1618–1648* (London, 1997).

Bahlcke, J., 'Calvinism and estate liberation in Bohemia and Hungary (1570–1620)', in K. Maag (ed.), *The Reformation in Eastern and Central Europe* (Aldershot, 1997), pp. 72–91.

Bireley, R., *Religion and Politics in the Age of the Counterreformation: Emperor Ferdinand II, William Lamormaini S.J. and the Formation of Imperial policy* (Chapel Hill, 1981).

Brightwell, P.J., 'Spain and Bohemia: the Decision to Intervene', *European Studies Review*, 12 (1982): pp. 117–41.

Brockmann, T., *Dynastie, Kaiseramt und Konfession. Politik und Ordnungsvorstellungen Ferdinands II. im Dreißigjährigen Krieg* (Paderborn, 2011).

Croxton, D., and Tischer, A. (eds), *The Peace of Westphalia. A Historical Dictionary* (Westport, 2002) (articles: 'Austria'; 'Chemnitz, Bogislaus Philipp von'; 'Edict of Restitution'; 'Ferdinand II'; 'Ferdinand III'; 'Jankov, Battle of','Trauttmansdorff and Weinsberg, Count Maximilian of').

Höbelt, L., *Ferdinand III. Friedenskaiser wider Willen* (Graz, 2008).

Mortimer, G., *Wallenstein. The Enigma of the Thirty Years War* (New York, 2010).

Parker, G., and Adams, S. (eds), *The Thirty Years' War* (2nd edn, London, 1997).

Schwarz, H.F., *The Imperial Privy Council in the Seventeenth Century* (Cambridge, MA., 1943).

Wilson, P., *Europe's Tragedy. A History of the Thirty Years War* (London, 2009).

The Spanish Monarchy and the Challenges of the Thirty Years' War

Gabriel Guarino

Recent studies on Spain's role in the Thirty Years' War have clearly shown that in order to comprehend the successes and failures of the Spanish military campaigns of the time it is necessary to consider the interaction of the following factors: the complex geo-political challenges posed by the vast territorial dispersal of Spanish territories, Spain's limited economic capabilities in relation to these challenges, and the widespread social malaise affecting many of the Spanish territories following the strains brought about by the war effort. Moreover, Spain's involvement in the Thirty Years' War has been assessed within such wider topics of debate as the 'military revolution', the 'general crisis' of the seventeenth century, and the alleged 'decline' of Spain. Accordingly, this chapter will trace the bellicose events in which Spain was involved against both foreign powers and rebellious provinces within the Spanish monarchy, as well as the various related scholarly debates, aiming to propose a balanced review of the state of the question.[1]

To begin with, the chronology of the Thirty Years' War doesn't apply well to the Spanish monarchy's reality when we take into consideration that the war with the Netherlands indeed ended in 1648, but its span encompassed 80 years. Similarly, the war with France had started in the midst of the conflict (1635) but went on until the signing of the Treaty of the Pyrenees in 1659. Moreover, according to Stradling, as far as Spain was concerned, it would be more accurate to speak of a 'fifty years war' (1618–68) if we also take into account the various conflicts that Spain was involved in, long after the signing of the Peace of Westphalia with Portugal (1640–68), England (1654–60), and again France (1667–68).[2] In this sense, Spain's deep military involvement throughout the best part of the seventeenth century reflects well its vast territorial commitments in Europe and in its colonies. Accordingly, it is fundamental to trace the extent of territorial possessions of the Spanish monarchy, and the strategic implications deriving from them on the eve of the Thirty Years' War. First, the Spanish monarchy held the entire Iberian Peninsula, including Portugal and its colonies. Territories around the French orbit included Roussillon, French Cerdagne in the Pyrenees, and Franche-Comté to the east of France. Alsace was in the orbit of the Holy Roman Empire. Territories in the Low Countries included Belgium and Luxembourg, Artois, and part of

---

[1] For some of the important general works on Spain, which also highlight her role in the war see: J.H. Elliott, *Imperial Spain, 1469–1716* (London, 1963); J. Lynch, *The Hispanic World in Crisis and Change, 1598–1700* (Oxford and Cambridge, Mass., 1992); the collection of essays by R.A. Stradling, *Spain's Struggle for Europe, 1598–1668* (London, 1994); H. Kamen, *Spain's Road to Empire: The Making of a World Power, 1492–1763* (London, 2002); and the collection of essays edited by G. Parker, *La crisis de la monarquía de Felipe IV* (Barcelona, 2006).

[2] R.A. Stradling, *Philip IV and the Government of Spain, 1621–1665* (Cambridge, 1988), p. 129.

Picardy, whereas the United Provinces, nowadays Holland, had been conducting an open rebellion against Spain since 1568. The Italian territories included the duchy of Milan, and the Kingdoms of Naples, Sicily and Sardinia. The extra-European colonies, augmented since 1580 by the Portuguese territories, included some posts in North and West Africa, large parts of present-day South, Central and North America, including Brazil, and various territories in the Asian Pacific including the Philippines and Goa.

The rule of these immense possessions by the Spanish 'composite monarchy' had some clear advantages like the potential availability of vast economic and human resources, and the resulting might that would deter other European powers from challenging Spain's position of supremacy.[3] On the other hand, this same territorial spreading in Europe was perceived as a constant threat by the other European powers – in particular France and England – a fact that turned Spain into a common enemy. Moreover, the great dispersal of lands meant very slow communication between the various parts, and the inevitable Spanish vulnerability when attempting to fend off military threats, particularly if these came from multiple fronts. In addition, the increasing expenses involved in maintaining the new military capabilities and forms of organisation, which constituted a 'military revolution' in early modern times, pushed Spain to spend well beyond its economic limits.[4] The combination of these reasons will be Spain's crucible in the 1640s as this chapter shall describe at length.

Spain's limitations were also manifested by the amount of revenues that the crown was able to extract from its vast possessions. In practice, the share of the burden between the various territories was uneven. The great burden of taxation and military conscription fell upon Castile. The Italian territories and the Spanish Netherlands came next in terms of contribution. Paradoxically, the other Iberian kingdoms – Valencia, Navarre, Catalonia, Aragon, and Portugal – contributed very little, if at all, by exercising their traditional privileges. Particularly important for the Spanish economy were the substantial quantities of silver dispatched from the New World, although the shipments were intermittent due to external attacks mostly perpetrated by English and Dutch privateers, or by such internal factors as corruption and fraud. The amount of bullion shrank considerably in the seventeenth century, and Spain was forced to turn to the debasement of coinage, a measure that consequently brought debilitating cycles of inflation and deflation in the Iberian Peninsula starting in the 1620s. As for the taxes collected in the Americas, much remained there to build defences against English, Dutch, and French encroachment, thereby using up the funds that the Spanish crown would otherwise have had available for its expenses in Europe.[5] In other words, there were clear limits to Spanish power. This fact was also accepted and acknowledged by the Spaniards themselves, and it is precisely this self-perception of vulnerability that conditioned their foreign policy during early modern times.[6]

---

[3] See J.H. Elliott, 'A Europe of Composite Monarchies', *Past and Present*, 137 (1992): pp. 48–71. For Elliott's earlier discussions concerning the composite nature of the Spanish monarchy see his *Imperial Spain*, especially pp. 156–8, 242–78.

[4] On Spain's disastrous financial policies during times of war see: G. Parker, *The Army of Flanders and the Spanish Road, 1567–659. The Logistics of Spanish Victory and Defeat in the Low Countries' War* (Cambridge, 1972); J. Alcalá-Zamora y Quiepo de Llano, *España, Flandes, y el Mar del Norte (1618–1639): la última ofensiva europea de los Austrias madrileños* (Barcelona, 1975); and J.H. Elliott, 'Foreign Policy and Domestic Crisis: Spain, 1598–1659', in J.H. Elliott (ed.), *Spain and Its World 1500–1700: Selected Essays* (New Haven and London, 1989), pp. 114–36.

[5] For the fiscal policies during this time see A. Domínguez Ortiz, *Política y hacienda de Felipe IV* (Madrid, 1960). For the Spanish economy in the Americas see S.J. Stein and B.H. Stein, *Silver, Trade, and War: Spain and America in the Making of Early Modern Europe* (Baltimore, 2000).

[6] For the Spaniards' self-awareness and related proposals for reform see J. H. Elliott, 'Self-perception and Decline in Early Seventeenth-Century Spain', in his *Spain and Its World*, pp. 241–61.

Hispanists agree on two general directives guiding the Spanish Habsburgs' foreign policy: the maintenance of Spanish power and its territories by way of military defence; and the protection, by force if necessary, of the confessional unity of Europe under the Catholic banner. To this we should add Spain's avowed responsibility in protecting the Mediterranean shores from the threat of Islam. These objectives, however, were pursued at different levels of intensity at different times, as can be seen from the apparent distinction between the policies of the two Spanish kings that ruled during the Thirty Years' War, Philip III (1598–1621), and his successor, Philip IV (1621–65). On the eve of the Thirty Years' War Spain's government was in a phase of transition, as the duke of Lerma, Philip III's chief minister and favourite (*valido*), was ousted from power in 1618. In terms of Lerma's foreign policy, the relatively peaceful relationship with France, the signing of a peace treaty with England (London, 1604), and particularly the 12 years' truce with the United Provinces (1609–21), marked his twenty years' rule (1598–1618) as a long period of peace for Spain.[7] That said, Lerma's policies were probably conditioned more by economic constraints than by outright 'pacifism'. In this sense, signing the truce with the Dutch in 1609 can be better understood within the context of Spain's declaration of bankruptcy in 1607.[8] However, since the truce was only valid for the Low Countries and did not include Spain's overseas territories, the Dutch took advantage of the situation by taking over outposts in Brazil and in South-East Asia.[9] In addition to the economic damage inflicted by the Dutch, Lerma's critics at home believed that his 'pacificist' policies were damaging Spain's international prestige. With Lerma out of the picture (although his son, the duke of Uceda, succeeded him for a brief period), and the death of Philip III in 1621, the stage was set for Philip IV and his new favourite, the duke of Olivares (count-duke starting from 1625), who promptly proposed a more assertive foreign policy to restore Spain's damaged reputation.[10]

In essence, according to Elliott, Olivares' foreign policy was not very different from that of his predecessor by being essentially defensive, only that his insistence on keeping Spain's reputation intact meant that 'whether in the Netherlands or elsewhere – peace and security could not be bought at the price of national honour.'[11] Moreover, as Olivares made clear in a later memorandum during the Thirty Years' War, prestige was not the only thing at stake. Showing weakness with the Dutch could set an example for others to rebel against Spain, thus creating a 'domino effect':

> *The first and greatest dangers are those that threaten Lombardy, the Netherlands and Germany. A defeat in any of these three is fatal for this Monarchy, so much so that if the defeat in those parts is a great one, the rest of the monarchy will collapse; for Germany will be followed by Italy and the Netherlands, and the Netherlands will be followed by America; and Lombardy will be followed by Naples and Sicily, without the possibility of being able to defend either.*[12]

---

[7] See B.G. Garcia, *La Pax Hispanica. Política exterior del Duque de Lerma* (Leuven, 1996).

[8] Elliott, 'Foreign Policy', p. 116.

[9] On the truce see P. Brightwell, 'The Spanish System and the Twelve Years Truce', *English Historical Review*, 89 (1974): pp. 270–92.

[10] On Olivares' stressing of reputation in foreign policy see J.H. Elliott, *The Count-Duke of Olivares: The Statesman in an Age of Decline* (New Haven and London, 1986), pp. 82, 681–2.

[11] Elliott, 'Foreign Policy', p. 123.

[12] Quoted in G. Parker, 'The Making of Strategy in Habsburg Spain: Philip II's "bid for mastery", 1556–1598', in W. Murray, K. MacGregor and A.H Bernstein (eds), *The Making of Strategy: Rulers, States, and War* (Cambridge, 1994), p. 122.

Spain's swift choice to get involved in the Thirty Years' War is a good testimony to the aforementioned preoccupations. Thus, closely after the 'defenestration of Prague' (23 May 1618) and the beginning of the Bohemian Revolt against Ferdinand of Habsburg, king of Bohemia and Emperor of the Holy Roman Empire from 1619, the Spanish Habsburgs intervened in assisting their Austrian relatives. Spain's motivation for aid was clear – a Protestant victory in the empire posed a direct threat to Spanish interests in the Spanish Netherlands and Italy. The aid started off with financial assistance. The first instalment comprised of 200,000 thalers which were sent in July 1618. The money kept streaming steadily from Madrid to Vienna and by the end of 1624 the Spanish financial assistance totalled 6 million thalers. A total of 7,000 Spanish troops were also sent to the rescue as soon as May 1619. By the end of Philip III's reign, in March 1621, there were 40,000 troops assisting the Austrian Habsburgs.[13] In these first years of the conflict, the Spaniards also deployed troops to secure their strategic interests, in particular the means of communication, supply, and flowing of troops to and from Italy to Flanders. For this reason, troops from Lombardy were sent to secure the 'Spanish Road' and the Alsace area in 1619, and a year later the Spanish governor of Milan occupied the Valtelline pass in the Alps. Similarly, the Low Countries army, led by Ambrosio Spinola, occupied the Lower Palatinate in order to control the strategic passage of the Rhine. In addition, Spain's support of the Emperor during the 1620s and 1630s was also done with the hope that he would be able to return the favour and support them against the Dutch once he got rid of his enemies. This was an expectation that would be met only partially, as the Emperor never fully committed to the Spanish cause, despite sending token military support to fight the Dutch.[14]

Clearly then, the imminent confrontation with the United Provinces was the major concern of Spain during the first years of the war. Olivares had no illusions of being able to bring back the Dutch under Spanish rule, but he aspired towards a favourable permanent peace settlement which would yield better results than the truce negotiated by his predecessor, the duke of Lerma. By 1621 the truce with the United Provinces expired and Olivares' belligerent intentions towards the Dutch were matched by the Council of State, which opted not to extend the truce further. Similarly, the Portuguese Council pressured towards a renewal of the conflict owing to the damages inflicted by the Dutch in Brazil. As stipulated by Lynch, if previously the conflict revolved around sovereignty, religious issues, and trade, by the time the truce terminated, Spain's main concern was its economic survival via the defence of the American trade.[15] Accordingly, the Spanish war on the Dutch was mostly done via economic means, like economic embargoes and privateering, with the aim of bringing Dutch trade to its knees. These objectives were to be met via a close collaboration with the Austrian Habsburgs. In fact, Olivares envisaged a Habsburg league to include Spain, the Emperor and the German Catholic princes. As a part of this alliance Olivares planned a Habsburg merchant base in the Baltic to rival the Dutch monopoly there, which he tried to activate in the years 1626–28. The scheme, however, failed to materialise because the various prospective partners either lacked the commitment or were unable to provide the needed resources for the design to work. Ironically, one of the undesired effects of the proposed scheme, from a Habsburg perspective, was that it pushed the Swedish ruler Gustav Adolph to join the anti-Habsburg coalition, as the Spanish machinations over the

---

[13] These sums are brought by G. Parker, *The Thirty Years' War* (London, 1984), p. 50.

[14] On Spain's involvement in Central Europe around the early stages of the war see: P. Brightwell, 'The Spanish Origins of the Thirty Years' War', *European Studies Review*, 9 (1979): 409–31; also by the same, 'Spain, Bohemia and Europe, 1619–1621', *European Studies Review*, 12 (1982): pp. 371–99; and M.S. Sánchez, 'A House Divided: Spain, Austria and the Bohemian and Hungarian Successions', *Sixteenth Century Journal*, 25 (1994): pp. 887–903.

[15] Lynch, *Hispanic World*, p. 98.

Baltic were perceived as a potential encroachment on Swedish interests. On the positive side, according to Israel, the Spaniards were able to effectively block the Dutch trade from the 1620s to the late 1640s, to the Iberian Peninsula, to Italy, and to the Levant – a fact that directly favoured English trade at the expense of the Dutch in the 1630s.[16]

Alongside the economic blockades the Spaniards conducted a successful military campaign in the early 1620s. In 1620 they helped the imperial troops to defeat the Bohemian rebels at the battle of White Mountain. Similarly, spectacular victories were achieved in 1625, enabled financially by a particularly remarkable delivery of bullion from the Americas in the previous year, like the rendition of Breda in the Low Countries, the recapture of Bahia in Brazil from the hands of the Dutch, the repulsion of the British fleet in Cadiz, and the repulsion of a French invasion in the Valtelline.[17] However, things took a turn for the worse during the years 1627–29 with the Spanish intervention in the duchy of Mantua – a decision that bore destructive results. With the death of the childless duke of Mantua, the best prospect of succeeding him went to the French claimant, the duke of Nevers. Fearing the strategic compromise of Spanish interests in northern Italy, Olivares sent the governor of Milan to occupy the Monferrat, a Mantuan region bordering Milan to the west. In reaction, a French army was sent to the occupied region, resulting in a long and inconclusive war that lasted until April 1631. Olivares' expectations of a short campaign were thus shattered, leaving Spain in greater financial ruin as the crown's share of the Indies bullion went to finance the Italian front.[18] In addition, in 1628 a heavy blow was inflicted on Spanish prestige and economic resources by the Dutch squadron of Piet Heyn, which was able to capture the entire Spanish silver fleet in Cuba. This string of misfortunes was prolonged by a Dutch fleet taking Recife in Brazil.[19] To the strain placed on the Spanish regime by these external events one needs to add internal strife in Castile, where the economy entered a new phase of recession following a string of poor harvests and rising food prices.[20]

On February 1631, in a desperate attempt to reverse Spain's fortunes, Olivares designed a new grand scheme involving Philip IV's two brothers: Charles was to go to Portugal and assemble a fleet to recapture the Brazilian possessions taken by the Dutch, while Ferdinand, the Cardinal-Infante, would be sent to the Southern Netherlands to lead the Spanish troops, aiming to restore the Spanish reputation after the many losses inflicted on Spain by the Dutch from 1629–33 in the Low Countries. In fact, according to Israel, 'by 1633 Spanish prestige in the Low Countries stood lower than at any time since the disastrous collapse of the late 1570s'.[21] Charles of Habsburg died en route in 1632 before reaching Portugal, and

---

[16] J.I. Israel, 'Spain, the Spanish embargos, and the struggle for the mastery of world trade, 1585–1660', in J.I. Israel (ed.), *Empires and Entrepots: The Dutch, the Spanish Monarchy, and the Jews, 1585–1713* (London, 1990), pp. 189–212. This view challenges Alcalá-Zamora's opinion that the Spanish blockades against the Dutch have been completely ineffective. See Alcalá-Zamora, *España, Flandes, y el Mar del Norte*. See also R.R. Villar, 'Un gran proyecto anti-holandés en tiempo de Felipe IV. La destrucción del comercio rebelde en Europa', *Hispania*, 22 (1962): pp. 542–58.

[17] For these events see M. Fernández Alvarez, 'El fracaso de la hegemonia Española en Europa', in F. Tomás y Valiente (ed.), *Historia de España Ramón Menédez Pidal, vol. 25: La España de Felipe IV. El gobierno de la monarquía, la crisis de 1640 y el fracaso de la hegemonía europea* (Madrid, 1982), pp. 694–9.

[18] For the War of Mantuan Succession see J. H. Elliott, *Richelieu and Olivares* (Cambridge, 1984), pp. 95–112; R.A. Stradling, 'Prelude to Disaster: The Precipitation of the War of the Mantuan Succession, 1627–1629', *The Historical Journal*, 33/4 (1990): pp. 769–85; and D. Parrott, 'The Mantuan Succession, 1627–1631: A Sovereignty Dispute in Early Modern Europe', *The English Historical Review*, 112 (1997): pp. 20–65.

[19] G. Parker, *Europe in Crisis, 1598–1648* (2nd edn, Oxford, 2001), p. 172.

[20] Elliott, 'Foreign Policy', p. 127.

[21] J. Israel, 'Olivares, the Cardinal-Infante and Spain's Strategy in the Low Countries (1635–1643): The Road to Rocroi', in R. Kagan and G. Parker (eds), *Spain, Europe and the Atlantic World: Essays in Honour of John H. Elliott* (Cambridge, 1995), p. 273.

the fleet that eventually set sail for Brazil in 1635 was defeated by the Dutch.[22] The Cardinal-Infante was considerably more successful. During 1633–34 he assembled a powerful army in Lombardy destined for Germany, where a new threat preoccupied Spanish interests – at the end of 1631 the Swedes, who had joined the Protestant cause in Germany the previous year, invaded the Lower Palatinate. The two Habsburg branches were now resolved to collaborate more closely to push back the Swedish menace as they signed a mutual collaboration treaty in early 1632. In 1634 the Cardinal-Infante's army invaded the Rhineland, and the joint forces of imperial and Spanish troops achieved an impressive victory at the Battle of Nördlingen against the Protestant army of Swedes and Germans (the Heilbronn League). Paradoxically, this victory made things worse for Spain's cause. Rather than serving as a propeller of a joint Habsburg effort against the Dutch and the Protestants in the north, the events at Nördlingen finally convinced the French to join the war against the Habsburgs, opening a particularly formidable front for Spain.[23]

In fact, taking into account the ever-present rivalry between Spain and France, it is surprising that overt warfare had not started earlier. The relatively amicable relations between the two during the first two decades of the seventeenth century ceased with the accession to power of Louis XIII's minister, the Cardinal of Richelieu, in 1624. From then on France started subsidising the various parties involved in the anti-Habsburg coalition. France's direct military involvement was eventually triggered by Spain's decision to support more vehemently their Austrian relatives, but Olivares' intervention in Mantua had already signalled to Richelieu the path to war, as it confirmed his mistrust in Spain, which he perceived as an aggressive and imperialist power that needed to be kept in check. Accordingly, in the 1630s both the French and Spanish governments started mobilising resources towards the imminent and inevitable clash. In Spain this translated into growing fiscal demands on Castilian tax-payers as well as on the nobility, which was called upon to provide voluntary contributions of funds towards the war effort. In fact, according to Stradling, starting from 1635, because of the direct and indirect bearing of the war effort on all aspects of social life throughout the Spanish territories, the Spanish monarchy entered a period of total war. This was manifested in Olivares' exploitative attempts at taxation throughout the Spanish possessions, as well as the battle zones themselves that extended all over the globe, owing to the sustained Dutch, French and English attempts to encroach on Spanish and Portuguese colonial interests.[24] The extent of Spain's want at these stages of the war is well exemplified by the degree of indiscrimination in its conscription policy. According to Parker, the Spanish army had no choice but to draft vagrants, disabled men, teenagers, old men, and even convicted criminals, pardoned in exchange for military service.[25]

A point of contention among historians regarding the Franco-Spanish war is the order of priority in which Spain placed it. According to Kennedy and Stradling, from a Spanish point of view, the war with the Dutch lost precedence to the new French challenge from the very outset – a claim supported by the strong Spanish offensive of 1636 against France.[26] Israel's assertion, on the other hand, is that this change in strategic emphasis took place only in the 1640s, while the Dutch front remained the main offensive stage for Spanish military operations throughout the 1630s and the early 1640s. Thus, the Cardinal-Infante's efforts

---

[22] Parker, *Europe in Crisis*, p. 173.
[23] For these events see Lynch, *Hispanic World*, pp. 108–10; Fernández Alvarez, 'El fracaso de la hegemonia Española', pp. 717–20.
[24] See Stradling, *Philip IV*, pp.129 onwards.
[25] Parker, *Europe in Crisis*, pp. 178–9. See also R.A. Stradling, 'Filling the Ranks: Spanish Mercenary Recruitment and the Crisis of the 1640s', in his *Spain's Struggle for Europe*, pp. 251–69.
[26] See respectively, P. Kennedy, *The Rise and Fall of the Great Powers: Economic Change and Military Conflict from 1500 to 2000* (London, 1989), p. 50, and Stradling, *Philip IV*, pp. 103–4.

concentrated on the Dutch from 1634 to 1636. The attack on France in the summer of 1636, rather than being part of a new Spanish grand scheme, was an improvised, secondary operation, that was taken by the Cardinal-Infante (contrary to his general directives from Madrid) as a response to the Emperor's sudden pressure to attack France. Both men believed that it was a rare opportunity to join imperial and Spanish forces in order to concentrate on the French after the withdrawal of the Swedes and the Protestant electors from the war. Accordingly, the Cardinal-Infante invaded France from the north, and after taking Corbie he had the route to Paris open. However, he was eventually stopped after strong French resistance. Apart from this ultimately unsuccessful parenthesis, for the rest of the decade the Spaniards remained focused on offensive efforts against the Dutch objectives, while limiting themselves to defensive attempts to repulse French initiatives.[27]

At this stage, however, shortly after the failed invasion, the Spaniards received a brief boost in confidence as the French were forced to pull forces from various fronts following internal rebellions. Similarly, the death of France's allies in northern Italy, the Mantuan and Savoiard rulers in 1637, in tandem with the Spanish seizure of the Valtelline, marked the breakdown of French aspirations in Italy. Consequently, Richelieu proposed a truce with Spain, which was rejected by Olivares, who felt that the French proposal came from a deep weakness that could be exploited to achieve a convincing victory. These hopes were to be frustrated as Spain subsequently suffered a string of painful defeats at the hands of the French and the Dutch. On this note, the decade came to a close with the Naval Battle of Downs (1639), where the Dutch effectively destroyed Spain's North Atlantic fleet.[28] Despite the grave losses, the Spaniards were still able to preserve the sea-link with the Spanish Netherlands. Moreover, according to Stradling, the frustration of Spain's aspirations to control the northern waters should be placed in context, as she remained in control of the Atlantic and the Mediterranean, consistently succeeding in repelling French maritime challenges throughout the 1640s.[29]

The year 1640 has been marked as an *annus horribilis* in Spanish history, for in this year the Spanish Habsburgs found themselves having to deal with the internal rebellions of Catalonia and Portugal on top of the existing military fronts. In order to understand the Iberian rebellions we need to take a step back and examine Olivares' conception of the Union of Arms (Union de Armas), which he aimed to implement starting from 1626. The idea was to create a closer cohesion and coordination between the Spanish monarchy's various parts, in a way that the burden of its defence would be shared by all more equitably. The existing arrangement whereby Castile carried most of the weight, somewhat supported by taxes wrung from the Italian States, the Spanish Netherlands, as well as the uneven streaming of American bullion, no longer sufficed to maintain the increasing military and fiscal demands of the Thirty Years' War. The end objective of the Union of Arms was to form a standing army of 140,000 soldiers made up of the total economic investment and draft of troops resulting from the quotas allocated to each Spanish territory. These numbers were to be allocated as follows: Castile and the Indies, 44,000; Aragon, 10,000; Catalonia, 16,000; Valencia, 6,000; Portugal, 16,000; Naples, 16,000; Sicily, 6,000; Milan, 8,000; The Low Countries, 16,000; Sardinia, the Balearic and the Canary Islands, 6,000. The Union of Arms was to be placed within Olivares' larger aim of reforming the Spanish economy as a means of bringing prosperity to an economically and psychologically exhausted nation.[30] Contrary

---

[27] Israel, 'Olivares, the Cardinal-Infante and Spain's Strategy', pp. 278–90.
[28] Fernández Alvarez, 'El fracaso de la hegemonia Española', pp. 730–2.
[29] R.A. Stradling, 'Catastrophe and Recovery: The Defeat of Spain, 1639–43', in his *Spain's Struggle for Europe*, p. 207.
[30] See Elliott, *Count-Duke of Olivares*, pp. 244–77.

to Olivares' intentions, however, the strong internal resistance to this plan within the Iberian kingdoms, ever jealous of their privileges, forced him to shelve it. When he tried to revive it in order to face the French threat it eventually contributed to trigger the revolts of Catalonia and Portugal.

The Catalan revolt started as an off-shoot of the conflict with France. In 1639 Richelieu decided to attack Spain from the poorly defended Catalan towns in the Pyrenees. Following the French seizure of the fortress of Salses, Olivares put pressure on the Catalans to aid with manpower and finances. Moreover, he seized this opportunity to revive his Union of Arms project, demanding to billet a Catalan force of 6,000 troops to aid in the military effort in Italy. These actions generated much local resistance. Various local groups, including villagers, agricultural seasonal workers and outlaws, clashed with Castilian troops during the early months of 1640. Emboldened by their successes and aided by urban supporters, they entered the capital, Barcelona, as well as other towns, where they attacked royal officials and local citizens loyal to the crown. These actions culminated in June, when the viceroy, the Count of Santa Coloma, was assassinated alongside other members of the royal bureaucracy. These clear acts of open rebellion were later backed by the local elites, which sought and received French support – a move which turned it into a French dependency by January 1641. The installed French regime, however, was met by the local population with the same antipathy as shown to the previous regime. Significantly, just as they had with Olivares, the Catalans refused to provide troops against Castilian attacks. The Spanish efforts paid off, and eventually in 1652 Barcelona was recaptured and Catalonia was reinstituted into the Spanish monarchy, minus the areas of Roussillon and Cerdagne, which remained in French hands.[31]

The Portuguese revolt started in a similar fashion to that of the Catalans. When Olivares ordered the Portuguese to aid the Castilian troops to recapture Catalonia in 1640, the duke of Braganza, the leading aristocrat in the country, headed the Portuguese nobility to fight for independence from Spain. The first acts of rebellion included the seizure of the royal palace in Lisbon, the execution of Spanish officials, and the proclamation of Braganza as King John IV. In fact, the Portuguese had various reasons to rebel. Like many of the Spanish territories in those years, they were suffering from high taxation and the resulting social discontent. The Portuguese were also annoyed by the growing numbers of Castilians taking up positions of power at the expense of the local elites, as well as by the steady decline of their overseas empire, encroached upon by the Dutch in the Americas and South-East Asia. After various abortive attempts to recover Portugal during almost three decades, Spain was eventually forced to acknowledge its independence in 1668.[32]

The persistence of the Catalan and Portuguese rebellions ultimately led to Olivares' demise, as he was forced to resign in January 1643 by Philip IV. The king yielded to the growing pressure coming from Olivares' numerous enemies at court, who protested against the disastrous results of his centralistic policies. According to Elliott, Olivares' fall can be interpreted as a kind of bloodless revolution achieved by the Castilian elites – one that supplanted the need for an outright revolt there. Indeed, Spain's ability to survive the multiple crises of the 1640s depended, to a large extent, on the fact that Castile remained loyal and cooperative. In fact, as in the case of Catalonia and Portugal, Castile showed clear signs of discontent, or preconditions for revolution, which could have easily led to a revolutionary

---

[31] For a broad contextual study of the revolt see J. H. Elliott, *The Revolt of the Catalans: A Study in the Decline of Spain, 1598–1640* (Cambridge, 1963). For a more recent historiographical evaluation see R.G. Cárcel, 'La revolución catalana: algunos problemas historiográficos', *Manuscrits*, 9 (1991), pp. 115–42.

[32] For some recent interpretations see R. Valladres, *La rebelión de Portugal. Guerra, conflicto y poderes en la monarquía hispánica (1640–1680)* (Valladolid, 1998); and D. L. Tengwall, *The Portuguese Revolution (1640–1688): A European War of Freedom and Independence* (Lewiston, 2010).

outburst.³³ Castile's economy had been constantly declining since the late sixteenth century – a fact supported by many studies clearly showing that the Castilian industry and exports virtually ceased to exist during the years of the war, agricultural production was seriously damaged, and the population was constantly reducing.³⁴

While the Iberian revolts engaged the Castilian forces, the Spanish army in the Low Countries continued battling on against the French. After the premature death of the Cardinal-Infante in 1639, the command of the army and the Spanish Netherlands passed to the Portuguese Francisco de Melo. His campaigns in 1641–42 were successful, in particular the victory of Honnecourt in which the French lost 3,000 men, and an equal number were captured. However, only a year later, Melo's army was to suffer a particularly painful loss. Aided by a superior cavalry, the French army achieved a prestigious victory at Rocroi, by decimating the legendary Spanish infantry, the *tercios*. The defeat at Rocroi has been perceived as marking the end of Spain's military power in Europe. This point has been disputed by Lynch, who denies the possibility of a meaningful impact based on a single battle in the middle of a long contest with France, one that would indeed go on for another 15 years. Moreover, despite Rocroi's resounding defeat, Spain was able to maintain her position in the Southern Netherlands.³⁵ Similarly, according to Stradling, the epic defeats of Downs and Rocroi can be regarded as symbols of Spain's collapse, but in fact, as they took place only half-way through the prolonged confrontation, 'they tell us more about Spain's strength than about her weakness, explaining her survival rather than her decline.'³⁶

Indeed, new challenges were to test Spain's fortitude as the 1640s unfolded. The fiscal burdens imposed on Spanish territories in order to finance the already numerous fronts that Spain was engaged in during this period caused deep discontent also in Naples and Sicily. In addition to the fiscal burden the Sicilian revolt was fed by environmental disasters. Torrential rains in 1645 and 1646 destroyed crops, leading to the rise of bread prices, and also caused destructive floods leaving numerous people homeless throughout the island. The massive rains were followed by draught from the autumn of 1646 to the spring of 1647. During these difficult years the local authorities subsidised the price of wheat in Palermo in order to alleviate the burden. But new orders from the king, arriving in the summer, firmly demanded a halt to this practice. As a consequence the viceroy instructed the city's bakers to reduce the size of bread rolls by 15 per cent, a decision that proved to be the last straw. Hundreds of people took to the streets, looting the property of wealthy citizens, burning down the treasury's archives, and freeing more than a thousand prisoners. The response of the viceroy, desperate to restore the peace, was to yield to popular demand by reinstating the subsidy of bread, abolishing the taxes on five basic victuals, and pardoning the rioters. The ease with which Palermo's citizens achieved these concessions encouraged most Sicilian urban centres to follow suit. Palermo then saw a series of subsequent revolts and would not be finally pacified before the autumn of 1648, when the Spaniards could send a relief fleet to reassert their rule.³⁷

---

³³ See J.H. Elliott, 'A non-revolutionary society: Castile in the 1640s', in J.H. Elliott (ed.), *Spain, Europe, and the Wider World, 1500–1800* (New Haven and London, 2009), pp. 74–5.
³⁴ See the collection of essays edited by I.A.A. Thompson and C.B. Yun, *The Castilian Crisis of the Seventeenth Century: New Perspectives on the Economic and Social History of Seventeenth-Century Spain* (Cambridge, 1994).
³⁵ Lynch, *Hispanic World*, p. 165.
³⁶ Stradling, 'Catastrophe and Recovery', p. 212.
³⁷ For a concise synthesis see Geoffrey Parker, 'Los problemas de la monarquía, 1643–1648', in G. Parker (ed.), *La crisis de la monarquía de Felipe IV* (Barcelona, 2006), pp. 109–12, 136–7. For more detailed studies see H.G. Koenigsberger, 'The Revolt of Palermo in 1647', *Cambridge Historical Journal*, 8 (1946): pp. 129–44; and G.L. Ribot, 'Las revueltas sicilianas de 1647–1648', in *La Monarquía Hispánica en crisis* (Barcelona, 1991), pp. 183–99.

The news from the May revolts in Sicily soon reached the Neapolitans who felt that given their heavy burden they had even better reasons to rebel against their Spanish rulers. In fact, the 1647–48 revolt had been brewing for some time. According to Villari in his classic study of the Neapolitan revolt, the crises of the Thirty Years' War changed the relations of power between the Spanish state and the local political and social forces. The monarchical government, entering an extended period of mounting economic and political crisis due to the simultaneous and extended wars it had to contend with between 1636 and 1647, allowed the aristocratic elite of the Kingdom of Naples to increase its pressure on the lower strata of the population, in a process which he labelled 'refeudalisation'. Eventually, the concerted oppression of the landed aristocracy and the fiscal burden imposed by the Spaniards exploded in a large-scale revolt that affected not only the city of Naples and its surrounding countryside, but the entire urban and rural south of Italy.[38] In a similar fashion to the Sicilian revolt, the scales were tipped by the imposition of a new tax on fruits in the capital. Led by Tommaso Aniello of Amalfi (popularly known as Masaniello), a charismatic fisherman, large crowds of Neapolitan plebeians rallied to the royal palace demanding from the viceroy the abolition of the abhorred taxes on basic foodstuffs. After initial attempts at negotiation the Spanish authorities were forced to leave the city, backed by a meagre army of 1,200 troops instead of the regular force of 5,000 troops and the squadron of galleys that were temporarily redeployed elsewhere. The revolt that had started in July 1647 continued until April 1648, when the Spanish managed to retake the city with the help of a Spaniards fleet headed by John of Austria, Philip IV's illegitimate son.[39]

Eventually, the Iberian and Italian revolts of the 1640s pushed the Spaniards to make concessions to the Dutch, fearing to lose the very core of the monarchy. A settlement with the United Provinces was also facilitated by the Portuguese revolt, since the restitution of the Brazilian territories taken by the Dutch was no longer a pressing matter for Spain. In 1648, after direct negotiations, and against the will of their French allies, the Dutch signed the Treaty of Münster with the Spaniards. According to the treaty, the Spanish were forced to formally recognise the United Provinces as an independent republic, and they officially accepted the Dutch occupation of Portuguese territories in the Americas.[40] With the signature of the treaty, Spain's role in the Thirty Years' War was officially over.

In sum, Spain's participation in the Thirty Years' War, after encountering some notable success in the 1620s and 1630s, eventually concluded with the victory of the anti-Habsburg coalition, led by the French and the Dutch. Kennedy effectively summarises the reasons for the Habsburgs' failure to keep their power intact: first, there was the increase in costs, scale and management brought about by the early modern 'military revolution' in Europe starting from the 1520s onwards. It is precisely the spiralling costs in military endeavours, coupled with a steep rate of inflation that kept the Habsburgs in a constant struggle for economic survival. Accordingly, Spain's military campaigns were constrained by its economic limitations. When she was able to wring enough taxes from her subjects or obtain bullion from the Americas, ambitious campaigns, like the Cardinal-Infante's intervention in Germany in 1634–35, could be organised. But the constant demands from her many fronts limited the effect of short-term victories, and constantly eroded Spain's capabilities. Moreover, the heavy tax burden placed on her various provinces eventually backfired when

---

[38] See R. Villari, *The Revolt of Naples*, (Cambridge, 1993).
[39] For the pioneering studies on the events of 1647 see M. Schipa, *La cosidetta rivolta di Masaniello da memorie contemporanee inedite* (Naples, 1918). A recent contextual political analysis is provided by A. Musi, *La rivolta di Masaniello nella scena politica barocca* (Naples, 1989). For an alternative interpretation see P. Burke, 'The Virgin of the Carmine and the Revolt of Masaniello', *Past and Present*, 99/1 (1983): pp. 3–21.
[40] See Fernández Alvarez, 'El fracaso de la hegemonia Española', pp. 765–9.

many of these turned rebellious. Ultimately, Spain's military challenges were simply too much to handle. The immense Spanish monarchy provided 'one of the greatest examples of strategical overstretch in history; for the price of possessing so many territories was the existence of numerous foes.'[41] In fact, for the Spaniards the war was far from being over after Westphalia, as their confrontation with the Catalans, the Portuguese, and the French continued to loom large into the next decade.

Selected Bibliography

Alcalá-Zamora y Quiepo de Llano, J., *España, Flandes, y el Mar del Norte (1618–1639): la última ofensiva europea de los Austrias madrileños* (Barcelona, 1975).

Elliott, J.H., *The Count-Duke of Olivares: The Statesman in an Age of Decline* (New Haven and London, 1986).

Fernández Alvarez, Manuel, 'El fracaso de la hegemonia Española en Europa', in F. Tomás y Valiente (ed.), *Historia de España Ramón Menédez Pidal, vol. 25: La España de Felipe IV. El gobierno de la monarquía, la crisis de 1640 y el fracaso de la hegemonía europea* (Madrid, 1982), pp. 635–789.

Israel, J.I., 'Olivares, the Cardinal-Infante and Spain's Strategy in the Low Countries (1635–1643): The Road to Rocroi', in R. Kagan and G. Parker (eds), *Spain, Europe and the Atlantic World: Essays in Honour of John H. Elliott* (Cambridge, 1995), pp. 267–95.

Kamen, H., *Spain's Road to Empire: The Making of a World Power, 1492–1763* (London, 2002).

Kennedy, P., *The Rise and Fall of the Great Powers: Economic Change and Military Conflict from 1500 to 2000* (London, 1989).

Lynch, J., *The Hispanic World in Crisis and Change, 1598–1700* (Oxford and Cambridge, Mass., 1992).

Parker, G., (ed.), *The Thirty Years' War* (London, 1984).

Parker, G., *Europe in Crisis, 1598–1648* (2nd edn, Oxford, 2001).

Parker, G., 'Los problemas de la monarquía, 1643–1648', in G. Parker (ed.), *La crisis de la monarquía de Felipe IV* (Barcelona, 2006), pp. 105–40.

Stradling, R.A., *Philip IV and the Government of Spain, 1621–1665* (Cambridge, 1988).

Stradling, R.A., (ed.), *Spain's Struggle for Europe, 1598–1668* (London, 1994).

---

[41] Kennedy, *Rise and Fall of the Great Powers*, p. 61.

Denmark

Paul Douglas Lockhart

On 30 July 1625, Christian IV – king of Denmark and Norway, duke of Schleswig and Holstein-Segeberg, and lately commander of military forces in the Lower Saxon Circle of the empire – suffered a terrible accident near his headquarters at the Weser River town of Hameln. His forces had been fighting a running battle against Jean 'tSerclaes, Count Tilly, and the army of the Catholic League, and had been doing a creditable job of it. But this evening, while the king was out riding along Hameln's decaying battlements, his horse stumbled and fell, sending horse and rider to the ground more than 20 feet below. The beast died, its neck broken, but the king was alive… barely. He would be in a coma for two days. Within a few hours of his fall, though, the rumours began to spread – the king of Denmark was no more. Christian's enemies, Tilly included, took heart. Only yesterday the Catholic commander had been amenable to peace talks, but now he lost all inclination to be accommodating. And while Christian's lieutenants fretted over their fallen leader, many of the king's German allies heard the news, despaired, and scrambled to make peace while they still could.[1]

It was, of course, not the end of Christian IV, nor was it the end of the rebellion in Lower Saxony. But the accident at Hameln, and the hyperbolic reaction to it, demonstrate something that may appear curious to modern students of the seventeenth century: that Denmark was once of pivotal importance in European international politics. The Danish monarchy does not fit neatly into the mainstream of early modern historiography, which tends to highlight the histories of Tudor-Stuart England and Valois-Bourbon France. But in the early seventeenth century, there was a broader constellation of powers at work in Europe, and in the Baltic region it was still Denmark – the greatest Lutheran kingdom in Europe at the time – that held sway.

What we must remember, though, is that it was not Denmark that entered the war in 1625. Though survey histories of the Thirty Years' War conventionally refer to the Lower Saxon War of 1625–29 as the 'Danish phase' or the 'Danish intervention', or – worst of all – as the 'Danish invasion' of the Holy Roman Empire – the truth is that Denmark did not enter the war, not voluntarily at least. For it was the king himself, Christian IV, who intervened in the Thirty Years' War, without the support of his own kingdom – as a German prince and not in his capacity as a Scandinavian king.

The state which Christian IV ruled in 1625 was – like so many early modern polities – a varied conglomerate of territories. It included Denmark itself, the island of Bornholm, the kingdom of Norway (including the provinces of Jämtland and Härjedalen, lost to Sweden in 1658), Norway's vassal-state of Iceland, the Færø Islands, the Scanian provinces bordering

---

[1] J. Kocí et al. (eds), *Documenta Bohemica Bellum Tricennale Illustrantia* (7 vols.) (Prague, 1976–81), vol. 4, p. 59; Paul Lockhart, *Denmark in the Thirty Years' War, 1618* (Selinsgrove, 1996), p. 135.

on southern Sweden (Skåne, Blekinge, and Halland), and the German patrimony, notably the duchy of Holstein-Segeberg. With the addition of desolate Greenland, the Oldenburg dynastic state was vast, second in expanse only to contemporary Spain. Vast, but sparsely populated: only about one-and-a-quarter million souls resided in the Oldenburg lands, most of them in Denmark or the German duchies.[2]

Denmark was not populous, nor was it wealthy. It could boast of a modest export trade in barley, rye, and hemp, and smoked and salted fish; Norwegian timber was in high demand in Dutch and English shipyards. These, however, were not the sources of Denmark's wealth, nor the reason that Danish kings exerted influence in foreign affairs. *That* came from geography. Denmark controlled all the sea-lanes connecting the Baltic and North Seas, and hence the Baltic trade itself. The main passage, the Sound (Øresundet), which funnelled to a narrow choke-point between Helsingborg and Helsingør, was the only viable thoroughfare for ships entering or exiting the Baltic. Northern Europe was thoroughly dependent on the Baltic trade; at the time of the Dutch Revolt, the Netherlands imported nearly two-thirds of locally consumed grain from Baltic sources. Possession of the narrow seas leading into the Baltic gave the Danish kings the power to levy tolls – the infamous and unpopular 'Sound dues' – on all Baltic traffic at Helsingør. It also bestowed upon them the power to shut off the Baltic trade altogether.

The Sound dues provided a lucrative and reliable income, and possession of it shaped the relationships that Denmark had with the states of Northern Europe, especially England and the Netherlands. Denmark's parasitical trade practices inspired both respect and envy among all those who depended on the Baltic trade. Possession of the Sound also meant that Denmark could not seal itself off from the rest of Europe. From the time that Denmark officially adopted the Lutheran faith in 1536 until the military catastrophes of 1658–60, Danish kings and statesmen pursued three distinct but overlapping sets of goals: first, the protection and expansion of Denmark's commercial sphere-of-influence, which meant a constant state of enmity with the cities of the Hanseatic League; second, guarding Denmark's Baltic prominence against encroachment by upstart kingdom Sweden; and third, the pursuit of dynastic aspirations in northern Germany. The house of Oldenburg was not far removed from its Low German roots; possession of Holstein-Segeberg made sure that the kings kept a hand in German politics. As a result, the Danish kings – Christian IV in particular – were accustomed to think of themselves as Nordic monarchs *and* German princes. The Reformation, which brought the Lutheran faith to Denmark on a tide of popular enthusiasm backed by a charismatic usurper, made the ties between Denmark and the Germanies especially close.[3]

The constituent elements of the power elite in Denmark were usually of one mind where it came to foreign policy. The term 'Crown of Denmark' – *Danmarks krone* – referred not to the interests of the royal house, but to those of the dynasty *and* those of the ruling aristocracy, whose power and authority were embodied in a Council of State (*Rigsråd*). The king, according to the political ideology that has come to be known in Danish as *adelsvælden*, was an equal partner with the Council, and hence should rule with the Council or through it but not over it. Clearly there would be points of friction, and overall the Oldenburg kings tended to be more warlike than their Councils were. A clever king, like Frederik II, could exploit this to his advantage, by emphasising the bonds of brotherhood (aided by hunting and binge drinking) that held king to aristocracy, and by dealing with the Council as individuals rather than as a body. But as matters of trade and dynasty attracted the gaze of Denmark's kings to

---

[2] See the sources listed in Paul Lockhart, *Denmark, 1513–1660: The Rise and Decline of a Renaissance Monarchy* (Oxford, 2007), pp. 83–103.

[3] Lockhart, *Denmark, 1513–1660*, pp. 104–23.

the south, to Germany and a larger Europe, it became all but inevitable that the interests of the king and those of his conciliar elite would begin to diverge sharply.[4]

This divergence was visible before the Thirty Years' War drew Denmark into the maelstrom, but until that point it was not genuinely damaging. The consensus between king and aristocracy, so vital to the cohesion of the Oldenburg state, would eventually fall apart because of the stresses of European politics after 1618, something that Denmark simply couldn't avoid – but also because of the personality of Christian IV.

Not quite 11 years of age when his father, Frederik II, died in 1588, Christian grew up at the feet of the Council of State – and hence what he learned about governance came from the aristocracy and not from a ruling monarch. Consequently, Christian never fully understood the kind of give-and-take leadership that had made his father's reign successful. But he made up for his inexperience with a boundless personal energy, a burning desire to make Denmark wealthy, powerful, great among nations. Those aspirations can be seen in all his attempts at commercial and agricultural reform prior to 1630. His energy was often undisciplined and directionless, and the king easily tired of projects that did not yield immediate results, but they did not compromise his position at home; the aristocratic Council of State tolerated the king's dilettantish activity with overall good humour. Moreover, the king could afford to experiment: largely because of the Sound dues, he had a massive personal fortune, and was very likely the wealthiest monarch in early seventeenth-century Europe.[5]

That same energy infused the king's foreign policy endeavours, too. The touchy relationship with the 'wicked neighbour' Sweden consumed much of Christian's time and resources. He sparred repeatedly with the usurper king Karl IX over a host of issues, mostly concerning the position of the Swedish-Norwegian border in the far north and the status of Swedish shipping in the Sound. Christian ached for an excuse to go to war with Sweden; the Council refused him again and again, hoping instead to resolve any differences through negotiation. By 1611, the king was no longer willing to tolerate the Council's reticence, and he issued the Council an ultimatum: if the Council would not support a bid for war, then the king would go ahead and attack Sweden on his own, in his private capacity as duke of Holstein-Segeberg. Faced with such a threat, conciliar opposition cracked. The result was the Kalmar War (1611–13), a nominal – albeit costly – Danish victory.

The Kalmar War ushered in a period of barely subdued hostility and infrequent crises in Danish-Swedish relations. This 'cold war' with Sweden still demanded the king's attention, but in the meantime Christian could focus his attention on affairs to the south. Here Christian was concerned mostly with practical matters: carving out a commercial sphere-of-influence in Lower Saxony and providing for his growing brood of children. The king was determined to control the Weser and Elbe estuaries, beating the Hanseatic towns into submission should they dare to stand in his way. With Hamburg he was especially brutal, nearly cutting them out of the Norwegian trade, excluding them from the Icelandic trade, and claiming suzerainty over Hamburg itself. His commercial policies went hand-in-hand with his attempts to acquire secularised bishoprics in Lower Saxony to support his younger sons. Frederik II had tried his hand at this before, with some limited success, but Christian IV proved to be a master at the dubious trade. Through a judicious combination of bribery, threats of force, and skilful negotiation, between 1621 and 1624 the king was able to secure important posts – two coadjutorships, a canonry, and a bishop-administrator –

---

[4] Ilsøe et al. *Dansk forvaltningshistorie*, vol. 1, pp. 50–1; P. Colding, *Studier i Danmarks politiske Historie i Slutningen af Christian III.s og Begyndelsen af Frederik II.s Tid* (Copenhagen, 1939), pp. 68–167; F. P. Jensen, *Bidrag til Frederik II's og Erik XIV's historie* (Copenhagen, 1978), pp. 13–44.

[5] S. Heiberg, *Christian 4. Monarken, mennesket, og myten* (Copenhagen: Gyldendal, 1988), pp. 10–49; K.J.V. Jespersen, 'Herremand i kongeklæder. Christian IV, rigsrådet og adelen', in S. Ellehøj (ed.), *Christian 4.s verden* (Copenhagen, 1988), pp. 123–45.

at Bremen, Verden, Schwerin, and Halberstadt. By providing for Christian's younger sons, these acquisitions did indeed help to settle a potentially thorny dynastic problem, but at a price: Christian's neighbours in Lower Saxony, and the Dutch too for that matter, resented Christian for his success. Danish–Dutch relations, already strained because of Christian's Baltic policies, became truly cold by the late 1610s.

Christian IV had never completely shared his father's affinity for the higher politics of the empire. Frederik II had immersed himself deeply in European confessional politics in the 1570s and 80s, working tirelessly to forge an international Protestant alliance to aid the beleaguered Calvinist communities in France and the Netherlands. Christian could not quite bring himself to do the same. He shared his father's ardour for the Lutheran faith but not his far-ranging concern for the welfare of Protestantism. Though many of the German princes looked to Christian for leadership, the king pointedly refused to get involved. And when the Bohemian rebels sought the king's aid in the summer of 1618, he haughtily spurned their advances.[6]

The spread of the conflict into the Germanies in 1621, though, was enough to draw Christian's concern. To him, Ferdinand II's actions in the empire, starting with the imperial ban on the Elector Palatine, signalled that the house of Austria was willing to trample on German liberties in order to advance a Catholic agenda and the emperor's own authority. An ill-advised Catholic 'incursion' into Denmark itself – a handful of Jesuit priests had managed to penetrate even the tight inner circle of Christian's court by 1623 – further convinced Christian that the threat from the south, from Vienna as well as from Rome, would have to be taken seriously. As if the king's worry was motivation enough, there were those who sought to sway Christian IV into embracing the 'Protestant cause'. The States-General was casting about for allies as the expiry of the Twelve Years' Truce loomed; James I of England, Christian's brother-in-law, relentlessly tried to prod the Dane into intervening on behalf of the Elector Palatine.

It has become commonplace to assert that Christian IV's interest in the conflict to the south was selfish and opportunistic, that the king sought merely to acquire more lands for his growing commercial empire at the expense of a beleaguered Germany. But what motivated Christian IV was, in this case, fear pure and simple. That he craved more land in Lower Saxony is beyond doubt, but by 1623 he had just about had his fill; and when he was most concerned about the extension of Habsburg authority and of militant Catholicism into Lower Saxony – *his* lands – he put his more aggressive policies to the side in favour of cooperation. At Segeberg in March 1621, he orchestrated and hosted a meeting of Danish, English, Dutch, and Protestant German delegates, who demanded that the emperor restore the Elector Palatine and remove all foreign troops from the empire. The coalition, a fragile one at best, was fated to fail, and while Christian despaired over its failure he did not give up. Intrusions of Catholic League troops into Lower Saxony in 1622 and 1623 further convinced the king that force – or at least the threat of force – would ultimately be necessary if the emperor were to be deterred. Renewed promises of support from James I and from the States-General set him on his course: Christian IV would accept the proffered role as Protestant champion.

What the king lacked was support from his own kingdom. The Council of State had repeatedly warned the king to stay out of imperial affairs. The rebellions in Bohemia and in Germany had nothing to do with Denmark, the councillors said, and it was both dangerous and unnecessary to provoke the emperor. A new, more aggressive diplomatic posture on the part of the Swedes made the situation especially perilous, for a Danish war in Germany

---

[6] Lockhart, *Denmark in the Thirty Years' War*, pp. 74–80; F.P. Jensen, 'Frederik II. og truslen fra de katolske magter', in *Historisk Tidsskrift*, 93 (1993), pp. 233–77.

might just afford Sweden the perfect opportunity to attack Denmark. When the king laid out before the Council his plans for an intervention in Lower Saxony for a final time, in February 1625, the members of the Council were well aware that he intended to go to war, with or without their support. They had learned their lesson from 1611 and the Swedish crisis. That time, they had given in to the king. This time they would call his bluff. If the king went to war in Germany, then the kingdom would not follow him. He would be left to his own devices.[7]

The war was on, and King Christian rushed to meet it. In the spring of 1625 his allies in northern Germany elected him military commander (*Kreisoberst*) of the Lower Saxon Circle, and with his newfound authority he began to recruit an army locally. Since the Council of State still refused its collective support, Christian was on his own, and hence the army he commanded in May 1625 was not a Danish one. Nor was his act an 'invasion' of the empire. Technically, the king of Denmark, acting in his capacity as duke of Holstein and military commander of the Circle, was a rebel against the emperor and nothing more. Emperor Ferdinand II, who thus far had beaten down all challenges to his authority, sent the Catholic League army under Count Tilly to quash this new threat. Brief clashes at Höxter (July 1625) and at Seelze (November 1625) gave neither side a distinct advantage, though a raid by Duke Johann Ernst of Sachsen-Weimar, Christian's cavalry commander, forced Tilly to disengage from Christian's main army. Thus far, the two armies had barely bloodied one another. The next year's campaign promised much bigger things, for – after negotiations at Braunschweig failed to end the war – other forces and other agendas were about to enter the fray.[8]

Annoyed that Tilly's army had not been able to do the job, late in 1625 the emperor allowed the recruitment of a new army, an imperial army, under the command of the ambitious and gifted Bohemian nobleman Albrecht von Wallenstein. Wallenstein's army was intended to rendezvous with Tilly's army of the Catholic League, something that would have probably put a quick end to Christian IV's rebellion. But Christian, too, would have more help in the coming campaign – or at least the promise of it. At The Hague in November–December 1625, Danish diplomats met with their Dutch, English, and French counterparts. The assembly, though cordial, proved unable to settle on a common strategy; the Danes, for example, would have been satisfied with the restoration of the Elector Palatine, while the English pressed for an all-out war against Spain. Yet for all the indecision, at The Hague Conference the king of Denmark secured earnest promises that soon Dutch and English troops would arrive in Lower Saxony to boost his waning numbers.

The creation of Wallenstein's army, though, posed a potentially fatal threat to the Lower Saxon army. Christian responded with characteristic boldness, in probably one of the most ingeniously planned campaigns of the Thirty Years' War: a multi-pronged offensive, in which one army (under the talented cavalry commander Johann Ernst of Sachsen-Weimar) was to raid Catholic territories in Westphalia and hence divert Tilly, while another (including the forces of the notorious mercenary commander Ernst von Mansfeld) would push south and east towards Bohemia and Moravia to keep Wallenstein occupied; a third force would join forces with rebels in Hessen, and Christian IV would remain with the main army in Lower Saxony. Brilliant, perhaps, but overly complicated, and fated to fail. Tilly easily crushed the Hessian uprising, and the south-eastern army nearly disintegrated after Wallenstein

---

[7] Lockhart, *Denmark in the Thirty Years' War*, pp. 78–108; L. Tandrup, *Mod triumf eller tragedie* (2 vols, Århus, 1979), vol. 1, pp. 355–493; K. Jockenhövel, *Rom – Brüssel – Gottorf. Ein Beitrag zur Geschichte der gegenreformatorischen Versuche in Nordeuropa 1622–1637* (Neumünster, 1989), pp. 18–50.

[8] For the following paragraphs, on the course of the Lower Saxon War, see the following: J.O. Opel, *Der niedersächsisch-dänische Krieg*, (3 vols, Halle and Magdeburg, 1872–74); F. Askgaard, *Christian IV: 'Rigets væbnede Arm'* (Copenhagen, 1988); A.L. Larsen, *Kejserkrigen* (Copenhagen, 1896–91); and Lockhart, *Denmark in the Thirty Years' War*, pp. 131–207.

pummelled Mansfeld's troops at Dessau Bridge (April 1626). The king sent Sachsen-Weimar to Mansfeld's rescue, and after rebuilding the army the two generals pushed towards the Habsburg hereditary lands once more, hoping to join forces with the Hungarian rebel Bethlen Gabor and his Ottoman allies.

It all fell apart in August 1626. Christian, nervous about Tilly and about the failure of England and the United Provinces to send the troops they had promised, decided to go on the offensive himself. His actual goal has never been determined with any degree of certainty – he may have intended to relieve the rebel garrison at Göttingen, and he may have planned a truly daring invasion of the Danube valley – but either way he marched his army south, towards the Harz Mountains, forcing Tilly to fall back in some confusion. At the eleventh hour, though, unexpected but long-requested reinforcements from Wallenstein reinforced the Catholic League army, which promptly executed an abrupt volte-face. Now it was Christian's turn to retreat, but heavy rains and muddy roads slowed the rebel retreat and compelled the king to make his stand near the village of Hahausen in the foothills of the Harz Mountains. At the battle of Lutter-am-Barenberge, Christian's army came within a hair's breadth of victory, repulsing Tilly's opening assault and then launching a promising counterattack. Tilly's hardened veterans, though, held firm, and sent the king's army into a panicked rout. About half of Christian's army was killed or captured, and the king himself barely escaped with his life.

One by one, Christian's German allies deserted him after Lutter, and neither England nor the Dutch made anything more than the most lukewarm effort to uphold their end of the bargain. The eastern army, still under the command of Sachsen-Weimar and Mansfeld, fell apart by the year's end. Only a handful of survivors straggled back to Lower Saxony the following year. Christian's hopes were dashed, and he knew that there was no use in prolonging the inevitable. All along, his Council of State had begged him, again and again, to give up and seek shelter at the mercy of the emperor. Now he would heed that advice.

The emperor, though, had no particular desire to show clemency. Wallenstein's army, finally free of Sachsen-Weimar and Mansfeld, headed north and joined with Tilly in August 1627, only a year after the disaster at Lutter. Ignoring Christian's overtures for peace, Tilly and Wallenstein pushed beyond the Lower Saxon territories and into the king's own lands: first Holstein, then Schleswig, and within a few days the League-Imperial army crashed across the border and into Denmark itself. What the king's Council of State had studiously avoided by withholding their support for the war in Lower Saxony had come to pass anyway: like it or not, the war in the empire had finally come to Denmark.

The kingdom was completely unprepared. Tilly and Wallenstein overran the weaker defence points in the duchies, and simply bypassed the stronger ones. Local defence forces, hurriedly mustered, evaporated before the inexorable flood of veteran troops. Within weeks, all of Jutland was under foreign occupation. The Council of State, shocked by the speed of the avalanche and furious with their king for disregarding their advice, made it plain: there must be peace, without delay, no matter the cost.

The king ignored the Council yet again. He had invested too much into the war to simply give up now, and he was convinced that a well-timed counteroffensive just might turn the tide. The king's reputation was at stake, the future of his dynasty too, and something else besides: the fate of the Baltic. For quite some time, the Habsburgs – Austrian and Spanish alike – had given much thought to plan to establish a naval presence on the Baltic's German shore. Wallenstein's gains in the region, most notably in Christian's erstwhile ally Mecklenburg, made a Habsburg Baltic fleet more than a possibility. Imperial warships were already under construction at several Baltic ports by the summer of 1627, and even in the Danish port of Ålborg. Such a fleet, if completed, would threaten all of Northern Europe. This Christian would not tolerate.

The war resumed in the spring of 1628. Putting Denmark's naval supremacy to advantage, Christian launched a series of amphibious strikes against targets in Jutland and Holstein, destroying imperial naval facilities while they were still vulnerable. An assault on the island of Usedom ended in a crushing defeat for Christian at the battle of Wolgast (August 1628), but even then the enterprise served the main purpose: it drew Wallenstein further and further away from Denmark. Christian IV did not defeat Wallenstein and Tilly outright in the 1628 campaign – but he made both commanders, and especially Wallenstein, think very seriously about the long-range implications of a prolonged war with Denmark.

Wallenstein found those implications troubling – if only because he had good reason to think that Sweden might come to Denmark's aid. Gustav II Adolf may have been Christian's chief rival a decade before, but the two men admired one another, and the Swedish king understood that a defeated Denmark was not in Sweden's best interests – not yet, at least. The two kings signed a mutual defence pact in the spring of 1628; Danish and Swedish naval squadrons jointly patrolled off the German shore of the Baltic; Danish and Swedish troops fought side-by-side to defend the port of Stralsund against Wallenstein's army. Wallenstein thought highly of Christian IV, and he understood that Sweden was not to be trifled with. A generous peace with Denmark, Wallenstein suspected, was far better than a disastrous war with both of the Nordic powers at once.

Wallenstein's fear gave Christian IV an edge when he finally sued for peace. The terms that Wallenstein and Tilly had first offered Christian, back in September 1627, were humiliating: Christian would have to give up all pretence to imperial office, and he would have to either cede Holstein and Glückstadt to the emperor or pay a two million *Reichsthaler* ransom against the return of Holstein, Schleswig, and Jutland. The Council of State would accept the demands as they stood. Christian IV would not. When imperial and Danish representatives sat down to negotiate at Lübeck at the beginning of 1629, Wallenstein insisted on even more concessions. Denmark would have to pay the emperor's war debt and cede Jutland and the duchies immediately. Christian's emissaries countered with their own: Denmark would accept nothing less than the restitution of all lands taken by the emperor, payment of damages incurred by the emperor, and the guarantee of religious and political liberties of the Lower Saxon princes.

The Danish counterproposal looks ridiculous and potentially explosive. Yet Christian meant every word, and he had the diplomatic wherewithal to support it. To make his point, Christian arranged a personal meeting with Gustav II Adolf at the Scanian frontier parsonage of Ulvsbäck to discuss an alliance. The meeting was a calculated sham. Christian virtually ignored Gustav Adolf at Ulvsbäck, and the Swedish king was utterly confused – later he surmised that Christian must have been in his cups – but Christian made sure that the meeting was well-publicised. Moreover, he continued to make preparations for an invasion of occupied Jutland while Wallenstein's negotiators contemplated the reversal of fortunes. On May 22, 1629, with Ferdinand's blessing, the imperial delegates accepted a slightly modified version of the Danish counteroffer.[9]

Of all the settlements that ended individual conflicts in the Thirty Years' War, the Peace of Lübeck must rank among the most lenient. Christian agreed to give up his claims to the Lower Saxon bishoprics, but there would be no other cessions of territory, no reparations, and no indemnities. Denmark would walk away from the war scot-free. It was, as Christian's loyal supporter Christen Thomesen Sehested put it, 'a miracle ... a direct gift from God'.

Lübeck was indeed a miracle. Almost alone among those who had opposed Habsburg power and lost, Denmark had lost virtually nothing as punishment. It had suffered heavily

---

[9] Jespersen, 'Kongemødet i Ulfsbäck præstegård februar 1629', pp. 420–39; E. Wilmanns, *Der Lübecker Friede* (Bonn, 1904).

during the war, to be sure, but far less than most belligerents in the Thirty Years' War would. Lübeck was a better ending than Denmark had a right to expect.

But in Denmark, there was little rejoicing over Lübeck, either. In the long term, of course, the end of the Lower Saxon War would signal the point at which Denmark began its irreversible decline into political insignificance and when Denmark's carefully maintained constitutional balance no longer functioned well. Neither of these things was visible in 1629, but the near-catastrophe of the Lower Saxon War had strained the once intimate relationship between king and ruling aristocracy to breaking point. Both parties saw in the war's end confirmation that their position, for or against the king's intervention in Germany, had been the correct one. To the Council, or at least to the opposition majority in the conciliar ranks, the king's 'royal adventure' in Germany caused the imperial invasion of Denmark in 1627; Christian IV, to their minds, had very nearly brought about Denmark's partition and destruction. To the king, the Council's refusal to follow his lead had hobbled the war effort in Lower Saxony; if the Council had supported their king, as loyal subjects should, then victory would have been assured and Denmark would never have been invaded. The bitter resentment manifested itself in a struggle between king and Council over war finance. Though the Council agreed to help once Jutland had been invaded, it set special conditions on its support: the creation of a special 'Commissariat' to collect and disburse funds, for example. King and Council clashed over a myriad of trivial issues, so that by war's end they had become opponents rather than partners in the stewardship of the realm.

Christian had no intention of relegating himself to a passive role in European politics after the war, and the unrelenting pacifism of the Council of State was not about to dissuade him. The king's determination drove him to commit an act of outright political blackmail. Before Christian ratified the final draft of the Lübeck settlement, he blankly informed the Council that he expected to be reimbursed for his wartime expenses – to the tune of one million *rigsdaler* – and that if the Council refused him then he could not be expected to sign the treaty. The Council was shocked and angry but the king gave it no choice, and so it agreed reluctantly to pay the king what would become known as the 'Ten Barrels of Gold'.

The Ten Barrels of Gold was perhaps the final blow to the notion of government by consensus in Denmark, but it allowed the king to act as a free agent, to provide for Denmark's defence and to follow whatever diplomatic course the king thought best without having to rely on the Council's assent and cooperation – something that the king would likely never have again. Indeed, Christian made a deliberate effort to sidestep the Council at every turn. During the Lower Saxon War, the king revived the long-defunct idea of a national diet as an alternative to reliance on the Council. Christian summoned his first full diet in 1627 – the first such body to be called together in nearly six decades – and it eagerly approved his demands for new taxes. The lesson was not lost on the king, who summoned full Diets four more times between 1627 and 1645, each time with overwhelmingly favourable results. Christian had also made a deliberate effort to create a royalist clique within the highest circles of the government. His morganatic union with Kirsten Munk had been a fruitful one, resulting in several daughters, who were approaching marriageable age by the late 1620s. He married these daughters off to the sons of high-ranking aristocratic families, thereby assuring their loyalty, and then promoted his sons-in-law to key positions within the upper administration.[10]

---

[10] E.L. Petersen, 'Defence, War and Finance: Christian IV and the Council of the Realm 1596–1629', *Scandinavian Journal of History*, 7 (1982), pp. 277–313 ; S. Heiberg, 'De ti tønder guld: Rigsråd, kongemagt og statsfinanser i 1630erne', *Historisk Tidsskrift*, 76 (1976), pp. 25–58; K. Mykland, *Skiftet i forvaltningsordningen i Danmark og Norge i tiden fra omkring 1630 og inntil Frederik den Tredjes död* (Bergen and Oslo, 1967), pp. 16–18.

Christian's purpose was to not impose princely absolutism; indeed, he found the idea of absolutism repugnant and could not imagine a political system in which the aristocracy did not share power with the monarch. Rather, Christian's ambitions were fairly conservative if ill-advised: to recoup, as much as possible, the losses suffered during the Lower Saxon War, in territory, influence, commerce, and prestige. This he aimed to accomplish through a policy of armed neutrality, playing the emperor and his allies off against the king of Sweden and those states that had come to Sweden's aid after 1630. This was a dangerous proposition, a treacherous and highly risky course to follow, but in the short term it paid off. Ferdinand II did not want to give Christian an excuse to make common cause with the Swedes; conversely, neither Gustav II Adolf nor Axel Oxenstierna wanted to contemplate a hostile Denmark threatening its German conquests. Against the advice of his Council, Christian went back to bullying Hamburg as he had in the years before the war. The emperor looked the other way, and in 1633 he granted Christian the exclusive right to levy tolls on maritime traffic on the lower Elbe. In 1634, Ferdinand II and the Swedish government allowed Bremen to elect Christian's son, Duke Frederick, as archbishop-administrator, and the following year Verden followed suit.

Christian IV had come very close to recreating Denmark's antebellum dominion over the Elbe and Weser estuaries, and its presence in Lower Saxony, despite the current war. It was an achievement that could not be sustained for very long. Armed neutrality was an expensive policy, nearly as expensive as a genuine war. After 1638, the kingdom maintained a national defence force of more than 18,000 men, and of course the fleet required constant upkeep and occasional rebuilding. The Ten Barrels of Gold could not take care of such expenditures indefinitely. Hence the king tried to milk commercial revenues for every shilling he could wring out of them. A new schedule for the Sound dues increased the tolls collected at Helsingør by as much as 300 per cent for some types of cargoes, and enforcement became more aggressive, too. The new duties fell hardest on Dutch and English merchants. Desperate for cash, Christian refused to make long-term accommodations for the Dutch and the English, and consequently alienated them.[11]

That was, indeed, the main shortcoming of Danish foreign policy in the 1630s and 40s: its acquisitiveness drove away Denmark's allies, and its boldness infuriated Christian's enemies. Christian could not flirt with both Sweden and the emperor simultaneously, expecting to profit from both relationships without giving anything in return, and yet this was exactly what he tried to do. When either Sweden or the emperor called Christian's bluff – as when Emperor Ferdinand III (1637–53) refused to renew Denmark's 1633 monopoly on the Elbe tolls – the king would react churlishly. In the case of the Elbe tolls, Christian's response to Ferdinand III was to strangle Hamburg's trade with a blockade, forcing the town to submit to Danish rule (1643). Alternately coquettish and brusque in his dealings with the emperor and Sweden, insensitive to the pleas of England and the United Provinces, Christian ultimately cut his ties with nearly all potential allies. By 1643, Denmark was without a friend in the world.

Hence Christian's policy of armed neutrality, clumsily executed, proved ultimately to be fatal. Christian had aspired to broker the eventual peace treaties between the emperor, Sweden, and the German princes, and he got his wish: he was the first official mediator of what would become the peace talks at Osnabrück. But it would not work out quite as Christian had planned. Danish advances in Lower Saxony compromised Sweden's strategic position in Germany, just as the Sound dues hurt the Swedish economy. A bizarre episode involving the erratic Dowager Queen Maria Eleonora, widow of the late Gustav II

---

[11] J.A. Fridericia, *Danmarks ydre politiske Historie i Tiden fra Freden i Lybek til Freden i Kjobenhavn (1629–1660)*, pp. 63–75; Lockhart, *Denmark, 1513–1660*, pp. 197–205.

Adolf – she fled Sweden and sought asylum with Christian IV – further antagonised Axel Oxenstierna and the Swedish government. In May 1643, Oxenstierna began preparations for a pre-emptive strike on Denmark; in December the Swedes struck. Lennart Torstensson's army raced from Bohemia to crash across the Holstein frontier, and then a second army under Gustaf Horn invaded the Scanian provinces the following month. Denmark was unprepared and overwhelmed, and only the strength of the Danish fleet kept the Swedes from invading the Danish islands and bringing the war to a swift and brutal conclusion. Denmark could not hold out indefinitely, especially after a privately funded Dutch fleet came to Sweden's aid. The Danish fleet gave a good account of itself at Listerdyb (May 1644) and Kolberger Heide (July 1644), but lost control of its territorial waters following a crushing defeat at Fehmarn (October 1644). When France and the Dutch offered to mediate a peace, Christian IV jumped at the chance, but found the price of peace too high for his liking. For France and the Dutch, like Sweden, wanted a Denmark stripped of its dominance of the Sound. During the negotiations at Brömsebro early in 1645 Denmark was presented with a series of demands that were truly crippling: the temporary loss of Halland, and the permanent cession of Jämtland, Härjedalen, Gotland and Øsel to Sweden, plus free passage of the Sound for all Swedish ships. When the Danes balked, the Dutch went to great lengths to show Christian that he was in no position to argue, sending a fleet to force its way into the Sound.

The Torstensson War, as the Danes came to call it, marked the point at which Denmark lost its claim to greatness. Brömsebro was the humiliating end to a humiliating war. Only three decades before, Denmark had defeated Sweden, if only by a slim margin; now Swedish armies had utterly crushed Denmark. Everything about the war was humbling, from a failed imperial attempt to intervene on Denmark's behalf to the appearance of the Dutch fleet in the Sound.[12]

The humbling was not merely symbolic, but very real. Danish power was shattered, Denmark's dominion of the Baltic a thing of the past. In a way, the political climate in Northern Europe became more cordial towards Denmark. Within four years of Brömsebro, Denmark concluded defensive alliances with France, England, and the Dutch Republic. Those treaties, though, were in themselves a measure of how far Denmark had fallen. The northern maritime states had been eager to make alliances with Denmark because now Sweden was the Baltic power to be feared.

Denmark's failure in the Thirty Years' War, at least in its direction, was the king's and the king's alone. To be sure, the defection of his allies in the Lower Saxon War was beyond Christian's control, but the decision to go to war – even if based on these hollow promises – was Christian's. He had gone entirely against the will of the Council. The actions that led to the catastrophe of 1645 were entirely the king's, too – though it could be argued that, as the sovereign of a powerful neutral land caught in the crossfire of two belligerents who were both hostile to Denmark, Christian did not have a lot of diplomatic options available to him after 1629. Perhaps Christian's greatest failing was in not seeing something that is clear in the perfect light of retrospect: that Denmark simply did not have the money, or the resources, or the manpower to maintain its exalted status for very long. It was a hard lesson to learn, but it was one that – less than seven decades later – even Sweden would be forced to accept.

That is not to argue, though, that Denmark's – or Christian IV's – role in the Thirty Years' War was bereft of significance. It was a pivotal moment in Danish history: the point at which Danish pretensions at Baltic dominance were ended, and the point at which government by consensus in Denmark began to fail. It is impossible to understand the creation of absolutism

---

[12] Askgaard, *Christian IV*, pp. 152–78; N. Probst, *Christian 4.s flåde* (Copenhagen, 1996), pp. 227–56; Fridericia, *Danmarks ydre politiske Historie*, vol. 2, 448–524.

by fiat in 1660 without first understanding the impact of *Kejserkrigen*. Within the context of the Thirty Years' War, too, the intervention of Christian IV, the 'royal adventure', was an important development. The late E. Ladewig Petersen, the great Danish historian of the late twentieth century, referred to Christian's intervention as 'the Danish intermezzo'.[13] It is an unfair characterisation, for 'intermezzo' implies brevity and a lack of gravity. Christian's involvement in the great European conflict, though ill-advised and ultimately full of tragic consequences for the Oldenburg lands, fulfilled an important function in the war. If nothing else, it kept the anti-Habsburg cause alive in the difficult years between the collapse of the Palatine cause and the interventions of France and Sweden.

Selected Bibliography

Bellamy, M., *Christian IV and his Navy: A Political and Administrative History of the Danish Navy 1589-1648* (Leiden, 2006).
Garstein, O., *Rome and the Counter-Reformation in Scandinavia* (4 vols, Oslo, Bergen and Leiden, 1963–1992).
Heiberg, S., *Christian 4. Monarken, mennesket, og myten* (Copenhagen, 1988).
Jespersen, L., *A Revolution from Above? The Power State of 16th and 17th Century Scandinavia* (Odense, 2006).
Lockhart, P., *Denmark in the Thirty Years' War, 1618–1648: King Christian IV and the Decline of the Oldenburg State* (Selinsgrove, 1996).
Lockhart, P., 'Political Language and Wartime Propaganda in Denmark, 1625–1629', *European History Quarterly*, 31 (2001): pp. 5–42.
Lockhart, P., *Frederik II and the Protestant Cause: Denmark's Role in the Wars of Religion, 1559–1596* (Leiden, 2004).
Lockhart, P., *Denmark, 1513–1660: The Rise and Decline of a Renaissance Monarchy* (Oxford, 2007).
Murdoch, S., *Britain, Denmark-Norway and the House of Stuart, 1603–1660: A Diplomatic and Military Analysis* (East Linton, 2000).
Opel, J.O., *Der niedersächsisch-dänische Krieg* (3 vols, Halle and Magdeburg, 1872–1874).
Petersen, E.L., 'Defence, War and Finance: Christian IV and the Council of the Realm 1596–1629', *Scandinavian Journal of History*, 7 (1982): pp. 277–313.

---

[13] Petersen, 'The Danish Intermezzo', pp. 64–73.

Sweden

Pärtel Piirimäe

Sweden's intervention in Germany, that was originally limited both in its aims and its scope, developed into a massive military engagement that lasted for 18 years. In the course of this period, the 'German war' transformed into what has been called a 'total war'[1] or a 'European war in Germany'.[2] The ability of a small and sparsely populated peasant state to sustain a war effort for such a long period of time, with a huge impact on the progression of the war and on its eventual outcome, has fascinated historians and laypeople alike. This chapter discusses some central issues related to the Swedish war in Germany, such as Sweden's reasons and justification for intervention, the shift of its war aims during its course, its collaboration with imperial estates in the context of the constitution of the empire, and the system of war finance created by Sweden during the conflict.

Reasons for Intervention

The question of Gustav Adolph's motives behind his intervention has been one of the perennial issues in historical scholarship. The eighteenth- and nineteenth-century romantic image of a Protestant hero who intervened in the German war in order to save his fellow Protestants and German liberties from imperial tyranny has long been replaced by a more sober assessment of his motives.[3] The prevailing account acknowledges that Gustav Adolph was a pragmatic 'Realpolitiker' who first and foremost acted in what he saw as the interest of his own state. This account coincides with the king's own interpretation of his motives. In October 1630 he wrote to Chancellor Axel Oxenstierna retrospectively that the chief reason and aim (*scopus*) of the war was 'the security of the fatherland against the designs of the enemy'. The king asserted that the best means to achieve security against this particular enemy, the expanding Habsburgs in co-operation with the counter-reforming Pope, was the restitution of the German Protestant princes to their former status, so that 'we could be safe in our fatherland through their security'.[4]

---

[1] G. Parker, *The Thirty Years' War* (London and New York, 1984), ch. IV.
[2] C. Kampmann, *Europa und das Reich im Dreißigjährigen Krieg* (Stuttgart, 2008), p. 1.
[3] For a survey of historiography see S. Oredsson, *Geschichtsschreibung und Kult. Gustav Adolf, Schweden und der Dreißigjährige Krieg* (Berlin, 1994). Arguments summarised in pro and contra format by J. Burkhardt, 'Warum hat Gustav Adolf in den Dreißigjährigen Krieg eingegriffen? Der Schwedische Krieg 1630–1635', in P.C. Hartmann and F. Schuller (eds), *Der Dreißigjährige Krieg. Facetten einer folgenreichen Epoche* (Regensburg, 2010), pp. 94–107.
[4] Gustav Adolf to Axel Oxenstierna, 8 October 1630, in C. Hallendorff (ed.), *Tal och skrifter av konung Gustav II Adolf* (Stockholm, 1915), pp. 119–20.

Thus, at least for a while, the Swedish interest coincided with that of German Protestant estates, which enabled the pro-Swedish propaganda to portray the intervention as a selfless pursuit of religious and political liberties in the Holy Roman Empire. The astonishing success of Swedish arms, moreover, brought along a flood of broadsheets and pamphlets of a more radical nature, which depicted Gustav Adolph as a Biblical warrior, a 'Lion of the North' or an 'Alexander redivivus', with a godly mission to save his co-religionists from the papist oppression.[5] This was certainly beneficial for Sweden as it helped to mobilise support for its war effort in Germany, but at the same time its government was careful to avoid the language of a holy war in its official justifications, focusing on political motives and war aims. The argument of religion plays only an indirect role, as the former 'status' of Protestant princes also entailed the religious liberties. This was pointed out by Chancellor Oxenstierna in 1636: '[Religion] was not our *principalis scopus* ... it was a question not so much of religion, as of *status publicus*, in which religion is comprehended.'[6] In the domestic propaganda, on the other hand, the argument that the Swedes had a moral duty to assist their 'religious brothers' in Germany had a considerably larger weight.[7]

The extant protocols of debates held at Swedish State Council (*Riksråd*) and the Diet (*Riksdag*) from 1627 to 1630 suggest that the concern for security was not just a convenient post-facto justification but the Council and the representatives of the estates were genuinely convinced, or at least let themselves be persuaded by the king, that the increase of imperial power in northern Germany at the cost of Protestant princes and cities constituted a threat for Sweden.[8] In January 1628 Gustav Adolph asked a Diet Committee of the Estates for their consent to military action in Sweden's defence, pointing to the 'dangerous situation' which arose from the fact that 'the Emperor and the papist League had conquered and subjected one imperial prince and city after another'. In the king's view, Sweden could expect in this situation only 'a total ruin or a long and difficult war'.[9] The specific event that most worried Swedish statesmen, who for several years had anxiously followed the advancement of the Catholic party in Germany, was the takeover of Mecklenburg's Baltic port of Wismar in October 1627. After this the imperial general Wallenstein, who was grandly nominated 'the General of the Baltic sea and of the Ocean', started preparations for building a navy worth his new title.[10] The establishment of an imperial power base at the Baltic coast was seen as a direct threat to Swedish *dominium maris Baltici*, by which the Swedes meant their role as guarantor of the 'tranquillity' of the Baltic sea – the role they assumed after Denmark was forced out of war in 1627.[11] Oxenstierna would reflect in 1636 that 'had His Late Majesty not

---

[5] Cf. S.S. Tschopp, *Heilsgeschichtliche Deutungsmuster in der Publizistik des Dreißigjährigen Krieges: pro- und antischwedische Propaganda in Deutschland 1628 bis 1635* (Frankfurt a. M., 1991).

[6] Quoted from M. Roberts, 'The Political Objectives of Gustavus Adolphus in Germany 1630–1632', *The Transactions of the Royal Historical Society*, 7 (1957): p. 22.

[7] S. Arnoldsson, 'Krigspropagandan i Sverige före trettioåriga kriget', *Göteborgs Högskolas Årsskrift*, 47 (1941): pp. 3–33; King to the Diet: 'våra religions-förvandter', *Arkiv till upplysning om Svenska krigens och krigsinrättningarnes historia*, vol. I (Stockholm, 1854), p. 3.

[8] *Svenska riksrådets protokoll*, vol. I; *Arkiv till upplysning*, vol. I, pp. 1–63; N. Ahnlund, 'Öfverläggningarna i riksrådet om tyska kriget 1628–1630', *Historisk tidskrift*, 34 (1914): pp. 108–23; M. Roberts, *Gustavus Adolphus*, vol. 2, pp. 370–5; M. Roberts, *The Swedish Imperial Experience 1560–1718* (Cambridge, 1979), pp. 26 et seq.; Cf. Kampmann, *Europa und das Reich*, p. 71.

[9] *Arkiv till upplysning*, vol. I, p. 3.

[10] S. Goetze, *Die Politik des schwedischen Reichskanzlers Axel Oxenstierna gegenüber Kaiser und Reich* (Kiel, 1971), pp. 42–8.

[11] Axel Oxenstierna argued thus in his concept to the Emperor on the problem of Stralsund: '... sique S.R.M:tas id impetraverit, datum id sibi putabit, ut quies et tranquillitas mari Balthico atque eius accolis sit restituta.' *Rikskansleren Axel Oxenstiernas skrifter och brefvexling* (Stockholm, 1888), I. afd., vol. I, p. 530; cf. N. Ahnlund, 'Dominium maris Baltici', in N. Ahnlund, *Tradition och historia* (Stockholm, 1956), pp. 114–30.

betaken himself to Germany with his army, the emperor would today have a fleet on the seas ... and here in Sweden we should never have enjoyed a moment's security'.[12]

The estates acknowledged that the emperor had demonstrated both the capacity and the intention to dominate the north and to advance further towards Sweden. His next aim in their view was to render Sweden's control of the sea void, then shut down its commerce and finally to subjugate it to the same kind of 'tyranny' which he was exercising against the German Protestants. Their recommendation was to 'transfer the war into some place conquered by the enemy, so that the frontiers of the fatherland may as long as possible be spared from the troubles of war and its inhabitants may preserve their current well-being'.[13] After this meeting, the debates in *Riksråd* were dominated by the view that the war with the emperor was inevitable, and the question was only when and how it would be waged.[14]

Legitimation

Having satisfied themselves that they had good reasons for intervention, the Swedish government subsequently made an effort to find convincing legal grounds for the intervention, as the argument of preventive war against imperialist designs would not have gone down well with international audiences.[15] Also, the Swedes were aware that the success of the intervention depended on the support of the German Protestants and as long as they were not prepared to go into an open conflict with the emperor, it made sense for Sweden as well to avoid the legal state of war against the empire. A declaration of war against the emperor would have alienated the moderate Protestants who were willing to cooperate with Sweden to a certain extent so as to force the emperor to an accommodation.[16] The deposition of Ferdinand was not on the agenda of the majority of German Protestants, who saw in the preservation of the imperial constitution their main protection against possible Catholic aggrandisement.[17]

This is the reason why Sweden did not publicly portray the emperor as a 'tyrant', which had become common in domestic debates.[18] Instead, Sweden drew on the legal framework established when it had assisted Stralsund against the imperialist siege in 1628. This was in fact the beginning of Swedish military engagement in the German war. The legal ground for the deployment of a garrison there after the Danes had retreated was a treaty concluded with the town which emphasised that it was not directed against the emperor but against his general Wallenstein, who was acting without authorisation. This enabled Sweden to maintain that it was still neutral towards the empire. Equally, at this time the emperor was

---

[12] P. Wilson (ed.), *Thirty Years War. A Sourcebook* (London, 2010), doc. 71, p. 133.
[13] *Arkiv till upplysning*, I, 4. A.A; Stiernman, *Alla Riksdagars och Mötens Besluth* (Stockholm, 1728), p. 808.
[14] *Svenska riksrådets protokoll*, vols. I–II, passim.
[15] On Swedish search for legitimating grounds, cf. P. Piirimäe, 'Just War in Theory and Practice: the Legitimation of Swedish Intervention in the Thirty Years War', *The Historical Journal*, 45/3 (2002): pp. 499–523.
[16] On the attitudes of German Protestants, see D. Böttcher, 'Propaganda und öffentliche Meinung im protestantischen Deutschland 1628–1636' [1953], in H.U. Rudolf (ed.), *Der Dreißigjährige Krieg* (Darmstadt, 1977), pp. 325–67.
[17] R.G. Asch, *The Thirty Years War. The Holy Roman Empire and Europe, 1618–1648* (London, 1997), pp. 18–21.
[18] *Arkiv till upplysning*, vol. I, p. 4; *Svenska Riksrådets Protokoll*, vol. I, p. 123.

not interested either in breaching the fiction of neutrality, and therefore did not conduct the ostensibly hostile acts, such as giving military assistance to Poland, in his own name.[19]

Despite its efforts, Sweden did not manage to receive 'invitations' from German Protestant estates to protect them against the emperor, which is why the fiction of neutrality was continued even after the landing in Pomerania in June 1630. Gustav Adolph's manifesto published immediately after this contained a long list of grievances about the violations of Sweden's rights by the imperial side, which, as the text argued, would have given sufficient grounds for war.[20] Nevertheless, the manifesto avoided direct confrontation with the emperor, presenting the intervention as a kind of police-action for the restoration of order in northern Germany, in the situation where Wallenstein was acting against imperial orders and the emperor was unable to bridle him.[21] The fiction of neutrality was very similar to the situation in 1635–36 when France had declared war against Spain but not against the emperor. Despite actual warfare, neither the emperor nor Richelieu were interested in a legal state of war and thus avoided mutually declaring it.[22] In the Swedish case, however, the emperor's tactics were different. The 1630 Electoral meeting in Regensburg decided to consider the conflict with Sweden as a state of war, which enabled it to denounce Sweden's German allies as 'hostes imperii' and thus discourage others from joining its alliance system.[23]

Sweden's initial success in Germany can be explained with various factors. First, it only intervened after it had concluded a truce with Poland in 1629 and was thus free from other military engagements. The truce of Altmark secured Sweden the income from Prussian Baltic ports, contributing substantially to the costs of waging war abroad. The situation in the empire had also turned in Sweden's favour, as the Edict of the Restitution demonstrated that the emperor was set to resolve the conflict in the empire with force rather than with a negotiated settlement with the Protestants.[24] In addition, the unity of the Catholic camp was harmed by the tensions between Vienna and Munich.[25] Finally, Sweden's capability of waging war in Germany was seriously underestimated by the Catholic side, whose confidence can be partly explained by its relatively easy victory over Denmark which had hitherto been considered the dominant military power in Scandinavia.

War Aims

Sweden's proclaimed war aims were limited by the reasons presented in its official justification but in the course of the war the objectives underwent some major changes. The central objective of Gustav Adolph, expressed already before the intervention, was 'assecuratio' or the security of the Baltic sea from future imperialist threats.[26] It quickly

---

[19] See H. Langer, 'Innere Kämpfe und Bündnis mit Schweden: Ende des 16. Jahrhunderts bis 1630', in H. Ewe (ed.), *Geschichte der Stadt Stralsund* (Weimar, 1984), pp. 137–67; Roberts, *Gustavus Adolphus*, vol. II, 358–67; N. Ahnlund, *Gustaf Adolf inför tyska kriget* (Stockholm, 1918), pp. 48–56.

[20] Recently republished in Wilson (ed.), *Thirty Years War. A Sourcebook*, pp. 122–30. See chapter 11 by Toby Osborne in this volume.

[21] Cf. Piirimäe, 'Just War in Theory and Practice', pp. 517–18.

[22] Kampmann, *Europa und das Reich*, p. 120.

[23] Debates of the meeting published in D. Albrecht (ed.), *Briefe und Akten zur Geschichte des Dreißigjährigen Krieges. Neue Folge: die Politik Maximilians I von Bayern und seiner Verbündeten, 1618–1651* (Munich, 1964).

[24] Cf. Kampmann, *Europa und das Reich*, p. 70.

[25] See chapter 10 by Ronald G. Asch in this volume.

[26] Gustav Adolph to Axel Oxenstierna, 12 May 1630, in P. Wilson (ed.), *Thirty Years War. A Sourcebook* (London, 2010), doc. 68, p. 131.

became clear that this entailed not just the withdrawal of the imperial armies from the Saxon circles but also Swedish possession or control over the invasion-ports of Pomerania and Mecklenburg. The decision to hold on to Stralsund even in the case of an accommodation with the emperor was taken already in May 1630, and a semi-permanent base at the Baltic coast desired by Gustav Adolph also included Wismar and possibly other areas.[27] Moreover, the demands of 'assecuratio' also extended to constitutional issues of the empire: Sweden's (and later also France's) peace conditions included the full restitution and amnesty for all Protestant princes in 'status quo ante bellum', including for those expropriated on the charges of rebellion.[28]

The war effort itself, ostensibly carried out for the achievement of this primary aim, added other demands to the list. The most important among them was 'satisfactio' (indemnity). Originally conceived as a monetary payment, it gradually transformed into a territorial demand. The coastal territories that prior to the intervention were thought of as 'assecuratio', now appeared in the guise of 'satisfactio', which implied a more permanent possession.[29] Satisfaction was a combination of claims to friends and allies to compensate Sweden for its war effort for their benefit, and of confiscations of lands from the enemy by the right of war (*iure belli*). Sweden's increasing demands were not only rejected by the Catholic side but created ill blood also with its Protestant allies. In particular, the Swedish wish to retain Pomerania after the death of its heirless duke was contentious, as according to an earlier treaty the dukedom was supposed to fall to Brandenburg. In addition to the territorial demands, Swedish war objectives also included the contentment of the army (or 'military satisfaction'), as it was clear that Sweden was unable to pay off its troops without external financial means.[30]

The unresolved question of Swedish indemnity can be considered the main obstacle to achieving the peace in Germany, and thus the reason for its prolongation until the late 1640s. The Peace of Prague of 1635 resulted from the hopes entertained by the emperor and the leading Protestant princes that a permanent settlement in the empire would be possible without the inclusion of the foreign powers, and that their joint effort would be sufficient to force Sweden out of 'the beloved fatherland of the most noble German nation' without any territorial gains.[31] Again, the emperor and the Electors underestimated both the capacity of Sweden to wage war without any significant German allies, and the resolve of its government to continue war until its major demands were met. For the Swedish government, the question of indemnity became a matter of reputation: a retreat without achieving adequate compensation was deemed by Oxenstierna as dishonourable.[32] The motive of reputation is significant, considering that the entire German affair has been explained as an effort by Sweden to raise its international esteem in the situation where the legitimation of the Vasa dynasty was contested by Poland and its Catholic allies.[33]

---

[27] Wilson, *Thirty Years War. A Sourcebook*, doc. 67, p. 130; Roberts, 'Political Objectives', pp. 20–3.
[28] Kampmann, *Europa und das Reich*, pp. 85 and 158.
[29] Roberts, 'Political Objectives', p. 41.
[30] P. Wilson, *Europe's Tragedy. A New History of the Thirty Years War* (London, 2009), pp. 463–4; Kampmann, *Europa und das Reich*, pp. 85–9, 158.
[31] The text of the Peace of Prague published in Wilson, *Thirty Years War. A Sourcebook*, doc. 103, pp. 194–206, quote p. 194.
[32] Goetze, *Die Politik*, p. 95; Kampmann, *Europa und das Reich*, pp. 89 and 116.
[33] For this argument see E. Ringmar, *Identity, Interest and Action. A Cultural Explanation of Sweden's Intervention in the Thirty Years War* (Cambridge, 1996).

Sweden and the Imperial Constitution

Whether or not Gustav Adolph had more far-reaching aims than restitution, amnesty and territorial and monetary compensation has been a contested issue. It has been suggested that after the victory in Breitenfeld the king changed his objectives and started to aspire towards a permanent hegemony over Protestant estates, or perhaps even the imperial crown.[34] It is, however, highly unlikely that the king entertained hopes of a fundamental reconstitution of the empire or the establishment of a Protestant emperor, in a situation where the Protestant estates still avoided open conflict with the emperor, and France was deeply concerned about the increase of Swedish power in the empire. The king's wish to create a Protestant 'corpus politicum' under his directorate can be explained by military and financial considerations, and it should be regarded as a means to achieve the Swedish primary war aims described above.[35] The creation of a 'corpus evangelicorum' was a continuation of the Swedish endeavour to create an effective system of alliances that would harness the resources of Protestant princes to its war engine. Sweden had used not just diplomatic means, but also military pressure and outright threats in 1630–31 to conclude a number of alliances with Protestant estates, in the situation where the disposition of north-German rulers and imperial city councils could be described as that of 'obstinate loyalty and neutrality'.[36] Several influential princes, such as Electors John George of Saxony and George William of Brandenburg dreaded, at least prior to 1631, foreign intervention more than they feared the emperor's troops and believed that German Protestantism could still effect its own deliverance. Even those who saw the advantages of the Swedish intervention thought that this would force the emperor to be more reasonable and thus render an alliance unnecessary.[37] Brandenburg and Saxony thus hoped to find a middle way between Sweden and the emperor but Gustav Adolph was adamant that there was no 'third way'. He presents this view quite plainly in a declaration to the Elector George William of Brandenburg in June 1631: 'I don't want to hear about neutrality ... This is a fight between God and the devil. If His Grace is with God, he must join me, if he is for the devil, he must fight me.'[38]

Eventually, Sweden managed to conclude treaties of alliance with all major north-German Protestant princes: Pomerania in July 1630, Hesse-Cassel in November 1630, Brandenburg in June 1631, Saxony in September 1631, and Mecklenburg in February 1632. In most of these treaties, Sweden acquired the superior position of a 'protector'.[39] Yet Sweden could not achieve a further aim of persuading its Protestant allies to declare war against the emperor, which would have given it an elevated role as a 'protector' of the whole empire. All treaties emphasised their defensive character against 'disturbers of the peace', sometimes explicitly maintaining that the alliance was not directed against the emperor. The treaty between Gustav Adolph and Bogislaus of Pomerania is an example of this language: 'In the third place, this union is not directed against the majesty of the emperor or the empire, but is rather designed to maintain the constitution of the empire in its ancient state of liberty

---

[34] So Goetze, *Die Politik*, p. 75; Gustav Adolph's wish to become an Emperor is refuted by Roberts, 'Political Objectives', p. 43; for an opposing view see Wilson, *Europe's Tragedy*, pp. 486–7.
[35] See e.g. Gustav Adolph's instruction for his envoy to John George of Saxony, 11 June 1632, published in M. Roberts (ed.), *Sweden as a Great Power 1611–1697: Government, Society, Foreign Policy* (London, 1968), pp. 144–5.
[36] Roberts, *Gustavus Adolphus*, vol. II, pp. 432–4.
[37] Ibid., p. 433.
[38] Wilson, *Thirty Years War. A Sourcebook*, doc. 74, p. 136.
[39] For an analysis of the Swedish role in these alliances, see Roberts, 'Political Objectives', pp. 26–38.

and tranquillity, and to protect the religious and secular settlement against the ravages of the disturbers of public peace.'[40]

Swedish success in south-western Germany prompted Oxenstierna to put renewed pressure on the Protestant estates to break openly with the emperor. In his proposal to the Heilbronn Convent in 1633, where a Protestant alliance under the Swedish leadership was formed, Oxenstierna suggested that the Convent should 'declare both the emperor and the Catholic League public enemies, who should be fought as long as Sweden and the injured estates have not received sufficient compensation.'[41] The Protestants declined the proposal to issue a declaration of war, as they were unwilling to destroy the final opportunity to reach a settlement with the emperor. Although they agreed to carry on fighting under Swedish leadership, they strongly preferred to abstain from the language of 'enemy'.[42] This stance seemed to pay off in 1635 when the majority of the Protestant estates were able to conclude the Peace of Prague with the emperor. This destroyed the Swedish system of alliances, leaving only a few princes, such as Hesse-Cassel who was excluded from the peace, at Oxenstierna's side. As shown above, contrary to general expectations, Sweden was able to carry on the war with only a limited number of allies. Also, in spite of widespread language of *Reichspatriotismus* and calls for unity against foreign invaders,[43] Sweden managed to acquire some new allies in the later stages of the war, such as the dukes of Braunschweig-Lüneburg and Braunschweig-Wolfenbüttel who joined the Swedish side in 1640.

War Finance

The remarkable capacity of Sweden to successfully wage a prolonged campaign abroad calls for an explanation. In 1955 Michael Roberts launched the thesis of a 'Military Revolution', arguing that the increased use of firearms and resultant tactical reforms of Maurice of Nassau and Gustav Adolph led to larger and more disciplined armies which in turn necessitated more effective logistics, bureaucracy, and fiscal mechanisms supporting the military.[44] More recent scholarship has cast some doubt concerning the novelty of Swedish tactics and strategy.[45] Also Denmark employed the new 'Dutch' tactics but had no success against the Catholics who relied on the old-style 'Spanish' tactics.[46] Similarly, Spanish tactics were used to annihilate the Swedes at Nördlingen in 1634.[47] If Swedes possessed any tactical

---

[40] Roberts (ed.), *Sweden as a Great Power*, p. 140.
[41] M.C. Lundorp (ed.), *Acta publica* (3 vols, Frankfurt a. M., 1629–1640), vol. 3, p. 266. Cf. J. Kretzschmar, *Der Heilbronner Bund 1632–1635* (3 vols, Lübeck, 1922), vol. 1, p. 217; J. Öhman, *Der Kampf um den Frieden: Schweden und der Kaiser im Dreißigjährigen Krieg* (Wien, 2005), pp. 48–54
[42] Cf. the resolution of the Protestant Estates, published in Lundorp, *Acta publica*, vol. 3, p. 267.
[43] On the patriotic discourse surrounding the conclusion of the peace, see A. Schmidt, *Vaterlandsliebe und Religionskonflikt. Politische Diskurse im Alten Reich (1555–1648)* (Leiden and Boston, 2007), ch. III.4.
[44] The 1955 inaugural lecture was published in M. Roberts, *The Military Revolution, 1560–1660* (Belfast, 1956); reprinted with some amendments in his *Essays in Swedish History* (London, 1967).
[45] For the criticism and development of Robert's thesis, see esp. G. Parker, 'The "Military Revolution," 1560–1660 – a Myth?', *The Journal of Modern History*, 48/2 (1976): pp. 195–214; G. Parker, *The Military Revolution: Military Innovation and the Rise of the West* (Cambridge, 1988); David Parrott, 'Strategy and Tactics in the Thirty Years' War: The "Military Revolution"', *Militärgeschichtliche Mitteilungen*, 18 (1985): pp. 7–25; J. Black, *A Military Revolution?: Military Change and European Society, 1550–1800* (London, 1991).
[46] J. Glete, *War and the State in Early Modern Europe. Spain, the Dutch Republic and Sweden as Fiscal-Military States, 1500–1660* (London and New York, 2002), p. 208.
[47] Parker, 'The "Military Revolution"', p. 205.

superiority during their campaigns, it was due to the more extensive use of artillery and cavalry, which were innovations compared to the Dutch methods.[48]

Yet rather than seeking the reasons for success in tactical superiority, which are often just *ad hoc* explanations of single events, historians now tend to emphasise more fundamental aspects of the Swedish military enterprise in Germany, which enabled them to recover even from serious setbacks on the battlefield. It was less the question of military tactics than of military organisation: the ability to raise, maintain and command large mercenary forces on a foreign soil. Jan Glete has argued that Sweden's superior ability to extract resources and to administer a permanent army organisation resulted in better training, discipline and motivation for both soldiers and officers. Sweden was remarkable for its permanent conscript army, centralised and government-controlled tax system, and an ability to find broad support among its own population despite huge burdens in both men and taxes caused by offensive wars abroad. During the German war, Sweden was able to transfer the experience of running an efficient national army onto a mercenary army of a much larger scale. The ability to create a 'temporary fiscal-military structure over large parts of Germany' has been called an 'organizational triumph'.[49]

Swedish war finance rested on three main pillars. First of all, the aim of Swedish government was to ensure that 'war should sustain war'.[50] Sweden created an extensive system of contributions which were extracted both by contracts with the Protestant allies (the Heilbronn League and bilateral treaties), and by raising local contributions from conquered territories which often amounted to plunder. The need to feed and pay the army was a key factor pushing Sweden to wage war offensively rather than defensively.[51] Nevertheless, it was not entirely realistic to shift the entire burden of war onto Germany, and the war placed a heavy toll on the state budget as well. It was extremely helpful in this respect that in 1629 Sweden managed to secure the customs revenues from Prussian ports which amounted to a third of its state budget. According to the 1635 Truce of Stumsdorf, however, Sweden was obliged to give up its possessions in Polish Prussia. Since then, Sweden depended more heavily on other sources, particularly on the third pillar of its war finance, namely the French subsidies. Both the treaty of Bärwalde from 1631, when France was waging war in the empire indirectly with Swedish hands, and the alliance treaty of Hamburg from 1638 stipulated that France had to pay substantial sums in return for Sweden continuing the war effort.[52] The price Sweden had to pay was the limitation of its sphere of action, such as the prohibition from concluding a separate peace with the emperor. This was yet another factor that helped to prolong the war until the Peace of Westphalia was finally concluded in 1648.

Selected Bibliography

Ahnlund, N., *Gustaf Adolf inför tyska kriget* (Stockholm, 1918).

---

[48] The important victory at Jankau in 1645 has been attributed to the superior artillery: Parker, *The Thirty Years' War*, p. 176; cf. Glete, *War and the State*, p. 208. On the limitations regarding the use of cavalry: F. Tallett, *War and Society in early-modern Europe, 1495–1715* (London and New York, 1992), pp. 30–31.
[49] Glete, *War and the State*, ch. 5, quote p. 178.
[50] Wilson, *Europe's Tragedy*, p. 464; Roberts, 'Political Objectives', p. 24.
[51] See Parker, *The Thirty Years War*, p. 160.
[52] On Swedish war finance, see Kampmann, *Europa und das Reich*, pp. 72–4; S. Lundkvist, 'Svensk krigsfinansiering 1630–1635', *Historisk Tidskrift*, 83 (1963): pp. 1–38.

Böttcher, D., 'Propaganda und öffentliche Meinung im protestantischen Deutschland 1628–1636' [1953], in H.U. Rudolf (ed.), *Der Dreißigjährige Krieg* (Darmstadt, 1977), pp. 325–67.

Glete, J., *War and the State in Early Modern Europe. Spain, the Dutch Republic and Sweden as Fiscal-Military States, 1500–1660* (London and New York, 2002).

Goetze, S., *Die Politik des schwedischen Reichskanzlers Axel Oxenstierna gegenüber Kaiser und Reich* (Kiel, 1971).

Kampmann, C., *Europa und das Reich im Dreißigjährigen Krieg* (Stuttgart, 2008).

Öhman, J., *Der Kampf um den Frieden: Schweden und der Kaiser im Dreißigjährigen Krieg* (Wien, 2005).

Oredsson, S., *Geschichtsschreibung und Kult. Gustav Adolf, Schweden und der Dreißigjährige Krieg* (Berlin, 1994).

Parker, G., *The Thirty Years' War* (London and New York, 1984).

Piirimäe, P., 'Just War in Theory and Practice: The Legitimation of Swedish Intervention in the Thirty Years War', *The Historical Journal*, 45/3 (2002): pp. 499–523.

Ringmar, E., *Identity, Interest and Action. A Cultural Explanation of Sweden's Intervention in the Thirty Years War* (Cambridge, 1996).

Roberts, M., 'The Political Objectives of Gustavus Adolphus in Germany 1630–1632', *The Transactions of the Royal Historical Society*, 7 (1957): pp. 19–46.

Roberts, M., *Gustavus Adolphus. A history of Sweden, 1611–1632* (2 vols, London, New York and Toronto, 1958).

Wilson, P., *Europe's Tragedy. A New History of the Thirty Years War* (London, 2009).

Wilson, P. (ed.), *Thirty Years War. A Sourcebook* (London, 2010).

France and the Thirty Years' War

Lucien Bély

The initial framework of the Thirty Years' War was the Holy Roman Empire. King Henri II of France did not sign a peace treaty with the emperor after the occupation of the Three Bishoprics in 1552. Although events in Bohemia in 1618 seemed far away to people in France, the links between the king of Spain and his cousin in Vienna were of major concern to the French monarch. The kingdom felt the Spanish presence to the south, east and north as a threat of encirclement, even though relations between Paris and Madrid had settled during the regency of the Queen Mother, Marie de Medici, widow of Henri IV (1610–1614). Indeed, they settled so far as to allow for the marriage of the young King Louis XIII and the Infanta, Anne of Austria (1615).

Yet Louis XIII did not approve of the revolt by the Bohemian nobility against its legitimate sovereign. He offered to act as mediator, sending the duc d'Angoulême[1] as his ambassador. The duke supported the Treaty of Ulm between the army of the Evangelical Union and the army of the Catholic League but Bohemia was not party to it. The imperial forces had an excuse to attack the new king, Frederick V; they defeated him at the Battle of White Mountain (1620).

The victories won by the Catholic cause could have been favourably received in a France marked by the Catholic Reformation that had been inspired by the Council of Trent but the French monarch's government was also concerned about the imperial victory and the new power of the Hapsburgs. The defeat of the German Protestant princes threatened the political balance in the empire and many of them had known since the sixteenth century that they could count on the support of France. The end of the ceasefire between Spain and the United Provinces in 1621 was a further concern for France, which had supported the Dutch efforts to obtain independence. The new king of Spain and his minister, Olivares, carefully defined a major strategy in Europe to put down this revolt.

The Covert War

For years, the French government hesitated to become directly involved in the European conflict because the king wanted to subdue the Protestants in France and he was also facing conspiracies fomented by leading members of the aristocracy. Nevertheless, tension in Europe spread and increased. Local and regional conflicts became international issues. Princes and ordinary people turned to the great powers, seeking assistance.

---

[1] He was the illegitimate son of Charles IX, of the Valois dynasty, king of France from 1560 to 1574.

The Valtellina was a case in point. The high-altitude Adda Valley in the north of Italy, in the heart of the Alps, was a strategic route for Spanish troop movements. The local, Roman Catholic, population was counting on the protection of the Spanish governor of the Milan area but the valley was dependent on the Grey Leagues which were Protestant, allied to the cantons of Switzerland and seeking aid from France. Eventually, papal troops were sent to occupy the area to prevent conflict breaking out between Louis XIII and Philip IV.

The kingdom of France was at risk of being drawn into the war spreading through Europe at any time, so Louis XIII brought Cardinal de Richelieu into the government in 1624 to define a consistent political strategy. Richelieu had been the main councillor of Marie de Medici and the king eventually appointed him 'Principal Minister' of the State in 1629. Until his death in 1642, the prelate continued to lead the government in France.[2]

Faced with Spain's ambitious policy, what attitude would Louis XIII take? He re-established his ties with the United Provinces (1624) and slowly did the same for relations with England. Yet France had to remain on its toes, especially as 1625 was an 'admirable year' for Spain. The dazzling Spanish success at Breda (June 1625) may have suggested the end of the Dutch revolt. The French Ambassador in Spain signed the Treaty of Monzón with Spain (1626).[3] The Spanish victories over the Dutch, however, did not last long.

While Emperor Ferdinand II attempted to turn the empire into a unified Roman Catholic monarchy, Louis XIII did not have the resources or, perhaps, the desire to become too deeply involved with the humiliated Protestant princes. He was too busy with civil unrest in his own country. Richelieu's arrival in the Council allowed him to re-establish the old principles of French diplomacy. The cardinal, when considering politics, believed that France should have loyal allies in Germany and Italy who could, if necessary, organise themselves into 'Leagues' to withstand pressure from the Hapsburgs – the Austrian branch in the empire and the Spanish branch in Italy.

France's maritime policy also upset England, which organised a landing on the Island of Ré (1627) and counted on the assistance of La Rochelle, the main centre of Protestantism in France. King Louis XIII took command of an army of 20,000 men himself and forced the English army to re-embark (November 1627). He decided to lay siege to La Rochelle and Richelieu took personal command of the operation, organising the town's blockade from land and sea. The town surrendered on 28 October 1628. The capture of La Rochelle, however, did not mark the end of Protestantism in France; rather it redefined its place in the kingdom. The Atlantic defences were strengthened, eliminating any breach that might be formed by the town.

At the same time as fighting within the country itself, France became caught up in a conflict against Spain in Italy. War had not yet been declared, there were no actual battles; instead historians have spoken of a 'covert war'. Richelieu believed that Italy was the 'very heart of the world' and that it was also the weak point in the Spanish empire.[4]

The Mantuan succession proved him right. The duke of Mantua, from the House of Gonzague, died with no direct descendants but he had a cousin, another Gonzague, the duc de Nevers who lived in France and was considered a subject of the king of France. The emperor, as sovereign of Mantua, refused Nevers the right to inherit the duchy but Nevers took it anyway. As the king of France was, at that time, busy with the siege of La

---

[2] S. de Franceschi, 'La genèse française du catholicisme d'Etat et son aboutissement au début du ministériat de Richelieu. Les catholiques zélés à l'épreuve de l'affaire Santarelli et la clôture de la controverse autour du pouvoir pontifical au temporel (1626–1627)', *Annuaire-bulletin de la Société de l'histoire de France*, année 2001 (Paris, 2003): pp. 19–63.

[3] The Valtellina was neutralised.

[4] S. Externbrinck, '"Le cœur du monde" et la "Liberté de l'Italie". Aspects of Richelieu's Italian policy 1624–1642', *Revue d'Histoire diplomatique*, 114/3 (2000): pp. 181–208.

Rochelle, Spain thought it would be possible to chase out the French intruder although two main towns remained loyal to him, Casale Monferrato defended by a French garrison, and Mantua itself. This was a major challenge for Spain. Casale controlled the road from Genoa to Milan and Mantua was on the only road between the Milan area and the Republic of Venice, as well as standing on the road to the Brenner Pass and Austria. The duke of Savoy (who also owned the Piedmont) took up arms with the Spanish after they promised him the Monferrat area. Olivares gave the order to besiege Casale. France and Spain were on the brink of war, drawn in by minor powers.

After the capitulation of La Rochelle, Richelieu advised intervention in northern Italy in December 1628. The French supporters of an alliance with Spain were, of course, hostile to the idea, behind Marie de Medici and the Keeper of the Seals, Marillac. In their opinion, the Casale business was a minor affair and not worth the sacrifice of the efforts at reform within the kingdom and the Catholic reconquest of Europe. According to them, Richelieu was recommending war to make himself irreplaceable in the king's eyes. Meanwhile, the policy burdened the people with higher taxes and led to general discontent. French troops crossed the Alps. Spain obtained assistance from the emperor who, as a result, had to draw troops away from the other fronts, seriously weakening them. This was the first time since 1527 that a German army had entered the Italian Peninsula.[5] Cardinal de Richelieu, in a note to the king dated 13 January 1629, set out the salient points of a political programme: 'France should think only of fortifications within its borders. It should build and open doorways allowing it access to all the neighbouring States so that it can guarantee them against oppression by Spain when the occasions arise.' The French forces captured the redoubtable fortress of Pignerol in the Piedmont on 22 March 1630. As to the imperial army, it took Mantua in July 1630 and sacked the town.

The situation in northern Italy was linked to the situation of the Holy Roman Empire and the Hapsburgs' ambitions were of concern to the whole of Europe. France and England favoured agreement between the two princes of the House of Vasa – the Roman Catholic King Sigismond III of Poland, and his Lutheran cousin, King Gustav Adolph of Sweden. The latter now had a free hand. He could intervene in northern Germany and provide backup for the Protestant princes who had been dispossessed by the emperor. A meeting of Electors was held in Regensburg in the summer of 1630. Father Joseph, Richelieu's right-hand man, encouraged the German princes to refuse the election of Ferdinand II's son as King of the Romans: that would have ensured he succeeded his father automatically, without an election, and would possibly have been one step towards the hereditary transmission of the imperial crown in the House of Hapsburg. Everything might go a different way, however. Gustav Adolph of Sweden landed in northern Germany in 1630, on the grounds that he was defending Protestantism.

When the imperial army captured Mantua, French negotiators took fright and agreed, on 13 October 1630, to sign a treaty that required the French and imperial troops to pull out of northern Italy. The situation in France was then very tense because, at the end of summer, Louis XIII had fallen seriously ill in Lyon and seemed likely to die soon. He had hardly recovered when he received news of the Treaty of Regensburg. Its ratification would mean the failure of Richelieu's policy since France would then abandon its allies and leave the way

---

[5] The historian David Parrott underlines the contrast between the Siege of La Rochelle (military resources were mobilised for the purposes of an achievable aim) and the campaign in northern Italy where the gap constantly widened between the military objectives on the one hand and, on the other, the resources and organisation set in place. This prefigures the situation after 1635 when France entered the war against Spain. Cf. D. Parrott, *Richelieu's Army. War, Government and Society in France, 1624–1642* (Cambridge, 2001).

free for the emperor. The cardinal advised Louis XIII not to ratify the treaty, claiming that the French envoys had overstepped their brief.[6]

The rejection of the Treaty of Regensburg led to lively controversy in France; Richelieu was immediately subjected to attacks by supporters of peace and by his political adversaries who feared a war against the Hapsburgs. The Queen Mother, Marie, launched an offensive against Richelieu who believed himself to be disgraced. This was the 'great storm' or the 'Day of Dupes' of 11 November 1630 when, in fact, Louis XIII asked his minister to continue 'steering the ship' and exiled his enemies. In France, Richelieu's political victory was greeted as a victory for 'good Frenchmen' and a defeat for the pro-Spanish faction. Soon, Queen Marie found herself on the road to exile.[7]

In Italy, while the French and Spanish forces were about to do battle at Casale, a papal envoy called Mazarin miraculously obtained a ceasefire on 26 October 1630. The negotiations at Cherasco then led to treaties that appeared to be favourable to France with Savoy giving it Pignerol in 1632. Thanks to this, Louis XIII obtained a 'gateway' halfway between Briançon and Turin, a gateway which, in those days, was seen as the entrance to Italy and a means of rapid intervention. In the end, the Spanish government felt it had been duped by this treaty, with the complicity of the negotiator, Mazarin.

The New International Scene

The Day of Dupes showed that the French monarchy would not change its political line. Setting aside internal reforms, Richelieu proposed to mobilise the kingdom and take action against the Hapsburgs, indirectly to begin with.

France occupied a central position on the chessboard that was Europe because it was able to intervene in the Holy Roman Empire, Italy or the Spanish Low Countries. The kingdom was also densely populated. This was not essential for the armies that still had many mercenaries but it was vital for the king's finances which relied on a huge population of taxpayers. At the same time, however, France had long borders and long coastlines to protect and the capital could easily be threatened by invasion from the north or east.

On 23 January 1631, the Treaty of Bärwalde obliged France to pay a huge subsidy to King Gustav Adolph of Sweden for five years after he had won great victories in Germany, settled in the Rhineland and been considered as the arbitrator of Europe. France also succeeded in negotiating an alliance with Bavaria (1631).

Richelieu and Father Joseph became concerned about the great successes of their Swedish ally, whose soldiers had entered Alsace. Lorraine in the east was an independent duchy in a strategic position; its duke, Charles IV, was an adventurous prince and supporter of the emperor. Military operations in 1632–1633 led to a number of treaties that allowed French forces to gradually control all the fortresses in Lorraine and guard the bridges over the River Meuse. The duke abandoned Lorraine and Louis XIII's armies took control of the roads leading to Germany. The king of France also sent an army to occupy fortresses that the elector of Trier entrusted to him in July 1632 (Ehrenbreitstein, Koblenz and Trier).

This military presence weighed heavily on village life in Lorraine as can be seen in the *Small Miseries* and the *Great Miseries of War*, engravings by a local man, Jacques Callot. Today,

---

[6] D.P. O'Connell, 'A Cause Celebre in the History of Treaty Making. The Refusal to Ratify the Peace Treaty of Regensburg in 1630', *British Yearbook of International Law*, XLII (1967): pp. 71–90.

[7] Warmly welcomed by the princes in countries neighbouring France, she attracted French malcontents and the enemies of Louis XIII and Richelieu.

historians see the engravings as a lesson about the need to limit the atrocities committed by soldiers. Each scene of horror ends with its own punishment; Callot's work is thought to have been part of the significant efforts made during the Thirty Years' War to regulate the conduct of war.

The death of the king of Sweden in Lützen in 1632 and the assassination of Wallenstein in 1634 plunged Germany into chaos. In the Rhineland countries, numerous princes were at a loss and turned to France for protection. During this time, there was permanent friction between French forces and Hapsburg troops, the latter possibly considering that the great victory won by the Spanish and imperial forces over the Swedes in Nördlingen on 6 September 1634 was the first step towards reconciliation between the emperor and the German princes.

While Spain was exhausted by war, France benefited from its relatively prudent attitude. It still had significant resources at its disposal. Mandatory taxation hit a French population that had already been through significant demographic crises in 1628–1632 and 1636–1638 – popular revolts against taxes broke out all over France.[8]

The Outbreak of War

The Swedish defeat at Nördlingen finally won Louis XIII and Richelieu over. French garrisons replaced the Swedes in Alsace and most of the area, including Colmar and Sélestat, was then occupied. Yet negotiations with the Swedes proved difficult. Chancellor Oxenstierna met Louis XIII and his prime minister before the Treaty of Compiègne was eventually signed on 28 April 1635. Both parties made a commitment to support the Protestant cause in Germany and not to sign a separate peace treaty or ceasefire. Negotiations with the United Provinces and Stathouder Frederick Henry of Nassau led to a treaty (8 February 1635) which was both defensive and offensive, allowing two armies, one French and the other Dutch, to enter the Low Countries.

The final military preparations were crucial. For 1635, Louis XIII had enough money to pay 165,000 men but the king's army deployed at the gateways to Germany seemed to be in very poor condition, weakened by disease and desertion. The Spaniards entered the Electorate at Trier and, on 26 March 1635, captured and imprisoned the elector, who had placed himself under French protection.[9] The event was enough to justify France's entry into the conflict. The declaration of war on Spain was solemnly taken to Brussels by a herald-at-arms on 19 May 1635 for the Cardinal-Infante, Governor of the Low Countries, in a procedure dating back to feudal times.

The French launched a three-pronged offensive against the Low Countries, Germany and northern Italy. Olivares's strategy was equally ambitious – a threefold invasion of France by Spanish troops from the Low Countries, imperial forces from Franche-Comté and by Philip IV himself from Catalonia. The French offensive in the Low Countries in 1635 began smoothly but did not produce the expected uprising against Spanish domination. The victorious army was not paid and it exacted so much from local populations that they revolted as it passed through. Disease and desertion decimated these brigand troops.

---

[8] Y.-M. Bercé, *Histoire des croquants. Etude des soulèvements populaires au XVIIe siècle dans le sud-ouest de la France* (Paris, 1974).

[9] H. Weber, 'Richelieu et le Rhin', *Revue historique*, CCXXXIX (1968): pp. 265–80; idem., *Frankreich, Kurtrier, der Rhein und das Reich, 1623–35* (Bonn, 1969).

Bernard of Saxe-Weimar carried French hopes in Germany. He was a member of the House of Saxony and a perfect example of a wartime entrepreneur, capable of recruiting and commanding an army but without any territorial base or financial resources. This meant that he had to seek contributions from people in occupied territories or place himself in the service of the rich and powerful. He signed an agreement with France in 1635 under which he was to receive four million *livres* a year, four times the payment made to Sweden. In return, he was to maintain 12,000 foot soldiers and 6,000 cavalry. The agreement was vital for France because the emperor's situation was improving. On 30 May 1635, the elector of Saxony signed the Treaty of Prague under which he changed his allegiance from the Swedes to the emperor. Most of the princes and imperial towns followed suit. Only a few obstinate allies of France continued the war.

The Spanish army was able to launch a major offensive in the north of France in 1636 while an imperial general entered Champagne. On 15 August, Corbie, the town that controlled the passage of the Somme, was captured; it was a mere 120 kilometres from Paris. The capital was rocked by panic. The 'year of Corbie' was to remain in people's minds for a very long time. The king and the cardinal travelled to Compiègne to take command of the situation. French military might (30,000 men), the difficulties experienced by the Cardinal-Infante when attacked to the north by the Dutch, and desertions from the Spanish army because of inadequate food enabled the French to take back the towns in the area, including Corbie. For their part, the Dutch advanced, relieving the pressure on the French camp. One army was sent to stop the imperial forces that were entering Burgundy and laying waste to the province. The fortress in Saint-Jean-de-Losne withstood imperial attack and, when the imperial army received news of a Swedish victory in Wittstock, it had to return to Germany.

The enemy armies had 'fouled' (i.e. laid waste) three provinces – Champagne, Picardy and Burgundy. To the south, the Spanish took the Lérins Islands offshore from Cannes without meeting any resistance (September 1635). Yet Spain was unable to push on with its offensive from the south which, at the time of the capture of Corbie, might have brought its plans to a successful conclusion.

The Franco-Swedish alliance then revealed its limits and ambiguities. As long as relations were not broken off between France and the emperor, Chancellor Oxenstierna did not consider himself bound by the Treaty of Compiègne. In January 1636, however, the emperor declared war on France. This was a major turning-point. On 30 March, under the Treaty of Wismar, France guaranteed that Sweden would receive Pomerania but Oxenstierna was careful not to ratify the treaty. Concerned with France's reversals of fortune, he kept this strategy up for some considerable time, not reneging on the French alliance but not committing to it too resolutely. What he wanted was favourable negotiations with the emperor so that his country could obtain permanent ownership of land on the south shores of the Baltic Sea, in the Holy Roman Empire.

Battles were fought at the gateways to France. In the south, the French recaptured the Lérins Islands (1637). In the north, the need to coordinate three army units along the border from Picardy to Burgundy was still as difficult. The situation in France depended on operations across the Rhine. At the end of 1637, the Swedes were pushed back on all fronts and, in 1638, only Saxe-Weimar had enough resources to undertake a victorious campaign in Germany. Assisted by a member of the Bouillon family, the Vicomte de Turenne who brought him reinforcements, Saxe-Weimar took Freiburg-in-Breisgau then, in December 1638, Brisach on the right bank of the Rhine which guarded one of the few bridges over the river.¹⁰ Saxe-Weimar died in July 1639 but his formidable army remained in the service of the king of France.¹¹

The Question of Alsace and the Rhine

Thanks to Brisach, the royal army protected Alsace and broke the line of communications between the Milan area and Franche-Comté, on the one hand, and the Low Countries, on the other. Brisach opened the door to the empire, enabling France permanently to intervene in German affairs.

The question of the Rhine was an important one, especially in German historiography. From Friedrich Schiller in the late eighteenth to historians in the twentieth century, there was an ongoing belief that Richelieu's entire policy was aimed at expanding French territory to the banks of this river, seen as the kingdom's natural border (and possibly beyond). By undertaking such an offensive, the French nation created an obstacle to the development of the German nation and Richelieu was therefore responsible for all the wars thereafter, including the Second World War.¹² Another point of view, though, had its supporters – Richelieu's policy had to be seen against the background of contemporary ideas and concepts. France, as part of its policy on protection and passages, was seeking to provide itself with bridgeheads. Neither the Rhine nor Alsace were included as such in the aims of French policy during the Thirty Years' War but the conflict showed that control of Alsace and access to the Rhine were both useful to France.¹³

The notion of reason of State that inspired Richelieu continues to be central to historians' analyses. In 1921, Friedrich Meinecke, in his *Idee der Staatsräson* [The Idea of the Reason of State], put national interest at the centre of Richelieu's political thinking. Devoid of any individual or private motive, it was driven purely and solely by a need to serve public interest. For many German historians, however, Richelieu remained a Machiavellian, or even demonic, figure.¹⁴ Yet a study of the cardinal's writings, notably instructions for the peace negotiators, was sufficient to change this view by showing that the cardinal had also considered ways of providing Europe with a collective security system. To counterbalance the excessive political weight of the Hapsburgs, the kingdom of France had to be able to intervene in Italy and the Holy Roman Empire and it needed solid allies on which it could count if the need arose.

---

¹⁰ Brisach was the only permanent crossing point on the river between Basel and the Palatinate. The other bridge was the one linking Strasbourg and Kehl, but it was in the hands of one of the Empire's free cities, reputed to be neutral, and it only granted a right of passage if it wished to do so. For Richelieu, Brisach was the gateway to Germany in the same way as Pignerol was the gateway to Italy.

¹¹ It fought like a corps decentralised, self-sufficient and, to a large extent, strategically independent, according to the historian David Parrott.

¹² On the other hand, the idea that the French nation gained strength to the detriment of the German nation led to outrageous statements: the Cardinal is thought to have wanted to weaken the German people and empire whose power was reduced by structural divisions and internal conflicts. In 1940, Adolf Hitler was even considered as the antithesis of Cardinal de Richelieu. This view was reversed after 1945.

¹³ A.V. Hartmann, 'La politique française à l'époque de Richelieu: interprétations allemandes de 1648 à 1998', in *1648, Belfort dans une Europe remodelée* (Belfort, 2000), pp. 103–12.

¹⁴ In 1996, Henry Kissinger, in his book *Diplomacy* (1994), expressed the same opinion: for him, Richelieu's influence on the history of Central Europe was the opposite of the successes that he achieved on behalf of France. He feared a unified Europe and prevented it from happening. In all likelihood, he delayed the unification of Germany by some two hundred years.

Richelieu's policy was one step in the strengthening of the concept of Nation-State in France. It was accompanied by an authoritarian government that did not accept political negotiations with the king's subjects. It was the system described by historians as 'absolutism'.

The French Army

It became increasingly common in France to accept the principle that the army was answerable solely to the monarch and was designed to serve him alone. Yet private initiative remained essential when it came to recruiting, paying, arming and feeding soldiers. The French army consisted of regiments, each with a variable number of companies of several dozen men each (an average of 42.2 men). Two of the ranks could be purchased – colonel or master of the camp, who commanded a regiment, and captain, who commanded a company. The price of a regiment, already high, continued to climb. Recruitment was conducted by captains and their 'lower officers' (we would say NCOs). Captains received a sum of money from the king to recruit and feed them.

As demonstrated by David Parrott, the financial burden of recruitment lay on the shoulders of the officers, which meant that a military career was extremely expensive and required personal income. The officers were drawn from the ancient nobility, a class from which a monarch could request this type of sacrifice because it still cherished the military values respected by society as a whole. Officers often found their soldiers in the area in which their families had been established for centuries, among the young peasants living on their lands. They would also use their local acquaintances and influence to recruit troops. However, although the general recruitment business did not exist, the French army nevertheless appeared to result from a number of individual businesses. Moreover, many soldiers in the French forces were still foreign mercenaries from the empire, Swiss cantons, Italy and the British Isles. Richelieu wrote, 'It is almost impossible to fight great wars with Frenchmen alone'.

Historians have much debated the question of the size of the French army. Before 1635, French troops would have consisted of little more than 45,000 foot soldiers and 3,000 or 4,000 cavalry. For the 1635 campaign, it was planned to raise 134,000 foot soldiers and 20,880 cavalry (or fewer according to a letter from Bullion in 1634: 115,000 and 9,500). In 1636, the number is thought to have increased to 172,000 infantry and 21,400 cavalry. It would appear plausible for the army to have had between 170,000 to 200,000 men until 1648 – Spain had some 300,000 men in 1635. These numbers remain uncertain as they are purely theoretical and were put forward during preparations for the campaign. David Parrott, setting aside the overall evaluations of French forces and, instead, finding the figures for each campaign and each front, believed that an army in a theatre of war was smaller than this, rarely more than 15,000 men.

An International Reversal

Military operations continued, with varying results. In Italy, Rohan failed to retain the Valtellina and the road into the Tyrol was again open to the Spaniards. In Savoy, Louis XIII's sister, the duchess, governed on behalf of her son who was still a minor and her authority was challenged. She requested assistance from France when civil war broke out.

In October 1636, the Dutch took Brazil.[15] In the hope of reconquering it, Olivares entered negotiations with France. The idea of a conference in Hamburg was accepted but, once there, French diplomats first and foremost obtained the signature of a new treaty with Sweden (15 March 1638). The two kingdoms could not sign separate peace treaties for three years and France granted the Swedes new subsidies. A joint policy with Germany, which was never really aimed at, took shape in the form of a draft. Yet in the Holy Roman Empire, where the war began, the emperor had repaired the damage while retaining pre-existing religious and political rights. He was ready for peace but had yet to free the empire from French and Swedish occupation, by force or negotiation. Attempts at achieving peace were not instigated by Olivares but, after a Dutch victory near Dover in Les Dunes on 21 October 1639, the Dutch controlled the Channel and the North Sea: independence seemed inevitable for the Low Countries. An international reversal of situation took place, at the expense of the Hapsburgs.

It was in the Iberian Peninsula that the tension caused by the war led to open rebellion, in Catalonia[16] and Portugal. On 23 January 1641, Louis XIII agreed to become count of Barcelona.[17] In fact, the war was waged mainly in Roussillon and the province of Lerida. Collioure surrendered in April 1642 followed by Perpignan in September. French troops marched south of the Pyrenees and, on 7 October 1642, at the Battle of Lerida, the Spanish army was defeated. A French viceroy ceremoniously entered Barcelona on 4 December 1642.

In 1640, Portugal also rebelled against Madrid. The War of Independence, then in its infancy, did not end until 1668. At the same time, French forces re-established the authority of the king's sister in Savoy. However, although Richelieu's foreign policy met with success, it was not enough to ward off dangers within the country – conspiracies and uprisings led by the nobility continued.

On 4 December 1642, Richelieu died. On the following day, Mazarin, who had settled in France and won Richelieu's trust,[18] was appointed to the council. Louis XIII died in his turn on 14 May 1643. Queen Anne of Austria became regent on behalf of her son, Louis XIV, who was not yet five years old. To everybody's surprise, she kept Cardinal Mazarin on as Principal Minister.

In the spring of 1643, a Spanish army of 28,000 men attempted to invade France from Flanders. The young duc d'Enghien, later the prince de Condé, who was in command of the army in Picardy, decided on a pitched battle outside Rocroi on 19 May 1643. 'Rocroi was a victory for the encirclement manoeuvre served by a mind able to take decisions and the offensive', said the historian André Corvisier. The French victory at Rocroi showed that the formidable Spanish infantry was no longer invincible. This victory, coming five days after the death of Louis XIII, who had defined the strategy for the campaign, showed that the policy upheld by the deceased king and Richelieu was bearing fruit. Mazarin suggested to the regent that the impetus should be maintained by besieging Thionville. The town was taken in August and the French soon controlled Moselle. Meanwhile, the French Navy scattered the main Spanish fleet. Thus, Anne of Austria continued the conflict begun by her husband despite contacts from Madrid because, although she wanted peace with Spain, she did not want it at any price. She wanted France, her son's kingdom, to be victorious.

---

[15] Jean-Maurice de Nassau-Siegen was appointed Governor of Brazilian New Holland in 1636 and remained there until 1644.
[16] Catalonia included the Roussillon area north of the Pyrenees.
[17] Louis XIII made a commitment not to introduce any innovation in the tax system and to leave Catalonia's towns to raise and use taxes as they saw fit.
[18] Richelieu even intended to entrust the negotiations planned in Westphalia to this cardinal.

The Path to Peace?

French policy was laid out in the great 'instruction' of 30 September 1643, prepared by Richelieu for French negotiators. It was simply taken up again by Mazarin who had already worked on it. France did not want to expand into Germany and Italy to the detriment of others. Only the fortified town of Pignerol seemed to be necessary as 'a gateway through which to succour Italy'. The French diplomats denounced 'the large number of invasions' through which the House of Austria had expanded and accused it of 'laying claim to universal monarchy'. France had to maintain its union with its allies – Holland, Savoy and Mantua in Italy, the elector of Trier and the German princes in the Holy Roman Empire, Catalonia and Portugal in the Iberian Peninsula and, of course, Sweden. A joint 'safety' device was implemented by setting up two leagues, one in Germany and the other in Italy, through which all powers would oppose any party attempting to contravene the treaty. France kept Lorraine, and its ownership of Metz, Toul and Verdun was an accepted fact. The king of France would keep his conquests in Artois and Flanders, as well as the county of Roussillon. He would retain the occupied fortified towns in Alsace, temporarily at least. This highlighted the moderation of France's territorial appetites. Satisfying its claims would be detrimental to Spain. Negotiators turned to the emperor, now Ferdinand III, seeking the support of the German princes. That 'instruction' actually laid down the outlines of a European settlement.

Meanwhile, war continued, even moving into new areas. In 1644, the French army occupied the entire left bank of the Rhine, from Basel to the Dutch border. In 1645, the army captured ten major towns in the Spanish Low Countries. In October 1646, the French took Dunkirk. Italy became a favourite target for Mazarin's manoeuvres. Savoy, now allied to France, retained the alpine passes, preventing any Spanish attack. French forces were therefore able to attack the State of Presides on the coast of Tuscany and the Island of Elba, both of which belonged to the Spanish empire (1646). The French remained there for four years, threatening Genoa and Naples. It was even easier for them to act after a popular uprising broke out in Naples on 7 July 1647, led by a fisherman named Masaniello. On 17 October 1647, Naples proclaimed itself a republic under the protection of France with the duc de Guise as 'Duke of the Republic'. In April 1648, however, the Spaniards took back control of the town.

The king of Spain's army regained the upper hand from 1644 onwards in Catalonia and even Condé was unable to prevent the recapture of the area. The victor of Rocroi, disgusted by this failure, believed that Mazarin had not provided him with enough support and this affront led to his first few murmurings of opposition to the cardinal. The Fronde revolt soon put an end to French efforts in Catalonia. In Portugal, the rebels retained John IV of Braganza as their leader and were united in their hatred of Castilians. They continued to receive aid from France and Holland.

In 1641, a Franco-Swedish treaty specified Münster and Osnabrück as the seats of negotiations with the empire. The French delegation consisted of Abel Servien and the Comte d'Avaux.[19] Mazarin controlled their actions but the two plenipotentiaries were in disagreement. D'Avaux was more sensitive to arguments in favour of a Catholic reconquest; Servien, on the other hand, was a loyal assistant to Mazarin, maintaining the alliance with Sweden and the Protestant powers. In 1645, Mazarin sent Henri d'Orléans, duc de Longueville, to head the delegation and put an end to the discord.

---

[19] A.Tischer, *Französische Diplomatie und Diplomaten auf dem Westfälischen Friedenskongress: Außenpolitik unter Richelieu und Mazarin* (Münster, 1999).

During these preparations, Bavaria, which had broken off ties with France, again went on the offensive – successfully.[20] It accepted assistance from the Swedes before Turenne was able to defeat Bavaria in August 1645 in Allerheim – it was also described as the second Battle of Nördlingen. In the following November, Turenne returned Trier to the elector, showing that the king of France upheld his commitment to defend German liberty. Five months earlier, the main Swedish army won a dazzling victory over the imperial army in Jankov to the south-west of Prague (6 March 1645). The emperor and his family had to flee Vienna. Ferdinand III played his hand in 1645 and lost everything. The Franco-Swedish alliance proved to be still solid. Despite the fears of a separate peace treaty Mazarin remained loyal to this decision and a joint strategy was eventually put in place, with the Swedish army relieving the French army in Germany.

For obvious tactical reasons, France declared that it was defending German liberty with an emperor who should be the leader of Germany but not its sovereign. From a religious point of view, French policy (which was actually favourable to Protestant princes) put it in a difficult position. The 'very Christian' king, the pious queen and the cardinal prime minister could not allow the weakening of Roman Catholicism. Within the kingdom, the Protestants had become less of a threat recently but might reverse this trend. This meant that France had to manoeuvre between preserving Catholic interests and showing loyalty to its allies. The first of these, Sweden, wanted to turn Germany into a vast territory governed by the Reformed Religion. Discussions therefore focused on the date that would serve as a reference in establishing the primary religion in the various regions of the empire. In 1618, the Protestant camp had seemed to be at the height of its expansionism; by 1629, it was the Roman Catholic faction which had succeeded in recapturing vast tracts of land. An intermediate date between these two extremes therefore had to be found and, eventually, agreement was reached on 1624.

Negotiations made progress but Mazarin then committed his greatest political mistake. He tried to obtain the whole of the Spanish Low Countries by abandoning the areas conquered by France. Spain, however, resisted in 1646 and, of course, the Spanish government used the French proposal as a weapon. The Catalans now knew that France would hardly support them and, more importantly, the Dutch realised that their long-standing ally might become their neighbour and that, instead of a far-off king of Spain, the neighbour would be the nearby, offensive king of France. This speeded up the negotiations between Spain and the United Provinces and led to a peace treaty. The Spanish government, having reached agreement with the Dutch, no longer seemed in a hurry to complete negotiations.

The Treaties of Westphalia

Towards the end, military operations and events cast a shadow over the peace negotiations, making the process a very fragile one. Ferdinand III recovered troops and negotiated with Maximilian of Bavaria and it was not until the crushing French victory in Zusmarshausen on 17 May 1648 that Maximilian was forced to lay down his arms. Königsmark, in the service of Sweden, delivered one final blow. He entered Prague by surprise on 26 July 1648. The unexpected event was fatal for Ferdinand and he agreed to sign the peace treaty. In Lens, on 20 August 1648, the Spaniards were also roundly defeated by Condé's army but Spain was still not ready to sign. The victories of 1648 precipitated events in Westphalia and, on 24

---

[20] On this, see chapter 12 by Tryntje Helfferich in this volume.

October 1648, the Treaties of Westphalia were signed, with Servien signing on his own on behalf of Louis XIV.

The empire sacrificed territory on a permanent basis. France was recognised as having sovereignty over the three bishoprics of Toul, Metz and Verdun. While France did not demand any 'satisfaction' from the German States, it demanded it from the Hapsburgs, particularly Alsace.[21] It therefore acquired two bridgeheads on the other side of the Rhine (Brisach and garrison rights in Philippsbourg) and lands belonging to the House of Austria in Alsace, i.e. the *'landgraviat'* of Upper Alsace, Lower Alsace and protection of the Decapolis (a league of ten towns – Landau, Wissembourg, Haguenau, Rosheim, Obernai, Sélestat, Kaysersberg, Colmar, Türckheim and Münster). Although the situation was clear as regards the Sundgau and Upper Alsace, the same could not be said for the remainder of the territories granted. Eventually, from the uncertainty rose the idea that the strongest party at the end would win the day. Thus a portion of the course of the Rhine was a natural border. The French presence cut the traditional routes to Spain. The king of France acquired complete sovereignty over the land in Alsace and this was undoubtedly satisfying for a great king who did not recognise any political authority above his own. It was, however, disappointing for Mazarin who had sought a vote at the diet for the king, a move that would have given him direct involvement in German affairs. Although the whole of Alsace did not become French, it was a first step in the right direction.[22]

France and Sweden acted as guarantors for the Treaties of Westphalia and obtained the right to keep a close watch on the affairs of the Holy Roman Empire.

Even though a large part of Central Europe had acquired stability, the treaties of 1648 did not bring peace to France, since no agreement was signed with Spain and the war continued. More importantly, the huge effort imposed on the population for decades led to a major political and social uprising in France, called 'the Fronde'. In France, the Treaty of Westphalia passed almost unnoticed.

Selected Bibliography

Bély, L., *L'Art de la paix en Europe. Naissance de la diplomatie moderne, XVIe–XVIIIe siècle* (Paris, 2007).
Bély, L. (ed.) (in collaboration with I. Richefort), *L'Europe des traités de Westphalie. Esprit de la diplomatie et diplomatie de l'esprit* (Paris, 2000).
Bercé, Y.-M., *Histoire des croquants. Etude des soulèvements populaires au XVIIe siècle dans le sud-ouest de la France* (Paris, 1974).
Bonney, R., *Political Change in France under Richelieu and Mazarin 1624–1661* (Oxford, 1978).
Bonney, R., *The King's Debts. Finance and Politics in France 1589–1661* (Oxford, 1981).
Church, W.F., *Richelieu and Reason of State* (Princeton, 1972).
Croxton, D., *Peacemaking in Early Modern Europe. Cardinal Mazarin and the Congress of Westphalia, 1643–1648* (Selingsgrove/Pa., 1999).
Elliott, J.H., *Richelieu and Olivares* (Cambridge, 1984).
Lynn, J., *Giant of the Grand Siècle. The French Army, 1610–1715* (Cambridge, 1997).
Nordman, D., *Frontières de France. De l'espace au territoire XVIe–XIXe siècle* (Paris, 1998).

---

[21] After the victories of 1645, this was the main French demand.
[22] There would be others, e.g. in 1679 the annexation of the towns in the Décapole, from 1680 to 1682 the annexation of various estates and in 1681 the occupation of the imperial town of Strasbourg. In fact, the province of Alsace did not really come into being until the Treaty of Ryswick in 1697.

Oresko, R., G. Gibbs and H.M. Scott, *Royal and Republican Sovereignty in Early Modern Europe. Essays in Memory of Ragnhild Hatton* (Cambridge, 1997).

Parker, G., *The Military Revolution. Military Innovation and the Rise of the West (1500–1800)*, 2nd edn (Cambridge, 1996).

Parrott, D., *Richelieu's Army. War, Government and Society in France, 1624–1642* (Cambridge, 2001).

Parrott, D., *The Business of War. Military enterprise and military revolution in Early Modern Europe* (Cambridge, 2012).

Sonnino, P., *Mazarin's Quest. The Congress of Westphalia and the Coming of the Fronde* (Cambridge, 2008).

Tischer, A., *Französische Diplomatie und Diplomaten auf dem Westfälischen Friedenskongress: Außenpolitik unter Richelieu und Mazarin* (Münster, 1999).

The Papacy

Guido Braun*

The early modern papacy was a celibate electoral monarchy with a sacred-secular double ruler at the top, who was at the same time head of Catholic Christendom and ruling prince of the Pontifical States.[1] The result of the dynastic discontinuity was regular social change within the papal Curia and a change of political leadership with almost each new pontificate. From this change, a social mobility developed at the Roman court which was unusual for Early Modern Europe. For the majority of curial functionaries including external representatives, i.e. legates and nuncios, certain group characteristics are discernible, namely all stemming from Italian patricians and all being clerically, humanistically, theologically and legally educated. High fluctuation gave social connections, patronage and nepotism in Rome a special functional relevance.[2] Micro-political aspects, i.e. the intentional use of social connections in the allocation of benefices and resources, also played a prominent role in external relations. However, the special position of the clergy became dysfunctional in the long term and prevented the formation of a modern civil service as well as a modern civil society.

Although certain basic principles of the Roman system of government (like the system of benefices) remained the same from the Late Middle Ages until the time of the Thirty Years' War, it demonstrated its productivity, flexibility and potential for renewal, especially from a culturalistic point of view. The Council of Trent had strengthened the Catholic Church and the papacy, which took the lead in the practical realisation of its decrees after 1563 and both Church and papacy had been able to recover parts of the territorial, social and symbolic terrain lost to the Protestants.

The State of the Church was the only Italian state which, as far as territory was concerned, succeeded in expanding during the period of the Thirty Years' War.[3] Its historic centre consisted of the *Patrimonium Sancti Petri* around Rome. Around 1600 it extended to large parts of central Italy between the Kingdom of Naples and the River Po, with exclaves in southern Italy and France (Avignon, Comtat Venaissin). In 1598 the vacant Fiefdom of

---

* I would like to thank Frank Meier for the translation of this chapter.

[1] P. Prodi, *Il sovrano pontefice. Un corpo e due anime: la monarchia papale nella prima età moderna*, Annali dell'Istituto storico italo-germanico, Monografia 3 (Bologna, 1982); English tr. by S. Haskins: *The Papal Prince. One body and two souls: the papal monarchy in early modern Europe* (Cambridge, 1987). Cf. for a further introduction A.D. Wright, *The Early Modern Papacy. From the Council of Trent to the French Revolution 1564–1789*, Longman History of the Papacy (London et al., 2000).

[2] Groundbreaking study by W. Reinhard, *Papstfinanz und Nepotismus unter Paul V. 1605–1621. Studien und Quellen zur Struktur und zu quantitativen Aspekten des päpstlichen Herrschaftssystems* (2 vols, Stuttgart, 1974).

[3] For an introduction cf. G. Hanlon, *Early Modern Italy. 1550–1800* (London et al., 2000), here pp. 201–4.

Ferrara had already been confiscated and integrated into the Papal States.[4] In 1625–1631 the Holy See was also able to reincorporate the duchy of Urbino as a papal legation into its territory. Urbino was not only rich in resources but also offered important ports to the Adriatic and connected the Marche with the Romagna. In contrast, the papal family Barberini failed to gain the duchy of Castro, a fiefdom of the Holy See, which lay inside the boundaries of the Papal States and was rich in crops, during the war with Odoardo Farnese, the duke of Parma and Piacenza, 1641–1644. This war was not only costly but also ended in bitter defeat for the Holy See and forced the Pope to accept the return to *status quo ante* in the Peace Treaty of Venice on 31 March 1644. He suffered not only politically but also militarily. The Holy See's reputation was greatly damaged and was not fully restored even by the successful confiscation of the fiefdom in 1649. These events should not hide the fact that during the Thirty Years' War (as opposed to the time around 1500), from a process of spiritualisation of its own concept of governance, the papacy consciously distinguished itself from secular powers and, in general, considered itself a spiritual, supranational force rather than a military power.

The administratively modernised organisation of the Curia was an inheritance from the sixteenth century and the Tridentinum, and it was part of the exemplary process of European state building since the return of the papal court from Avignon in 1420. Between 1566 and 1590 the popes of the Trent reforms extended and consolidated the network of permanent nunciatures,[5] and at the Curia itself a 'Secretariat of State' was now in charge of external relations, and permanent assemblies of cardinals (congregations) took over certain areas of responsibility in the course of an administrative differentiation. Thus the influence of the general assembly of cardinals, the Consistory, decreased. The cardinal-nephew as the alter ego of the Pope posed a continuous, leading role. The congregational system which was developed during the sixteenth century, namely by Sixtus V, was reformed during the Thirty Years' War and extended to over half a dozen new congregations. This affected the internal administration of the church and the Papal States (from issues of territorial integration to health matters) as well as matters of foreign policy and not least the organisation of the world mission. The world church and world mission in particular gained a growing relevance for the Holy See from the 1620s, even though Europe and particularly Italy remained the most important points of reference for papal action. One of the most important areas of renewal was the reform of the Gregorian Conclave in 1621/22, which fixed the process of the secret election of the Pope until 1904.[6] Its aim was to favour concerns of public welfare and personal suitability of candidates over social and political loyalties. In spite of the enormous difficulties (not least in financial politics) which they faced in the Thirty Years' War, the Roman Curia and governing system of the Papal States as a whole emerged in the end institutionally and structurally strengthened from this period of change.

---

[4] Cf. B. Emich, *Territoriale Integration in der frühen Neuzeit. Ferrara und der Kirchenstaat* (Cologne et al., 2005), with results as to the Roman system of government, which go beyond the topics dealt with here.

[5] For papal politics during the Thirty Years' War the editions of main instructions and the nunciature reports form an important source. For the years 1605–1623 the former were edited by S. Giordano (ed.), *Le istruzioni generali di Paolo V ai diplomatici pontifici. 1605–1621* (3 vols, Tübingen, 2003) and K. Jaitner (ed.), *Die Hauptinstruktionen Gregors XV. für die Nuntien und Gesandten an den europäischen Fürstenhöfen. 1621–1623* (2 vols, Tübingen, 1997). An overview of the series of nunciature reports from several countries and views of their examination is offered in A. Koller (ed.), *Kurie und Politik. Stand und Perspektiven der Nuntiaturberichtsforschung* (Tübingen, 1998).

[6] Including insightful scientific approaches like symbolic communication in detail examined by G. Wassilowski, *Die Konklavereform Gregors XV. 1621/22. Wertekonflikte, symbolische Inszenierung und Verfahrenswandel im posttridentinischen Papsttum* (Stuttgart, 2010).

The strengthening of central papal power and the achievement of consistent (disciplinary but also liturgical) norms were the main aims of church organisation as well as the administration of the Pontifical States; in both respects the papacy of the Thirty Years' War adhered to earlier traditions.

The resources of the popes lay on one hand in spiritual revenues which included external (also non-Italian) sources. Their contribution decreased considerably during the early modern period. On the other hand the popes gained revenue from their own territory. Through an increase of the tax burden and an extension of sales of offices, these sources were now increasingly exploited. In addition, the Curia used an established system of direct state loans – a necessity since the budget was in deficit. After a temporary consolidation until approximately 1620, the financial situation of the Papal States subsequently deteriorated dramatically during the Thirty Years' War, especially around 1640, and the papacy became economically dependent on Genoese banks. A further increase of revenue was attempted to meet those needs, in particular by increasing or introducing more than 60 taxes on consumption, mainly during the periods of 1625–30 and 1640–44 (Valtellina and Mantua conflict and Castro war). Still, the total debt of the Pontifical States rose between 1623 and 1644 from an estimated 17–19 million scudi to about 36–40 million, the exact composition of which needs closer research,[7] and peaked in 1655 at approximately 48 million in the seventeenth century.[8]

Besides papal spending policy, a lingering economic crisis in the State of the Church during the last decade of the Thirty Years' War seems to have been responsible for this debt. In addition to a rise in the price of gold, the taut economic situation in connection with a beginning agrarian crisis in the 1620s led to several food shortages, e.g. after crop failures in 1621/22, partly accompanied by social unrest (especially in the summer of 1648). Hunger now became a formative experience while in comparison the first two decades of the seventeenth century with its successful, protective agrarian policy would be viewed by later generations as a veritable 'golden age', even for the poorer classes. The Papal States now had to import grain from Castro, Savoy, Sicily and western Europe. Securing an affordable price of bread was only possible with heavy losses in papal finances. Thanks to consistent quarantine measures, the Papal States remained largely untouched by the devastating wave of plague which haunted Italy because of the war between 1629 and 1632.

In spite of all these financial problems, patronage of the arts by the popes – in a highly competitive social climate in Rome – was, however, continued. The main focus was the interior of the St Peter's Basilica consecrated in 1626 and in particular the works of Bernini, who also designed the Fountain of the Four Rivers, which was finished in 1651, for the Piazza Navona, and was central to the urban planning concepts of the Pamphili.[9]

As a rule, the popes tried to provide for the well-being of their families by micro-political means. During the Thirty Years' War, the term 'nepotism' was coined to describe the system of conscious promotion of the popes' relatives. According to credible estimations millions

---

[7] G. Lutz, 'Urbano VIII', in *Enciclopedia dei papi*, ed. Istituto della Enciclopedia Italiana, vol. 3 (Rome, 2000), pp. 298–331, here p. 314. In spite of its brevity this biographical article is probably the best presentation of Urban VIII and his pontificate and compensates for an absent monograph. As to the position in the system of powers, idem, 'Rom und Europa während des Pontifikats Urbans VIII.', in *Rom in der Neuzeit. Politische, kirchliche und kulturelle Aspekte*, ed. R. Elze (Rome and Vienna, 1976), pp. 72–168; also A. Kraus, 'Die auswärtige Politik Urbans VIII. Grundzüge und Wendepunkte', in *Mélanges Eugène Tisserant*, vol. 4 (Rome, 1964), pp. 407–26.

[8] O. Poncet, 'Innocenzo X', in *Enciclopedia dei papi*, ed. Istituto della Enciclopedia Italiana, vol. 3 (Rome, 2000), pp. 321–35, here p. 328.

[9] Cf. for an introduction T. Magnuson, *Rome in the Age of Bernini*, vol. 2: *From the Election of Innocent X to the Death of Innocent XI* (Stockholm, 1986).

were spent on this.[10] Although the Barberini nepots from 1644 were temporarily exiled to France and the Pope's sister-in-law Olimpia Maidalchini was banned from Rome in 1655, this model, which considered relatives the basis of a stable rule of the Pontifical States and did not necessarily seem largely dysfunctional, remained unchallenged at the time and escaped any kind of structural reform.

The period of the Thirty Years' War was an era in which the papacy had to position itself in a changing world, and not only politically. The contemporary scientific view of the world was also in upheaval and these changes challenged Rome, which reacted mostly with rejection and an insistence on traditional positions: the Holy Office answered the latest heliocentric theses of Galilei from 1632 by banning his works in June 1633.

Four popes ruled the Pontifical States between 1618 and 1648[11]: the war started during the last years of the pontificate of Paul V (1605–1621) from the House of Borghese. It was followed by Gregory XV (1621–1623), whose rule coincided with the victories of the emperor and the Catholic League in the Bohemian-Palatine War. For more than two decades Urban VIII (1623–1644) directed the fate of the Papal States and its external relations, while the conflict between the Catholic Spanish and French monarchies, which had been threatening for some time, escalated towards open war. After the peak of imperial Catholic power in the late 1620s, Lutheran Sweden intervened successfully in Germany, to the advantage of the Protestants. Finally Giovanni Battista Pamphili gained the papal throne in 1644 as Innocent X (1644–1655), when the negotiations for the Peace of Westphalia to allay European and German hostilities were already under way. Innocent, however, was never to see the desired peace between Spain and France, and the Peace of the Pyrenees of 1659 was gained without papal mediation by direct bilateral negotiations during the pontificate of Alexander VII, the former peace nuncio of Münster.

When a series of military conflicts which was finally categorised under the collective term 'Thirty Years' War' was chimed in by the Defenestration of Prague, Rome was ruled by Paul V, whose pontificate is rightly considered as the best researched in early modern papal history, mostly through the work of Wolfgang Reinhard and his students.[12] Paul V supported the course of the war, which in particular in its first decade was highly confessional, on the Catholic side. But only a third of a million scudi was paid in subsidies to Catholic states since 1618, about half of which went directly to the Catholic armies in the Thirty Years' War.

---

[10] Estimates (contemporary and historical) vary widely. E.g. Lutz, 'Urbano VIII', pp. 309–10 considers 30 million scudi a reliable figure for the pontificate examined by him. Computations by the Curia in 1691 came to 900,000 scudi; for the following pontificate 1.4 million; Poncet, 'Innocenzo X', p. 328. The latter figures presumably refer only to direct payments, excluding return etc.

[11] Very precise presentations of the individual pontificates, with extensive information on sources and research, in *Enciclopedia dei papi*, here the articles by V. Reinhardt, 'Paolo V', in *Enciclopedia dei papi*, ed. Istituto della Enciclopedia Italiana, vol. 3 (Rome, 2000), pp. 277–92; A. Koller, 'Gregorio XV', in *Enciclopedia dei papi*, ed. Istituto della Enciclopedia Italiana, vol. 3 (Rome, 2000), pp. 292–7; Lutz, 'Urbano VIII'; Poncet, 'Innocenzo X'. The latest presentation of Innocent X with further information on research, G. Braun, 'Innozenz X. – Der Papst als *padre comune*', in M. Matheus and L. Klinkhammer (eds), *Eigenbild im Konflikt. Krisensituationen des Papsttums zwischen Gregor VII. und Benedikt XV.* (Darmstadt, 2009), pp. 119–56. L. von Pastor remains indispensable with his wealth of facts, *Geschichte der Päpste seit dem Ausgang des Mittelalters*, 8–13th edn (16 vols, Freiburg, 1955–1961); Italian tr.: *Storia dei Papi. Dalla fine del medio evo* (16 vols, Rome, 1942–1955).

[12] After many preliminary studies from his own pen and recently from his students the monumental summary by W. Reinhard, *Paul V. Borghese. 1605–1621. Mikropolitische Papstgeschichte*, Päpste und Papsttum, 37 (Stuttgart, 2009).

This was raised by tithes put on the congregations. Considerably more money was spent by the Curia on the defences of the Papal States.[13]

Putting aside the bitter conflict with Venice at the start of his pontificate, the foreign policies of Paul V can be described as highly cautious, hesitant and even passive at times.[14] The neutrality kept by the Pope between the competing powers Spain and France in Europe and the Apennine peninsula, is consistent with this defensive orientation. Paul V tried hard to retain Catholic interests in the hotly contested Lower Rhine area and intervened diplomatically on the eve of the Thirty Years' War, mainly through his nuncio Antonio Albergati in Cologne. But his support of the Catholic League, founded in 1609, was very moderate and his dealings of the political and confessional conflicts in Grisons and the Valtellina largely followed the principle of non-intervention. Rome cannot, therefore, be ascribed a leading role in the formation of a unified Catholic camp in the empire as sometimes suggested in confessionally tinted earlier research. The diplomacy of the Holy See was much more targeted on de-escalation.

After all, Paul V granted the new emperor Ferdinand II in 1619/1620 temporary monthly subsidies of 10,000 scudi. Although gaps and discrepancies of the sources do not allow reliable computations of Paul's total payments for the League, their proven slightness stands out, which is contrasted with the far greater generosity of Clement VIII (1592–1605) for the Turkish War by Volker Reinhardt. Reinhardt does not exclude the possibility of an underestimation of the raging conflicts in the empire and their consequences for Catholicism at the Curia, but stresses the general primacy of internal politics (including clientelism) of spending in the entire pontificate.[15]

In spite of limited papal support, the Catholic forces managed to win resounding victories in the first phase of the war: the victory at Bílá Hora on 8 November 1620 was extensively celebrated by Paul V, who was now marked by serious illness. The political consequences were drawn later with much greater verve by his successor.

On 8 February 1621 the 67-year-old Alessandro Ludovisi was elected Pope as Gregory XV. He enjoyed the support of the pro-Habsburg as well as the pro-France parties in the Conclave. This double promotion of his candidacy was due to his obvious mediatory skills. Like his first patron Gregory XIII (1572–1585) he came from Bologna. Similarities between the two pontificates do not, however, end here, since Gregory XV, who attended the *Collegium Germanicum* in Rome from 1567 to 1569, and his predecessor Gregory XIII were the only popes in the early modern period who commanded a veritable Germano-political programme.[16]

Shortly before the election of Ludovisi, the Bohemian Winter King Frederic V had been decisively beaten and a ban declared on him by Ferdinand II (29 January 1621). Gregory XV heartily embraced the offered opportunity to confer the electoral powers of the Calvinist Palatine to a Catholic prince. For this he initiated several diplomatic missions at the Spanish court, beginning with the empire. In addition to the ordinary nuncio at the imperial court,

---

[13] Figures concerning this pontificate according to Reinhardt, 'Paolo V'. The higher subsidies of his successor have been examined by D. Albrecht, 'Zur Finanzierung des Dreißigjährigen Krieges. Die Subsidien der Kurie für Kaiser und Liga 1618–1635', *Zeitschrift für bayerische Landesgeschichte*, 19 (1956): pp. 534–67.

[14] Different facets of the Curia's external relations under Paul V are now being considered by A. Koller (ed.), *Die Außenbeziehungen der römischen Kurie unter Paul V. Borghese (1605–1621)* (Tübingen, 2008).

[15] Cf. also Reinhardt, 'Paolo V'.

[16] Accurate observations by Koller, 'Gregorio XV'. As to the German politics of the pope, D. Albrecht, *Die deutsche Politik Papst Gregors XV. Die Einwirkung der päpstlichen Diplomatie auf die Politik der Häuser Habsburg und Wittelsbach. 1621–1623* (Munich, 1956) remains significant.

Fabrizio Verospi became extraordinary nuncio and furthermore, the Capuchin padre Giacinto da Casale was entrusted the task of maintaining curial interest with Ferdinand II. Possible candidates from the House of Wittelsbach were Count Wolfgang Wilhelm of Neuburg and Duke Maximilian I of Bavaria. Gregory supported Maximilian in his electoral candidacy in recognition of the outstanding achievements of the Bavarian dukes in fighting Protestantism and supporting Catholic reform since the sixteenth century as well as holding the leading military and political position among the Catholic princes in the empire. The conferment of the Palatine electoral graces on the Bavarian duke was accomplished *ad personam* on 14 February 1623.[17] Maximilian gave the Holy See the former *Bibliotheca Palatina*, which had come into the hands of the League's forces with the taking of Heidelberg a year earlier.

In spite of the shortness of the pontificate, which ended on 8 July 1623, the Holy See scored an important political victory with the electoral conferment, since the number of votes in the Council of Electors increased in favour of the Catholics, as opposed to previously when four Catholics had faced three Protestants and a Protestant majority had repeatedly been within reach (especially during the War of Cologne in the 1580s).

Since the beginning of his pontificate, Gregory XV had dedicated himself wholly to the support of the Habsburgs and the Catholic League in the empire. The preservation of the Catholic empire, the consolidation of Habsburg authority in the Hereditary Lands as well as the strengthening of the imperial position within the empire seemed to guarantee the future of Catholicism.

Gregory insistently supported the continuation of the war through the emperor and the League with the aim of reclaiming the empire for Catholicism. He contributed his share in the cost of war and increased subsidies which had already been granted by Paul V. This papal contribution was mainly raised by the Apostolic Camera and the tithes on German benefices and Italian monastic orders. The papal general Pietro Aldobrandini was ordered to create a regiment in Bohemia, which was financed by these means. The counter-reformatory character of Gregory XV's pontificate was not least underlined by the canonisation of Ignatius of Loyola on 12 March 1622, the Feast of Gregory the Great.

The recatholicisation by quite violent means was only one side of the coin; the reformatory church politics of Gregory in Germany was the other. Special attention was paid to the bishops and cathedral chapters by the Curia and the nuncios. The practices adopted in co-opting new capitulars and electing new bishops were meant firstly to create new diocesan leaders who would be competent spiritually and in terms of pastoral care as well as administratively and governmentally, and secondly would make them bearers of Catholic reform in the empire. Carlo Carafa, nuncio at the imperial court (1621–1628), was particularly active in achieving church reform in Bohemia and Prague, where prospects were especially favourable because of the imperial Catholic victory and Ferdinand II's position of power as local ruler. The recatholicisation of Bohemia and throughout the empire was further served by the *Congregatio de Propaganda Fide*, a congregation established during the pontificate of Gregory XV for the spreading of Catholic belief.[18] It was founded on Epiphany 1622. This congregation still exists today and is dedicated to world mission. Since its founding, it was comprised of overseas missions so that Spain, worried about its own influence, viewed this creation rather critically. During the Thirty Years' War, however, an important area of activity of the new congregation lay in the supervision and promotion of Catholic restoration

---

[17] Ibid. As well as the single case study, D. Albrecht, 'Der Hl. Stuhl und die Kurübertragung von 1623', *Quellen und Forschungen aus italienischen Archiven und Bibliotheken*, 34 (1954): pp. 236–49.

[18] As to its history, very extensively with further significant contributions, see J. Metzler (ed.), *Sacrae Congregationis de Propaganda Fide Memoria Rerum. 350 anni a servizio delle missioni. 1622–1972* (3 vols, Rome et al., 1971–1976).

in Europe's Protestant countries. The advance of Ferdinand II in the empire to the north and the Baltic, and the superiority of Catholics over Protestants connected with it, created ideal conditions in the 1620s to regain lost territories. Gregory himself took part in congregational sessions at least once a month. Cardinal Barberini, Gregory's successor in the Chair of Saint Peter, was a member since 14 January 1622, but, from 1628 onwards his attendance in the meetings, *coram Sanctissimo* decreased. The first secretary, Francesco Ingoli, stayed in office until 1648 and thus guaranteed continuity. The Roman Curia was rarely as well informed, particularly about Germany, and was able to absorb incoming information as it had in the 1620s, thanks especially to the work of the new congregation and reliable reporters in the empire such as Carlo Carafa.[19]

The recatholicisation and Catholic reform of Styria was considered finished at the beginning of the 1620s. Therefore, the nunciature of Graz, created by Gregory XIII in 1580, could be dissolved on 8 March 1622. The number of ordinary nunciatures at Catholic courts was thereby reduced to 11. Giovanni Battista Agucchi, the Secretary of State, had great influence on the relationship between the Curia and the nuncios.

A further trouble spot from a confessional and geostrategic point of view, which kept papal diplomacy busy for years, was the Valtellina[20] in the far north of the Appenine peninsula, which had been a vassal state of Grisons and so part of the Swiss Confederation since 1513. The conflict around the Valtellina, which came to a head in the 1620s, was important to the papacy in terms of confessional politics because it had stayed true to Catholicism whereas the majority of Grisons had become Protestant after the Reformation. Tensions had increased markedly in 1618–1620. When, in August 1620, the Valtellina was occupied by Spanish and Austrian troops, the religious problems of the Swiss Alpine region became closely connected with the European antagonism between Habsburg and France. At the core of the conflict was the control of the Valtellina Alpine passes, which had enabled the Habsburgs to relocate their troops along the 'Spanish Road' from its possessions in northern Italy, namely Milan, to Tyrol and the Upper Rhine area and further to the war zone in the Low Countries, where in 1621 the Twelve Years' Truce between the Spanish king and the States-General of the Netherlands came to an end. France opposed Spanish control of the Valtellina and the Alpine passes, as well as of Savoy and Venice.

Gregory XV was very interested from a power-political point of view in keeping peace on the Apennine peninsula, which was threatened by the Valtellina conflict. After several peace missions had failed in 1621 and 1622 and France had allied itself with Venice and Savoy with the Treaty of Paris in an offensive union on 7 February 1623, the dramatically worsening conflict could at first be mitigated by putting the Valtellina fortresses under the Pope's control as a token of neutrality in the Treaty of Madrid on 14 February. A month before Gregory died, on 6 June, the fortresses were indeed given over to papal forces. Almost 3,000 soldiers were needed for this task – a great effort for the Holy See's weak military. Gregory entrusted his own brother Orazio, duke of Fiano, with the execution of this task. In accepting the deposit, he determined papal politics concerning the Valtellina question, which was by no means permanently solved, beyond the end of his pontificate and left Urban VIII a difficult inheritance.

In 1623 Urban VIII was the first Pope in the Chair of Saint Peter who had been born after the end of the Council of Trent in 1568. Like Gregory he had passed his law studies

---

[19] For his nunciature and the perception of the Empire cf. G. Braun, 'Kaiserhof, Kaiser und Reich in der *Relazione* des Nuntius Carlo Carafa (1628)', in R. Bösel, G. Klingenstein and A. Koller (eds), *Kaiserhof – Papsthof (16.–18. Jahrhundert)* (Vienna, 2006), pp. 77–104.

[20] S. Giordano, 'La Santa Sede e la Valtellina da Paolo V a Urbano VIII', in *La Valtellina crocevia dell'Europa. Politica e religione nell'età della guerra dei Trent'Anni*, ed. A. Borromeo (Milan, 1998), pp. 81–109.

with a doctoral degree *in utroque*. In spite of having similar views of the world, which were typical for the Curia including the popes, Urban by no means followed the prerogatives of his predecessor in his political direction. Several diplomatic missions on behalf of the Curia since 1601 had familiarised Maffeo Barberini (Urban VIII) with French politics and culture, long before the beginning of his pontificate.

At first, Urban VIII influenced government business very intensively, as proven by numerous additions in his own hand to correspondence with nuncios and legates, particularly in Italy and France. From the late 1620s he continued to be briefed by the Secretary of State about current state business, but now confined himself to declaring his decisions and directions verbally. The degree of personal participation of the Pope in making decisions remains an open scientific problem, as he was increasingly marked by illness from 1639 onwards. The same goes for the political and cultural assessment of an ambiguous pontificate ending in disaster.[21] The four Secretaries of State, chosen personally by Urban, each competed with the cardinal-nephew Francesco Barberini. He took over responsibility for internal administration and politics of the Pontifical States as well as external affairs based on his position as Superintendent (*sovrintendente generale e speciale*) of the Holy See, and from 1632 ran his own *in proprio*-office parallel to the Secretariat of State.

Urban had to turn immediately to the Valtellina problem, which was unsolved under Gregory XV. Urban, when he was still cardinal, had refused to honour the commitment to occupy the fortresses along the Valtellina Valley entered into by his predecessor, in consideration of the military weakness of the papacy and his ideal of keeping equal distance from the Catholic crowns. At the beginning of his pontificate, the Spanish–French conflict indeed turned out to be irreconcilable as far as transit rights were concerned. An agreement, reached in January 1624 through Urban's mediation, was rejected by France, who invaded the Valtellina and expelled the papal garrisons in late 1624/early 1625. In spite of this affront, Urban tried to promote a peaceful resolution of the conflict. Apart from this European dimension, it was important for the Holy See to prevent the return of Catholic Valtellina to the rule of mainly Protestant Grisons, who were allied to France. However, while a legation of the cardinal-nephew to France and Spain failed and demonstrated the 'political impotence' of the papacy, the two crowns found a bilateral resolution with the Treaty of Monzón on 5 March 1626 which excluded the Holy See. The treaty granted the Valtellina a pragmatic administrative and confessional autonomy, which, nevertheless, was not in accordance with the strict ideas of Rome, and stipulated the demolition of the fortresses, which was then consequently accomplished in early 1627. The papal garrisons had to return there in the meantime and the total cost of the protective forces, estimated at approx. 670,000 scudi, had to be borne by the Holy See in the end.[22]

At first, the French-Spanish conflict seemed indeed settled: both powers even considered a joint invasion of England supported by the Roman Curia. But the common understanding was only superficial: The next disputed inheritance in Italy led to war over the succession of the duchy of Mantua and the margraviate of Monferrato. During the War of the Mantuan Succession, the Holy See undertook extensive diplomatic measures to secure peace, the cost of which has been estimated at 100,000 to 200,000 scudi, but they did not always follow clear guidelines. One the one hand, Urban postulated the role of the papacy as the common father of Christendom (*padre comune*).[23] On the other hand, his politics may have been a result of the

---

[21] In Lutz's view, 'Urbano VIII', pp. 314 and 316 (citation, see also for further desiderata in research).

[22] Ibid., pp. 304–5.

[23] Not undisputed but still worth considering is the classic study by A. Leman, *Urbain VIII et la rivalité de la France et de la maison d'Autriche de 1631 à 1635* (Lille and Paris, 1920) which deals with

fear that the Spanish-Habsburg position of power in Italy could threaten the independence of Church and Papal States. Therefore it was vital not only to re-establish peace between the Catholic princes but also to prevent, as much as possible, the rise of Spanish power. In order to oppose a threatening invasion of the Pontifical States which was feared primarily from the Habsburg side, Urban spent more than 3.5 million scudi on the military. Georg Lutz assumes that the Barberini Pope, who has often been described as francophile, would have opposed the French in a similar way had there been the same hegemony on the Apennine peninsula as Spain. At its core, papal politics from 1628 to 1633 showed an understanding between the Holy See and France against the arch-Catholic House of Habsburg, which is clearly distinct from the principle of absolute papal impartiality. Urban not only supported several French diplomatic missions like the negotiations for a union with Bavaria, mainly through the Paris nunciature, he also did not oppose French treaties with Protestants, particularly the Union of Bärwalde with Sweden in January 1631.[24] Even though these pro-French gestures existed, the Pope was at no time ready to support one side openly and the relationship with France deteriorated noticeably at the end of the 1630s.[25]

Since as liege lord, the emperor was also involved in the Mantuan conflict of succession, the most important nunciatures (Paris, Madrid, and Vienna) were entrusted with missions of peace. Moreover, the Pope's nephew Antonio Barberini was appointed legate to establish peace between the Catholic crowns. The young Giulio Mazzarini was sent on a mission of peace and so met his later mentor, the leading French minister Richelieu, who had been made a cardinal by Gregory XV. Richelieu later had Mazarin come to Paris and provided him the opportunity to become the cardinal's successor, which led to the former papal messenger of peace ending the war against the emperor as French Cardinal minister in 1648.

The Mantuan conflict, settled in the Peace of Cherasco in April 1631, left the Papal States militarily unharmed in the end and was resolved with a positive result in the eye of the Holy See: The conferment of Mantua-Monferrato on the French candidate, the duke of Nevers, and the surrender of the fortress of Pinerolo to France seemed to shift the ratio of power in Italy and a Spanish hegemony became more improbable.

Urban held imperial intervention in the Italian conflict responsible for heavy defeats of Catholic armies against the Lutheran Gustav Adolph of Sweden, who had entered the war with resounding success in 1630. At first Urban VIII, who, unlike Paul V or even Gregory XV, was uninterested in the conditions in Germany, absolutely refused to support the imperial party with subsidies and his interest was largely confined to controlling the recatholicisation of territories reclaimed by the victorious Catholic armies which had been particularly successful in Bohemia and Moravia. In 1632, the advance of the Swedes on Prague, one of the most important centres of imperial power, seemed threatening enough to raise a total of 477,000 scudi for the German Catholics until 1634, which was paid for by tithes on the Italian clergy.[26]

Criticism of the Pope's imperial politics erupted at a consistory on 8 March 1632. The speaker of the Spanish faction of cardinals, Cardinal Borgia, claimed that the Pope's apathy would ruin German Catholicism. The Pope took disciplinary measures against the cardinals

---

Urban's politics of impartiality.

[24] Lutz, 'Urbano VIII', pp. 305–6 (see also for details of the expenditure for the military and peace diplomacy).

[25] To learn more about the relationship between the Pope and France with special regard to the Paris nunciature cf. the fundamental work by G. Lutz, *Kardinal Giovanni Francesco Guidi di Bagno. Politik und Religion im Zeitalter Richelieus und Urbans VIII.* (Tübingen, 1971).

[26] Lutz, 'Urbano VIII', p. 306 particularly for this figure as well as the assessment of the politics of Ferdinand II by Urban VIII.

involved but also intensified his peace efforts by sending extraordinary peace nuncios to the courts of Paris, Madrid and Vienna in May 1632, followed by plans for a peace conference in 1634–1635, which however could not prevent the outbreak of open war between France and Spain in May 1635.

In spite of their intensity, the papal mediation efforts of the 1630s showed only little promise of success since they lacked a pragmatic view: they excluded the Protestant world with tacit approval of Catholic-Protestant peace talks at the margins of the general peace conference or even led to an intervention of France against its Swedish allies. From the summer of 1636 the Cardinal legate Marzio Ginetti spent four years in vain in Cologne with the intention of opening the Cologne Conference, which the Holy See had promoted. Once again in May 1639, three special nuncios were appointed. The Preliminary Peace of Hamburg on 25 December 1641 finally paved the way for a conference by naming two towns as conference locations, Münster for the Catholics, Osnabrück for the Protestants. The Holy See and Venice, which sent Alvise Contarini, were meant to mediate peace. Finally, after a few substitutions, Fabio Chigi, the Cologne nuncio, represented the Pope in Westphalia and was instructed for this in April 1644.[27]

In Urban VIII's crucial decisions the scales were often tipped by canonists. The Pope himself was a rigorous jurist. Most decisions made were against innovative movements both inside and outside the Church, hence, presumably, the sentence against Galilei, who in fact admired, and since 1611 was admired by, Maffeo Barberini. After all, the Pope did not have a solely political programme. His central concerns were his projection as *padre comune*, the strengthening of the Pontifical States and a wariness about an increase of Spanish predominance in Italy. Beyond these, there are no further ideas of order to be found in his politics – as can be stated with Georg Lutz – which could really accommodate the confessional schism of Western Christianity. It can be claimed that even the Catholic world was only partly familiar to him since he mistrusted Spain as a perceived threat to the 'libertà d'Italia' and remained a stranger to the empire.[28]

Urban's successor Innocent X followed a strict policy of impartiality and balance in Italy. Canon law and peace were also central to the Pope's politics after the election of the 70-year-old Giovanni Battista Pamphili on 15 September 1644. Innocent, who had long been an ambassador for peace, promoted the negotiations between the Catholic powers (France vs. Spain and the emperor) through his mediation in Münster; at the same time the local peace nuncio Chigi was a negotiating party in the religious disputes with the Protestants. Even though he did not directly participate in these peace negotiations, he still tried to influence the Catholic envoys in the spirit of the Pope's canonistic, intransigent attitude. Eventually, the papacy even opposed the Peace of Westphalia in 1648, which put an end to

---

[27] For the history of papal politics preceding the peace conference of Westphalia cf. the detailed study by K. Repgen, *Die römische Kurie und der Westfälische Friede. Idee und Wirklichkeit des Papsttums im 16. und 17. Jahrhundert* (2 vols, Tübingen, 1962–1965); for papal mediation and politics in Münster, idem, *Dreißigjähriger Krieg und Westfälischer Friede. Studien und Quellen*, F. Bosbach and C. Kampmann (eds), Rechts- und Staatswissenschaftliche Veröffentlichungen der Görres-Gesellschaft, new series 81, 2nd edn (Paderborn et al., 1999), pp. 458–86. The *Acta Pacis Westphalicae*, M. Braubach (†), M. Lanzinner and K. Repgen (eds), published on behalf of the Nordrhein-Westfälische Akademie der Wissenschaften in connection with the Vereinigung zur Erforschung der Neueren Geschichte e.V. (45 vols, Münster, 1962–2011), represent the great collection of sources of the conference, in it the diary of the mediator: vol. III C 1/1: *Diarium Chigi. 1639–1651*, ed. K. Repgen (Münster, 1984). The papal mediation between France and Spain is more closely examined in G. Braun, 'Päpstliche Friedensvermittlung am Beispiel von Piombino und Porto Longone', *Quellen und Forschungen aus italienischen Archiven und Bibliotheken*, 83 (2003): pp. 141–206.

[28] As presumed in Lutz, 'Urbano VIII', pp. 307 and 316.

the Thirty Years' War but not the Franco-Spanish conflict (in the view of many participants, not least the Curia, the main conflict).

The clear contradiction between the intensive papal efforts to make peace between the Catholic princes on the one side, which was already under way in the pontificate of Urban VIII and emphatically continued under Innocent X, and the curial protest against the eventual peace treaty on the other side had been the central point in Leopold von Ranke's assessment of papal politics. Through 'relentless insistence on unrealistic demands' it had put itself 'outside the viable and effective interests of the world' with the instructions for the cardinal legate Ginetti as early as 1636.[29] Konrad Repgen, who has thoroughly examined papal politics before 1648, concludes that the unnamed Pope 'had so been excluded from the international political system of the whole of Europe for the future' with the treaty.[30] This conclusion cannot be doubted with regard to the European significance of the papacy even if taking into account that it pretended to be a mediator for peace during the second half of the century at the negotiations in Aachen and Nijmegen.[31] All in all, the papacy had changed from a central figure in the European system of power and its peace-making mechanisms to a marginal one. The Peace Treaties of Westphalia had set the course for a secularisation of law and politics and it became 'acutely clear that the Christian union of states of the Middle Ages, which even in times of its worst humiliation had respected the central role of the head of the church, had ceased to exist'.[32]

We know, however, in particular through Repgen's studies of papal politics since 1521, that the protest was a conscious decision on the part of Innocent X and had not, as claimed by earlier research, been forced on him by previous commitments of the papacy as an absolute necessity. Innocent positioned himself with the protest as a canonist, from the point of view of Church law, in view of a future caveat. However, contrary to Chigi's demand, the Pope and the Secretariat of State avoided a theological examination of the Peace of Westphalia by the Holy Office and thus a theologically binding positioning to its canonistic provisions. Even the nuncio was keen on making sure that Rome with its legal and theological reservations would not endanger the realisation of peace. Although Chigi registered a written protest in 1648 against the stipulations in question,[33] the caveat of Innocent X, dated back to 26 November 1648, was only made public at the end of August 1650 in a *breve* ('Zelo domus Dei' – 'a key document of modern papal history'[34]) sent to the nuncios.[35] By then the peace had come into effect with the signing of the Nuremberg Agreements with Sweden (26 June) and France (2 July), and the withdrawal of Swedish troops had already begun.

---

[29] L. von Ranke, *Die römischen Päpste in den letzten vier Jahrhunderten*, Sämtliche Werke 37–39, 6th edn (3 vols, Leipzig 1874), vol. 2, pp. 372–3.

[30] K. Repgen, 'Der päpstliche Protest gegen den Westfälischen Frieden und die Friedenspolitik Urbans VIII.', *Historisches Jahrbuch*, 75 (1955): pp. 94–122, quotation p. 95.

[31] On this theme M. Rohrschneider, 'Friedensvermittlung und Kongresswesen: Strukturen, Träger, Perzeption 1643–1697', in C. Kampmann, M. Lanzinner, G. Braun and M. Rohrschneider (eds), *L'art de la paix: Kongresswesen und Friedensstiftung im Zeitalter des Westfälischen Friedens* (Münster, 2011): pp. 139–65.

[32] Repgen, 'Der päpstliche Protest', pp. 96–7.

[33] There is a total of five protest notes by Chigi in 1648/49; to be found in Repgen, *Dreißigjähriger Krieg und Westfälischer Friede*, pp. 539–61, esp. p. 546.

[34] Ibid., p. 614. Poncet, 'Innocenzo X', p. 330 judges more cautiously, even if the papacy had consciously left the international stage with it.

[35] The *breve* is edited by M. F. Feldkamp, 'Das Breve "Zelo domus Dei" vom 26. November 1648. Edition', *Archivum Historiae Ponitficiae*, 31 (1993): pp. 293–305. Additions to its printing history in Repgen, *Dreißigjähriger Krieg und Westfälischer Friede*, pp. 621–42.

The French historian Olivier Poncet moreover stresses rightly that the parameter regarding the two 'natures' of popes as spiritual leader and as secular ruler shifted during Innocent X's pontificate in favour of the religious – which was not least due to the fact that the road to a more decisive assertion of the Holy See as a political player of European stature was closed in Westphalia.[36]

In their expectation and self-image the popes, first of all Innocent, who finally opposed peace, continued to see themselves as peace-makers and placed themselves as *padre comune* within the Catholic family of princes. This formula defined papal self-perception and papal representation in discourse and performance not only outwardly, but also in the internal writings of the Curia which makes a process of self-assessment of the Curia recognisable in its outlines and stood it in a complex relationship with the practical politics of the Holy See, which can by no means be reduced to a purpose of legitimation.

The term *'padre comune'*, as Johannes Burkhardt rightly points out, has not been 'examined in context, but is without doubt a central term for the political ideology of the papacy in early modern times'.[37] It is probable that the term was sometimes 'topos',[38] but indeed represented a guiding image in the papacy's efforts for peace at the end of the Thirty Years' War. One of the crucial interests of the papacy around that time and also other times was to maintain the Pope's reputation as *padre comune*. Even competing political aims of the Papal States had to take second place, and the mediation of peace was one of the most important manifestations of this prestigious position.

For long periods of the Thirty Years' War peace and quiet in Italy ('quiete d'Italia') as well as political order on the Appenine peninsula, which prevented non-Italian powers – particularly Spain – from establishing a hegemony, took precedence for the Holy See over confessional conflicts beyond the Alps. However, the papacy of the time was characterised most of all by the 'primacy of canonistic norms over political considerations'[39] and the insistence on dogmatic principles. In this regard the papacy in its central attitude is in accordance with Heinz Schilling's thesis of the existence of a 'confessional fundamentalism' in Europe around 1600.[40] Even if confessional politics was not always guiding the actions of the Curia during the entire war, in 1648–50 the papacy did not shift from this attitude and thereby caused its own decline as a political and moral reference, even in the Catholic states.

Selected Bibliography

(a) Editions

Acta Pacis Westphalicae, M. Braubach (†), M. Lanzinner and K. Repgen (eds), published on behalf of the Nordrhein-Westfälische Akademie der Wissenschaften in connection with the Vereinigung zur Erforschung der Neueren Geschichte e.V. (45 vols, Münster, 1962–2011), in particular vol. III C 1/1: *Diarium Chigi. 1639–1651*, ed. K. Repgen (Münster, 1984).

---

[36] Poncet, 'Innocenzo X', p. 334.
[37] J. Burkhardt, *Abschied vom Religionskrieg, Der Siebenjährige Krieg und die päpstliche Diplomatie* (Tübingen, 1985), p. 370.
[38] Ibid.
[39] Repgen, *Dreißigjähriger Krieg und Westfälischer Friede*, p. 495.
[40] Cf. H. Schilling (ed.), *Konfessioneller Fundamentalismus. Religion als politischer Faktor im europäischen Mächtesystem um 1600* (Munich, 2007).

(b) Research Literature

Albrecht, D., *Die deutsche Politik Papst Gregors XV. Die Einwirkung der päpstlichen Diplomatie auf die Politik der Häuser Habsburg und Wittelsbach. 1621–1623* (Munich, 1956).

Braun, G., 'Innozenz X. – Der Papst als *padre comune*', in M. Matheus and L. Klinkhammer (eds), *Eigenbild im Konflikt. Krisensituationen des Papsttums zwischen Gregor VII. und Benedikt XV.*, (Darmstadt, 2009), 119–56.

Hanlon, G., *Early Modern Italy. 1550–1800* (London et al., 2000).

Koller, A. (ed.), *Kurie und Politik. Stand und Perspektiven der Nuntiaturberichtsforschung* (Tübingen, 1998).

Lutz, G., 'Urbano VIII', in *Enciclopedia dei papi*, ed. Istituto della Enciclopedia Italiana, vol. 3 (Rome, 2000), 298–331.

Pastor, L., *Geschichte der Päpste seit dem Ausgang des Mittelalters*, 8–13th edn (16 vols, Freiburg, 1955–1961); Italian tr.: *Storia dei Papi. Dalla fine del medio evo* (16 vols, Rome, 1942–1955).

Prodi, P., *Il sovrano pontefice. Un corpo e due anime: la monarchia papale nella prima età moderna*, Annali dell'Istituto storico italo-germanico, Monografia 3 (Bologna, 1982); English tr. by S. Haskins: *The Papal Prince. One body and two souls: the papal monarchy in early modern Europe* (Cambridge, 1987).

Reinhard, W., *Paul V. Borghese. 1605–1621. Mikropolitische Papstgeschichte* (Stuttgart, 2009).

Repgen, K., *Die römische Kurie und der Westfälische Friede. Idee und Wirklichkeit des Papsttums im 16. und 17. Jahrhundert* (2 vols, Tübingen, 1962–1965).

Repgen, K., *Dreißigjähriger Krieg und Westfälischer Friede. Studien und Quellen*, F. Bosbach and C. Kampmann (eds), Rechts- und Staatswissenschaftliche Veröffentlichungen der Görres-Gesellschaft, new series 81, 2nd edn (Paderborn et al., 1999), 458–86.

Wright, A. D., *The Early Modern Papacy. From the Council of Trent to the French Revolution 1564–1789* (London et al., 2000).

Non-splendid Isolation: The Ottoman Empire and the Thirty Years' War

Maria Baramova

Introduction

At the beginning of the eighteenth century, at the height of the War of the Spanish Succession, the Habsburg resident in Constantinople, Anselm Franz Fleischmann, indicated in his reports to the Hofkriegsrat one of the principles of Ottoman foreign policy with respect to the Holy Roman Empire and the other adversaries of the Sublime Porte: not to attack rulers while they were waging war against each other. 'At such times', he wrote, 'when Christians are well armed and ready to fight, the Sultan feared that, if he chose to strike, all their troops may unite and turn against him'.[1] Fleischmann was apparently referring to the Ottomans' neutrality in one of the greatest armed conflicts in Europe in Early Modern History – the Thirty Years' War. The Ottomans' behaviour was not much different in the first half of the seventeenth century when they maintained neutrality in the massive war despite the attempts of various parties to win their alliance. In the last years of the conflict the Ottoman Empire took no part in the peace negotiations, not signing the peace treaties of either Münster or Osnabrück, clearly keeping a distance from the 'World War of the Early Modern Times'. At the same time it was impossible to raise a thick wall separating the Ottomans from the fierce clashes in Europe and the sparks occasionally reached the Sultan's empire. Therefore it can hardly be argued that the Sublime Porte lived in complete isolation from Europe's most burning issues between 1618 and 1648. It would seem that the empire vacillated between complete neutrality and a sporadic swing to the brink of formal military intervention without ever crossing the line. Figuratively speaking, it was a case of 'non-splendid isolation' that forms the subject of this chapter.

The roots of the conflict between the Habsburg Empire and the Ottoman Empire go back to the mid-1520s. From its earliest emergence on the political scene their confrontation was not unfolding in isolation and was largely influenced by their respective relations with France. Remembering that 'my enemy's enemy is my friend', a number of sixteenth-century contemporaries in Europe suspected that Paris and Constantinople might see eye to eye and force the Habsburgs to face war on two fronts. It remains controversial whether such an 'unholy alliance' of the Crescent and the Fleur-de-Lys was indeed sealed between the Sublime Porte and the French king François I and his successors in the 1540s–1550s, or whether it

---

[1] HHStA, Türkei I–180, 1714–1716, Fasz. 86b.

was the outcome of counterfeit documents and powerful – and very efficient – propaganda against the French.[2] The temptation of joining forces against the common Habsburg enemy can hardly be underestimated both for the Ottomans and for the French court. The realities, however, were different and at least until the end of the seventeenth century France never sent its armies against the emperor while he was engaged against the Ottomans.[3]

Nonetheless, France had a special role in the Habsburg–Ottoman relations throughout the sixteenth and the seventeenth centuries. The Sublime Porte's 'non-splendid isolation' during the Thirty Years' War was to an extent mirrored by the position of the Parisian court. For 200 years, the French kings hesitated in their stance towards the Habsburg–Ottoman conflict between complete neutrality and 'the brink of formal military intervention', and never crossed the line.

Suspicions of French–Ottoman political cooperation against the Habsburgs had persisted ever since the 1520s and inevitably shaped strong anticipations – shared in equal measure by sixteenth-century public opinion and the research community – that the Ottomans would most likely interfere after the outbreak of the European conflict in the 1620s. For reasons I will elaborate on below, however, the sultans at the Bosporus confounded these expectations, not letting their empire be entangled in the major conflict raging in Europe.

Like the *Rois très Chrétien*, Protestants were the other Habsburg enemies that were harangued and accused of entering a 'pact' with the Sultan. Setting aside the rampant anti-Protestant propaganda of the Habsburgs, it is common knowledge that the Thirty Years' War was fundamentally the teeming armed conflict between Protestants and Catholics that was forestalled in the sixteenth century. Another piece of common knowledge is that the conflict was forestalled in direct consequence of the looming Ottoman menace in Central Europe.[4]

Historiographical Notes

The problem of Ottoman (non-)participation in the Thirty Years' War and the policy of the rulers in Constantinople towards the Christian monarchs fighting each other for three decades is a topic in historiography which has not yet attracted much scholarly attention. What was the actual role played by the Ottomans in that European conflict? Is there any difference between the official position of neutrality of the Sublime Porte and the actual reality in political and military affairs? Was the time of the Thirty Years' War a period of peace which was desired by the Ottomans or, on the contrary, was it enforced on them by

---

[2] Cf. K.M. Setton, *The Papacy and the Levant (1204–1571)*, 4 vols (Philadelphia, 1984), vol. 4, pp. 346–93; M. Hochedlinger, 'Die Französisch-osmanische "Freundschaft" 1525–1792. Element antihabsburgischer Politik, Gleichgewichtsinstrument, Prestigeunternehmung – Aufriß eines Problems', *Mitteilungen des Instituts für Österreichische Geschichtsforschung* 102 (1994), pp. 108–64; G. Poumarede, 'Justifier l'injustifiable: l'alliance turque au miroir de la chrétienté (XVIe-XVIIe siècles)', *Revue d'histoire diplomatique* 111.3 (1997): pp. 217–46; K.-P. Matschke, *Das Kreuz und der Halbmond. Die Geschichte der Türkenkriege* (Düsseldorf and Zürich, 2004), pp. 269–72.

[3] Hochedlinger, 'Die Französisch-osmanische "Freundschaft"', pp. 123–5; see further details in G. Veinstein, 'L'Europe et le Grand Turc', in H. Laurens et. al. (eds), *L'Europe et l'Islam. Quinzes siècles de l'histoire (Paris, 2009)*, pp. 120–270.

[4] Although it is difficult to prove that the reformists consciously tried to use the Ottoman power in their struggle against the Emperor and the Pope, they certainly took maximum advantage of the Ottoman expansion by upholding the principle 'support in return for concessions'. Cf. S. A. Fischer-Galati, *Ottoman Imperialism and German Protestantism, 1521–1555*, Reprint (New York, 1972); K. Setton, 'Lutheranism and the Turkish Peril', *Balkan Studies* 3 (1962): pp. 133–68; K. M. Setton, *Western Hostility to Islam and Prophecies of Turkish Doom* (Philadelphia, 1992).

circumstances? Did the Christian powers try to break the unwritten 'Gentlemen's agreement' that a ruler fighting the Ottomans would never be attacked by his Christian neighbour in an attempt to use, as early as the middle of the seventeenth century, the power potential of the sultans for their own purpose and political goals?[5] The problem of Ottoman neutrality during the war is the central theme of several studies.[6] Some scholars are trying to find answers by examining different case studies connected to diplomatic residents' activities in the Ottoman capital.[7] The majority of authors have argued that the Porte refrained from intervening in the war as it deliberately preferred to maintain neutrality.[8]

According to the opposite view put forward in other studies, the Sublime Porte quite effectively supported the Habsburg enemies during the Thirty Years' War. Claiming an alliance between Protestants and the Ottomans since the sixteenth century, Dorothy Vaughan, for example, has dedicated a chapter of her book *Europe and the Turk. A Pattern of Alliances 1350–1700* to the European attempts to provoke Ottoman intervention in the conflict.[9] Suraya Faroqhi goes even further, claiming that the Sublime Porte's support for the Protestant ruler of Transylvania, Gabor Bethlen, and for the Bohemian revolt against Habsburg rule, made Sultan Osman II 'the one and only ally of great-power status which the rebellious Bohemian states could muster after they had shaken off Habsburg rule and had elected Frederick V as a Protestant king'.[10]

The official Ottoman histories of the seventeenth century pay special attention to the Sublime Porte's stand vis-a-vis the Thirty Years' War and Joseph von Hammer relies heavily upon them.[11] This cannot be said however for some popular twentieth-century Turkish works on that period, which only briefly mention the conflict without going into any particular details.

---

[5] 'Gentlemen's agreement' is a term used by some scholars to describe the unwritten rule which provides that a Christian ruler would not be attacked by his Christian neighbours as long as he is fighting the Ottomans. According to this view this 'agreement' was in force between the middle of the fifteenth century and the end of the seventeenth century. See I. Parvev, '"Krieg der Welten" oder "Balance of Power". Europa und die Osmanen, 1300–1856', in I. Dingel and M. Schnettger (eds), *Auf dem Weg nach Europa: Deutungen, Visionen, Wirklichkeiten* (Mainz, 2010), pp. 131–46.

[6] K. M. Setton, *Venice, Austria, and the Turks in the Seventeenth Century* (Philadelphia, 1991), pp. 28–136; Matschke, *Das Kreuz und der Halbmond*, pp. 321–25.

[7] I. Hiller, 'Feind im Frieden. Die Rolle des Osmanischen Reiches in der europäischen Politik zur Zeit des Westfälischen Friedens', in H. Duchhardt (ed.), *Der Westfälische Friede: Diplomatie, politische Zäsur, kulturelles Umfeld, Rezeptionsgeschichte* (Munich, 1998), pp. 393–404; E.D. Petritsch, 'Fremderfahrungen kaiserlicher Diplomaten im Osmanischen Reich (1500–1648)', in M. Rohschneider and A. Strohmeyer (eds), *Wahrnehmungen des Fremden. Differenzerfahrungen von Diplomaten im 16. und 17. Jahrhundert* (Münster, 2007), pp. 345–66; A. Strohmeyer, 'Politische Leitvorstellungen in der diplomatischen Kommunikation: kaiserliche Gesandte an der Hohen Pforte im Zeitalter des Dreißigjährigen Krieges', in C. Kampmann et al. (eds), *L'art de la paix. Kongresswesen und Friedensstiftung im Zeitalter des Westfälischen Friedens* (Münster, 2011), pp. 409–39.

[8] M. Köhbach, 'Warum beteiligte sich das Osmanische Reich nicht am Dreißigjährigen Krieg?', in W. Leitsch and S. Trawkowski (eds), *Polen und Österreich im 17. Jahrhundert* (Vienna, 1999), pp. 277–94. The classical histories of the Ottoman Empire of the nineteenth and early twentieth century written by J. v. Hammer-Purgstall, J. . Zinkeisen and N. Jorga should not be forgotten. They contain detailed narratives which confirm the thesis of Ottoman neutrality during the war.

[9] D.M. Vaughan, *Europe and the Turk: A Pattern of Alliances, 1350–1700* (Liverpool, 1954), pp. 191–204.

[10] S. Faroqhi, 'Crisis and Change, 1590–1699', in Halil İnalcık and Donald Quataert (eds), *An Economic and Social History of the Ottoman Empire*, 2 vols (Cambridge, 1997), vol. 2, p. 424.

[11] For example Tarih-i Naima: *Ravzat ül-Hüseyn fi hulasat-i ahbar el-hafıkayn* (Istanbul, 1863). Cf. *Annals of the Turkish Empire: from 1591 to 1659* (London, 1832).

Ottoman Neutrality

The end of the 'Lange Türkenkrieg' (1593–1606) marked the beginning of a long period of peaceful relations between the Habsburg Empire and the Ottomans. For almost 60 years (until 1663–1664) the two old foes avoided direct military confrontation in order to put pressure on solving problems and conflicts elsewhere.[12] This seemingly strange attitude can be explained by the new political situation which the Habsburgs and the Ottomans faced after the Peace of Zsitvatorok (1606).[13] The long war ended with a stalemate, which was a surprise and a cause of dismay for the Sultan. As a consequence the diplomatic tradition of negotiating and signing peace agreements between the two powers changed and the Sublime Porte had to make certain concessions not completely in line with the rules of Muslim law that had been strictly followed until that time.[14] The Ottomans agreed to the title 'Emperor' for the Habsburg rulers instead of the rather pejorative 'King of Vienna' which was used during the sixteenth century; the annual payments which the Habsburgs had to send to the Sublime Porte between 1547 and 1593 were virtually abandoned after 1606.[15]

According to the Muslim understanding of international relations, any peace with an infidel ruler had to be in the form of an armistice, or a ceasefire agreement, for a fixed number of years, and the Ottomans adhered to that principle in the peace treaties with the Habsburg Empire. The Sublime Porte's ability to enforce its own interpretation of interstate relations was undoubtedly a function of its power potential not only in Central and South-Eastern Europe, but also in Asia and North Africa. At the beginning of the seventeenth century, however, the power of the sultans' empire had reached its natural geopolitical limits, hence every Ottoman plan for further territorial expansion in Europe had to be 'synchronised' with the power balance between the Christian rulers. During the conflict of 1593–1606 the Ottomans had to face the real danger of waging war on two fronts – a nightmare that the sultans had been trying to avoid since the rise of their empire. It is hardly surprising that Zsitvatorok ushered in a relatively long peace between the Sublime Porte and the Habsburg Empire – obviously both sides could no longer sustain an armed conflict without adapting their politics to the new strategic and geopolitical realities.

The gruelling conflict with the Habsburg rulers at the end of the sixteenth century, the internal problems of the Ottoman Empire and the war with the Safavids in the East

---

[12] Cf. J.P. Niederkorn, *Die europäischen Mächte und der 'Lange Türkenkrieg" Kaiser Rudolfs II. (1593–1606)* (Vienna, 1993); see also H. Heppner, 'Der lange Türkenkrieg (1593–1606). Ein Wendepunkt im Habsburgisch-Osmanischen Gegensatz', *Osmanlı Araştırmaları: Journal of Ottoman Studies*, 2 (1981): pp. 133–46.

[13] Cf. G. Bayerle, 'The Compromise of Zsitvatorok', *Archivum Ottomanicum* 6 (1980), pp. 5–53; K. Nehring, *Adam Freiherrn zu Herbersteins Gesandtschaftsreise nach Konstantinopel. Ein Beitrag zum Frieden von Zsitvatorok (1606)* (Munich, 1983), pp. 15–67.

[14] K.-H. Ziegler, 'The peace treaties of the Ottoman Empire with European Christian powers', in R. Lesaffer (ed.), *Peace Treaties and International Law in European History. From the late Middle Ages to World War One* (Cambridge, 2004), pp. 342–7.

[15] Nonetheless, one-off payments were made upon each renewal of the peace treaty after 1606. Even though the Ottomans traditionally regarded this as a payment of tribute, the Habsburg emperors preferred to see their obligation as 'sending a gift'. Cf. E.D. Petritsch, 'Der habsburgisch-osmanische Friedensvertrag des Jahres 1547', *Mitteilungen des Österreichischen Staatsarchivs*, 38, (1985): pp. 73–4; E.D. Petritsch, 'Tribut oder Ehrengeschenk? Ein Beitrag zu den habsburgisch-osmanischen Beziehungen in der zweiten Hälfte des 16. Jahrhunderts', in E. Springer and L. Kammerhofer, (eds), *Archiv und Forschung. Das Haus-, Hof- und Staatsarchiv in seiner Bedeutung für die Geschichte Österreichs und Europas* (Vienna, 1993), pp. 53–7.

(1603–1639)[16] were among the main reasons for Osman II and his successors, Murad IV and Ibrahim, to abstain from full-scale intervention in the Thirty Years' War. In part, the Ottoman neutrality was also the result of effective conflict management by the Habsburg diplomacy in Constantinople. The seven renewals of the treaty of Zsitvatorok between 1606 and 1649 clearly indicate the Ottomans' will to keep the peace and Vienna's desire not to challenge the fragile co-existence that could benefit both sides.[17]

Bohemian Revolt, Transylvanian Question and the Ottomans

Regardless of the Sublime Porte's policy of neutrality, the Ottomans' political actions in some events during the Thirty Years' War differed from the officially proclaimed stance of non-intervention.

At the end of 1619 the leaders of the revolt against Habsburg rule and the newly crowned ruler of Bohemia, the Elector Palatine Frederick V (1619–1620),[18] faced difficulties in organising the new state and its defence. They soon engaged in diplomatic activities to secure financial and military aid. Even though the majority of the states that recognised the Palatine as ruler showed sympathy towards the revolting Bohemians, they were reluctant to offer significant military assistance.[19] Therefore Frederick did not shun the possibility of looking for political support even from the Ottoman Sultan. It was not a secret that since the sixteenth century many Protestants believed they could count on the Sublime Porte in order to oppose their Catholic foes. Such reasoning had its grounds: knowing that the Ottoman enemies in the Eastern Mediterranean, as well as in Southern and Central Europe over the previous century had been only Catholic states and rulers, it seemed logical to assume that the Sultan in Constantinople would look with sympathy on the Protestant cause.

The new King of Bohemia did not even have to establish initial contacts with the Sublime Porte single-handedly because he could rely on the mediation of the ruler of Transylvania, Gabor Bethlen. At least in theory the prince was supposed to be a vassal of the Ottoman Empire: this was the political course laid down in 1541 for Transylvania whose creation as an autonomous principality was approved by the Ottomans.[20]

Gabor Bethlen (1613–1629) is an interesting and controversial political figure. During the 'Long Turkish War' he supported Emperor Rudolf II (1576–1612) in his struggle against the Ottomans, but the collaboration was refracted through Bethlen's own political objectives. His aim was twofold: he wanted to defend the rights of Protestants without losing sight of any possibility that could expand his power and influence as a ruler. An able diplomat and military commander, and an ardent champion of Protestantism, during his two decades as prince of Transylvania Gabor Bethlen managed to keep for a long time non-hostile relations

---

[16] The Ottoman Empire experienced a series of social riots in the sixteenth and the seventeenth centuries known as the *Celâli Revolts*.

[17] Cf. G. Noradoughian (ed.), *Recueil d'actes internationaux de l'Empire ottoman. Traités, conventions, arrangements, déclarations, protocoles, procès-verbaux, firmans, bérats, lettres patentes et autres documents relatifs au droit public extérieur de la Turquie*, 4 vols (Paris, 1897), vol. 1, pp. 33–53.

[18] Frederick V was called also the Winter king (Zimní král). Cf. B.C. Pursell, *The Winter King: Frederick V of the Palatinate and the Coming of the Thirty Years' War* (Aldershot, 2003); see chapter 2 in this volume.

[19] Ibid., pp. 107–12.

[20] For more details about Gabriel (Gabor) Bethlen see D. Angyal, 'Gabriel Bethlen', *Revue Historique*, 53/158 (1928): pp. 19–80.

both with the Ottomans and the Habsburgs.[21] When the Bohemian revolt broke out, he even offered military aid to the emperor, but later changed sides and aligned forces with the rebels against Vienna, probably alarmed by the extreme anti-Reformist attitude of the Habsburgs. At the same time Bethlen did not fail to see the chance of broadening his own power base in Central Europe after a possible dissolution of the domains of the House of Austria.[22] Quite naturally, he set his eye on the western parts of Medieval Hungary, which after 1541 came under Habsburg rule. These lands could come under Bethlen's sceptre, who could thus recreate the old Hungarian kingdom. With this vision in mind, he sought Ottoman political support and with the consent of the Sublime Porte was proclaimed King of Hungary in 1620. That 'political matrix' had already worked in the wake of the battle of Móhacz (1526), when John Zápolya ascended the Hungarian throne with the approval of Suleiman the Magnificent, and was acceptable both to the Sublime Porte and to Bethlen and his supporters.[23]

After becoming King of Hungary and after reaffirming his vassal status vis-à-vis the Sublime Porte, Gabor Bethlen actively supported Frederick V in establishing contacts with the Ottomans.[24] At the beginning of 1620 the ruler of Bohemia sent his envoy, Heinrich Bitter, to Constantinople in order to seek support against Ferdinand II and his allies.[25] It seems that the visit was rather successful, since a couple of months later a certain Mehmed Aga was sent to Prague with the mission to inform the Bohemians that the Sublime Porte was ready to send a cavalry corps of 60,000 men as auxiliary troops. The Sultan was also prepared to attack Poland with an army of 400,000 men as a reprisal raid for the Cossack incursion in Bohemia, which the Poles had approved. An annual tribute, which Prague should pay to the Ottomans, was agreed upon, as well as a subsidy that the Bohemians were to forward to Gabor Bethlen so that he could fight Bavaria and Saxony.[26]

One can definitely speculate about the accuracy of these numbers and to what extent they were a declaration of good will, or conveyed the Porte's genuine intention to actively intervene in the Thirty Years' War and side with the Habsburg enemies. Scepticism seems rather justified because, irrespective of the diplomatic contacts between Prague and Constantinople and the option of military cooperation against the Habsburgs, none of it

---

[21] Vaughan, *Europe and the Turk*, pp. 192–3. See also Setton, *Venice, Austria and the Turks*, pp. 33–5.

[22] J. v. Hammer-Purgstall, *Geschichte des Osmanischen Reiches*, 10 vols (Pesth, 1829), vol. 5, pp. 91–2.

[23] See Fischer-Galati, *Ottoman Imperialism and German Protestantism*, passim.

[24] *Extract Eines Relationschreibens Herrn Bethlehem Gabors/ Fürsten in Siebenbürgen/ an den Türckischen Kayser/ wegen glücklich Occupirten Königreichs Hungarn abgangen (1619)*. See also *Copia eines Sendschreibens / So von Bethlem Gabor vor dem Fürsten in Sibenbürgen / auaß Weissenburg / sub dato den 20 Augusti dieses abgelauffenden Jahrs/ An die Herrn Directores des Königreichs Böheim abgelauffen … (1619)*, fol. 2r-v.

[25] 'The Wars growing hot in Bohemia against the Protestants, and the Emperor raising what force he could, to suppress them, the Governors of the Country, wrote their Letters to Bethlem Gabor Prince of Transilvania, to acquaint him with the State of their affairs; to whom he made answer that his Country lying even in the Jaws of the Turks, was necessitated to take his measures from them, and having to that end sent an Ambassador to the Sultan, who assur'd him of his Favour, he resolv'd notwithstanding the opposition of the House of Austria, the Pope, and others Bohemians, promising in September next, to be upon the confines of Moldavia, unless he found some stay in Hungary'. Paul Rycaut, *The Turkish History, Comprehending the Origin of that Nation, and the Growth of the Othoman Empire, with the Lives and Conquests of their several Kings and Emperors. Written By Mr. Richard Knolles an Continu'd by the Honorable Sir Paul Rycaut, to the Peace at Carlowitz, in the Year 1699* (London, 1701), pp. 57–8.

[26] Pursell, *The Winter King*, p. 112–13. See also H. Forst, 'Der türkische Gesandte in Prag 1620 und der Briefwechsel des Winterkönigs mit Sultan Osman II.', *Mittheilungen des Instituts für Oesterreichische Geschichtsforschung*, 16 (1895), pp. 566–81.

materialised. The unsuccessful Ottoman war with Poland (1620–1621),[27] which led to a forceful change of rulers at the Bosporus, may indeed be interpreted as indirect help for the Protestant cause because it prevented the Polish troops from helping their fellow Catholic forces in Vienna. But with the exception of this small episode, the neutrality of the Sublime Porte in the great European conflict could hardly be questioned.

Another important factor for keeping the Ottoman neutrality in the early phase of the Thirty Years' War was the Habsburg diplomacy.[28] The work of the Habsburg residents and extraordinary envoys greatly contributed to the fact that the relations between Vienna and Constantinople remained peaceful and without great tensions between 1618 and 1648.

At the outbreak of the Bohemian revolt the Habsburg envoy, Baron Ludwig von Mollard, was sent to Constantinople with the special mission to thwart possible negotiations between the Protestant rebels and the Sublime Porte for Ottoman support.[29] Although he could not prevent the Sultan from receiving the Bohemian envoy and although, at least officially, the Sublime Porte was inclined to aid Prague, Mollard successfully 'encouraged' the Ottomans ultimately to prefer neutrality over a political adventure with an uncertain outcome.

Habsburg Strategy vis-à-vis Constantinople

During the Thirty Years' War the diplomatic activity of the Habsburg court in regard to the Ottoman Empire focused mainly on keeping and, if necessarily, prolonging the Peace of Zsitvatorok.[30] A number of issues had to be negotiated due to differences in the language variants of the peace agreement of 1606, but a compromise was not easy to achieve. The talks were accompanied by constant military tension along the Habsburg–Ottoman border which inevitably permeated the bilateral relations, dominated for more than a century by wars and ideological hostility. Yet the fact that the treaty of Zsitvatorok was renewed several times with some of the problems remaining unsolved and pending future negotiations, clearly demonstrates the will of both sides to avoid or at least postpone direct military confrontation.[31]

Two extensions of the treaty of Zsitvatorok in 1627 and 1642 turned out to be of special importance for Habsburg–Ottoman relations. In 1628 a 'Großbotschaft' headed by Baron Hans Ludwig von Kuefstein was sent to Constantinople,[32] while Receb Pasha's reciprocal mission set out for Vienna. The renewal of the treaty and the exchange of diplomatic envoys were rightfully seen as a gesture of good will on both sides and an expression of their desire to keep the peace. Quite remarkably, these events coincide with Gabor Bethlen's vigorous

---

[27] The Ottoman-Polish conflict was called the 'Chocim war'. On Ottoman-Turkish relations during the Thirty Years' War see D. Kołodziejczyk, 'Polen und die Osmanen im 17 Jahrhundert', in W. Leitsch, S. Trawkowski (eds), *Polen und Österreich*, pp. 261–76; D. Kołodziejczyk, *Ottoman-Polish Diplomatic Relations (15th–18th Century). An Annotated Edition of 'Ahdnames and Other Documents* (Leiden, 2000), pp. 129–41.

[28] Cf. Strohmeyer, 'Politische Leitvorstellungen'. For negotiations during the Bohemian rebellion, see R. R. Heinisch, 'Habsburg, die Pforte und der Böhmische Aufstand (1618–1620)', *Südostforschungen*, 33–34 (1974–1975): pp. 125–65; 79–124.

[29] Pursell, *The Winter King*, p. 112.

[30] C. Finkel, *Osman's Dream. The History of the Ottoman Empire* (New York, 2005), pp. 218–22.

[31] Hammer, *Geschichte des Osmanischen Reiches*, pp. 96–7.

[32] K. Teply, *Kaiserliche Großbotschaft an Sultan Murad IV. 1628. Des Freiherrn Hans Ludwig von Kuefsteins Fahrt zur Hohen Pforte* (Vienna, 1976), pp. 29–48.

efforts to ensure Ottoman intervention in the war that led to one of the greatest outbursts of tension along the Habsburg–Ottoman border in the late 1620s.[33]

The Transylvanian question was extensively discussed by the European diplomats in Constantinople.[34] Due to Bethlen's constantly shifting position the fighting powers used the 'Transylvanian connection' as leverage to influence the Sublime Porte to intervene in the conflict. The Habsburg resident, Johann Rudolf Schmid (1590–1667),[35] complains in his dispatches about the intrigues of the other diplomats in Constantinople against him. The English ambassador Sir Thomas Roe (1622–1629) was an ardent supporter of Bethlen and his letters report on the talks between the Transylvanian ruler and the Ottomans.[36] Several months after the renewal of the treaty of Zsitvatorok at Gyarmath, Gabor Bethlen dispatched Paul Keresztessy as his envoy to Murad IV to ask for permission for Transylvania to make an alliance with the Christian powers fighting against the emperor. The prince even managed to convince France, Venice, England and the Netherlands to help him with funds to pay his annual tribute to the Sultan.

The death of Gabor Bethlen in 1629 deprived the 'Case of Transylvania' of the political explosive force that could bring the Ottomans to intervene more clearly in the affairs of Central Europe.[37] Gabor was, by the way, well aware that the new ruler of the Ottomans, Murad IV, was not inclined to undertake any adventurous enterprises in Europe until the war with his dangerous enemy in the East, Shiite Persia, had ended with a decisive victory. The Sultan's stand was clear and logical: during the Long Turkish War (1593–1606) the Sublime Porte was for the first time forced to fight a very dangerous war on two fronts. In order to prevent such crisis from ever happening again in the future, the only solution was to fight (and defeat) the two enemies one by one. Murad IV was a pragmatic politician and he reasonably started war with his weaker foe and neighbour, the Persians. It was in the Sultan's interest that peace with the Habsburg Empire remained inviolable – at least until Persia was eliminated as an important geopolitical factor.[38]

It was perhaps good luck for the emperor that the Ottoman victory in the Persian war coincided with the death of Murad IV. The new ruler in Constantinople, Sultan Ibrahim (1640–1648), not only suffered from serious mental problems but also had difficulties identifying clear priorities in his European policy. A Habsburg resident, Johann Rudolf Schmid, remarked in his letters that even though the moment for Ottoman intervention in the European war was opportune after the end of the Persian campaigns, the Sublime

---

[33] In 1626 Gabor Bethlen managed to convince the Sublime Porte to replace the beglerbeg of Buda with the militant Bosnian commander Murtesa Pasha. N. Zahirović, *Murteza Pascha von Ofen zwischen Panegyrik und Historie: eine literarisch-historische Analyse eines osmanischen Wesirspiegels von Nergisi (El-vasfü l-kāmil fi-ahvāli l-vezīri l-ʾādil)* (Frankfurt am Main, 2010).

[34] Hiller, 'Feind im Frieden'.

[35] Cf. B. Spuler, 'Die Europäische Diplomatie in Konstantinopel bis zum Frieden von Belgrad (1739)', 3. Teil, *Jahrbücher für Kultur und Geschichte der Slaven, Neue Folge*, 11 – 3/4 (1935), pp. 313–66; P. Meienberger, *Johann Rudolf Schmid zum Schwarzenhorn als kaiserlicher Resident in Konstantinopel in den Jahren 1629–1643. Ein Beitrag zur Geschichte der diplomatischen Beziehungen zwischen Österreich und der Türkei in der ersten Hälfte des 17. Jahrhunderts* (Bern, 1973). See also Strohmeyer, 'Politische Leitvorstellungen', p. 412.

[36] T. Roe, *The negociations [...] in his Embassy to the Ottoman Porte, from the year 1621 to 1628 Inclusive*. Now first publ. from the originals (London, 1740); see also Rycaut, *The Turkish History*, pp. 61–8.

[37] Gabor was succeeded by his brother Stephen Bethlen, but was later expelled by György Rákóczi I (1593–1648). At the beginning the new prince was supported by the Emperor, but soon the Habsburgs had to realise that Rákóczi followed the example of his predecessor Gabor Bethlen by politically balancing between Vienna and Istanbul. Cf. Hammer, *Geschichte des Osmanischen Reiches*, pp. 126–7.

[38] For more about the reign of Sultan Murad IV see Cavid Baysun, 'Murad IV', in *İslâm Ansiklopedisi*, (Istanbul, 1979), vol. 8, pp. 625–47.

Porte preferred to stay calm and maintain neutrality. In his opinion the Sultan's empire faced serious internal problems and its military resources were depleted after the long war with Persia.[39]

The Sublime Porte retained some of its political influence in Transylvania, but the rulers of the principality gradually drifted away from the Ottoman gravitational pull and in various degrees pursued their own policy in the course of the Thirty Years' War. The intention of the Ottoman Empire to avoid military engagements in Central Europe had a direct impact on the outcome of the revolt of György Rákóczi I (1593–1648) in 1644.[40] When in 1645 an unexpected accident led to the outbreak of an Ottoman–Venetian war which lasted until 1669, the problems of the great European conflict which was drawing to a close faded away in the minds of Ottoman politicians.[41]

Conclusion

The important question in historiography of whether the Ottoman Empire was or was not involved in the Thirty Years' War, is clearly linked to the rulers of Transylvania. Even though the Sublime Porte lent some informal support to its vassal principality, the fact remains that in the end the Ottomans did not intervene with troops in the conflict against the Habsburg Empire. Furthermore, the campaign of György Rákóczi I in 1644, which was intended to be a joint Transylvanian–Swedish military effort against Emperor Ferdinand III, was halted on orders from the Sublime Porte.

For his part, the emperor showed similar unwillingness to intervene in the Venetian–Ottoman war, which broke out in 1645. According to some scholars, Vienna was trying at any cost to keep the quite acceptable bilateral relations with the Sublime Porte in order to block a possible increase of French influence in Constantinople.[42] It seems that both the Habsburgs and the Ottomans deemed it necessary to keep the peace, and this necessity was more powerful than the dream of claiming revenge on the battlefield.

Selected Bibliography

Eickhoff, E., *Venedig, Wien und die Osmanen. Umbruch in Südosteuropa 1645–1700* (Munich, 1970).
Finkel, C., *Osman's Dream. The History of the Ottoman Empire* (New York, 2005).
Heinisch, R.R., 'Habsburg, die Pforte und der Böhmische Aufstand (1618–1620)', *Südostforschungen*, 33–34 (1974–1975): pp. 125–65; 79–124.
Hiller, I., 'Feind im Frieden. Die Rolle des Osmanischen Reiches in der europäischen Politik zur Zeit des Westfälischen Friedens', in H. Duchhardt (ed.), *Der Westfälische Friede: Diplomatie, politische Zäsur, kulturelles Umfeld, Rezeptionsgeschichte* (Munich, 1998), pp. 393–404.

---

[39] Meienberger, *Johann Rudolf Schmid*, pp. 176–80; Strohmeyer, 'Politische Leitvorstellungen', p. 416.

[40] Hammer, *Geschichte des Osmanischen Reiches*, pp. 345–52.

[41] About the Ottoman-Venetian War, the so called 'Cretan War" (1645–1669), see Setton, *Venice, Austria, and the Turks*; E. Eickhoff, *Venedig, Wien und die Osmanen. Umbruch in Südosteuropa 1645–1700* (Munich, 1970).

[42] Hiller, 'Feind im Frieden', pp. 402–3.

Hurewitz, J.C., 'Ottoman Diplomacy and the European State System', *Middle East Journal*, 15, No. 2 (1961): pp. 141–52.
İnalcık, H. and Quataert, D. (eds), *An Economic and Social History of the Ottoman Empire* (2 vols, Cambridge, 1997), vol. 2.
Köhbach, M., 'Warum beteiligte sich das Osmanische Reich nicht am Dreißigjährigen Krieg?', in W. Leitsch, S. Trawkowski (eds), *Polen und Österreich im 17. Jahrhundert* (Vienna, 1999), pp. 277–94.
Kołodziejczyk, D., *Ottoman-Polish Diplomatic Relations (15th–18th Century). An Annotated Edition of 'Ahdnames and Other Documents* (Leiden, 2000).
Murphey, R., *Ottoman Warfare, 1500–1700* (London, 1999).
Setton, K.M., *Venice, Austria, and the Turks in the Seventeenth Century* (Philadelphia, 1991).
Vaughan, D.M., *Europe and the Turk: A Pattern of Alliances, 1350–1700* (Liverpool, 1954).
Ziegler, K.-H., 'The peace treaties of the Ottoman Empire with European Christian powers', in R. Lesaffer (ed.), *Peace Treaties and International Law in European History. From the late Middle Ages to World War One* (Cambridge, 2004), pp. 342–7.

PART III
Different Stages and Theatres of the War

1618–1629

Ronald G. Asch

The Outbreak of the War

Germany, as opposed to France, which had been torn apart by civil war between 1562 and 1598, had been largely spared the chaos of large-scale domestic conflict in the later sixteenth century. The Peace of Augsburg (1555) despite its shortcomings had provided the empire, at least for the time being, with the means to defuse the religious tensions which threatened to undermine order and stability. Moreover the fact that both the Habsburg dominions and the empire itself were threatened by the powerful Ottoman Empire in the late sixteenth century created a bond which united both Protestants and Catholics. The contest with the Ottomans had culminated in the so-called 'Long Turkish War' of 1593–1606. The treaty of Zsitvatorok (1606) ended the conflict and marked the beginning of a protracted period when the Sultan concentrated his forces on the east and the fight against Persia.[1] However, the fact that the threat from the old enemy now receded into the background had not only beneficial consequences. Mutually hostile political and religious factions both in the Habsburg dominions and in the empire at large could now feel free to pursue their grievances with far less restraint than in the past. The situation was exacerbated by the fact that the aged Emperor Rudolph II, who ruled both Bohemia and its dependent principalities and Upper and Lower Austria as well as Hungary (insofar as it was not occupied by the Turks), increasingly lost his grip on events – and Rudolph had never been the most energetic of rulers. He had, however, been determined to prolong the war against the Turks and to subdue the Protestants in Hungary in 1606 but had been forced by his brother Matthias to abandon this policy. He subsequently not only lost control over most of his dominions to Matthias, he also had to pacify the unruly Protestant Estates of Bohemia by granting them extensive privileges and official religious toleration. When he died in 1612 imperial authority had not only been fatefully weakened within the Habsburg monarchy but also and probably even more so in the empire as a whole. With the power vacuum at the top other players had begun to dominate the field in the empire, in particular the ambitious duke of Bavaria, Maximilian, who had become the leader of the Catholic princes and the Electors Palatine in Heidelberg, first Frederick IV (d. 1610) and then his son Frederick V, both Calvinists who organised an alliance of Protestant imperial cities and princes (the Union of 1608) against the perceived threat of a Catholic roll-back. The Electors Palatine enjoyed good relations with the Dutch Republic and the French Huguenots whom they had supported in the French Wars of Religion. Moreover the young Elector Frederic V had in 1613 married Elizabeth, the daughter of James I of England. He and his advisors certainly saw the Palatinate as a

---

[1] J.P. Niederkorn, *Die europäischen Mächte und der 'Lange Türkenkrieg' Kaiser Rudolfs II. (1593–1606)* (Vienna, 1993).

serious player not just on the German but on the European stage. In Heidelberg a sense of a providential mission and dynastic ambition formed a heady brew, as the years to come were to show.[2]

Nevertheless, tensions within the empire had slightly diminished in the years after Rudolph II's death; men like Johann Georg the elector of Saxony – though a Lutheran, a staunch supporter of the Emperor's authority – but also a number of Catholic princes pursued a moderate course. But there was still more than enough combustible material to turn a local conflict in the empire into a major conflagration.[3]

This local conflict was to be the revolt of the Bohemian Estates in 1618. Having reasserted their rights during the years 1608–1612, when Rudolph II was no longer capable to resist them, the Bohemian Protestants who dominated the assembly of estates saw their position under threat during the new regime of Emperor Matthias who succeeded his brother as king of Bohemia in 1612. Bohemia had a long history of resistance against royal power; it was considered as an elective monarchy not a hereditary one (although the kings had been Habsburgs ever since 1526) and in the early fifteenth century the revolt of the Hussites – precursors of the Reformation in many ways – had broken the power of the dynasty ruling Bohemia at the time, the House of Luxemburg. The church had lost most of its property and the remaining bishops and prelates no longer took part in the sessions of the diet in Prague which was dominated instead by the higher nobility. The great majority of noblemen and of the population at large were either Protestants or had at least strong Protestant sympathies. The German-speaking burghers and peasants were often Lutherans, the Czechs were members of the Utraquist Church – going back to the Hussite revolt. Most Utraquists (some continued to lean towards the Catholic Church) had adopted the *Confessio Bohemica* in 1575 which was influenced by the Lutheran *Confessio Augustana* of 1530. Strong as the Protestant position was in Bohemia, a small circle of Catholic noble families, many of them converts, had begun to reassert their influence both at court and to a lesser extent at the local level from the 1590s onwards with the Emperor's support.[4] They presented a political and cultural *avantgarde* inimical to the values of the Protestant Estates. The vibrant culture of late renaissance and early baroque Italy proved to this group of noblemen clearly more attractive than the somewhat dour humanism of the leading Protestant scholars and theologians.[5]

Already on the defensive, the leaders of the Protestant Estates dreaded the moment when Matthias – strongly Catholic but nevertheless not radical – would be succeeded by his nephew Ferdinand of Styria who had been elected as his successor designate in 1617. Ferdinand had shown in Inner Austria that he was determined to destroy Protestantism, regardless of what privileges the estates claimed to have obtained in the past.[6] Within the Protestant Bohemia nobility there was a strong group which was resolved to defend religious liberty and political freedom – as they saw it – at all costs and to anticipate whatever measures Ferdinand might take by a preventive strike. They decided to depose Emperor Matthias's governors in Bohemia, Martinitz and Slawata. Officially this was an answer to

---

[2] B.C. Pursell, *The Winter King: Frederick V of the Palatinate and the Coming of the Thirty Years War* (Aldershot, 2003), pp. 17–35.

[3] On confessional alliances before 1618 see A. Ernst and A. Schindling (eds), *Liga und Union 1608/09: Konfessionelle Bündnisse im Reich. Weichenstellung zum Religionskrieg* (Stuttgart, 2010).

[4] On Bohemia see T. Winkelbauer, *Ständefreiheit und Fürstenmacht. Länder und Untertanen des Hauses Habsburg im Konfessionellen Zeitalter* (2 vols, Vienna 2003), vol. 2, pp. 18–29, and R.J.W. Evans, *The Making of the Habsburg Monarchy* (Oxford, 1979), pp. 47–57.

[5] H. Louthan, *Converting Bohemia: Force and Persuasion in the Catholic Reformation* (Cambridge, 2009), p. 81.

[6] On Ferdinand see T. Brockmann, *Dynastie, Kaiseramt und Konfession. Politik und Ordnungsvorstellungen Kaiser Ferdinands II. im Dreißigjährigen Krieg* (Paderborn, 2011).

the infringement of Protestant rights in some Bohemian towns and local communities, but essentially what was at issue was Habsburg rule over Bohemia as such. On the morning of 23 May 1618 the assembly of the Bohemian Protestants met near the royal castle, the Hradshin, in Prague. Following a brief discussion, the members of the assembly went to the castle where they insisted on seeing the governors. After a heated exchange of words between members of the assembly led by Heinrich Count Thurn, and the imperial representatives, Thurn and his friends declared two of the governors, Martinitz and Slawata, traitors because they had undermined the rights and privileges of the estates. To the applause of the angry crowd Martinitz and Slawata were thrown out of the windows of the Council Chamber of the Hradshin, and one of the Clerks of the Council, a certain Frabricius, shared their fate for full measure. However the 'execution' was bungled. Martinitz and Slawata, and Fabricius too, miraculously survived.

The defenestration of May 1618 was the beginning of a movement which ultimately meant to destroy Habsburg power and to block the advance of the Counter Reformation, not just in Bohemia but also in Moravia, Silesia and Austria. Imperial and royal authority was largely to be replaced by a new political order based on a federation of all dominions belonging to the Bohemian crown, Bohemia itself, Moravia, Silesia and Upper and Lower Lusatia.[7] Politically the rebels subscribed to a sort of monarchical republicanism. They saw themselves as the king's partners not his obedient subjects and their support for Protestantism was one way of expressing these values. While the revolt was still gaining strength the elderly Emperor died in March 1619. Matthias's death, weak as he may have been as a ruler, made a peaceful solution of the Bohemian crisis even less likely than before. The Bohemians were faced with the alternative of either accepting Ferdinand as their king after all, or taking the ultimate step of deposing him. On 19 August 1619 they did indeed pass a resolution deposing him with the assent of delegates from Moravia, Silesia and Lusatia. It should be stressed that despite the serious religious and political tensions in the Holy Roman Empire there seemed at first to be a chance of containing the Bohemian crisis and preventing a general conflagration. The attitude of most Protestant princes in Germany was cautious. The fact that the crisis was not contained was ultimately due to the fact that Frederick V, the Elector Palatine, who was also lord of the Upper Palatinate, an area directly bordering on Bohemia, decided to intervene. The Elector Palatine and in particular his regent in Amberg (the capital of the Upper Palatinate), Prince Christian of Anhalt, had been in touch with the Bohemian opposition right from the start. What Anhalt had been trying to bring about before 1618 was an international coalition with a leading role for the Palatinate and himself, uniting all opponents of the House of Habsburg and of Counter-Reformation Catholicism. Now the hour for bringing these plans to fruition seemed to have struck. Anhalt certainly encouraged the Bohemian estates' decision to depose Ferdinand in August 1619. Their further decision to proceed to the election of Frederick V, the Elector Palatine, as the new king of Bohemia, barely two weeks later on 26/27 August, had also initially been in accord with Anhalt's wishes, although at this stage he had already begun to doubt the wisdom of his own radical policy.[8] However, whatever doubts Anhalt may have harboured, Frederick accepted the Bohemian crown and was thereby irrevocably committed to open war against Ferdinand of Austria. This decision finally transformed the Bohemian crisis if not into an all-embracing European conflict, then certainly into a war in which the future of the Holy Roman Empire was at stake.

---

[7] J. Bahlcke, *Regionalismus und Staatsintegration im Widerstreit: Die Länder der böhmischen Krone im ersten Jahrhundert der Habsburgerherrschaft (1526–1619)*, (Munich, 1994), pp. 430–45.

[8] M. Ritter, *Deutsche Geschichte im Zeitalter der Gegenreformation und des Dreißigjährigen Krieges* (3 vols., Stuttgart, 1889–1908), vol. 3, p. 50.

Frederick V and his advisors seem to have believed that Ferdinand would not muster the strength on his own to suppress the rebellion in Bohemia. Spain, however, governed by the senior branch of the Habsburg dynasty, potentially a powerful ally for Ferdinand, had withdrawn from active involvement in Central Europe during the preceding decade. Full-scale Spanish support for Ferdinand appeared therefore unlikely to many observers. Should the revolt in Bohemia succeed in creating a lasting new settlement this would not only have made Frederick V a king in his own right as opposed to being merely a king's son-in-law, as he was until 1619, it would also have made him the natural leader of all Protestants in Europe or at least of those who showed sympathy for Calvinism, a position which had become vacant with the death of Henry IV of France 1610, if not in fact with his conversion to Catholicism in 1593. But such ambitious plans soon proved to be unrealistic.

Spain had already granted Ferdinand considerable financial assistance in 1618 contrary to expectations in Heidelberg, and within a few months of the fall of the duke of Lerma (the royal favourite at the Spanish court) in autumn 1618 the advocates of an active Spanish policy north of the Alps were able to overcome the last opposition to intervention in Bohemia and the Holy Roman Empire.[9] In many ways the Elector Palatine had chosen the worst possible moment for a confrontation with Ferdinand. On the one hand Spain had already decided to give her interests in Central Europe a higher priority than in the preceding years but on the other hand the war with the Dutch Republic which had been suspended by a 12-year truce in 1609 had not yet been resumed, so that the Spanish monarchy still had enough resources available to support Ferdinand in Bohemia and in Germany.

Bavaria, the most powerful Catholic principality in Germany both in financial and military terms, was as important an ally for Ferdinand as Spain despite earlier tensions between the Bavarian Wittelsbach and the Habsburgs. In October 1619 Duke Maximilian and the reconstituted Catholic League (originally founded in 1609 and led by Maximilian) agreed to send their army to support Ferdinand. Maximilian was not only a militant Catholic who saw a Protestant Bohemia as a threat to his authority in his own duchy of Bavaria where Protestantism had successfully been eradicated but also considered the Elector Palatine as one of his main rivals for a pre-eminent place among the princes of the empire. A royal crown for his Heidelberg kinsman (both the Electors Palatine and the Dukes of Bavaria belonged to the Wittelsbach dynasty) meant that Maximilian's own ambitions would be thwarted for the foreseeable future. Relations between Vienna and Munich had not been free of tensions before 1618 and these tensions were to resurface in the late 1620s but for the time being both Ferdinand II and Maximilian were determined to defeat their common enemy the Elector Palatine. In recognition of his support Ferdinand also assured Maximilian that he, Maximilian, would be rewarded with substantial parts of the Palatine dominions and a transfer of the electoral dignity from the Palatine branch of the Wittelsbach dynasty to Maximilian's own Bavarian branch.[10]

Ferdinand was able to make such promises because he had been elected Emperor in Frankfurt on 28 August 1619, hardly two weeks after his deposition as king of Bohemia. Palatine policy in spring and summer 1619 had really been based on the assumption that the election of a new Emperor after Matthias's death in March could be postponed until the

---

[9] In May 1619, 7,000 Spanish or Spanish-paid soldiers were sent from Flanders to Vienna to help the German Habsburgs. See H. Ernst, *Madrid und Wien 1632–1637. Politik und Finanzen in den Beziehungen zwischen Philipp IV und Ferdinand II.* (Münster, 1991), p. 18, and P. Brightwell, 'Spain and Bohemia 1619–1621', *European Studies Review*, 12 (1982): pp. 371–91.

[10] D. Albrecht, *Maximilian I. von Bayern 1573–1651* (Munich, 1998), pp. 489–538. On the conflict between the two branches of the house of Wittelsbach see also A.L. Thomas, *A House Divided: Wittelsbach Confessional Court Cultures in the Holy Roman Empire, 1550–1650* (Leiden, 2010), pp. 187–294.

Bohemian crisis had been resolved and Habsburg power in the empire destroyed or at least severely curtailed. However, it was the empire's arch-chancellor, the archbishop of Mainz, who organised the election. Mainz and the other two archbishops who were members of the Electoral College (Trier and Cologne) were determined to go through with the election regardless of the crisis in the empire. Ferdinand was allowed to cast the Bohemian vote for himself – his deposition as king was not accepted as valid by the Electoral College – and the outcome was largely a foregone conclusion. Thus the archduke and recently deposed king of Bohemia was elected not only by the spiritual members of the college but also by Protestant Saxony and Brandenburg. Even the Palatine representative ultimately had to concur with the majority decision of the *Kurkolleg*, which traditionally tried to achieve a unanimous election.[11] From the moment he was elected and crowned Ferdinand had an enormous political capital at his disposal. Without the Emperor's assent no legitimate political settlement could ever be reached in Germany. Ferdinand, on the other hand, could outlaw his enemies for breach of the empire's peace and high treason and felony. Never clearly defined and often fragile, the Emperor's authority was nevertheless a factor of considerable significance.

Moreover the system of alliances which the Palatine politicians had built up before 1618 now started to disintegrate. Saxony, the most powerful Lutheran principality and no ally of the Palatinate in any case had never been sympathetic to the idea of a confrontation with the house of Habsburg and sided with the Emperor,[12] and other Protestant princes were at least reluctant to oppose the recently elected ruler of the Holy Roman Empire on the field of battle. They knew that their own authority was based on the legal framework of the empire which for all its shortcomings had in the past always safeguarded the rights of the estates and princes. Not a few Lutherans also showed a tendency to see radical Calvinism – which seemed to deny the sacramental character of the Eucharist – as a far worse enemy than Tridentine Catholicism, and the Emperor and his advisors had been careful to give moderate Protestants assurances that this was not be a war of religion but merely a campaign against an unlawful rebellion. The culprits were to be punished but the Peace of Augsburg on which the rights of Protestants rested was not to be called into question as such. Influenced by such assurances the members of the Protestant Union (founded in 1608 under Palatine leadership) and the princes of the League signed a treaty of neutrality in Ulm in July 1620. Under its terms neither side was to attack the other, so that the war would be limited, in theory, to Bohemia and the Habsburg dominions. This was an arrangement which strongly favoured Ferdinand II, Maximilian of Bavaria and their allies. Maximilian remained free to intervene in Bohemia and the Rhine Palatinate was in no way protected against a Spanish invasion.

The Triumph of the Catholic League

With the Union neutralised Maximilian was free to send his and the League's troops into Bohemia. Frederick V, the Elector Palatine, had been crowned king of Bohemia in November 1619. A year later his troops were defeated by the Catholic army in the Battle of the White Mountain near Prague on 8 November 1620. Frederick V's rather inept foreign policy and his failure to win allies had certainly considerably hampered all efforts to defend Bohemia. However, internal dissension among the Bohemian Estates, and the fact that the system of taxation and administration in the Kingdom remained as inefficient under the new

---

[11] Cf. A. Gotthard, *Säulen des Reiches. Die Kurfürsten im frühneuzeitlichen Reichsverband* (2 vols, Husum, 1999), vol. 1, pp. 86–100, vol. 2, pp. 704–11.

[12] F. Müller, *Kursachsen und der böhmische Aufstand 1618–1622* (Münster, 1997).

government as under the Habsburgs, had also undermined the Bohemian army's ability to fight. After the Battle of the White Mountain, Moravia, and even more so Bohemia, were subjected to a savage campaign of repression which was to last for several years. The leaders of the Bohemian Estates who had not been able to escape were executed. Protestantism was suppressed during the 1620s. Moreover the estates of larger sections of the old established elite were confiscated and their possessions distributed among Ferdinand's supporters or sold off to loyal noblemen at bargain prices. For the next two centuries the Austrian duchies – Upper Austria had actively participated in the rebellion, which had also received some support from Protestants in Lower Austria – as well as Moravia and Bohemia were to be dominated by a Catholic aristocracy of noble magnates with close links to the imperial court. In the two latter countries many members of this aristocracy were of foreign origin, hailing from other parts of the Habsburg monarchy, from southern Germany, Italy, or even Spain or Ireland although a number of native families who had always remained loyal to the old church, or had converted to Catholicism before 1618, continued to hold their own.[13]

Such were the long-term consequences of the Battle of the White Mountain. The more immediate problem facing Ferdinand and his allies after the victory, however, was how to deal with Frederick V. The elector and temporary king had fled Bohemia immediately after the battle, but he was not yet prepared to abandon his claim to the Bohemian crown. Although Spanish troops had already started to advance on the Lower Palatinate in 1620 and had occupied a number of towns west of the River Rhine, Frederick and his councillors could hope that their military position would improve once the main theatre of operations shifted away from Bohemia towards the Rhine valley. In spite of the gradual dissolution of the Protestant Union, Frederick could still count on a number of allies in this area, in particular, the Margrave Georg Frederick of Baden-Durlac and the Landgrave Moriz of Hesse-Cassel, who was himself a Calvinist. In 1621 Count Ernst of Mansfeld, a well-known military entrepreneur who had already fought for Frederick in Bohemia, managed to recruit more than 40,000 soldiers in Alsace to defend the Palatinate. Mansfeld's army was supported by smaller contingents under the command of the Margrave of Baden and Christian of Brunswick, the Protestant administrator of the bishopric of Halberstadt, who was a reckless adventurer.

Nonetheless the Protestant troops were no match for the army of the Catholic League commanded by Count Jean Tserclaes Tilly. Tilly, a veteran who had served his military apprenticeship in the Spanish army of Flanders, had already beaten the Protestant forces in Bohemia in 1620 and had occupied the Upper Palatinate around Amberg in 1621.[14] As the various Protestant commanders proved incapable of co-ordinating their operations, the Margrave of Baden and Christian were defeated separately in the battles of Wimpfen (6 May 1622) and Höchst (22 June 1622). Mansfeld's position became untenable. Officially dismissed by the Elector Palatine, he decided to retreat to the Netherlands together with Christian and the remnant of his troops. The Lower Palatinate was now lost. Whereas the western part of the Electorate beyond the Rhine was occupied by Spanish troops, the eastern districts came under the control of Maximilian of Bavaria, the head of the League. Maximilian had already occupied the Upper Palatinate the year before.

---

[13] T. Winkelbauer, 'Krise der Aristokratie? Zum Strukturwandel des Adels in den böhmischen und niederösterreichischen Ländern im 16. und 17. Jahrhundert', *Mitteilungen des Instituts für österreichische Geschichtsforschung*, 100 (1992), pp. 328–53; Evans, *Making*, pp. 201–13, cf. pp. 169–80; T. Knoz, 'Die Konfiskationen nach 1620 in (erb)länderübergreifender Perspektive. Thesen zu Wirkungen, Aspekten und Prinzipien des Konfiskationsprozesses', in P. Mat'a and T. Winkelbauer (eds), *Die Habsburgermonarchie 1620 bis 1740* (Stuttgart, 2006), pp. 99–130.

[14] M. Kaiser, *Politik und Kriegführung. Maximilian von Bayern, Tilly und die Katholische Liga im Dreißigjährigen Krieg* (Münster, 1999).

The Elector Palatine had in fact been officially outlawed by the Emperor in early 1621.[15] This entitled Ferdinand to confiscate Frederick's forfeited fiefs, possessions and dignities. It gave the Emperor a chance to reward his allies, in particular Maximilian of Bavaria, but also created a precedent for punishing other 'rebels' later. The imperial sentence against the Elector Palatine in January 1621 showed that the war had decisively changed the constitutional balance in the Holy Roman Empire in the Emperor's favour. During the years that were to follow Ferdinand deliberately used his position as supreme judge within the empire – which he exercised mostly through the imperial Aulic Council (Reichshofrat) – to reclaim dominions for the Catholic Church and to reward his followers, both Catholics and to a lesser extent loyal Lutherans as well, by adjudging disputes in their favour.[16]

For the time being Maximilian of Bavaria benefited most from this policy and from Frederick V's defeat. Ferdinand had transferred Frederick's electoral dignity to him in secret in September 1621. In February 1623 Maximilian was officially invested with the title of prince elector in Regensburg, where an assembly of princes, a *Deputationstag* had met. However, Ferdinand did not yet dare to grant the dignity of elector to the Bavarian Wittelsbachs in perpetuity. For the time being Maximilian was to bear the new title only during his life time.[17] There was little Frederick could do to counter the imperial decision. He did manage to assemble an army once more with Dutch support. While Mansfeld advanced eastwards from the Netherlands and took up a position in Eastern Frisia near the Dutch border, Christian of Halberstadt tried to move southwards with about 21,000 men. He planned to enter Bohemia, where he hoped to join forces with the prince of Transylvania, Gabor Bethlen. Bethlen had taken up the fight against the Habsburgs once again and, supported by troops which the Turks had supplied, managed to invade Hungary and Moravia. However, Tilly had already moved to northern Germany with superior forces before the fresh Protestant offensive got off the ground. Christian of Halberstadt was confronted by Tilly's forces at Stadtlohn near the Dutch border, on 6 August 1623. Christian's army was totally defeated and only a few thousand of his troops managed to escape into the Netherlands. In Eastern Frisia Mansfeld was wise enough to disband his army early in 1624 before a lack of supplies and money made his position untenable.

After Stadtlohn the war in Germany was, or so it seemed, over for the time being. On the other hand, the calm which returned in 1624 was deceptive. The balance of power in the Holy Roman Empire had changed so drastically since 1618 that this in itself was likely to provoke other European powers to intervene. Moreover, during the years 1619 to 1622 the theatres of operation had been areas traditionally under imperial control or the Emperor's influence. Northern Germany where Tilly's troops were garrisoned in 1624, and the areas east of the River Elbe were a different matter. Here armies fighting for the Roman Catholic Church and imperial authority were moving on more difficult ground than in the south.

The Danish War and the Road to the Edict of Restitution

While the theatre of war had moved north the conflict which had begun in 1618 was increasingly internationalised. Powers such as England and Denmark, and ultimately, after 1627/28, France, too, which so far had mostly stayed on the sidelines took up arms and

---

[15] C. Kampmann, *Reichsrebellion und kaiserliche Acht. Politische Strafjustiz im Dreißigjährigen Krieg und das Verfahren gegen Wallenstein 1634* (Münster, 1992), pp. 47–100.
[16] Brockmann, *Kaiseramt*, p. 252.
[17] Albrecht, *Maximilian*, pp. 569–71.

tried to redress the military and political balance in Central Europe. Among the European monarchs who had watched the Catholic triumph in Germany in the early 1620s with dismay was James I of England. He could not ignore the fact that the ill-fated Winter King was his own son-in-law, however much he had disapproved of the Bohemian adventure. James's prestige and honour as a king were at stake if he allowed his daughter and her husband to be driven not just from Prague but also from Heidelberg, their native capital, and be forced to take refuge in the Netherlands as exiles; moreover there were many people in England who felt strongly that it was the king's duty to defend both his family and the Protestant cause. James had initially tried to come to a peaceful accommodation with Spain. A dynastic marriage between his son and heir and a Spanish Infanta was to bring peace to Europe and was to ensure that the Prince Palatine could return to his native lands (though not to Bohemia of course). But James had overestimated both the Spanish will to come to an agreement with England and the influence Madrid wielded in Vienna and in Germany in general. In 1623 the Prince of Wales, Charles, tried to force the issue by travelling to Madrid to woo the Infanta who was to be his bride.[18] The journey was a complete disaster. The Spanish were clearly unwilling or unable to make concessions regarding the Palatinate but demanded full-scale toleration for Catholics in England. Charles returned infuriated from Spain and England was soon on its way to open war against Philip IV. James, who was still trying to avoid an outbreak of hostilities, conveniently died in early 1625 and Charles could have the revenge he had sought ever since being snubbed during his visit to Madrid. The English soon recognised that neither their fleet not their hastily recruited troops were up to a real war against the country which was still Europe's most formidable military power. But the mere fact that England declared war on Spain in 1625 gave encouragement to those Protestant powers in Central and Northern Europe who had so far refrained from openly entering the war, because they lacked allies outside Germany.

Foremost among this group of princes was Christian IV of Denmark, who was not just a ruler over a powerful composite monarchy, comprising Denmark, Norway, Schleswig and Scania, but also as duke of Holstein a prince of the empire.[19] Denmark was traditionally at odds both with the Dutch, who resented Danish control of the Sound, and with Sweden, its main rival for hegemony in the Baltic, so Christian was not cut out to be the ideal leader of a pan-Protestant alliance. In fact Spanish–Danish relations had traditionally been amicable, but the king was concerned about the Catholic triumphs in the empire. They seemed to threaten, in the long run at least, the survival of Protestantism itself, even in the north, and moreover Christian IV was not only a staunch Lutheran but also an ambitious man. He was the only prince of the empire to wear a royal crown, if one does not count the Winter King, and he hoped to secure some of the church lands in northern Germany which were on their way to becoming secular principalities for his own sons as permanent possessions. It was unlikely that an Emperor who had an army at his disposal to intervene in northern Germany would agree to such arrangements. The presence of Tilly's troops in northern Germany was therefore a matter of great concern for Christian IV. But he only decided to confront the League and the Emperor when a wider alliance against Ferdinand II seemed to take shape in 1625. At the end of this year his envoys signed a treaty at The Hague with the Dutch Republic and England which promised Denmark ample financial support for a war against the Catholic armies in Germany. Moreover, and this was equally important, the estates of the

---

[18] G. Redworth, *The Prince and the Infanta: the Cultural Politics of the Spanish Match* (New Haven, Conn., London, 2003); A. Samson (ed.), The Spanish Match: Prince Charles's Journey to Madrid, 1623 (Aldershot, 2006).

[19] P.D. Lockhart, *Denmark In the Thirty Years' War, 1618–1648. King Christian IV and the Decline of the Oldenburg State* (Selinsgrove, 1996), pp. 126–41, see also chapter 5 in this volume.

imperial Circle of Lower Saxony (as duke of Holstein, Christian was a member of the circle) elected Christian as their military commander (Kreisoberst) in May 1625, so that the king could now officially mobilise troops to defend Lower Saxony against Tilly's encroachments.

As it turned out, Christian himself received only a small part of the subsidies England had promised him in the Hague treaty and very little of this after 1626. Dutch and even more so French payments – which had also been part of the agreement with Denmark – were made more promptly and came closer to the sum, much smaller than the English share, initially promised. However, this could not disguise the fact that Christian IV's position was comparatively weak. His main supporters were the troops of the Lower Saxon Circle and even their support was only half hearted. The first military encounters between the troops of the League under Tilly's command and Christian IV's army in summer 1625 remained inconclusive. When hostilities recommenced in 1626, however, Tilly's position had improved considerably while Christian's had deteriorated, as the Emperor now took a much more active part in the military conflict in the north. So far Ferdinand had limited his own military activities mostly to his own hereditary lands and their eastern border in Hungary. He now took a much greater interest in the war at large. At some stage Ferdinand even thought about joining Spain in the war against the Dutch Republic, but his councillors advised him to reject Spanish demands to impose the imperial ban on the Dutch while attacking them from the east.[20] He nevertheless decided to send an army of his own to Lower Saxony to fight the Danes and their allies.

He entrusted the Czech nobleman, Albrecht von Wallenstein, with the command of this new imperial army. Born in 1583, Wallenstein had belonged to the minority of Bohemian and Moravian noblemen who had supported the Habsburgs in their fight against the Protestant Estates in 1618–20. Thanks to his enormous fortune – which he had partly amassed during the confiscations and the currency manipulations of the early 1620s in Bohemia – he was able to draw on an ample supply of loans for the initial recruitment of his troops.[21] Wallenstein's new army, growing within a short time to strength of about 50,000 men decisively changed the balance of military forces. Wallenstein's men were initially often ill-trained and many of them were Protestants including not a few of the regimental colonels so this was definitely not the army of a religious crusade. However this somewhat motley crew was sufficiently effective to beat Count Mansfeld. In April 1626 Mansfeld attempted to prevent Wallenstein's troops from crossing the Elbe by taking the imperialists' bridgehead at Dessau, but failed. Wallenstein turned the battle into a disastrous and bloody defeat for Mansfeld. With the remainder of his regiments Mansfeld tried to move to Silesia, but Wallenstein forced him to retreat to the Turkish-controlled Balkans where he died on his way to the Adriatic coast in Bosnia.

Meanwhile, Christian of Denmark had been beaten decisively by Tilly at Lutter am Barenberge on 26 August 1626. A number of strong fortresses in Holstein and in the archbishopric of Bremen garrisoned by Christian's troops delayed the final Danish defeat, but in 1627 when Wallenstein's forces, moving north-westwards from Silesia and growing all the time in numbers, advanced into Holstein, Christian's fate was sealed. The imperial forces occupied Jutland. For a time it seemed feasible to impose a peace settlement on the Danish king which would have forced him to abandon at least Holstein (and thereby his position within the empire) and possibly even Schleswig and Jutland as well, which would have come under imperial control. But such dreams which some imperial councillors

---

[20] Brockmann, *Kaiseramt*, p. 262.
[21] On Wallenstein see now G. Mortimer, *Wallenstein: The Enigma of the Thirty Years War* (Basingstoke, 2010).

entertained in early 1628 soon proved to be elusive.[22] At a merely military level, the Danish Islands, not to mention Norway and Danish Scania, were beyond Wallenstein's reach because he had no real fleet. In political terms the fear of a direct Swedish intervention in Germany and the outbreak of war in northern Italy in 1628, which required imperial intervention, also dampened Ferdinand's appetite for further adventures in the north. These factors explain why Christian ultimately managed to gain comparatively favourable terms in his negotiations with the Emperor. The prince-bishoprics which he had tried to claim for members of his family in northern Germany were lost, but the peace of Lübeck, signed in July 1629, left Christian's possessions north of the Elbe, that is Holstein, Schleswig and Jutland intact. Christian's allies were not all so lucky. The Dukes of Mecklenburg, an old and venerable dynasty going back to the twelfth century, were singled out for punishment. The Emperor pronounced their fiefs forfeited because of their treasonous alliance with Denmark. As supreme liege lord Ferdinand II created Albrecht von Wallenstein, his commander-in-chief and also his most important creditor, duke of Mecklenburg in June 1629, although the duchy had already been assigned to him in February of the previous year. This sudden rise of a mere Bohemian nobleman to a status that entitled him to consider princes from families who had provided the empire with rulers in the Middle Ages as his equals was highly controversial. Even Catholic princes resented this decision which they saw as an attack on the traditional political and social hierarchy, and Wallenstein hardly made himself any more popular by seeking quarters and supplies for his troops throughout the empire, including dominions ruled by Catholic princes. The resentment provoked by his high-handedness and the extortionate methods he employed in finding supplies and financial resources for his army fed into the political campaign led by Bavaria which forced Ferdinand to dismiss Wallenstein as commander of his armies in 1630. But two years earlier the greatest military entrepreneur of the Thirty Years' War was to all appearances at the height of his power.[23] Not only was he now a member of the *Reichsfürstenstand* (the exclusive estate of princes of the empire) ruling a large principality of his own, he was also appointed (in February 1628) 'General of the Oceanic and Baltic Seas', that is imperial Lord High Admiral. In this capacity he was to organise a naval offensive against Dutch trade in the Baltic. This was an idea which the Spaniards had successfully sold to Ferdinand II; if the Dutch Republic could be cut off from the supplies of grain, fish, wood and other raw materials imported from the Baltic it might be forced to sign a peace treaty with Madrid, which would allow Spain to declare that the long war against the Dutch rebels had ended in victory.[24] However, Wallenstein, personally no great friend of Spain even at this stage, pursued this project only half-heartedly. He did besiege the old Hanseatic city of Stralsund in Pomerania to gain a harbour for the imperial fleet which was to control the Baltic in the future in summer 1628, but abandoned the siege when the town garrison was re-enforced by Swedish troops.

The attention of the ruler he served, Ferdinand II, was about to move from the coast of the Baltic to northern Italy anyhow. The conflict between France and Spain about the inheritance of the last duke of Mantua who had died in December 1627 moved the Emperor to send some of his own troops to Italy in May 1629 and thus weakened his position in Germany. Shortly before the seriousness of the situation in Italy became visible he had, however, decided to use his military power in Germany and that of the League to enforce

---

[22] Brockmann, *Kaiseramt*, pp. 286–7.
[23] Wilson, *War*, pp. 399–407, 420–1.
[24] J. Alcala Zamora, *España, Flandes y el mar de norte (1618–1639)* (Barcelona, 1975), pp. 229–42, 267–82; J. I. Israel, 'The Politics of International Trade Rivalry during the Thirty Years' War: Gabriel de Roy and Olivares' Mercantilist Projects 1621–45', in idem, *Empires and Entrepots: The Dutch, The Spanish Monarchy and the Jews, 1585–1713* (London, 1990), pp. 213–46.

a revision of the prevailing interpretation of the Peace of Augsburg (1555). The Edict of Restitution which he enacted in March 1629 forced Protestant princes and cities to restore church property which they had acquired after this date (or rather after the date of the preliminary peace of Passau, 1552) to the Catholic Church, that is to the various monasteries, priories and bishoprics which had once owned these estates and lordships. This was a highly controversial decision which brought the empire much nearer to an all out religious war than it had ever been since 1618.

Thus in 1629, the year which marked the greatest triumph of the Emperor's armies over the Protestant 'rebels', the situation in the empire was far less stable then it seemed. The alliance between Ferdinand and Bavaria – the real foundation for the series of Catholic victories from 1620 onwards – suffered from severe strains, as Maximilian of Bavaria was seeking contacts and ultimately an alliance with France to counterbalance the potential drive for imperial 'absolutism' which seemed to threaten the 'Teutsche Libertet' (German freedom) of the princes which he cherished as much as his Protestant rivals and enemies.[25] Moreover, the moderate Lutherans led by the elector of Saxony who had so far silently and sometimes not so silently backed many of Ferdinand's decisions became increasingly restless, feeling threatened by the Edict of Restitution. Nevertheless, without outside intervention nobody within the empire would be capable of arresting the triumphant Catholic offensive against the strongholds of Protestantism let alone of redressing the balance of power in Central Europe. It was left to Gustav Adolph of Sweden to provide this outside intervention in 1630.

Selected Bibliography

Brockmann, T., *Dynastie, Kaiseramt und Konfession. Politik und Ordnungsvorstellungen Kaiser Ferdinands II. im Dreißigjährigen Krieg* (Paderborn, 2011).

Ernst, A., and Schindling A. (eds), *Liga und Union 1608/09: Konfessionelle Bündnisse im Reich. Weichenstellung zum Religionskrieg* (Stuttgart, 2010).

Evans, R.J.W., *The Making of the Habsburg Monarchy* (Oxford, 1979).

Gotthard, A., *Säulen des Reiches. Die Kurfürsten im frühneuzeitlichen Reichsverband* (2 vols, Husum, 1999).

Kaiser, M., *Politik und Kriegführung. Maximilian von Bayern, Tilly und die Katholische Liga im Dreißigjährigen Krieg* (Münster, 1999).

Knoz, T., 'Die Konfiskationen nach 1620 in (erb)länderübergreifender Perspektive. Thesen zu Wirkungen, Aspekten und Prinzipien des Konfiskationsprozesses', in P. Mat'a and T. Winkelbauer (eds), *Die Habsburgermonarchie 1620 bis 1740* (Stuttgart, 2006), pp. 99–130.

Lockhart, P.D., *Denmark In the Thirty Years' War, 1618–1648. King Christian IV and the Decline of the Oldenburg State* (Selinsgrove, 1996).

Louthan, H., *Converting Bohemia: Force and Persuasion in the Catholic Reformation* (Cambridge, 2009).

Mann, G., *Wallenstein: His Life Narrated*, transl. by C. Kessler (London, 1976).

Mortimer, G., *Wallenstein: The Enigma of the Thirty Years War* (Basingstoke, 2010).

Pursell, B.C., *The Winter King: Frederick V of the Palatinate and the Coming of the Thirty Years War* (Aldershot, 2003).

Thomas, A.L., *A House Divided: Wittelsbach Confessional Court Cultures in the Holy Roman Empire, 1550–1650* (Leiden, 2010).

---

[25] Albrecht, *Maximilian*, pp. 715–28.

11 1629–1635

Toby Osborne

The Dance of Europe's Princes, 1629–1630

> Pasquino: 'What news do you have, Marforio'.
> Marforio: 'They're dancing as usual in the house of Lady Europe'.[1]

Pasquino and Marforio were Rome's 'talking statues', antique sculptures that were news hubs, on which political satires were posted about Roman politics and international events. The 'Dance of Europe's Princes' was a commentary on Europe's wars in which various princes and states danced according to their fortunes. Written between 1634 and 1645, it understandably focused on Italy, though not exclusively, as Marforio satirised most of Europe's powers. Even the imperial *generalissimo* Albrecht von Wallenstein got a mention. What does this tell us about the Thirty Years' War? The war captured public imagination, even if it would be unwise to think that Europeans shared a single news culture.[2] Events in the Holy Roman Empire were narrated and glossed to German audiences, and also to others further afield, from England to Italy.[3] Equally, Germans and Europeans joined the dots of regional and international conflicts to see different political permutations of alliances and disputes, centred on the empire. As the war was partly a media event, so it was also a series of inter-connected military theatres. From the Atlantic and North Sea to the Baltic and Mediterranean, across Northern Europe and the empire to Italy, dynastic interests, territorial claims, constitutional disputes and religious rivalries were entwined in the dance of war and diplomacy.

That was certainly the case in 1629, a pivotal year for Europe and the empire in particular. In one sense it was a year of peace settlements, and indeed we should remember that war and peace, or at least the willingness to negotiate, went hand-in-hand throughout the conflict. As seen in the previous chapter, 1629 marked the resolution of Denmark's imperial war, following the peace of Lübeck. Christian IV's nephew, Charles I, had already settled his war with France that dated back to 1627, in a peace agreement signed at Susa on 24 April 1629. Charles I's appetite for conflict had largely dissipated following the assassination in September 1628 of his favourite, the duke of Buckingham, and the French peace marked the scaling down of England's direct European commitments. Later in the

---

[1] The National Archives, Kew SP 85/7/279–280, 'Ballo di Principi d'Europa'.
[2] N. Malcolm, *Reason of State, Propaganda and the Thirty Years War. An Unknown Translation by Thomas Hobbes* (Oxford, 2007), pp. 30–31.
[3] That was true for England until 1632, when the politically sensitive nature of the war forced the Caroline regime to censor news of foreign affairs. K. Sharpe, *The Personal Rule of Charles I* (New Haven and London, 1992), pp. 78–9, 646–7.

year, in September 1629, Denmark's Scandinavian rival, Sweden, agreed to a five-year truce with Poland, mediated by France, giving Sweden a share of toll dues from Polish ports, together with control of Livonia and parts of Prussia. France's settlement with England and mediation of the Swedish-Polish Peace of Altmark, coupled with the resolution of France's domestic Huguenot problem, were part of a process of enabling the regime to pressurise the Spanish and imperial Habsburgs, as we will see. But while Richelieu reached the goal of an English peace first, his Spanish counterpart, Olivares, was not far behind. On 15 November 1630 an Anglo-Spanish peace was eventually finalised, partly through the mediation of the artist-diplomat Peter Paul Rubens, working on behalf of the regime in the Spanish Netherlands, and also through the Savoyard ambassador, Alessandro Scaglia.

Why was a north Italian diplomat so closely involved in the Anglo-Spanish peace? For Savoy, as for France and Spain, England was a potential lever in international power politics, for so long as England continued to fight either France or Spain, that power would be constrained elsewhere, to the advantage of the other. In short, Savoy wanted to prolong England's French war to limit any involvement in the war over Mantua and Monferrato that followed the death in December 1627 of the last Gonzaga duke. Savoy had a dynastic claim in the region, though its principal rival, the duke of Nevers, was looking for French aid in support of his claim. When the Anglo-French war was settled first, it correspondingly became imperative for Savoy to resolve the Spanish war.[4] Given the sensitivity of north Italy to Spain's composite monarchy and its logistics between the Mediterranean and Northern Europe, the conflict threatened to draw France and Spain into a direct war. The dispute, which continued until 1631, furthermore involved the emperor. Savoy was an imperial fief, like Mantua and Monferrato, and the conflict was grounded on a disputed succession in theory subject to a settlement by the feudal overlord. The emperor was compelled to intervene, in part to support Spain, though also because of his feudal responsibilities, not least because of the meddling of France, a power outside the Holy Roman Empire and because of requests for arbitration from rival claimants.[5]

Not that Ferdinand II's intervention was welcomed in the empire. Wallenstein, who was instructed to dispatch troops to Italy, understood that the war, seemingly fought to protect Spanish interests, would do little for the German portion of the empire. For different reasons, the emperor's Jesuit confessor, and one major (though not the only) influence at the imperial court, William Lamormaini, also wished to see a resolution of the north Italian war. If Europe's Catholic powers could settle their differences, then they might at last cooperate to address definitively Protestantism in the empire, in what he believed was a holy war against heresy.[6] Lamormaini failed to neutralise north Italy as an imperial concern, but he was a strong advocate of one of the most significant – and contentious – decisions of Ferdinand II's imperial reign. The Edict of Restitution, issued in March 1629, was in part borne out of Ferdinand II's confidence, following the military successes of the 1620s, and convictions partly fuelled by his confessor. Here, so it seemed, was an opportunity to assert his rightful authority as emperor. Yet a belief in rights was not his prerogative alone. The edict was a grievous body-blow to imperial Protestants, a breach of trust on the

---

[4]   T. Osborne, *Dynasty and Diplomacy in the Court of Savoy. Political Culture and the Thirty Years' War* (Cambridge, 2002), part III.

[5]   D. Parrott, 'The Mantuan Succession, 1627–31: A Sovereignty Dispute in Early Modern Europe', *The English Historical Review*, 112/445 (1997): pp. 20–65. On north Italy and the Thirty Years' War, see Sven Externbrink's chapter in this volume.

[6]   The emperor's relationship with his Jesuit confessor has been a long-standing theme of R. Bireley's work, in particular: *Religion and Politics in the Age of the Counterreformation: Emperor Ferdinand II, William Lamormaini, S.J., and the Formation of Imperial Policy* (Chapel Hill and London, 1981); *The Jesuits and the Thirty Years War: Kings, Courts, and Confessors* (Cambridge, 2003).

emperor's part, and evidence of the apparent extent of his ambitions in rolling back the Reformation. Even Catholic rulers harboured concerns. Ferdinand II had issued the edict unilaterally, without consulting the empire's princes. As we saw previously, Maximilian of Bavaria, the leading Catholic prince and effective leader of the Catholic League, may well have felt ambivalence towards Ferdinand II, while Wallenstein too saw the edict as folly; it generated additional political problems for the emperor when he had enough on his plate as it was.[7] This gross political miscalculation on Ferdinand II's part was all the worse because at this same moment he sought the goodwill of the electors to support the election of his son, Ferdinand of Hungary, as King of the Romans. In fact, if the papal nuncio in Vienna, Giovanni Battista Pallotto, is to be believed, the emperor himself wanted to resolve north Italy, in part to secure the election.[8]

Accordingly, the emperor called an electoral meeting, which convened at Regensburg between July and November 1630. In fact this was closer to a general diet of the empire's rulers, though the Protestant electors refused to attend in person, instead sending delegates. It was equally evident that the emperor would not obtain a *carte blanche* for his son's election, which in any case was not even a formal issue on the meeting's agenda. Whatever the emperor's successes during the 1620s, or possibly because of them, imperial princes were wary of Ferdinand, and also of his generalissimo's power. In the first place, they wanted Wallenstein removed. Additionally, they were reluctant to endorse interventions in support of Spain in Italy and the Netherlands, and were concerned about constitutional developments in the empire. Perhaps surprisingly, Ferdinand complied with calls against Wallenstein, and in August 1630 he was dismissed. However, even this did not secure the election of his son – that only happened in 1636, and not before further meddling from France, who saw this as an opportunity to unsettle Habsburg power by suggesting alternative candidates.

Enter Sweden, 1630–1632

While attention in the empire was to a degree fixed on Regensburg, events further north, on the Baltic coast, would shortly determine the war's direction. During the 1620s, Sweden had become increasingly agitated by events in the empire. The confluence of Denmark's defeat and Spain's continuing war with the Dutch raised the prospect of a joint Spanish and imperial Habsburg campaign of economic warfare in the Baltic to squeeze the rebellious Netherlands, as mentioned in the previous chapter. It was also possible that the imperial forces might side with Poland to exert further control in the region, a particular concern for Sweden, given Poland's claims to the Swedish throne dating back to the deposition in 1599 of the Polish king Sigismund III Vasa as king of Sweden. Despite Wallenstein's reluctance to pursue Spain's Baltic Design, and its eventual failure, these prospects were far from welcome in Sweden. Indeed, by 1628 Sweden had already become embroiled in the empire, following the decision in June to send reinforcements to the besieged Baltic port of Stralsund.

In the wake of protracted discussions within Sweden's governing regime, and some continuing attempts to negotiate with Wallenstein (exhausting the route of peace), the Swedish king, Gustav Adolph, took the decision to intervene more forcefully in the empire. On 6 July 1630 he landed on the island of Usedom off the Pomeranian coast, albeit with a

---

[7] G. Mortimer, *Wallenstein. The Enigma of the Thirty Years War* (Basingstoke, 2010), p. 113.
[8] R. Becker (ed.), *Nuntiaturberichte aus Deutschland nebst ergänzenden Aktenstücken. Vierte Abteilung, 17. Jahrhundert, 4. Bd.: Nuntiaturen des Giovanni Battista Pallotto und des Ciriaco Rocci (1630–1631)* (Tübingen, 2009), p. 64.

relatively modest force of around 14,000 troops, with reinforcements coming from Stralsund and others arriving later in the summer. His precise reasons for doing so remain debatable. Was it part of a wider strategy to create a Swedish *imperium* in Northern Europe? Was it for economic ambitions? Was it, rather, to uphold German liberties, or to protect Protestant co-religionists? After all, the landing coincided with the centenary of the Lutheran Augsburg Confession, and according to Pallotto, writing in August 1630, Gustav Adolph was motivated 'only for zeal of Lutheranism and to free the people from the oppressions of soldiers'.[9] None of these explanations alone seems entirely credible, though not for want of evidence. The Swedish king was attuned to the need to explain himself, though he did so to different audiences – both domestic and international – with different reasons. Perhaps the most widely known justification was the Manifesto, published in June 1630. Remarkably it appeared in 5 languages and 23 editions, with a clear eye on a European readership, reminding us of the Thirty Years' War as a media war. In the document, which varied slightly for different audiences, Gustav Adolph catalogued his grievances, in particular the push of imperial forces to the Baltic, the treatment his delegates had received when they sought to attend the Danish-imperial peace talks at Lübeck, the interception of Swedish courtiers, and the aggression against the Swedish garrison at Stralsund, arguably a declaration of war by itself. There was, on the other hand no mention in this document of religion, nor much about German liberties. Nor did the Manifesto articulate an over-arching strategy – the Swedes had indeed landed without extensive maps of the empire. The decision to intervene was, so it seems, taken in self-defence, perhaps even to uphold Sweden's national identity deserving of international respect.[10]

Sweden's broader propaganda campaign targeted international Protestant sentiments, but this did not mean that Lutheran princes were supportive, as Sweden's intervention provoked an ambivalent response. Most strikingly, the two leading Protestant powers, George William, the Calvinist elector of Brandenburg and John George, the Lutheran elector of Saxony, were unwilling to ally with the Swedes. John George's position was, at best, one of 'nervous apathy'.[11] Gustav Adolph, despite being a co-religionist, was not an imperial prince; he was an unwelcome foreign presence threatening to complicate the crisis provoked by the Edict of Restitution. The Saxon elector might even have been duty-bound to oppose him. Ferdinand II's apparent determination to stand by the edict nevertheless left John George in a difficult position, unwilling to support Sweden, yet deeply concerned by the emperor's high-handed policies. In fact, the Catholic position was potentially open to moderation, and we should be cautious about assuming that unbending confessional ideology shaped all the empire's princes. Attempts to resolve the conflict over Mantua and Monferrato had resulted

---

[9] J.R. Paas, 'The Changing Image of Gustavus Adolphus on German Broadsheets, 1630–3', *Journal of the Warburg and Courtauld Institutes*, 59 (1996), pp. 209–10; Becker (ed.), *Nuntiaturberichte aus Deutschland*, p. 243. On Sweden's reasons for intervening consult, for example, P. Piirimäe, 'Just War in Theory and Practice: The Legitimation of Swedish Intervention in the Thirty Years War', *The Historical Journal*, 45/3 (2002), pp. 499–523; P.D. Lockhart, *Sweden in the Seventeenth Century* (Basingstoke, 2004), pp. 39–44. For an older view see also M. Roberts, *Gustavus Adolphus. A History of Sweden 1611–1632* (2 vols, London, New York, Toronto, 1953), vol. 2, Chapter VI, and for a historiographical assessment see W. Bucholz, 'Der Eintritt Schwedens in den Dreißigjährigen Krieg in der schwedischen und deutschen Historiographie des 19. und 20. Jahrhunderts', *Historische Zeitschrift*, 245/2 (1987): pp. 291–314. See also the chapter by Pärtel Piirimäe in this volume.

[10] The Manifesto can be read in English in two accessible recent collections of documents: P.H. Wilson (ed.), *The Thirty Years War. A Sourcebook* (Basingstoke, 2010), pp. 122–30, and T. Helfferich (ed.), *The Thirty Years War. A Documentary History* (Indianapolis, 2009), pp. 98–107. On the idea of national identity as a motive for intervention consult E. Ringmar, *Identity, Interest and Action. A cultural explanation of Sweden's intervention in the Thirty Years War* (Cambridge, 1996).

[11] Lockhart, *Sweden*, p. 50.

in a treaty, agreed at Regensburg on 13 October 1630, but this was repudiated by France. The resumption of war may have persuaded some Catholic powers that the emperor would need to offer concessions to Protestants in order to fend off further difficulties in the empire, and accordingly invited Protestant counterparts to a meeting in Frankfurt early in 1631. For their part, the Saxon and Brandenburg electors sought a third-way, independent of both Gustav Adolph and Ferdinand II, and met in February 1631 at Leipzig in a conference involving the empire's Protestant powers. The aim was in part theological, to seek a Lutheran-Calvinist accommodation, though also to establish a more unified response to the proposed meeting at Frankfurt and the Edict of Restitution, and indeed to form a viable military force in the empire that could defend collective interests. The Leipzig Manifesto, issued on 12 April 1631, set out the plan to raise an army of 40,000 troops, ostensibly for defensive purposes, to protect the constitutional rights of the Protestant signatories.[12]

While German Protestants were generally ambivalent towards Sweden, aside from those who had little to lose, the Swedish king received backing from beyond the empire. On 23 January 1631, he entered a five-year alliance with France, providing subsidies in return for the continuation of the campaign in the empire. Reflecting the sensitivity of France's alignment with the Lutheran Swedes, the alliance stipulated that in lands occupied by Sweden, imperial law would be recognised and freedom of worship (including Catholicism) would be exercised. Evidently, this was not a full endorsement of Gustav Adolph. Indeed, in another alliance clause, Sweden was obliged not to attack members of the Catholic League – principally Bavaria – so long as the League did not attack Sweden or her allies. The French regime was engaged in a delicate act of juggling potential allies in a strategy of pressurising the Habsburgs. On 30 May 1631, France ratified a notionally secret treaty at Fontainebleau with Maximilian of Bavaria, an eight-year mutual defensive alliance with recognition of Bavaria's imperial title, which had the potential for France of splitting the leading member of the Catholic League from the Habsburg Emperor. Maximilian's motives, by contrast, should be understood as analogous to those of John George of Saxony. He too was wary of the emperor's seeming ambitions cutting against constitutional rights, of Wallenstein as a rival commander, and of Gustav Adolph. Furthermore, Maximilian's acquisition of the Upper Palatinate and part of the Lower Palatinate remained to a degree fragile, not least as the Spanish seemed willing to negotiate with England over the Palatinate. The French treaty, though, ultimately proved fruitless; however reluctantly, the French were to prove more consistent in supporting Sweden, principally because of the Swedes' remarkable successes rather than a commitment to their cause, underlining the fundamental incompatibility of the contrary alliances.

Still, Sweden's military fortunes until early 1631 were muted. Swedish forces were initially hemmed into the relatively poor territory of Pomerania by a strong imperial cordon, although the need to breakout was precipitated by the requirement to secure territories that could sustain those forces and by the growing threat to the city of Magdeburg, which had declared for Sweden by August 1630. Eventually Gustav Adolph managed to push westwards towards the Elbe and south along the Oder river, capturing Frankfurt-an-der-Oder in Brandenburg on 3 April 1631. He also acquired a significant new ally, Brandenburg, who reluctantly sided with the Swedes when Gustav Adolph forced the issue by massing troops outside the electoral capital of Berlin in May 1631. But while the Swedes spread their operations through Pomerania and Mecklenburg (eventually reinstating its deposed dukes), and southwards, the fortunes of Magdeburg came to a violent end. The Protestant bastion that in 1550–1551 had stood against Emperor Charles V, fell to imperial troops on 20

---

[12] Roberts, *Gustavus Adolphus*, vol. 2, pp. 483–90.

May 1631. An estimated 20,000 of its inhabitants died among the flames and violence that came as Tilly's troops ransacked the city. It was quite possibly the bloodiest episode for civilians of the entire Thirty Years' War, and sent shockwaves around Europe.[13] The papacy expressed its jubilation. Understandably, the mood was different among Protestants, though some had been reluctant to endorse what had arguably been a rebellion against the emperor. In blunt terms it was a serious embarrassment to Gustav Adolph, who had impotently pledged to support the city as one of his few German allies. Still, it confirmed to some the emperor's brutal ambitions, and Tilly made matters worse by moving troops towards Saxony's borders, in part to secure much-needed resources for his troops, though also to exert pressure on the electorate in the wake of Ferdinand II's repudiation of the Leipzig Manifesto. By September 1631, John George, inherently conservative as he was, and still wary of Gustav Adolph, had little option than to ally with the Swedes, given this direct threat to his dynastic territory. It was clear that this would have dreadful consequences: 'Germany will have a cruel and bloody war', as the nuncio Pallotto put it.[14]

These words soon became painfully true for the Catholic cause. The outcome of Tilly's threat to Saxony and of Saxony's reluctant alliance with Sweden was a battle that transformed the war. On 17 September 1631, Tilly's estimated 37,000 troops, including soldiers back from north Italy following the conclusion of the war there in March 1631, met a combined Swedish and Saxon force of 39,000 troops at Breitenfeld, near Leipzig. The result was a spectacular victory for Gustav Adolph and a hammer blow to the morale of Catholic forces.[15] For some Protestants, it was just retribution for Magdeburg. Indeed, Gustav Adolph's stunning successes thereafter confirmed for them his providential role, reflected in the steady stream of hagiographic polemics that eventually peaked in 1632. The 'Lion of the North' was a new Alexander or Hercules, or a hero of biblical resonance, a Judas Maccabeus, Gideon, or a King David, ironic, given he had landed in 1630 with little sense of a long-term strategy.[16] After Breitenfeld, the Swedish king was nevertheless faced with the question of what to do next. He could have pursued Tilly, or even have pushed towards Vienna, as some imperialists feared; instead he moved to the Rhine-Main valley, partly to secure winter quartering for his troops, capturing Würtzberg and Frankfurt-am-Main on his way. On 23 December 1631, he took control of Mainz, which became his principal Rhenish headquarters. Meanwhile, a Saxon force under the command of the former imperial general, Hans George von Arnim, augmented by Swedish forces, had pressed into Silesia and Bohemia, taking Prague in November 1631. Still, Gustav Adolph harboured greater ambitions for the following year, for which he envisaged coordinating several independent forces across the empire, partly because no single territory would have been able to sustain his entire army.

When campaigning resumed, 1632 was to prove the most intensive year of the entire Thirty Years' War. Gustav Adolph had to balance competing needs: defending his Baltic flank; keeping the unreliable Saxons from settling with the emperor; and pressing his advantage where he could. He also had to respond to circumstances as they changed. The

---

[13] H. Medick and P. Selwyn, 'Historical Event and Contemporary Experience: The Capture and Destruction of Magdeburg in 1631', *History Workshop Journal*, 52 (2001): pp. 23–48.

[14] Becker (ed.), *Nuntiaturberichte aus Deutschland*, p. 522.

[15] For a detailed account of the battle consult W. P. Guthrie, *Battles of the Thirty Years War. From White Mountain to Nordlingen, 1618–1635* (Westport CT, 2002), Chapter 1. Figures for the sizes of armies involved vary, though here I have used P. H. Wilson, *Europe's Tragedy. A History of the Thirty Years War* (London, 2009), pp. 472–3.

[16] Paas, 'The Changing Image of Gustavus Adolphus', pp. 205–44. See also S.S. Tschopp, *Heilsgeschichtliche Deutungsmuster in der Publizistik des Dreißigjährigen Krieges. Pro- und antischwedische Propaganda in Deutschland 1628 bis 1635* (Frankfurt am Main, Bern, New York, Paris, 1991), especially part 2.

decision in the previous year not to pursue Tilly enabled the general to regroup. The city of Bamberg had been occupied following a unilateral action taken by the Swedish general Gustav Horn in February 1631, but Tilly, augmented by support from Bavaria, moved against Bamberg, in effect nullifying the Treaty of Bärwalde's clauses of non-aggression between Sweden and her allies and the Catholic League. Gustav Adolph's counter-moves forced the imperial commander to retire to the Upper Palatinate, and perhaps more importantly left the Swedes free now to attack League territories. Gustav Adolph decided to move against Bavaria, on 31 March 1632 entering the city of Nuremberg. On 15 April 1632, he met Tilly again on the battlefield, at the River Lech, as the Swedes looked for a crossing into the Bavarian heartland. The battle was a second major victory for the Swedes, and Tilly left the field mortally wounded. The victory also left Bavaria exposed to Sweden's full force. With a sense of historical irony, on 17 May 1632 Gustav Adolph entered Munich in the company of Frederick of the Palatinate, whose electoral title and a swathe of territory had been ceded to Maximilian. Bavaria's effort to stand aside from war in the empire, underscored by the Treaty of Fontainebleau, had evidently failed.

Sweden's unexpected successes from late 1631 had the potential to transform power relations in the empire. The landgrave of Hesse-Kassel, for one, hoped that a re-working of the imperial constitution might yield an electoral title as a reward for supporting Sweden. From others, Sweden expected feudal dues as if Gustav Adolph were a new overlord, and indeed expected the emperor's own mandates to be ignored.[17] It also seemed, from England's perspective, that Gustav Adolph might provide the crucial key to finally resolving the fate of the Palatinate. In the period after the settlement of the Anglo-Spanish war, Charles I had pinned what hopes he still had on negotiations with Spain, grounded on the possibility that England might re-enter the European war against the Dutch. However, nothing came of the Anglo-Spanish initiative, in part because of the perennial problem that whatever the Spanish might have wished regarding the Palatinate, the imperial Habsburgs had other priorities, and England had no leverage with Bavaria or the emperor.[18] Given Sweden's providential progress, it was therefore hardly surprising that Charles I of England turned to Gustav Adolph as an alternative. In fact in 1630, Charles I had given permission for levies to be raised for the Swedish army, reminding us that a significant proportion of Gustav Adolph's fighting force were mercenaries, including a large number of Scotsmen.[19] Moreover, Frederick had clearly thrown his lot in with the Swedes, though he was to die in November 1632 frustrated in his hopes of restoring the Palatinate, not least because of Gustav Adolph's heavy conditions for support.[20]

Exit Gustav Adolph, 1632–1635

Breitenfeld might have transformed the fortunes of Protestantism, and definitively marked Sweden's emergence as the leading Scandinavian power, supplanting Denmark, but Sweden was not always successful militarily. The aspiration of a coordinated series of campaigns

---

[17] Wilson, *Europe's Tragedy*, pp. 484–7.
[18] L.J. Reeve, 'Quiroga's Paper of 1631: A Missing Link in Anglo-Spanish Diplomacy during the Thirty Years War', *The English Historical Review*, 101/401 (1986): pp. 913–26.
[19] A. Grosjean, 'Scotland: Sweden's Closest Ally?', in S. Murdoch (ed.), *Scotland and the Thirty Years' War, 1618–1648* (Leiden, 2001).
[20] B.C. Pursell, *The Winter King. Frederick V of the Palatinate and the Coming of the Thirty Years' War* (Aldershot, 2003), chapter 9.

in 1632 proved too difficult to manage. At the same time, imperial opponents were still a threat – as Tilly's forces had regrouped and had sought to regain some initiative, Field-Marshal Pappenheim's imperial forces continued to harry the Swedes in north-western Germany. Nevertheless, it was evident to the emperor that if he were to challenge the Swedes seriously he would have to recall the general who had the skills to muster and command a sufficiently large army: Wallenstein. While he was far from enthusiastic – exhausted, physically and financially, by military command – Wallenstein eventually agreed to return, albeit officially for only three months from December 1631, a position restated in April 1632. Over the course of the winter of 1631–32 he thus began regrouping his forces, and by the spring of 1632 Wallenstein had managed to re-take both Bohemia and Silesia from Arnim's Saxon troops, with whom Wallenstein had earlier engaged in informal talks (something that raised the possibility of Saxony reneging on the Swedish alignment). Again, Gustav Adolph faced difficult strategic dilemmas. While he might have wished to push towards the emperor's territorial heartlands, his freedom of action was constrained by the challenges of the Catholic League and Wallenstein's forces, and of potential threats to his logistical routes to the Baltic. He was also aware of the threat to Saxony itself, a key, if unreliable, ally, as Wallenstein's parleys suggested. Still, it proved difficult to force Wallenstein to a decisive engagement. Gustav Adolph established his forces at Nuremberg, while Wallenstein moved into heavily defended positions to squeeze the Swedes. Seeking to break the stalemate, in September 1632, a Swedish force under Gustav Adolph met Wallenstein at an old fortress, Alte Veste, around which the imperial general had dug in. Wallenstein triumphed, and the defeat was a blow to the morale of the Swedes, who were forced to retreat.

Fearing Wallenstein's threat to Saxony and to the Baltic logistical routes, Gustav Adolph had little choice but to confront the imperial general again. On 16 November 1632 they met on the battlefield, at Lützen, near the city of Leipzig recently occupied by Wallenstein – in fact it was the only time Wallenstein personally took to the field, though he had taken part in the action at the fortress of Alte Veste. While Wallenstein had not expected the battle, assuming that winter would bring an end to campaigning, on the day, his estimated 19,000 troops matched those under Gustav Adolph's command. The outcome of the battle, though, was not entirely clear – it was at best a tactical victory for the Swedes, given the withdrawal of imperial forces from the field (Wallenstein retreated to Bohemia).[21] However, just as Breitenfeld had transformed the fortunes of Protestantism in the empire, so Lützen itself had dramatic consequences: Gustav Adolph, the 'Lion of the North', was killed, shot twice by an imperial musketeer. The Swedish regency regime, under the direction of Gustav Adolph's former chancellor, Axel Oxenstierna (the heir, Christina, was aged six at the time), needed to reassert control of a potentially dangerous political and military situation. On 9 April 1633, France effectively renewed the terms of the Treaty of Bärwalde, a prelude to the formation of a league of Protestants, agreed at Heilbronn, including powers from the Franconian, Swabian and Rhenish Circles. The Protestant league would finance the war effort, under Sweden's overall command, until its aims and Sweden's 'satisfaction' were met, though more problematically it was not clear if it could meet all the army's financial requirements, and it did not include either of the Protestant electors – Brandenburg, in particular, had deepening grievances over the future of Swedish-controlled Pomerania, to which it had a dynastic claim. Oxenstierna nevertheless found himself one of Europe's most powerful political figures.[22]

---

[21] Guthrie, *Battles of the Thirty Years War*, Chapter 7.
[22] M. Roberts, 'Oxtenstierna in Germany, 1633–1636', *Scandia* (1982): pp. 61–105.

Despite the need to regroup after Lützen, it should not be assumed that Protestant forces were spent in 1633. Rather, the military situation seemed to be in the balance for both the Swedes and imperialists. Command of the Swedish forces was divided between rival commanders, while campaigning continued in separate theatres, though providing for these troops remained difficult – indeed, Oxenstierna had to fall back on a customary but problematical policy of promising lands to officers as payment, while allowing commanders to extract contributions from occupied territories, in part as a response to a mutiny of unpaid troops in April 1633. However, the imperial cause was not secure itself, as Wallenstein was once again the focal point of deepening hostility and resentment among Catholics in the empire, and indeed further afield. To Maximilian of Bavaria, Wallenstein remained a rival. To others, Wallenstein seemed more concerned with his own interests, at crucial moments slow to engage with the enemy. Prior to his dismissal in 1630, he had won few friends by his failure to take Stralsund. His apparent reluctance to pursue a campaign after Gustav Adolph's death only furthered speculation against him, despite his victory over a Swedish force at Steinau in September that resulted in the recapture of Silesia. Moreover, his decision after Steinau to spend the winter of 1633–34 quartering his troops on imperial lands in Bohemia and Moravia, with Pilsen as his headquarters, generated further hostility at the imperial court, not least as Bavaria was still partly occupied and Regensburg had been captured by Bernard of Saxe-Weimar on 14 November 1633. Eventually, in February 1634, Ferdinand II issued the order to have Wallenstein taken, dead or alive, on the charge of treason. While attempting to elude arrest, on 25 February Wallenstein was killed by a group of Scottish and Irish officers. Rome's Marforio astutely observed that Maximilian 'throws off his cares to dance, totally captivated, looking from the chamber's room with great joy at Wallenstein dead in the street'.[23] Nor was his murder unwelcome beyond the empire. As the previous chapter noted, the Spanish regime was losing patience with the general. After all, Wallenstein had proved unreliable in supporting the Baltic Design, and had disapproved of the emperor's Italian intervention – as early as 1628, the marquis of Aytona, a leading figure in the regime in the Spanish Netherlands, had come to see Wallenstein as capricious, while Spanish ambassadors in Vienna reported back their lack of faith in him, even if Olivares for one still harboured hopes of the *generalissimo* until the last moment.[24]

To be sure, the war had become a growing concern to the Spanish, not least Sweden's advances to the Rhineland. From the later sixteenth century, Spanish policy-making had been grounded on resolving the insoluble war with the Dutch – the rebels proved seemingly impossible to defeat entirely, yet the Spanish felt compelled to assert claims to what they saw as their rightful territory. This strategy depended on maintaining lines of communication between north Italy and the Netherlands, an immense drain on Spain's resources. It was also coupled with a belief – often misplaced – that both branches of the Habsburgs should cooperate. That had in part underpinned the Baltic Design and the war for Mantua and Monferrato. Yet this too proved difficult. As we have seen, the emperor faced foot-dragging from Wallenstein and hostility from some of his Catholic princes over the apparent willingness to support Spain. The Swedes' intervention made matters all the worse, because not only did they directly threaten the Spanish Road, but also because they effectively forced the French themselves to engage more actively in protecting their interests along their eastern borders. French foreign policy-making under Richelieu was seemingly guided by principles of self-defence, and of the fears of Habsburg hegemony, whatever its reality. France's principal aim, it has been argued, was to bring peace to Christendom, grounded on a new conception

---

[23] TNA SP 85/7/279v, 'Ballo'.

[24] R. Vermeir, *En estado de guerra. Felipe IV y flandes 1629–1648* (Córdoba, 2006), p. 24; J.H. Elliott, *The Count-Duke of Olivares. The Statesman in an Age of Decline* (New Haven and London, 1988), pp. 467–70.

of European power, which by definition entailed confrontation with the Habsburgs.²⁵ This was to be achieved in part by supporting third parties such as the Dutch Republic, Sweden and Bavaria, though also by ensuring that France maintained strategic influence in north Italy and the Rhineland. Accordingly, during the early 1630s the French offered 'protection' to a series of Rhenish powers, including the archbishop of Trier, and later the archbishop of Cologne, in return for the right to garrison troops in a string of fortresses.²⁶ The duchy of Lorraine also came under this strategic posture. The duke had been far from trustworthy as a neighbour, at times seeming to offer support to Richelieu's various domestic opponents, and to Spain. In January 1632, Duke Charles IV of Lorraine and France had nevertheless signed a treaty, at Vic, by which the French would garrison troops in the duchy, and would be able to use the duchy for passage through to the Rhine. Despite Charles IV's attempts to preserve his independence, and indeed his willingness to continue supporting Richelieu's enemies, by the end of the summer of 1634, the duchy was under French control.

France's support of the Dutch, the intervention in north Italy, and the policies towards the Rhineland and Lorraine predictably provoked the Spanish. The 1630s were marked by a growing polemical campaign on both sides that targeted both domestic and international audiences, playing on the competing rhetoric of French support of heretics or of Spanish ambitions. Indeed, it seems that the French and Spanish had come to see war as probable, if not entirely inevitable, whatever the attempts by the papacy to mediate.²⁷ The Spanish also took more practical action. In September 1633 the duke of Feria crossed the Alps to undertake a successful, but relatively small-scale, campaign at the head of his army of Alsace, culminating in the recapture of Breisach and the safeguarding of Alsace (a campaign that had diverted imperial forces elsewhere and had allowed Bernard of Saxe-Weimar to take Regensburg). In May 1634, Philip IV's younger brother, the Cardinal-Infante Ferdinand, made his formal entry into Milan, as a prelude to his planned progress from the Italian peninsula northwards. The Spanish wanted the cardinal-infante to secure the Road and to take command of the Spanish Netherlands, and accordingly, he moved northwards at the head of an army of around 15,000 troops. Although Sweden and her allies had resumed campaigning in July 1634, pushing once more into Bohemia, imperial forces under the command of the emperor's son, Ferdinand of Hungary, recaptured Regensburg in July 1634, followed by Donauwörth in August, and then moved to besiege the city of Nördlingen. There, he was joined by the cardinal-infante, and on 6 September 1634, their combined force of around 33,000 troops met an army of 23,000 troops from Sweden, Saxe-Weimar and the Heilbronn League. The result was a major victory for the Catholic forces that effectively ended Sweden as a leading combatant in the empire and which ensured the security of the Spanish Road, albeit on a route further east from French-protected territories.²⁸

---

²⁵ For this view see, for example, K. Malettke, 'France's Imperial Policy during the Thirty Years' War and the Peace of Westphalia', in K. Bussmann and H. Schilling (eds), *1648. War and Peace in Europe* (2 vols, Münster, Osnabrück, 1999). The theme has been explored also by H. Weber. For example, '"Une bonne paix". Richelieu's foreign policy and the peace of Christendom', in J. Bergin and L. Brockliss (eds), *Richelieu and his Age* (Oxford, 1992).

²⁶ On France's Rhenish strategy consult H. Weber, 'Richelieu et le Rhin', *Revue historique*, 239 (1968): pp. 265–80.

²⁷ J.M. Jover, *1635. Historia de una polémica y semblanzaa de una generacion* (Madrid, 2003 edn). On the road to war see R.A. Stradling, 'Olivares and the Origins of the Franco-Spanish War, 1627–35', *The English Historical Review*, 101 (1986), pp. 68–94; D. Parrott, 'The Causes of the Franco-Spanish War of 1635–59', in J. Black (ed.), *The Origins of War in Early Modern Europe* (Edinburgh, 1987); A. Leman, *Urbain VIII et la rivalité de la France et de la Maison d'Autriche de 1631 à 1635* (Lyon and Paris, 1920).

²⁸ Guthrie, *Battles of the Thirty Years War*, On the cardinal-infante see A. van der Essen, *Le Cardinal-Infant et la politique européenne de l'Espagne 1609–1641* (Leuven: Bibliothèque de l'Université 1944).

The battle also precipitated moves towards a settlement in the empire between the emperor and at least some disgruntled Protestant princes. That prospect had in any case increased following Gustav Adolph's death, or at least a settlement between the emperor and Saxony – never a committed ally of Sweden. Saxony may well have seen the peace as the best means of marking an end to Sweden's presence in the empire. Following a provisional settlement, known as the 'Preliminaries of Pirna', involving the emperor and Saxony in November 1634, a wider settlement was agreed at Prague which aimed to restore peace and stability to the empire. The Peace of Prague is invariably seen as a pivotal moment, the end of the 'Holy War', according to Robert Bireley, as the Edict of Restitution was effectively suspended. Just as this chapter began with a series of peace agreements in 1629, so it concludes, appropriately, with another, where the emperor settled with his Protestant princes. But even if 1635 represented the scaling down of the confessional dimension of war, and despite the genuine attempts in the empire to negotiate throughout the period 1629–35, it did not mean that a lasting settlement was at hand. War was rarely distant from peace, as competitors sought honourable terms on which to settle.[29] On 19 May 1635, a French herald arrived in Brussels carrying a declaration of war against Spain, triggered by the arrest on 25 March of the French-protected elector of Trier.[30] While written probably before the outbreak of the Franco-Spanish war, Pasquino and Marforio's Dance of Europe satirised France and Spain before all others. According to Marforio, 'these French dance as if they are in a frenzy', while Spain 'dances in his habit, though is beginning to be annoyed by so many dances.'[31] A new phase of the Thirty Years' War, as a European conflict, had begun.

Selected Bibliography

Bireley, R., *Religion and Politics in the Age of the Counterreformation: Emperor Ferdinand II, William Lamormaini, S.J., and the Formation of the Imperial Policy* (Chapel Hill/London, 1981).

Guthrie, William P., *Battles of the Thirty Years War. From White Mountain to Nordlingen, 1618–1635* (Westport CT, 2002).

Lockart, P.D., *Sweden in the Seventeenth Century* (Basingstoke, 2004).

Medick, Hans and Selwyn, P., 'Historical Event and Contemporary Experience: The Capture and Destruction of Magdeburg in 1631', *Historical Workshop Journal*, 52 (2001): pp. 23–48.

Mortimer, G., *Wallenstein. The Enigma of the Thirty Years War* (Basingstoke, 2010).

Osborne, T., *Dynasty and Diplomacy in the Court of Savoy. Political Culture and the Thirty Years' War* (Cambridge, 2002).

Paas, J.R., 'The Changing Image of Gustavus Adolphus on German Broadsheets, 1630–3', *Journal of the Warburg and Courtauld Institutes*, 59 (1996): pp. 204–44.

Parrott, D., 'The Mantuan Succession, 1627–31: A Sovereignty Dispute in Early Modern Europe', *The English Historical Review*, 112/445 (1997): pp. 20–65.

Piirimäe, P., 'Just War in Theory and Practice: The Legitimation of Swedish Intervention in the Thirty Years War', *The Historical Journal*, 45, 3 (2002): pp. 499–523.

---

[29] Wilson, *Europe's Tragedy*, p. 424; C. Kampmann, 'Peace Impossible?: The Holy Roman Empire and the European State System in the Seventeenth Century', in O. Asbach and P. Schröder (eds), *War, the State and International Law in Seventeenth Century Europe* (Farnham and Burlington, 2010).

[30] For a detailed discussion on the declaration of war see R. Lessafer, 'Defensive Warfare, Prevention and Hegemony. The Justifications for the Franco-Spanish War of 1635', *The Journal of the History of International Law*, 8, parts 1–2, (2006), pp. 91–123, 141–79.

[31] TNA SP 85/7/279, 'Ballo'.

Ringmar, E., *Identity, Interest and Action. A cultural explanation of Sweden's intervention in the Thirty Years War* (Cambridge, 1996).
Roberts, M., *Gustavus Adolphus. A History of Sweden 1611–1632* (2 vols, London, New York, Toronto, 1953).
Wilson, P.H., *Europe's Tragedy. A History of the Thirty Years War* (London: Allen Lane, 2009).
Wilson, P.H. (ed.), *The Thirty Years War. A Sourcebook* (Basingstoke, 2010).

12

ASHGATE RESEARCH COMPANION

The Long War (1635–1648)

Tryntje Helfferich

With the Peace of Prague, the war ended in the empire. Finally, Emperor Ferdinand, the elector of Saxony, and all the other signatories to the peace had come together, in the words of the peace, so 'that the bloodletting be ended once and for all, and the beloved fatherland, the most noble German Nation, be rescued from final ruin.'[1] This, at least, was the aim and design of the peace, and at the time many believed it had succeeded. Across the empire people celebrated the news with religious ceremonies, feasts of thanksgiving, and expressions of public joy. Such festivities were a reflection of the extraordinary destruction inflicted on Central Europe by 1635. From Bohemia and Bavaria in the south-east, to the Netherlands and Denmark in the north-west, the war had already caused the deaths of many hundreds of thousands, and the suffering of even more. Entire cities, such as the great medieval jewel of Magdeburg, lay in ruins, and innumerable small towns or villages had suffered similar fates, or had been abandoned by their frightened residents. In June 1635, for example, after marauding soldiers had taken what they wanted, the pleasant town of Altheim, which had once had over 120 homes, was set on fire and reduced to two houses, three barns, and the church.[2]

Similar scenes had played out across the empire over the past years, and now, even with the peace, many ordinary people faced an uncertain future. Plague and disease were rampant, spread by soldiers and the vast numbers of displaced or fleeing peasants, and made more deadly by the general weakness and infirmity of the population. In Baden-Württemberg, for example, a 1635 outbreak of the plague brought a ten-fold increase in the number of dead to the small towns of Bietigheim and Bönnigheim. By the end of the year over a third of the population of the towns had perished, and the pastor begged God to 'say to the Angel of Ruin: it is enough, now remove your hand, for the sake of Jesus Christ'.[3] In December 1635, the ecclesiastical superintendent at Ulm, Conrad Dieterich, reported that over 15,000 people had died that year of the pestilence in the city, primarily the poor and refugees from the countryside, but also ordinary residents. Famine too had become an everyday occurrence, and also one not resolved by the peace. One diarist recorded in late 1635 that the poor were driven by such hunger that they ate 'many hideous and loathsome things … that did not make sense: dogs and cats, mice and dead livestock' along with 'all kinds of weeds from the open country … thistle, nettle, water hemlock, buttercup'.[4]

---

[1] Peace of Prague, 12 June 1635, copies at the Universitätsbibliothek Augsburg, Signature 02/IV.13.4.183 angeb. 06 and 02/IV.13.4.183 angeb. 07.

[2] T. Helfferich (ed.), *The Thirty Years War: A Documentary History* (Indianapolis, 2009), p. 318

[3] G. Bentele, *Protokolle einer Katastrophe: zwei Bietigheimer Chroniken aus dem Dreißigjährigen Krieg* (Bietigheim-Bissingen: Stadtarchiv Bietigheim-Bissingen, 1984), pp. 64–5.

[4] Helfferich, *Thirty Years War*, p. 320.

An even more horrifying depiction of the condition of the common man in the empire at this time came from the journal of the Englishman William Crown, travelling as part of an official embassy to the imperial court. As he travelled across the empire, he saw first-hand the many burnt or abandoned villages, and described the places where famine was so severe that 'poore people are found dead with grasse in their mouthes'. In one place the starving peasants had 'scraped out of the grave' their own dead to eat. And everywhere the refugees: sick, starving, so poor and desperate that they fought like dogs for the scraps of food handed out by the English travellers.[5]

Still, not everyone welcomed the Peace of Prague, as it was significantly favourable to imperial power and Catholicism and, on the contrary, damaging to the German Liberties and Protestantism. Not only had the emperor gained territories for his own family, he had also fulfilled his main goals of severing the foreign powers of Sweden and France from their German allies, ending almost all internal military opposition, and rallying his forces by a significant military reform that both enlarged the imperial army and saw to its ongoing financial support. Furthermore, all alliances among princes of empire, as well as their treaties with foreign powers, were henceforth banned. Although it is hard to argue, as some past historians have done, that the peace was a victory for imperial absolutism, there is no doubt that it considerably strengthened the emperor vis-à-vis both the imperial princes and the foreign crowns.[6] As for the religious angle, although the emperor had agreed to a 40-year pause in the implementation of the Edict of Restitution, the new normal year of 1627 for all ecclesiastical properties benefited Catholic princes far more than Protestant ones. Calvinists in particular were uneasy, as they were not explicitly included in the peace and had to take on faith that they would not be molested in the future. The suspicious Calvinist landgrave of Hesse-Cassel argued that the authors of the peace intended nothing less than 'a suppression of the evangelical religion and of German freedom'. His councillor agreed, stating that 'Johann Georg [of Saxony] has put his co-religionists into disgraceful chains'.[7] Given such opposition, it is not surprising that the landgrave was one of a small handful of princes and estates of the empire who had found the terms of the peace too difficult, and so had refused to join. Others, such as the duke of Württemberg and the exiled heir of the Elector Palatine, had been excluded from the peace, since, in the words of the emperor, they were 'so tightly bound to Sweden and France ... that they have made themselves into vassals of the crowns.'[8]

Yet while the peace was a high point for imperial power, it did not mark the emperor's final victory, for the dramatic military advantages the emperor gained at Prague were almost simultaneously countered by the new involvement of France. And yet at first the advantage seemed to be Ferdinand's. The emperor's army was joined by the troops of the signatory German princes, including the duke of Bavaria and the elector of Saxony, and on 16 October 1635, the latter, eagerly embracing his new role as imperial field marshal, declared war against his former Swedish allies. Leading a large force of imperial and Saxon troops, the elector advanced against the Swedish general Johan Banér, whose semi-mutinous army was steadily driven back to Pomerania, and was saved only by the fortuitous arrival of

---

[5] F. Springell and W. Crowne, *Connoisseur and diplomat: the Earl of Arundel's embassy to Germany in 1636...* (London, 1963), pp. 59–76.

[6] H. Haan, 'Kaiser Ferdinand II. und das Problem des Reichsabsolutismus: Die Prager Heeresreform von 1635', *Historische Zeitschrift*, 207/2 (1968): pp. 297–345. On this peace see the contribution by Martin Espenhorst in this volume.

[7] D.C. von Rommel, *Geschichte von Hessen* (vol. 8) (Cassel, 1843), pp. 362–75.

[8] Ferdinand II Instructions for his Delegates, 12 March 1635, published in K. Bierther, *Die Politik Maximilians I. von Bayern und seiner Verbündeten 1618–1651: 2. Teil. Bd. 10: Der Prager Frieden von 1635* (Munich and Vienna, 1997), pp. 241–89.

additional Swedish forces under Lennart Torstenson. Meanwhile, the inexperienced French army floundered along the Rhine, struggling to counter a joint imperial-Bavarian offensive against Lorraine. French attacks against Spain in Italy and in the Spanish Netherlands were similarly unsuccessful. Embarrassed and worried about a possible Habsburg invasion of the homeland, the French Prime Minister, Cardinal Richelieu, now approached Duke Bernard of Saxe-Weimar, one of the few to reject the Peace of Prague. Bernard was ready to listen, as without the support of either his former German allies or the foreign crowns, he had been forced to retreat, allowing the imperialists to capture Heidelberg and besiege Mainz, which they would reclaim by the end of the year. With both Bernard and Richelieu in desperate need of support, therefore, the two struck a deal at St. Germain-en-Laye on 27 October 1635, by which Bernard agreed to field an army of 18,000 men in return for hefty annual subsidies.

The months after the Peace of Prague thus saw a significant turn in the shape of the war, with imperial forces having great success at holding off the French while pushing the Swedes to the borders of the empire. And yet as 1636 dawned, the war was no closer to a resolution and its outcome was still entirely in doubt. The peace had failed both to provide a permanent religious solution and to resolve the problem of those princes and estates that were still, either voluntarily or involuntarily, excluded from its amnesty. This posed a danger to peace, both because these rebel princes remained a dangerous source of internal conflict, and because they served the propaganda purposes of the foreign crowns, who continued to use their alienation as justification for intervention in the empire. Then, on 20 March 1636, the Swedes and French signed the Treaty of Wismar, by which they agreed to unite their armies against the Habsburgs. The Swedish army, bolstered by French subsidies, would proceed against Habsburg hereditary territories in Bohemia and Silesia, while the French army, reinforced by Saxe-Weimar's men, would redouble its efforts along the Rhine. The Treaty of Wismar, struck as it was between the Lutheran Swedes and the Catholic French, and waged now against a mixed-confessional body of German princes, was long seen along with the Peace of Prague as marking the end of the religious phase of the war and the beginning of its purely political phase. However, cross-confessional alliances had existed since the beginning of the war, and all parties tended to focus their primary concerns not on the general well-being of their co-religionists, but on their own territorial power and territorial churches. For most rulers of this era, in other words, political and religious motivations were intertwined, and they found it relatively easy to justify their actions in terms of both expediency and piety.[9]

It is in this respect that one can view the concerns of the Lutheran Johann Georg of Saxony, who found himself entirely dissatisfied with the progress of events by early 1636, as the quick victory he had hoped for failed to materialise. The Swedes, rather than simply cutting their losses and sailing back across the Baltic, had stubbornly refused to lay down their arms until their few remaining allies in the empire were granted a general amnesty.[10] The exclusion of these princes had been a mistake, the elector argued in a letter to Emperor Ferdinand in March, and he complained that he had now repeatedly 'appealed to your majesty for a rebuttal of the pretexts by which the foreign troops justify their persistent residence and evil start in the empire.'[11] More trouble for Johann Georg was to come, for in June the Calvinist

---

[9] For French justifications, see P. Sonnino, *Mazarin's Quest: The Congress of Westphalia and the Coming of the Fronde* (Cambridge, 2009), pp. 17–9. For the argument that the Peace of Prague, in particular, marked the de-confessionalisation of the war, see R. Bireley, 'The Peace of Prague (1635) and the Counterreformation in Germany', *Journal of Modern History*, 48 (1976): pp. 56–60. See also P. H. Wilson, *The Thirty Years War: Europe's Tragedy* (Cambridge/Mass., 2009), pp. 565–6.

[10] HHStARK Friedensakten 17a, fol. 24–34, Oxenstierna Memorial, 12 December 1635.

[11] HHStARK Friedensakten 17a, fol. 78–83, Johann Georg to Ferdinand, Hall, 15 March 1636.

landgrave of Hesse-Cassel announced his decision to side with the foreign crowns with a bold attack against the elector's son-in-law, the landgrave of Hesse-Darmstadt, and with a valiant, if short-lived, relief of the imperial siege on the Swedish-controlled city of Hanau. Then, in September, Banér began to advance once again, sweeping south along the Elbe and badly defeating the imperial-Saxon army at the battle of Wittstock in October. This allowed the Swedes open access into Brandenburg and then Saxony, where they besieged the city of Leipzig in a failed attempt to bring the elector to terms. The French and Weimarian troops, meanwhile, were also advancing in Upper Alsace, though this success was overshadowed by the extraordinary offensive of the Spanish and imperialists deep into French territory, an advance that almost reached Paris before it was finally rebuffed.

The victories and defeats of 1635–1636 thus set the pattern for the remaining years of the war, which would be characterised by a continual back-and-forth between the two almost evenly matched sides. It was, perhaps more than anything, this delicate balance of forces that would contribute to the war's painful and frustratingly long duration. Battles won or lost, smaller allies gained or forfeited, leading princes dying or rising to power, all contributed to a sense that a single roll of the dice, a single Providential moment, might restore the fortunes of one side or another and so lead to victory. Nothing was inevitable, either the progress of the war or its ultimate result. 'One sees only how fortune miraculously changes', one German ruler noted with wonder. 'The ball is round – quickly good, quickly otherwise'.[12] February 1637, for example, saw the death of Ferdinand II, but the successful transfer of the imperial title to his son Ferdinand III – something in doubt only a few months before. The campaign of 1637 also yielded major advances for the imperialists, who managed to hold the French to the left bank of the Rhine and drive the Swedes back to the Baltic coast. A further victory came in the banning and flight into exile of the landgrave of Hesse-Cassel, and the occupation of his territories by the Bavarian general Götz, who allowed his men free rein to pillage. According to a report by the local Hessian Estates, Götz's troops 'had cut off noses, ears and tongues. They had gouged out eyes, and poured liquid lead and tin into people's mouths and ears. The women had been raped, their breasts had been cut off and children had been baked in ovens like bread'.[13] While the landgrave managed to escape with most of his army, which he then used to occupy the neutral territory of East Frisia, his death at the end of the year effectively knocked Hesse-Cassel out of the war.

The only bright spot for the allies in 1637 were the advances by Bernard of Saxe-Weimar along the Rhine, which put him in position, by March 1638, to seize Rheinfelden. Then in May, joined by the French commander Guébriant, Bernard attacked Breisach, the mighty and strategic fortress on the right bank of the Rhine. But the emperor had anticipated this move, and Bernard's siege was quickly broken. The Swedes under Banér also advanced in early 1638, and were able to reinforce Pomerania and then move south, pushing the imperialists back yet again to Bohemia and Silesia. Bernard, meanwhile, had not given up his designs on Breisach and, defeating the imperialists under General Götz, once again besieged the city, which finally submitted in December. The siege had been so bad, the food shortages so extreme, that there were reports of cannibalism by the defenders.[14]

---

[12] HStAM4d Nr. 50, fol. 6-8, Amalia Elisabeth (own hand letter sent) to Vultejus, Early September 1638.

[13] R. Asch, '"Wo der Soldat hinkombt, da ist alles sein": Military Violence and Atrocities in the Thirty Years War Reexamined', *German History*,18 (2000): p. 293.

[14] G. Benecke. (ed.), *Germany in the Thirty Years War* (New York, 1979), pp. 56–7; G. Zillhardt, *Der Dreißigjährige Krieg in zeitgenössischer Darstellung. Hans Heberles 'Zeytregister' (1618–1672)* (Ulm and Stuttgart, 1975), pp. 175–7.

The victory over Breisach gave the allies renewed confidence, and the French used this victory to try to gain new German supporters, especially the widowed landgravine of Hesse-Cassel, who, angered by the emperor's continued refusal to grant explicit legal protections for Calvinism, finally agreed to join the allies in August.[15] This was a principled stand by Ferdinand, but it cost him the large and experienced Hessian army, which would instead now bolster the French-Swedish side until the end of the war. The death of Bernard of Saxe-Weimar a few weeks before this only strengthened the anti-Habsburg coalition, as the directors of his army continued their relationship with the French – and proved themselves far less unpredictable and uncontrollable allies. Meanwhile, the Swedes under Banér battled the Saxons and imperialists, defeating the one at Dresden and the other at Chemnitz, and then advanced again into Habsburg territories in Bohemia, reaching even to the city of Prague before being forced to retreat once again. In February 1640, in a desperate effort to end this war, the imperial Electoral College met at Nuremburg. But tension among the electors, and especially between Bavaria and the emperor, limited the meeting's utility and led Ferdinand reluctantly to call the first full meeting of the imperial diet since before the war's beginning. This was a sign of both his weakness and his desperation to rally all the forces of the empire, without which he saw no way finally to eject the foreign crowns.[16]

Indeed, even before the diet opened in Regensburg in September 1640, events were already getting away from the emperor. In the beginning of that year, the combined forces of the French, Weimarians, Hessians, and Swedes began to mass outside of Erfurt, prepared for a major new advance designed to bring the emperor and his allies to their knees. Yet the imperialists under Ottavio Piccolomini refused to engage, and so the 1640 campaign was surprisingly indecisive, resulting in nothing more than bruised feelings among the quarrelling allied generals, along with a newly devastated section of the empire, picked clean of supplies and rations by the thousands of hungry and miserable soldiers.[17] Still, the emperor and his allies had little to be happy about, for on the one side, the events of 1639, and especially the loss of the Hessians, had tilted the military advantage slightly in favour of the foreign crowns, and on the other side, the Spanish Habsburgs were facing enormous difficulties, culminating in open revolt in both Catalonia and Portugal.

It was thus with some urgency that the emperor came together with representatives of most of the German princes at Regensburg, ready to offer as concessions both a complete revocation of the Edict of Restitution and amnesty for excluded states willing to join the war against the foreign crowns. But while the delegates discussed the ongoing disagreements over imperial constitutional, religious, and judicial matters, the war continued outside the walls of the city, though not too far outside, as in January 1641 Banér attempted a feint across the frozen Danube River to try to capture the emperor himself. Imperial troops were able to fend off this attack, but Banér then moved on to terrorise Bavaria, from which, according to a local account, he 'took immense booty, and led away many captives'.[18] Yet Banér's death in May left the Swedish army again on the brink of total mutiny, and Ferdinand, hoping to take advantage of this sudden weakness, now secretly offered the Swedes all of Pomerania in return for peace. The Swedish chancellor Oxenstierna was suspicious, however, and instead

---

[15] For the French use of the victory of Breisach see HStAM 4f Frankreich, No. 1312, La Boderie to Amalia Elisabeth, January 23, 1639.

[16] K. Bierther, *Der Regensburger Reichstag von 1640/1641* (Kallmünz OPF, 1971), pp. 25–43. For more on Maximilian of Bavaria, see K. Pfister and G. Stetter, *Kurfürst Maximilian I von Bayern* (Munich, 1980).

[17] Banér to Queen Christina, 14 July 1640, publ. in A. Oxenstierna., *Rikskansleren Axel Oxenstiernas Skrifter och Brefvexling: Johan Banérs bref 1624–1641* (ser. 2, vol. 6) (Stockholm, 1893), pp. 758–65.

[18] M. Friesenegger, *Tagebuch aus dem 30jährigen Krieg, Nach einer Handschrift im Kloster Andechs*, ed. by P. W. Mathäser (Munich, 1974), p. 71.

agreed in June to the Treaty of Hamburg with the French, which strengthened their alliance and bound them to keep fighting until both were satisfied and the war was over.

At Regensburg, meanwhile, the diet was shaken by the actions of the new elector of Brandenburg, the 20-year-old Friedrich Wilhelm. While his father had agreed to the Peace of Prague in return for vague assurances for his Calvinist faith and for the eventual restoration of Pomerania (seized from him by Gustav Adolph in 1630), Friedrich Wilhelm was both less trusting and embittered by the devastation of his lands after years of war. Through his delegates, he now proclaimed the Peace of Prague an invalid basis for negotiations, claimed the diet discriminated against Protestants, and insisted on the inclusion of Calvinists in all diet resolutions. He also began secret negotiations with the Swedes, which resulted in a truce in July 1641. By this time many other smaller imperial princes had also begun to question the utility of the diet and to challenge the emperor's leadership. As the Regensburg diet had failed to restore imperial unity, failed to resolve the empire's institutional problems (such as a mis-functioning judicial system), and, in sum, failed to end the war in the empire, the emperor dissolved it in October. Unwilling to give up on peace, the delegates voted before disbanding to call for additional negotiations through a more limited form of imperial meeting known as a Deputations Diet, to be held in Frankfurt in May 1642. Due to the usual delays, however, the talks would not actually begin until February 1643.[19]

Meanwhile, on 25 December 1641, after years of diplomatic wrangling, representatives of the French, Swedes, and emperor finally agreed to a framework for a general peace congress to resolve the international aspects of the war. Given the various interests and disagreements among the powers, the diplomats agreed to split the negotiations in two, with the Swedes and imperialists meeting for direct talks in the city of Osnabrück, and the French and imperialists meeting in the nearby city of Münster. The talks were scheduled to begin in March 1642, and both cities, which were in the region of Westphalia, would be declared neutral zones for the duration of the congress. The Spanish and Dutch were also soon invited, but the inclusion of the imperial estates was a more contentious question. The delegates at Regensburg, in a show of support for the German Liberties and rebellion against imperial power, had voted before dissolving that 'each and every imperial prince' be at least allowed to send delegates, but the emperor was adamantly opposed. Accepting the right of the imperial estates to attend and vote would validate the arguments of those who argued that sovereignty in the empire lay with the princes, not with the emperor and electors alone.[20]

A means for a negotiated end to the war was now available, but still the various parties delayed, hoping to establish more favourable military circumstances from which to begin their diplomatic efforts. Thus the date for the opening of the Westphalian congress was pushed back to July 1643, and the armies of the emperor and the foreign crowns readied themselves for the campaign season of 1642. Beginning in January, with a victory against the imperialists by the French general Guébriant outside Kempen, the unified French-Hessian army swept along the Lower Rhine, taking territories in Cleves, Berg, and Jülich and putting them under contribution. Meanwhile, strengthened by the addition of new troops from Sweden and by larger financial assistance from the French, the reinvigorated Swedish army also saw early successes. General Lennart Torstenson, Banér's gifted successor, led his army deep into the Habsburg hereditary lands of Silesia and Moravia, and almost to the gates

---

[19] Bierther, *Der Regensburg Reichstag*, pp. 96–109, 195–7; E. Opgenoorth, *Friedrich Wilhelm, Der Große Kurfürst von Brandenburg, I. Teil 1620–1660* (Frankfurt and Zürich, 1971), pp. 95–9; L. Hüttl, *Friedrich Wilhelm von Brandenburg, der Große Kurfürst 1620–1688. Eine politische Biographie* (Munich, 1981), pp. 76–99, 110–13.

[20] Bierther, *Der Regensburg Reichstag*, pp. 231–43.

of Vienna itself. Pushed back into Saxony by the imperialists, he then besieged the great city of Leipzig. There, on 2 November, only a few miles from the city at Breitenfeld, his army met the imperial forces under Archduke Leopold Wilhelm and Piccolomini. Like the first battle of Breitenfeld 11 years before, the Swedes were once again entirely victorious. With 46 cannon lost and as many as 10,000 imperial soldiers killed, wounded, or captured, the imperial army was crushed, and Leipzig itself soon fell to the Swedes. The shock of this horrible defeat caused 'a general terror' among residents of Catholic southern Germany, and spurred renewed demands from both Catholics and Protestants that the emperor reach peace quickly.[21] Of particular concern to the emperor, however, were the Catholic electors of Bavaria, Mainz, and Cologne, whose lands had now been devastated many times by French and Swedish occupation or invasion, and who began making overtures to the French for a possible separate peace.

But the emperor was not the only one with troubles. In December 1642 Richelieu died, and was succeeded by the Italian Cardinal Jules Mazarin. Then, in May 1643, King Louis XIII also died. As the king's heir was only a child, his mother, the Habsburg princess Anne of Austria, became regent. This abrupt change stunned France's allies, who feared this might usher in a new pro-Habsburg foreign policy. Yet both Anne and Mazarin, who continued on as her prime minister and close confidant, were determined to uphold the honour and might of their adopted country. They were also lucky, as a surprise victory by the duke d'Enghien over the Spanish at Rocroi, in the Spanish Netherlands, helped them solidify their domestic position. Resolved to continue Richelieu's policies, therefore, Mazarin quickly revitalised the relationship of the French crown with its German and Swedish allies, releasing the temporarily delayed subsidy monies that were so necessary to keeping the entire allied war effort afoot.[22]

By autumn 1643, the foreign crowns and their few remaining German allies were on the offensive, the imperialists on the defensive. Yet the very successes of the Swedes now encouraged the Swedish Chancellor Axel Oxenstierna to plan a new attack against their old enemy, the Danes. This was designed primarily to wrest control of the Baltic from King Christian IV, but also to forestall any Danish meddling in the imperial theatre (including a proposed mediation at Westphalia). In September, therefore, Torstenson was secretly ordered to leave the Habsburg hereditary territories and march northwards. The attack against Danish positions in Holstein, Bremen, and Verden began in December, and by the end of January 1644 Torstenson held the entire Jutland peninsula. This offence was matched by the Swedish General Gustav Horn's occupation of the Danish provinces of Scania and Halland. The Swedish advance was thus brilliantly successful, but it left the French and Hessians aghast, especially as their position on the Rhine had recently been severely damaged. Although the French General Rantzau had captured Rottweil on 19 November, he was unprepared for a surprise attack a few days later at nearby Tuttlingen by the Bavarian general Franz von Mercy. Thus instead of advancing through Swabia and into a poorly protected Bavaria, as they had planned, the French army was totally crushed, its remnants fleeing across the Rhine to Alsace.[23]

The humiliating defeat of the French, combined with the distraction of the Swedes, left their sole remaining German ally, the landgravine of Hesse-Cassel, in serious trouble. Yet with extraordinary efforts by Mazarin, by the spring Marshal Turenne was able to lead a partially rebuilt Army of Germany across the Rhine to counter the large imperial-

---

[21] Friesenegger, *Tagebuch*, p. 75.
[22] Sonnino, *Mazarin's Quest*, pp. 31–3.
[23] AAECP *Hollande 30*, fol. 108–9, Krosigk to Mazarin, 25 January 1644.

Bavarian army under Mercy and the Bavarian commander Jan van Werth. But Turenne's forces were still too small to provide an effective counter-weight, and the imperialists easily advanced into allied-controlled territory in south-western Germany, then moved through the Black Forest to the city of Freiburg im Breisgau, which they took in July 1644. In August, however, reinforced by new troops under the duke d'Enghien, the French engaged Mercy in a horrifically bloody, but indecisive, battle near Freiburg. Mercy now retreated back to Bavaria, while the French were free to move north along the Rhine and into the Lower Palatinate, seizing the major fortresses of Philipsburg, Speyer, Worms, and then, without a fight, the city of Mainz.[24]

The emperor, meanwhile, had sent General Matthias Gallas to aid the Danes, but the general had been slow to arrive, and once there was unable to stop Christian from signing a truce with the Swedes. Gallas was then ordered back to manage a revolt in Hungary sparked by Prince George Rákóczy of Transylvania.[25] Torstenson, now unencumbered due to the Danish truce, took up the pursuit, and Gallas was forced to retreat through territories already picked clean of every possible source of provisions. By the time they reached Saxony, in December, Gallas's army was shattered, unable to block the Swedes as they turned south towards Bohemia. The disgraced Gallas was relieved of command and replaced by Melchior von Hatzfeldt, who rushed to meet the advancing enemy, bolstered by reinforcements under Werth and Götz, whose troops had been freed by the emperor's timely arrangement of a truce with Rákóczy. On 5 March 1645 the imperialists met the Swedes at Jankau, some 35 miles from Prague. Although the two armies were roughly equal in size, Torstenson won the field decisively, killing Götz and capturing Hatzfeldt. With this stunning victory, the emperor's territories were wide open to the Swedes, who advanced again towards Vienna, burning and pillaging as they went.

While Torstenson had moved into Bohemia and Austria, the French and Hessians had pressed into southern Germany, and on 3 August 1645 at Allerheim, near Nördlingen, they met the imperialists under Mercy. Although both sides suffered heavy losses, Mercy was killed, his army forced to retreat, and Maximilian of Bavaria now began more serious discussions with the French over a separate peace. Meanwhile, other Swedish troops under Hans Christoff von Königsmarck had advanced into Saxony. Victorious against the elector's forces, on 6 September Königsmarck compelled the elector to sign the Truce of Kötzschenbroda, which took Saxony out of the war.[26] Still, the war was not over, as Torstenson was unable to take either Vienna or Brünn, in Moravia, and by the end of the year, seriously ill, he retreated north and handed command of the Swedish army over to Gustav Wrangel. The French too were unable to build on their success at Allerheim and also retreated back to the Rhine.

At Westphalia, the congress had opened on schedule in July 1643, but as the French and Swedish delegations only arrived in March and April 1644, nothing was accomplished until then.[27] And even so, the first months would be entirely taken up by matters of honour and precedence, and only in December 1644 did the foreign crowns issue their first vague diplomatic proposals. The problem of the inclusion of the imperial estates, which had seemed so impossible, in the end resolved itself, for the military setbacks faced by Ferdinand in 1645 emboldened increasing numbers of princes to defy the imperial prohibition and

---

[24] Wilson, *Thirty Years War*, pp. 678–84.
[25] G. Rákóczi, *The Declaration or, Manifesto of George Racokzkie, Prince of Transylvania...* (London, 1644).
[26] Wilson, *Thirty Years War*, pp. 704–5.
[27] Imperial instructions are in HHStA RK, Friedensakten, 46i, fol. 24–30.

send delegates to Westphalia.[28] In August the emperor acquiesced and agreed to accept both the princes' inclusion and their right of suffrage. This was an extraordinary concession, as it gave a clear precedent to the constitutional argument that the emperor was not absolute, but ruled only in conjunction with the princes. The emperor's weakness also encouraged the French and Swedes, who demanded enormous territorial compensation (including Alsace, Breisach, and other areas along the Rhine for the French; Pomerania, Verden, Bremen, and other areas in the northern part of the empire for the Swedes). To resolve the satisfaction of the foreign crowns and to address the demands of the princes and the Protestants, Ferdinand, severely shaken, now sent his close confidant Count von Trauttmansdorff to Westphalia with secret instructions to agree to almost anything if necessary for peace.[29]

The campaigns of 1646 and early 1647 did nothing to improve the emperor's negotiating position. In 1646 the French and Swedes, avoiding the imperial army under Archduke Leopold Wilhelm, made a joint assault on Bavaria, which they ravaged. Leopold Wilhelm resigned in frustration and was replaced by Gallas, who did no better. Maximilian of Bavaria, discouraged by the emperor's inability to protect his lands from repeated assaults, agreed in March 1647 at Ulm to a truce with the allies, and was joined in this defection by the electors of Cologne and Mainz.[30] Even worse, in July 1647 the Swedes under Wrangel, who had advanced once again to Bohemia, took the city of Eger despite the fevered efforts of the new imperial commander, Peter Melander, who had replaced Gallas in April. And yet, as was characteristic of this war, nothing ever remained static, for that same month the Spanish, having reached a ceasefire with the Dutch at the beginning of the year, prepared to attack the French on their northern border. To counter this, Mazarin ordered Turenne to move his forces to northern France, but these troops, including the remaining Weimarian soldiers, refused to leave the empire and mutinied en masse. Such a humiliating disaster, added to serious financial difficulties and growing popular discontent at home, weakened the French diplomatic position and spurred Maximilian of Bavaria to re-enter the war in September 1647. Maximilian's forces then advanced north into Bohemia, pushing Wrangel and the Swedes to retreat once again.

While the war continued to teeter back and forth between the two sides, with the emperor clearly weakening but his enemies never managing to gain a decisive military advantage, at Westphalia matters had slowly and painfully begun to reach some resolution. By the end of 1647, the diplomats at Münster and Osnabruck had come to a general agreement on many major issues, such as the question of amnesty, the disposition of religious territories within the empire, and the fate of the Palatinate, and there were also understandings on the Swedish and French demands for territorial satisfaction. Furthermore, the cold calculus of the war to date – which had for so long encouraged many rulers to judge that the possible territorial, political, religious, and financial rewards were worth the risks of further warfare – had begun to look less reasonable to larger and larger numbers of the war's participants. The elector of Brandenburg, for example, had decided in early 1647 to cut his losses, accepting the forfeiture of Western Pomerania to the Swedes in return for Magdeburg and some other small territories, and thus resolving what might have been a major stumbling block to a final treaty. The most striking demonstration of the new move for peace, however, came on 30 January 1648, when the Dutch plenipotentiaries at Münster signed a treaty with the Spanish, thereby ending their 80-year war and establishing Dutch independence. This was a nasty

---

[28] D. Albrecht, 'Die Kriegs- und Friedensziele der deutschen Reichsstände', in K. Repgen (ed.), *Krieg und Politik 1618–1648. Europäische Probleme und Perspektiven* (München, 1988), p. 249.

[29] F. Dickmann, *Der Westfälische Frieden* (7th edn) (Münster, 1998), pp. 163–89; HHStA, StK. Friedensakten 1, fol. 210–17, Ferdinand III Instructions for Trauttmansdorff.

[30] Dickmann, *Der Westfälische Frieden*, pp. 396–8.

blow to the French, and one that severely damaged their diplomatic and military position towards the Spanish, but it was also a clear sign that neither the patience nor the financial resources of the warring parties was infinite.[31]

Yet another sign soon came from the princes of the empire, who, angry and tired of a seemingly unending conflict that had devastated their lands and decimated their populations, decided to seize the initiative in early 1648. Rather than wait for the emperor's plenipotentiaries to shape the remaining negotiations, the princes' delegates at Osnabrück, with the support and leadership of Maximilian of Bavaria and the elector of Mainz, instead successfully undertook a major diplomatic push to resolve on their own many of their outstanding differences, including the problem of Calvinism. Still unresolved, however, were such thorny issues as the emperor's insistence on the special treatment of the Habsburg hereditary territories and the Swedes' demand for large sums of money in order to disband their troops. Yet while the imperial princes and estates were now more than ready for peace, and while an agreement was almost within the grasp of the combatants, the French, Swedes, and Habsburgs still stubbornly refused to give up the faint hope that a decisive military victory might yet advance their diplomatic agendas. Thus by the spring of 1648 the French had once again painfully re-created the Army of Germany, and now sent it, under Turenne, to join forces with the Swedes under Wrangel for another assault on Bavaria. Moving south, the allied army crossed the Danube and on 17 May 1648 met the imperial-Bavarian army under General Melander and Count Gronsfeld at Zusmarshausen, near Augsburg. The battle was a major defeat for the imperialists, as Melander was killed and his army barely escaped intact. Gronsfeld was forced to fall well back, leaving almost all of Bavaria open for vicious looting by the triumphant allies. Only the great efforts of Piccolomini, appointed by the emperor to replace Melander, kept the allies from proceeding into Austria and subjecting it to similar devastation. Adding to the pressure on the emperor, in July further Swedish forces under Königsmarck marched into Bohemia and took a portion of the city of Prague.[32]

This was yet another major setback for the Habsburgs, but the Swedes, who had expended enormous manpower and treasure in this war, and the French, whose costly military adventures had now sparked open insurrection at home, were also exhausted and ready to deal. And so finally, on 24 October 1648, the plenipotentiaries at Münster and Osnabrück signed the two treaties that together comprised the Peace of Westphalia.[33] The peace was both an imperial peace and a peace between the empire and the foreign powers, though the Spanish–French conflict would drag on until 1659. In many ways the peace was a compromise. Within the empire, the princes were still understood to be subjects of the emperor and bound by the empire's laws and institutions, but otherwise regained many of their cherished German Liberties, including the right to make war and peace, to make foreign alliances (though not against the empire), to assent to taxation, and to oversee the churches in their own territories. This maintained the empire as an aristocratic, decentralised body, rather than the centralised absolutist state the Habsburgs had so dearly desired. Yet princely sovereignty was limited both by the princes' legal and traditional ties to the empire, and by the acceptance of a new normal year of 1 January 1624, which fixed the religious

---

[31] For more on Dutch–Spanish negotiations and the impact on the French, see Sonnino, *Mazarin's Quest*, pp. 152–71; M. Rohrschneider, *Der Gescheiterte Frieden von Münster: Spaniens Ringen mit Frankreich auf dem Westfälischen Friedenskongress (1643–1649)* (Münster, 2007).

[32] J.P. Abelinus and M. Merian, *Theatrum Europæum, oder Warhaffte Beschreibung aller denckwurdigen Geschichten* (6 vols) (Frankfurt am Main, 1643–1652), vol. 6, pp. 346–7.

[33] *Die Westfälischen Friedensverträge*; Helfferich, (ed.), *The Thirty Years War*, pp. 252–73; H. Duchhardt (ed.), *Der Westfälische Friede: Diplomatie, politische Zäsur, kulturelles Umfeld, Rezeptionsgeschichte* (Munich, 1998). See also the chapters by Axel Gotthard and Heinz Duchhardt in this volume.

makeup of the empire as of that date. In the future, no prince or ecclesiastical ruler would be able to convert his territories or oppress protected religious minorities. Individual residents of the empire were also given freedom of conscience (a radical new idea), dissenters were given the right of emigration, and Calvinists were given the same legal rights and privileges as Lutherans and Catholics. Only in the Habsburg hereditary lands was the normal year modified, as the emperor had insisted that he be allowed to maintain these areas as Catholic. Protestants elsewhere in the empire were mollified, however, by the agreement to grant them parity in certain imperial institutions, which meant they could never again be outvoted in matters of religion by their Catholic colleagues.

In addition to these adjustments, the Peace of Westphalia redrew the map of the empire and resolved numerous internal dynastic and territorial conflicts that had radicalised princes such as the landgraves of Hesse-Cassel. The requirements of the new normal year also meant a considerable number of ecclesiastical territories necessarily changed hands, while the promises made to Maximilian of Bavaria by the emperor earlier in the war were satisfied by granting him the Upper Palatinate and the Palatine electoral title. Karl Ludwig, the heir of Frederick of the Palatinate, was allowed to recover the Lower Palatinate and was given a new, eighth electorate. Other transfers were required to deal with the satisfaction of the foreign crowns. The Swedish demand for Pomerania was resolved by giving them the western, richer half as a fief of the empire, along with Bremen, Verden, and Wismar, while the elector of Brandenburg was compensated for this loss with lands including the archbishopric of Magdeburg and the bishopric of Halberstadt. The French too got a foothold in the empire, as they were granted territories in Alsace and along the Rhine. The nature of French control over these territories – as sovereign lands or as fiefs – was left deliberately vague to appease all sides, a provision that ensured peace in 1648, but caused numerous conflicts over this land in the future.

As news of the peace spread across the empire, the people celebrated with extraordinary relief and joy. Yet there was still quite a lot of work to be done, as the troops had to be disbanded, the terms of the peace executed, and a few remaining problems worked out at a future diet. It is difficult to know exactly how many were killed in this war, though some estimates put it as high as seven or eight million, mostly Germans, and of course many millions more were either injured or displaced. Some areas of the empire had emerged relatively unscathed or even prospered, but many had suffered massive losses from war, famine, and disease, and others had been completely destroyed, never to be rebuilt. It would take decades for the empire to recover, and in the meantime the people of Central Europe slowly began to pick up the pieces. 'The 28th day of November', wrote a resident of the little village of Neenstetten, 'we, the entire countryside, returned home with every joy and moved back home and to our houses, which we tidied up and put back together, for they were, in part, badly smashed and the windows, ovens, and doors were destroyed'.[34]

Manuscript Sources

AAECP = Archives du Ministère des Affaires Etrangères, Correspondance Politique, Paris Hollande 30.

HHStA = Haus- Hof- und Staatsarchiv, Vienna, Staatskanzlei Friedensakten 1; Reichskanzlei Friedensakten 17a, 46i.

---

[34] Helfferich, *Thirty Years War*, p. 324.

HStAM = Hessische Staatsarchiv Marburg, 4f Frankreich.

Selected Bibliography

Asch, R., *The Thirty Years War: The Holy Roman Empire and Europe, 1618–48* (New York, 1997).
Bireley, R., 'The Peace of Prague (1635) and the Counterreformation in Germany', *Journal of Modern History*, 48 (1976): pp. 31–70.
Bussmann, K., and H. Schilling (eds), *1648, War and Peace in Europe* (3 vols) (Münster, 1998).
Lockhart, P.D., *Denmark in the Thirty Years' War, 1618–1648: King Christian IV and the Decline of the Oldenburg State* (Selinsgrove, 1996).
Lockhart, P.D., *Sweden in the Seventeenth Century* (Basingstoke, 2004).
Parker, G., and S. Adams (eds), *The Thirty Years' War* (2nd edn) (London, 1997).
Parrott, D., *Richelieu's Army. War, Government and Society in France, 1624–1642* (Cambridge, 2001).
Roberts, M., *Gustavus Adolphus. A History of Sweden 1611–1632* (London, New York and Toronto, 1953).
Sonnino, P., *Mazarin's Quest: The Congress of Westphalia and the Coming of the Fronde* (Cambridge, 2009).
Sreenivasan, G.P., *The Peasants of Ottobeuren, 1487–1726. A Rural Society in Early Modern Europe* (Cambridge, 2004).
Wedgwood, C.V., *The Thirty Years War* (Gloucester/Mass., 1967).
Wilson, P.H., *The Thirty Years War: Europe's Tragedy* (Cambridge, Mass., 2009).

13

ASHGATE
RESEARCH
COMPANION

The Dutch–Spanish War in the Low Countries 1621–1648

Olaf van Nimwegen

The Thirty Years' War lives on in popular memory as one of Europe's most barbarous and destructive conflicts in which although pitched battles, the sacking of towns, and the looting of the countryside may not have been everyday occurrences, they were at least common ones. The war simultaneously waged in the adjacent Low Countries – the Dutch Republic, the Spanish or Southern Netherlands, and the duchy of Luxemburg, an area that corresponds roughly to the modern Benelux countries – stands in stark contrast to this picture. The second round (1621–1648) of the 80-year struggle (1568–1648) between the Dutch and the king of Spain is as much renowned for its restrained violence as the Thirty Years' War is notorious for its excesses. By 1600 the wholesale slaughter of towns was already a bad memory for the Netherlanders. The Dutch leadership was appalled by the wanton destruction of the Thirty Years' War, and the idea that armies should be risked in daring undertakings was totally alien to them. The military command and the regents, the members of the ruling bodies in the Dutch Republic, agreed that warfare should be methodical and the outcome of operations as near predictable as possible: in short, Dutch strategy was concerned first with the conquest of towns and fighting battles was seen as a last resort.

By adhering to this view the Dutch made sure that their highly disciplined and skilled armed forces were not put in jeopardy, their provinces spared from predatory raids, and newly conquered towns and tracts of land could be added to the territory of the Dutch Republic with their populations and wealth largely intact. However the costs incurred in this type of warfare were immense and not even the wealthy Dutch Republic could support these indefinitely. Contemporaries were well aware of the dilemma posed by siege-orientated warfare. The well known French soldier Henri duke of Rohan wrote that the Ancients had staked everything on battles, and in his opinion rightly so because only battles resulted in quick conquests. But today, he complained, wars were waged more with cunning than with bravery, seeing that they were based rather on sieges than on battles.[1] Dutch officers underscored Rohan's judgement that too much circumspection in war undermined fighting effectiveness. In 1644 a Dutch colonel worried:

> [T]here are hardly any officers, whether of foot or of horse, who have seen any event in the field, but only sieges, where one is solidly entrenched and out of danger of being

---

[1] Henri duc de Rohan, *Le parfaict capitaine* (Paris, 1636), p. 257.

attacked, which is a wholly different thing to fighting in the field, where one must act well and pay heed to all occurrences and events and not be neglectful.[2]

It would be unfair however to conclude from the foregoing that the slow pace of the second half of the Eighty Years' War should be blamed simply on the Dutch being too cautious. After all, the Spanish crown adhered to the same strategy. The great captain Ambrogio Spinola (1569–1630), commander-in-chief of the Army of Flanders from 1604, may very well have been an avid advocate of all-out offensive war to force the Dutch to comply with Spanish peace terms, his master Philip IV (1605–1665), king of Spain since 1621, decided to heed the advice of his chief minister, Gaspar de Guzmán (1587–1645), duke of Olivares, and limit the war in the Low Countries to a *guerra defensive*. Since the resumption of hostilities, Spinola had only made limited headway against the Dutch. In 1622 he had failed in taking Bergen op Zoom, and although he succeeded in capturing Breda in 1625, a victory immortalised by Velázquez in his painting *Las Lanzas*, the conquest of this outpost was of limited consequence for the overall strategic situation in the Low Countries. Breda had value as a base for exacting Spanish contributions from the inhabitants of the border regions of the provinces of Holland, Zeeland and Gelderland, and its capture was also of symbolic value, being a prized possession of the house of Orange-Nassau, but, as a Dutch contemporary laconically observed, although the territory of the Dutch republic had been reduced by the loss of Breda, her 'vastigheid' (solidity) was not compromised.[3] Breda did not open a gateway for further Spanish conquests. The Dutch even consoled themselves that the nine-month blockade (28 August 1624 to 5 June 1625) had sent thousands of Spanish soldiers to their graves (mostly through illness). Spinola could point out that the Dutch relief army had suffered no less during the winter and that all attempts by Maurice of Nassau to come to the succour of the town had been thwarted by him, but the fact remained that the siege of Breda had been very costly, an expense the Spanish Monarchy could hardly afford. Olivares was therefore adamant that the Spanish offensive in the Low Countries had to be shelved. Spinola protested against this decision whereupon the king had him suspended and had the command over the Army of Flanders temporarily assigned to Count Hendrik van den Bergh (1573–1638), Stadholder of Upper Gelderland. According to Olivares, Spanish interests would be better served by containing France.[4]

Under the leadership of Prince Frederick Henry of Orange-Nassau (1584–1647) the Dutch were intent on exploiting the removal of Spinola to mount a carefully planned counter-offensive. Frederick Henry had been appointed commander-in-chief of all Dutch land and sea forces upon the death of his famous half-brother Maurice of Nassau in April 1625, besides being elected Stadholder of five of the seven provinces constituting the Dutch Republic. Frederick Henry was of the opinion that the Republic would never be able to exact a peace agreement from Spain unless she demonstrated her military might. He could count on the Remonstrant or Arminian factions in the Republic supporting this viewpoint, given that they had sustained serious economic setbacks from the resumption of the struggle with Spain. Particularly in Amsterdam, where the Remonstrants had gained full control of city government in 1622, there was a stark contrast between the commercial interests of the Arminians and the staunchly Calvinist Counter-Remonstrants. The latter invested heavily in trade with the East and West Indies and therefore benefited from a long-

---

[2] J. Visser (transcription) and G.N. van der Plaats (ed.), *Gloria Parendi. Dagboeken van Willem Frederik stadhouder van Friesland, Groningen en Drenthe 1643–1649, 1651–1654* (The Hague, 1995), p. 74.

[3] A. Montanus, *'t Leven en bedrijf van Frederik Hendrik* (Amsterdam, 1652), pp. 127–28.

[4] J. Israel, *The Dutch Republic and the Hispanic World 1606–1661* (Oxford, 1982), pp. 103, 109 and 162–3.

lasting conflict with Spain to strengthen their overseas positions further, while the former were largely dependent on cargo trade with European destinations for their income. As long as war between the Republic and Spain continued, the trade in staple goods was seriously complicated.[5] The fisheries also suffered a great deal from the strife with Spain flaring up again, especially after a new admiralty had been established at Dunkirk in 1626, an admiralty that was wont to issue many letters of marque.

The outcome of the Dutch–Spanish struggle depended however on more than the relative military strength of the two main protagonists. Until the 1620s the Habsburg Emperor and the German princes had refrained from taking sides in the Dutch Revolt. They had had no intention of getting involved in the religious hornets' nest of the Low Countries which could easily upset the Augsburg settlement of 1555. The outbreak of the Thirty Years' War changed everything. The Spanish Habsburgs gave full support to their Austrian cousins, and the Dutch offered sanctuary to the defeated protestant king of Bohemia, Frederick V of the Palatine.[6] Frederick Henry and the Dutch regents had therefore every reason to anticipate an imperial attack on the Dutch provinces bordering the Holy Roman Empire. Thousands of Dutch soldiers had to be garrisoned along the frontier to guard against this eventuality, diminishing the number of troops that could be used for conquering towns in the Spanish Netherlands. The States-General also had to take into account the possibility that the Emperor would join forces with the Army of Flanders and attack the main Dutch field army. It should not come as a surprise then that Frederick Henry was loath to leave anything to chance.[7]

The military-political worries Madrid and Brussels laboured under were even greater than those of The Hague. The outbreak of a full-scale war with France seemed only a matter of time. Huguenot leaders had supported the Dutch Revolt from the start, but as long as the French civil wars lasted, Spain's position as the greatest European power was not really threatened. By the 1620s France had sufficiently recovered to look beyond her frontiers again. Armand Jean Duplessis (1585–1642), Cardinal Richelieu – chief minister since 1624 – had set himself the objective of making King Louis XIII (1601–1643) 'the world's most powerful monarch'.[8] For Spain the timing could not have been worse. With fighting in the Netherlands resumed, Philip IV was now also threatened by an outbreak of war in Italy where Spain and France supported rival claimants in the disputed Mantuan succession. On paper Spain's armed forces numbered 300,000 men, but because of financial exhaustion the real strength was about half that number.[9] In the 1630s and 40s the French army had an actual size of 80,000 men,[10] while the effective strength of the Dutch army was approximately 60,000 troops.[11] If France and the Dutch Republic joined forces, Spain would be very hard pressed to defend the Southern Netherlands and the rest of her empire as well.

---

[5] J.E. Elias, *Geschiedenis van het Amsterdamsche regentenpatriciaat* (2nd rev. edn, The Hague, 1923), pp. 36–7, 45–6 and 86–7; J. Israel, *Empires and Entrepots. The Dutch, the Spanish Monarchy and the Jews, 1585–1713* (London and Ronceverte, WV, 1990), p. 65.

[6] See the chapter by Ronald Asch in this book.

[7] O. van Nimwegen, *The Dutch Army and the Military Revolutions 1588–1688* (Woodbridge, 2010), pp. 120–22.

[8] R. Bonney, *The King's Debts. Finance and Politics in France 1589–1661* (Oxford, 1981), p. 151.

[9] G. Parker, *The Military Revolution. Military Innovation and the Rise of the West, 1500–1800* (2nd rev. edn, Cambridge, 1996), p. 45.

[10] D. Parrott, *Richelieu's Army. War, Government and Society in France, 1624–1642* (Cambridge, 2001), p. 220.

[11] Van Nimwegen, *The Dutch Army*, p. 46.

The Dutch Counter-Offensive (1626–1632)

Ably assisted by his cousin Field-Marshal Ernst Casimir count of Nassau-Dietz, Stadholder of Friesland and Groningen, Frederick Henry recaptured in 1626 and 1627 Oldenzaal and Groenlo, towns that had been lost to Spinola 20 years earlier. With Groenlo captured the States-General felt enough had been achieved that year and urged Frederick Henry to disband as many troops as possible. The Dutch commander-in-chief wanted to hear nothing of this, pointing out that it would give Hendrik van den Bergh a free hand to besiege any town he desired. The turn of events within the Holy Roman Empire and Italy also made it imperative to keep the Dutch army up to strength. In 1626 the imperial troops under the command of Wallenstein as well as the Catholic League's forces under Count Tilly, had won great victories over the Danes and the German Protestants. In December 1627 troops from the Catholic League and the imperial army were encamped in East Friesland. In the Republic this raised the fearful spectre that the king of Spain 'shall endeavour to raid these lands with the assistance of the soldiers of the popish League'.[12]

Frederick Henry pointed out to the regents that Spain could only be forced to make peace on Dutch terms if they gave him the means to prosecute the war with vigour. He proposed laying siege to 's-Hertogenbosch (Bois-le-Duc). The loss of this important town of approximately 11,000 inhabitants would constitute a serious blow to Spanish prestige, and no less importantly give the States-General lordship over the Meierij, the sizeable territory belonging to it. Frederick Henry did not believe Brussels would be able to relieve 's-Hertogenbosch. The Mantuan war drained the greatest portion of Spanish receipts, and to make matters worse the entire Spanish treasure fleet, heavily laden with silver, was lost in September 1628, having been surprised by Admiral Piet Heyn in a bay near Cuba. The Dutch army invested 's-Hertogenbosch on 1 May 1629. The governor of this town, Anthonie Schetz, baron of Grobbendonk, put up a determined resistance. His garrison was not very substantial – 2,500 to 3,500 men – but the food stores were amply stocked and 4,000 to 5,000 bellicose burghers fought alongside the troops. Brussels was moreover determined not to abandon 's-Hertogenbosch to its fate. The peace that had been concluded with Denmark at Lübeck on 22 May 1629 made it possible for Ferdinand II to do his Spanish cousins a favour in return for their earlier assistance in his struggle against the Protestants.[13]

At the end of July 1629 Hendrik van den Bergh with 15,000 to 16,000 Spaniards and approximately 8,000 imperial troops under the command of Ernesto Count Montecuccoli (ca. 1580–1633) crossed the River IJssel into Gelderland.[14] Ernesto was an older cousin and tutor of Raimondo Montecuccoli (1609–1680), the future great captain of Emperor Leopold I. The invasion then stalled for more than a week, affording the Dutch the opportunity to take countermeasures. They hired thousands of new troops increasing the number of soldiers in their pay to 120,000 on paper and perhaps 80,000 to 90,000 in reality. Not only Spain but also the Dutch Republic profited from the Peace of Lübeck that left thousands of Danish, German, Swedish, Scottish, English and French soldiers out of work. All were not immediately deployable, of course, since their transportation and preparing them for battle would take several weeks. It is therefore a question of great importance why Hendrik van den Bergh and Ernesto Montecuccoli failed to take advantage of their head start to push on to Utrecht immediately.

---

[12] Van Nimwegen, *The Dutch Army*, pp. 212–17.
[13] Israel, *The Dutch Republic*, p. 172; J. Israel, *Empires and Entrepots*, p. 43; J. Lynch, *Spain under the Habsburgs*, 2 vols (2nd edn, Oxford, 1981), vol. 2, pp. 82 and 84; G. Parker (ed.), *The Thirty Years' War* (2nd edn, London and New York, 1997), pp. 71, 95–6.
[14] On the 1629 campaign see Van Nimwegen, *The Dutch Army*, pp. 219–22.

In 1629 the Spanish and imperial generals faced a complex logistical problem. The Spanish-Imperial army's main depot was located in Wesel, but this town's milling and baking capacity was inadequate to be able to meet the daily bread requirements of all the troops so some food had to be requisitioned locally. However, the poor reputation of the imperial troops caused Gelderland's country folk to take flight en masse, and in addition Ernst Casimir had threatened to have anyone who supplied food to the enemy 'shot dead immediately'. This meant food had to be purchased elsewhere, which then had to be transported to Wesel, and from there to the army. The great convoy from Wesel eventually arrived in the second week of August. Montecuccoli pushed on in the direction of Utrecht, capturing Amersfoort without a struggle on 14 August. Van den Bergh with the Spanish force stayed behind to guard the bridgehead on the River IJssel. The loss of Amersfoort sowed panic in Utrecht. Frederick Henry was under increasing pressure to raise the siege of 's-Hertogenbosch and use his main army to drive the enemy out of the Republic. He summarily dismissed this plan. He pointed out that there was already a garrison of almost 4,000 men in Utrecht and more troops were on their way, so the city was not in danger. Frederick Henry was right about this, but this did not alter the fact that the situation was extremely perturbing. The enemy had, after all, penetrated into the heart of the Republic and was already imposing contributions to the sum of 600,000 guilders. Ernst Casimir had too few soldiers available to him to be able to attack Hendrik van den Bergh directly, so the only way to force the Spanish-Imperial troops to leave the Republic's soil was by severing their supply lines. It was Colonel Otto van Gendt (ca. 1580–1640), Lord of Dieden, who extricated Frederick Henry from this thorny position. He launched a surprise attack on Wesel with 2,500 soldiers on 19 Augustus 1629. The garrison put up hardly any resistance.

The loss of Wesel heralded the end of the Spanish-Imperial invasion. On 21 August Montecuccoli left Amersfoort and headed for the Holy Roman Empire with the bulk of the imperial force. Hendrik van den Bergh retreated to Brabant. Without any hope of relief the defenders of 's-Hertogenbosch capitulated on 14 September 1629.

The Spanish-Imperial attack had transformed the 1629 campaign into a battle of prestige that was splendidly won by the Republic. The Dutch had demonstrated that they had access to sufficient financial reserves to simultaneously bring a major siege to a successful conclusion and to withstand a sizeable enemy counterattack, all without foreign assistance! The joy over the triumph of 1629 was, however, short-lived. The regents were all too aware that the Republic could not afford a financial exertion of such proportions again. The 1629 campaign had cost no less than 18 to 19 million guilders.

Frederick Henry shared the concerns of the regents but developments in Italy made him hopeful that the Republic would not need to raise such a large force again. In February 1629 France had intervened in the War of the Mantuan Succession and in December of that year Richelieu told The Hague that the king of France was contemplating an invasion of the Spanish Netherlands together with the Republic. Frederick Henry urged the States-General to consent to an attack on Antwerp, the capture of which would decide the war. It would provide the Dutch with access to the rivers Scheldt, Leie, Dijle and Demer, waterways which would allow the Dutch to transport their siege artillery and provisions into the heart of the Spanish Netherlands.[15]

French military assistance was however less certain than Frederick Henry believed it to be. Richelieu was willing to furnish an annual subsidy of 1 million guilders, but as yet he did not send any troops.[16] Without being forced to wage war on two fronts, Brussels had

---

[15] Ibid., 223, 225.
[16] F.J.G. ten Raa and F. de Bas, *Het Staatsche leger 1568–1795*, 5 vols (Breda, 1911–21), vol. 4, p. 44.

sufficient troops to successfully withstand the Dutch. Not being able to besiege Antwerp, Frederick Henry set his sights in 1631 on the important naval base of Dunkirk but this operation could not be executed either because in March the Army of Flanders received a reinforcement of some 1,200 men from Spain and in the summer an additional 11,000 troops arrived from Lombardy where on 19 June 1631 the Treaty of Cherasco ended the War of the Mantuan Succession.[17] With the road to Dunkirk and Antwerp barred Frederick Henry decided to attack in the east along the Meuse. Hendrik van den Bergh had informed the States-General in The Hague in secret that the dissatisfaction with Spanish rule among the nobility of the Spanish Netherlands had become so great that they wished to switch their allegiance.[18] As Stadholder of Upper Gelderland he could give the assurance that the garrisons of Venlo, Stralen and Roermond would put up minimal resistance and that the Dutch army would therefore be able to press on to Maastricht swiftly. It would then be possible to move into Brabant. Based on this information the States-General endorsed the besieging of Maastricht. The Dutch army arrived before Maastricht on 10 June 1632.

The siege of Maastricht was plagued by difficulties.[19] The line of circumvallation was very long and because the defenders fired their artillery incessantly the approach trenches could advance but slowly. A setback more serious for the Dutch than the stout resistance from the garrison was the arrival of a Spanish relief army under the command of Alvarez de Bazán, marquis of Santa Cruz. The Spaniards established a position to the north-west of Maastricht. Frederick Henry started to become increasingly concerned about his lines of communication with Nijmegen, all the more because there was reason to fear that Brussels would summon the assistance of an imperial army under the command of Gottfried Heinrich, count of Pappenheim (1594–1632).

By purchasing enormous quantities of flour in Liège the Dutch army was assured of bread for more than a month, but in early August the campaign coffers were running dry. At around the same time Pappenheim's army, approximately 12,500 strong, crossed the Rhine and encamped to the north-east of Maastricht thus completely blocking the communication with Nijmegen. Mid-August, however, the besiegers achieved two important military successes from which they could take heart. On 17 August Pappenheim ordered a storm assault on the circumvallation, but the Dutch troops stood their ground and repelled Pappenheim's men, inflicting heavy losses (1,500 to 1,600 dead and wounded). Four days later the besiegers exploded a mine beneath Maastricht's main rampart. English troops in Dutch pay stormed the breach. The garrison managed to drive the Englishmen away, but the following day (22 August) the Spanish governor surrendered the town. The Dutch discovered that the reason the garrison had given up the fight with such unexpected swiftness was the shortage of gunpowder. Frederick Henry remained in Maastricht until the damage to the fortifications was repaired. In early September 1632 Pappenheim left for Saxony with his troops, while the Spaniards took up positions in Brabant.

---

[17] Lynch, *Spain under the Habsburgs*, vol. 2, p. 84; G. Parker, *The Army of Flanders and the Spanish Road 1567–1659. The logistics of Spanish victory and defeat in the Low Countries' Wars* (rev. edn, Cambridge, New York and Melbourne, 1990), p. 279; R. Vermeir, *In staat van oorlog. Filips IV en de Zuidelijke Nederlanden 1629–1648* (Maastricht, 2001), p. 45.

[18] Israel, *The Dutch Republic*, p. 184; J.J. Poelhekke, *Frederik Hendrik prins van Oranje. Een biografisch drieluik* (Zutphen, 1978), p. 374.

[19] On the siege of Maastricht see Van Nimwegen, *The Dutch Army*, pp. 230–34.

The Dutch Offensive Stalls (1633–1634)

The Meuse campaign had required an expansion of the Dutch army by no fewer than 15,600 men. Frederick Henry insisted that the States-General should retain the extra troops so that he could continue the offensive in 1633. The provinces consented to this, as there was no prospect of the war being ended soon.[20] Frederick Henry had in the meantime made plans for an incursion into Brabant 'yet to do this with certainty and profit the enemy ought to be drawn into a *bataille* and defeated in order to prevent the vivres being cut off'. However, the new Spanish commander in the Netherlands, Francisco de Moncada (1586–1635), count of Osona and marquis of Aytona, refused to oblige Frederick Henry. 'He [Aytona] is always positioning himself in advantageous places, withdrawing from one to the other, so it was not advisable to go and attack him', the Dutch field deputies complained.[21] Frederick Henry urged the regents to vote him the financial means so that he could break the deadlock in the following year, but the Amsterdammers would hear nothing of it. This convinced Frederick Henry that Spain could only be defeated if France joined the fray. A French declaration of war would, after all, force the Spaniards to divide their forces between two fronts. Holland's Grand Pensionary, Adriaen Pauw (1585–1653), and Johan de Knuyt from Zeeland were instructed to devise an offensive and defensive alliance with Paris. The rift between Frederick Henry and Amsterdam had grave consequences for the Dutch war effort. The paradox was that Frederick Henry was duly aware that the powers of the Republic were inadequate to bring the Spaniards to their knees, which was precisely why he considered an alliance with France indispensable. However, among the regents favourably disposed to peace, the alliance with France reinforced the impression that the captain-general of the Union wanted to pursue the struggle with Spain to the death.

The Franco-Dutch alliance was signed on 8 February 1635.[22] The signatories were bound to make available 25,000 infantry and 5,000 cavalry for a joint campaign of conquest in the Spanish Netherlands. If the Southern Netherlanders revolted against Spain then the king of France would be satisfied with the Flemish seaports, Namur and Thionville and the Republic with Breda, Gelder and Hulst, while the remnants of the Spanish Netherlands would, following the Swiss example, be transformed into a league of independent cantons. On the other hand, should the inhabitants remain loyal to Philip IV, then Luxemburg, Namur, Hainaut, Artois and West Flanders would fall to France, while Antwerp, Hulst, Mechelen, Ghent and Bruges would fall to the Republic.[23]

The Dutch–French Invasion (1635–1646)

On 2 June 1635 a French army of 29,000 men under the command of *maréchals* Gaspar III de Coligny (1584–1646), duke of Châtillon, and Urbain de Maillé (1597–1650), marquis of Brézé, arrived at Maastricht, the rendez-vous agreed upon with Frederick Henry. The Dutch force numbered approximately 20,000 men so that the combined Dutch–French invasion army numbered 50,000 men.[24] In the meantime some 350,000 pounds of bread had been baked

---

[20] Israel, *Empires and Entrepots*, p. 94.
[21] Van Nimwegen, *The Dutch Army*, p. 236.
[22] Ibid., pp. 237–40.
[23] Israel, *The Dutch Republic*, p. 527; Ten Raa and F. de Bas, *Het Staatsche leger*, vol. 4, p. 78.
[24] Van Nimwegen, *The Dutch Army*, p. 243. According to Parrott, *Richelieu's Army*, p. 190, the French field army dispatched to the Spanish Netherlands was 26,500 strong.

in Maastricht and at Aix-la-Chapelle for the troops, and in addition 200,000 pounds of rusk had been loaded onto waggons. This stockpile was intended to feed the Dutch–French army until it reached Tienen (Tirlemont), and from then on this town would serve as the logistical base for the onward push to Brussels.[25]

The prospects for the Spaniards were, however, less gloomy than they seemed on the face of it. On 4 November 1634, Ferdinand of Austria (1609–1641), the Cardinal-Infante, had arrived in Brussels. The appointment of Philip IV's younger brother as Governor-General of the Spanish Netherlands was one aspect of the change in strategy decided on in Madrid. The war against the Republic would once again be waged offensively. The Cardinal-Infante had therefore brought along reinforcements of 11,500 troops from Italy,[26] and in June 1635 a further 1,400 to 1,500 Spaniards arrived in Dunkirk. The combined Dutch–French army was still much stronger than the military force at the Cardinal-Infante's disposal, but the circumstance that Brabant was highly suitable for a defensive war largely compensated for this drawback.

At the start of June 1635 the allied forces set out on their advance to Tienen. The Cardinal-Infante withdrew to Louvain, where his troops established new positions on the far side of the River Dijle. Frederick Henry ordered Tienen's defenders to open the gates, but they refused to comply. So on the morning of 10 June he ordered the storming of Tienen. The garrison of approximately 1,200 men put up very little resistance.

However, what occurred thereafter was a cause of serious embarrassment to Frederick Henry. Not only was the town looted, a fire broke out reducing most of Tienen to ashes. Tienen's devastation denied the allies an essential logistical base. The Dutch army's commissioner of the victualling left for Diest together with his French colleague to arrange the transportation of provisions from Maastricht via the River Demer. It was evident, however, that the invasion could now be successful only if Frederick Henry managed to capture Louvain as swiftly as possible. Without control of this major town it would be impossible to safeguard the supply of provisions during the onward push into Brabant.

The situation was deteriorating by the day. The poorly paid French soldiers were melting away: by the end of June 1635 the French contingent counted just 17,000 men.[27] The Spaniards were in the meantime industriously reinforcing their positions and assistance from the Emperor was close at hand as well. General Ottavio Piccolomini (1599–1656), prince of Melfi, was heading for the Low Countries with approximately 12,000 imperial troops. If Piccolomini established a position between the allied forces and Maastricht, their supply lines would be completely blocked. The Dutch–French army made a half-hearted attempt to capture Louvain, but as soon as news arrived that the imperial force was close by, the allies withdrew. The fiasco of the Dutch–French invasion was complete when Schenkenschans, a Dutch fort guarding the River Rhine, was surprised by 500 Spaniards on 28 July 1635. This unexpected setback forced Frederick Henry to beat a hasty retreat to Nijmegen to prevent the Spanish-Imperial army following up this important success with a foray into Gelderland. Schenkenschans was not retaken until 29 April 1636. The remnants of the French army – less than 9,000 men[28] – had in the meantime returned to France.

The disappointing course of the 1635 campaign led to a sharp clash between Frederick Henry and the States of Holland. The attitude of Paris during the siege of Louvain had, if anything, further reinforced the distaste of many Hollanders for the alliance with France.

---

[25] On the 1635 campaign see Van Nimwegen, *The Dutch Army*, pp. 244–50.
[26] Vermeir, *In staat van oorlog*, pp. 105 and 109; Parker, *Army of Flanders*, p. 279.
[27] Parrott, *Richelieu's Army*, p. 190.
[28] Van Nimwegen, *The Dutch Army*, p. 249.

During this siege the Dutch had urged Louis XIII to create a diversion in Picardy to lure away Piccolomini towards the south of the Spanish Netherlands, but instead of promising to do his very best to arrange this the French envoy in The Hague had responded that, based on the alliance treaty, his king was not obliged to do this. This reaction seemed to indicate that Richelieu was not intending to attack Spain with all the means available and that he primarily wanted to shift the financial burden of the war in the Low Countries onto the Republic's shoulders. The war effort required of the Republic was, however, already greater than Holland's finances could bear. The Hollanders therefore considered it necessary to make it clear to Frederick Henry that things could not continue like this. They demanded cuts in military spending. Frederick Henry refused to comply. The disagreement between the captain-general and the States of Holland prevented any Dutch campaigning in 1636.[29] To end the political deadlock Frederick Henry proposed the following year to attack Dunkirk, a plan that could reliably gain broad support within Holland, as Dunkirk's privateers were devastating the herring fleet.[30] Louis XIII promised Frederick Henry moreover that the French army would create a diversion.

The siege of Dunkirk failed to materialise because of adverse weather conditions that delayed the shipping of the Dutch siege force thus giving the Cardinal-Infante the time to amass a substantial force in Flanders. Frederick Henry was hard pressed to find an alternative campaign objective to parry the critique that it were only the French who benefited from the 1635 treaty. Frederick Henry had Breda invested. The siege turned out to be more difficult than expected, with the defenders putting up a stout resistance. The Cardinal-Infante assembled an estimated 20,000 men, but instead of relieving the garrison, he marched to the River Meuse and recaptured Venlo and Roermond, thus severing the lines of communication between the Republic and Maastricht. Breda did not capitulate until 7 October 1637, after a siege of 79 days. Between 700 and 800 Dutch soldiers had lost their lives during the siege. Compared with the massive losses suffered by Spinola in 1624–25, Frederick Henry had retaken Breda with a minimal loss of life, but whether the capture of this town compensated for the loss of Venlo and Roermond is debatable. Without these two towns the Dutch could not threaten the Spanish Netherlands from the east, so the Cardinal-Infante could in future employ all his might against them for the defence of Antwerp and Flanders.[31]

The remaining nine campaigns (1638–46) of the Eighty Years' War were wholly dominated by Antwerp. Frederick Henry staked his military reputation on the taking of this city. It was a daring venture that ill-suited this cautious general, but as a politician he knew that only Antwerp's capture would convince the regents disposed to peace to continue fighting the Spaniards. An attack on Antwerp called for a military force of at least 30,000 men: 20,000 to 22,000 men were needed to hem in the city on the Brabant side; the remaining 8,000 to 10,000 men were needed on the Flanders side. Because of the proximity of Bergen op Zoom, the Republic enjoyed the fortunate advantage that provisions for 30,000 men could be conveyed with ease during such an operation, but the need to commit tens of thousands of Dutch soldiers to garrison duties in frontier towns made it questionable whether the Republic would be able to collect such a number of troops. The Spaniards, moreover, enjoyed the advantage of the inner lines, so they could swiftly shift troops between the Flanders and Brabant sides of the River Scheldt.[32]

---

[29] Ibid., p. 251.
[30] J.R. Bruijn, *Varend verleden. De Nederlandse oorlogsvloot in de zeventiende en achttiende eeuw* (n.p., 1998), p. 62; Israel, *The Dutch Republic*, pp. 264–5.
[31] On the 1637 campaign see Van Nimwegen, *The Dutch Army*, pp. 252–5.
[32] Ibid., p. 272.

The danger of attacking Antwerp with less than the required number of troops was made abundantly clear in 1638. In June of that year Field-Marshal Willem of Nassau-Siegen dug in with about 5,700 men on the Flanders side of the River Scheldt near Kallo, a village facing Antwerp. In the night of 20/21 June the Spaniards managed to break through the Dutch lines and took more than 2,000 Dutch soldiers prisoner.[33] The defeat at Kallo was largely the blame of panic among the Dutch soldiers, but the more deep-seated reason for this fiasco must be that the Republic could not attack with superior numbers. About 22,000 field troops had been available to Frederick Henry. The Cardinal-Infante had assembled approximately 18,000 men to face the Dutch, while the remaining Spanish field troops and the imperial supporting army under Piccolomini were being deployed against the French.[34] This meant the Dutch army was about a quarter stronger than the Spanish, a numerical superiority wholly negated by the strategic advantage of access to interior lines enjoyed by the Cardinal-Infante. The lesson to be drawn from the events of 1638 was crystal clear: Antwerp, Ghent and Bruges could not be besieged unless the Cardinal-Infante was obliged to dispatch the majority of his field troops to the border with France by a large-scale French offensive. Since 1635 France had brought strong armies into the field each year, but due to a lack of money and food these evaporated into thin air. In the autumn the Spaniards could undo most of the French conquests,[35] so the Cardinal-Infante accepted losses along the border with France during the summer months and deployed the bulk of his field troops to check the Dutch army.

From 1639 to 1643 Frederick Henry assembled each year a powerful army, but without achieving anything of note against the Spaniards. The French made some headway, but the new Spanish commander in the Netherlands, Francisco de Melo (1597–1651) – the Cardinal-Infante was seriously ill – managed to protect Lille, Douai and Saint-Omer and on 29 May 1642 he joined battle with the French at Honnecourt. The French army of 10,000 men suffered a heavy defeat: 1,200 Frenchmen lost their lives and the Spaniards took about 2,000 of them as prisoners of war.[36]

The year 1643 started more promisingly for the Dutch, because Melo advanced on Paris with the bulk of his troops. Richelieu had died on 4 December 1642 and Louis XIII was seriously ill. Melo hoped that the uncertain political situation would make the queen of France willing to reach a peace settlement with Madrid before the Spaniards had reached the gates of the French capital. Louis XIII died on 14 May 1643. However, the volte-face in French foreign policy that Melo was expecting failed to materialise, because the queen-dowager, together with her chief minister, Cardinal Jules Mazarin (1602–1661), continued down the political course plotted out by Richelieu. Only five days after Louis XIII's death Melo suffered a serious defeat at the battle of Rocroi (19 May 1643).[37] The French followed up on their victory by laying siege to Thionville.

The Spanish defeat at Rocroi did not benefit the Dutch, because Melo amassed all his remaining field troops (14,000 infantrymen and no fewer than 136 cavalry companies) for the defence of the towns in Flanders and Brabant. For him retaining control of these provinces was of much greater importance than the relief of the outlying fortress of Thionville. It fell into French hands on 10 August 1643. The French army continued its offensive in 1644 by laying siege to Gravelines (taken 28 July). Melo deployed again his

---

[33] Ibid., p. 256.
[34] Vermeir, *In staat van oorlog*, pp. 144–7.
[35] Parrott, *Richelieu's Army*, p. 129.
[36] Ibid., p. 157; Vermeir, *In staat van oorlog*, pp. 244–9; Israel, *The Dutch Republic*, p. 316.
[37] Bonney, *The King's Debts*, pp. 190–91, 193 and 195; Vermeir, *In staat van oorlog*, pp. 252–3.

best troops for the defence of Antwerp, Ghent and Bruges, even at the cost of abandoning the fortresses along the Westerscheldt estuary to their fate. Finally Frederick Henry was presented with the opportunity to attack. In late July the Dutch laid siege to Sas van Gent. This town would provide the Dutch Republic with a second strong base, in addition to Sluis, on the Westerscheldt. Melo advanced with approximately 20,000 men to relieve Sas van Gent, but he did not dare launch an assault on the strongly entrenched Dutch army. When Melo received news that a French cavalry force of 6,000 troopers was plundering Flanders, he broke camp and left for Ghent to take countermeasures. Sas van Gent capitulated on 5 September 1644.[38]

The reduction of Sas van Gent was an important success but Frederick Henry was not in the least satisfied with the outcome of the 1644 campaign: for him all that counted was Antwerp. In 1645 he therefore wanted to undertake a new attempt to invest Antwerp. This would require a temporary augmentation of the Dutch army with 13,000 men so that 30,000 men could take the field. Frederick Henry declared that if the provinces did not wish to consent to this then the States-General would have to be satisfied with an assault on Hulst. He was also willing to attack Ghent or Bruges but this would require French assistance. The majority of the regents had no desire to see the French penetrate into the heart of Flanders, and they therefore agreed to the siege of Antwerp. In the spring of 1645 30,000 Dutch troops were ready for the big offensive. Finally Frederick Henry had a force at his disposal that was big enough for the task at hand, but the Dutch commander-in-chief's enthusiasm for laying siege to Antwerp flagged considerably on receiving spy reports that indicated that the Spaniards had a numerical superiority of cavalry. The States-General at The Hague urged Frederick Henry to act offensively, but he believed it to be irresponsible to divide his forces. The French, however, advanced deeper and deeper into the Southern Netherlands and in late September seemed to have put their sights on Bruges. There was huge consternation about this in the Dutch headquarters, because on the basis of the 1635 alliance this town appertained to the Republic. The French assured Frederick Henry that the only purpose of their advance had been to make it possible for him to act offensively whereupon the Dutch commander-in-chief asked them to remain close to Ghent to 'give a diversion', while he with the Dutch army would approach Hulst. This town was taken on 3 November. In December the Spaniards recaptured Fort Mardyck from the French, but this success would not halt the French advance.[39] Developments in the political arena did, however, give Madrid hope of better prospects.

The Holy Roman Emperor had from 1641 been working on a diplomatic solution for the war in Germany. His efforts were formally limited to the lands involved in the Thirty Years' War, but because the Republic was allied to France she was also approached to participate in the negotiations. Frederick Henry had his doubts about sending Dutch diplomats to Münster, but was willing to consent in exchange for the Hollanders agreeing that in 1646 a final attempt would be made to capture Antwerp. Everything seemed now to be cut and dried, but then events in France threatened to frustrate the siege of Antwerp. In February 1646 it became common knowledge in The Hague that the seven-year-old Louis XIV (1638–1715) had purportedly married the eldest daughter of Philip IV, Maria Theresia (1638–1683), also aged just seven, 'and that the King of Spain would … be giving his daughter as a wedding gift the Netherlandish provinces that he still has under his authority, to be annexed to the crown of France for all eternity'.[40] The rumour of the French–Spanish betrothal caused great

---

[38] On the 1643–44 campaigns see Van Nimwegen, *The Dutch Army*, pp. 268–72.
[39] On the 1645 campaign see Ibid., pp. 272–8.
[40] Ibid., pp. 279. See also Poelhekke, *Vrede van Munster*, pp. 241–2.

alarm in the Republic. Mazarin swore to the Dutch ambassador in Paris that there was no question of a marriage with the Spanish Infanta. He was, however, forced to acknowledge that there had been talks with the king of Spain about the possibility of an engagement and that it was correct that the Spanish Netherlands had been mentioned as dowry.[41] To reassure the Dutch about France's good intentions, Frederick Henry received the commitment from Paris that 6,000 French troops would assist him in the siege of Antwerp, and that the main French army would in the meantime threaten Dunkirk and thereby tie the majority of the Spanish field troops to the coast.

In June 1646 25,000 Dutch troops were in readiness to invest Antwerp.[42] At long last Frederick Henry's main prize seemed to be in his grasp, but then an unexpected demand from the French threw everything into the air again. As a precondition for providing troops they stipulated 'that in this place [Antwerp] which we [the Dutch] are taking with their assistance, one would allow the Catholic religion'. This stipulation was in accordance with the alliance of 1635, but over the previous decade the French had not even mentioned it. The Amsterdammers were not adamantly against the allocation of a few churches to the Catholics, but then their city had to be allowed 'to build two papist churches in Amsterdam in order to keep the [Catholic] merchants in Amsterdam who would otherwise move to Antwerp'.[43] For the staunch Calvinist faction in the Dutch Republic this solution was, however, unacceptable. The siege of Antwerp was again shelved.

In Münster the negotiations between the Republic and Spain had by now reached a decisive phase. The growing distrust between The Hague and Paris gave the Spanish plenipotentiaries a wonderful opportunity to elaborate a separate peace settlement with the Republic. On 17 May they had already hinted that Philip IV was prepared to recognise the independence of the Republic and would assent to the permanent 'closure' of the River Scheldt (the relevance of this was that all shipping to and from Antwerp would be regulated by Dutch tariffs and trade stipulations), would permit the levying of import duties in the Flemish seaports as high as those on the River Scheldt, and would agree to cede the Meijerij of 's-Hertogenbosch. The provision concerning the seaports offered the Hollanders and Zeelanders guarantees against Antwerp's possible plans to transform Ostend into an out port by digging canals, thus re-establishing her former trading status.[44] The king of Spain and his new chief minister, Don Luis Mendez de Haro (1598–1661), were prepared to grant these concessions because they thought they offered the only means of retaining the Spanish Netherlands. Because of the uprisings in Catalonia and Portugal, Madrid could no longer contend with France and the Republic simultaneously.[45] In the summer of 1646 the French captured Fort Mardyck and Veurne, and then pressed on to Dunkirk. This fortress fell on 10 October. The Dutch–Spanish negotiations in Münster gained momentum. Philip IV removed the last obstacles to a Dutch–Spanish peace when he intimated to recognise all the conquests won by the Dutch East and West India Companies in America and Asia since 1641 as Dutch possessions. The king of Spain had opted for this remarkable step because the loss of these territories did not affect Spain but hit the rebellious Portuguese, and in exchange the Republic promised to suspend trade with the Spanish colonies forthwith. The preliminary points were signed by the Dutch and Spanish negotiators on 8 January 1647.[46] The formal signing

---

[41] Poelhekke, *Vrede van Munster*, p. 242.
[42] Van Nimwegen, *The Dutch Army*, p. 281.
[43] Visser, *Gloria Parendi*, pp. 250–51.
[44] Israel, *The Dutch Republic*, p. 360; V. Enthoven, 'Zeeland en de opkomst van de Republiek. Handel en strijd in de Scheldedelta c. 1550–1621', PhD diss., Leiden University 1996, pp. 109–10.
[45] Lynch, *Spain under the Habsburgs*, vol. 2, pp. 125–9; Vermeir, *In staat van oorlog*, p. 287.
[46] Poelhekke, *Vrede van Munster*, pp. 271, 308–10; Israel, *The Dutch Republic*, pp. 366–7 and 369–70.

of the peace between the Republic and Spain took place on 30 January 1648. Frederick Henry did not witness the conclusion of the peace between the Republic and Spain: he passed away on 14 March 1647, aged 63.

Selected Bibliography

Bruijn, J.R., *Varend verleden. De Nederlandse oorlogsvloot in de zeventiende en achttiende eeuw* (n.p., 1998).
Israel, J., *The Dutch Republic and the Hispanic World 1606–1661* (Oxford, 1982).
Israel, J., *Empires and Entrepots. The Dutch, the Spanish Monarchy and the Jews, 1585–1713* (London and Ronceverte, WV, 1990).
Lynch, J., *Spain under the Habsburgs*, 2 vols (2nd edn, Oxford, 1981).
Nimwegen, O. van, *The Dutch Army and the Military Revolutions 1588–1688* (Woodbridge, 2010).
Parker G., *The Army of Flanders and the Spanish Road 1567–1659. The logistics of Spanish victory and defeat in the Low Countries' Wars* (rev. edn, Cambridge, New York and Melbourne, 1990).
Parker G., *The Military Revolution. Military Innovation and the Rise of the West, 1500–1800* (2nd rev. edn, Cambridge, 1996).
Parker G. (ed.), *The Thirty Years' War* (2nd edn; London and New York, 1997).
Parrott, D., *Richelieu's Army. War, Government and Society in France, 1624–1642* (Cambridge, 2001).
Poelhekke, J.J., *Frederik Hendrik prins van Oranje. Een biografisch drieluik* (Zutphen, 1978).
Raa, F.J.G. ten, and F. de Bas, *Het Staatsche leger 1568–1795*, 5 vols (Breda, 1911–21), vol. 4.
Vermeir, R., *In staat van oorlog. Filips IV en de Zuidelijke Nederlanden 1629–1648* (Maastricht, 2001).
Visser, J. (transcription), and G.N. van der Plaats (eds), *Gloria Parendi. Dagboeken van Willem Frederik stadhouder van Friesland, Groningen en Drenthe 1643–1649, 1651–1654* (The Hague, 1995).

14

The Thirty Years' War in Italy 1628–1659

Sven Externbrink

Italy, Europe, and International Relations, ca. 1560–1618

In the first half of the seventeenth century, Italy has to be considered as the 'cœur du monde', to quote a famous phrase of Richelieu's *Testament politique*.[1] Richelieu's comment alludes to two areas that establish Italy's importance. First, Italy is the place where the head of Catholic Christianity resides, and secondly it is the centre of the Spanish empire in Europe – a view central also for Spanish officials. The Spanish ambassador at the imperial court, the Marquis d'Aytona, characterised Italy in 1628 as 'the heart of Spanish empire'.[2] There are further reasons for this: in the first half of the century, Italy was still the heart of the European economy; Lombardy was still one of the most productive regions in Europe; and Italy commanded the trends in all fields of arts, be it literature, art and architecture, or music.

Politically, after half a century of almost continuous warfare in the sixteenth century, the peace of Cateau-Cambrésis established a solid order founded on Spanish dominance. The peace ended a period of more than 50 years of permanent invasions of French armies into Italy.[3]

The king of Spain ruled as duke of Milan in Lombardy, and as king of Naples and Sicily. As such, he controlled almost half of the area of Italy. Contrary to Risorgimento historians of the late nineteenth and early twentieth centuries, foreign rule did not mean oppression or 'decadence'. Spanish rule in its territories was well established and based on a system of collaboration and control of the local elites. Italian rulers and nobles were orientated toward Spain.[4] The other actors of the political scene in Italy had to arrange themselves with this Spanish hegemony in Italy. Only the republic of Venice and the duke of Savoy retained a certain independence from Spanish tutelage.

We must also consider that the affiliation of northern Italy to the Holy Roman Empire had an impact on the political order of the region. Savoy, Tuscany, Mantua, and Milan were all imperial fiefs, and their rulers had to demand their investiture by the emperor when they came to the throne. Although the relations between the emperor and Italy had

---

[1] Richelieu, *Testament politique*, ed. L. André (Paris, 1947), p. 414.
[2] H. Kiewning (ed.), *Nuntiaturberichte aus Deutschland 1628–1635. Nuntiatur des Pallotto 1628–1630*, (2 vols, Berlin, 1895–1897), vol. 1, p. 6.
[3] On the peace of Cateau-Cambrésis, see now B. Haan, *Une paix pour l'éternité. La négociation du traité du Cateau-Cambrésis* (Geneva, 2010).
[4] On Spanish Italy, see T.J. Dandelet and J.A. Marino (eds), *Spain in Italy. Politics, Society, and Religion 1500–1700* (Leiden and Boston, 2007) and T. J. Dandelet, *Spanish Rome, 1500–1700* (New Haven and London, 2001).

lost the intensity they had had during the Middle Ages, the Emperors never gave up their rights there.[5]

To return to Richelieu's deliberation, Italy was of the greatest strategic importance for the Spanish empire. Not only did it serve as a reservoir to fill the ranks of the Spanish *Tercios*, as they left from the duchy of Milan to the battlefields north of the Alps; it was of the greatest strategic importance for the king of Spain's interests that the main roads to the Habsburg territories in the empire and in the Netherlands should never be closed. Unfortunately, the Franco-Savoyard war that ended in 1601 with the treaty of Lyon closed the western route to the Franche-Comté. This blockade increased the importance of the routes through the Swiss Cantons and the Grisons.[6]

The treaty of Lyon also signifies Henri IV's intention to oppose Spanish hegemony in Europe and Italy. Henri intervened in Italy during the conflict between Venice and Rome about Church rights in the republic. Thus, Henri signalled to other Italian rulers the return of France to Italian affairs. In the spring of 1610, Henri assembled a large army and prepared to intervene in the Jülich-Cleves Succession crisis. As is well known, this army never marched, because Henri IV was assassinated on 14 May of that year. What is less well known is that he had also prepared an attack on the duchy of Milan. He had concluded a treaty with Charles Emanuel I of Savoy that envisaged setting up an army of almost 30,000 men and the transferral of the duchy of Milan to the duke of Savoy. After Henri's assassination, Charles Emanuel I hastened to apologise to Philip III for his collaboration with the French.[7]

Prelude to War: the Mantuan Succession and the Uskoks War 1612–1618

The war that had been avoided in Italy finally broke out two years later. When Francis III, duke of Mantua and Monferrato, died in 1612, the ambitious Charles Emanuel claimed the possession of Monferrato for himself. He justified his pretensions by means of the alliance of the Savoyard dynasty with the former owners of the duchy, the Paleologi family. Now Charles Emanuel saw a new chance to acquire this small territory, which was of the greatest strategic importance, because its capital Casale, the most sophisticated fortress of the early seventeenth century, controlled the road from Genoa to Milan.

Charles Emanuel believed himself strong enough to challenge the Gonzagas and the Spanish Crown. He invaded Monferrato in April 1613 and tried to occupy Casale. The Spanish reacted promptly on behalf of the Gonzaga, and a first truce was concluded in 1615 (the Treaty of Asti). This was the beginning of a limited war in Piedmont and Monferrato that lasted until 1617. The French politics during the war reflect the complicated distribution of power inside France. Marie de Medici, the regent, wanted to avoid a conflict with Spain.

Acting on his own, the Governor of the Dauphiné, the Connétable de Lesdiguières, a friend of the duke of Savoy, had already sent military aid to Piedmont. Marie de Medici and her young Secretary of State for foreign affairs and war, a certain Armand Jean du Plessis de Richelieu, feared serious repercussions with Spain, but they were not able to prevent Lesdiguières's solo action. But, in April 1617, Louis XIII, who had freed himself from the

---

[5] M. Schnettger and M. Verga (eds), *L'Impero e L'Italia nella prima età moderna* (Berlin and Bologna, 2006).

[6] G. Parker, *The Army of Flanders and the Spanish Road, 1567–1659*, 2nd edn (Cambridge, 1990).

[7] For details see S. Externbrink, *'Le Cœur du monde' – Frankreich und die norditalienischen Staaten (Mantua, Parma, Savoyen) im Zeitalter Richelieus 1624–1635* (Münster, 1999), pp. 70–74.

tutelage of his mother, decided to back Charles Emanuel I and accused the Governor of Milan of the violation of the Treaty of Asti. This was a first sign that Louis wanted to return to the anti-Habsburg policy of his ancestors. The stalemate that followed led to the peace treaty of Pavia (9 October 1617) and the return to the *status quo ante*. Monferrato remained in the possession of the Gonzagas.

This first war of the Mantuan succession can be regarded as a blueprint for the events that followed over the next decades in Italy. Not only Savoyard and Spanish forces fought in the war, but also French and (French-paid) German forces intervened. The duke of Savoy challenged the Spanish domination of northern Italy and he gained a reputation for his resistance against the Spanish. Publicists praised him as the defender of Italian liberty. In search of allies, Charles Emanuel also contacted the Protestant Union in Germany and negotiated with envoys from the Palatinate about the recruitment of German soldiers.

French politics returned to the paths of the Valois and of Henri IV's policies, presenting France as the protector of the small states against Spanish oppression. On the other side, Madrid had to face – for the first time since the 1530s – an attempt against the strategic Italian 'heart' of the Spanish empire.

There was another war at the same time as the Mantuan war, on the eastern frontier of Italy. Venice fought, with the help of Dutch and English mercenaries, against the Adriatic pirates called the Uskoks, who were backed by the Archduke Ferdinand (later Emperor Ferdinand II), who employed them as allies in his fight against the Ottoman Empire. The war lasted from 1615 to 1617 and ended with an agreement between Venice and Ferdinand, mediated by Spanish and French negotiators. It ended the Uskoks' piracy in the Adriatic, but the main significance of this war was the rapprochement between Ferdinand and his Spanish cousins.

For now, however, all attention turned to Bohemia, where a revolt against the Habsburg Emperor broke out on 23 May 1618, when members of the Protestant Estates of Bohemia carried out the famous defenestration, throwing three imperial representatives out of the window of the royal palace in Prague.

The Bohemian Rebellion and Charles Emanuel I of Savoy

The Bohemian Rebellion was a European affair from the outset, as can be seen by the Spanish intervention in the Palatinate and papal aid for the Habsburg war efforts. Less known is the Savoyard involvement. When the revolt broke out, Charles Emanuel I offered to help the insurgents by subsidising a regiment of German mercenaries, commanded by Count Mansfeld, whom he had hired for the Mantua War.[8]

The duke of Savoy thus continued his anti-Habsburg policy, but his aim was to use the weakness of the Habsburgs for the elevation of his rank within the European 'society of princes' (L. Bély). He launched his candidature for the Bohemian, as well as for the imperial crown, as the Catholic alternative to the Protestant Frederick V, prince elector of the Palatinate. This might seem audacious and unrealistic, but viewed from the duke's perspective, it fits in well with his quest for the revaluation of his dynasty.[9]

---

[8] See R. Kleinmann, 'Charles Emanuel of Savoy and the Bohemian Election of 1619', *European Studies Review* 5 (1975): p. 3–29 and B. Erdmannsdoerffer, *Herzog Karl Emanuel I. von Savoyen und die deutsche Kaiserwahl von 1619. Ein Beitrag zur Vorgeschichte des Dreißigjährigen Krieges* (Leipzig, 1862).

[9] On the Savoyard dream of gaining royal honours: R. Oresko, 'The House of Savoy in Search for a Royal Crown in the Seventeenth Century', in R. Oresko, G.C. Gibbs and H.M. Scott (eds), *Royal and*

Nevertheless, Charles Emanuel had no chance of being elected. Even his ally, Christian of Anhalt, *spiritus rector* of the Calvinist party in the empire, did not regard his candidature as convincing. Surprisingly, the open opposition to the Austrian Habsburgs and to his feudal overlord, the emperor, was not followed by any sanctions after the repression of the Bohemians in the aftermath of the Battle of White Mountain. The Bavarian councillor Wilhelm Jocher, commissioned to edit the papers of the rebels captured at the Battle of White Mountain, advised against mentioning Charles Emanuel's name in the publication.[10] Finally, Charles Emanuel quickly changed sides and tried to approach the emperor.

Although one might consider Charles Emanuel's involvement in the Bohemian revolt as secondary, this does show that Spain had lost its overwhelming dominance in Italy, and that enterprising actors in the Italian 'theatre' would try to use their new room to manoeuvre for the pursuit of their own interests.

The Valtellina Affair

While Spanish troops helped to defeat the Palatinate in Germany, a new conflict arose in Italy that again affected the most important political actors of the Italian peninsula and led to a first confrontation between France and Spain. The closing of the Spanish road via Savoy and the Franche-Comté highlighted the geo-strategic importance of a small corridor in the Alps, the Valtellina valley.[11] Coming from the duchy of Milan, Spanish troops passed through this corridor (under the government of the Protestant Grisons) to enter Habsburg lands in Tirol. In 1620, the Catholic population, encouraged by the Spanish governor at Milan, Feria, revolted in a 'holy slaughter' (*sacro macello*) against their Protestant government. In the following months, Spanish troops occupied the valley.

This provoked a reaction: France, as ally and protector of the Grisons sovereignty, decided to intervene and formed an alliance with Savoy and Venice (Treaty of Lyon 1623). But before the joint army was prepared, France and Spain agreed to a neutralisation of the valley under the surveillance of papal troops. An open war appeared to have been avoided. But with the appointment of Cardinal Richelieu in the *conseil d'en haut* in 1624, the French disposition for a peaceful solution yielded to confrontation. At the end of the year, a French corps dispersed the Spanish and papal troops and took possession of the valley for the Grisons. The alliance with Savoy was confirmed, and, with French assistance, Charles Emanuel attacked Genoa, under the pretext of a quarrel over the possession of the fief of Zuccarello. If Genoa could be captured, this would be a terrible blow to the Spanish hegemony in Italy, because Madrid not only depended on the Genoese bankers, but Genoa also served as the principal port for the communication between Madrid and Milan. Here the troops landed to march to the battlefields north of the Alps.

But soon it became clear that the Savoyard army was incapable of forcing the Genoese to surrender. The situation also became critical for the French in the Valtellina when the Spanish counter attack began. Now it was revealed that Richelieu's position in the *conseil*

Republican Sovereignty in Early Modern History. Essays in Memory of Ragnhild Hatton (Cambridge, 1997), pp. 272–350.

[10] *Briefe und Akten zur Geschichte des Dreißigjährigen Krieges, N. F.: Die Politik Maximilians I. von Bayern und seiner Verbündeten 1618–1651*, Part I, vol. 2: Januar 1621–Dezember 1622, ed. by A. Duch (Munich and Vienna, 1970), p. 38 and pp. 86–7.

[11] For details see A. Wendland, *Der Nutzen der Pässe und die Gefährdung der Seelen. Spanien, Mailand und der Kampf ums Veltlin (1620–1641)* (Zürich, 1995); Externbrink, *Cœur du monde*, pp. 78–84.

d'en haut was far from uncontested. Revolts by powerful nobles, the armed Huguenot party, and opponents such as Gaston, the brother of Louis XIII, threatened Richelieu, who began to search for a compromise in the Valtellina. Richelieu gave priority to internal French problems, but this did not mean that he gave up his plan to confront and block what he thought was the Spanish will to erect a universal monarchy. Thanks to papal mediation, French and Spanish envoys concluded the treaty of Monzón in Spain (5 March 1626). The French retreated from the Valtellina and were replaced by papal troops. The authority of the Grisons in the valley was restored, but the population was allowed to practise their Catholic faith. The Savoyard army retired from Genoese territory.

The outcome of this conflict marked a severe blow to Richelieu's ambition to reinstall France as an actor and as a counterweight to Spain in Italy. For the next two years, he was occupied with the fight against England and the Huguenot strongpoint La Rochelle. The treaty of Monzón seriously harmed the French reputation in Italy, especially in Turin, where the duke began to make approaches to the Spanish court.

The War of the Mantuan Succession: A Turning Point of the Thirty Years' War

The years from 1628 to 1631 mark the turning point of the Thirty Years' War. The German war escalated in these years irrevocably into a European conflict. In the 1620s the branches of the Habsburg family were on the brink of victory over their opponents. The Spanish army had conquered the Dutch stronghold of Breda, and in 1629 the emperor seemed to have defeated Protestant opposition in Germany and to have achieved the Catholic roll-back with the issue of the Edict of Reconstitution. In 1631, however, both branches of the Habsburg family had to face a series of severe defeats all over Europe.

In the centre of these events we find the war of the Mantuan Succession.[12] The question of who would succeed the last duke of the Gonzaga family brought the war to northern Italy, and, with the war, a terrible plague epidemic struck Italy, with grave consequences for the local economic system. All 'great powers' intervened in the conflict, France, Spain, and the Habsburg Emperor, and the question of how to act in this conflict caused a great domestic crisis, especially at the French and Spanish courts. As John H. Elliott observes, the war of the Mantuan succession was 'a confrontation that would transform the political configuration of Europe'.[13]

---

[12] There is a renewed interest in this war; its significance for the history of the Thirty Years' War has been acknowledged to an ever greater extent, see the remarks in P. Wilson, *Europe's Tragedy. A New History of the Thirty Years War* (London, 2010), pp. 424, 438–46, 457–8. Cf. D. Parrott, 'A *prince souverain* and the French Crown: Charles de Nevers 1580–1637', in G.C. Gibbs, R. Oresko and H.M. Scott (eds), *Royal and Republican Sovereignty in Early Modern Europe. Essays in Memory of Ragnhild Hatton* (Cambridge, 1997), pp. 149–87; idem, 'The Mantuan Succession, 1627–1631: a Sovereignty Dispute in Early Modern Europe', *English Historical Review*, 112/445 (1997), pp. 20–65. On the Duchy of Monferrato in general see R. Oresko, D. Parrott, 'The Sovereignty of Monferato and the Citadel of Casale as European Problems in the Early Modern Period', D. Ferrari (ed.), *Stefano Guazzo e Casale tra Cinque e Seicento. Atti del convegno die studi nel quarto centenario della morte. Casale Monterrato, 22–23 ottobre 1993* (Rome, 1997), pp. 11–86. Richelieu's policy is analysed in Externbrink, *Cœur du monde*, pp. 87–201. For all details of the war, see the basic studies of R. Quazza, *Mantova e Monferrato nella politicaeuropea alla vigilia della guerra per la successione (1624–1627)* (Mantua 1922), and idem, *La guerra per la successione di Mantova e del Monferrato (1628–1631)* (2 vols, Mantua, 1926).

[13] J.H. Elliott, *Richelieu and Olivares*, 4th edn (Cambridge, 1991), p. 95.

On 25 December 1627, Duke Vincenzo II of Mantua died. With him expired the main line of the Gonzaga family that had ruled Mantua since the fourteenth century. The main pretender was Charles de Nevers, head of the French branch of the Gonzaga. He was the son of Louis Gonzaga, who had settled in France in the sixteenth century, and since then had been integrated into the French high nobility. There were also other pretenders, like the duke of Guastalla, from an Italian branch of the Gonzaga. The most powerful was the duke of Savoy. Savoyard princesses had married Gonzaga Dukes, and Charles Emanuel was especially interested in Monferrato, claiming that this duchy could pass via the female line. The possession of Monferrato would considerably increase Savoyard power over, and influence on, Italian affairs.

The question of who was to succeed in Mantua was of the greatest concern for Madrid. The strategic importance of Monferrato in particular has already been mentioned. A French duke in Mantua and Monferrato could and would endanger the Spanish position in northern Italy. Consequently, the Governor of Milan, Don Gonzalo de Córdoba, transcending his instructions, occupied Monferrato in the spring of 1628 and besieged Casale, where Charles de Nevers had managed to reinforce the garrison some weeks before. Córdoba concluded an alliance with Charles Emanuel I, who claimed the Monferrato territory north of the Po River as his heritage.

Meanwhile, Nevers arrived in Mantua and took over the government. He immediately asked for investiture in Vienna. Both duchies belonged to *Reichsitalien* and, as they were imperial fiefs, it was the emperor who gave the ultimate legitimation to their rulers. However, Ferdinand II denied the investiture and named Count Nassau as sequestrator of the two duchies. He did so not because he contested the rights of Nevers, but out of consideration for the interest of his Spanish cousins. His councillors saw clearly the dilemma. Nevers's rights to the succession were incontestable, but they had to be denied 'on grounds of reason of state, to exclude the French from Italy' on behalf of the Spanish king.[14] The Spanish pressure on the emperor was high. Without Spanish help, the imperial triumph in the Bohemian revolt and in the following conflict would not have been possible, but 'now, in the matter of Mantua and Italy, Spain made clear that payment was due'.[15] But the emperor also pursued interests of his own. The Mantuan succession offered a perfect opportunity to strengthen the emperor's position in *Reichsitalien* and Ferdinand was prepared to seize it.

On the other hand, Nevers rejected all possibilities that could have led to a compromise. He appealed to Louis XIII for protection, referring to the French view of themselves as protectors of the Italian states, and to the concept of *Libertá d'Italia*, 'invented' by Machiavelli, who, in the last chapter of his *Prince*, called on the Italians to banish the Spaniards from the peninsula.[16]

Louis XIII and Richelieu answered in the affirmative to Nevers's appeal, although, at that moment, they gave priority to the Huguenot revolt and the siege of La Rochelle. But immediately after the defeat of the Huguenots in October 1628, they began preparations for an armed expedition to Italy. Already, in March 1629, the French army, headed by the king and Richelieu, crossed the Alps, dispersed the Savoyard army at Susa, and forced Duke Charles Emanuel to capitulate. In a series of treaties concluded at Susa, the abandonment of

---

[14] H. Kiewning, *Nuntiatur des Pallotto*, vol. 1, p. 12. Externbrink, *Cœur du monde*, p. 94.

[15] R. Bireley, *Religion and Politics in the Age of Counterreformation. Emperor Ferdinand II, William Lamormaini, S.J. and the Formation of Imperial Policy* (Chapel Hill, 1981), p. 68.

[16] Cf. V. Di Tocco, *Ideali d'indipendenza in Italia durante la preponderanza spagnuola* (Messina, 1927). S. Externbrink, '*Le cœur du monde et la Liberté de l'Italie*: Aspects de la politique italienne de Richelieu 1624–1642', *Revue d'Histoire diplomatique*, 114 (2000): pp. 181–208.

the siege of Casale was resolved and an alliance between France, Savoy, Mantua, and Venice was founded. For a moment, it seemed as if France had re-established the peace in Italy.[17]

But the Habsburgs, and especially the emperor Ferdinand, were not ready to accept French mediation. Because all enemies in the empire were on the retreat (except the town of Stralsund, besieged in vain by Wallenstein), Ferdinand decided to send an army to Italy. In the late summer of 1629, an imperial army crossed the Alps and laid siege to Mantua.

The appearance of the imperial army in Italy marks a new step in the escalation of the conflict. Richelieu and Louis XIII could ignore neither the failure of their system of alliances created at Susa, nor leave Nevers without support. Thus, after the definitive victory over the Huguenots in the south of France in the summer of 1629, preparations for a return of the army to Italy began.

As in 1629, but without the king, Richelieu arrived at the head of an army in Italy in March 1630. Charles Emanuel of Savoy changed sides again and looked for help to the emperor and Spain. This was his last volte-face; he died on 26 July, leaving his successor Victor Amadeus I in a terrible situation. But neither Madrid nor the emperor were in a position to help. The Spaniards were still besieging Casale, and the imperial army renewed their siege of Mantua after a first attempt had failed in December 1629. The war now reached its climax. The French again defeated the Savoyard army and occupied the fortress of Pinerolo, which guarded the Chisone Valley and the pass of Mount Genèvre. This was Richelieu's real aim. Pinerolo opened a passage for the French army south of Turin. If the French could guard it, it would be possible for them to enter Italy whenever they wanted. Needless to say, this was unacceptable to Madrid.[18] In the late summer, the French army approached Casale, where the garrison was still defending the citadel against the Spaniards headed by Ambrogio Spinola, the conqueror of Breda.

Meanwhile, in Mantua the situation of Nevers became hopeless. With no chance of relief from the outside, he desperately defended Mantua against the imperial army. On the night of 16 July, German lansquenets entered the town and a three-day pillage of the town began that resurrected the memory of the *sacco di Roma*. The German mercenaries and their generals, Aldringen and Collalto, took what remained of the splendours of the Gonzaga.[19] Nevers and his family sought refuge in the territory of the Church State. He had to accept what French, Spanish, imperial, and papal diplomats would negotiate in the following months.

As always during early modern wars, the opponents did not stop negotiating. The emperor, in particular, had a growing interest in a settlement in Italy, because on 6 July 1630, the Swedish king Gustav Adolph landed with 13,000 men at Usedom in Pomerania.[20] Encouraged by France and Venice, the Swedish force represented a massive threat to the emperor's position in northern Germany, and gave Protestants new hope.

What was worse was the growing opposition of Catholic Electors to the military power of the emperor. This, and the Italian affairs, were negotiated at the Regensburg Electoral Congress from July to October 1630. Instead of finding backing for his Italian policy, the emperor was forced to enter into peace negotiations with the French delegation.

The Peace of Regensburg, concluded on 13 October 1630, did not pacify Italy. Because of the domestic crisis that paralysed Richelieu from September onward, culminating in the 'day

---

[17] Externbrink, *Cœur du monde*, pp. 105–15.

[18] For a detailed account, see Externbrink, *Cœur du monde*, pp. 116–32.

[19] See Quazza, *Guerra di successione*, vol. 2, pp. 119–81, S. Externbrink, 'Die Rezeption des *Sacco di Mantova* im 17. Jahrhundert. Zur Wahrnehmung, Darstellung und Bewertung eines Kriegsereignisses', in M. Meumann and D. Niefanger (eds), *Ein Schauplatz herber Angst. Wahrnehmung und Darstellung von Gewalt im 17. Jahrhundert* (Göttingen, 1997), pp. 205–22.

[20] See Wilson, *Europe's Tragedy*, pp. 459–65.

of the Dupes' in November, the French envoys were in Regensburg without instructions from France for weeks, and thus agreed to a treaty that not only settled the Mantuan succession (the investiture of Charles de Nevers as duke of Mantua, compensations for the pretenders, mutual retreat of foreign armies from northern Italy), but also obliged the French king to stop all support for the opponents of the emperor, such as the Protestant Electors and *Reichsstände*, or the king of Sweden. This turned out to be unacceptable for Richelieu, who refused the ratification.[21]

Nevertheless, the news of the treaty sufficed to stop the confrontation in Italy. The French and Spanish commanders concluded – with the mediation of a young papal diplomat named Giulio Mazzarino – a truce that avoided a direct confrontation between the Spanish and the French armies. The siege of Casale was lifted and the Spanish could enter the town, but not the citadel. In November, both armies retired from Casale and control of the town was assigned to representatives of the duke of Nevers. This marked the end of the hostilities of the War of the Mantuan Succession; now negotiations began for a peaceful settlement of the conflict that lasted until 6 April 1631, when, in Cherasco, a peace treaty was signed by the envoys.

The articles concerning Italy in the treaty of Regensburg served as the basis for the new peace treaty. Nevers was invested with Mantua and Monferrato, but he was forced to cede almost half of the latter territory to the new duke of Savoy, Victor Amadeus I, and to pay compensation to him and to other pretenders. The most difficult question concerned the retreat of French and imperial troops from Italy. After further negotiations, the opponents reached an agreement in June that foresaw a gradual retreat of the armies until all occupied territories and fortresses were returned. In mid-September, the foreign troops had left Italy and Nevers was officially recognised as duke of Mantua and Monferrato.[22]

Did this war really 'transform the political configuration of Europe', as John H. Elliott asserts?[23] Let us answer this question by looking at the winners and losers of the war.

Charles de Nevers certainly counts among those who paid a terrible price for the recognition of his rights as heir to the Gonzaga. His territories, and especially Mantua, an architectural and cultural jewel among north Italian cities, were ravaged by war and the plague. He paid for the peace by ceding parts of Monferrato to Savoy and by according a high sum of compensation to other pretenders. He also lost the fortresses of Luzzara and Reggiolo to the Guastalla-Gonzaga, and even if during the peace negotiations of Munster it was decided that they had to be returned to Mantua (IPM § 97), they finally returned only in the 1660s.[24] Spain also counts among the losers. Madrid had to accept a duke of Mantua of French origins – although weak – at the frontier of the duchy of Milan. It was France, not Spain, who more or less dictated the peace conditions, and the peace in general served more French intents than Spanish. As John Elliott points out, the Spanish 'intervention in Mantua had antagonised Europe, driven the papacy into the arms of the French, strained Madrid's relations with Vienna almost to a breaking point, and wrecked Olivares's grand design for securing peace with the Dutch on better terms than those of 1609. Above all, the breathing-space that looked like being gained in 1627 had been recklessly thrown away'.[25]

This was also true for the emperor. Urged by Madrid to intervene, Ferdinand II and his councillors hoped to strengthen imperial authority in *Reichsitalien*, but the results were poor

---

[21] D.P. O'Connel, 'A *cause célèbre* in the History of Treaty Making: the Refusal to ratify the Peace Treaty of Regensburg in 1630', *The British Year Book of International Law*, 42 (1967): pp. 71–90.

[22] Details of the negotiations: Externbrink, *Le cœur du monde*, pp. 133–53.

[23] Elliott, *Richelieu and Olivares*, p. 95.

[24] C. Mozzarelli, *Mantova e i Gonzaga dal 1382 al 1707* (Turin, 1987), p. 121.

[25] Elliott, *Richelieu and Olivares*, p. 112.

compared to the commitment and the losses. The imperial army conquered Mantua, but perished of the plague in the aftermath. What was worse, Ferdinand did not have the army at his command when Gustav Adolph started his triumphal campaigns through Germany. All the success of the 1620s perished under the attack of the Swedish army.

Although his possessions south of the Alps were also ravaged by war and the plague, in a long-term view the duke of Savoy must be counted among the winners. In 1630/31, Victor Amadeus I was forced into an alliance with France (Richelieu was helped by the duke's wife, Christine de France, sister of Louis XIII) that would last almost for the rest of the seventeenth century. As compensation, he obtained half of the duchy of Monferrato (unfortunately without Casale) and extended the frontiers of the duchy to the shores of the River Po.

Undoubtedly France and Cardinal Richelieu were the winners of the war. The risk taken by Richelieu in advising Louis XIII to wage the war was rewarded. Inside France, Richelieu defeated all his opponents in a plot that could serve as a scenario for a Hollywood film. After 1631, he controlled the *conseil d'État*. Outside France, the Habsburgs were generally weakened as we have seen, the emperor haunted by the Swedish; his Spanish cousins had to face serious setbacks caused by the Dutch, and their hegemony in Italy was questioned by the French presence there.

This was Richelieu's masterpiece in this conflict: he re-opened a passage for the French armies, for in a secret treaty of alliance concluded with Victor Amadeus I in Cherasco, the latter ceded the fortress of Pinerolo and the valley of Chisone. Even the restitution of Pinerolo – in the presence of Spanish and imperial witnesses – was a subterfuge; while the commissioners visited the fortress only briefly, in a cursory way, because they feared contagion (maybe a rumour spread by the French), French soldiers were hidden in the casemates. After the retreat of the armies, Victor Amadeus I and the French envoy, Abel Servien, continued to play out the 'comedy' for the public by concluding a series of treaties that led to the cession of Pinerolo to the king of France. But every treaty contained a secret article, referring to the alliance treaty of 1631 as the only valid one.[26]

This was probably the most severe blow to the Spanish in Italy. The presence of a French garrison in Pinerolo formed a constant threat to the duchy of Milan, as well as the communication lines in northern Italy. In the worst case, the French could cut the Spanish road to the Netherlands in Italy. On the other hand, Richelieu justified the acquisition of Pinerolo with his will to 'defend the liberty of Italy', threatened by Spanish troops in Milan.[27] This would be the 'leitmotif' in the negotiations with Italian princes in the following years.

Cold War: Italy 1631–1635

The new constellation created by the outcome of the War of Mantuan Succession weighed heavily on Italy: northern Italy had suffered terribly from the plague and war; the economy of Lombardy and northern Italy had collapsed;[28] Richelieu was continuing to explore the new situation;[29] and since 1631 Pinerolo had remained fortified.[30] Servien and other French

---

[26] See Externbrink, *Cœur du monde*, pp. 158–89. R. Quazza, 'Una pagina di storia diplomatica franco-sabauda' *Convivium*, 8 (1936): pp. 292–331.
[27] Count Solar de Marguerite (ed.), *Traités publics de la royale Maison de Savoie avec les puissances étrangers depuis la paix de Cateau-Cambrésis*, 6 vols (Turin, 1836–1844), vol. 1, p. 437.
[28] D. Sella, *Italy in the Seventeenth Century* (New York, 1997), p. 35.
[29] For the following Externbrink, *Cœur du monde*, pp. 202–325.
[30] Externbrink, *Le Cœur du monde*, p. 182.

diplomats were courting the rulers in Turin, Mantua, Parma, Modena, Florence, and Venice to enter into Richelieu's 'grand design' of an anti-Spanish league. Richelieu's dream was the conquest of Milan and the expulsion of Spain from (northern) Italy. His councillors wrote expertises to justify French claims on Milan, thus building on the Valois tradition of the first half of the sixteenth century. But in the negotiations this objective was abandoned: Milan was offered as a prize to the Italian princes, especially Savoy.

But all these diplomatic efforts showed, in the end, only limited success. In July 1635, Victor Amadeus I and the French envoy Bellièvre signed an alliance treaty, known as the 'League of Rivoli'. In the following months, only the Dukes of Mantua and Parma joined in. But meanwhile – as a result of the battle of Nördlingen and the capture of the Bishop-Elector of Trier, a French protégé – Louis XIII had already declared war on his brother-in-law Philippe IV. Nevertheless, the League of Rivoli, flanked by the occupation of the Valtellina valley by French troops headed by the duke of Rohan, again threatened the communication between Spain and its armies operating north of the Alps.

War in Italy 1635–1659

The open war that began in Italy in summer 1635 lasted until the Peace of the Pyrenees in 1659. Italy became a kind of training ground for French public servants – some of the great ministers of Louis XIV's reign passed some months or years in Italy in the 1640s, such as Michel Le Tellier as *intendant de l'armée*, and we already mentioned the importance of the 'Italian Years' for Hugues de Lionne. They all met in and around Turin and Piedmont between 1640 and 1643, and all came in contact with the young Giulio Mazzarino. For a French commander-in-chief, the Italian theatre of war was dangerous: Marshal Toiras, defender of Casale in 1630 and the duke of Créquy were killed in action in 1636 and 1638, while the Cardinal de La Valette died of fever as commander-in-chief of the French army in Italy in 1639. The young Turenne showed his skill as commander during the campaigns between 1639 and 1643.[31]

Comparable to the events north of the Alps, no warring party could win a noteworthy advantage. Sieges and attacks to relieve the beleaguered characterised the war. France was not able to make war on three fronts on the same level – since 1635 and since the Spanish advance to Corbie in 1636 it was clear that the emphasis of the French war efforts had to be located north of the Alps, in Flanders and on the frontier to the empire. The difficulties in providing the promised strength of the army for Italy caused discontent in Victor Amadeus I of Savoy. A real offensive against Milan was not possible. This meant also that the joint French-Savoyard forces would not be able to support the duke of Rohan who had successfully closed the Valtellina to Spanish troops in 1635, but was under double attack in 1636, by the Spaniards and by his former allies, the Grisons, who searched reconciliation with Madrid to end the war. The Grisons changed sides in 1637 and Rohan was finally forced to surrender and to retire with his remaining troops to Zürich and then to Germany. This failure was a severe blow to the French plans in Italy.[32]

---

[31] M. Baudier, *Histoire du Marechal de Toiras* (Paris, 1644), J. Humbert, *Le marechal de Crequi, gendre de Lesdiguières (1573–1638)* (Paris, 1963), A. H. R. Vicomte de Noailles, *Le Cardinal de La Valette* (Paris, 1906), J. Bérenger, *Turenne* (Paris, 1987), pp. 147–61, for Le Tellier see A. Corvisier, *Louvois* (Paris, 1983), pp. 31–5.

[32] See Wendland, *Der Nutzen der Pässe*, pp. 151–214.

Viewed from Milan, French failure gave Spain the occasion to counter the French plans against Milan and to carry the war into the Savoyard territories and to keep the war away from the duchy of Milan. Until 1640/1641 this strategy was successful. First Odoardo Farnese who had joined the alliance of Rivoli in 1635 was attacked – without French help, after serious defeats and heavy pressure from the Pope, the duke was forced to retire from war in 1637. Thus in 1637, the anti-Spanish alliance broke to pieces. The duke of Mantua, Charles de Nevers, although a member, did not take part in the fighting (but he agreed to a French garrison in Casale). After his death in 1637, the regent, Maria Gonzaga, led the duchy into the Habsburg camp.[33]

The death of Victor Amadeus I in 1637 plunged the French-Savoyard coalition into crisis. A 'civil war' broke out over the regency question – the brothers of the late duke, Prince Tommaso and Cardinal Maurizio, paid by the Spanish, contested the regency established by Christine with French help. The war between *madamisti* and *principisti* would last until the summer of 1642. For Richelieu and Louis XIII it was clear that their whole Italian policy and all their objectives were at stake if Savoy should change the camp or retire from war as did the duke of Parma. Consequently Richelieu put the screws on Christine de France, the widow of Victor Amadeus and the regent for the minor Charles Emanuel II. Slowly the duchy of Savoy passed from alliance to French protection.[34] Probably the French arms benefitted from the Spanish breakdown in the 1640s beginning with the rebellions of Catalonia and Portugal. The able commander Henri de Guise-Lorraine, Count d'Harcourt managed – with the help of his young regimental commander Turenne – to secure the fortresses of Turin and Casale. Prince Tommaso and Cardinal Maurizio joined – for adequate remuneration – the French camp.[35] The war in Italy continued and when Richelieu died in December 1642, none of his objectives of 1635 had been achieved.

The outbreak of the Castro war in 1642 complicated the situation. At its origins was the quarrel between the duke of Parma and Pope Urban VIII over the duchy of Castro, a papal feudal state ruled by Parma. When, in 1642, Urban VIII decided to seize it as compensation for the duke's debts, Odoardo called for help from the other Italian courts. A league was formed against the Pope, composed of Parma, Florence, Modena, and Venice.[36] After a year of skirmishing along the frontiers of the Papal State, France mediated a peace based on the *status quo ante*. In 1649, a new war broke out when Pope Innocent X wanted to appoint a new bishop in Castro without the consent of the duke of Parma. The murder of the bishop by agents of the duke led to the 'second Castro war' and the complete destruction of the city. Parma ceded the duchy to the Papal State.

When Mazarin managed in 1643 to assert himself against the other *créatures* of Richelieu as 'prime minister', not only did an Italian take over the direction of French foreign policy, but also a politician whose apprenticeship as diplomat coincided with the French intervention in

---

[33] There is no research comparable to that on the events north of the Alps on the Italian war theatre. For an overview, see Externbrink, *Cœur du monde*, pp. 326–38, with comments on the literature. Still useful: R. Quazza, *Preponderanza spagnuola (1559–1700)*, 2nd edn (Mailand, 1950), pp. 478–522. Wilson, *Europe's Tragedy*, pp. 645–50. See also: G. Hanlon, *The Twilight of a Military Tradition. Italian Aristocrats and European Conflicts 1560–1800* (London, 1997), pp 106–34; D. Parrott, *Richelieu's Army. War, Government and Society in France, 1624–1642* (Cambridge, 2001), pp. 110–63.

[34] Externbrink, *Cœur du monde*, 335–6, see also G. Ferretti, 'Au nom du droit (de conquête). La politique italienne de la France au XVIIe siècle', *La Pierre et l'Écrit. Revue d'histoire et du patrimoine en Dauphiné*, 23 (2012): pp. 101–25 and G. de Mun, *Richelieu et la maison de Savoie. L'ambassade de Particelli d'Hémery en Piemont (1635–1639)* (Paris, 1907).

[35] P.P. Merlin and C. Rosso, *Il Piemonte sabaudo: Stato e territori in età moderna* (Turin, 1994), pp. 236–42.

[36] Hanlon, *Twilight of a Military Tradition*, pp. 135–42.

Italian affairs from the mid-1620s onwards. Thus Mazarin learned the French political aims in Italy from scratch and he proved to be a devoted follower of Louis XIII and Richelieu's ambitions. He managed to get the duke of Modena, Francesco d'Este, into the war against the Spaniards. The latter's fate resembled the fate of Odoardo Farnese. Without effective help he soon withdrew from war and changed sides.[37] But what counted for Mazarin was the new diversion of Spanish forces in Italy.

French maritime raids were made against the western coast of Tuscany, especially the Spanish Stato di Presidio. When in 1647, a revolt broke out in Naples, Mazarin seized the occasion to intervene, but this was more aimed to divert Spanish forces than really to support the rebellion or the ideas of the French commander, the duke of Guise who dreamed of being the new king of Naples. Mazarin wanted to encourage the Neapolitans to revolt against their suzerain, but he was not interested in supporting a Neapolitan republic. The fear of losing the kingdom of Naples and Sicily should help to bring the Spanish to accept the French ideas for the peace treaty negotiated at the same time in Munster.[38] But in vain, the French–Spanish war in Italy as well in Flanders continued until 1659. Nevertheless the peace of Westphalia concerned Italy as well.

Epilogue: Italy and the Peace Congress in Westphalia

The peace congress in Westphalia was a European congress and dealt with European questions. Besides the papal and Venetian intermediators, Italian envoys came from Genoa, Savoy, Mantua, and Tuscany.[39] For the participants, especially for the 'great powers' France and Spain, Italy stood in the centre of the agenda of negotiations: 'His Majesty regards it as absolutely necessary to begin with the Italian affairs ... because the origin of this war lay in the attempted oppression against the duke of Mantua'.[40] This remark can be found in the French instruction, and the Spanish contains similar considerations.[41] In contrast to the importance of Italy for the negotiations as far as the two main opponents at the congress were concerned, the Italian question has never been analysed, and this research cannot be accomplished here.[42] The guarantee of the possession of Pinerolo counted among the principal negotiation goals of the French envoys, and the negotiations were a long and difficult matter because of the incompatibility of the French and Spanish territorial goals. It was a great step forward in the general negotiation when the emperor's envoy, Trauttmannsdorff, finally agreed to the acquisition of Pinerolo by France, and after some hesitation, Madrid accepted this.[43]

The articles concerning Italy in the peace treaty of Muenster repeat the arrangements of the peace of Cherasco concerning the partition of Monferrato (§ 92–93 IPM). The imperial

---

[37] L. Simeoni, *Francesco I d'Este e la politica italiana del Mazzarino* (Bologna, 1922).

[38] A. Hugon, *Naples insurgée, 1647–1648. De l'événement à la mémoire* (Rennes, 2011).

[39] K. Repgen (ed.), *Acta Pacis Westphalicae*, Abt. D: *Varia*, vol. 1: *Stadtmünsterisches und Vermischtes*, ed. by H. Lahrkamp (Münster, 1964), p. 347.

[40] *Acta Pacis Westphalicae*, Serie I: *Instruktionen*, vol. 1: *Frankreich-Schweden-Kaiser*, ed. by F. Dickmann, K. Goronzy, E. Schieche, H. Wagner and E.M. Wermter (Münster, 1962), p. 73.

[41] M. Rohrschneider, *Der gescheiterte Friede von Münster. Spaniens Ringen mit Frankreich auf dem Westfälischen Friedenskongreß (1643–1649)* (Münster, 2007), p. 88.

[42] Concerning the Savoyard embassy, there is some information in: D. Carutti, *Storia della diplomazia della corte di Savoia* (4 vols, Turin, 1875–1880), vol. 2, pp. 448–97; G. Claretta, *Storia della reggenza di Chistina di Francia, duchessa di Savoia*, (3 vols, Turin, 1868), vol. 2, pp. 77–82, 110–16; 128–32; 134–50; 161–3; 170–75; 184–7; 192–200; 281–4; several documents are printed in vol. 3, pp. 213–25.

[43] Rohrschneider, *Der gescheiterte Friede*, pp. 315–17, 320, 322.

feudal lordship over *Reichsitalien* was confirmed, and the emperor ceded his right to Pinerolo and the adjacent territories to the French king (§ 72 IPM). Other articles concerned the question of feudal dependency of fiefs in the Langhe (§ 95–96 IPM). Savoy and Modena (the duke joined the French camp in the late 1640s) were integrated into the amnesty article (§ 119 IPM).

As already mentioned, the peace of Westphalia did not end the war in Italy. The duke of Savoy ratified the peace treaty on 22 December 1648, in contrast to the duke of Mantua, who protested against it.[44] At the diet (*Reichstag*) of 1653/54, the envoys again discussed the Monferrato question and the Mantuan protest, but without a final resolution. Until his death in 1675, Duke Charles Emanuel II did not obtain the investiture of the Savoyard Monferrato (and paid no compensation for it to the duke of Mantua, as stipulated in the treaties). But apart from this protest, the Savoyard possession of the Monferrato was not contested.[45] Peace returned to Italy only after the Peace of the Pyrenees in 1659. A Thirty Years' War came to an end. It may be a minor point, but we should mention the fact that both French main negotiators, Abel Servien and Claude de Mesmes, Comte d'Avaux, were not only experienced diplomats, but both had had their 'diplomatic apprenticeship' in Italy. Servien was responsible for the Cherasco treatises and the cession of Pinerolo, Avaux was France's resident in Venice during the Mantuan war. Not to forget, Hugues de Lionne, French Secretary of State for Foreign Affairs, was the nephew of Servien, and served as his secretary during his embassy in Turin, before he assumed his first diplomatic missions in Italy in 1642. Finally, French government and foreign policy were conducted by an Italian: Guilio Mazzarino, naturalised as Jules Mazarin, who made his first appearance on the political stage in 1629.

Until now, Italy has usually not been considered part of the conflicts subsumed under the term 'Thirty Years' War', and only recently has more attention been paid to Italy's role in this war. It was the aim of this overview to show that the *European* dimension of the Thirty Years' War is only understandable if Italy is included in the account.

Selected Bibliography

Dandelet, T.J., *Spanish Rome, 1500–1700* (New Haven and London, 2001).

Dandelet, T.J. and J.A. Marino (eds), *Spain in Italy. Politics, Society, and Religion 1500–1700* (Leiden and Boston, 2007).

Externbrink, S., *'Le Cœur du monde' – Frankreich und die norditalienischen Staaten (Mantua, Parma, Savoyen) im Zeitalter Richelieus 1624–1635* (Münster, 1999).

Hanlon, G., *The Twilight of a Military Tradition. Italian Aristocrats and European Conflicts 1560–1800* (London, 1997).

Elliott, J.H., *Richelieu and Olivares*, 4th edn (Cambridge, 1991).

Kleinmann, R., 'Charles Emanuel of Savoy and the Bohemian Election of 1619', *European Studies Review*, 5 (1975): pp. 3–29.

---

[44] *Traités publics*, vol. 1, p. 600. J. DuMont (ed.), *Corps universel du Droits des Gens ...* , (8 vols, Amsterdam and Den Haag, 1725–1731), vol. 6/1, p. 493.

[45] A. Müller, *Der Regensburger Reichstag von 1653/54. Eine Studie zur Entwicklung des Alten Reiches nach dem Westfälischen Frieden* (Frankfurt/M., Bern, New York and Paris, 1992), pp. 325–38; G. Tabacco, *Lo stato sabaudo nel sacro Romano imperio* (Turin, 1939), pp. 129–33.

Oresko, R., 'The House of Savoy in Search for a Royal Crown in the Seventeenth Century', in R. Oresko, G.C. Gibbs and H.M. Scott (eds), *Royal and Republican Sovereignty in Early Modern History. Essays in Memory of Ragnhild Hatton* (Cambridge, 1997), pp. 272–350.

Oresko, R., Parrott, D., 'The Sovereignty of Monferato and the Citadel of Casale as European Problems in the Early Modern Period', D. Ferrari (ed.), *Stefano Guazzo e Casale tra Cinque e Seicento. Atti del convegno die studi nel quarto centenario della morte. Casale Monterrato, 22–23 ottobre 1993* (Rome, 1997), pp. 11–86.

Parrott, D., 'A prince souverain and the French Crown: Charles de Nevers 1580–1637', in G.C. Gibbs, R. Oresko and H.M. Scott (eds), *Royal and Republican Sovereignty in Early Modern Europe. Essays in Memory of Ragnhild Hatton* (Cambridge, 1997).

Parrott, D., 'The Mantuan Succession, 1627–1631: a Sovereignty Dispute in Early Modern Europe', *English Historical Review*, 112/445 (1997): pp. 20–65.

Parrott, D., *Richelieu's Army. War, Government and Society in France, 1624–1642* (Cambridge, 2001).

PART IV
Religion and Politics

15

ASHGATE RESEARCH COMPANION

The Peace of 1555 – A Failed Settlement?

Matthias Pohlig

It has long been common historiographic practice to include the Augsburg Peace of 1555 in the discussion of the reasons, causes, or determining factors of the Thirty Years' War. This assumption sometimes leads scholars to the conclusion that the Peace of 1555 was a failure. But what is a 'failed peace'? Was the Peace of 1555 a failure because it failed to prevent the outbreak of the Thirty Years' War almost 65 years later? How plausible is it to point to the Augsburg Peace when trying to explain the outbreak of the Thirty Years' War?

I would like to answer these questions in four steps: first, I shall explain the political and religious situation that led to the settlement. In a second step, I shall discuss the Peace provisions. Then I shall point out some of the political problems that ensued from the Peace, particularly starting in the 1580s, and show how the destabilisation of the imperial constitutional order made war not inevitable but more likely. Finally, I shall discuss various directions of scholarship and show that while several interpretations are broadly shared, fundamental disagreements remain. The hardly original argument I want to make is that the Augsburg Peace did not 'fail', but was the only possible solution to the Holy Roman Empire's religious problems, and for the first decades after 1555 worked surprisingly well. It even proved remarkably influential on the cultural and intellectual history of the following centuries. At the same time, however, the Peace entailed a number of systematic problems, which from the beginning, but particularly after political leaders became less inclined toward a pragmatic interpretation, burdened the politics of the empire. In this sense, the Peace of Augsburg is the most important determining factor for the collapse of the empire's political structure that finally led to the outbreak of war.

The Political and Religious Context of the Peace

After the Reformation and the resulting religious schism had reached the level of imperial politics in the 1520s, several attempts were made to solve the problem of two religions within a unified polity. An important player in this process was Emperor Charles V who, due to his ideal of a universal empire, was determined to preserve the unity of the church. The religious question was a political issue for the Protestant princes as well who wanted to strengthen their power and were also striving to acquire property owned by the Catholic Church. After the failed attempt to outlaw the Reformation through the Edict of Worms of 1521, Charles, beginning in the 1530s, tried various strategies to get the religious division under control. He repeatedly called for a general council, but most importantly he fought the Protestants first legally and later by military means.¹ The Schmalkaldic War 1546–47 brought Charles to the apex of his Imperial power; at the same time, it was a turning point because the Protestant princes – and not only those – in an alliance with France, saw a serious threat to their own position in Charles's expanded power. The princely uprising that led to the Treaty of Passau in 1552 marked the end of Catholic universalism under Charles V: with regard to important issues, the territorial princes emerged as the winners of the conflict. Thus, the various short-term settlements between 1532 and 1555 eventually culminated in the Augsburg Peace.² One of the main characteristics of this settlement was a political solution that did not attempt to solve the problem of religious division, but accepted it and even made it into a permanent arrangement. The religious dissent was institutionalised and became part of a process of politicisation and, most importantly, of legal codification. The goal was, first and foremost, to secure peace. Charles V did not want to support this settlement that meant the end of the universal Christian empire, and did not participate in the negotiations; he abdicated in 1556. imperial universalism had failed and the Augsburg Peace was the beginning of a new era in the empire's history.³

The Provisions of the Peace

The solution to the problem of religious division that the Augsburg imperial diet of 1555 found was very simple: religious decisions in each territory were left to the territorial rulers.⁴ This settlement established the bi-confessional state of the empire and admitted Protestantism – called the 'Augsburg Confession' – as the second legitimate faith. Thus, the so-called *ius reformandi* authorised the princes either to introduce the Reformation in their territories, or to keep them under the Catholic faith; their subjects were not free to make their own religious

---

[1] H. Rabe, 'Karl V. und die deutschen Protestanten: Wege, Ziele und Grenzen der kaiserlichen Religionspolitik', in H. Rabe (ed.), *Karl V. Politik und politisches System: Berichte und Studien aus der Arbeit an der Politischen Korrespondenz des Kaisers* (Konstanz, 1996) – I thank Katharina Kaliardos for the translation.

[2] A. Kohnle, 'Nürnberg – Passau – Augsburg: Der lange Weg zum Religionsfrieden', in H. Schilling and H. Smolinsky (eds), *Der Augsburger Religionsfrieden* (Gütersloh, 2007), pp. 5–15; Herbert Immenkötter, 'Augsburg, Peace of', in H.J. Hillerbrand (ed.), *The Oxford Encyclopedia of the Reformation* (New York and Oxford, 1996), vol. 1, pp. 91–3; H. Tüchle, 'The Peace of Augsburg: New Order or Lull in the Fighting?', in H.J. Cohn (ed.), *Government in Reformation Europe 1520–1560* (New York, 1971), pp. 145–65.

[3] On the Empire, see P.H. Wilson, *The Holy Roman Empire, 1495–1806* (New York, 1999).

[4] On the religious negotiations of 1555 see most recently R. Aulinger, E.H. Eltz and U. Machoczek (eds), *Deutsche Reichstagsakten unter Karl V.: Der Reichstag zu Augsburg 1555* (Munich, 2009), vol. 3, pp. 1679–2134. An easily accessible edition of the original document can be found in: *Kaiser und Reich: Klassische Texte zur Verfassungsgeschichte des Heiligen Römischen Reiches Deutscher Nation vom Beginn des 12. Jahrhunderts bis zum Jahre 1806*, trans., pref. and ed. by A. Buschmann (Munich, 1984), pp. 215–83 (for the text of the settlement itself see pp. 215–31). On the Augsburg Peace and its reception in the Empire see the authoritative study by A. Gotthard, *Der Augsburger Religionsfrieden* (Münster, 2004), for shorter overviews in English: Th.A. Brady, Jr., 'Settlements: The Holy Roman Empire', in Th.A. Brady, Jr., H.A. Oberman and J.D. Tracy (eds), *Handbook of European History 1400–1600: Late Middle Ages, Renaissance and Reformation* (Leiden, New York and Cologne, 1995), vol.2, pp. 349–83; Th.A. Brady, Jr., 'Augsburg, Religious Peace of (1555)', in J. Dewald (ed.), *Europe 1450 to 1789: Encyclopedia of the Early Modern World* (6 vols, New York and Munich, 2004), vol. 1, pp. 168–70; F. Brendle and A. Schindling, 'Religious War and Religious Peace in the Age of Reformation', in R.J.W. Evans, M. Schaich and P.H. Wilson (eds), *The Holy Roman Empire 1495–1806* (Oxford and New York, 2011), pp. 174–8; J. Whaley, *Germany and the Holy Roman Empire. Vol. I: Maximilian I to the Peace of Westphalia 1493–1648* (Oxford, 2012), pp. 383–427.

choice, but had to submit to that of their ruler. The decision about religious matters, which in the sixteenth century was seen as a hallmark of political power, was transferred from the Emperor to the territorial rulers. This solution strengthened the relatively strong autonomy of territorial rulers and reinforced the tendency toward decentralised political administration. From the 1580s on, Protestant jurists used the phrase 'cuius regio, eius religio' (he who rules, decides the religion) to describe this important provision. Therefore, the Augsburg settlement is the starting point of a process usually described as confessionalisation: the connection between the doctrinal and organisational integration of the church and the formation of the early modern territorial state.[5] The consequence was that at the imperial level, two different confessions had to negotiate; the Peace was therefore a political settlement that avoided the question of religious truth. But which were the religious faiths that the settlement defined as legitimate? It prohibited any 'sects' besides Catholicism and the Augsburg Confession. Since during this time the 'Lutheran' and the 'Reformed' confessions were still in the process of self-differentiation, it is debatable whether the Peace included the Reformed (or 'Calvinist') faith. The process of clarification regarding the question of who belonged to the Augsburg Confession and who did not, is closely linked to a process of religious differentiation that necessitated this very clarification. Both the development of a Calvinist confession, as well as the consolidation of the Lutheran faith in the Book of Concord of 1580 are steps in a process of confessional definition that was inextricably linked to the legal framework of the empire at the time. Calvinism's legally precarious position indeed fostered the political-religious militancy of, for example, the Electoral Palatinate. But the Palatinate as well as other Calvinist imperial estates certainly still participated in the politics of the empire and were accepted as part of German Protestantism at a political level.[6]

Besides the bi-confessional structure of the empire and the *ius reformandi*, the diet also passed a provision confirming the Eternal Peace of 1495 – the religious settlement was thus part of a comprehensive programme aimed at preserving public peace in the empire. Contrary to some of the settlement attempts of the preceding decades, the Peace was meant to last. Moreover, article 25 decreed that while attempts at religious reunification should continue to be made, the settlement was still valid, should these attempts fail. Even if Protestants placed greater emphasis on this idea of permanence than Catholics, and Catholic authors around 1600 claimed that the settlement was rendered obsolete by the Tridentine reform, the Peace was largely interpreted as a permanent settlement during the first decades after its conclusion.[7]

One provision in latent contradiction to the *ius reformandi* and therefore a perpetual source of discontent was the so-called 'normative year': with regard to the secularisation of clerical properties, the confessional assets were frozen at the state of 1552 – a provision that would be taken up aggressively by the Catholic side during the Thirty Years' War and which

---

[5] H. Schilling, 'Confessionalization: Historical and Scholarly Perspectives of a Comparative and Interdisciplinary Paradigm', in J.M. Headley, H.J. Hillerbrand and A.J. Papalas (eds), *Confessionalization in Europe, 1555–1700: Essays in Honor and Memory of Bodo Nischan* (Aldershot, 2004), pp. 21–35.

[6] H.J. Cohn, 'The Territorial Princes in Germany's Second Reformation, 1559–1622', in M. Prestwich (ed.), *International Calvinism 1541–1715* (Oxford, 1985), pp. 135–65; V. Press, 'Außerhalb des Religionsfriedens? Das reformierte Bekenntnis im Reich bis 1648', in G. Vogler (ed.), *Wegscheiden der Reformation. Alternatives Denken vom 16. bis zum 18. Jahrhundert* (Weimar, 1994), pp. 307–35; I. Dingel, 'Augsburger Religionsfrieden und "Augsburger Konfessionsverwandtschaft". Konfessionelle Lesarten', in H. Schilling and H. Smolinsky (eds), *Der Augsburger Religionsfrieden* (Gütersloh, 2007), pp. 157–76.

[7] Chr. Strohm, 'Konfessionsspezifische Zugänge zum Augsburger Religionsfrieden bei lutherischen, reformierten und katholischen Juristen', in H. Schilling and H. Smolinsky (eds), *Der Augsburger Religionsfrieden* (Gütersloh, 2007), pp. 127–56.

even saw political implementation in the Edict of Restitution of 1629.[8] Another provision was that the subjects of a territorial ruler, while obliged to submit to the confessional stance of their prince, were permitted to sell their property at a profit and emigrate – the *ius emigrandi*. This provision, however, was phrased as a right and not as an obligation, and at least Protestants increasingly saw the *ius emigrandi* also as a 'Recht der Nichtauswanderung' (right not to emigrate).[9] Another equally controversial point was the provision that imperial cities that had been bi-confessional before 1555 should retain this status. The *ius reformandi* of the cities, which would have accorded them the same rights as the princes, was highly contentious. Furthermore, it was predictable that serious problems could ensue from bi-confessionalism within a community during times of religious discord.[10]

These contradictory provisions were further complicated by two exceptions: the 'ecclesiastical reservation' and the Declaratio Ferdinandea. The ecclesiastical reservation decreed that a ruler of an ecclesiastical territory could not become Protestant without losing his lands. This provision was the most obvious sign that the two confessions were not completely equal.[11] To compensate for this discrimination of Protestantism, King Ferdinand made a secret agreement with the Protestants, the so-called Declaratio Ferdinandea – which was not disclosed to the imperial Chamber Court and therefore never became official. This agreement promised religious freedom to Protestant knights and cities in territories under – Catholic – clerical rule.

The text of the Peace used 'deliberately ambiguous, dissimulative formulaic compromises'[12] typical of imperial contracts and legal statutes, which became increasingly problematic in the context of the increasing confessional strife toward the end of the sixteenth century. Almost all provisions of the treaty became contentious over time.[13] There were arguments about the legal status of Calvinism within the empire – an issue that for political reasons was solved only de facto. Especially on the part of the Calvinists, the *ius reformandi* provoked demands to grant religious freedom to all subjects; the term they used was *Freystellung*. There were arguments about every act of secularisation, when a Protestant territorial ruler who enforced his *ius reformandi* ignored the 'normative year'; arguments about the *ius reformandi* for city councils; arguments about the Declaratio Ferdinandea, which was impossible to enforce; arguments about the status of the settlement: how permanent, how temporary should it be? And finally the most highly charged point of contention: the ecclesiastical reservation, which the Protestants saw as a serious discrimination.

Martin Heckel has discussed the complexity of the situation that resulted from the settlement's simple basic idea, namely the settlement created three levels of law: the non-confessional law of public peace at the imperial level, which was limited by the partially confessional law of the ecclesiastical reservation, and the confessional law of the individual territories.[14] The Peace did not solve the issue of the relationship between religion and

---

[8] On this, see chapters by Ralf-Peter Fuchs and Marc Forster in this volume.

[9] W. Schulze, *Deutsche Geschichte im 16. Jahrhundert* (Frankfurt a.M., 1987), p. 175.

[10] G. Pfeiffer, 'Der Augsburger Religionsfriede und die Reichsstädte', *Zeitschrift des historischen Vereins für Schwaben*, 61 (1955): pp. 213–321.

[11] F. Dickmann, 'Das Problem der Gleichberechtigung der Konfessionen im Reich im 16. und 17. Jahrhundert', in F. Dickmann (ed.), *Friedensrecht und Friedenssicherung. Studien zum Friedensproblem in der neueren Geschichte* (Göttingen, 1971), pp. 7–35.

[12] Strohm, 'Konfessionsspezifische Zugänge', p. 127.

[13] On the following, see Gotthard, *Augsburger Religionsfrieden*.

[14] M. Heckel, 'Autonomia und Pacis Compositio: Der Augsburger Religionsfrieden in der Deutung der Gegenreformation', in M. Heckel, *Gesammelte Schriften: Staat, Kirche, Recht, Geschichte*, vol. 1, ed. by K. Schlaich (Tübingen, 1989), pp. 40–2.

politics. It just silenced the problem on the imperial level in order to turn it into a virulent matter for the territories. Ending the conflict on the imperial level paved the way for territorial confessionalisation.

What is truly surprising is that the settlement with its complicated structure, after the religious upheaval of the first half of the century, was able to pacify at all – not the fact that it did not solve all the problems. Certain problems were obvious from the start, but the fact that the political leaders were tired of war and that the princes saw advantages in the settlement contributed to a peace that lasted several decades.

Political Problems Resulting From the Settlement

The Augsburg Peace worked quite well until the 1580s; however, the accelerating process of confessional confrontation eventually led to its erosion. In this new context the settlement's formulaic compromises made the problems clearly evident around 1600. This precipitated a constitutional crisis of the empire, which converged with emerging conflicts outside its borders, even if it is impossible to determine whether one of these factors would have been able to trigger a 30-year international religious and political war by itself.

During the first decades after 1555 the imperial estates tended to exploit the settlement's potential advantages, fighting with it rather than against it. As a result, during the 1560s and 70s, the empire went through a period of intensified unity and a multitude of Diets where religious questions and matters of domestic politics as well as funding for the defence against the Ottomans were discussed.[15] Only from the 1570s or 1580s did Catholics increasingly start to argue that the Peace of Augsburg was only an external, fake peace and that a true peace would require the termination of all heresy. Nonetheless, it was the Catholic side that during the decades around 1600 demanded a literal enforcement of the settlement, because 'the Peace had given Lutherans legal equality, but left Catholics with a political majority'.[16] Therefore, Catholics for instance demanded the principle of majority rule in all votes at the diet. The Protestants, on the other hand, tended to declare all kinds of contentious questions to be religious and thereby – with reference to the Protestation at Speyer of 1529 – rejected the majority principle.[17] But even though at the Diets Protestants and Catholics often ignored the traditional structure of the estate councils in order to cooperate with their confessional allies, contrary to the Peace of Westphalia with its *itio in partes* principle, the Augsburg Peace did not allow for the formation of official confessional parties.[18]

Those politicians who favoured pragmatic, 'political' solutions gradually lost influence.[19] With the enigmatic figure of Emperor Rudolf II and a new generation of territorial rulers entering the stage in the 1580s, the Augsburg Peace was increasingly viewed as old fashioned, inconsistent, and unrealistic – an assessment that did not prevent anybody from using it to

---

[15] Schulze, *Deutsche Geschichte*, p. 164.

[16] P.H. Wilson, *Europe's Tragedy: A History of the Thirty Years War* (London, 2009), p. 45.

[17] W. Schulze, 'Majority Decision in the Imperial Diets of the Sixteenth and Seventeenth Century', *Journal of Modern History*, 58, Supplement (1986): pp. 46–63; K. Schlaich, 'Die Mehrheitsabstimmung im Reichstag zwischen 1495 und 1613', *Zeitschrift für Historische Forschung*, 10 (1983): pp. 299–340.

[18] M. Heckel, 'Die Krise der Religionsverfassung des Reiches und die Anfänge des Dreißigjährigen Krieges', in M. Heckel, *Gesammelte Schriften: Staat, Kirche, Recht, Geschichte*, vol. 2, ed. K. Schlaich (Tübingen, 1989), pp. 970–98.

[19] W.E.J. Weber, 'Politische Integration versus konfessionelle Desintegration. Das Problemlösungsangebot der *Politiques* im europäischen Kontext', in C.A. Hoffmann et al. (eds), *Als Frieden möglich war: 450 Jahre Augsburger Religionsfrieden* (Regensburg, 2005), pp. 131–45.

their political advantage. While turning the religious question into a political and legal one was one of the settlement's undeniable achievements, this very accomplishment became problematic once the legal debate again became an expression of a more fundamental dispute over confessional truth.[20] The conversion of the religious issue into a legal one could only work if those involved accepted the law as the appropriate means to deal with these issues, and this was less and less the case. Particularly during the first decades after 1555, the imperial Chamber Court seems to have played a pacifying role, not so much by means of its often delayed rulings, but by virtue of its mere existence – if only by silencing the disputes for the duration of the proceedings.[21]

As has been said before, almost all provisions of the settlement were potential sources of dispute; nonetheless, I shall now discuss a few particularly contentious issues in more detail. One serious problem was the ecclesiastical reservation, which the Protestants saw as discriminatory because it most clearly marked the legal limits of the spread of the Reformation. In the early 1580s, three conflicts emerged that demonstrate the urgency of this dispute: the Cologne War, the Strasbourg Bishops' War, and the dispute over the Magdeburg bishop's legal status. The Cologne War began in the early 1580s with the aim of turning the Electorate of Cologne into a Protestant territory, which violated the ecclesiastical reservation. This attempt was thwarted with military force. Just as important for the politics of the empire, however, was that during the Cologne War, the solidarity of the electoral imperial estates yielded to confessional polarisation.[22] Similarly, the Strasbourg Bishops' War, which started in 1580, erupted over the possible election of a Protestant bishop, but the Catholic side eventually prevailed. The Magdeburg case was more complex.[23] Magdeburg was an old bishopric, which had long ago become Protestant. The Catholic side had for a long time tolerated the situation and it was only in 1582 that a dispute arose about the bishopric's administrator. Should he be granted a seat and a vote at the diet, a question also relevant for the majority votes in the princely council. This conflict became especially dramatic because in 1588 Magdeburg was scheduled to take the chairmanship of the annual Visitation of the Imperial Chamber Court. According to the Catholic side, this would have equalled an official acceptance of the bishopric's secularisation. What followed was a process of evasive manoeuvres at the end of which the Visitation was entrusted to a (Catholic dominated) Imperial Deputation in 1594. At this point the conflict converged with the so-called Four Monasteries Dispute, which centred on the secularisation of clerical property and the *ius reformandi* of the imperial knights, and which had become the most virulent religious lawsuit at the imperial Chamber Court. In 1601, the Four Monasteries Dispute paralysed the Imperial Deputation, which made the Visitation of the imperial Chamber Court impossible; and this in turn meant that the imperial Chamber Court lost its appeals procedure.[24] This crippling of the imperial judiciary was one of the most serious aggravating factors of the constitutional crisis around 1600, and possibly even a reason for the conflict's escalation to war due to the failure of legal mechanisms of resolution.

---

[20] Gotthard, *Augsburger Religionsfrieden*, p. 585.

[21] Rabe, 'Augsburger Religionsfriede'; Ruthmann, 'Religionsprozesse'.

[22] A. Gotthard, '"Macht hab ehr, einen bischof abzusezen". Neue Überlegungen zum Kölner Krieg', *Zeitschrift der Savigny-Stiftung für Rechtsgeschichte, Kanonistische Abteilung*, 82 (1996): pp. 270–325.

[23] J. Leeb, *Der Magdeburger Sessionsstreit von 1582: Voraussetzungen, Problematik und Konsequenzen für Reichstag und Reichskammergericht* (Wetzlar, 2000).

[24] D. Kratsch, 'Decision oder Interpretation. Der "Vierklosterstreit" vor dem Reichskammergericht', in B. Diestelkamp (ed.), *Die politische Funktion des Reichskammergerichtes* (Köln, Weimar and Wien, 1993), pp. 41–58.

Two major conflicts centred on the *ius reformandi* of the city councils and the question of multi-confessional imperial cities. In the case of Aachen, which had become bi-confessional partly due to immigrants from Western Europe, an imperial ban was imposed in 1593, and in 1598 Catholicism was restored with military force.[25] Even more serious was the case of Donauwörth. After conflicts arose over a Catholic procession, the second central court of the empire, the imperial Aulic Council, in 1607 assigned the execution of the imperial ban to the elector of Bavaria – despite Donauwörth being part of the Swabian Imperial circle. Donauwörth was re-catholicised by force and was degraded to the rank of a Bavarian territorial city.[26] At least since the case of Aachen, the imperial Aulic Council was perceived as confessionally Catholic and was therefore eliminated as an instrument of conflict resolution just like the imperial Chamber Court.

As a reaction to the fate of Donauwörth, at the diet of 1608 the Protestant estates demanded a formal confirmation of the Augsburg settlement. The Catholics countered this request by stipulating that any confirmation of the Peace would have to include the restitution of the complete Catholic assets that had been appropriated by the Protestants after the 'normative year' of 1552. Now even the formal validity of the settlement was called into question. The Protestants left the diet, which ended without passing a resolution. Thus, even the imperial diet was paralysed by confessional controversy.

The failure of this diet marked, as Axel Gotthard has argued, the start of the pre-war period.[27] Immediately after the diet, the constitutionally problematic confessional associations were founded, first the Protestant Union, then the Catholic League. Especially the smaller imperial estates sought protection in these associations, because Emperor and empire increasingly failed to fulfil their protective role.[28] The diet of 1613 also ended without a resolution. Confessional conspiracy theories flourished, and the anniversary of the Reformation in 1617 offered lots of opportunities for confessional polemics.[29]

While the constitutional crisis during the years after 1600 is obvious, it has been argued that around 1600 confessional partisanship in the imperial Aulic Council was past its peak and was decreasing from around 1612 onwards. This means that the crippling of the imperial judiciary as a reason for war, which cannot be underestimated, must nevertheless be considered with caution.[30] On the political level, the pre-war years saw downright desperate attempts to resolve the impasse that were often described with the term 'compositio'.[31] Therefore, the path to war cannot solely be attributed to the confessional, judicial and political crisis of the empire. International politics also played a role.

It is hardly accidental that the failed diet of 1608 was the first after the end of the Long Turkish War (1593–1606). The fight against the Ottoman Empire had created a potential for

---

[25] W. Schmitz, *Verfassung und Bekenntnis: Die* Aachener Wirren *im Spiegel der kaiserlichen Politik (1550–1616)* (Frankfurt a.M., 1983).

[26] C. Scott Dixon, 'Urban Order and Religious Coexistence in the German Imperial City: Augsburg and Donauwörth, 1548–1608', *Central European History*, 40 (2007): pp. 1–33.

[27] Gotthard, *Augsburger Religionsfrieden*, p. 461.

[28] C. Kampmann, *Europa und das Reich im Dreißigjährigen Krieg: Geschichte eines europäischen Konflikts* (Stuttgart, 2008), p. 25.

[29] V. Leppin, '"… das der Römische Antichrist offenbaret und das helle Liecht des Heiligen Evangelii wiederumb angezündet": Memoria und Aggression im Reformationsjubiläum 1617', in H. Schilling (ed.), *Konfessioneller Fundamentalismus: Religion als politischer Faktor im europäischen Mächtesystem um 1600* (Munich, 2007), pp. 115–31.

[30] S. Ehrenpreis, 'Die Tätigkeit des Reichshofrats um 1600 in der protestantischen Kritik', in W. Sellert (ed.), *Reichshofrat und Reichskammergericht: Ein Konkurrenzverhältnis* (Köln, Weimar and Wien, 1999), pp. 27–45.

[31] Wilson, *Europe's Tragedy*, pp. 244–5.

solidarity that slowed confessional polarisation, but this solidarity only lasted until the end of the Turkish War in 1606.[32] This conflict was now replaced by the empire's destabilisation through the struggle for hegemony in the Baltic region after the rise of Sweden, which provoked the involvement of Denmark and Poland, and through the Habsburg engagement, for instance in Poland. Even more important were the conflicts in Western Europe; even though the French Religious Wars were over, the Protestant Union entered into an alliance with France and thereby joined an anti-Spanish coalition. In the conflict between the Netherlands and Spain a truce had been reached in 1609, which offered Spain, the Netherlands, and also France free rein for greater political and military engagement in the empire. As early as 1598, Spanish soldiers had been stationed in the empire; overall, their presence in the Netherlands created recurring potential for conflict.[33] Spain transferred its movement of troops to the Netherlands onto the 'Spanish Road', guaranteeing it enormous military resources in the empire and in immediate proximity to the rival French.[34] These issues are beyond the scope of this chapter, but the Spanish hegemonic position of the *pax hispanica* was certainly one of the most serious threats to the Protestants. The Spanish–French conflict culminated in the Jülich-Kleve succession crisis (1609–1614). The territorial rulers vying for the inheritance made pacts with the Netherlands, France, and Spain and thereby imported an international conflict into the empire. In the spring of 1614, Spanish and Dutch troops arrived at the lower Rhine; the outbreak of war could only narrowly be averted.[35]

It was in Bohemia, however, a Habsburg territory, that war finally erupted. With the tense domestic situation in the Habsburg territories, and the conflict of the estates typical for Central and Eastern Europe with its resulting religious concessions, it was the Bohemian attempt to break free from Habsburg rule which was finally the catalyst for the start of the war. Whether this was only an excuse to start the war, however, or if it was an actual cause, remains controversial.

Directions of Scholarship

Recent scholarship no longer draws a clear connection from 1555 to the outbreak of war in 1618. While a connection between the Augsburg Peace and the Thirty Years' War is seldom denied, the idea of a 'failed peace' is replaced with more nuanced interpretations. We know a lot more about the second half of the sixteenth century today than just a few decades ago,[36] even if many questions remain unanswered. The time between 1555 and 1618 has therefore become much more complex. Teleological interpretations, which interpret this entire time span as prehistory of the war, are no longer offered. Overall, a broad consensus has emerged: the Peace is largely seen as burdened by specific problems that were evident early on, and that created the framework for the empire's crisis around 1600. This tendency

---

[32] Schulze, *Deutsche Geschichte*, p. 165; see chapter by Maria Baramova in this volume.

[33] M. Lanzinner, 'Das römisch-deutsche Reich um 1600', in N. Hammerstein and G. Walther (eds), *Späthumanismus: Studien über das Ende einer kulturhistorischen Epoche* (Göttingen, 2000), pp. 19–45; see chapter by Olaf van Nimwegen in this volume.

[34] Kampmann, *Europa*, p. 8.

[35] A.D. Anderson, *On the verge of war: international relations and the Jülich-Kleve succession crises (1609–1614)* (Boston, 1999).

[36] A milestone of the older scholarship, which because of its many details is still very useful: M. Ritter, *Deutsche Geschichte im Zeitalter der Gegenreformation und des Dreißigjährigen Krieges 1555–1648* (3 vols, Stuttgart, 1889–1908), especially the first two volumes.

is apparent in the most recent comprehensive study of the Thirty Years' War, Peter Wilson's *Europe's Tragedy*, published in 2009. Wilson speaks of the 'success of the 1555 settlement'[37], referring, like many other authors, to the Peace which worked pretty well at least into the 1580s; he describes the contradictions of the settlement, but points out that these are typical for compromises within the empire, and under different historical circumstances might well have worked for a longer time. As Wilson puts it, 63 years without a 'major war' do not support the argument that the settlement was a failure and immediately responsible for the outbreak of war in 1618.[38]

This assessment is consistent with a large part of recent scholarship, which has generally stressed the fact that during Ferdinand I's and Maximilian II's reigns, even in the early years of Rudolf II, the most influential parties – the imperial court and the Electors of Saxony and Bavaria – interpreted the settlement in a constructive and pragmatic way, and thus kept the political system alive.[39] It was only a new generation of princes and theologians who, starting around 1580, saw less the advantages of the Peace than its disadvantages for their confessional and political interests. The hardening of confessional fronts changed the political climate in the empire, and the confessionally heated situation at the empire's western border, especially in the Netherlands and France, tended to undermine peaceful imperial politics.[40] If the Peace left a lot of questions unanswered or ambiguous from the beginning, it could still – if interpreted benevolently – have served its purpose, and must actually be seen as a milestone of the political institutionalisation of religious dissent. Maximilian Lanzinner and Dietmar Heil have concisely summed up the consensus of research: 'There was no self-organised escalation from conflict to war that gave history between 1555 and 1618/48 a logical determination.'[41] Similarly, Winfried Schulze stresses that there was 'certainly no continuous rise of tension in the Empire; rather, we can discern an astonishingly long phase of a quite functional imperial order, which by no means inevitably led to the great conflict.'[42]

Maybe it is not accidental that a dissenting voice comes from a discipline whose method is as much systematic as it is historical: the legal historian Martin Heckel argues that the systematic legal problems inherent in the settlement, while not necessarily precipitating its failure, were an enormous burden for imperial politics. Therefore, Heckel cautions against overestimating the 1580s as a turning point.[43] In his view, it was not so much the confessional fundamentalism of individual political figures that led to the constitutional crisis; instead, the problems were ultimately inherent in the settlement itself and hardly avoidable under the circumstances of the period. But even Heckel points out that, at least for a while, the settlement preserved peace in the empire. Heckel's provocative conclusion is: the Peace has prevented an imperial St. Bartholomew's Day Massacre.[44]

While there is a broad consensus that the Peace worked until about 1580, disagreement remains regarding the decades before the war: some authors stress the role of confessional antagonism, while others place greater importance on the constitutional crisis that the

---

[37] Wilson, *Europe's Tragedy*, p. 10.
[38] Ibid., p. 43.
[39] Lanzinner, 'Reich', p. 19.
[40] H. Schilling, 'Die Konfessionalisierung im Reich: Religiöser und gesellschaftlicher Wandel in Deutschland zwischen 1555 und 1620', *Historische Zeitschrift*, 246 (1988), pp. 1–45.
[41] Lanzinner and Heil, 'Augsburger Reichstag', pp. 626–7.
[42] Schulze, *Deutsche Geschichte*, p. 166.
[43] M. Heckel, 'Politischer Friede und geistliche Freiheit im Ringen um die Wahrheit: Zur Historiographie des Augsburger Religionsfriedens von 1555', *Historische Zeitschrift*, 282 (2006): pp. 391–425, here p. 414.
[44] Heckel, 'Autonomia', p. 37.

contradictory provisions of the Augsburg settlement provoked. A third group of scholars, while not denying an internal crisis, weighs the factors differently and points to the entanglement of the empire's domestic problems with a European power struggle. The Western European wars, the hegemonic position of Spain, the Spanish–French rivalry, the Dutch Revolt, as well as the struggle for political and economic hegemony in the Baltic Sea and finally the situation in Bohemia should be considered factors at least as important as the imperial and religious crisis: 'The outbreak of war … cannot be explained by confessional division.'[45] 'The great conflict of the Thirty Years War cannot be directly attributed to the state of the Empire.'[46] The most extreme position is held by Johannes Burkhardt in the context of a very positive, modernist interpretation of the empire. Burkhardt argues that the war did not have its roots in the empire itself, but was solely caused by external factors: 'The degree of institutionalisation of the Empire was in an advanced state, but the continent as a whole, as backward in its religious politics as in its constitutional development, now exported its problems into this early modern Empire.'[47]

A comparison with other religious peace treaties of the period heightens the scepticism regarding a close connection between the Augsburg Peace and the Thirty Years' War, because the problems are similar throughout Europe. It seems as if the deliberate exclusion of doctrinal goals and arguments was the hallmark of religious settlements in the confessional age. Admittedly, the issue of religious settlements in the sixteenth and seventeenth century has not been sufficiently investigated comparatively.[48] All peace treaties – from Denmark in 1527 to Switzerland in 1529–31 to the Edict of Nantes and the Peace of Westphalia – tended to disregard questions of religious doctrine and focused on political issues. Apparently, however, decentralised countries such as Switzerland, the empire, or Poland could handle confessional plurality better than more centralised countries such as France. All these agreements limit individual religious freedom to a greater or lesser degree; they grant limited religious freedom to certain groups – usually the nobility – and more or less territorialise confessional distinction.[49] When there was a strong nobility and a weak central power – the typical situation in Eastern Europe – a more comprehensive solution, which embraced a greater number of faiths, was usually possible.[50] The Eastern European peace agreements are usually marked by a highly privileged position of the nobility and a relatively large degree of confessional tolerance, which probably had its roots in the late medieval experience of religious plurality in these territories; the most famous example being the Letter of Majesty of 1609.[51]

---

[45] Lanzinner, 'Reich', p. 36.

[46] Schulze, *Deutsche Geschichte*, p. 193.

[47] J. Burkhardt, *Das Reformationsjahrhundert: Deutsche Geschichte zwischen Medienrevolution und Institutionenbildung 1517–1617* (Stuttgart, 2002), p. 199.

[48] Exceptions are: E. Wolgast, 'Religionsfrieden als politisches Problem der frühen Neuzeit', *Historische Zeitschrift*, 282 (2006): pp. 59–96; E. Wolgast, '"Cuius regio, eius religio" als Modell zur Fixierung von Grenzen', in F. Schweitzer (ed.), *Kommunikation über Grenzen* (Gütersloh, 2009), pp. 90–103; A. Kohnle, 'Konfliktbereinigung und Gewaltprävention: Die europäischen Religionsfrieden in der frühen Neuzeit', in I. Dingel and C. Tietz (eds), *Das Friedenspotenzial von Religion* (Göttingen, 2009), pp. 1–19; T. Brockmann, 'Die frühneuzeitlichen Religionsfrieden – Normhorizont, Instrumentarium und Probleme in vergleichender Perspektive', in Christoph Kampmann et al. (eds), *L'art de la paix: Kongresswesen und Friedensstiftung im Zeitalter des Westfälischen Friedens* (Münster, 2011), pp. 575–602, and in parts also O. Christin, *La paix de religion: L'autonomisation de la raison politique au XVIe siècle* (Paris, 1997).

[49] See Christin, *La paix de religion*, p. 44.

[50] See Wolgast, 'Cuius regio', p. 94.

[51] See Schulze, *Deutsche Geschichte*, pp. 194–202.

Another line of interpretation that emphasises the pacifying aspects of the settlement and those that had the potential to impact future developments – whether in a perspective of *longue durée* or with regard to more microhistorical phenomena – is more pertinent to a discussion of the importance of the Peace itself than for the question of the outbreak of the Thirty Years' War. Without losing sight of the settlement's problems, Winfried Schulze, for instance, points out that the new experience of religious schism generated new political solutions; this could lead to pragmatic tolerance in a political and secular sense. In this regard, the sixteenth century was very modern, Schulze argues, maybe to a degree that in the end exceeded the period's ability to accept dissent.[52] This is true both for coexistence on the imperial level, which temporarily worked, and coexistence in everyday life, for instance in the bi-confessional imperial cities.[53] Maybe it is an exaggeration to see the right to emigrate as the first fundamental right of German history, as some authors have suggested. Nevertheless, the Peace may be seen as an almost avant-garde legal order, which – but this is far beyond the horizon of contemporaries – played a special role for the development of tolerance and human rights, as well as for the privatisation of religion and the development of secular politics.[54]

In conclusion, we can discern a relatively broad consensus among scholars: the Peace of 1555 is seen as successful on many levels; the systematic legal problems that were inherent in it from the beginning are weighed differently, but it is clear that it was only a deliberately polemical interpretation of this inherently contradictory document that steered the imperial institutions into a crisis. 'The Peace of Augsburg, which had been formulated with a view to preserving the mid-century status quo, had limited application once the confessional dynamic gathered pace, and in the end it was the very clauses and the provisions of the settlement that provided the basis for further conflict.'[55] Scholars disagree, however, whether this confessional and constitutional crisis was enough to trigger a war. Some see the reasons for the outbreak of war in the empire itself; they postulate the increasing confessional fundamentalism around 1600 as a root cause, diagnose seriously flawed communication on the part of the political leaders[56] or argue that contemporaries were overwhelmed by the Peace's partial separation of politics and religion.[57] Other interpretations, without denying the crisis of the empire, place greater importance on the international situation and argue that its impact was at least as important as the domestic problems. The question of the role of the Augsburg Peace and the imperial constitutional crisis is therefore also a question about the character of the Thirty Years' War: Was it a religious war? A war caused by a constitutional crisis and waged over different ideas of what the empire should be?[58] Was it a war of emerging states?[59] Was it triggered by a crisis of the empire itself, or was the war imported to Germany?

---

[52] Ibid., p. 163.

[53] P. Warmbrunn, 'Toleranz im Reich vom Augsburger Religionsfrieden bis zum Westfälischen Frieden: Kirchen- und Landesordnungen und gesellschaftliche Praxis', in H. Lademacher, R. Loos and S. Groenveld (eds), *Ablehnung – Duldung – Anerkennung: Toleranz in den Niederlanden und in Deutschland: Ein historischer und aktueller Vergleich* (Münster et al., 2004), pp. 99–116.

[54] See Gotthard, *Augsburger Religionsfrieden*, pp. 500–578.

[55] Dixon, 'Urban Order', pp. 32–3.

[56] A. Gotthard, 'Der deutsche Konfessionskrieg seit 1619: Ein Resultat gestörter politischer Kommunikation', *Historisches Jahrbuch*, 122 (2002): pp. 141–72.

[57] Gotthard, *Augsburger Religionsfrieden*, pp. 582–4.

[58] P.H. Wilson, 'The Thirty Years War as the Empire's Constitutional Crisis', in R.J.W. Evans, M. Schaich and P.H. Wilson (eds), *The Holy Roman Empire 1495–1806: A European Perspective* (Oxford and New York, 2011), pp. 95–114.

[59] Burkhardt, 'The Thirty Years' War'.

Thus, was the Augsburg Peace a 'failed' peace? An examination of the text of the settlement itself and its contextual analysis within the general history of the half century before 1618 show that this label is too simplistic. Linking the Peace to the Thirty Years' War, however, and considering it a prerequisite or determining factor of this war – a position that is, as has been shown, by no means inevitable – entails several new answers and many new questions.

Selected Bibliography

Brady, Jr., T.A., 'Settlements: The Holy Roman Empire', in Th.A. Brady Jr., H.A. Oberman and J.D. Tracy (eds), *Handbook of European History 1400–1600: Late Middle Ages, Renaissance and Reformation*, vol. 2 (Leiden, New York and Cologne, 1995), pp. 349–83.

Brady, Jr., T.A., 'Augsburg, Religious Peace of (1555)', in Jonathan Dewald (ed.), *Europe 1450 to 1789: Encyclopedia of the Early Modern World* (6 vols, New York and Munich, 2004), vol. 1, pp. 168–70.

Brendle, F., and A. Schindling, 'Religious War and Religious Peace in the Age of Reformation', in R.J.W. Evans, M. Schaich and P.H. Wilson (eds), *The Holy Roman Empire 1495–1806: A European Perspective* (Oxford and New York, 2011), pp. 165–81.

Burkhardt, J., 'The Thirty Years' War', in Ronnie Po-Chia Hsia (ed.), *A Companion to the Reformation World* (Oxford, 2004), pp. 272–90.

Gotthard, A., *Der Augsburger Religionsfrieden* (Münster, 2004).

Immenkötter, H., 'Augsburg, Peace of', in H.J. Hillerbrand (ed.), *The Oxford Encyclopedia of the Reformation* (New York and Oxford, 1996), vol. 1, pp. 91–3.

Schilling, H., 'Confessionalization: Historical and Scholarly Perspectives of a Comparative and Interdisciplinary Paradigm', in J.M. Headley, H.J. Hillerbrand and A.J. Papalas (eds), *Confessionalization in Europe, 1555–1700: Essays in Honor and Memory of Bodo Nischan* (Aldershot, 2004), pp. 21–5.

Whaley, J., *Germany and the Holy Roman Empire. Vol. I: Maximilian I to the Peace of Westphalia 1493–1648* (Oxford, 2012).

Wilson, P.H., 'The Thirty Years War as the Empire's Constitutional Crisis', in R.J.W. Evans, M. Schaich and P.H. Wilson (eds), *The Holy Roman Empire 1495–1806: A European Perspective* (Oxford and New York, 2011), pp. 95–114.

16

The Edict of Restitution (1629) and the Failure of Catholic Restoration

Marc R. Forster

Promulgation and Origins

The Edict of Restitution, promulgated in March 1629, at the height of Catholic military success, was the most ambitious attempt by Emperor Ferdinand II and the Catholic Church to restore German Catholic institutions lost to the Protestants during the previous century. The Edict sought to enforce a strict interpretation of the Ecclesiastical Reservation of the Peace of Augsburg of 1555, returning to Catholic possession a large number of monasteries, convents, and other institutions that had been secularised by Protestant states between 1552 and the outbreak of the Thirty Years' War. Interpreted strictly, the Edict required that the archbishoprics of Magdeburg and Bremen, 13 bishoprics, and over 500 monasteries be returned to the Catholic Church.[1]

The Edict was discussed in secret in Vienna and Munich for months before its promulgation and it reflected both the confidence of the Catholic party in Germany in the late 1620s and the experience of Catholic reform and Counter-Reformation policies over the previous decades. On the one hand, the Edict was firmly in the tradition of the religious Peace of Augsburg, since much of it was couched in legalistic and constitutional arguments. Ferdinand insisted that his goal was to properly and consistently enforce the Peace and that the Edict did not create any new laws. On the other hand, the Edict was, at least partly, couched in strong providential language, that the 'emperor's God-given victories enabled him to restore peace in the Empire and, beyond that, to uproot the source of so much civil strife through the return to the observance of the Peace of Augsburg'. The notion, expressed in this period by some Catholic leaders, particularly the emperor himself and his Jesuit confessor and advisor William Lamormaini, that they were leading a successful Catholic holy war, put the Edict in an aggressive and strongly Counter-Reformation context.[2]

Above all, the Edict was a carefully argued assertion of a strict Catholic interpretation of the Peace of Augsburg.[3] While reaffirming the basic clauses of the Peace, for example the

---

[1] P.H. Wilson, *The Thirty Years War. Europe's Tragedy* (Cambridge, MA, 2009), p. 448. 1552 was the 'normative date' used in the Peace of Augsburg, that is, the date that determined the possession of ecclesiastical institutions under the Peace.

[2] R. Bireley, *Religion and Politics in the Age of the Counterreformation. Emperor Ferdinand II, William Lamormaini, S.J., and the Formation of Imperial Politics* (Chapel Hill, 1981), p. 75; Wilson, *The Thirty Years War*, p. 447.

[3] The text of the Edict can be found in P.H.Wilson, *The Thirty Years War. A Sourcebook* (Houndsmills, 2010), pp. 114–17.

principle of *cuius regio, eius religio*, the Edict asserted that the Ecclesiastical Reservation of the Peace, which forbade Protestants from taking over bishoprics and abbeys, was an integral part of the Peace. As a consequence of this interpretation, the Edict stated that the Protestants must allow Catholic prelates and orders to reclaim lost institutions and that Protestants could not in the future be elected or appointed as bishops, abbots, or abbesses. It further asserted that Protestants had no right of legal complaint against the enforcement of religious uniformity in Catholic territories, another disputed aspect of the Peace of Augsburg. Finally, after considerable debate in Catholic circles, the Edict also outlawed Calvinism, stating unequivocally that it was not protected under the Peace of Augsburg.

The Edict had potentially far-reaching consequences. It provided for the appointment of imperial commissioners who were authorised to call on imperial soldiers to overawe any resistance to the restoration of Catholic institutions. Implementation, which got underway immediately in 1629 and lasted until the Swedish invasion in 1631, caused enormous difficulties. Of course Protestants, from local villagers to town councils and territorial authorities, protested, stalled, and sometimes openly resisted the Catholic takeover of monasteries, convents, hospitals, and schools. While bishops, canons, and episcopal officials could be found to manage the recovered episcopal sees, the religious orders had neither the manpower nor the organisation to staff hundreds of restored monasteries scattered across Germany.[4] Divisions among Catholics, particularly between the older orders (Benedictines, Cistercians, and Premonstratensians) and the Jesuits, who sought to take over many of the restored monasteries, further hindered implementation of the Edict.

Protestant Resistance

The Edict provoked strong Protestant resistance, since Protestants correctly suspected that some Catholics saw it as a first step toward the full restoration of Catholicism and the total suppression of Protestantism. The Edict also had economic and fiscal consequences for Protestant states and towns, since these institutions were usually large landowners. The impact of Catholic restoration had particularly serious effects in some Protestant territories. In Württemberg, where Catholics claimed 14 large monasteries and 36 convents, the resources of these houses had been used by the duchy to fund churches, schools, hospitals, and orphanages and their loss seriously threatened the income of the Lutheran Church and the State.[5] Württemberg's monasteries also held as much as one-third of the duchy's wealth.[6]

Württemberg officials were particularly tenacious in their resistance to the Edict, partly because the stakes were so high and partly because of how intertwined the former monastery property was with the State.[7] The duke himself was willing to resist imperial demands for enforcement of the Edict, despite the proximity of victorious Catholic armies. When in August 1629 Benedictine monks, accompanied by imperial commissioners, sought to take control of the Abbey of St. Georgen, they were met by Württemberg officials and troops and

---

[4] M.R. Forster, *Catholic Germany from the Reformation to the Enlightenment* (Houndsmills, 2007), pp. 88–90.

[5] Bireley, *Religion and Politics*, p. 86; Forster, *Catholic Germany*, pp. 88–9; W. Seibrich, *Gegenreformation als Restauration. Die restaurativen Bemühungen der alten Orden im deutschen Reich von 1580 bis 1648* (Münster, 1991), pp. 340–77.

[6] Wilson, *The Thirty Years War*, p. 449.

[7] See Seibrich, *Gegenreformation als Restauration*, pp. 340–77 for an extensive discussion of the restoration of monasteries in Württemberg.

forced to back down. Imperial commissions met similar resistance in the autumn of 1629 in Württemberg, while the orders hesitated, fearing expensive legal proceedings in Vienna.

In January 1630, Württemberg participated with other members of the Swabian *Kreis* in protesting the Edict.

> Moreover, thanks to the Imperial Edict, we and other Evangelical princes and Estates are threatened with juridical punishments the like of which has neither been heard nor used before in the Empire, [and] are being de facto deprived of our property that we have held for many years through legal entitlement and inherited from several generations of ancestors.[8]

Neither this protest, nor another formal Württemberg protest in August 1630, changed the emperor's mind of course, but they delayed implementation of the Edict for months.[9] Meanwhile, the situation on the ground changed in the summer of 1630, as imperial troops moved into Württemberg in support of imperial commissions. In September Cistercian monks moved into Maulbronn, the ancient Cistercian Abbey converted to a Lutheran Seminary in the late 1550s, held mass in the abbey church and announced that they would be appointing Catholic priests for the surrounding parishes.[10] The same process took place in many of the Württemberg monasteries, feeding Protestant fears of a more extensive Counter-Reformation. The orders, however, were usually unable to place more than four or five monks in each house, although there were ten monks at Maulbronn in the fall of 1630.[11] Württemberg officials sought to undermine the religious influence of the monks by telling their subjects that the monasteries were only landlords (*Grundherren*).[12]

The methods of resistance to the Edict employed in Württemberg were used across Germany. Protestant authorities filed lawsuits, refused to turn over documents, demanded negotiations before relinquishing properties, harassed monks and episcopal officials, and refused to cooperate with imperial commissions.[13] Important Protestant leaders who had been loyal to the emperor, particularly John George of Saxony, demanded that their territories be exempted from the Edict. The Edict alienated Protestants and proved to be difficult to enforce; it was also a major political blunder that led most Protestants to greet Gustav Adolph of Sweden as a liberator.

Conflicts Among Catholics

The Edict brought to the surface a variety of conflicts among Catholics, particularly between the Jesuits, who wanted to use the resources of the restored institutions for pastoral and educational purposes, and the older orders (such as the Benedictines and the Cistercians) who hoped to restore old monasteries to their (imagined) medieval glory. There were also conflicts between the Papacy and the emperor and between the German bishops and the

---

[8] Wilson, *The Thirty Years War. A Sourcebook*, p. 118.
[9] Bireley, *Religion and Politics*, p. 124.
[10] Seibrich, *Gegenreformation als Restauration*, pp. 369–70.
[11] Ibid., p. 377.
[12] Ibid., p. 376.
[13] Wilson, *The Thirty Years War*, pp. 453–4.

Jesuits and their supporters, all of which reflected the competing visions Catholics had about how to exploit the success of Catholic arms.

The Papacy had pushed the emperor to restore Church property for quite some time and the Edict seemed to support that policy.[14] A letter from Urban VIII to Ferdinand in May 1629 expressed enthusiasm for the Edict.

> Our soul has been filled with a marvelous joy by the recent Edict of Your Majesty which orders the sectaries to return to the priestly estate the ecclesiastical lands they have long held and in which are contained other provisions (which we bless) that remove obstacles that have up to now held back the Catholic restoration ... Thus heresy will have learned that the gates of hell do not prevail against the church which legions of angels and the arms of powerful Austria so defend.[15]

This militant tone, however, did not prevent conflicts between the Curia and the imperial court over implementation of the Edict. Papal officials wanted the nuncio in Cologne to take an active role in the restoration of the monasteries in order to protect papal authority in appointments to restored benefices. As Robert Bireley points out, 'Papal policy on the Edict was subtle, complex, and sometimes simply unclear'.[16] The emperor and his officials often found papal policy irritating and sometimes infuriating, especially when the Pope repudiated the Edict completely once it was clearly a failure.[17]

The Edict also highlighted the less than militant policies and strategies of most of the German Church. Bishops and their officials favoured a legalistic and gradual restoration of ecclesiastical property, with a focus on recovering rights and incomes. This outlook had become part of the culture of the German Church over the previous century, as it had struggled to survive the Protestant onslaught. In many places this attitude had meant the toleration of Protestant minorities in Catholic territories, the presence of Protestants in cathedral chapters, and the employment of Protestant officials in ecclesiastical territories. Efforts to enforce religious uniformity and the decrees of the Council of Trent, especially after 1580, did have success in some places, particularly in Bavaria and some southern German ecclesiastical territories. On the other hand, more traditional and moderate policies, including a willingness to compromise with Protestant neighbours, continued to characterise the German imperial Church in much of western and northern Germany.[18] This element within German Catholicism viewed the Edict with some scepticism and certainly did not consider it as the first step in a re-conquest of Germany for Catholicism.

Bishops had a mixed view of the Edict. On the one hand, some of them expected they would gain control over the restored monasteries, given the stronger episcopal authority supported by the decrees of the Council of Trent. At the same time, they feared that the restored monasteries would demand ancient exemptions and privileges, thereby undermining episcopal authority. Furthermore, powerful existing monasteries, such as Weingarten and Ochsenhausen in Upper Swabia, sought to take a strong role in the restoration and bishops feared they would incorporate the restored houses, expanding their already strong exempt positions.[19]

---

[14] Bireley, *Religion and Politics*, p. 81.
[15] Wilson, *The Thirty Years War. A Sourcebook*, pp. 117–18.
[16] Bireley, *Religion and Politics*, p. 83.
[17] Ibid., pp. 81–4.
[18] Forster, *Catholic Germany*, chapters 1 and 2.
[19] Seibrich, *Gegenreformation als Restauration*, pp. 405–24.

At New Year, 1630, Lamormaini presented the emperor with a list of 90 possible Jesuit houses, most of which were to use the resources of restored monasteries. He also proposed creating four new Jesuit provinces in northern Germany. Lamormaini believed that these new Jesuit houses would be bases for missionary work in Protestant regions and that the Jesuits were the most effective force for the re-conquest of Germany for Catholicism.[20] Lamormaini's position was not shared by the Jesuit leadership in Rome, which urged him to oppose attempts to turn monasteries over to the Jesuits.[21] The emperor's views were less clear. Politically, he was well aware of the difficulties of taking monasteries from the old orders. On the other hand, he seems to have recognised that the Jesuits were probably the only group within the Church with the ability and manpower to convert the population to Catholicism, a process he recognised would take time.[22]

The resulting 'monastery controversy' engulfed the Catholic camp during 1630 and 1631. Polemics were exchanged, with the supporters of the Jesuits arguing that the old orders' claims had lapsed when monasteries had sat vacant for decades. Lamormaini made the mistake of telling one abbot that, 'only the Society of Jesus had stood firm against the onslaughts of the heretics, whereas the older orders had failed in the crisis'.[23] This remark was then used against the Jesuits by polemicists on the other side of the controversy.

In the Rhenish Palatinate, conquered by Catholic armies early in the war, efforts were underway to restore monasteries to Catholic authority even before the Edict. In this region, conflicts erupted between imperial officials, the Bishop of Speyer, and the Jesuits took over control of the resources of the monasteries.[24] Imperial generals wanted to use the incomes to support their troops, while the Bishop wanted resources for an episcopal seminary and to support his political aims in both Speyer and Trier. The Jesuits did gain possession of the former Cistercian convent of Heilsbruck, using it as a base for missionary work in the surrounding Protestant countryside. Here too, Jesuit success was precarious, since the fathers had to flee Protestant armies on several occasions. They eventually lost control of Heilsbruck to the Cistercian nuns, who won a lawsuit in 1644.

It is perhaps a simplification to say that the monasteries controversy reflected the tensions between the older, more traditional culture of imperial Church and the more militant Catholicism of the Jesuits and their supporters, most of them in the service of the emperor and Bavaria. Yet this tension was real enough, even if the two sides shared aspects of post-Tridentine Catholic culture. These divisions did much to make implementation of the Edict difficult. As Bireley points out, the controversy also had a long afterlife and anti-Jesuit polemicists continued to refer to it into the eighteenth century.[25]

The Edict of Restitution as Religious Policy

Historians have long argued about whether the Edict represents an effort by the emperor to increase his authority within the empire, or if it is an indication of the religious and ideological aspects of the war. Evans attempts to split the difference by arguing that the

---

[20] Bireley, *Religion and Politics*, chapter 7; Wilson, p. 451.
[21] Bireley, *Religion and Politics*, p. 135.
[22] Seibrich, *Gegenreformation als Restauration*, pp. 446–51.
[23] Bireley, *Religion and Politics*, p. 136.
[24] M.R. Forster, *The Counter-Reformation in the Villages. Religion and Reform in the Bishop of Speyer, 1560–1720* (Ithaca, 1992), pp. 158–61.
[25] Bireley, *Religion and Politics*, p. 148.

Edict reflected above all Ferdinand's 'confessional absolutism'.[26] This notion was never an 'abstract political idea', nor, says Evans, was it theocracy. Nevertheless, Church and State were closely tied and often indistinguishable in the Habsburg lands (and in Bavaria) and Ferdinand clearly believed that he should support the Catholic Church in as many ways as possible. Confessional absolutism did not, however, mean unquestioning support of the Papacy, nor did it look like the absolutism later practised by Louis XIV. For Evans, then, 'The Edict of Restitution made perfect sense, as an expression of the sovereign Imperial will'.[27]

The concept of 'confessional absolutism' usefully leads to a complex understanding of interactions between religion and politics that led to the Edict, particularly at the courts in Vienna and Munich. It is, however, also important to point out that there were Catholics in Germany who saw the Catholic victories of the 1620s as an opportunity to re-conquer Germany for Catholicism. These religious militants injected an ideological component to the war that contributed greatly to its duration and destructiveness.

Thomas A. Brady Jr. sees the Edict as the result of the triumph of militant Catholics in the courts in Munich and Vienna. The Jesuit confessors of both Ferdinand and Maximilian 'pressed for an aggressive policy of Catholic restoration'.[28] Already in 1627 Maximilian had urged the emperor to restore the Swabian monasteries, stating 'We think the opportunity presented to us by God should be accepted and the course pointed out by him continued.'[29] Bireley points out that the initial push for the Edict came from Bavaria and the Catholic League, not the emperor, and these princes advocated for such a policy strongly at the Mühlhausen Congress in late 1627.[30]

Catholic militants considered the restitution of the monasteries a step in the direction of a full restoration of Catholicism in Germany. While in retrospect this appears to have been an unrealistic goal, they had reason to believe that it was possible. Catholic leaders of the 1620s had experienced not only the military victories of the previous years, but had also witnessed the success of aggressive Counter-Reformation policies in the decades around 1600. These included the restoration of Catholicism in the region around Würzburg under Bishop Julius Echter von Mespelbrunn, the enforcement of Catholic uniformity in Bavaria, and the destruction of noble Protestantism in the Habsburg lands between 1580 and the 1620s. The conversion of the population of the Upper Palatinate and Bohemia to Catholicism was also well under way by the late 1620s, with the eventual effect of turning both regions into Catholic strongholds for centuries to come.

The Jesuits played a powerful role in each of these regions, leading efforts to convert local elites, educate their children, and form a more active Catholic leadership.[31] In Germany the Jesuits frequently sought out locations on the confessional front lines, founding houses in Protestant cities or in locations where Catholicism was threatened. This policy led, as was intended, to conflicts with Protestants. It also led to conflicts with more moderate and traditional Catholics. Thus, in the 1570s the Jesuits supported a new and aggressive reforming Abbot of Fulda, who confronted both the traditionalist canons of his chapter and

---

[26] G. Parker (ed.), *The Thirty Years War* (London, 1984), chapter III (R.J.W. Evans), pp. 85–6.

[27] Parker, *The Thirty Years War*, chapter III (R.J.W. Evans), p. 86.

[28] T.A. Brady Jr., *German Histories in the Age of Reformations, 1400–1650* (Cambridge, 2009), p. 380. Wilson follows this interpretation as well.

[29] Quoted in Bireley, *Religion and Politics*, p. 54.

[30] Bireley, *Religion and Politics*, p. 56.

[31] L. Châtellier, *Europe of the Devout. The Catholic Reformation and the Formation of a New Society* (Cambridge, 1989).

the mostly Protestant nobles of his secular territory.[32] Abbot Balthasar's 'mission' to fully restore Catholicism in Fulda ultimately failed, but the conflict he ignited showed a deep generational and ideological divide between the militant, international Catholicism of a younger generation influenced by the Jesuits, and an older, regionally flavoured, traditional Catholicism that was still strong in the imperial Church.

The militants were not strong enough to dominate the German Church in the 1570s. In the 1620s they were stronger and they saw their chance. They had precedents to draw on, successful restorations and re-conquests over the previous 50 years. They had methods and strategies that had worked and they had an active Catholic elite led by the Jesuits who were willing to do the hard work. For these people, the Edict was the next step in the ongoing triumph of the church militant.

Many German Catholics disagreed with this policy. The leadership of the imperial Church was not opposed to the restoration of the monasteries and the return of Church property, but these men generally favoured a policy that emphasised the legal rights of the Church. Furthermore, the leaders of the imperial Church, the electors/archbishops of Mainz, Cologne, and Trier as well as the other prince-bishops, saw an opportunity to increase their authority and incomes by taking the monasteries for their own use.[33] As Peter Wilson states, 'They [the bishops] wanted to recover Church property, not eradicate Protestantism.'[34]

The Edict itself reflected this viewpoint. Much of the Edict was couched in juridical and constitutional language, presenting a hardline Catholic interpretation of the Religious Peace of 1555. The Edict asserted in particular the Catholic interpretation of the 'ecclesiastical reservation', which did not allow bishops and prelates to keep their positions if they converted to Protestantism, and did not allow them to convert their secular territories to Protestantism.

> *Certain Protestant Estates have broken the express words of the Religious Peace, not least in retaining their bishoprics, prelacies and prebends and renouncing the Catholic faith, but also those who were not entrusted with such have striven for such bishoprics and prelacies under this pretext and excuse, claiming this paragraph that appears so clear to them was never part of the Religious Peace, because they never agreed to it, but instead have protested against it. However, we regard this paragraph, that is commonly called the ecclesiastical reservation, as an actual constitution.*[35]

This kind of legal language set the tone for much of the Edict. The arguments themselves were based on the work of Paul Laymann, an influential Jesuit professor at Dillingen. Laymann's book, *Paciscompositio* (*The Way of Peace*) was commissioned by the Bishop of Augsburg, published in January 1629, and widely read in Vienna and Munich. According to Bireley, 'it was a rigidly Catholic commentary on the Peace of Augsburg and was to the Edict of Restitution as theory is to practice'.[36] Laymann argued that 'Whatever is not found to have been explicitly granted [to Protestants] should be considered forbidden'.[37] This interpretation of the Peace of Augsburg obviously threatened many Protestant holdings

---

[32] G. Walther, *Abt Balthasars Mission. Politische Mentalitäten, Gegenreformation und eine Adelsverschwörung im Hochstift Fulda* (Göttingen, 2002).

[33] R.G. Asch, *The Thirty Years War. The Holy Roman Empire and Europe, 1618–48* (Houndsmills, 1997), p. 96.

[34] Wilson, *The Thirty Years War*, p. 447.

[35] Wilson, *The Thirty Years War. A Sourcebook*, p. 115.

[36] Bireley, *Religion and Politics*, p. 76.

[37] Quoted in Parker, *The Thirty Years War*, chapter III (R.J.W. Evans), p. 99.

with restitution. In Laymann's work we also see the place where the legally minded bishops and prelates could agree with the more militant Catholics at the secular courts.

At the same time, bishops and other leaders of the *Reichskirche* found it difficult to support this extreme interpretation of the Religious Peace. While it fitted with their general and long-standing policy of shoring up legal arguments and appealing to tradition and constitutional arrangements, it clashed with the local and regional culture of the imperial Church. For much of the sixteenth century, the Catholics had been on the defensive and Catholic institutions often survived Protestant attacks because of legal protection. Furthermore, the secular role of many Church institutions, especially the bishops, had contributed in important ways to the survival of Catholicism in Germany during the sixteenth century, and the first priority of many Church leaders was to protect their secular rights rather than pursue risky religious policies. In addition, cathedral chapters were usually filled with members of the regional nobility, from both Catholic and Protestant families, making them sceptical of reforms or initiatives coming from Vienna or Rome. The result of these conditions was an imperial Church that reacted to the crisis of the Edict in a decidedly sceptical and conservative way. The Edict did not fit well with the culture of the ecclesiastical leadership.[38]

The bishops and their officials also faced a clash with the monasteries. In many ways the German monasteries shared the culture of the imperial Church and were indeed part of it. Many monasteries were also secular lords and free imperial estates. Like the bishops, they also owed their survival to their constitutional status within the empire. German monasticism, however, had been greatly damaged by the Reformation. In many regions almost all monasteries had been secularised in the sixteenth century and even where monasteries survived, there were few monks and declining revenues. This general decline was not universal, however, and starting in the 1570s there was a revival led by the Benedictine Abbey of Weingarten in Upper Swabia.[39] Monks from Weingarten went to Jesuit universities to study, then worked to reform other monasteries across southern Germany. Wolfgang Seibrich's study of 'the restorative efforts of the old orders in the German Empire from 1580 to 1648' emphasises the broad goals of the Benedictines, Cistercians, Augustinians, Premonstratensians, and Carthusians.

> *The goal of the orders (Ordensleute) themselves was more than just a recovery of the monasteries. Particularly in the conflict with the opposing powers, bishops, Curia, and Jesuits, the goal developed: a (total) restoration of the Imperial Church, a reestablishment of the ecclesiastical and ecclesio-political conditions of the High Middle Ages, as they imagined them, more as a wish than from historical knowledge.*[40]

Seibrich recognises that such a goal was 'utopian', but points to the long-standing reform or restorative tradition within the orders. The idea of returning to medieval traditions was, in Seibrich's view, an effort to look for the 'essence' of Catholicism. This perspective contrasted with the 'absolute dominance' of pastoral care and the goal of conversion of Protestants in the Tridentine Church, which left no room for the contemplative orders and certainly not for female convents. 'So the older orders and the Jesuits became the poles, between which the tension over the character of post-Tridentine Catholicism was played out.'[41]

---

[38] Forster, *Catholic Germany*, esp. pp. 12–3, 36–7, 105–8.
[39] R. Reinhardt, *Restauration, Visitation, Inspiration. Die Reformbestrebungen in der Benediktinerabtei Weingarten von 1567 bis 1627* (Stuttgart, 1960).
[40] Seibrich, *Gegenreformation als Restauration*, p. 2.
[41] Seibrich, *Gegenreformation als Restauration*, pp. 4–6; quote p. 6.

Seibrich argues that in the conflict over the Edict the orders were able to prevent the destruction of the monastic tradition and the takeover of the Church by the Jesuits and their allies. The orders also prevented the full implementation of a hierarchical model of Church governance, with bishops fully controlling each diocese. Finally, Seibrich presents the monasteries and convents as 'carriers of the popular religious and traditional element' in Catholicism, against the institutional Church (*Amtskirche*) of the bishops.[42]

Although Seibrich certainly overstates his argument, he has identified another cultural divide with German Catholicism that was brought to the surface by the conflict over the Edict of Restitution. The Edict clearly did not reflect a particular or well thought-out Catholic religious policy. Even the advocates of the Edict were divided – there were militants who saw a chance to convert Protestants, bishops who hoped to establish greater authority, and monastic leaders hoping to restore the glory of their orders. Even without the arrival of Swedish armies, the Edict would have been hard to implement.

The Edict as Political Policy

The Edict was not just religious policy. By issuing the Edict in his own name, Ferdinand claimed authority to make a definitive ruling on a constitutional issue. As C.V. Wedgwood, in her classic 1939 history states, 'An Edict of Restitution properly carried out could be advantageous to the sovereign power of his dynasty.'[43] Even if Ferdinand was not an absolute monarch and had no plan to move in that direction, the Edict asserted imperial authority that went beyond the political and constitutional practice of the previous century.

Historians have debated whether the Edict was the result of, as Evans calls it, a kind of 'confessional absolutism', or something even less coherent. Brady presents Ferdinand's ruling style as a rejection of the rule of his predecessors, who he characterises as 'unsteady temporisers'. 'And no more conciliatory imperial Catholicism, for Ferdinand was the first Habsburg monarch to adopt Munich's forward Catholic policy.'[44] Whatever Ferdinand's motives, both Catholic and Protestant political leaders considered the Edict a grab for power by the emperor.

The Edict was, of course, a great blunder. Its political goals were unachievable, in the sense that the emperor did not have the clout to enforce his authority. In fact, Maximilian and the other electors used the conflict over the Edict to force Ferdinand to dismiss Wallenstein, weakening the imperial army. Moderate Protestants, led by John George of Saxony, were alienated by the Edict and their support for the emperor weakened and in some cases evaporated. Important prelates, such as the Bishop of Vienna and two Austrian cardinals, protested the Edict. Even the Spanish opposed the Edict, since they supported compromise with the German Protestants in order to focus on the Dutch War.[45]

As Wilson emphasises, the Edict did not bring the Swedish into the war. Gustav Adolph had a variety of motives for intervention and was initially little interested in the plight of German Protestants. But, the Edict and the long controversy over its implementation meant that German Protestants welcomed the king and his army when it arrived in Germany. The Edict seemed to many to end any chance of compromise or mediation of disputes. 'By

---

[42] Seibrich, *Gegenreformation als Restauration*, p. 7.
[43] C.V. Wedgwood, *The Thirty Years War* (New Haven, 1939), p. 239.
[44] Brady, *German Histories*, p. 378.
[45] Wilson, *The Thirty Years War*, pp. 448–53.

insisting on wholesale restitution without adequate regard to individual circumstances, Ferdinand rendered the entire process untenable and increased the number of embittered German Protestants.'[46]

The Edict floundered partly because it did not fit with the religious culture of much of German Catholicism. It also failed because it clashed with the political culture of the empire.[47] This political culture included the notion that disputes, and particularly disputes involving the Religious Peace of 1555, needed to be resolved through negotiation and compromise among the imperial estates. As Wilson points out, 'the majority favored judging each case on its merits'; sweeping edicts were not part of this culture.[48] The result, predictably, was a wave of protests, legal challenges to the Edict, and demands for negotiation.

Brady brings a slightly different perspective to the discussion of the political culture of the Holy Roman Empire. Brady argues that the Peace of Augsburg had enshrined a kind of *convivencia* in the German-speaking lands. Reminiscent of the coexistence of Jewish, Muslim, and Christians in medieval Iberia, the German *convivencia* meant that Protestants and Catholics coexisted, sometimes in the same cities, cooperated as necessary within carefully laid-out legal and constitutional arrangements.[49] This coexistence was regularly threatened and challenged in the empire, especially after about 1580, when a more militant Catholicism clashed with Calvinism, but it held strong in most of Germany.[50] The Thirty Years' War was, according to Brady, the greatest challenge of all to the imperial *convivencia*, and the Edict of Restitution was exemplary of the different political culture the war promoted. When the war ended, the Peace of Westphalia restored the older political culture to dominance. 'Its ethos promoted a general practice of regulating conflict and difference through arbitration and judicialization, a hallmark of Imperial governance until the end.'[51]

Conclusion

The Edict of Restitution was an important moment in the war. It brought to the surface the conflicting motivations and goals of the different forces on the Catholic side, while driving the divided Protestants into opposition to imperial policy. In retrospect it was a great blunder and Ferdinand lost a chance to negotiate a peace from a position of strength. Yet, with France and Sweden committed to preventing imperial domination of the empire, was such a peace really a possibility in the late 1620s?

Selected Bibliography

Asch, R.G., *The Thirty Years War. The Holy Roman Empire and Europe, 1618–48* (Houndsmills, 1997).

---

[46] Wilson, *The Thirty Years War*, p. 453.
[47] This point is made particularly well by Peter Wilson: *The Thirty Years War*, pp. 453–4.
[48] Wilson, *The Thirty Years War*, p. 453.
[49] Brady, *German Histories*, pp. 233–4.
[50] Brady, *German Histories*, pp. 334–6.
[51] Ibid., p. 408.

Bireley, R., *Religion and Politics in the Age of the Counterreformation. Emperor Ferdinand II, William Lamormaini, S.J., and the Formation of Imperial Politics* (Chapel Hill, 1981).

Bireley, R., *The Jesuits and the Thirty Years War. Kings, Courts, and Confessors* (Cambridge, 2003).

Brady, T.A. Jr., *German Histories in the Age of Reformations, 1400–1650* (Cambridge, 2009).

Châtellier, L., *Europe of the Devout. The Catholic Reformation and the Formation of a New Society* (Cambridge, 1989).

Forster, M.R., *The Counter-Reformation in the Villages. Religion and Reform in the Bishop of Speyer, 1560–1720* (Ithaca, 1992).

Forster, M.R., *Catholic Revival in the Age of the Baroque. Religious Identity in Southwest Germany, 1550–1750* (Cambridge, 2001).

Forster, M.R., *Catholic Germany from the Reformation to the Enlightenment* (Houndsmills, 2007).

Parker, G. (ed.), *The Thirty Years War* (London, 1984).

Wedgwood, C.V., *The Thirty Years War* (New Haven, 1939).

Wilson, P.H., *The Thirty Years War. Europe's Tragedy* (Cambridge, MA, 2009).

Wilson, P.H., *The Thirty Years War. A Sourcebook* (Houndsmills, 2010).

17

Lutherans, Calvinists and the Road to a Normative Year

Ralf-Peter Fuchs

Protestantism Devastated? After the Edict of Restitution

In spite of bitter religious disputes that separated Lutherans and Calvinists, they were nevertheless still united after 1566 when necessary in their controversies with the Catholics during the imperial diets.[1] From then on they pursued common aims as a Protestant religious party,[2] and struggled against the Catholics for denominational parity with the supporters of the *Confessio Augustana*. Together they repelled Catholic attempts to withhold legal acceptance of the Calvinist Estates. They rejected the ecclesiastical reservation (*reservatum ecclesiasticum*)[3] and were consequently able to resist the Catholic demand to surrender the mediate church property in their own territories, which had been taken over after 1552.[4]

Behind the legal question of church property there existed a concealed struggle for those areas which had formerly belonged to the medieval imperial church and had been increasingly lost by Catholics as the result of conversions of imperial estates to Protestantism after the Religious Peace of Augsburg. Both religious parties, Catholics and Protestants, regarded them as essential. The Catholics had tried to protect 'their' possessions before the great war by referring to the ecclesiastical reservation and to 1552 as a key year. This was supposed to hinder the Protestants from secularising more and more church property. On the other hand, the Protestants had claimed 'autonomia' ('Freistellung der Religion'). With this term they had attempted to circumscribe the principle of freedom of conscience as well as the right to peacefully gain further possessions within the empire despite the ecclesiastical reservation.[5] And in fact, after 1555 considerable parts of the empire had become Protestant through the conversions of territorial princes, especially in the north.

---

[1] For the beginnings of the Calvinists' presence at the imperial diets cf. A. Edel, *Der Kaiser und Kurpfalz. Eine Studie zu den Grundelementen politischen Handelns bei Maximilian II. (1564–1576)*, (Göttingen, 1997).

[2] F. Dickmann, 'Das Problem der Gleichberechtigung der Konfessionen im Reich im 16. und 17. Jahrhundert', in F. Dickmann, *Friedensrecht und Friedenssicherung. Studien zum Friedensproblem in der neueren Geschichte* (Göttingen, 1971): pp. 7–35, here p. 9.

[3] A. Gotthard, *Der Augsburger Religionsfrieden* (Münster, 2004), pp. 393–7; see the chapter by Matthias Pohlig in this volume.

[4] Ibid., pp. 250–51.

[5] For the term of 'Freistellung' as used by the Lutherans see N. Paulus, 'Religionsfreiheit und Augsburger Religionsfriede', in H. Lutz (ed.), *Zur Geschichte der Toleranz und Religionsfreiheit* (Darmstadt, 1977), pp. 17–41. For the Calvinist project of 'Freistellung' during the 1580s see

After decades of struggles between the two religious parties, the emperor had made a decision solely in favour of the Catholics by proclaiming the Edict of Restitution in 1629.[6] The ecclesiastical reservation was again explicitly confirmed, and during the initial restitutions Protestant imperial estates were expropriated. Lutheran and Calvinist preachers were expelled by imperial commissioners and soldiers, thus causing central political positions of Protestantism to be forfeited. What is more, followers of the Protestant faith must have felt existentially threatened by the recatholicisation of large areas of the empire. Under these circumstances, was there actually a future for Protestantism, considering the decrease of possessions and the prohibition of further seizure of church property? It was not only, however, the ecclesiastical reservation that appeared to determine the minority of Protestants on imperial diets in the future. The prohibition of Calvinism, which was proclaimed at the same time by the emperor, meant a complete reorganisation of the empire. Although the existence of the *Confessio Augustana* had not been questioned in the Edict of Restitution, the fear of a Holy Roman Empire without Protestants was not unfounded and continued to spread increasingly among them.

Electoral Saxony and Electoral Brandenburg – A Lutheran and a Calvinist Prince on the Road to Cooperation

All Protestants had been shocked by the Edict of Restitution. It was, however, especially those imperial estates that had promoted ways of agreement and cooperation with the emperor and the Catholics in the past which felt snubbed. Above all, the policy of the Lutheran electoral prince of Saxony, Johann Georg I, a former ally of Emperor Ferdinand II in the war against the Bohemian confederates, seemed – retrospectively considered – to have damaged and weakened the Protestant position. Loyalty to the Catholic emperor and fidelity to Protestantism had not been regarded as a contradiction by Johann Georg and his councils before. They had contributed to the expansion of the Lutheran denomination in their territory and simultaneously maintained good relationships with the emperor. In contrast to the electoral prince of the Palatinate, they had repeatedly tried to act as bridge builders between Protestants and Catholics.[7] Now, after the proclamation of the Edict of Restitution by the emperor – a measure which could only be interpreted as a breach of trust – Electoral Saxony contemplated a change of policy. Whereas on the one hand, Johann Georg and his councillors in Dresden did not want to evoke the impression of open enmity against the emperor and the Catholics, on the other hand, a closer political connection with the Calvinist electoral prince, Georg Wilhelm of Brandenburg, was gradually being taken into consideration.

The electoral prince of Brandenburg ruled over a vast association of territories in which many Protestants lived, although his Calvinist brothers in faith constituted a small minority compared to the Lutherans. Since 1609, after the death of Johann Wilhelm of Jülich-Kleve, the electoral princes of Brandenburg had also laid claim – among other competitors – to

---

H. Duchhardt, *Protestantisches Kaisertum und Altes Reich. Die Diskussion über die Konfession des Kaisers in Politik, Publizistik und Staatsrecht* (Wiesbaden, 1977), p. 105.

[6] See M. Heckel, 'Das Restitutionsedikt Kaiser Ferdinands II. vom 6. März 1629 – eine verlorene Alternative der Reichskirchenverfassung', in G. Köbler and H. Nehlsen (eds), *Wirkungen europäischer Rechtskultur. Festschrift für Karl Kroeschell zum 70. Geburtstag* (Munich, 1997); see also the chapter by Marc Forster in this volume.

[7] See also G. Parker, *The Thirty Years' War* (London and New York, 1987), p. 115.

the United Territories of Jülich, Kleve, Berg, Mark and Ravensberg and in 1614 they had acquired, at least provisionally, a part of these countries by the Treaty of Xanten. The population of this region was denominationally mixed, with Lutherans as well as Calvinists and Catholics. Georg Wilhelm recruited one of his most important advisors from the County of Mark. Adam of Schwarzenberg was an aristocrat and a Catholic, but was always loyal to his Calvinist sovereign and to the Brandenburgian aspirations during the Conflict of the Jülich succession. He became a member of the elector's privy council, where he faced a Calvinist majority.

In the opinion of the historian Cicely Veronica Wedgwood, Georg Wilhelm of Brandenburg was the 'most harmless ruler in Germany'[8] during the Thirty Years' War. This harsh judgement is based on the fact that he and his privy council had followed a very erratic course during the first decade of the war. During the Bohemian War (1619–1622) Brandenburg had pursued neutrality. After 1622 – following an alliance with the United Netherlands – the troops of the elector had conducted a war against Spain and the duke of Palatine-Neuburg to gain control of the Jülich-Kleve territories.[9] That had evoked the enmity of the emperor. But four years later, in 1626, during the Danish-Lower Saxon war, Georg Wilhelm also made an alliance with the emperor, on the advice of Schwarzenberg. These political manoeuvres had bad consequences for his territories. During this time, and even after the Peace of Lübeck (1629), his home territory, the Margraviate of Brandenburg, was devastated by friends and enemies alike.

After the Edict of Restitution Georg Wilhelm's situation became precarious. The only remaining Calvinist elector after the dismissal and flight of Friedrich V of the Palatinate, he had to assume the worst, namely not only the loss of substantial possessions, but also the end of the latent toleration of his faith, a toleration on which he had relied for many years. And it was not only the relationship to the emperor that had worsened, because Ferdinand II had intervened in the Conflict of the Jülich-Kleve succession, trying to gain control of those countries for himself. Since 1628, propagandistic pamphlets had promoted a closer Lutheran and Calvinist cooperation against the Catholic Habsburg Emperor, and the failure of Schwarzenberg's pro-imperial politics increased the plausibility of such an alliance. In particular Levin von dem Knesebeck, a member of the privy council in Cölln and a firm opponent of Schwarzenberg, campaigned for this position.[10]

With the invasion of the Swedish troops already imminent,[11] Electoral Saxony and Electoral Brandenburg began closing ranks.[12] Georg Wilhelm of Brandenburg, in particular, needed support. Although family bonds existed with the House of Wasa – Gustav II Adolph, king of Sweden, was married to a sister of the electoral prince – the Swedish troops were feared throughout the territories. They had already destroyed the duchy of Prussia in the year 1626, during their war against Poland. In view of the state of his territories, the

---

[8] See C.V. Wedgwood, *The Thirty Years' War* (New Haven, 1949), p. 221.

[9] H. Gabel, 'Sicherheit und Konfession. Aspekte niederländischer Politik gegenüber Jülich Berg vor und während des Dreißigjährigen Krieges', in S. Ehrenpreis (ed.), *Der Dreißigjährige Krieg im Herzogtum Berg und in seinen Nachbarregionen* (Neustadt/Aisch, 2002), pp. 132–79, here p. 155. See also R.-P. Fuchs, 'Der Dreißigjährige Krieg und die Grafschaft Mark', *Märkisches Jahrbuch für Geschichte*, 100 (2000): pp. 103–38, here pp. 110–22.

[10] B. Nischan, *Prince, People and Confession. The Second Reformation in Brandenburg* (Philadelphia, 1994), pp. 250–51.

[11] For the motives of Gustav II Adolph to invade the Empire see J. Burkhardt, 'Warum hat Gustav Adolf in den Dreißigjährigen Krieg eingegriffen? Der Schwedische Krieg 1630–1635', in P.C. Hartmann and F. Schuller (eds), *Der Dreißigjährige Krieg. Facetten einer folgenreichen Epoche* (Regensburg, 2010), pp. 94–107.

[12] Parker, *Thirty Years' War*, p. 115.

Brandenburgian elector made every effort to avoid a further war. In April 1630 he proposed a joint Saxon-Brandenburgian deputation, which was to convince Gustav Adolph to give up his plan to invade the empire. But Johann Georg refused even to get in contact with the Swedish king, and the Brandenburgian had to take the initiative alone, only to discover that Gustav Adolph was determined to intervene and expected his support as an ally in the war to come.

When the Lutheran king of Sweden, Gustav Adolph, landed on Usedom on 6 July 1630 and began his campaign against the emperor and the Catholics, the two most important Protestant princes of the empire, Johann Georg of Saxony and Georg Wilhelm of Brandenburg, were not enthusiastic. Although they felt threatened, both initially refused military resistance against the Edict of Restitution and still tried to find political ways to end the conflict with the emperor. In the meantime, Gustav Adolph was performing his role as the 'Saviour' of Protestantism. In his manifesto of war he declared that he was moved to intervene by many imperial estates ('von vielen Ständen'[13]) and that he was supporting divine law by defending his fellow believers.[14] Whereas some Protestant estates were willing to believe his propaganda and were hoping to improve their positions, neither the Lutheran prince elector of Saxony nor the Calvinist prince elector of Brandenburg were willing to give up their critical attitude towards the campaign.

War Avoidance Strategies. The Invention of the Normative Year at the Electoral Diet of Regensburg 1630

At the first imperial convent after the Edict of Restitution in Regensburg in the summer of 1630, the emperor and the Catholics expected the two Protestant electoral princes to condemn the Swedish campaign. Johann Georg of Saxony and Georg Wilhelm of Brandenburg did not, however, appear personally, intending to express their protest against the Edict of Restitution by sending only envoys.[15]

At this electoral diet, which began just three days before the invasion by Gustav Adolph, Emperor Ferdinand II acted with greater strength, but Catholic estates like Electoral Bavaria were already suspicious of this increasing power and tried to operate against it. One result was to be the dismissal of Wallenstein, the emperor's military leader.[16] Saxony and Brandenburg had not been involved in this operation. They had instead tried to put the complete dissolution of the huge armies of the League and the emperor onto the agenda, but without success.[17]

The negotiating position of the two Protestant electoral estates was very weak in 1630. They not only faced a Catholic majority, but were also suspected of having made secret agreements with the Swedish king. Neither was the hope of negotiating the revocation of the Edict of Restitution fulfilled, because it was blocked by concerted Catholic and imperial

---

[13] H. Schilling, 'Das schwedische Kriegsmanifest vom Juli 1630 und die Frage nach dem Charakter des Dreißigjährigen Krieges', in R. Hohls, Iris Schröder and H. Siegrist (eds), *Europa und die Europäer, Quellen und Essays zur modernen europäischen Geschichte* (Stuttgart, 2005), pp. 376–7.

[14] Ibid.

[15] For the Convention of Regensburg in 1630 see P.H. Wilson, *Europe's Tragedy. A History of the Thirty Years' War* (London, 2009), pp. 454–8.

[16] Ibid., pp. 454–5.

[17] U. Kober, *Eine Karriere im Krieg. Graf Adam von Schwarzenberg und die kurbrandenburgische Politik von 1619 bis 1641* (Berlin, 2004), p. 248.

action. The envoys of the electoral prince Johann Georg of Saxony presented a protest note and demanded the annulment of the Edict.

In the long run, even more important was another associated demand. The electoral prince of Saxony also required restitution of lands and property. As he put it, the conditions before the Bohemian War should be restored.[18] This new attempt was to mark the beginning of a big shift in Protestant positions. Whereas they had formerly categorically rejected the Catholics' claims to make restitution of those territories that had become Protestant after 1552, they were now willing – after heavy losses in the latest years of war – to claim restitution for themselves.

However, Johann Georg's appeal to re-establish the pre-war situation was not discussed by the Catholics in Regensburg at all. Attention was given instead to another envoy of a Protestant imperial estate. Anton Wolff, Chancellor of the Lutheran Landgrave of Hessen-Darmstadt, presented a peace proposal, in which both Catholic and Protestant restitutions should be granted. In his concept, the year 1555 was the key year. Protestants and Catholics were to mutually restore the controversial lands of which they had gained possession during and since that year.[19]

The year 1555 was only three years after 1552, the year of the Peace of Passau, which was proposed as the restitution year by the Catholics. The 1555 arrangement would have meant many unfavourable consequences for most of the Protestants, as many of those lands which had belonged to them before the war would have been irretrievably lost. But for the Protestants, the year 1555 also had symbolic importance. It was the year of the Peace of Augsburg, which established the legal existence of Protestantism in the empire. Furthermore, the acceptance of this key year by both sides would have also revoked the hated Edict of Restitution which had been forced on the Protestants and would have secured the coexistence of Catholicism and Protestantism for the future. In fact, the electoral diet of Regensburg was a turning point. In the long run, it would lead to the solutions of the Peace of Westphalia in 1648, in which a normative year would be fixed, granting denominational plurality by the allocation of territories between Catholics and Protestants.[20]

Anton Wolff's proposal did not, however, meet with the consent of the Protestant estates in 1630, although he had suggested it in combination with another key year, the year 1621. This more favourable year was only meant to count for the two Protestant electoral princes, but even the elector of Saxony and the elector of Brandenburg objected to the peace efforts of the chancellor of Hessen-Darmstadt, and the Catholic reaction was disappointing, too. It was merely a friendly appreciation of his and his prince's intention to make peace. Instead of negotiating about a key year, the Edict of Restitution was affirmed by a large majority at the end of the diet of Regensburg. Further negotiations were nevertheless promised. Emperor Ferdinand II and the Catholic estates announced a composition meeting, which was to take place in Frankfurt, in order to elaborate the exact execution of the Edict of Restitution.

Thus, it can be assumed that in the summer of 1630 substantial Protestant estates still believed in the possibility of finding a peaceful way to abandon the Edict of Restitution. On the other hand, given the refusal of the Catholics to cooperate and given the presence of the

---

[18] M.C. Lundorp, *Der Römischen Kayserlichen Majestät Und Deß Heiligen Römischen Reichs Geist- und Weltlicher Stände, Chur- und Fürsten, Grafen, Herren und Städte Acta Publica Und Schrifftliche Handlungen, Außschreiben, Sendbrieff, Bericht, Unterricht [...] so in Friedens- und Kriegeszeiten gegeneinander ergangen und gewechselt*. Part 4 (Frankfurt/M., 1668), p. 73: 'alles in Religion und Prophan-Sachen in den Stand zu stellen / wie es vor dem Böhmischen Krieg gewesen'.

[19] J.H. Gebauer, *Kurbrandenburg und das Restitutionsedikt von 1629* (Halle, 1899), pp. 115–17.

[20] R.-P. Fuchs, *Ein 'Medium' zum Frieden. Die Normaljahrsregel und die Beendigung des Dreißigjährigen Krieges* (Munich and Oldenbourg, 2010), pp. 86–94.

troops of the Swedish king, which were already in the empire, it became increasingly urgent to think about other measures. Protestantism stood at a crossroads.

Peace or War? From the Convention of Leipzig to the Frankfurt Composition Meeting

The Protestant imperial estates met again in Leipzig in February 1631 to confer about the possibilities of achieving a sustainable peace, as well as to consider the establishment of a corporate army to withstand the emperor's and the Catholics' troops.[21] At this convention, which was the largest assembly of Protestants after the dissolution of the Union (1621), Wolff's proposals appeared again on the agenda, and again they were rejected by the majority. However, Johann Georg's proposal to restore the pre-war situation by means of restitution was brought to light and was then discussed in detail. The crucial point was to determine when exactly the war had begun. The Electorate of Brandenburg referred to the year 1620, indicating that even after the Battle of White Mountain it would have been possible to avoid war with the Catholics and that only afterwards had the Protestant estates been forced into the conflict.[22]

At this point, Georg Wilhelm of Brandenburg himself and his envoys no longer expected successful peace negotiations with the emperor and the Catholics and preferred the organisation of a Protestant army. In the end, the convent of the Protestant estates in Leipzig made the decision to set up a defensive constitution on the basis of the imperial circles with the intention of creating a third party between the emperor and the Swedish king. Although a direct alliance with Gustav Adolph was avoided, the manifesto of the convent of Leipzig from May 12, 1631, displayed a determination to resist even by military force. Only eight days later this position would be affirmed after the Protestants had been shocked once more: On May 20, 1631, after several months of siege, the troops of the Catholic League under Tilly sacked and pillaged the Protestant city of Magdeburg, causing a destructive fire to which tens of thousands of inhabitants fell victim.[23]

The majority of the Protestant estates attending the Composition Meeting in Frankfurt therefore had little hope of coming to an agreement with the Catholic estates.[24] Nevertheless, the electoral prince of Saxony made a last-ditch effort to avert armed conflict with the Catholics. His negotiators presented the idea of using the year 1620 as normative year for achieving peace. Johann Georg of Saxony and his envoys described it as a 'medium' of peace. The aim was to regain all the property that had belonged to the Protestants in that

---

[21] For the Leipzig Convention see Parker, *The Thirty Years' War*, pp. 116–8 and Wilson, *Europe's Tragedy*, pp. 465–7.

[22] SächHStA Dresden, Geheimes Archiv 8097/1, fol. p. 147.

[23] See for example H. Medick, 'Historisches Ereignis und zeitgenössische Erfahrung: Die Eroberung und Zerstörung Magdeburgs 1631', in H. Medick and B. von Krusenstjern (eds), *Zwischen Alltag und Katastrophe. Der Dreißigjährige Krieg aus der Nähe* (Göttingen, 1999), pp. 377–407.

[24] See also R.-P. Fuchs, 'Für die Kirche Gottes und die Posterität – Kursachsen und das Friedensmedium eines Normaljahres auf dem Frankfurter Kompositionstag 1631', in *Mitteilungen des Sonderforschungsbereichs 'Pluralisierung und Autorität in der Frühen Neuzeit'* (2007): pp. 19–27.

year.[25] On the other hand, according to the same principle, the Catholics were to keep their property for eternity.[26]

At first the proposal made by the electorate of Saxony provoked strong objections among the other Protestant estates. What remained of the principle of autonomia ('Freistellung der Religion'), the freedom to choose one's own religion? Wouldn't the Protestants be giving up the chance of further increasing Protestant property and more than that, wouldn't they be giving up the obligation to propagate their true religion? The delegates of the Electorate of Brandenburg especially expressed concern over the proposal, as they found that it threatened the expansion of evangelical belief and insisted on the principle of 'Freistellung'. Giving this up would forever hinder the subjects of the Catholic princes and their descendants from finding the way to real belief and truth even if their rulers converted to Protestantism.[27] Nevertheless, the proposal of Johann Georg of Saxony was accepted, because the delegates of the electorate of Saxony were able to convince the other Protestant estates that a normative year of 1620 was the only possibility of saving the Protestant religion in a very threatening situation. Thus, for the first time, Lutheran and Calvinist agreed on a common proposal for a normative year, which was subsequently submitted to the Catholics.

However, the Protestant offer failed due to the rigid attitude of the Catholics. They insisted on the Edict of Restitution and called the offered 'medium' an 'extremum'. What many of the Protestant delegates had foreseen then occurred. Considering the military successes during the Bohemian and the Danish-Lower Saxon wars, the Catholics did not want to relinquish the advantages they had gained.

It was not only because of the dissension of the religious parties that the Composition Meeting in Frankfurt ended turbulently in October 1631. The Catholic delegates found themselves in the unpleasant situation of having to flee from the congress because Swedish troops were approaching Frankfurt after the battle of Breitenfeld. But despite its unhappy ending, the meeting had not been a meaningless episode,[28] as has been claimed in older studies. The idea of achieving peace by means of a normative year, which would be obligatory for Catholics as well as for Protestants, was soon to be taken up again during peace negotiations between the Emperor and the electorate of Saxony. And in the long term, this idea would lead to the termination of the war at the Westphalian Congress. Unfortunately in September 1631 the proposal enjoyed little support. Essentially this was because the Catholics still assessed the prospects for success of the Swedish king and a Protestant army as limited. However, as it turned out, even the Protestant estates that actually wanted to avoid military confrontation were overwhelmed by the events and saw no other alternative than to join Gustav Adolph.

---

[25] SächHStADresden, Geh. Archiv, Friedensschlüsse 8098/1, Frankfurter Kompositionstag, fol. 80: 'was sie anno 1620 inngehabt, beseßen, genoßen undt gebraucht und folgende zeiten durch postulationen oder sonsten erlangt'.

[26] SächHStADresden, Geh. Archiv, Friedensschlüsse 8098/1, Frankfurter Kompositionstag, fol. 80–81.

[27] See J.H. Gebauer, *Kurbrandenburg und das Restitutionsedikt von 1629*, pp. 184–5.

[28] A. Gindely, *Geschichte des Dreißigjährigen Krieges in drei Abtheilungen. Abth. 2: Der niedersächsische, dänische und schwedische Krieg bis zum Tode Gustav Adolfs 1622 bis 1632* (Prag, 1882), p. 204.

Confrontation of the Religious Parties in the Empire?

Already during the Composition Meeting in Frankfurt on 11 September 1631, Johann Georg of Saxony, the strongest supporter of peace in the empire, had decided to enter into a formal war alliance with the Swedish king.[29] This change of mind was a reaction to the invasion of the League's armies under Tilly in the electoral prince's territory which took place on the very same day, 11 September.[30] Only six days later, on 17 September, a Swedish-Saxonian army defeated the armies of the Emperor and the League near Breitenfeld and forced them to flee. The events of autumn and winter 1631 marked a military turning point which no one had considered possible before. The military superiority of the Emperor and the League was replaced by the hegemony of Gustav Adolph of Sweden.[31]

In addition to the military cooperation with the electorate of Saxony on 27 July 1631 the Swedish king had also found another supporter, the Calvinist Landgrave of Hessen-Kassel, Wilhelm V.[32] At the same time the Lutheran Dukes Bernhard and Wilhelm of Saxe-Weimar joined the Swedish king. And since June 1631 even the prince elector of Brandenburg, Georg Wilhelm, had been participating in the anti-Catholic alliance.[33] The prince elector had not, however, surrendered unconditionally to the supreme command of Gustav Adolph, but had stipulated his independence.[34]

Protestant historians later interpreted the triumphal march of the Swedish king and his allies as a heroic deed of saving the Protestant faith in the empire – with the brilliant climax of seizing Munich, the residence of the leader of the League, the prince elector Maximilian I, on 17 May 1632. Protestant contemporaries also celebrated the anti-imperial and anti-Catholic alliance. For example, the two Lutheran leaders, Gustav Adolph of Sweden and Johann Georg of Saxony were pictured together with Martin Luther as victors in the 1632 pamphlet 'Triga heroum'.[35] The initiator of this pamphlet was Johann Georg himself, who feared that his part in the heroic military success might not be sufficiently appreciated. Gustav Adolph and Johann Georg turned out to be rivals for the leadership of the Protestant cause, and Gustav Adolph cooperated more with the Calvinist Landgrave of Hesse-Kassel than with his Lutheran brother in faith.

Although he always emphasised the common Protestant concern, Gustav Adolph also had other motives for being at war in the empire, and they did not always correspond with the interests of his allies. Christoph Kampmann has stressed the openness of his actions.[36] By trying to take possession on the south coast of the Baltic Sea he was engaged in conflict with several Protestant sovereigns, among others the prince elector of Brandenburg. On the other hand he broke up imperial structures by handing over previously Catholic territories to his Protestant allies. But he also made an effort to maintain a good relationship with the Lutheran Landgrave of Hesse-Darmstadt, Georg II, who was a true believer in the idea of a unified empire. Even if the large Protestant war alliance against the emperor and the

---

[29] Wilson, *Europe's Tragedy*, p. 472.
[30] C. Kampmann, *Europa und das Reich im Dreißigjährigen Krieg. Geschichte eines europäischen Konflikts* (Stuttgart etc., 2008), p. 78.
[31] Ibid.
[32] Wilson, *Europe's Tragedy*, p. 471.
[33] Ibid.
[34] See Kober, *Eine Karriere im Krieg*, p. 281.
[35] W. Harms, 'Das illustrierte Flugblatt als meinungsbildendes Medium in der Zeit des Dreißigjährigen Krieges', in K. Bußmann and H. Schilling (eds), *1648: Krieg und Frieden in Europa*, vol. 2, (Münster, 1998), pp. 323–7.
[36] Kampmann, *Europa und das Reich*, pp. 86–7.

Catholics suggests a religious war, some very different aims within the Protestant war party can be revealed on a closer view.

Moreover, Gustav Adolph was linked to a political power which forced him to respect Catholic interests as well. It had been the Catholic kingdom of France which had created the basis for the Lutheran king of Sweden to rise up as the saviour of Protestantism in the empire by the contract of Bärwalde. This contract contained not only a declaration of alliance but also the commitment of large subsidies for Gustav Adolph, who was already having problems keeping an appropriate number of soldiers. By supporting Sweden, the French Prime Minister Richelieu followed the plan of weakening the Habsburg Monarchies, which were threateningly surrounding France. Richelieu's aim was to conduct a 'secret' war, i.e. a war without direct military intervention. Louis XIII and Richelieu even stuck to that strategy when the establishment of a Swedish hegemony became apparent in September 1631. They did not even follow the appeal of the Catholic electoral princes to intervene as a protecting power of the whole League, but only offered help to two Catholic princes, the duke of Lorraine and the prince elector of Trier, Philipp Christoph of Sötern. The contract of protection with these princes assured a military presence in the fortresses of Ehrenbreitstein and Philippsburg. Although it allowed the passage of the Swedish troops it was a clear signal that further Swedish conquests would not be tolerated in this region.[37]

After the death of Gustav Adolph in the battle of Lützen (1632) the conflicts between the Protestant electoral princes and Sweden became evident. In the winter of 1632/33 the Swedish chancellor Oxenstierna fixed the military and political rules of future Swedish engagement. He revealed that the troops under his command should fight in the empire until they had gained satisfaction by tangible benefits and the delivery of imperial lands. To reduce the vast costs of war he proposed a stronger military involvement by the Protestant estates. This led to the establishment of the 'Heilbronner Bund' in spring 1633,[38] a federation of the Protestant estates of the Franconian, the Swabian and the Upper-Rhenish circles under Swedish command. Neither the electorate of Saxony nor the Electorate of Brandenburg joined this war alliance. Both princes refused to accept the Swedish supreme command. Suspicion and rivalry between Sweden and the electorate of Saxony nearly caused a military conflict in Silesia in the winter of 1633/34.[39] The electoral prince of Brandenburg had feared at least since August 1634 that his own plans to incorporate Pomerania into his dominion were at risk, because the Swedish were claiming the same territory.[40]

It can therefore be concluded that in the first period of the alliance between the two electoral princes and Gustav Adolph which began in summer 1631, there was indeed a temporary revival of the ideal of Protestant solidarity. If nothing else, the close cooperation of the Lutheran king of Sweden and the Calvinist landgrave of Hesse-Kassel had proven that differences in faith could be bridged to follow common aims. At the same time it is obvious that the concept of a common operating Protestant war party was ultimately an illusion. The leading electoral princes in particular remained reserved towards Sweden, which could not convince its partners that its ambition was congruent with that of the imperial estates and the ideals of the empire.

---

[37] See H. Weber, 'Richelieu und das Reich', in H. Lutz, F.H. Schubert and H. Weber, *Frankreich und das Reich im 16. und 17. Jahrhundert* (Göttingen, 1968), p. 44.

[38] See J. Kretzschmar, *Der Heilbronner Bund 1632–1635*, vol. 1 (Lübeck, 1922).

[39] Kampmann, *Europa und das Reich*, p. 92.

[40] Ibid.

Negotiating a Normative Year and the Peace of Prague

The hope of pacifying the empire and making possible a coexistence of Catholics and Protestants was never given up by the two Protestant leading powers. Although they had participated in the war against the Emperor and the League – the electorate of Brandenburg since June and the electorate of Saxony since September 1631 – the electoral princes of Brandenburg and Saxony remained in permanent contact in order to work out opportunities for peacemaking. After the experience with the Edict of Restitution, the basic question now was how the right to exist as imperial estates could be permanently secured for the Protestants.

In February 1632 the two electoral princes and their delegates discussed the situation again at a meeting in Torgau. They considered whether the idea of individual freedom of religion for the empire's subjects, independent from the denomination of the territorial princes, should be included in the negotiations with the emperor and the Catholics.[41] However, Johann Georg of Saxony stuck to the concept of a normative year of 1620, which he had also presented to the Swedish.[42] Further debates between the electorate of Saxony and the Electorate of Brandenburg in Dresden in February 1633 produced another date of restitution which led to the revival of peace negotiations with the Catholics.[43] The suggestion was to fix 1612, the year of the death of Emperor Rudolf II, as a normative year. This was meant to memorialise his reign as a peaceful one and was associated with the hope of very favourable restitution conditions for the Protestants, even in Bohemia.

The triumphal march of the Swedish king and the Protestants had led Ferdinand II and his councillors in Vienna to think about negotiations as well. Since 1631 even suspending the Edict of Restitution had been considered because this could break up the alliance between Sweden and the Protestant estates. Given the hegemony of a foreign power in the empire, with disastrous consequences for the population, which had already suffered from contributions, troop passages and plagues on both the Protestant and Catholic sides, imperial patriotism was increasingly regarded as a basis for a common political language.[44] The saving of the 'fatherland' had become an important item in the peace negotiations conducted since June 1634 between the delegates of Emperor Ferdinand II and of the prince elector Johann Georg of Saxony.

At that time Ferdinand II was willing to suspend his Edict of Restitution for a while. The prerequisite for this was to be the relinquishing of the Protestant war gains achieved after the intervention of the Swedish king. From the perspective of the emperor, the year 1630 seemed to be the best normative year. Restitutions were to restore the empire to the way it had been before Gustav Adolph's invasion. The electorate of Saxony however promoted setting the normative year at 1612, which had been worked out in cooperation with the Electorate of Brandenburg, as a point of departure. But in July 1634 this suggestion had already been dropped. Since then the delegates of Johann Georg held the position to establish 1620 as the normative year, in the hope of regaining the territories for the Protestants which had been lost during the Danish-Lower Saxon war.

---

[41] Gebauer, *Kurbrandenburg und das Restitutionsedikt*, p. 222.

[42] M. Ritter, *Deutsche Geschichte im Zeitalter der Gegenreformation und des Dreißigjährigen Krieges (1555–1648). Vol. 3: Geschichte des Dreißigjährigen Krieges* (Darmstadt, 1962), p. 514.

[43] Kretzschmar, *Der Heilbronner Bund*, pp. 176–77. For the 'Dresdner Punkte' see H. Knapp, *Matthias Hoë von Hoënegg und sein Eingreifen in die Politik und Publizistik des Dreißigjährigen Krieges* (Halle, 1902), pp. 52–5.

[44] See A. Wandruszka, *Reichspatriotismus und Reichspolitik zur Zeit des Prager Friedens von 1635. Eine Studie zur Geschichte des deutschen Nationalbewußtseins* (Cologne etc., 1955).

On the other hand, the imperial delegates did not accept this date because they considered the Danish-Lower Saxon war as finished definitively by the Peace of Lübeck in 1629. They attached importance to the interpretation that the Swedish king had initiated a new war in 1630 when he invaded the empire. Nevertheless, they proposed another compromise with the year 1627 as a normative year. Their suggestion included the restitution of those areas which had been wrested from the Protestants as the result of the imperial Edict of Restitution.

What was the point of debating which year should be selected? Firstly, the two negotiation parties could affirm their requirements by proposing dates which were advantageous for the one or the other side. Secondly, their political scope was widened because imperial patriotism was always central to the negotiations. By discussing the central starting point of reorganising the empire Ferdinand and Johann Georg operated as spokesmen for all the imperial estates which had suffered from the long war. Their extensive particular interests were postponed for the benefit of a general 'patriotic' ('vaterländische') solution. Because not all of those particular interests could be taken into consideration, it was necessary to develop a concept for reorganisation which all warring parties could accept as a viable and fair compromise. Discussing a new peaceful beginning on the basis of a normative year, which was usually referred to as 'terminus a quo' during the negotiations, always implied the mutual affirmation of preserving the Holy Roman Empire and retaining the idea of the empire as a common value. The specific dates not only marked the tenure of the two religious parties, but also indicated those times when Catholics and Protestants lived together in peace.

Moreover, the different figures proposed at the negotiating table made a rapprochement possible by simple arithmetic means. The willingness to compromise and peaceful intentions could soon be seen in the change of positions. The electorate of Saxony proposed the year 1620 instead of 1612, and the emperor suggested the year 1627 instead of 1630. For a short time Emperor Ferdinand II aimed for the year 1623, which was the arithmetical mean between 1620 and 1627.[45] The delegates of the electorate of Saxony proposed the year 1622 a little later.[46] Using patriotic rhetoric, the two negotiating parties appealed to each other to demonstrate their desire for peace by 'conceding a little'.[47] These conversations about a fair, constructive normative year and the apparent ability to give up former positions indicated that the two parties were now interacting with one another in ways that created trust.

The victory of the imperial and Spanish troops in the battle of Nördlingen on 5 September 1634 changed the military balance of power once again. The Swedish position within the Protestant alliance was weakened. On the one hand, Johann Georg of Saxony could now act as sole partner in sealing a peace contract between the empire and Saxony which could be a first step towards the realisation of a universal peace. On the other hand, the emperor and the Catholics were in a much better military position than before. The emperor's delegates still accepted the idea of a normative year but were no longer willing to abandon the year 1627. They also insisted that they would accept this year as a normative year only if it was considered as a temporary solution. The suspending of the Edict of Restitution should be temporary as well. This was the context in which the negotiations were carried on after Nördlingen, in an attempt to specify a precise day in the year 1627 as the appointed date.

The imperial delegates were eager to set the *terminus a quo*, which should now become a normative day, in the month of November 1627. In the end, they achieved the adoption

---

[45] Fuchs, *Ein 'Medium' zum Frieden*, p. 132.
[46] Ibid., p. 136.
[47] See the writs of the negotiations: 4 vols, K. Bierther (ed.), *Der Prager Frieden von 1635. Briefe und Akten zur Geschichte des Dreißigjährigen Krieges*, N. F. 2, 10 (Munich and Vienna, 1997), vol. 3, p. 1420.

of 12 November 1627 as a normative day in the Peace of Prague. This was exactly the date on which Ferdinand II had been challenged by the Catholic electoral princes at the electoral diet of Mühlhausen to enact the Edict of Restitution.[48] This again immensely enhanced the role of the emperor as a decision-making authority in property conflicts between the religious parties. In the wording of the Peace of Prague it was also fixed that the normative day, 12 November 1627 should only be valid for 40 years. Thereafter, the imperial courts, the imperial Chamber Court and the Aulic Council were to decide on disputed areas in the name of the emperor.[49]

The Meaning of the Normative Day (Year) of the Peace of Prague for Protestants in the Empire

It is obvious that the Peace of Prague, which was finally passed in 1635, accorded more with the interests of the emperor than with the demands of the Protestants. As the historian Friedrich Dickmann has pointed out, the emperor was now at the peak of power.[50] The settlement secured the Catholics' war gains of the early 1620s. Moreover, the normative date of 12 November 1627 did not protect the interests of the Protestant free imperial cities, because the prince elector of Bavaria had intervened against such an arrangement. It also entailed a risk for the Protestants that the Edict of Restitution might be reinstated in 40 years' time.

In 1635 all this was not, however, necessarily inevitable for the future. In fact, the text of the treaty stipulated that after 40 years Protestants and Catholics should submit to the judgement of the supreme courts of the empire, the imperial Aulic Court und the imperial Chamber Court, which would then be represented equally by Catholic and Protestant judges. In the meantime the two religious parties were to settle matters amicably. Moreover, the normative day secured the existence of Protestantism in the empire for the period of validity and the immediate restitution of lands and properties. For the time thereafter, the general framework of legal proceedings at least indicated that the empire should be an empire in which followers of the two faiths could live.

The right of existence for the Calvinists was not formally included in the Peace of Prague, and although the emperor had tried to involve only the Lutherans, the Calvinists, like the elector of Brandenburg, could not be prevented from declaring themselves members of the *Confessio Augustana* and from maintaining their imperial statehood. This openness of the Peace of Prague was a prerequisite for the acceptance of the treaty by nearly all Protestant estates, including the Electorate of Brandenburg. Moreover, after the dissolution of the Catholic League was included in the wording of the contract, the Protestants' trust went so far that most of them agreed with it, although the treaty contained many unfavourable regulations. Among the few who did not, was Wilhelm V, Landgrave of Hesse-Kassel, who was still receiving money from France to keep an army and to continue the war.[51] One cause for the failure of the Peace of Prague was in the end the intention of France to intervene militarily in imperial affairs. In addition, the emperor's hope of excluding Sweden, as an enemy of the empire, proved illusory.

---

[48] See M. Frisch, 'Die Normaltagsregelung im Prager Frieden', *Zeitschrift der Savigny-Stiftung für Rechtsgeschichte, Kanonistische Abteilung*, 87 (2001): pp. 442–4.

[49] See the text of the Peace of Prague: *Der Prager Frieden von 1635*, vol. 4, pp. 1609–10.

[50] F. Dickmann, *Der Westfälische Frieden* (Münster, 1998), p. 73.

[51] Ritter, *Deutsche Geschichte*, vol. 3, p. 600.

With regard to imperial Protestantism it is important to stress that the intensive war phase, which began with the invasion by Gustav Adolph of Sweden, was at the same time a phase in which ways to bring about peace were being ceaselessly explored. Although the readiness to exert military resistance increased considerably after the shock of the Edict of Restitution, under the principle of Protestant solidarity, and although Lutherans and Calvinists joined forces, they simultaneously considered means of establishing amicable arrangements with the emperor and the Catholics.

The central idea was for the opponents to come to an agreement about a date for determining and settling the boundaries of religious property in the empire. Politicians in the two Lutheran princedoms of Saxony and Hesse-Darmstadt realised that such a *terminus a quo*, which coming generations would call a normative year, or in fact a normative day, could also legally secure religious plurality in the empire. In this regard, the Peace of Prague took up the ideas of the electoral diet of Regensburg in 1630, which would lead to future developments. While the normative day in the Peace of Prague, due to the resistance of the emperor's delegates, was only valid for a limited period, at the Westphalian Peace Congress the Protestants would finally achieve acceptance of the year 1624 as a perpetual normative year. This normative year would ultimately assure the restoration of many territories which had been lost during the Thirty Years' War. Furthermore, it constituted a permanent acknowledgement of a bi-denominational imperial constitution.

Selected Bibliography

Frisch, M., 'Die Normaltagsregelung im Prager Frieden', *Zeitschrift der Savigny-Stiftung für Rechtsgeschichte, Kanonistische Abteilung*, 87 (2001): pp. 442–54.
Fuchs, R.-P., *Ein 'Medium' zum Frieden. Die Normaljahrsregel und die Beendigung des Dreißigjährigen Krieges* (Munich and Oldenbourg, 2010).
Gotthard, A., *Der Augsburger Religionsfrieden* (Münster, 2004).
Kober, U., *Eine Karriere im Krieg. Graf Adam von Schwarzenberg und die kurbrandenburgische Politik von 1619 bis 1641* (Berlin, 2004).
Nischan, B., *Prince, People and Confession. The Second Reformation in Brandenburg* (Philadelphia, 1994).
Parker, G., *The Thirty Years' War* (London and New York, 1987).
Ritter, M., *Deutsche Geschichte im Zeitalter der Gegenreformation und des Dreißigjährigen Krieges (1555–1648). Vol. 3: Geschichte des Dreißigjährigen Krieges* (Darmstadt, 1962).
Wedgwood, C.V., *The Thirty Years' War* (New Haven, 1949).
Wilson, P.H., *Europe's Tragedy. A History of the Thirty Years' War* (London, 2009).

The Thirty Years' War – A Religious War? Religion and Machiavellism at the Turning Point of 1635*

Cornel Zwierlein

The debate about whether the Thirty Years' War was a religious war at all, whether before or after 1635, is a very old one and it echoes similar questions for the other Western wars of religion. For example, the French wars of religion were treated for a long time, from the 1960s to the 1980s, exclusively as 'Civil Wars', prompting Denis Crouzet to become the scholar who finally 'put religion back into the wars of religion' in 1990.[1] This refers to a historiographical situation which also has its parallels for the Thirty Years' War, where many scholars used to deny the importance of religion for the war at all or – in a not very hidden Marxist way – conceived religion only as the 'opium' for the masses used by a political elite who had other aims.[2] However, if there is something like a modern 'war of religion / religious war', the Thirty Years' War has to be one – if not, which other war should match that definition?[3] The question of the religious character of the war implies a question of chronology or epochal differentiation: in Europe, Medieval Wars and Renaissance Wars are succeeded by the religious wars of the late sixteenth and seventeenth century and are followed by eighteenth-century (enlightened) warfare which is no longer characterised predominantly by religion. In medieval times, the crusades are marked by religious motives, aims and themes such as the campaigns against heretics (Albigenses, Hussite Wars), seen

---

*   Many thanks to Philip Benedict for important suggestions.

[1]   M.P. Holt, 'Putting Religion back into the Wars of Religion', *French Historical Studies*, 18/4 (1993), pp. 524–51. The dating of the 'religious turn' around 1990 is true only for the French historiography. In the Anglo-American historiography, that turn took place more than a decade earlier. Cf. G. Murdock, P. Roberts and A. Spicer (eds), *Ritual and Violence. Natalie Zemon Davis and Early Modern France* (Oxford, 2012). For the French Wars of Religion as preparation for the Thirty Years' War cf. C. Zwierlein, *Discorso und Lex Dei. Die Entstehung neuer Denkrahmen im 16. Jahrhundert und die Wahrnehmung der französischen Religionskriege in Italien und Deutschland* (Göttingen, 2006).

[2]   J.V. Polišensk, *Der Krieg und die Gesellschaft in Europa 1618–1648* (Prague, 1971), p. 141; S.H. Steinberg, 'The Thirty Years' War. A New Interpretation', *History*, XXXII (1947), pp. 89–102; idem, *Der Dreißigjährige Krieg und der Kampf um die Vorherrschaft in Europa 1600–1660* (Göttingen, 1967), p. 59. From a very different point of view, P.H. Wilson, *The Thirty Years War: Europe's Tragedy* (Cambridge/Mass., 2009) also stresses rather the secular tendencies.

[3]   Earlier contributions to that question are, among others, K. Repgen, 'Was ist ein Religionskrieg?', *Zeitschrift für Kirchengeschichte*, XCVII (1986): pp. 334–49; J. Burkhardt, 'Religionskrieg', *Theologische Realenzyklopädie*, XXVIII (1997): pp. 681–7, and more generally on the character of the epoch P. Benedict, 'Religion and Politics in the European Struggle for Stability, 1500–1700', in P. Benedict and M.P. Gutman (eds), *Early Modern Europe. From Crisis to Stability* (Newark, 2005), pp. 120–37.

as 'holy wars', but they are normally held to be of a different character from the sixteenth/seventeenth-century religious wars. A holy war is constituted by the idea that one has to campaign with violence against heretics and unbelievers with the mandate and the help of God.[4] Modern religious wars are characterised by the conflation of those motives – normally only to be found with regard to the suppression of religious minorities in one territory or to the confrontation of Christendom and Islam – with the configuration of early modern civil and inter-state wars. Perhaps the phenotypes of the Albigenses and the Hussite Wars are most difficult to distinguish from, for example, the Huguenot and Dutch wars of religion. But in the latter cases it is always also a war about rule and the entire reign or about independence from foreign rule, while with the Hussites and Albigenses the idea of an action mainly organised by the Church and the Pope, executed only by the secular power (and conflated with inquisition), is predominant. But the differences of the sixteenth/seventeenth-century religious wars from prior ones are as difficult to establish as is a clear-cut difference from the later wars of the eighteenth century and even the Napoleonic Wars, where one can still find many religious motives.[5] The question itself, as well as its answers, needs some preparatory clarifications and systematisation. First we should ask when and how there arose a contemporary notion and reflection about 'religious wars'. We will detect here two different notions, a normative and a functional-analytical one. Secondly we will take a look at the crucial turning point of 1635 when Catholic France entered the war on the side of the Protestant forces: how was that decision embedded in the self-understanding of France's political culture at that time? Thirdly, taking into account how and to what extent 'religion' was (if at all) neutralised at the level of the European State System as well as at the level of the empire, we should come to a conclusion as to how we can define a religious war in general and the Thirty Years' War in particular.

Two Contemporary Notions of 'Religious War'

It has been stressed that the notion of 'religious war' was discussed 'already' during the period of the Thirty Years' War.[6] But in fact, there are much older traditions where we find explicit reflections on a 'war of religion'. We can discern an early normative and an early functionalist and analytical conception of 'war of religion' from the middle of the sixteenth century.

For the normative notion, it is the Swiss-German (rather than the Calvinist-Geneva) tradition of reformed theology where we find it: such legitimations were present very early among those theologians who fled from Germany after the Interim of 1548 to England (Vermigli, Bucer) and their main Swiss correspondent Bullinger: Vermigli introduced religion as one of the just causes to legitimate 'justa bella' in his *loci communes*, his commentaries on the Book of Judges and on Samuel.[7] Zwingli's successor in Zurich, Heinrich Bullinger,

---

[4] R. Bireley, 'The Thirty Years' War as Germany's Religious War', in K. Repgen (ed.), *Krieg und Politik 1618–1648*, (Munich, 1988), pp. 85–106, here pp. 85–6 and 95–100.

[5] Cf. for this D. Onnekink (ed.), *War and Religion after Westphalia, 1648–1713* (Aldershot, 2009); the contributions of A. Fuchs, E. Godel, C. Muller, G. Maier and U. Planert in F. Brendle and A. Schindling (eds), *Religionskriege im Alten Reich und in Alteuropa* (Münster, 2006), pp. 313–431.

[6] J. Burkhardt, *Der Dreißigjährige Krieg* (Frankfurt am Main, 1992), pp. 128–76 ('War der Dreißigjährige Krieg ein Religionskrieg?'), here p. 136.

[7] J.P. Donnelly, 'P. Martyr Vermigli's Political Ethics', in E. Campi (ed.), *Peter Martyr Vermigli. Humanism, Republicanism, Reformation* (Geneva, 2002), pp. 59–66, here pp. 60–65.

treated the theory of just war in the ninth sermon of the second Decade of his *Decades*. This collection of sermons, first written and published in 1549/1550, was reprinted in 38 Latin, German, Dutch, French and English editions until 1622 and was something like the Zurich equivalent of Calvin's *Institution*.[8] Here we find the explicit legitimation of a religious war if bad princes are oppressing real Christian worship. This theory had a direct impact right up to the beginning of the Thirty Years' War because it was received authoritatively in the Palatinate. In 1567 when the second son of Frederic III of the Palatinate (who introduced reformed Calvinism into the territory), John Casimir, led his first military expedition to France in support of French Huguenots, the court chaplain Johann Willing wrote a *Simple reminder of how a Christian prince with his Christian troops should behave against the enemies of the church of Christ*.[9] Three years later, in 1570, Willing published another text, a reformed mirror for princes: *Instruction what the prince's estate is, I. how the lords of that rank should behave, II. what is their office, III. and power, IV. in times of peace and war [...]*.[10] Both texts reveal themselves as a patchwork of (not explicitly cited) passages from other texts, especially from the Bullinger *Decades*, where the legitimation of a war for religious causes is in question. That passage bears the title 'War that is to be waged for the religion':

> ... this is also the case of the wars that are fought against the idolaters and suppressors of the true and just Christian faith. Because those do err who think that one should not make war because of the faith. Our Lord has told St. Peter to put back his sword when he wanted to fight [Mt 26, 52; John 18, 11]. But that does not mean that he commanded the magistrate not to bother about the religion and not to guard and defend the pureness of faith. ... So if the magistrate is commanded to punish the apostates with war it follows that he should defend the right and true faithful church by and through war when a foreign faithless prince would undertake to lead them from true to false faith.[11]

Bucer, Vermigli, Bullinger, Willing and others also developed a theory of alliances with princes and magistrates of the same confession for the aims of a religious war, referring to the Old Testament (Joshua 10; I Samuel 11; Judges I, 3).[12] Willing's sermon and his mirror for princes were both reprinted exactly in 1617, right on the eve of the Palatinate's Bohemian adventure: It is not fallacious to take that theological justification of 'religious wars' as the official stance on the side of the Calvinists, and it encompasses the times of resistance to the emperor's Interim after the Schmalkaldic War, the French and Dutch Wars of Religion until the Thirty Years' War.

But we do not find in this Calvinist (or rather: reformed) theory the consciousness that the sixteenth-century wars of religion were something new, belonging to a special historical epoch. Such a consciousness is only possible in the context of an analytical point of view external to theological reflections. We do find such an analytical view of the phenomenon

---

[8] H. Bullinger, *The Decades*, 5 vols (Cambridge, 1849).

[9] J. Willing, *Einfaltige erinnerung Wie sich ein Christlicher Fürst mit seinem Christlichen Heerzeug wieder die feind der Kirchen Christi verhalten solle* [...] (Heidelberg, 1567; newly pr. 1617).

[10] J. Willing, *Vnterricht Was der Fürsten Stand sey. I. Wie sich die Herren in solchen stand schicken sollen. II. Was jhr Ampt III. vnd Gewalt sey IV. Zu Friedes vnd Kriegeszeiten.* [...] (Heidelberg, 1570) (I am citing the reprint Frankfurt am Main, 1617).

[11] 'Krieg so von der Religion wegen fürgenommen werden' – Willing, *Vnterricht*, p. 35s. = Bullinger, *Decades*, vol. 1, pp. 376–9.

[12] M. Bucer, 'In librum Iudicum enarrationes', in idem, *Psalmorum libri quinque* [...] *eivsdem commentarii in librum Iudicum, & in Sophiniam Prophetam* (Geneva, 1554), pp. 473–519, here p. 474.

of 'religious wars' in the new sixteenth-century Italian method of political reflection which we could brand as 'Machiavellian': Machiavelli himself did not reflect explicitly on something like 'guerre di religione'. But he analysed in a previously unknown empirical way the political functionalist use of religion of the Romans and the destructive power of the medieval Catholic church of the Popes (*Discorsi* I, 11–15).[13] In 1567 a remarkable academic discussion took place in Rome in the *famiglia* of the Venetian cardinal Marcantonio da Mula (1506–1572), where the Machiavellian perspective was applied to the wars of religion.[14] Da Mula had put forward three questions:

> (1) Why can we not read in all the histories of the Assyrians, Medians, Persians, Greeks, Romans and all other pagan powers throughout the centuries of one case where they fought a war because of religion?
> (2) Why had the Romans persecuted the Christians so hard?
> (3) Why do the Christians currently make war among themselves between Catholics and heretics?

As 'wars of religion' in the sense of point (3), da Mula and his respondents counted the war of the peasants (1525), the war of Kappeln (1531/32), the siege of Münster (1535), the Schmalkaldic War (1547) and the 'revolutions' in France, the Netherlands and Scotland. We know of at least nine responses by eight political councillors and intellectuals to these questions. One of them, Fabio Benvoglienti's, was printed in three editions in 1570 and 1575; the others remained in manuscript but belonged to the canonical texts copied by the professional copyists in Venice and Rome from the late sixteenth to the eighteenth century for the needs and purposes of politicians during their Grand Tour and generally for their political education. Da Mula's councillors asked how it was possible that there were more than 300 sects and religions in the Roman Empire without any civil or external war that would have had religion as a main content. They answered it by pointing to the private status of religion under Roman rule: the Romans tolerated the other religions in their empire as private beliefs as long as they did not touch the sphere of public government. Religion was 'part of politics' and 'located under the government of the Republic'. The Romans would have treated their own religion in a real 'Machiavellian' way just for the masses while a prudent elite knew that everything was invented. Christianity was only perceived as a threat by the Romans because that religion had a universalist authoritative pretension and tended to undermine the obedience to the empire by demanding first of all obedience to the Christian faith and the emerging church. That is why the late emperors persecuted the Christians so heavily 'per ragione di stato',[15] not because the Romans insisted on their religion as the only permitted one. When they realised that they could not stop the spread of Christendom, they just converted to the new faith to retain obedience mainly among the soldiers on which their military success and the rule of the empire was built. Now that, in the sixteenth century, a multiplication of Christian beliefs had taken place, the competing universalist pretensions had created inter-Christian wars. That is why the wars of religion were happening now. This

---

[13] Cf. E. Cutinelli-Rèndina, *Chiesa e religione in Machiavelli* (Pisa and Rome, 1998).

[14] Cf. for more details C. Zwierlein, 'Intention und Funktion, Machiavellismus und Konfessionalisierung: Zum militärischen Eingreifen Papst Pius' V. in die französischen Religionskriege 1569', in M. Kaiser and S. Kroll (eds), *Militär und Religiösität in der Frühen Neuzeit* (Münster, 2004), pp. 145–66.

[15] Bibliothèque nationale de France Ms. italien 251, f. 182r–184v: 'Discorso del Riccioli perche auanti la uenuta di x.rini non si guerreggiasse per conto di religione', f. 183r – this is one of the earliest uses of the formula 'ragione di stato' after Guicciardini and before the first print of Botero's treatise with that title in 1589.

discussion shows clearly that the sixteenth-century contemporaries judged the wars of their time as belonging to a new epoch different from the situation of antiquity and different from medieval crusades and campaigns against heretics. And it also shows how it was already possible to apply something very similar to the 'Marxian' perspective cited above from twentieth-century historiography, in Machiavellian terms, to the same wars of religion in the sixteenth century.

The co-presence of such analytical approaches to the phenomenon on the one hand, with the normative legitimations of 'wars of religion' on the other, is perhaps the best characterisation of the confessional age with regard to this question. If we are thinking of the confessional age and the wars of religion as the effect of a 'religious fundamentalism' we should always specify that the terms 'confessionalism' or 'early modern religious fundamentalism' are well applied only to those types of communication which are not 'purely' religious, but where *under the conditions of early modern empiricism and methodical political analysis* and of an already quite strong differentiation between religious and political affairs, religion is re-enforced in a new way as a contested element or directive force of politics.[16] This is why the confessional age is marked by the dispute between Machiavellism and Antimachiavellism, why Machiavelli was the 'Marx of premodernity' as Benedetto Croce has coined it: As long as the relationship between religion and politics was as has been characterised, Machiavelli could serve as the polarising indicator for that paradoxical liaison.[17]

The different forms of reasoning – (reformed) theology, early Italian political discourse – mark the possibilities of how to speak of 'wars of religion' in the confessional age. Political reasoning did develop further forms – treatises, pamphlets, printed discourses – which replaced the discussion in academic circles such as that of da Mula and their handwritten copy distribution. But putting subtleties aside, until 1648 there are no great innovations with regard to the content of reasoning about 'wars of religion' – although Grotius's natural international law would perhaps be a candidate for such an innovation, it did not gain dominant status before the second half of the seventeenth century. So, the contemporary reflections on the Thirty Years' War had necessarily to be expressed in those forms inherited from the century before. And indeed, in all the reflections concerning crucial decisions during the war we find repetitions of the systematic reflections of the above kind. We will concentrate now on the moment of France's entry into the Thirty Years' War in 1635: traditionally in the discussion about the character of the war as a whole, one points to that moment when the Catholic monarchy of Louis XIII entered an alliance with the Protestant German princes and Sweden as a turning point: at least from that moment on, the war cannot be easily characterised as a 'war of religion'.[18]

---

[16] Cf. C. Zwierlein, '*convertire tutta l'Alemagna* – Fürstenkonversionen in den Strategiedenkrahmen der römischen Europapolitik um 1600: Zum Verhältnis von *Machiavellismus* und *Konfessionalismus*', in M. Pohlig et al. (eds), *Konversion und Konfession in der Frühen Neuzeit* (Gütersloh, 2007), pp. 63–105.

[17] S. Anglo, *Machiavelli. The first century* (Oxford, 2006); C. Zwierlein and A. Meyer (eds), *Machiavellismus in Deutschland. Chiffre von Kontingenz, Herrschaft und Empirismus in der Neuzeit* (Munich, 2010); C. Zwierlein, 'Machiavellismus / Antimachiavellismus', in H. Jaumann (ed.), *Diskurse der Gelehrtenkultur in der Frühen Neuzeit* (Berlin and New York, 2010), pp. 903–51.

[18] Burkhardt, *Dreißigjähriger Krieg*, p. 139.

Turning Point of the War's Character? – France's Entry into the War in 1635

The succession of events leading to the French declaration of war of 19 May 1635 is well known: while Sweden and the Netherlands had for quite a long time pressed France to change its hidden participation (foremost by subsidies and diplomatic means) into an open war, it was only in August 1634 – and perhaps enforced by the impression of the great defeat of the Swedish at Nördlingen in September – that Louis XIII declared his explicit will to enter the war openly. Richelieu did not judge this opportune at the moment and delayed the process for nearly a year until the declaration of May 1635. The mutual support treaties between the Netherlands and Sweden were signed between February and April 1635. The official reason for entering the war was the capture of the elector of Treves by the Cardinal-Infante on 26 March 1635: after an ultimatum sent to the Cardinal-Infante (who refused to free the elector), the French government could formulate a declaration of war which responded to all the requirements of early modern international law: the aggressor was not France, but Spain; France acted only as the legitimate protector of the elector of Treves; it was therefore a just war according to contemporary conditions. From the French point of view, they did not enter the war to help the Protestants but only the elector; Richelieu even deleted the mention of the king of Sweden in the official manifesto that explained the French position.[19] This is the version of the event if we look at the level of the diplomatic fabric of official 'wording'.

But as we have seen, the decision had already been taken and the different reasons for or against it had been in the air since the beginning of the war, had been present during the first Monferrato War and later on. If we take – as did most thinkers, political actors and diplomats at that time if not currently involved in the construction of a war justification – the perspective of the *longue durée*, the decision to enter the European war in 1635 was something like the reversal of the 1572 decision. In 1572, only the Huguenots, then seemingly close to the king, had advised him to start a war against Spain in the Netherlands as well as in northern Italy to pacify his kingdom internally and thus avoid civil war and to regain France's deserved status in Europe in the everlasting competition with the Habsburgs after the unfortunate peace of Cateau-Cambrésis (1559). But at that moment, the crown – it will always be a disputed question to what extent – decided not to act in favour of the option of a divertive external war but to kill the Huguenot leaders and by that means to purify the kingdom of the competing religion.[20] It is known now that this decision prolonged the wars of religion in France, which were pacified only for a first time in 1598, and perhaps more importantly, for a second time after the siege of La Rochelle in 1627/28 when Louis XIII and Richelieu finally triumphed over the Huguenot military forces and their English support. Now it was not the Huguenots but the Catholic councillors and authors of political pamphlets and treatises close to the crown who advised leaving the Huguenots to their

---

[19] Cf. H. Weber, 'Zur Legitimation der französischen Kriegserklärung von 1635', *Historisches Jahrbuch*, CVIII (1985), pp. 90–113 and *APW*, I, t. 1, p. 17–20; R. Lesaffer, 'Defensive Warfare, Prevention and Hegemony. The Justifications for the Franco-Spanish War of 1635 (Part I/II)', *Journal of the History of International Law*, VI (2008): pp. 91–123 and 141–79, here p. 163–5 (also for the Spanish rejection of that casus belli).

[20] Cf. D. Crouzet, *La nuit de la St Barthélemy* (Paris, 1994); A. Jouanna, *La Saint-Barthélemy: les mystères d'un crime d'État* (Paris, 2007); cf. for the important place that this event had in European memory on all political and confessional sides, also during the Thirty Years' War: C. Zwierlein, 'Die Genese eines europäischen Erinnerungsortes: die Bartholomäusnacht im Geschichtsgebrauch des konfessionellen Zeitalters und der Aufklärung', in F. Bezner and K. Mahlke (eds), *Zwischen Wissen und Politik. Archäologie und Genalogie frühneuzeitlicher Vergangenheitskonstruktionen* (Heidelberg, 2011), pp. 91–129.

religion and starting a war instead against Spain in Germany and the Netherlands: only in this way could France regain its position in Europe equal to or above that of Spain.[21] First of all, it was Richelieu in 1629 who advised the king after the conquest of La Rochelle in this sense:

> *Concerning foreign policy, we need to be constantly worried about stopping the rise of Spain and, unlike that nation, whose goal it is to enhance its domination and expand its borders, France must only think about fortifying itself and build and open gateways to enter the states of its neighbours in order to be able to save them from the oppression of Spain when the moment arises.*[22]

If we discuss the question to what extent the Thirty Years' War 'was' a war of religion by focusing on the 1635 decision, it is important to concentrate on the perceptions and intentions present in France at that time and how they were rooted in the long-term experience of the Huguenot wars of 1562 to 1629.

Already in 1629 under the impact of the final peace with the Huguenots, Jean-Louis Guez de Balzac had begun to write his treatise *Le Prince* which was published in 1631 and which finished again with a reference to La Rochelle. The worst thing for a state is a civil war 'which tears the state into pieces and abolishes the monarchic government'. The treatise is full of accusations against the Spanish who would always use religion as a pretext for tyrannical, expansive, imperialist politics. The Spanish have become arrogant and ambitious because of their military successes in Germany. The text praises the Dutch for resisting for such a long time against the Spanish[23] and is in favour of a trans-confessional alliance:

> *It is necessary that on that occasion Italy, England, the Catholics and the Protestants and the Armenians ally against their common enemy, against him who does not attack the heretics from religious zeal but only from interest of state. … Necessity divides brothers and unifies strangers. She unites the Christian and the Turk against the Christian. She excuses and justifies everything she does. The law of God has not abrogated the laws of nature. And self-conservation is the most ancient of all the obligations.*[24]

Finally he cites Machiavelli's chap. XXVI of the *Principe* (without mentioning Machiavelli's name): the Italians should take that author to be a prophet of Henri IV's marriage with Maria de' Medici and of the coming of Louis XIII who would finally be the liberator of Italy from Spanish servitude.[25] So, in its composition, Balzac's *Prince* echoes Machiavelli's *Principe* by concluding with the appeal for Italy's liberation – but from the point of view of the supposedly new liberator France instead of Lorenzo de' Medici. Balzac's treatise instantly

---

[21] For the anti-Spanish propaganda in France at that time cf. R. Babel, 'Frankreichs Gegner in der politischen Publizistik in der Ära Richelieu', in F. Bosbach (ed.), *Feindbilder. Die Darstellung des Gegners in der politischen Publizistik des Mittelalters und der Neuzeit* (Köln et al., 1992), pp. 95–116; N. Poujade de Lassus, 'Richelieu and anti-Spanish propaganda', *Revista de Historia Universal*, XV (2006): pp. 195–219.

[22] *Advis donné au roy après la prise de la Rochelle* (Jan 13, 1629), in: D.-L.-M. Avenel (ed.), *Lettres, instructions diplomatiques et partiers d'état du Cardinal de Richelieu*, vol. IV (Paris, 1861), p. 179, 181, transl. by Lesaffer, 'Defensive Warfare', p. 173.

[23] "Ne connoissons nous pas ceux-là qui meslent Dieu parmy toutes leurs passions […]? S'ils vsurpent vn Royaume, sur lequel ils n'ont aucun droit […] ils disent que c'est pour empescher que les ennemis de l'Eglise ne s'en saisissent […]' (J.-L. Guez de Balzac, *Le Prince* (Paris, 1631), pp. 95, 171, 375).

[24] Ibid., p. 372.

[25] Ibid., p. 391.

created a controversy because of its Machiavellian flavour and did not find Richelieu's full acceptance.[26] But nevertheless it demonstrated how the Janus-like bi-polar co-presence of religious and analytical political perspectives was common in the 1630s. Already in the *Catholique d'État* in 1625, which was re-edited right at the moment of France's entry into the war, one could read that 'it is a war and a dispute of state and not of religion that is happening in Germany'.[27] In his *Ministre d'État* Jean de Silhon, who was closer to Richelieu than Balzac, underlined the principles of sovereignty and of the division between domestic and external affairs. If the subjects of a prince rebel against him, other princes are not allowed to help the rebels. The English did not respect that rule by helping the Huguenots in France, nor did the Spanish when they started to help the League against Henri III in the 1580s.[28] Long parts of the treatise are reserved for the horrible memory of the Huguenot and League wars which had, for the author (differently from most modern historians who locate the French wars of religion before 1598), finished just some months before. This is not in opposition to France's entry into the war if one accepts the official version of the 1635 declaration, because France would not help 'rebels' but did protect a Catholic prince, even an archbishop, the elector of Treves. But even if one were to take everybody's perspective in 1635 who saw the treaties with the Dutch and with Sweden, alliances with forces of different religions were again plainly defended in the anonymous pamphlet *The Free War* in 1640, which Thuau called 'the Marseillaise de la raison d'état'.[29] So, the French authors and pamphleteers in Richelieu's orbit did produce stronger and milder legitimations for the war decision; in any case, the competition with Spain was inevitable and too menacing. If in 1633 an anonymous pamphlet was called *Réveil-Matin de l'Anti-Espagnol*, this was clearly an echo of the *Reveille-matin des François et de leurs voisins* published in 1573 after the St. Bartholomew's massacre: the once-committed error of supporting Spanish politics should not be repeated; now France should act as the liberator of Christendom. In 1634, some months before the official declaration of war when French troops had already gathered close to the Rhine, the emperor's resident in Paris, Lustrier, who apparently was very familiar with the French reasoning, handed out a reminder to Louis XIII in which Ferdinand II complained about the effects of those gatherings which would lead to 'a not anymore hidden but open war'; the king should be aware that the 'reason of state' was only an 'imagined whiff of state [soupçon imaginative d'estat]' which would not have any force above in heaven.[30]

Research has already pointed for a long time to the importance of 'reason of state' as the directing principle of Richelieu and his entourage and his direct collaborators Boisrobert, Hay du Chastelet, Chapelain, the above-treated authors as well as Cardin Lebret (*De la souveraineté du roi*), Philippe de Bethune (*Le conseiller d'État ou recueil général de la politique moderne*), and Hersent (*De la souveraineté du Roi à Metz*), who all formed something like the Richelieu 'think tank' of foreign politics. One has even re-situated the foundation of

---

[26] Cf. *Discours sur le Liure de Balzac intitulé le Prince, & sur deux Lettres suiuantes* (s.l., 1631); I.P.D.D.B.M., *Apologi [sic] pour le livre de Monsieur de Balzac Intitulé le Prince* (s.l. 1632).

[27] *Le Catholique d'État ou discours politique des alliances du roi très chrétien contre les calomnies de son État*, s.l. 1625, in P. Hay du Chastelet: *Recueil de diverses pièces pour servir à l'histoire*, Paris 1643 [1st edn, 1635], p. 149.

[28] So it is inconsistent that the *Declaration* of 6 June 1635 included as a cause for the war France's assistance to the Dutch as oppressed people under Spanish 'servitude', Lesaffer, 'Defensive War', p. 166.

[29] É. Thuau, *Raison d'Etat et pensée politique à l'époque de Richelieu* (Paris, 1966), p. 316.

[30] *Les Papiers de Richelieu. Section politique Extérieure. Correspondance et Papiers d'Etat. Empire Allemand*, vol. II (1630–1635), ed. by A.V. Hartmann (Paris, 1997), No. 292. A.V. Hartmann, *Von Regensburg nach Hamburg. Die diplomatischen Beziehungen zwischen dem französischen König und dem Kaiser vom Regensburger Vertrag (13. Oktober 1630) bis zum Hamburger Präliminarfrieden (25. Dezember 1641)* (Münster, 1998), p. 187.

Renaudot's *Gazette* (1631) and of the *Academie française* (1635) in the larger context of a cultural politics which aimed also at the legitimation of France's politics in the war and at least at clearing the ground for her successful re-entry into European politics. The Tacitean culture of France's political elite has been recently stressed and the importance of the library culture, the gathering of historical manuscripts and the rest of the government's 'information system' have been underlined.[31] The writings of Gabriel Naudé and Louis Machon[32] have been analysed in this way and it has been shown that Richelieu's own writings, his *Maximes d'État* and the *Testament politique* – even if their authenticity has been contested since the eighteenth century[33] – built upon the texts of Balzac, Silhon and others.[34] Richelieu himself defined the goals of the French war enterprise as 'helping to render liberty to her ancient allies, restituting peace in Germany and reordering affairs in a just balance' because otherwise the Austrian dynasty would take France as the next military target when there was nothing more to gain in Germany.[35] By that Richelieu played the card of France as the protector of the German princes' liberty, which had been a recurring argument since medieval times, but enforced – because it applied also to the Protestant princes – at least since the so-called 'princes' rebellion' of 1552 when Elector Maurice of Saxony sold Metz, Toul and Verdun in return for French support against Charles V. During that war, the chancellery of Henri II already advertised France as protector of the estates' liberty.[36] The repertoire of foreign policy strategies was refined in seventeenth-century France, mainly in line with reason of state discourse, but they did rely still on older fundaments.

So, at the level of the French political culture of decision-makers and the political elite in 1635, there is indeed very little or no reference to religion or religious schemes of war legitimation concerning its attitude to the Thirty Years' War. Internal politics are strongly directed by the fear of another 'rebellion' of Huguenot nobles, and the entry into the external war can be seen as something like appeasement politics with an implicit satisfying and pacifying effect on domestic affairs. At the level of political discourse, such proceeding is rendered possible by a certain hierarchisation between the two levels of approach discussed

---

[31] J. Soll, *Publishing 'The Prince': History, Reading and the Birth of Political Criticism, 1513–1789* (Ann Arbor, 2005); idem, *The Information Master: Jean-Baptiste Colbert's Secret State Intelligence System* (Ann Arbor, 2009) – what is said here of Colbert could also be said of Richelieu and Mazarin, cf. E. Thomson, 'Commerce, Law, and Erudite Culture: The Mechanics of Théodore Godefroy's Service to Cardinal Richelieu', *Journal of the History of Ideas*, LXVIII/3 (2007): pp. 407–27.

[32] Cf. G. Naudé, *Considérations politiques sur les coups d'État. Précédé de 'Pour une théorie baroque de l'action politique' par Louis Marin* (Paris, 1988); G. Naudé, *Bibliografia politica*, ed. by D. Bosco (Rome, 1997); J.-P. Cavaillé, *Dis/simulations. Jules-César Vanini, François La Mothe Le Vayer, Gabriel Naudé, Louis Machon et Torquato Accetto. Religion, morale et politique au XVIIe siècle* (Paris, 2002).

[33] P. Sonnino, 'The Dating of Richelieu's *Testament Politique*', *French History*, XIX/2 (2005): pp. 262–72 has convincingly dated the text to late 1640; for the famous Voltaire controversy about the text's authenticity cf. L. Avezou, 'Autour du *Testament Politique* de Richelieu. À la recherche de l'auteur perdu (1688–1778)', *Bibliothèque de l'École des chartes*, CLXII (2004): pp. 421–53.

[34] R. v. Albertini, *Das politische Denken in Frankreich zur Zeit Richelieus* (Zurich, 1951); Thuau, *Raison d'Etat*; Anna Maria Battista, *Politica e morale nella Francia dell'età moderna* (Genova, 1998), pp. 130, 205, 211–4; J. Wollenberg, Richelieu et le système européen de sécurité collective, *Dix-septième siècle*, CCX (2001), pp. 99–112.

[35] "[…] aider à rendre la liberté à ses anciens alliés, restituter la paix à l'Allemagne et y remettre les choses en une juste balance que si l'on n'y pourvoyait présentement, la maison d'Autriche, dans six ans au plus tard, lorsqu'elle n'aurait plus rien à conquérir en Allemagne, tâcherait de s'occuper en France à nos dépens.' (A.-J. Cardinal de Richelieu, *Mémoires*, vol. V 1625–1626 (Paris, 1921), p. 193).

[36] Cf. e.g. W.E. Winterhager, '*Verrat des Reiches, Sicherung deutscher Libertät* oder pragmatische Interessenpolitik? Betrachtungen zur Frankreich-Orientierung deutscher Reichsfürsten im Zeitalter Maximilians I. und Karls V.' in K. Malettke and C. Kampmann (eds), *Französisch-deutsche Beziehungen in der neueren Geschichte* (Berlin, 2007), pp. 17–66.

above: it may also be possible to detect forms of strongly upheld confessionalist normativity beneath the Catholic clergy and Huguenot ministers in France, but at least at the level of governmental decision-making, reason of state is now, de facto and sometimes explicitly, ranked above confessional normativity.

Conclusion

How much religion was in the Thirty Years' War? If we look closely at one political decision such as that of 1635, the number of religious elements often seems to shrink down to zero. Spain and some Catholic princedoms, such as Bavaria, used to legitimate their actions in the war by referring to the necessity of repulsing the heretics. At the beginning of Sweden's entry into the war, Gustav Adolph was fashioned as a Protestant Godly Warrior – but that was almost exclusively at the level of propaganda.[37] Even if we look more closely at the empire and its confessional order, it has only recently been stated that even at the point of his highest powers (1629, at the moment of the edict of restitution), Ferdinand II and his entourage did not plan openly or covertly the reversal of the confessional order in the empire; they always came back to the peace of Augsburg of 1555.[38] Anton Schindling has underlined the fact that officially both parties, the emperor and the Protestants, had always dissimulated the perhaps present religious causes of their wars since the Schmalkaldic War: they were presented in the framework of the empire's legal order as wars to keep up the Eternal Land Peace of 1495 (*Ewiger Landfriede*) – a 'model of dissimulation' and juridification present from the sixteenth century onwards, which was not part of the highly reflexive Machiavellian culture of reason of state, but nevertheless also an effective late medieval way to hierarchise religion under the empire's customary law.[39] It has also been argued that on the level of everyday life and on the level of the fighting soldiers, religious convictions did not play a great role or at least were not present in the sense that the armies were really armies of Godly Warriors, of 'fundamentalists' who would fight primarily not for money but for the sake of religion. The opposite reveals itself to be mostly true.[40]

On the other hand it is clear that strong confessional identity-building had taken place on all levels of society since the Reformation and Counter-Reformation, that also major political actors like Richelieu and Ferdinand II were personally and privately devoted

---

[37] S. Oredsson, *Geschichtsschreibung und Kult. Gustav Adolph, Schweden und der Dreißigjährige Krieg* (Berlin, 1994).

[38] T. Brockmann, *Dynastie, Kaiseramt und Konfession. Politik und Ordnungsvorstellungen Ferdinands II. im Dreißigjährigen Krieg* (Paderborn, 2009).

[39] A. Schindling, 'Gab es Religionskriege in Europa? Landfrieden und Völkerrecht statt Glaubenskampf und *Strafgericht Gottes*' in A. Gotthard et al. (eds), *Studien zur politischen Kultur Alteuropas* (Berlin, 2009), pp. 275–98.

[40] Some contributions in B. v. Krusenstjern and H. Medick (eds), *Zwischen Alltag und Katastrophe. Der Dreißigjährige Krieg aus der Nähe* (Göttingen, 1999) and in A. Schindling and M. Asche (eds), *Das Strafgericht Gottes. Kriegserfahrungen und Religion im Heiligen Römischen Reich Deutscher Nation im Zeitalter des Dreißigjährigen Krieges*, 2nd edn (Münster, 2002) show, surely, religious consolation and interpretations of events in times of war – but only slightly differently to other epochs; M. Kaiser, 'Cuius exercitus, eius religio? Konfession und Heerwesen im Zeitalter des Dreißigjährigen Krieges', *Archiv für Reformationsgeschichte*, XCI (2000), pp. 316–53; cf. also the very little attention the famous *Landsknecht* discovered by Jan Peters paid to religious affairs: J. Peters (ed.), *Ein Söldnerleben im Dreißigjährigen Krieg. Eine Quelle zur Sozialgeschichte* (Berlin, 1993); F. Kleinhagenbrock, 'Die Wahrnehmung und Deutung des Westfälischen Friedens durch Untertanen der Reichsstände', in I. Schmidt-Voges et al. (eds), *Pax perpetua. Neuere Forschungen zum Frieden in der Frühen Neuzeit* (Munich, 2010), pp. 177–93.

Catholics,[41] just as the Protestant leaders were devoted Lutherans and Calvinists, and that a good deal of the political disputes negotiated at Münster and Osnabrück were rooted in the bi- or triconfessional and even religiously pluralised societies and their constitutional framework of the empire and also the Netherlands. The way to pacify those conflicts was a multiple neutralisation of the religious question. On the level of diplomacy and foreign politics, the powers tended to fade out the religious question, as we can read very explicitly in the instructions and the dispatches: the Secrétaire d'État des Affaires Étrangères, Loménie de Brienne, instructed the French representatives in Münster, d'Avaux and Servien in 1645 that the union of the crowns would serve the principal goal to 'diminish the much too great power of the house of Austria' and to help some allied princes, but that they should avoid any situation where France could be blamed for a direct violation of the Catholic religion; France would just tolerate the advantages of the Protestants enabled by the French forces as something like an unintended by-product. If a Protestant prince were restituted in his land and reintroduced the heresies, France would not feel guilty for that.[42] This is what Paul Sonnino has called the 'Pontius Pilate position' of Mazarin's France concerning religious policies.[43] As is known, the only power who really held up the religious cause openly at the level of international politics as something not to be negotiated was the Pope.[44] By doing this, he lost his status as arbiter of Christendom. The last peace where he had played that role was the peace of Vervins and Lyon in 1598/1601 – only between Catholic powers.[45] The important issue of Protestant or Catholic land ownership in the empire was neutralised by the abstract solution of the 'Normaljahr' in 1618/1624.[46]

We have seen that the decision about the religious or non-religious character of the Thirty Years' War leads to many follow-up questions and to many levels of society and discourse being taken into account. For the concluding remarks let us gather some clarifications and defining elements:

1. If we take 'war of religion' to be something characteristic of the so-called confessional age, we have to find differences between those religious wars, the medieval crusades and 'wars' against heretics; we should also try to differentiate between the Western European and the mid-European wars of religion, and we have to distinguish these wars from the later eighteenth-century wars.

---

[41] R. Bireley, *Religion and Politics in the Age of the Counterreformation. Emperor Ferdinand II, William Lamormaini, S.H., and the Formation of Imperial Policy*, (Chapel Hill 1981), pp. 14–6; M. Rohrschneider, *Der gescheiterte Frieden von Münster. Spaniens Ringen mit Frankreich auf dem Westfälischen Friedenskongress (1643–1649)* (Münster, 2007), p. 66.

[42] APW II B 2 No. 113, pp. 378–84, cit. 379 – cf. O. Chaline, 'Le facteur religieux dans la politique française des congrès', in C. Kampmann et al. (eds), *L'art de la paix. Kongresswesen und Friedensstiftung im Zeitalter des Westfälischen Friedens* (Münster, 2011), pp. 555–73.

[43] P. Sonnino, *Mazarin's Quest. The Congress of Westphalia and the Coming of the Fronde* (Cambridge/Mass. and London, 2008), p. 5.

[44] K. Repgen, *Die römische Kurie und der Westfälische Friede*, 2 vols (Tübingen, 1962, 1965); Chigi to Francesco degli Albizzi, Aachen, 10 Sept 1650: 'Si eseguisce la pace d'Imperio, ma sono tanti pregiuditii contro la religione Cattolica, contro la S. Sede, e contro tutto lo Stato Ecclesiastico' (idem, 'Die Proteste Chigis und der päpstliche Protest gegen den Westfälischen Frieden (1648/50)', in idem, *Dreißigjähriger Krieg und Westfälischer Friede*, ed. by F. Bosbach and C. Kampmann (Paderborn, 1998), pp. 539–61, here p. 560).

[45] B. Barbiche, 'Les instructions de deux papes florentins aux légats et aux nonces: des témoignages privilégiés sur l'évolution de la diplomatie pontificale du traité de Vervins à la paix de Westphalie', in Kampmann, *L'art de la paix*, pp. 517–28.

[46] Cf. R.-P. Fuchs, *Ein 'Medium zum Frieden'. Die Normaljahrsregel und die Beendigung des Dreißigjährigen Krieges* (Munich, 2010).

2. In doing that, we have to distinguish between the contemporary perception and notion of what might have been called a 'war of religion' in the sixteenth and seventeenth century and our own historiographical term.
3. In analysing the perception of contemporaries, we have to distinguish the different levels and groups of society concerned, the different modes of speech (propaganda, private memories, and diplomatic exchange).
4. In analysing the character of the actions during the wars, we have to be highly careful not to confound any war-like or military violence with religious violence.

Starting with that last point, one might say that perhaps the French and Dutch wars fit even better under the rubric 'religious war' because they show a high amount of 'bottom-up' exercised religious violence. The pattern of civil war mixed up with the religious issue seems a bit more explosive: the religious massacres undertaken not in explicit war situations and *not necessarily by soldiers* in France, in the Netherlands and also later in England and Ireland are a type of event which is known to research on the Western European 'wars of religion' but not so much on the Thirty Years' War.[47] The opposite decisions in 1572 and in 1635 might also be revealing at the level of governmental decision. This is due to the different religious and confessional constitutions of the regions: the Western European situation is characterised rather by intra-confessional and intra-dominion conflicts while – at least formulated in ideal terms – in the empire the borders of confessions and dominions should have been identical after 1555 (with the exception of biconfessional cities), so the war was rather an inter-confessional and inter-territorial war. Even if that was disputed, the relative autonomy of German princes and territories was very different from the situation in Western Europe. This led to an intermediary status between civil and international war, and apparently also to different forms of violence. We can find in the context of all the sixteenth/seventeenth-century wars apocalyptic consciousness and religious convictions with some individuals and in some pertinent pamphlets, but it seems to have been only in some extreme situations (mostly sieges) that those apocalyptic visions had the power to unify greater groups for a certain time. The defence of one or the other religion/confession was sometimes to be found in official declarations of war, but much rarer than one would perhaps expect. So, in the end, what distinguishes the sixteenth/seventeenth-century wars from the Middle Ages is the above-developed co-presence of the normativity of religious legitimation of just wars and of the political-analytical point of view. In the Middle Ages one may say that the latter 'Machiavellian' view of *functional* analysis was not yet at hand, at least in a methodically developed, written way. And in the eighteenth century, the first option – religious legitimation – ceased to apply. This co-presence could be explosive on every level of society and discourse. The way to stop its explosiveness was by hierarchisation of importance ('international balance of powers is more important than confession' – the French way) or by fading out, juridification, neutralisation (the empire's way), implicit or explicit oblivion.[48] One important epochal indicator of that co-presence in a given time and European region is the cyphering of politico-religious conflict in the terms of Machiavellism vs. Antimachiavellism present in all forms of private and public writings. So, the Thirty

---

[47] Cf. only N.Z. Davis, 'The Rites of Violence: Religious Riot in Sixteenth-Century France', *Past and Present*, LIX (1973): pp. 53–91; D. Crouzet, *Les guerriers de Dieu. La violence au temps des troubles de religion vers 1525 – vers 1610*, 2 vols (Paris, 1990); M. Levene and P. Roberts (eds), *The Massacre in History* (New York, 1999); D. El Kenz (ed.), *Le massacre, objet d'histoire* (Paris, 2005).

[48] Cf. for this C. Zwierlein et al. (eds), *Forgetting Faith. Negotiating Confessional Conflict in Early Modern Europe* (New York and Berlin, 2012); A. Höfele et al. (eds), *Representing Religious Pluralization in Early Modern Europe* (Berlin, 2007); S.C. Dixon et al. (eds), *Living with Religious Diversity in Early Modern Europe* (Aldershot, 2009).

Years' War, in this restricted sense, was a religious war and a war between Machiavellism and religion.

Selected Bibliography

Benedict, P., 'Religion and Politics in the European Struggle for Stabiliy, 1500-1700', in P. Benedict and M. P. Gutman (eds), *Early Modern Europe. From Crisis to Stability* (Newark, 2005), pp. 120–37.

Bireley, R., 'The Thirty Years War as Germany's Religious War', in K. Repgen (ed.), *Krieg und Politik 1618–1648*, (Munich, 1988), pp. 85–106.

Burkhardt, J., *Der Dreißigjährige Krieg* (Frankfurt am Main, 1992).

Lesaffer, R., 'Defensive Warfare, Prevention and Hegemony. The Justifications for the Franco-Spanish War of 1635' (Part I/II), *Journal of the History of International Law*, VI (2008): pp. 91–123 and 141–79.

Repgen, K., 'Was ist ein Religionskrieg?', in *Zeitschrift für Kirchengeschichte*, XCVII (1986): pp. 334–49.

Sonnino, P., *Mazarin's Quest. The Congress of Westphalia and the Coming of the Fronde* (Cambridge/Mass. and London, 2008).

Thuau, É., *Raison d'Etat et pensée politique à l'époque de Richelieu* (Paris, 1966).

Zwierlein, C., *Discorso und Lex Dei. Die Entstehung neuer Denkrahmen im 16. Jahrhundert und die Wahrnehmung der französischen Religionskriege in Italien und Deutschland* (Göttingen, 2006).

Zwierlein, C. et al. (eds), *Forgetting Faith. Negotiating Confessional Conflict in Early Modern Europe* (New York and Berlin, 2012).

19

The Material Conditions of War

John Theibault

'For war you need three things: 1) money, 2) money, 3) money.'
(Raimondo Montecuccoli)

'War feeds itself.'
(Livy)

As the name indicates, the Thirty Years' War lasted thirty years; a long time for a society to be at war. And unlike in earlier and other contemporary long wars, such as the Dutch Revolt, French Wars of Religion, or Hundred Years War, armies were almost constantly active for all thirty of the years of conflict during the Thirty Years' War. Such constant warfare placed unprecedented strains on the European economy and society, both because military activity required money and materiel and because war disrupted ordinary economic activity through occupation and troop movements. This chapter will explore the material conditions that made thirty years of constant deployment possible as well as the most dramatic material impact of the war, a level of death and destruction that made the Thirty Years' War notorious from the seventeenth century to the present day. The subject complements other chapters in this volume, which address the conduct of war, and how the people of Europe experienced and interpreted the impact of war.[1] For the most part, the focus will be on the Holy Roman Empire, where the war took place, though the experiences of other parts of Europe and the world undoubtedly impinged on the empire in various ways.

The two epigrams cited at the start of this chapter point to the paradoxical nature of how the war was sustained. Money was indeed essential to the conduct of war and the inability to raise sums limited how territorial rulers pursued their policies. But at the same time, once armies were in the field, they often became self-sustaining enterprises, drawing in the resources to stay alive even if the fiscal system had collapsed. In assessing the material conditions of war it is helpful to distinguish several aspects of the problem. First, there are the basic characteristics of the European economy on the eve of the war, which give a measure of its potential for production. Second, there are finance and logistics for raising and maintaining an army. And finally, there are the ways in which the course of war actually consumed and altered production. Although modern economic statistics favour aggregate economic measures such as population and GDP, these numbers are difficult to come by in the seventeenth century. On the other hand, the emergence of the early modern 'financial state' during the sixteenth century means that fiscal measurements of state assets and sources of taxable income are more common. For that reason, some of the impacts this chapter will be analysing can only be approached in local contexts rather than generalised for all of Central Europe.

---

[1] See the chapters by Peter Wilson and Sigrun Haude in this volume.

Structures of the European and Central European Economy on the Eve of War

Early seventeenth-century Europe was an agricultural and thus rural society. About 80 per cent of the European population lived in the countryside, and most of those in villages of fewer than 500 inhabitants. Food production was by far the largest economic sector, consuming about three-quarters of a typical household's budget. Basic agricultural techniques were unchanged from the medieval period, with crop yields hovering around 5:1. There were few independent self-sufficient farms. Peasants held the use right to land subject to a noble lord. Some portion of the agricultural produce was sold in regional markets to generate cash to pay seigneurial dues, taxes, and to purchase goods and services. Although barter still played some role within village commerce, for the most part villages operated in a money economy, both in coin and in moneys of account noted in account books. The lack of innovation in the sector that employed the overwhelming majority of the population and produced most of the output of the economy placed practical limits on how many people could be supported.[2]

Though village-based agriculture was the foundation of the economy, most commerce and manufacturing was based in regional towns and cities. Towns in Central Europe were numerous, but small. Only a handful had as many as 40,000 inhabitants. Although villagers did some rudimentary manufacturing for basic needs, anything requiring special skills was purchased from small artisan shops in towns, usually associated with a craft guild. Towns also held weekly markets and were the seats for courts and other administrative functions which tied them to their neighbouring villages. A town combined with anywhere from three to twenty surrounding villages formed a common fiscal and economic unit.

By far the largest manufacturing sector in most towns was textiles and clothing trades. Luxury goods were produced in a few major cities, while most smaller towns sold mostly to regional customers. Specialised industries shaped by the availability of raw materials gave distinctive character to some regions. Important centres for the manufacturing of armaments were Suhl in Thuringia, which manufactured firearms, Solingen in the Rhineland, which manufactured swords and daggers, and Danzig in Prussia, which was the main European source for saltpetre, an essential ingredient in gunpowder.

Those long-standing structural elements of European society provide limited information about underlying trends on the eve of the Thirty Years' War. It has now been more than half a century since the British Marxist historian E.J. Hobsbawm suggested that Europe confronted a 'General Crisis' caused by social and economic changes prompted by the emergence of capitalism in the first half of the seventeenth century.[3] The ensuing historiographical debate ranged widely, and the Thirty Years' War figured sometimes prominently, sometimes in the background as a symptom (and sometimes as a cause) of crisis. In assessing what may have prompted the outbreak of war and what made 30 years of continual warfare possible, it matters whether we perceive Europe as being on the verge of crisis for reasons external to the course of the war itself or whether war caused the crisis.

While not written as a direct response to the General Crisis debate, T.K. Rabb analysed writings about the Central European economy prior to and during the war and identified two principal schools of interpretation: a 'disastrous war' school, which argued that war descended on an essentially prosperous and growing economy and destroyed it and an 'earlier decline' school, which argued that however disruptive the war might have been,

---

[2] For criticism of the pure Malthusian explanation of seventeenth-century demographic crises see A.E.C. McCants, 'Historical Demography and the Crisis of the Seventeenth Century', *Journal of Interdisciplinary History*, 40 (2009): pp. 195–214.

[3] E.J. Hobsbawm, 'The Crisis of the Seventeenth Century', *Past and Present*, 6 (1954): pp. 44–65.

symptoms of social and economic trouble were already apparent prior to the outbreak of war, so not all negative post-war circumstances can be directly attributed to the war.[4] Within the 'earlier decline' school, there were some who treated the war as an external force that merely accelerated social and economic disruptions that were bound to happen in any case while others viewed the outbreak of war as a logical consequence of increasing social and economic difficulties. There also emerged a school of thought related to the 'earlier decline' school that suggested that the whole idea that the war was notably disruptive is misguided, that claims of widespread death and destruction are for the most part exaggerations or self-serving attempts to protect local interests from state intervention. That notion has been thoroughly debunked by historians. The war was severely disruptive. The general consensus of economic historians today is that Central Europe was neither 'flourishing' nor 'in decline' as the war approached. Instead, it was showing unmistakable signs of stagnation after a century of steady expansion.

Still, that consensus does not resolve the underlying conflict between the destructive war and earlier decline schools. It remains difficult to assess what direction the Central European economy would have gone in the absence of war. Some parts of Europe that were not in the direct path of the war, such as Spain, experienced as sharp or even sharper economic contractions than did Central Europe. It is certainly possible that the balance of population and economic capacity was reaching a point where instability was likely no matter what the specific trigger for that instability. It is also difficult to determine how much of the sixteenth-century expansion can be attributed to improvements in productivity per capita and how much is due to increasing aggregate production because of increasing population. There is ample evidence of increasing inequality, as the percentage of the population that had little or no land to farm and the percentage of urban artisans in the lowest tax categories grew, but that too might be a sign of increasing productivity per capita. The rural land-poor turned increasingly to wage labour and small crafts production as a substitute for income from crops. One factor that almost certainly reduced per capita productivity in the largest economic sector was a steady drop in average annual temperatures beginning in the sixteenth century and reaching its nadir between 1640 and 1660. The weather pattern is often given the title the 'Little Ice Age,' and its effects may have been compounded by the fact that it arrived at a post-Black Death population peak.[5]

Overall, then, the economic foundations of Central Europe appeared to be at a crossroads just as the Thirty Years' War arrived. Heiner Haan has even argued that it is precisely the scramble to maintain economic status as this long period of expansion began to wane that was one of the main causes of the political tensions that produced the Thirty Years' War.[6] At the very least, the sixteenth century expansion produced two things that would be of central importance for sustaining 30 years of war: a large pool of land-poor men who could be employed in the armies and a century's worth of accumulated capital that could be diverted to fund the war machine.

---

[4] T.K. Rabb, 'The Effects of the Thirty Years War on the German Economy', *Journal of Modern History*, 34 (1962): pp. 40–51.

[5] G. Parker, 'Crisis and Catastrophe: The Global Crisis of the Seventeenth Century Reconsidered', *American Historical Review*, 113 (2008): pp. 1053–79.

[6] H. Haan, 'Prosperität und Dreißigjähriger Krieg', *Geschichte und Gesellschaft*, 7 (1981): pp. 91–118.

The Kipper und Wipper

One case that underlines the difficulty of separating the war's effects from broader social and economic forces is the so-called 'Kipper und Wipper' inflation of 1620–1623. As noted above, urban and rural economic life were thoroughly integrated into markets that relied on money as a measure of value and medium of exchange. The exchange value of those coins was determined by their precious metal content by weight and fineness. Coins were produced at local mints to specifications laid out in various coinage ordinances. The creation of large silver and gold coins like *Thalers* and *Gulden* was restricted to a handful of producers and those coins rarely appeared in everyday transactions because their value far exceeded most local purchases. Everyday coins in copper and bronze were produced in great numbers and could be found in every town and village. Indeed, they were essential for local commerce. Well before the outbreak of the war, unscrupulous minters had learned that they could cheat on the specification on weight and fineness of coins by shaving small bits off existing coins and adulterating alloys with more base metals. Basic assaying techniques were limited to a very small population and few would have scales sensitive enough to note the small amount clipped from a coin. By the outbreak of the war, the effects of constant manipulation of the precious metal content of small coins was beginning to be felt in local commerce. Prices began to rise sharply for food and other necessities, even though there was no external production shock to drive the price change.

The costs of fighting and the actions of rulers in the early stages of the war clearly inflamed the situation. Frederick of the Palatinate encouraged the minting of new currency in Prague to pay for the upkeep of the rebel army. After White Mountain, Ferdinand leased the right to mint coins in Prague to a consortium of private investors led by Karl von Liechtenstein, the head of the Bohemian treasury Paul Michna, and two prominent Prague financiers, Hans de Witte and Jacob Bassevi. The consortium members profited from their control over the delivery of silver to the mint and added millions more debased coins into the already fragile economy.

The effects of coin clipping and debasement were not restricted to the towns with mints. Debased coins flooded local economies all across the Holy Roman Empire. Anyone with the ability to save hoarded their high-value coins that had not been diluted while spending the low-quality coins. Particularly hard hit were townspeople whose regular wages were paid in increasingly debased coinage while the price of bread rose rapidly. Cities had to intervene to make grain available at subsidised prices to fend off riots. But that shifted the costs of the inflation onto town budgets. Meanwhile, the economic relationship between creditors and debtors was thrown out of balance. Debtors paid off outstanding debts in debased currency, removing the incentive to lend. Wealth that had accumulated during the expansion of the sixteenth century was wiped out and some property owners were forced to sell at a loss. The result was a massive redistribution of wealth, with speculators gaining and stable investors losing, which inflamed a vigorous pamphlet war in 1622/23.[7]

Yet despite the ongoing impact of the war, the effects of the inflation went away almost as quickly as it had come. With the smaller coins now virtually worthless, they were formally abandoned and new coin ordinances issued which fixed the weight and fineness of small coins at about three-quarters of their previous value. Towns and districts tried as best they could to mitigate the local effects of redistribution by fixing new official prices for essential goods. By 1625, the new price system was stabilised and there would be no serious debasement for the rest of the war.

---

[7] U. Rosseaux, *Kipper und Wipper als Publizistisches Ereignis (1620–1626)* (Berlin, 2001).

Raising and Maintaining an Army

A key point to understand in evaluating the material conditions of the Thirty Years' War is that armies were run as businesses. They were raised when a territorial ruler issued patents to raise a specific number of regiments of troops to trusted military enterprisers, the overwhelming majority of whom were nobles.[8] The decision to issue patents depended on how large a force was required and what the territory's budget could support. The patent to recruit essentially gave the military enterpriser ownership of the regiment he raised, though of course decisions about how the regiments were to be used in campaigns were made by the commanding general. Regiment commanders sub-contracted to others in their entourage to raise the individual companies that made up the regiment.

Patents to raise a regiment specified where the forces were to be recruited. They included a promise of payment for recruiting and continuing costs, but it was often expected that the noble military enterprisers would have to use their own sources of cash and credit to raise and support the forces for some time until the ruler could deliver payment, so enterprisers usually worked with a financier to raise funds, using the familial estates and future booty as collateral. Once the regiment was raised, the patent issuer was expected to provide regular support for it via taxes or territorial revenues, with the regiment owner taking responsibility for maintaining the regiment in full fighting strength. But territorial rulers often found it difficult to uphold their promises of support, so various fiscal expedients had to be found. Regiment owners often found themselves using their own credit to support their forces and adding the arrears to the unpaid recruiting costs. The interdependence of military enterprisers and financiers grew deeper as arrears grew.

The outbreak of war provided military enterprisers with an opportunity to be more entrepreneurial. Rather than wait for the Emperor or other rulers to issue patents, which they were reluctant to do because of their tight budgets, regimental commanders forwarded offers to recruit forces on their own account, hoping that military success would give them access to favours later on. These enterprisers were still dependent on territorial rulers to issue the patent, for without it they could not legally muster, but the promise to use one's own resources to build the force reduced strain on the ruler's treasury. Despite the dangers of non-payment and reliance on one's own credit to sustain forces, there was a great deal of money to be made in forming a successful regiment. When territorial rulers, especially the Emperor, could not fulfil their obligations to army commanders from regular budgets, they tapped extraordinary sources to help repay. One such expedient was 'lien administration,' the temporary alienation of seigneurial prerogatives over a district to a creditor. The most conspicuous and consequential example of lien administration was Emperor Ferdinand's grant of Upper Austria to Duke Maximilian of Bavaria to help cover the 12 million fl. costs of sending the army of the Catholic League against the Bohemia rebels.[9] Another expedient was to elevate the status of commanders' estates, hoping that social capital would substitute for real capital. Again, Maximilian of Bavaria was a primary beneficiary of this option, being invested with an electoral title confiscated from Frederick of the Palatinate.

No military enterpriser better illustrates the underlying fiscal and economic considerations that drove the war or had a more profound role in shaping those considerations than the Bohemian nobleman Albrecht Wenzel Eusebius von Wallenstein. Wallenstein first came to prominence in the war as one of the minority of Bohemian nobles to actively back the Habsburgs in response to the Bohemian revolt. Already in October 1618 Wallenstein offered

---

[8] F. Redlich, *The German Military Enterpriser and his Work Force* (2 vols, Wiesbaden, 1965).
[9] H. Rebel, *Peasant Classes: The Bureaucratization of Property and Family Relations under Early Habsburg Absolutism 1511–1636* (Princeton, 1983).

to raise a cavalry regiment for Ferdinand, backed by his own fiscal resources, and was granted a patent as a colonel in the imperial army. His offer was backed by little more than 20,000 fl. he had been able to raise from his own estates and a loan of an additional 20,000 fl. If the regiment he raised had been defeated, his financial situation would certainly have been ruined. But strong organisational skills and a bit of good fortune in campaigns solidified his place among the Emperor's leading commanders. After the Battle of White Mountain, Ferdinand confiscated the property of Bohemian nobles and townspeople of Prague who backed Frederick's kingship. Perhaps 1,000 families and half the land of Bohemia were affected by the confiscations. The Emperor remained short on cash and relied on various expedients to raise funds quickly, including selling confiscated properties or using them as collateral for loans and leasing the Prague mint to the consortium that became involved in the Kipper und Wipper debasement. Wallenstein, appointed as military governor of Prague in the wake of White Mountain, was exceptionally well positioned to benefit from this situation. As part of the coinage consortium, he reaped a profit of 290,000 fl. and became acquainted with the Flemish émigré financier Hans de Witte, who became his personal financial liaison with the Habsburg court. Between purchases of confiscated properties and a strategic marriage, he was able to build his relatively small noble estates into one of the largest and most profitable in all of Bohemia by 1624. In all, Wallenstein acquired nearly 2,000 square miles of land, centred on the lordship of Friedland in northern Bohemia. Eventually, Wallenstein was given the title duke of Friedland. In 1623, Wallenstein was able to lend 3.5 million fl. to the Emperor using his estates as collateral, a far cry from the 40,000 he raised in 1618.

Wallenstein introduced two important innovations in the military enterpriser's system. The first was his decision to use his home properties not just as collateral to finance military activities, but to turn it into a supply hub of war materiel for the forces that he raised. He built grain magazines, powder mills, and small arms manufacturing centres. His forces were consistently better equipped than the others. Wallenstein was the only military enterpriser capable of carrying out such a large scale operation, and this innovation found no imitators. The second innovation was a new way of paying for the upkeep of armies in the field. This was a tax called the contribution. It was to become the standard way that all revenues for the armies were raised for the rest of the war. In 1625, Wallenstein proposed raising not just a regiment, but a whole army for the Emperor. Like other speculative military enterprisers, he offered to raise the force entirely from his own resources. For maintenance of the army once it was raised, he asked for a special tax that could be collected directly by army paymasters on both allied and enemy territories. Prior to the contribution, armies were paid directly from the treasuries of the patent issuer, or more likely, for subsidies paid to the patent issuer from allies. Taxes were also levied by agreement of allies and assessed and collected on the basis of a sixteenth-century imperial defence tax called *Römermonate*. Before the institution of the contribution, commanders had relied on a more ad hoc method of collecting revenues from the regions being occupied called a *salva guardia*. The *salva guardia* was essentially a letter of protection issued by a regimental commander or commanding general. It regulated temporary quarters and marches through a territory, promising good behaviour backed by the signature of the commanding general in exchange for free passage, lodging, and money. If the terms of the *salva guardia* were not adhered to, the commander was in theory required to compensate the occupied territory for damage. Beyond the fairly transparent extortion that it represented, the *salva guardia* was inefficient as a regular source of revenue because it had to be negotiated for each occupation or passage. The contribution brought greater system to collection and disbursement of money, making armies less dependent on the fiscal balance of the treasuries of individual rulers.

As the case of Wallenstein makes clear, what was good for the armies was not necessarily good for the rulers supposedly directing the war. The synergy of Wallenstein's personal wealth from his extensive estates, fiscal hold on the Emperor because of money lent since the outbreak of the war, reorganisation of his estates into a personal supply depot to support armies in the field, and mastery of the contribution system to shift its impact from his own lands to those of both enemies and allies nearly made it possible for him to operate his army independently of any input from the Emperor and his allies. This prospect was frightening enough that he was dismissed from his command in 1630 and when he renewed his generalship in 1632 was viewed with such suspicion that the Emperor tacitly accepted Wallenstein's assassination rather than risk the danger that he might conclude an independent peace with the Swedes.

Wallenstein's Friedland was unique among military enterprisers for turning the outfitting and supply of soldiers into a source of profit instead of expense for the commander. His estates delivered up to 5,000 Zentner (approx. 280 metric tons) of gunpowder per year during the time of his supreme command. But overall, surprisingly little has been written about the production of weapons and gunpowder within the Holy Roman Empire during the war. Amsterdam and Hamburg acted as the main finance and distribution centres for international arms for the war.[10] The Netherlands had become a major producer of armaments during the course of the Dutch Revolt and were thus well positioned to dominate the weapons trade during the Thirty Years' War. But there are no estimates of how many guns were produced to equip armies of over 100,000 soldiers.

Similarly, there is no overall estimate of the vast sums of money raised by the contribution. Existing registers from district levies and individual towns are in the tens of millions of fl., and that must represent the tip of the iceberg. The overwhelming majority of the money collected went to pay for the troops. In the Lower-Rhine-Westphalian Circle in 1643–1645 for example, 87 per cent of contributions collected went to pay salaries of troops and another 6.5 per cent went to the high command. Of the other seven categories noted in the accounts, 'unspecified extraordinary expenses' were the only other category to take more than 2 per cent of the money collected. A total of 1.5 per cent went to the purchase of military equipment and 1.2 per cent to recruiting costs. The remaining 1.7 per cent was divided among extra purchases of food and supplies, sending messages, gifts and ransom money, and uncollectible contributions that were carried over to expenses.[11] Somehow that money had to be extracted from the rural economy and circulated.

The Costs of Staying, the Costs of Flight

Just as the system for raising and maintaining armies could bring generals like Wallenstein great riches to the detriment of patent-issuing rulers, it also brought few benefits to the common soldier and could devastate local economies. The logistical challenges faced by the armies in turn imposed logistical challenges on the local population. Relations between soldiers and villagers and townspeople during occupation and the movement of troops were supposed to follow a legal framework. 'Supply ordinances' specified both what localities were obligated to supply to the troops and how troops were obligated to behave in the quarters. Like the contribution, supply ordinances were negotiated and promulgated in advance.

---

[10] J. Zunckel, *Rüstungsgeschäfte im Dreißigjährigen Krieg* (Berlin, 1997).

[11] H. Salm, *Armeefinanzierung im Dreißigjährigen Krieg: Der Niederrheinisch-westfälische Reichskreis 1635–1650* (Münster, 1990), pp. 123–5.

Despite that, there were many opportunities for controversy over the fair distribution of those burdens, not to mention over what should be done if one member failed to fulfil their obligation once it was set. Indeed, one of the most common forms of complaint from towns and villages to territorial rulers during the war was when they perceived an inequity in the distribution of soldiers during an occupation or a tax burden – when a significantly wealthier town or district was asked to support the same number of troops as a smaller one.

An important factor that increased the economic pressure on communities quartering troops is that armies were accompanied by a large number of camp followers. Wives, children, servants, prostitutes, and peddlers of all kinds marched with the baggage train. The real burden on a community might be half again as great as the official numbers posted in the agreement specified. Typical soldier's pay was 4 fl. a month. From that, they were expected to pay for their own food and supplies, though supply ordinances usually obligated the places where soldiers lodged to provide light and heat. The fact that soldiers had to buy their own food complicates how one assesses the economic burden imposed by contributions, since a substantial proportion of the money collected re-circulated in the local economy from purchases of goods and services. But there is almost no evidence to tell us how much. Surviving contribution registers indicate how much was collected, but give only hints about how some of the money stayed in the community. Certainly some cash paid to soldiers was disbursed to camp followers rather than locals and so eventually left the community, but one should not infer massive losses from a large tax bill. For the community, the larger problem may not have been how much money remained in local circulation but how much of the produce that could be easily transported to the area was eaten up by troops and camp followers. Also, soldiers valued the resources of a village differently from the villagers. One of the pillars of household wealth in the village was livestock. Animals were very desirable for an army for transportation and meat and they were among the easiest things for troops to requisition because they could transport themselves. The mere presence of troops, even if they adhered scrupulously to the supply ordinances and paid for everything they consumed, was likely to be highly disruptive to local production.

As the war went on, it was less and less likely that the legalistic framework of the supply ordinances would stand. The formally illegal but widely practised plunder economy became a primary way that soldiers acquired supplies and income. Croatian light cavalry were particularly feared for their ability to sweep in and carry off valuables. In many regions, there was a well-developed local information network, which provided warning to towns and villages about when troops approached so that assets could be protected. Escalating incidents of plunder and violence led villagers to flee to nearby towns rather than contend with violations of another supply ordinance. Occasionally, such as in the Harz mountains around 1627, peasants took up arms to harass invading troops. More frequently, groups of peasants took revenge on straggling soldiers as civilian–military relations became almost entirely antagonistic. The problem with long-term flight to escape the depredations of soldiers was that absence from fields and crops undermined productivity, leaving less for both villagers and soldiers the next time troops came through. A downward spiral of agricultural production continued throughout the war. Ironically, the negative impact on production in the countryside also detached more of the land-poor from their communities, making it easier for them to join the armies or camp followers when they moved on and reducing the local population.

Disruptions in villages caused different disruptions to the urban economy. As long-term flight became the most common response to the threat of troops, tensions developed in the towns that served as refuges. The number of refugees often exceeded the number of regular residents, causing intense crowding and stretching demand on local resources and increasing the likelihood of devastating diseases. Meanwhile, villagers who fled to towns with all of their goods feared having them requisitioned by the town or taken away from them by sharp dealers. Animals were useful to townspeople in just the same way that they were useful for soldiers and harder to hide in the town.

Death and Population Loss

The Thirty Years' War is notorious for its destructiveness. Yet most histories of the war have not placed the destructiveness of the war in the centre of the discussion, perhaps because the bewildering military and diplomatic gyrations require such close attention that also addressing the direct material effects makes it impossible to assemble a coherent narrative. Most of the best-regarded recent general histories of the war such as those by Wilson, Asch, Burkhardt, and Parker, treat economic disruption, death, and destruction in a separate chapter at the end of the book, after discussing the Treaties of Westphalia.[12] The implication of that placement of the topic is that the war's destructiveness matters primarily in retrospect, with 1648 as a kind of *Stunde Null*, and is unrelated to its course. That impression is reinforced by the fact that there has been no comprehensive overview of the social and economic impact of the war since Günther Franz's influential but highly problematic book, *Der Dreißigjährige Krieg und das deutsche Volk*, first published in 1940.[13]

Demographic historians estimate that the population within the boundaries of modern Germany numbered about 17 million in 1618 and about 10 million in 1650, a decline of about 40 per cent.[14] But that general figure of decline masks substantial variation in demographic impact. First, there is a distinction between regions that saw frequent and severe military action and those that remained relatively protected. Wherever the main theatre of war went, depopulation went with it, but when the war arrived was at least as important as how long or intensely the war came. Regions such as Lower Austria and East Frisia, which were the scene of early battles but avoided the later stages of the war, did not suffer as severely. The most significant population declines took place on a rough axis from Alsace in the south-west to Prussia in the north-east, where troops passed repeatedly during the war. Second, the economic and demographic character before the war affected how the war made its impact. Günther Franz estimated that about 33 per cent of the urban population and 40 per cent of the rural population was eliminated in the course of the war, suggesting that rural areas were more susceptible to population decline. Christian Pfister has shown that that interpretation is deceptive. People migrated constantly from the countryside to towns and almost never from towns to the countryside during the war, so the overall proportion of the pre-war urban population that died probably far exceeded that of the rural population. Finally, there is the question of how closely any particular depopulation was directly related to the war. As brutal as soldiers were on the battlefield and in quarters, most of the people who died did not do so by sword or gun. Estimates of military casualties from combat and

---

[12] P. Wilson, *The Thirty Years War* (Cambridge, MA, 2009), R. Asch, *The Thirty Years War: The Holy Roman Empire and Europe, 1618–48* (New York, 1997), J. Burkhardt, *Der Dreißigjährige Krieg* (Frankfurt a.M., 1992), G. Parker, *The Thirty Years War* (2nd edn, London, 1997).

[13] G. Franz, *Der Dreißigjährige Krieg und das deutsche Volk* (Jena, 1940) with three additional editions. On the reception of Franz's work see J. Theibault, 'The Demography of the Thirty Years War Re-revisited: Günther Franz and his Critics', *German History*, 15 (1997): pp. 1–21 and W. Behringer, 'Von Krieg zu Krieg. Neue Perspektiven auf das Buch von Günther Franz 'Der Dreißigjährige Krieg und das deutsche Volk' (1940)', B. v. Krusenstjern and H. Medick (eds), *Zwischen Alltag und Katastrophe: Der Dreißigjährige Krieg aus der Nähe* (Göttingen, 1999), pp. 543–91.

[14] C. Pfister, *Bevölkerungsgeschichte und Historische Demographie 1500–1800* (Munich, 1994), p. 10.

disease range from 600,000 to 1.8 million. The number of civilians to die at the hands of soldiers is pure guesswork and would be dominated by a handful of famous massacres such as the plundering of Magdeburg in 1631 which overshadow myriad local accounts of atrocities that list casualties in single or low double digits. The biggest killers during the war were disease and famine. Major epidemics struck repeatedly during the war. And, as we have seen, poor harvests, both as a direct result of disruptions caused by the presence of troops and simply the vagaries of a climate entering the Little Ice Age were particularly prevalent in the 1630s.

Quentin Outram has analysed three different models for understanding how disease and hunger may have acted to reduce civilian populations: a 'synergy model,' where hunger increases susceptibility to disease; a 'hunger model,' where people die directly of starvation; and a 'transmission model,' in which the movement of troops spreads disease.[15] He shows that the movement of troops and what he calls the 'socio-economic relations of warfare' played a central role in causing high mortality. Even within a relatively small region, the effects of depopulation could vary widely, so some of the impact is probably due to chance. But overall, Outram makes a strong case that hunger is the principal driver of population decline, not merely because of bad harvests or the amount of food diverted to the military, but because of the disruption of traditional production caused by civilian–military relations.

The Course of War from the Perspective of Material Conditions

Students of the Thirty Years' War are familiar with the traditional phases of the war, defined by the principal belligerents on the anti-Habsburg side. What does the course of the war look like if we focus not on the changes in the belligerents but on fiscal and economic indicators? While some of the landmark years are similar, the fiscal and economic conditions followed a different rhythm from the political situation.

Although belligerents had been on a near war footing even before the outbreak of the Bohemian rebellion, no one had prepared for 30 years of war. Thus, the early phase of the war followed familiar paths of early modern warfare. Civilian–military relations, while not frictionless, mostly conformed to legal expectations on both sides. The proliferation of minor German princes able to raise forces in support of the Protestant cause indicates that the credit system functioned. There were, to be sure, some indications of underlying economic tensions which would make it harder to scale back the war in coming years. The Emperor's empty treasury and dependency on the army of the duke of Bavaria led to a scramble for expedients to discharge debts that became politically impossible to retract. The Kipper und Wipper inflation showed that the fiscal system was fragile. But the most notable material change in the early years of the war was the great transfer of wealth that came with the confiscation of the property of the Bohemian rebels and their sale to loyalists of the Emperor. Interestingly, there was no comparable redistribution of property within the nobility in any other part of the empire, though the right of confiscation and redistribution was invoked against rebellious princes later on in the war.

The first significant change in the underlying material conditions of the war was the emergence of Wallenstein's self-funded army for the Emperor in 1625. The innovation was two-fold. Wallenstein's system significantly increased the size of the armies fighting in the war. And the finance system he established to support the army, the contribution,

---

[15] Q. Outram, 'The Socio-Economic Relations of Warfare and the Military Mortality Crises of the Thirty Years' War', *Medical History*, 45 (2001): pp. 151–84.

spread the burden of payment much more widely on the general population. The system for apportioning and collecting contributions bypassed a central treasury, allowing armies to acquire their own revenues as they marched. Larger armies consumed more resources. Repeated fighting over and occupation of the same areas had made the search for winter quarters with sufficient resources a central logistical challenge. From 1626 to 1629, Tilly complained vociferously that Wallenstein's soldiers monopolised the best districts, fatally weakening his own forces. Wallenstein's ruthless system for ensuring his troops were adequately supplied aroused the ire not just of Protestant princes, but many of the Emperor's closest allies, especially Duke Maximilian of Bavaria. Alarm that the contribution system would make Wallenstein's force impervious to political direction was one of the primary motivations for Maximilian's insistence that he be dismissed and a unified imperial/League army be placed under the command of Tilly. There was much uncertainty about whether Wallenstein would actually accept his dismissal and what could be done about it if he refused. But in the end, he acquiesced quietly. He was well situated on the extensive properties he acquired since the outbreak of the war, but his financier Hans de Witte was not so fortunate. Without the Emperor's direct patronage the sums de Witte had lent out could not be recovered and he quickly became bankrupt. Rather than face the consequences of his bankruptcy, he committed suicide in 1630.

Nearly contemporaneous with the introduction of Wallenstein's contribution system was another change that shaped the material conditions of the war: a wave of plague that swept through Central Europe in 1626. When combined with the ongoing strains of supplying soldiers, the sudden depopulation caused severe local economic disruptions. Most regions responded to this demographic crisis of the old type in the traditional manner, with an increase in marriages and births to try to rebuild the population. But the response was not robust. In many places, the mortality rate was so high that even with a small but noticeable rise in per capita fertility, the absolute numbers of new births were not sufficient for a quick return to the pre-crisis population.

The next noticeable change in the material conditions of war coincided with Wallenstein's dismissal and Sweden's entry into the war. As a result of changing fortunes of war, two resource-rich territories that had been spared the direct impact of fighting and occupation for the first decade of the war, Saxony and Bavaria, ceased to be safe havens. At the same time, civilians became more direct targets of military activity. In the first decade of the war, plunder and the threat of plunder were sometimes used as a means of forcing the enemy to quit or as a form of vengeance. The sack of Heidelberg in 1622 is a notable example. It was also not uncommon for armies to deliberately choose quarters in a way that would shift the burden of supporting the army on to the enemy in an effort to destroy the territory's fiscal capacity to fight. Tilly, for example, slowly strangled the resources of Hessen-Kassel in 1624 and 1625 by taking quarters there, forcing the abdication of the Landgrave in 1627. But until the rapid turning of the tide after the Swedish victory at Breitenfeld in 1631, armies did not undertake the deliberate and systematic destruction of the enemy's lands. That changed when Swedish forces reached Bavaria. Unable to lure Maximilian's forces from the safety of the city of Ingolstadt, Gustav Adolph gave his forces free rein to destroy the productive capacity of the region, so that the Emperor's army could no longer be supplied. Eventually, Gustav was forced to retreat from Bavaria to secure his own supply lines back to Sweden, but a precedent for retaliatory military actions against a whole territory rather than an army was established. Whereas villagers in the early years of the war could be uncertain whether to flee when troops approached, by the 1630s flight was the normal response.

Even before the Peace of Prague in 1635 there were unmistakable signs that the ability of Central European society to support continued fighting was beginning to fade. After growing steadily for the first half of the war, the size of the belligerent armies began to shrink. Indeed, it was not until well after the Thirty Years' War was over that the size of armies began to grow again. But fighting continued, even as the capacity for regeneration of the civilian economy began to collapse. The years of 1636 and 1637 were probably the nadir for the civilian economy. A second major plague struck, shattering communities that had yet to recover the population lost in the previous wave a decade earlier. In the most severely affected regions, the normal mechanisms of the demographic crisis of the old type broke down. After the period of intense mortality passed, the survivors were strong enough that mortality rates plunged dramatically, but nuptiality and fertility also hovered near zero. Migration became the main mechanism of population regeneration. Prior to the Peace of Prague there had been occasional notices about the devastating impact of warfare on the civilian population. After 1636, pamphlets and travel accounts that described intense suffering and whole districts virtually devoid of people exploded – not just in the empire but in Britain as well. All semblance of regular economic activity ceased in large areas of Central Europe. Fields were overrun with vermin and there were occasional sensationalised stories of cannibalism, and more plausible stories of people surviving by eating dogs, cats, rats, and animal fodder. A series of better harvests in the 1640s began to alleviate some of the most intense suffering, prompting the first signs of what the post-war recovery would look like. Notice of the negotiations for peace in Westphalia gave optimism that the war would indeed end.

The structural problem of war finance also emerged as a barrier to ending the war. In the course of their 17 years of campaigning, the Swedish army had accumulated massive arrears that could no longer be collected. But without a final settlement with the troops, the Swedes argued, they could not effectively demobilize the force. How to apportion Swedish 'satisfaction money' was one of the issues that slowed the peace negotiations in Osnabrück. It proved easier for war to feed itself than to be sated.

Selected Bibliography

Asch, R. 'Wo der Soldadt hinkömbt, da ist alles sein': Military Violence and Atrocities in the Thirty Years War Re-examined', *German History*, 18 (2000): pp. 291–309.
Friedrichs, C., *Urban Society in an Age of War: Nördlingen 1580–1720* (Princeton, 1979).
Glete, J., *War and the State in Early Modern Europe: Spain, the Dutch Republic, and Sweden as Fiscal-Military States, 1500–1660* (London, 2002).
Ogilvie, S. 'Germany and the Seventeenth-Century German Crisis', *The Historical Journal*, 35 (1992): pp. 417–41.
Outram, Q., 'The Socio-Economic Relations of Warfare and the Military Mortality Crises of the Thirty Years' War', *Medical History*, 45 (2001): pp. 151–84.
Parker, G., 'Crisis and Catastrophe: The Global Crisis of the Seventeenth Century Reconsidered', *American Historical Review*, 113 (2008): pp. 1053–79.
Parrott, D., *The Business of War: Military Enterprise and Military Revolution in Early Modern Europe* (Cambridge, 2012).
Polisensky, J.V., *The Thirty Years War* (Berkeley, 1971).
Rebel, H., *Peasant Classes: The Bureaucratization of Property and Family Relations under Early Habsburg Absolutism 1511–1636*, (Princeton, 1983).
Redlich, F., *The German Military Enterpriser and his Work Force* (2 vols, Wiesbaden, 1965).
Theibault, J., *German Villages in Crisis: Rural Life in Hesse-Kassel and the Thirty Years War, 1580–1720* (Atlantic Highlands, 1995).
Theibault, J., 'The Demography of the Thirty Years War Re-revisited: Günther Franz and his Critics', *German History*, 15 (1997): pp. 1–21.

20

The Experience of War

Sigrun Haude

The previous chapters have highlighted the extraordinary political and military dimensions of the Thirty Years' War. How did people experience a war of such magnitude, length, and severity? In the last few decades scholarship has increasingly focused on the war 'up close'. The first spate of studies in this respect coincided with the 350th anniversary of the Peace of Westphalia (1998). The event induced many archivists and historians to mine local archives for testimonies regarding the war, which stimulated the publication of a great many accounts – from short excerpts of parish records to lengthy diary-style manuscripts. Furthermore, historians of everyday life (*Alltagsgeschichte*), micro history, and historical anthropology, such as Hans Medick, Benigna von Krusenstjern, Anton Schindling, Matthias Asche, and Geoff Mortimer, have capitalised on the rich narrative accounts produced during the war in an attempt to learn more about how people experienced and dealt with these horrific events.[1] This included a realignment in military history, where the major focus had been on battles, strategies, arms, and generals, to incorporate studies on regular soldiers and their experience of war.[2]

Moreover, scholars have debated intensely both the subject of 'experience' and the terminology of sources that might provide access to it. Is it possible to recover or know anything about how early modern people experienced certain events or situations?[3] And do we define and delineate documents that narrate something about the self as autobiographical accounts, testimonies about or to oneself (*Selbstzeugnisse*), Ego-documents, self-narratives, personal accounts, or any variation of the above?[4] The most important development in this

---

[1] B. von Krusenstjern and H. Medick (eds), *Zwischen Alltag und Katastrophe. Der Dreißigjährige Krieg aus der Nähe* (Göttingen, 1999); M. Asche and A. Schindling (eds), *Das Strafgericht Gottes. Kriegserfahrungen und Religion im Heiligen Römischen Reich Deutscher Nation im Zeitalter des Dreißigjährigen Krieges* (Münster, 2001); G. Mortimer, *Eyewitness accounts of the Thirty Years War, 1618–1648* (New York, 2002); H. Berg, *Military Occupation under the Eyes of the Lord. Studies in Erfurt during the Thirty Years War* (Göttingen, 2010). See also H. Medick and B. Marschke, *Experiencing the Thirty Years War: A Brief History with Documents* (Boston and New York, 2013), which focuses on documents of the war up close.

[2] W. Wette (ed.), *Der Krieg des kleinen Mannes. Eine Militärgeschichte von unten* (Munich, 1992); J. Peters (ed.), *Ein Söldnerleben im Dreißigjährigen Krieg. Eine Quelle zur Sozialgeschichte* (Berlin, 1993); M. Meumann and D. Niefanger (eds), *Ein Schauplatz herber Angst. Wahrnehmung und Darstellung von Gewalt im 17. Jahrhundert* (Göttingen, 1997); P. Burschel, 'Himmelreich und Hölle. Ein Söldner, sein Tagebuch und die Ordnungen des Krieges', in B. von Krusenstjern and H. Medick (eds), *Zwischen Alltag und Katastrophe. Der Dreißigjährige Krieg aus der Nähe* (Göttingen, 1999), pp. 181–94.

[3] J. Scott, 'The Evidence of Experience', *Critical Inquiry*, 17 (1991): pp. 773–97; P. Münch (ed.), *'Erfahrung' als Kategorie der Frühneuzeitgeschichte* (Munich, 2001).

[4] J.S. Amelang describes autobiographical texts as 'any literary form that expresses lived experience from a first person point of view' ('*Vox populi*: popular autobiographies as sources for early modern urban history', *Urban History*, 20 [1993]: p. 33). See also K. von Greyerz's assessment

debate has been the spotlight on the collective dimension of the experience expressed in personal accounts: '… personal narratives, both in reproducing and in creating discourse, are deeply embedded in a collective context'.[5] Kaspar von Greyerz thus finds the term 'Ego-documents' inadequate in capturing the broader implications of such accounts.[6] In terms of experience, while in the 1990s scholars with different agendas and approaches have warned against the dangers of essentialism and early constructivism, most studies are now situated somewhere in the 'middle ground between pure constructivism and the evidence of experience offered by their sources'.[7]

Scholars have emphasised that, in the first half of the seventeenth century, the lines between the literary forms of autobiographies, diaries, and other chronological accounts were fluid.[8] 'Autobiographical' texts, unlike their post-Enlightenment counterparts, focused little on self-reflection or the construction of an individual personality. Rather than confidently arranging one's personal history from hindsight, these texts frequently listed events or experiences chronologically, without explanatory connections or transitions. With the adoption of such a *Reihenstruktur*, seventeenth-century 'autobiographies' were still indebted to the medieval recording tradition.[9] Often the author stepped back, while he or she recounted events of the day and other facets of life around him or her.[10] Early modern

---

of autobiographical sources (in this case autobiographies and diaries) in 'Religion in the Life of German and Swiss Autobiographers (Sixteenth and Early Seventeenth Centuries)', in K. von Greyerz (ed.), *Religion and Society in early modern Europe 1500–1800* (Winchester/Mass., 1984), pp. 223–41; and B. von Krusenstjern, 'Was sind Selbstzeugnisse? Begriffskritische und quellenkundliche Überlegungen anhand von Beispielen aus dem 17. Jahrhundert', *Historische Anthropologie*, 2 (1994): pp. 462–71. W. Schulze, following the Dutch scholars J. Presser and R. Decker, prefers the term 'Ego-Dokumente' to 'Selbstzeugnisse'. The argument is that 'Ego-Dokumente' include both free and forced testimonies. Thus, tax records, interrogations, visitations, and court records can also be utilised as documents pointing toward the self. See his 'Vorbemerkung' and his *Ego-Dokumente: Annäherung an den Menschen in der Geschichte* (Berlin, 1996), pp. 9–30. See also the special issue of *German History*, 28, 3 (2010) that is dedicated to ego-documents.

[5] K. von Greyerz, 'Ego-Documents: The Last Word?' *German History*, 28 (2010), p. 276. See also M. Fulbrook and U. Rublack's comment: '(o)ne does not have to follow down a post-modernist route to realize the significance of the fact that no account of the self can be produced which is not constructed in terms of social discourses: that the very concepts people use to describe themselves, the ways in which they choose to structure and to account for their past lives, the values, norms, and common-sense explanations to which they appeal in providing meaning to their narratives, are intrinsically products of the times through which they have lived.' M. Fulbrook and U. Rublack, 'In Relation: The "Social Self" and Ego-Documents', *German History*, 28 (2010): p. 267.

[6] For this and a discussion of the history of the term 'Ego-document', see Greyerz, 'Ego-Documents'.

[7] Greyerz, 'Ego-Documents', p. 176.

[8] K. von Greyerz, *Vorsehungsglaube und Kosmologie: Studien zu englischen Selbstzeugnissen des 17. Jahrhunderts* (Göttingen, 1990), p. 16.

[9] I. Schiewek , 'Zur Manifestation des Individuellen in der frühen deutschen Selbstdarstellung. Eine Studie zum Autobiographen Bartholomäus Sastrow (1520–1603) ', *Weimarer Beiträge*, 13 (1967): p. 893.

[10] See S. Pastenaci's pithy comment: 'Die Lektüre früneuhochdeutscher Autobiographien ist aufgrund der Heterogenität der Texte, oberflächlich betrachtet, gewiß kein Lesevergnügen. Intimes, Persönliches wechselt mit unpersönlichen Berichten aus der Ereignisgeschichte, es werden Anekdoten aus der Stadt, Biographien von anderen Persönlichkeiten breit ausgemalt. Private Briefe wechseln mit der ausführlichen Wiedergabe zeitgenössischer Dokumente. Es dominiert das Faktische vor der Reflektion.' S. Pastenaci, 'Probleme der Edition und Kommentierung deutsch-sprachiger Autobiographien und Tagebücher der Frühen Neuzeit, dargestellt anhand dreier Beispiele', in J. Golz (ed.), *Edition von autobiographischen Schriften und Zeugnissen zur Biographie*, Beihefte zu Editio, vol. 7 (Tübingen, 1995), p. 11.

German testimonies until the end of the seventeenth century, therefore, narrated personal facts in their external contexts.[11]

The Thirty Years' War produced a plethora of narrative accounts. These texts are immensely valuable to historians who are interested in people's perceptions, and in how contemporaries reacted to the world around them.[12] In looking at experiences through these narrative accounts, one has to bear in mind that many authors at some point in their testimony state the impossibility of articulating what happened to them. On one hand, writing down occurrences was one way of coming to terms with them. Placing one's thoughts outside of oneself on paper could alleviate the heavy burden. On the other, authors continuously pushed against the limits of language since some of their experiences could not be put into words. They repeatedly broke off in the middle of a painful description and declared they were unable to narrate the full extent of the outrage. Words could not convey, nor could human understanding grasp, the true magnitude of horror and pain. Such utterances reflect both the constraints and the power of language. Writing down the details of an ordeal meant having to endure the suffering all over again. There was, then, a fine line between easing the burden of one's experience and being overwhelmed by it anew.

At a time when literacy was still largely confined to the upper and middle classes, some of the most prolific recorders of the days' events could be found among the *Religiosi*, members of religious orders. Their position encouraged and sometimes demanded a daily record, and a good part of these writings survived due to the preservation by their orders. Clergy also often left diary-style accounts in addition to general parish records, as did some nobility and government officials and even the occasional artisan and soldier. Benigna von Krusenstjern's *Selbstzeugnisse der Zeit des Dreißigjährigen Krieges* broadened our access to a host of narrative accounts and provides an invaluable tool by locating 240 self-testimonies of the Thirty Years' War, often published in obscure, nineteenth-century regional journals.[13]

The vivid accounts and graphic images of both personal and official records convey the relentless devastation in the German lands and beyond. The forcefulness of their combined testimony suggests a homogeneous experience of loss, destruction, and desperation. A sense of utter ruin indeed pervades most documents, but beneath this profound reality lies a more complex and variegated web of experiences that was shaped by multiple factors. It is widely known that the greatest number of deaths did not result from the battles themselves but from the repercussions of war, such as forced contributions, inflation, famine, disease, pestilence, plundering, and violence. These effects were more intensely felt along the paths of troop movements than in areas further removed from the army routes. Thus the war did not hit every region equally. A place like Hamburg on the North Sea not only had a very low death toll, but also profited greatly from the conflict. The war's uneven visitation on the populace is only part of the explanation for the diversity of experiences. Other aspects played a role as well, among them one's gender, social and occupational group, personality, upbringing, networks, and whether one lived in the city or in the countryside. This chapter will provide a selection of windows on the breadth and depth of contemporaries' experiences.

One experience runs constant throughout these accounts: fear. Fear permeated everything. At the rumour of approaching armies, entire peasant communities panicked and took flight into the cities. Even though overlords often tried to force the peasants back into

---

[11] Amelang, 'Vox populi', p. 33.

[12] See also J. Held, 'Kulturgeschichte, Geschlechtergeschichte, Friedensforschung', in K. Garber et al. (eds), *Erfahrung und Deutung von Krieg und Frieden: Religion – Geschlechter – Natur und Kultur* (Munich, 2001), p. 329.

[13] B. von Krusenstjern, *Selbstzeugnisse der Zeit des Dreißigjährigen Krieges. Beschreibendes Verzeichnis* (Berlin, 1997).

the countryside, they remained behind walls until the danger had passed.[14] The possibility of losing everything they left behind and the inability to plant next year's crop became secondary concerns.

Mariastein, a convent of Augustinian nuns near Eichstätt, Franconia lay in the line of troop movements and experienced the destruction of their convent in the early 1630s. The *Verzaichnus* of its prioress, Klara Staiger, offers a detailed record of the convent's day-to-day happenings.[15] Descriptions of chores, religious rituals, hardships, finances, and the weather follow each other with no interpretive frame although the prioress does include the occasional comment. Staiger's writing offers insight into the larger context of her convent, the wider monastic world, and war times, as well as into her own more personal experiences and reactions. Fear was a collective experience. As Staiger tells it, their frightening encounter with war during the first half of the 1630s made the prioress and her nuns shrink back in horror at the mere mention of a troop's approach.[16] But she also discloses something about her own personal fear. The continuous attacks wore her down and brought her to the brink of what she could endure. She experienced anxiety of varying intensity. Certain events almost drove her out of her mind. When the Swedes took Eichstätt in 1633 and then, for 10 consecutive days, bombarded the castle where the sisters had sought protection and from where they watched the destruction of their cloister, the prioress felt a deadly fright that threatened to overcome her: 'I am so deeply afraid that I thought I would lose my body and my life, yes even my sanity (*Verstand*) since no one knows the outcome (of the siege).'[17] Evidently, more than death itself, Staiger dreaded losing control of her mind.

In March of 1648, the enemy entered Eichstätt's territory once again. Staiger and her nuns had fled via Eichstätt to St. Willibald's Castle high above the city. On the way the prioress witnessed how soldiers broke into her cloister. More agonising than seeing their just rebuilt home threatened anew with destruction was her fear for those who had stayed behind at Mariastein:

> *The concern for my twenty sisters in the cloister made me so anxious that I did not know how I felt. I dragged myself up the mountain (to St. Willibald's Castle) and thought I could not stop myself from falling down ... I was then carried and guided rather than that I walked myself.*[18]

Not only was *she* afraid for the lives of those who had remained behind to look after the cloister and do the baking, washing, and other necessary chores; she was also aware that *they* were extremely frightened – 'more so ... than they could ever tell us'.[19] Having to suffer such fear, her words suggest, leaves an indelible mark upon one's life, one that was shared by many but could not be communicated.

---

[14] For example, see the peasant population around Munich during the early 1630s and late 1640s.

[15] *Klara Staigers Tagebuch. Aufzeichnungen während des Dreißigjährigen Krieges im Kloster Mariastein bei Eichstätt*, ed. by O. Fina (Regensburg, 1981).

[16] See also A.E. Imhof, *Die Verlorenen Welten: Alltagsbewältigung durch unsere Vorfahren – und weshalb wir uns heute so schwer damit tun* (Munich, 1985), pp. 95–6 and 100–101; Imhof discusses the traumatisation of a local population and the difference between concrete fear and latent anxiety.

[17] *Klara Staigers Tagebuch*, p. 83.

[18] Ibid., p. 316.

[19] 'Haben versehen mit bachen (Backen) waschen und aller notturfft / aber Layder vilmer angst und schreckhen haben eingenomen / als sy uns in jar und tag erzelen kinden .' *Klara Staigers Tagebuch*, p. 51.

It is not surprising that chronicles and diaries of *Religiosi*, whose monasteries lay in the thick of military action or in the line of troop movements and thus had intimate knowledge of the war, are filled with references to the great fright they experienced as soon as they heard news or rumours about an approaching army or a negative military turn of events nearby. But the converse – distance from the war – did not provide calm either. The *Geschicht Buech* of Maria Magdalena Haidenbucher, abbess of the Benedictine Abbey of Frauenwörth on the island of Lake Chiemsee in Bavaria (also called Frauenchiemsee), shows that even when sisters were situated far removed from military action and troop movements, they could not shake the fear.[20] In many ways they had a much easier lot than the nuns of Mariastein. Although the war eventually took all the Frauenwörthers' financial resources, the nuns did not experience the continuous dearth and the push to the very edge of livelihood that other sisters did. Nor did they lie in the line of action but for most of the war witnessed its horrors from afar. The war, nevertheless, came to the sisters in the form of the many refugees they took in.

The fear of harm, then, could be as debilitating as the harm itself. It could paralyse men and women, and only the most resourceful were able to overcome its poison. It took a realistic mind to assess and react to these reports in an appropriate manner and to keep the paralysing elements of fear at bay. And, indeed, one of the most striking characteristics of people successfully dealing with the war was their keen sense of reality. Making informed judgements about what kind of action a situation required, they glanced – often with concern but sometimes with surprising optimism – toward the future. The many losses and the constant fear could not deter Klara Staiger from continuing her work and from being hopeful about what lay ahead. Even though her cloister's horses and other animals were perpetually raided and confiscated, she purchased new livestock whenever possible.[21] Despite the fact that countless supplies were robbed while in transit, she continued to organise shipments.[22] When, in early 1634, her cloister was finally entirely destroyed, she surveyed the ruins and began to plan the construction of a new cloister. Some of the sisters moved back in between the ruins to start the spring crop.[23]

A second prevalent experience was a profound sense of vulnerability and lack of protection. Complaints about plunderers and their brutality pervade the war's official and personal records. Just as evident is the authorities' inability to protect their subjects against such violent excesses. Villagers and citizens, tradesmen and merchants petitioned to overlords and magistrates, who appealed to local military leaders and then to the commanders in chief. Sympathetic to the problem, the military leadership passed edicts that promised harsh justice for plundering soldiers. This cycle of offence, complaint, resolution, and the occasional showcase against marauders repeated itself endlessly throughout the war, yet official actions were striking for their failure to curb violence.

Strapped for resources and faced with a war whose atrocities mounted with every year, Nuremberg's city council pursued a course of realism that verged on resignation. On 12 July 1632 a butcher sent a complaint to Nuremberg's council. On his way into the city, he had been robbed by eight Swedish cavalrymen of one calf and eight pounds of lard. Since many who were carrying victuals to the market were robbed on the streets, he requested that the council pass an ordinance against such crimes and see to their elimination. The council's response was noted on the letter: the matter should be put to rest since nothing could be

---

[20] G. Stella (ed.), *Geschicht Buech de Anno 1609 biß 1650. Das Tagebuch der Maria Madgalena Haidenbucher (1576–1650), Äbtissin von Frauenwörth* (Amsterdam and Maarssen, 1988).
[21] *Klara Staigers Tagebuch*, pp. 94 and 130.
[22] Ibid., pp. 97–8, 141–2.
[23] Ibid., p. 128.

done to remedy the miserable situation during these difficult times. Instead the butcher should be advised to be patient.[24] The inability to protect its own people is underlined by the mockery of the soldiers in the neighbouring margraviate Brandenburg-Ansbach, who were robbing Nuremberg's peasants and then ridiculing them by saying: 'Nuremberg's subjects had a very fine government that not only failed to protect them against hardships but turned them into beggars as well.'[25]

Peasants were particularly vulnerable to attacks by armies and the violence of marauders. If they managed to flee into a nearby city or forest, they invariably lost whatever they left behind. Enemy and 'friendly' troops destroyed their crops, demanded increasingly astronomical pay, and robbed them of the seeds that may have ensured a better future.[26] Left to take matters into their own hands, villagers organised themselves to defend their lives and livelihood. Indeed, their neighbourhood initiatives became the most successful strategy of protection. Many local communities maintained a warning system that alerted the villagers of impending danger. Since their authorities seemed unable to provide safety, the roughly three hundred peasants of Grevenberg, Franconia helped themselves. One hundred kept watch daily and secured the area; the other two hundred worked the fields.[27] In certain cases, Nuremberg's political leadership explicitly allowed self-help measures, the so-called *Glockenschlag*, by which the local bell was struck to gather the villagers for collective action. Such behaviour obviously only worked in cases of smaller groups of marauders. When armies made their way through the territory, particularly during the latter part of the war, flight was often the only sensible course of action.

City dwellers were less exposed than the peasants since they lived in walled communities that provided some protection – and, in the case of select cities like Nuremberg, state of the art fortifications. But the cities' more secure nature was a mixed blessing for its inhabitants. Once frightened subjects made for more fortified places, these turned into uncontrollable hazards. They were not equipped to accommodate thousands of peasants and others complete with their belongings and farm animals. Some refugees were able to rent a room in a burgher's house, but the rest had to contend with the streets. The almost inevitable results of invasions from the countryside were price increase, hunger, and epidemics. These consequences are palpable in the diary of Hans Heberle, a shoemaker in a village near Ulm, who over a period of 18 years fled 28 times into Ulm (1631–1648). During his third flight he noted: 'There is distress and misery, starvation and death. There we lay on top of each other in great wretchedness. Then price increase and hunger broke in on us, after these the evil disease, pestilence. Many hundreds of people died during this year, 1634.'[28] Heberle lost his second son as well as three of his sisters and a brother on this flight.

---

[24] 'Dies Ansag vff Sich ruhen, vnd weil diesem vnheil bey diesen leidigen beschwerlichen leuffen nicht zu remedirn, Jhn zu gedult weisen laßen.' Staatsarchiv Nürnberg, Reichsstadt Nürnberg, Ratskanzlei, B-Laden, Akten 82, Nr. 16, fol. 1 (12 July 1632).

[25] The soldiers of the margraviate plundered Nuremberg's peasants '(m)it dem spöttlichen Zuesprechen, das sie, die Nürnbergischen Vnterthanen, eine sehr schöne Herrschaft hetten, so sie nit allein wider keine Trangsal schützen, sondern gar an den Bettelstab lauffen ließen.' Staatsarchiv Nürnberg, Reichsstadt Nürnberg, Ratskanzlei, B-Laden, Akten 82, Nr. 3, fol. 77 (2 May 1632).

[26] For a discussion of the peasants' lack of protection see also B. von Krusenstjern, 'Das Schiff, der Steuermann und die Kriegsfluten. Staatserfahrung im Dreißigjährigen Krieg', in P. Münch (ed.), *'Erfahrung' als Kategorie der Frühneuzeitgeschichte* (Munich, 2001), pp. 425–32.

[27] Staatsarchiv Nürnberg, Reichsstadt Nürnberg, Ratskanzlei, B-Laden, Akten 86, Nr. 6 (6 April 1632).

[28] G. Zillhardt (ed.), *Der Dreißigjährige Krieg in zeitgenössischer Darstellung: Hans Heberles 'Zeytregister' (1618–1672). Aufzeichnungen aus dem Ulmer Territorium* (Ulm, 1975), p. 152.

Pastors were even more vulnerable than the peasants who could at least organise and pool their resources to defend themselves. Their parsonage did not afford the little shelter a monastery might. With the dwindling population, their livelihood was endangered since the parishioners could no longer pay their pastors. As a result and because of their diminishing numbers, ministers often had to serve several parishes, which involved considerable travel on treacherous roads. They were also expected to hold out and serve the parish rather than flee to safety. And when the enemy took over their territory, they typically lost their job and either had to convert or move to a region of their own confession.

Monks and nuns lived in walled surroundings, but these offered only limited protection. Not only did neighbouring peasants flock behind these walls for safety, thus turning monasteries into crowded and dangerous places; monasteries also became magnets for marauders since subjects stored their valuables and livestock there. Nor were most of these places particularly well fortified. Consequently many *Religiosi* fled to safer havens. A curious pattern is visible in all of this moving about: the reshuffling of living arrangements is reflective of society's hierarchy of power, social class, and gender. Nuns moved into the quarters that monks had just vacated on their flight to more secure places; and peasants made for the city from which the better-off citizens had fled.[29] Safety was a relative term in any case, but evidently it could also only be attained proportional to one's gender and station in society.

For a variety of reasons, the clergy and *Religiosi* were prime targets of attack. In some cases, they were suspected of being more affluent; in others, they were taken hostage to extract money from cities and communities. Confessional animosities also added to the antagonism toward them. To avoid harassment, they frequently opted for dissimulation and disguise. Monks and nuns regularly fled in secular clothes. Ministers kept silent about their profession when they were arrested. When pastors travelled to their far-flung parishes, many concealed themselves to be less noticeable. Camouflage was also the critical tactic when it came to holding services.

Rather than using the more conspicuous churches, pastors often held services in private homes. Similarly, other ecclesiastical services, such as baptisms and weddings, were relocated into the privacy of the parishioners' houses.[30] Catholic ministers were in a situation comparable to their Protestant counterparts. Stephan Mayer described his experiences in Unteregg, Windelheim during the Swedish War. He had to flee 10 times and hide out for long periods of time without being able to live in the parsonage. When he was arrested, he did not admit to being a minister because 'they treated the ministers very severely'.[31]

The lack of protection could be especially traumatic for women. Many females, whether young or old, were raped. Nuns were not safe from rape either, but some authors gratefully recorded that the enemy left them their 'honour'. Several aspects set nuns apart from other women. Often they were under a male guardianship. The extent of the protection that this term suggests, however, was quite modest. Every time soldiers were sighted in Eichstätt's vicinity, Mariastein's guardian of the Augustinian monastery in nearby Rebdorf ordered Staiger and her sisters to take their belongings and flee either to Eichstätt, St. Willibald's Castle, or Ingolstadt. Safety, however, could not be guaranteed at these places. Notably, the

---

[29] *Klara Staigers Tagebuch*, p. 312; M. Friesenegger, *Tagebuch aus dem 30jährigen Krieg*, ed. by P.W. Mathäser (Munich, 1974), p. 163.

[30] R. Großner and B. Frhr. v. Haller, 'Zu kurzem Bericht umb der Nachkommen willen. Zeitgenössische Aufzeichnungen aus dem Dreißigjährigen Krieg in Kirchenbüchern des Erlanger Raumes', *Erlanger Bausteine zur fränkischen Heimatforschung*, 40 (1992): p. 37.

[31] M. S. Mayer, 'Kurze Aufzeichnungen aus den Zeiten des Schwedenkrieges, 1625–45', *Deutsche Gaue*, 11 (1910): pp. 26–31, p. 29.

enemy conquered both Eichstätt and its castle while the nuns resided there. Even though the protection the status of *Religiosi* could offer women proved often doubtful, nuns had one advantage over other members of their sex: they were part of a group and could rely on a network. They could plan and act together, and the communal reality as well as the network of religious women in other cities often became essential to their survival, both physically and mentally.

For some the terrifying experience of war with its repercussions proved too much to endure. A particularly graphic example of the literally overwhelming pressures of war comes from the Brigidine cloister in Altomünster, Bavaria. Most nuns had been able to flee to Munich before the enemy advanced on their cloister in late April 1632, but two nuns who had been unable to travel starved to death. When the others returned, they found their market ruined and burned-down – even though the flames had spared their cloister. Shortly after their arrival in 1634, the plague hit the cloister and killed 15 sisters. When, in early May 1635, the abbess was unable to find food for her charges, she finally snapped and hanged herself.[32] This is a striking example of the lacking protection even of nuns. After the suicide Bavaria's elector, Maximilian, admonished the state institutions to keep a better watch over the cloister and render more timely assistance in case of economic dearth so that, in the future, such desperate actions could be forestalled.[33] Vulnerability and the absence of protection was thus a common experience, but it varied according to gender, location, and social group.

A third experience of the war was that of life's vicissitude. Many of the above examples testify to the instability and changeability of life during the conflict. With pillaging soldiers, disastrous poverty, and epidemic diseases, everything from the next harvest to one's life and religion was in question. The unpredictability of life is brought home by the experience of Pastor Dietwar and his colleagues in Kitzingen in the margraviate Brandenburg-Ansbach, Franconia, whose town was captured by a party of another confession. Kitzingen experienced both the quartering of troops and the repeated takeover by a power of another religious confession. When the town fell to the bishop of Würzburg in January 1629, the evangelical pastors had to convert or leave and lose their jobs. Dietwar decided to depart, and other evangelical ministers were eventually chased out of the city as well.[34] While Dietwar took over the parish of Höchstätten, the Swedes drove the bishop and his men out of Franconia. The Catholic ministers fled disguised in secular clothes since they feared what the Swedes might do to them, and the evangelical pastors returned.[35] Even though the Lutheran ministers were again in control of their parishes, they now had to contend with troops in their territory since the Swedish and imperial forces converged on nearby Nuremberg. Ministers were robbed on their journeys to their parishes, and plundering was endemic. In 1634 Kitzingen went again to the Catholics. This time the evangelicals were promised that they could remain with their religion but before long the Lutheran sermon was again discontinued, and the evangelical ministers were pushed out of their homes.[36] On 9 April 1635 Dietwar went once more into exile.[37] Incessant change seemed the only certainty.

---

[32] W. Liebhart, *Altbayerisches Klosterleben. Das Birgittenkloster Altomünster 1496–1841* (St. Ottilien, 1987).

[33] Liebhart, *Altbayerisches Klosterleben*, p. 41.

[34] Landeskirchliches Archiv Nürnberg, Markgräfliches Dekanat [MD] Uffenheim, Akten 95, Chronik Bartholomæus Dietwar, pp. 22–39.

[35] Ibid., pp. 53, 59–63.

[36] Ibid., pp. 78–82.

[37] Ibid., p. 93.

Soldiers, too, experienced the changeability of fate during the war. Even though they were the ones typically perpetrating violence and destruction, their lot was not an enviable one. Much of their aggression was prompted by the fact that they were paid insufficiently, infrequently, or not at all. Cities tried to bar their gates against them, and maltreated peasants sometimes paid marauding soldiers back atrocity for atrocity. In his journal, the soldier Peter Hagendorf continuously underlines the volatility of a soldier's life: one day is a feast, the next famine.[38]

Closely related to these apperceptions and occurrences is a fourth, the experience of disorder and disruption. War disrupted life on many levels. In its most extreme form, it took one's life or that of members of one's family, household, and neighbourhood. When a village became the victim of troop movements or quartering or when marauders terrorised the countryside, these actions had other severe consequences, including keeping peasants from performing their work, ruining the harvest, destroying the new crop, and thus breaking the chain of steps it took to ensure survival. Moreover, the war and its repercussions brought disorder to rural and civic life and had a restraining effect on vital communal rituals. The mounting deaths made customary funeral arrangements impossible. Other celebrations of life were scaled back. The death, migration, and dispersal of parishioners disrupted parish life. Frequently Sunday services were discontinued for weeks and months, sometimes years.[39] The flights into cities destabilised the already fragile social system within urban walls. But refugees, too, resented these forced travels. The prioress Klara Staiger dreaded the flights, which were often not of her own choosing but ordered by their guardian.[40] At times, she would have liked to hold out a little longer in her cloister. Flights did not simply mean a possible escape from violence, but entailed leaving behind what was familiar, enduring great discomfort, and fleeing 'into misery,' *ins Elend*, as she and her contemporaries called the place away from home.[41] Moreover, the flights separated the nuns since some had to stay behind to look after the cloister and take care of the farming. These only fled when the enemy was all but upon them. Rituals provided stability, comfort, and reassurance as the world around seemed to disintegrate. Staiger and her fellow nuns adhered to a soothing routine of religious acts and words and kept up with their chores even when they were in exile. By continuing to spin, wash, cook, and make soap, they remained busy and brought order to days and weeks of disorder.

The experience of war was also disruptive on a psychological level. It invalidated firmly entrenched ways of understanding the world. Many made sense of the war by casting it as

---

[38] Peters, *Ein Söldnerleben*.

[39] Carsten Kohlmann posits for Württemberg that the ministrations continued uninterruptedly throughout the war, but this was not the case in Franconia nor in many other areas of Germany. C. Kohlmann, '"Von unsern Widersachern den Baptisten vil erlitten und ussgestanden". Kriegs- und Krisenerfahrungen von lutherischen Pfarrern und Gläubigen im Amt Hornberg des Herzogtums Württemberg während des Dreißigjährigen Krieges und nach dem Westfälischen Frieden', in M. Asche and A. Schindling (eds), *Das Strafgericht Gottes. Kriegserfahrungen und Religion im Heiligen Römischen Reich Deutscher Nation im Zeitalter des Dreißigjährigen Krieges* (Münster, 2001), p. 128.

[40] *Klara Staigers Tagebuch*, p. 66.

[41] 'Going into Misery' was at the time a common expression for having to leave one's place for a region that was not home. This strange land could be a distant county or a foreign country but it could also be as close as the nearby forest or the next city. In short, it was an area beyond the immediate boundaries of one's home. See Renate Blickle who discusses boundaries and space from a social point of view (R. Blickle, 'Das Land und das Elend. Die Vier-Wälder-Formel und die Verweisung aus dem Land Bayern. Zur historischen Wahrnehmung von Raum und Grenze', in W. Schmale and R. Stauber (eds), *Menschen und Grenzen in der frühen Neuzeit* (Berlin, 1998), pp. 131–54). The opportunity to live in one's own homeland is juxtaposed with being sent 'into misery' (*ins Elend*), that is, outside the country, beyond the borders, away from everything that was familiar.

a battle of religions or confessions. One's own religion represented that of the true believers, while the enemies were followers of the devil. Catholics and Protestants respectively boosted their religious confession and righteousness by denigrating the opponents'. Propaganda went a step further by portraying it as a cosmic, apocalyptic struggle between good and evil, between the forces of Christ and Antichrist. It was a means to mark and reinforce one's identity, to provide comfort to followers, and to claim religious, if not necessarily military, victory. This strategy worked fairly well during the early years of the conflict but the mounting violence and a seemingly unending war also led to a profound questioning of identity. With the build-up of unspeakable atrocities on both sides over three decades, religion's content, function, and justification came under review.

Moreover, what happened when one could no longer neatly separate enemies and friends, when the purpose behind the suffering was no longer clearly discernible? What if one could not trust one's own troops, if they plundered your homestead or monastery or village as furiously as the enemy troops did? What, indeed, if one's own troops were worse than the enemy's? References to appalling behaviour of 'friendly' troops pervade many personal and official accounts. Such incidences of maltreatment shattered people's worldview. The sociologist Peter Sloterdijk calls these experiences 'Stör-Erfahrungen', a term that denotes occurrences 'that explode hitherto experiences, convictions, or behaviours that have been taken for granted'.[42] How can one make sense of a war if the basic principles with which one understands the world no longer apply? How can one maintain hope if one's own troops have become the enemy, and there is no recourse left?

Maurus Friesenegger, abbot of the Benedictine cloister Andechs on the Ammersee, Bavaria, commented on the atrocities carried out by 'friends'. Describing the destruction in the Bavarian countryside following the Swedish takeover of Munich in 1632, he acknowledged that 'one really cannot tell who plundered the most – the foreigners or the native thieves'.[43] By the end of 1633, Friesenegger equated riders (*Reiter*) with robbers (*Räuber*).[44] The Benedictine also criticised the idleness of their own troops in the face of widespread looting and their exploitation of the situation. While the Swedes executed all kinds of atrocities and amassed a large amount of booty, 'our army sat calmly in Munich and across the Isar and listened to everything evenly, while it procured its own spoils everywhere'.[45] The dragoons who were hired to guard the bridge across the Ammer from incoming robbers were themselves no better than the thieves, just as the *Salva Guardia* (a military guard for protective purposes) guarded and increased nothing but the hunger. Indeed, the (Catholic) peasants helped the (Protestant and presumably enemy) Swedes against the allied Croats since the latter plundered worse than the former.[46] Such experiences eroded conceptions people relied on in navigating their world.

While cognisant of the multiplicity and diversity in contemporaries' experiences with the war, this study focused particularly on the experience of fear, vulnerability, volatility, and disruption. These occurrences were a reality among many social groups and thus could be called common phenomena, but the analysis also revealed the variations and the more personal dimensions within these experiences. Fear, for example, even though universal,

---

[42] 'Stör-Erfahrungen' are 'such experiences … that break through past experiences, convictions, or things that have been taken for granted and that are at odds with these experiences.' P. Sloterdijk, *Literatur und Organisation von Lebenserfahrung. Autobiographien der Zwanziger Jahre* (Munich, 1978), p. 113.

[43] Friesenegger, *Tagebuch*, p. 28.

[44] 'Den 26. [November 1633] waren wiederum 20 Reiter, oder vielmehr Räuber da …'; Friesenegger, *Tagebuch*, p. 53.

[45] Friesenegger, *Tagebuch*, p. 43.

[46] Friesenegger, *Tagebuch*, pp. 48, 50, 68, 74.

manifested itself in diverse forms. It was specific to the individual and his or her situation. A person's circumstance and location could lessen or intensify the dread. Vulnerability was also a reality experienced by most contemporaries, but a look at a broad array of social agents shows that lack of protection meant different things to different people.

The reality of experiences during the Thirty Years' War was certainly more varied and layered than this short survey can reflect. It was also more complex in another respect. The above discussion has addressed largely the negative and unsettling encounters with the war. However, for some people, like military contractors and those who made a living from the armament industry, the war provided opportunities. Naturally the conflict had a very different impact on contemporaries who profited from the war, especially if they were situated far removed from military action and troop movements. But even people in locales that suffered the debilitating effects of the war cannot be described wholly in these dark terms. Narrative accounts give us a sense that communities who repeatedly became targets of the war's destructive effects were made up of more than fear and flight and misery. Some negative experiences had the positive side effect of welding people together and forging essential support groups.[47] Personal experiences and reactions certainly depended on individual and communal circumstances. For some the negative components proved overwhelming; others did not let the misery engulf them entirely, and they could gather strength from these lighter moments. While contemporaries tell us much about the agony of war, they also rejoice in a good harvest, a good wine, or times of companionship. The fact that they articulated these facets of life suggests that the dismal experience of war did not invalidate the positive aspects of their life, and that they experienced light within darkness.

Selected Bibliography

Asche, M., and A. Schindling (eds), *Das Strafgericht Gottes. Kriegserfahrungen und Religion im Heiligen Römischen Reich Deutscher Nation im Zeitalter des Dreißigjährigen Krieges* (Münster, 2001).

Berg, H., *Military Occupation under the Eyes of the Lord. Studies in Erfurt during the Thirty Years War* (Göttingen, 2010).

Friesenegger, M., *Tagebuch aus dem 30jährigen Krieg*, ed. by P.W. Mathäser (Munich, 1974).

Fulbrook, M., and U. Rublack, 'In Relation: The "Social Self" and Ego-Documents', *German History*, 28 (2010): pp. 263–72.

Großner, R., and B. Frhr. v. Haller, 'Zu kurzem Bericht umb der Nachkommen willen. Zeitgenössische Aufzeichnungen aus dem Dreißigjährigen Krieg in Kirchenbüchern des Erlanger Raumes', *Erlanger Bausteine zur fränkischen Heimatforschung*, 40 (1992): pp. 9–107.

Klara Staigers Tagebuch. Aufzeichnungen während des Dreißigjährigen Krieges im Kloster Mariastein bei Eichstätt, ed. by O. Fina (Regensburg, 1981).

Krusenstjern, B. von, *Selbstzeugnisse der Zeit des Dreißigjährigen Krieges. Beschreibendes Verzeichnis* (Berlin, 1997).

Krusenstjern, B. von, and H. Medick (eds), *Zwischen Alltag und Katastrophe. Der Dreißigjährige Krieg aus der Nähe* (Göttingen, 1999).

Mortimer, G., *Eyewitness accounts of the Thirty Years War, 1618–1648* (New York, 2002).

Peters, J. (ed.), *Ein Söldnerleben im Dreißigjährigen Krieg. Eine Quelle zur Sozialgeschichte* (Berlin, 1993).

---

[47] Klara Staiger notes that they could expect much more support from those who had experienced similar deprivation than from others who had not; cf. *Klara Staigers Tagebuch*, p. 142.

Stella, G. (ed.), *Geschicht Buech de Anno 1609 biß 1650. Das Tagebuch der Maria Madgalena Haidenbucher (1576–1650), Äbtissin von Frauenwörth* (Amsterdam and Maarssen, 1988).
Wette, W. (ed.), *Der Krieg des kleinen Mannes. Eine Militärgeschichte von unten* (Munich, 1992).
Zillhardt, G. (ed.), *Der Dreißigjährige Krieg in zeitgenössischer Darstellung: Hans Heberles 'Zeytregister' (1618–1672). Aufzeichnungen aus dem Ulmer Territorium* (Ulm, 1975).

21

Strategy and the Conduct of War

Peter H. Wilson

The Issues

The Thirty Years' War has long assumed a central place in European military history, through its duration and destructiveness, and its perceived significance for the development of warfare. Yet little has been written since the nineteenth century on how the war was fought, because more recent historians concentrated on the material and human impact instead. The relative dearth of new research has allowed a number of poorly founded assumptions to distort the overall interpretation of the strategy and conduct of the war.

Most see it as 'meaningless conflict',[1] because 'warfare seemed to escape from rational control; to cease indeed to be "war" in the sense of politically motivated use of force by generally recognised authorities, and to degenerate instead into universal, anarchic, and self-perpetuating violence'.[2] Logistical problems are usually cited to explain this. Armies, so the argument runs, had grown beyond the capacity of states to support them, forcing generals to keep moving into fresh areas just to support their troops, rather than to engage the enemy.[3] This standard perception of futile operations sits at odds with another assumption that the war was waged by 'Great Captains' who sought victory through decisive battles.[4] The focus on prominent commanders is deeply embedded in all military history, but has been emphasised for early modern Europe in the influential Military Revolution thesis which explains both success and change in warfare by reference to wider technological innovations, as well as the brilliance of individuals like Maurice of Nassau and Gustav Adolph.[5]

These two perspectives are generally harmonised within a two-stage chronology with an initial period of decision allegedly giving way around 1635 to a long, indecisive war of attrition. The turning point is marked by the Peace of Prague, but conveniently coincides with the deaths of those generals traditional military history thought worthy of commemoration: Tilly and Gustav (both 1632), and Wallenstein (1634). It also fits the standard paradigm of the war spiralling out of control, ceasing to be a 'German' or a 'religious war', and broadening into a general international conflict in which 'many of the military commanders and most of

---

[1] C.V. Wedgwood, *The Thirty Years War* (London, 1938; 1957 edn), p. 460.
[2] M. Howard, *War in European History* (Oxford, 1976), p. 37.
[3] M. van Creveld, *Supplying War. Logistics from Wallenstein to Patton* (Cambridge, 1977), pp. 5–18.
[4] For example, R.F. Weigley, *The Age of Battles. The Quest for Decisive Warfare from Breitenfeld to Waterloo* (London, 1993).
[5] C.J. Rogers (ed.), *The Military Revolution Debate* (Boulder, 1995).

those they had led had all but forgotten the lofty – if often misguided – ideals for which they or their predecessors had originally gone to war'.[6]

Contemporaries were well aware of the distinction between the strategies of decision and attrition,[7] but we need to recognise that subsequent discussion has been distorted by how these were debated in the wake of the wars of Italian and German unification, the American Civil War, and colonial conflicts like the Boer War. Military historians, like the nineteenth-century public, celebrated commanders who appeared able to bring wars to swift, successful conclusions with minimal casualties for the victor. The strategy of attrition has become associated with weaker, supposedly more 'backward' forces incapable of defeating their better-armed and trained opponents in formal battles which have been the yardstick for measuring success in the western way of war since ancient Greece.[8]

Logistics, Military Organisation and Political Structure

The received interpretation rests on the cliché of the 'mercenary' as a soldier of fortune who served the highest bidder. Unable to organise sufficient forces directly, early modern states allegedly contracted professional 'military enterprisers' to raise and command troops for them.[9] War-making became semi-privatised in the hands of men whose primary interest was to win fame and fortune and so conducted operations accordingly. The actual situation was far more complex, and in order to understand how logistics constrained strategy we need to investigate how soldiers were paid and maintained.[10]

Early seventeenth-century governments prioritised the pay and provisioning of the ordinary soldiers who, unlike their officers, lacked the personal means to sustain themselves. Plunder was an unauthorised supplement, or an emergency substitute to ensure material survival in the event of disruption of official pay and provisions. The consequences of failing to pay soldiers regularly were obvious from the start of the war. The Bohemian Confederate army's operations were repeatedly disrupted by mutinies as its unpaid soldiers refused to move until the government made good its promises. The soldiers did not act from disloyalty, despite being hired to fight and despite the large number of foreigners in their ranks. Their protests stemmed from desperation common to all unpaid soldiers: early seventeenth-century armies rarely provided their men with rations directly, expecting them instead to buy food from sutlers or villagers. No pay meant no food.

This problem decreased as belligerents stopped trying to pay their men directly or in full through a centralised administrative system by the mid-1620s, and moved over to more decentralised systems which have entered history as 'contributions'. These were often extorted with threats of violence, but essentially entailed methods to feed and pay soldiers at local expense, rather than raising sufficient taxation centrally to do this. Force was used or threatened, because contributions were demanded at much higher levels than peacetime

---

[6] D. Stone, *Fighting for the Fatherland. The Story of the German Soldier from 1648 to the Present Day* (Washington DC, 2006), p. 26.

[7] For example, H. duc de Rohan, *Le parfait capitaine* (Cologne, 1642), chapter 7.

[8] Writing in the fifth century BC, Herodotus idealises the pitched battle by suggesting barbarians could not understand why the Greeks did not use less 'honourable' tactics: *Histories*, ch.7, section 9.

[9] F. Redlich, *The German Military Enterpriser and his Workforce* (2 vols., Wiesbaden, 1964–65).

[10] For further discussion of the fiscal and economic dimensions see P.H. Wilson, 'Military Finance, Organisation and State Development', in D. Parrott and A. Waldron (eds), *The Cambridge History of War*, vol. 3: *War and the Early Modern World* (Cambridge, forthcoming).

taxes, and because they were levied in neutral or enemy territory as well. Usually, existing tax and tithe systems were harnessed to provide whatever was required by the troops in the immediate vicinity, with any surplus remitted to the central command for redistribution to other units, or pocketed as profit by various officers. Regular taxation and foreign subsidies were henceforth reserved to purchase specialised war material, like artillery, or as collateral to raise additional loans.

Contributions were regulated through pay and provision ordinances stipulating what each rank was entitled to receive. Soldiers could thus still accumulate arrears of pay and other entitlements, making it difficult to disband regiments until these obligations had been settled. However, this rarely affected strategy and was insignificant compared to the problem of officers' pay. Senior officers' entitlements were much larger. The monthly pay bill of the imperial artillery in July 1618 was 3,582 florins, of which the commanding general was to receive 1,400 and the remainder distributed among the 239 gunners and other personnel.[11] Pay arrears accumulated correspondingly more rapidly, but their significance lay in the officers' political, not material survival. The senior officers were drawn from the social and political elite. This generalisation holds true for the few commoners who rose to the top ranks, like Jan van Werth and Peter Eppelmann (also known as Melander) who were originally both peasants, since they were given titles and married noblewomen. Such men were well-connected, with friends and relations in high church and state offices. Their cooperation was essential for the functioning of army, church and state and, indeed, their high pay was intended to enable them to carry out these functions, since they were expected to pay secretaries and other assistants themselves.

No government could afford to ignore their interests, yet none was able to pay them in full. The problem was compounded by the inability to write off arrears in the event of their death – something which regularly occurred in the case of ordinary soldiers – since officers' heirs and creditors always pressed for payment. Taxation and loans never yielded sufficient cash, obliging each government to pay officers only irregularly, always favouring those whom it needed to please at any given moment. The methods employed to make up the shortfall, rather than the general problems of feeding large concentrations of men, are what really affected strategy.

Here we need to note the subtle differences between the belligerents. The emperor held two major advantages over his opponents. He directly ruled lands which were far larger, richer and more populous than those of any of his opponents bar France. Additionally, he was the recognised head of the Holy Roman Empire (even the elector Palatine voted for Ferdinand II in 1619), and his enemies never entirely escaped his stigmatisation of them as 'rebels'. Thus, he was able to reward officers by means other than cash. He could ennoble or bestow new titles, like naming Wallenstein 'duke of Friedland' in 1625. He could also confiscate 'rebel' property and distribute it in lieu of pay. This began in Bohemia in the wake of the imperial victory at White Mountain (1620), and was extended to the rest of the empire from 1621, culminating in the transfer of Mecklenburg to Wallenstein in 1628. The emperor could also call on the German territories, as imperial Estates, to contribute men, food and other resources to combat his enemies as outlaws. This proved difficult to enforce before 1630, because many rejected Ferdinand II's claims that his opponents were 'notorious rebels' whose behaviour denied them the right to a trial. Most of them, however, accepted his argument that Swedish intervention constituted a breach of the peace, and the electors, meeting in Regensburg in 1630, agreed to a regular levy to be paid by all imperial Estates

---

[11] K. Oberleitner, 'Beiträge zur Geschichte des Dreißigjährigen Krieges mit besonderer Berücksichtigung des österreichischen Finanz- und Kriegswesens', *Archiv für Österreichische Geschichte*, 19 (1858): pp. 5–6.

to fund the imperial army. Subsequent meetings in 1636–37 and 1640–41 renewed this levy, though many territories refused, or were unable to pay.

Ferdinand's use of the imperial constitution was not without drawbacks. Imperial law entitled those combating outlaws to recoup their expenses at the law-breakers' expense. This formed the basis of the subsequent transfer of Lusatia to recompense Saxony for its support against the Bohemian Confederates and, far more significantly, brought the transfer of the Palatine lands and electoral title from the defeated Frederick V to Duke Maximilian of Bavaria in 1623.

These arrangements affected strategy. Bavarian operations were directed at conquering and securing the Palatine lands in 1620–23, but these objectives were also in line with imperial policy. Thereafter, Bavaria was keen to garrison Heidelberg as capital of the Lower Palatinate which (unlike the Upper Palatinate) was associated with possession of the imperial title. Heidelberg assumed an importance in operations from 1631 far above its purely military significance as a second-rate fortress. The same applied to nearby Frankenthal which was garrisoned by Spain from 1623 to ensure it retained a say in any negotiations on the Palatinate's fate. These were all recognisably political objectives, and there is little evidence that commanders' personal motives affected imperial strategy. For example, Wallenstein was not preoccupied during the 1632–33 campaigns with reconquering Mecklenburg lost to Sweden in 1631. Imperial generals could be more sanguine about the fate of individual possessions than their opponents, given the emperor's ability to provide alternatives. Far from proving dependency on mercenaries, Wallenstein's example indicates that ultimate authority still lay with monarchs. Though Wallenstein persuaded many colonels to swear personal loyalty in January 1634, all but two abandoned him the next month, recognising that only the emperor could legitimate their possession of lands and titles.

The situation was rather different for the emperor's enemies. France had no formal presence within the imperial constitution, but did possess the means to offer German princes and officers significant honours and rewards, such as the pensions paid to Hessen-Kassel from 1636. However, intervention in the empire was never a French priority, since it was intended just to keep Austria busy and prevent it assisting Spain. The Palatinate was never able to offer patronage and remained dependent on unreliable foreign backers. Denmark was part of the empire through its possession of Holstein and used its position in the Lower Saxon imperial circle (*Reichskreis*) to rally local assistance. However, like Sweden, it only possessed sufficient resources to start, not finish its war, and so also relied on German support. The Catholic and some Lutheran princes backed the emperor, with the rest preferring to remain neutral. Support for Denmark and Sweden was reduced to those who were disadvantaged within the constitution, like the imperial counts and knights, or who hoped to benefit from changing it, like the Calvinist Palatinate and Hessen-Kassel. It is only the subsequent application of the anachronistic concept of a centralised, sovereign national state that renders their political goals as 'private interests'.

Thus, operations against the emperor always involved bargains between a primary belligerent, like France or the Palatinate, and a varying number of German aristocrats who generally provided the bulk of the actual forces in the hope that victory would advance their own objectives. The relative lack of legitimacy and the uncertainty surrounding their masters' positions in the empire forced these German officers to place less faith in promises and to divert operations towards their own ends. For example, Mansfeld spent much of 1621–22 trying to secure Alsace as a possible principality for himself, as well as a base from which to recover the Lower Palatinate for Frederick V. Bernhard von Weimar deliberately diverted part of Sweden's army in Germany to conquer Bamberg, Würzburg and Eichstätt in 1633, while orchestrating a mutiny to force Chancellor Oxenstierna to grant him these as his own principality. His operations in French service (1635–39) were also largely directed at securing Austrian lands in Alsace and the Breisgau as a substitute for these Franconian possessions which had been lost at the end of 1634. Likewise, Hessen-Kassel pursued its own war in Westphalia intermittently from 1631 to enlarge its possessions at the expense of Catholic church lands and, once this plan had been defeated by 1635, to secure Westphalian towns as bargaining chips to be exchanged for Marburg and Hersfeld which the emperor had sequestrated as a punishment.

Middle-ranking officers had lesser, but still important objectives. The successive defeats of Bohemia, the Palatinate, Denmark and (by 1635) Sweden, left a large number of dispossessed Bohemian, Moravian and German nobles little choice but to fight on. They were determined not to leave the war empty handed and insisted on compensation, not only for their lost possessions, but also their years of (largely unpaid) service. As company and regiment commanders, their cooperation was indispensable. Having already demonstrated their power in backing Weimar's mutiny in 1633, the officers forced Sweden to mortgage its strategy in the Powder Barrel Convention of August 1635.[12] A further mutiny in 1641 forced Sweden to confirm that it would not make peace without securing their 'contentment'. In addition to securing its own territorial 'satisfaction', subsequent Swedish operations mainly aimed at forcing the emperor and his allies to increase their offer of compensation and allow Sweden to safely disband its army. Only as peace became imminent did Swedish operations slip towards the plundering expeditions invoked by the mercenary cliché. Wrangel attacked the Tirol in January 1647 to secure supplies and capture booty. News that peace negotiations were nearing completion prompted Swedish generals to converge on Prague in summer 1648 in a desperate attempt to capture more booty before the war ended.

Strategic Goals

These large-scale plundering operations were at least still reconcilable with official strategy, since they pressured the emperor to improve his offer at the Westphalian peace congress. Plundering by individual officers or their men was generally condemned as contrary to military efficiency and political legitimacy. The prevailing 'laws of war' distinguished between illegal *violentia* and the demonstration of power by a legally constituted authority (*potestas*). The purpose of a just war was to overturn the injustice perceived as causing it. The objective was not to destroy the enemy, but compel him to be more reasonable and accept an honourable settlement.[13] All belligerents subscribed to this concept, despite disagreeing fundamentally over the political and religious order in the empire. Consequently, operations remained subordinate to diplomacy from the outset, with peace talks already held in June 1618, and continuing with varying intensity in different venues thereafter.

No belligerent fought unaided, obliging all to consult allies and imparting the characteristic of a coalition war. Additionally, all legitimised objectives by reference to the imperial constitution which also served to coordinate the mobilisation of resources from the

---

[12] O.S. Rydberg and C. Hallendorf (eds), *Sveriges Tractater med främmande magter jemte andra dit hörande handlingar* (5 vols., Stockholm, 1902–09), vol. 5, part 2, pp. 330–33.

[13] R. Pröve, 'Violentia und Potestas', in M. Meumann and D. Niefanger (eds), *Ein Schauplatz herber Angst* (Göttingen, 1997), pp. 24–42; M. Kaiser, 'Maximilian I. von Bayern und der Krieg', *Zeitschrift für Bayerische Landesgeschichte*, 65 (2002): pp. 69–99, and his '"Sed vincere sciebat Hanibal". Pappenheim als empirischer Theoretiker des Krieges', in H. Neuhaus and B. Stollberg-Rilinger (eds), *Menschen und Strukturen in der Geschichte Alteuropas* (Berlin, 2002), pp. 201–27.

imperial Estates. Differences in strategy can be explained by variations in the belligerents' relationship to the constitution and the degree of their dependency on allies.

The Palatinate and Bohemian Confederation were unable to develop a viable framework. The Palatine-led Protestant Union was already near collapse in 1618 and never managed to harmonise the divergent interests of its disparate membership. Few welcomed Frederick V's acceptance of the Bohemian crown in 1619, and Union forces remained separate from those of the Bohemians. The latter's fragmented command reflected their state's federal structure where each province's contingent served under its own general to ensure its political influence. Likewise, Mansfeld operated separately in western Bohemia as a way for Frederick to preserve his autonomy: the bulk of foreign aid and auxiliaries went to Mansfeld, rather than the Confederate army only loosely under royal control. The allied Transylvanian contingents also served under their own generals, answerable to Prince Bethlen Gabor who pursued his own objectives in loose concert with Frederick. A clash of personalities among the senior generals certainly undermined central control still further, but disagreements also reflected underlying arguments over the direction the revolt should take.

The Catholic League proved far more effective, despite its large membership which did not always agree with Bavaria. Strategy was debated in regular League congresses from 1619, but the details always remained with Maximilian as undisputed Director and Generalissimo. Maximilian undoubtedly put his own ambitions first, but was also concerned with the general security of all League members. His innate caution further reinforced the League's generally defensive character, and he consistently opposed widening the war beyond what was necessary to secure and defend his initial gains of 1620–23.[14] Maximilian's younger brother, Ferdinand of Cologne, was de facto leader of the League members in Westphalia in north-west Germany. Their geographical separation from the core membership in Bavaria, Swabia and Franconia encouraged them to raise their own forces which acted as an autonomous adjunct to the main League army after 1621 and became a separate organisation anchored on the constitutional framework of the Westphalian circle in 1644.[15]

Military autonomy was vital to political influence and all German princes were keen to preserve it when they allied with the emperor or his enemies. Bavaria and Saxony delayed active involvement until they received mandates in 1620 as imperial commissioners to assist against Bohemia. These arrangements not only legitimated their later claims for territorial recompense, but also ensured their forces acted separately from the small imperial army.[16] Maximilian also waited until July 1620 when the Union agreed not to attack him. He then asserted control over operations by insisting that Tilly and the League army were not subordinate to the imperial commander Bucquoy.[17]

Ferdinand II had to accept this as the only way to obtain help, but it also broadly conformed to his conception of the empire in which he was – naturally – pre-eminent, but shared certain powers with the electors and other leading princes. He refused to summon the imperial diet for fear this could challenge his interpretation of the war as rebellion, but he remained prepared to consult the electors whom Bavaria officially joined thanks to the transfer of the Palatine title in 1623. The electors could influence strategy, most notably

---

[14] M. Kaiser, *Politik und Kriegführung. Maximilian von Bayern, Tilly und die Katholische Liga im Dreißigjährigen Krieg* (Münster, 1999); D. Albrecht, *Maximilian I. von Bayern 1573–1651* (Munich, 1998).

[15] J.F. Foerster, *Kurfürst Ferdinand von Köln* (Münster, 1976); H. Salm, *Armeefinanzierung im Dreißigjährigen Krieg. Der Niederrheinisch-Westfälische Reichskreis 1635–1650* (Münster, 1990).

[16] F. Müller, *Kursachsen und der Böhmische Aufstand 1618–1622* (Münster, 1997), and the sources in n.14 above.

[17] P. Broucek, 'Feldmarschall Bucquoy als Armeekommandant 1618 bis 1620', in *Der Dreißigjährige Krieg* (issued by the Heeresgeschichtliches Museum, Vienna, 1976), pp. 44–7.

in 1630 when they forced Ferdinand to dismiss Wallenstein, reduce the imperial army and entrust it to Tilly as new commander.

Contrary to the impression conveyed in the general literature, the two armies were not merged, placing Tilly in a difficult position. His personal preference for an offensive to drive the Swedes into the sea was supported in Vienna, but not in Munich where Maximilian insisted that League units were not used against Gustav who had promised France he would only fight Austria. The sudden collapse of the imperial detachments defending the lower Oder rendered this impossible after early 1631, while League 'neutrality' was further compromised by Tilly's siege of Magdeburg which had openly allied with Sweden.

The League army remained distinct after Tilly's death, despite Wallenstein's reinstatement as imperial commander a few months earlier. Maximilian struggled to maintain his autonomy by appointing Duke Charles IV of Lorraine as his field commander in 1634. By choosing a fellow imperial prince, Maximilian hoped Charles's status would ensure Bavarian interests were respected. Similar motives guided Ferdinand II's choice of his son Archduke Ferdinand (III) to replace Wallenstein as imperial commander. Maximilian accepted that Archduke Ferdinand was the senior general, but argued his full authority was tactical, not strategic. The archduke could issue orders to League units attached to an army under his immediate command, for example during a battle, but all operational orders and directives to League units elsewhere depended on prior consultation with Bavarian representatives. These differences reflected disagreements over the legitimate extent of imperial authority and caused considerable friction. Though Archduke Ferdinand agreed strategy with Bavarian and Spanish representatives at the start of the 1634 campaign, he refused to accept the stream of advice and requests from Munich. Maximilian's anxiety was heightened, because he could not trust Duke Charles who clearly wanted to shift operations towards recovering Lorraine from France, which Maximilian did not want to antagonise. The underlying tensions are clear in the conflicting imperial and Bavarian accounts of their combined victory at Nördlingen in September 1634, where each sought to cement its influence by claiming the greatest share of the credit.[18] Throughout, Maximilian was aware the emperor was negotiating with Saxony to abandon its temporary alliance with Sweden and wanted to ensure Bavaria was not eclipsed in any new arrangement.

The immediate departure of the Spanish for the Low Countries after Nördlingen reinforced the emperor's dependency on his major German partners. Consequently, Maximilian's distinction between tactical and strategic command was upheld in the arrangements associated with the Peace of Prague in May 1635. Both Bavaria and Saxony ensured their armies remained separate under their own generals who would only have to accept direct orders from Archduke Ferdinand (or his later replacements) if he was personally with the army. Though the League was formally disbanded, Bavaria was assigned the imperial taxes from its former members to sustain its own army as a separate corps. Likewise, Saxony was granted the contributions from north German territories within its sphere of influence.[19] Though the emperor was able to assert greater control over the other forces which joined the imperial army, those of Bavaria, Saxony and, by 1644, Westphalia remained distinct. Each

---

[18] G. Rystad, *Kriegsnachrichten und Propaganda während des Dreißigjährigen Krieges* (Lund, 1960). For the disagreements over command and strategy, see L. Höbelt, *Ferdinand III. (1608–1657)* (Graz, 2008), pp. 69–76; R. Rebitsch, *Matthias Gallas (1588–1647)* (Münster, 2006), pp. 104–9, 112–33; S. Haberer, *Ott Heinrich Fugger (1592–1644)* (Augsburg, 2004), pp. 295–305 in addition to the sources in note 14.

[19] A. Kraus, 'Zur Vorgeschichte des Friedens von Prag', in H. Dickerhoft (ed.), *Festgabe Heinz Hurten* (Frankfurt/M., 1988), pp. 265–99; H. Haan, 'Kaiser Ferdinand II. und das Problem des Reichsabsolutismus. Die Prager Heeresreform von 1635', *Historische Zeitschrift*, 207 (1968): pp. 297–345; C. Kapser, *Die bayerische Kriegsorganisation in der zweiten Hälfte des Dreißigjährigen Krieges 1635–1648/49* (Münster, 1997), pp. 10–29.

used its military autonomy to oblige the emperor to respect its objectives when formulating strategy and in the peace negotiations.

The emperor's opponents were also influenced by the empire's political culture, though to a lesser extent. Denmark was the most constrained. Its intervention was preceded by long negotiations in the Lower Saxon circle assembly to foster legitimacy and secure allies. King Christian IV even appeared in person before the Holstein territorial diet in 1627 to plead for additional troops.[20] However, he retained control over strategy, not least because the Hague Alliance never established a viable framework to coordinate action with Denmark's foreign backers.

Sweden paid far less attention. Gustav Adolph clearly intended to amalgamate his conquests and allies within a Swedish empire. This plan was diluted after his death to become the League of Heilbronn in April 1633; a device to channel German resources to sustain Sweden's army in the empire. Sweden dominated the League council which had little influence on strategy that was now a matter for Oxenstierna and the principal Swedish generals. However, despite Gustav's insistence on his 'absolute direction' of the war, even he was obliged to respect the interests of major German allies, notably Saxony (1631–34), Hessen-Kassel, and the Guelph dukes, whose forces served under their own generals. The situation mirrored the emperor's relationship with Bavaria, Saxony and Westphalia in distinguishing between strategic and tactical command.[21]

France paid the least attention to imperial political culture since it never intended to establish itself in the empire. Even after Sweden's temporary collapse after Nördlingen, France tried to avoid direct involvement by assuming control over the remnants of the League of Heilbronn's army under Bernhard von Weimar. The Weimar army was gradually absorbed into that of France only because it failed to fulfil the role allocated it by Richelieu to keep imperial forces east of the Rhine. Once Richelieu decided to retain Alsace for France, it became imperative that Weimar establish himself east of the river, both to protect France's new province and to sustain his army without devastating French territory. French troops had to be sent to reinforce him, because he could not force his way across unaided. Though French involvement grew incrementally, its goals in Germany remained limited and it tailored its force size and structure to suit these. France's *Armée d'Allemagne* was to remain a small, mobile and self-sustaining force to lend weight to its diplomats' demands once the peace congress opened in 1643.[22]

The Institutional Framework

The personal nature of early seventeenth-century monarchy exerted considerable influence on the formulation of strategy. Christian IV and Gustav were not constitutionally obliged to lead their armies in person, but *chose* to do so from personal inclination. However, even they sought advice. War councils provided the framework for consultation at two levels. Court war councils were already emerging as permanent institutions in most monarchies around 1600, but still functioned on an ad hoc basis with fluctuating membership. They

---

[20] G. Knüppel, *Das Heerwesen des Fürstentums Schleswig-Holstein-Gottorf, 1600–1715* (Neumünster, 1972), pp. 16–31, 101.

[21] This and the following are based on the discussion in P.H. Wilson, *Europe's tragedy. A History of the Thirty Years War* (London, 2009), pp. 459–747 and the sources cited there.

[22] D. Croxton, *Peacemaking in Early Modern Europe. Cardinal Mazarin and the Congress of Westphalia, 1643–1648* (Selinsgrove, 1999).

were usually convened by the ruler, or his representative, and comprised senior military and civil advisors, plus sometimes invited allied envoys. They were forums for goal-setting, with their conclusions summarised in written instructions issued to the field commander at the start of each campaign. Field war councils were convened by the commander to consult his senior officers as necessitated by events or new information. They were method-setting to decide how best to achieve the assigned goals, and often a representative of the court war council was present to ensure the commander did not deviate from his instructions.

The general staff emerged during the war, not as a forum for strategic planning, but to assist the commander and maintain communications with the political centre. It evolved from the personal assistants initially paid by the general himself. Wallenstein created his own staff to manage the dramatic increase in the imperial army and cope with the relatively wide autonomy granted him by Ferdinand II. He relied on trusted senior generals like Aldringen, Schlick and Arnim for advice and to command major sections of the army. An equivalent development was inhibited in Denmark and Sweden by the fusion of political and military authority in the king-commander, as Christian and Gustav simply took their existing secretaries with them to maintain records and correspondence. The imperial general staff continued to grow after Wallenstein's death, and especially from early 1640 when Archduke Leopold Wilhelm was appointed field commander. Official pay and provision lists now contained a separate sheet for support staff, not just generals. The number of posts increased steadily to reach about 40 by 1647, and included senior legal, medical, engineering, logistical, administrative, postal and transport personnel, and a number of staff officers. The latter were already present by at least 1635. They normally held middling rank (usually colonels) and acted as personal advisors to the field commander and his envoys for sensitive missions. This system was replicated in the Westphalian army by 1644.[23] Additional administrative support was provided by other agencies, often subordinated to the court war council, which maintained records and offered some help with logistics and arms procurement.

Choice of field commander was the ruler's prerogative. A field commander exercised full tactical command in battle and other engagements, but rulers retained the final decision over strategy. This remained true even for Wallenstein whose autonomy lay in his choice of method, not objective. Commanders could also advise on the appointment and promotion of senior officers and generals. Such matters impinged on patronage and their sensitivity explains the controversy surrounding Wallenstein's influence in this area. Commanders could also receive plenipotentiary powers, as in the case of Tilly and Wallenstein who were empowered to negotiate with Denmark from 1627. Religion and social status affected choice, but rulers generally picked men they trusted. Maximilian had complete confidence in Tilly, but still sent detailed instructions. Others, notably Oxenstierna, remained anxious their commander might exceed his instructions or make a fatal mistake, and so divided command among several generals. Wallenstein only commanded imperial forces in the empire, with those in Hungary, Italy and elsewhere serving under other generals who reported directly to the emperor.

Methods

Operations had to be reconciled with the laws of war to avoid damaging a ruler's legitimacy and the commander's personal reputation. The furore following the infamous sack of

---

[23] E. Höfer, *Das Ende des Dreißigjährigen Krieges* (Cologne, 1997), pp. 69–73; Rebitsch, *Gallas*, pp. 240–50; Salm, *Armeefinanzierung*, pp. 93–5, 182–3.

Magdeburg in 1631 obliged the normally reticent Tilly to publish a denial that he had intended the city's destruction and rebut Swedish propaganda depicting it as imperial tyranny.

Commanders showed the least inhibition in using extreme force when facing rebellious peasants, partisans and others not associated with a recognised government. Armies routinely took brutal reprisals, including burning entire villages and massacring their inhabitants. Despite Ferdinand's characterisation of Frederick V and other opponents as rebels, however, he generally pardoned those he defeated, provided they accepted his authority.

Terror was excused as a lesser evil to bring operations to a swifter conclusion, but its application still conformed to accepted conventions. For example, Wallenstein had the 500 defenders of Breitenburg killed in September 1627 to intimidate other Danish garrisons into capitulating, but only after they refused his earlier offer to accept their surrender and resisted his initial attack.[24] Though relatively rare, such deliberate killing soon descended into a vicious cycle of atrocity, notably in 1631 when the Swedes and imperialists successively justified massacres as reprisals for the other's behaviour.[25] Most recognised that this was counter-productive, and systematic destruction was usually limited to demolishing dwellings, burning crops, and uprooting vines and fruit trees. Pappenheim deliberately destroyed the area around Stade in Lower Saxony before he withdrew in May 1632 to deny food and supplies to the enemy and thus hinder their pursuit. More usually, this scorched earth strategy was used offensively as added pressure on an opponent to negotiate; for example, Wallenstein against Saxony (1632), the imperialists against Hessen-Kassel (1637), Banér during his invasion of Bohemia (1639), and the Swedes in Westphalia (1646). It is noteworthy that all these efforts failed, not least because this strategy hit the common folk, not the princes who had usually fled to safety. It only succeeded when it coincided with general war-weariness and disillusionment, especially after the second battle of Breitenfeld in November 1642 dispelled the last hopes that the emperor could eject the Swedes. The Swedes then targeted key territories in turn, intimidating Brandenburg, Würzburg, Saxony and others into neutrality.

This represented a successful, if slow strategy of attrition which undermined the emperor's ability to resist Swedish demands at the peace congress by reducing the number of territories maintaining the imperial army. However, attrition and decision never stood as stark alternatives. Battles were not necessarily more 'decisive' than sieges which have been associated in subsequent military history with the strategy of attrition as practised by the Spanish in Flanders. The Swedish triumph at Hessisch-Oldendorf (1633) was one of the most complete battlefield victories, yet brought no lasting results, while the main imperial army ended the war advancing in Bavaria, despite having lost at Zusmarshausen five months before. Decisiveness was not measured by 'rational' criteria, such as the scale of enemy losses, but in the event's psychological impact. White Mountain, first Breitenfeld and Nördlingen proved turning points by shattering the confidence of the defeated side, whereas Jankau (1645), Zusmarshausen and other major reverses did not. Sieges could produce similar results. Weimar won three of the four battles he fought during 1638, but it was his capture of Breisach that created despondency in Vienna. Indeed, sieges could be strategically more significant, because possession of fortified places enabled an army to hold territory, whereas the lack of a secure base often obliged a retreat despite a victorious battle. For this reason, the defence and capture of politically or strategically important places featured prominently in strategic planning. It assumed even greater importance after 1643

---

[24] J. Polisensky and J. Kollmann, *Wallenstein* (Cologne, 1997), p. 138.
[25] P.H. Wilson, 'Atrocities in the Thirty Years War', in M. O'Siochrú and J. Ohlmeyer (eds), *Plantation and Reaction: the 1641 Rebellion* (Manchester, 2013), pp. 153–75.

when military success or failure directly affected belligerents' bargaining positions at the peace congress.

Generals knew that a successful battle or siege required the concentration of superior numbers, yet recognised inadequate resources made this hard to sustain for long. Armies grew in size, not because generals wished to find food by occupying more land, but because they wanted superior numbers and were expected to operate in several regions simultaneously. Contemporaries considered 25,000 men to be a 'formidable army' (*exercitus formatus*), but Wallenstein consistently pushed the emperor to sanction far more, eventually securing authorisation for 100,000 in May 1627, because he was obliged to fight both in northern Germany (against Denmark) and Silesia and Hungary (against Mansfeld and Bethlen), and because he wanted to end the war quickly by confronting the enemy with overwhelming force. The failure to concentrate such numbers for a single battle was not due to a lack of strategic understanding. True, armies were not organised into subdivisions like corps, and the brigade was only a tactical, not an operational formation. However, it is often forgotten that Napoleon was able to muster and manoeuvre such large armies, not only thanks to vastly stronger state structures, but also Europe's much larger population and greatly improved agricultural output and transport network.

In the Thirty Years' War dispersal paradoxically facilitated concentration, though it took time for this method to emerge. During the first decade, each side operated with a single principal field army of 25,000 men or less, one or two sizeable detachments, and a number of garrisons in key towns. The development of Wallenstein's army after 1625 added a second major field force on the emperor's side, but the real proliferation occurred after Sweden's victory at Breitenfeld (1631) allowed it to recruit German allies and collaborators across the empire. Whereas the war had been waged in only one or two regions simultaneously, it now became general, obliging each side to muster two to four field armies, several detachments and a far larger number of garrisons. Overall combined numbers peaked at about 250,000 men in the early 1630s, but no more than 88,000 were ever concentrated for a single battle (Alte Veste, 1632). Commanders now had to balance the political imperative of pursuing objectives in several regions at once, with the military requirement of concentrating forces for particular engagements. A flexible system evolved whereby each field army contested control of a specific region with its opponent. Temporary concentrations could be achieved by draining forces from one region and rushing them to another. Garrisons were left to secure vital areas and to continue resistance until more troops could be detached to resume offensive operations in their area. Garrisons also acted as reserves, reinforcing a major army in their vicinity if needed, or combining with new recruits to rebuild defeated field forces.

The emergence of this system contributed to the widespread devastation of the 1630s and early 1640s, since it enabled the war to be waged throughout the empire. It also left the impression of aimless, futile operations which has filled the pages of subsequent historical writing, because the demands of operations in one region constantly drew forces from other areas. One side often took several towns in rapid succession in the spring as the enemy diverted his main force from that area to assist elsewhere, only to lose their gains when the opposing troops returned in the autumn. If both sides despatched their field forces from the same region, operations were restricted to a 'little war' of raids between the remaining garrisons.

The composition of field forces changed to compensate. The proportion of infantry declined from between three-quarters and two-thirds to half or less, contrary to the assumption of the Military Revolution thesis of a growth in infantry with the adoption of linear, firepower tactics. The larger proportion of cavalry by the early 1640s improved mobility, because horsemen could travel faster, forage more widely and carry more provisions in their saddlebags. A further innovation was the introduction of the flying column of cavalry, dragoons and often additional infantry mounted on horses by 1642. Cavalry and dragoons had always preceded a field army as an advance guard, and had been used for short-term raiding or surprise attacks on camps or small garrisons. The flying column was a more permanent, substantial force that could be sent as a rapid reinforcement from one region to another, or used for its own special operations. A Swedish column under Königsmarck successfully intimidated Saxony into neutrality in 1645, and then assisted operations across southern, central and north-eastern Germany, before attacking Prague in 1648.

Mobility allowed the army to respond to the dictates of diplomacy, but did not necessarily bring greater decision, because both sides employed the same methods. Armies perceiving themselves to be weaker tried to evade and join garrisons or allied forces elsewhere. Failure to escape was the most common reason for battle during the war.[26] Commanders who ruthlessly abandoned their baggage train and camp followers usually got away, like Banér's retreat from Torgau in 1637, but this only worked if they had a well-garrisoned and supplied area to go to. Otherwise, lack of food and shelter meant half or more of the soldiers died or deserted, making a retreat often more costly than a battle. Less commonly, battles resulted from an encounter, either where neither side knew the other was so close, or more often as one laid a trap for the other.[27] Set-piece battles occurred where both sides felt sufficiently confident to fight, though some of these developed from a pursuit.[28] Such engagements could involve large numbers, because generals only accepted them when they felt sufficiently strong. The scale of the victory was determined less by the tactics employed by the victor, than whether the defeated side retained sufficient cohesion to evacuate its wounded and make an orderly retreat. More complete victories could be achieved by the rapid concentration of superior numbers to surprise and encircle an enemy. Since this required the enemy to be lax (Thionville, 1639) or incompetent (Tuttlingen, 1643), it rarely produced the defeat of a large army. More usually, a secondary detachment or besieging force was surprised by a more mobile, but still small force.[29]

Generals who sought to delay their opponents, either for political reasons, or because they felt too weak to fight, placed their armies in inaccessible terrain which they often strengthened with earthworks and other fortifications. Similar entrenchments were dug to protect armies as they besieged important towns. Attacking such positions could be costly and often resulted in defeat.[30] Attackers often entrenched nearby and tried to starve their opponents by raiding their supply lines (Waidhaus, 1621), or hoping they would throw themselves in a futile counter-assault (Alte Veste, 1632). More usually, one side ran out of supplies or left to assist hard-pressed allies elsewhere.

---

[26] Major battles arising from pursuit include Mingolsheim, Höchst, Fleurus (all 1622), Stadtlohn (1623), Lutter (1626), Kosel, Heiligenhafen (both 1627), Vlotho (1638), Chemnitz (1639), Neunburg (1641) and Zusmarshausen (1648).

[27] Záblati (1619), Rössing (1626), the opening phase of Nördlingen (1634), first Rheinfelden, Wittenweier (both 1638), Melnik (1639), Schweidnitz (1642).

[28] The latter case includes White Mountain (1620) and Lützen (1632). Other set-piece actions include Wimpfen (1622), Wolgast (1628), first Breitenfeld (1631), first Steinau, Alte Veste (both 1632), Hessisch-Oldendorf, Pfaffenhofen (both 1633), the second stage of Nördlingen (1634), Wittstock (1636), Thann (1638), Kempen, second Breitenfeld (both 1642), Freiburg (1644), Jankau, Allerheim (both 1645).

[29] Weingarten (1622), Seeze (1625), Bamberg, Höxter, Volksmarsen (all 1632); second Steinau, Geltolfing (both 1633), second Rheinfelden (1638), Herbsthausen (1645), Triebl (1647), Dachau (1648).

[30] Dessau (1626), Werben (1631), Breisach (1638), Wolfenbüttel (1641). Successful assaults include Lech, first Steinau (both 1632) and Freiburg (1644), but the latter almost destroyed the victorious French army.

Rather than stark alternatives, it is clear that the strategies of attrition and decision were combined differently depending on circumstance and a commander's preference. Tilly operated and fought offensively, consistently achieving success over less well-organised and often out-numbered foes in the 1620s. Wallenstein's strategy was offensive, but his battles (other than second Steinau) were defensive. Gustav had to operate and fight offensively because he lacked the resources for a protracted war. His successors, especially Banér, pursued a strategy of attrition to compel the emperor to grant better terms by forcing his German allies to leave the war. As the strategic balance shifted slowly in their favour, and as their diplomats secured viable cooperation with France, generals like Torstensson, Wrangel and Königsmarck resumed the offensive with smaller, more mobile armies. The imperial and Bavarian armies still scored successes, but the accumulative impact of battlefield defeats and the loss of further towns obliged the emperor's diplomats to give ground until France and Sweden finally accepted their terms in the Peace of Westphalia.

Selected Bibliography

Barker, T.M., *The military intellectual and battle. Raimondo Montecuccoli and the Thirty Years War* (Albany, NY, 1975).

Guthrie, W.P., *Battles of the Thirty Years War from White Mountain to Nordlingen, 1618–1635* (Westport, CT, 2002).

Guthrie, W.P., *The later Thirty Years War from the Battle of Wittstock to the Treaty of Westphalia* (Westport, CT, 2003).

Mortimer, G., *Wallenstein. The enigma of the Thirty Years War* (Basingstoke, 2010).

Murdoch, S., Zickermann, K. and Marks, A., 'The Battle of Wittstock 1636: Conflicting Reports on a Swedish Victory in Germany', *Northern Studies*, 43 (2012): pp. 71–109.

Parrott, D., *Richelieu's army. War, government and security in France 1624–42* (Cambridge, 2001).

Parrott, David, *The business of war: military enterprise and military revolution in early modern Europe* (Cambridge, 2012).

Wilson, P.H., 'The Causes of the Thirty Years War 1618–48', *English Historical Review*, 123 (2008): pp. 554–86.

Wilson, P.H., 'Dynasty, Constitution and Confession: The Role of Religion in the Thirty Years War', *International History Review*, 30 (2008): pp. 473–514.

Wilson, P.H., *Europe's tragedy. A history of the Thirty Years War* (London, 2009).

Wilson, P.H., (ed.), *The Thirty Years War: A Sourcebook* (Basingstoke, 2010).

Wilson, P.H., 'Meaningless Conflict? The Character of the Thirty Years War', in F.C. Schneid (ed.), *The Projection and Limitation of Imperial Powers 1618–1850* (Leiden, 2012), pp. 12–33.

Wilson, P.H., 'Was the Thirty Years War a "Total War"?', in E. Rosenhaft, E. Charters and H. Smith (eds), *Civilians and War in Europe 1640-1815* (Liverpool, 2012), pp. 21–35.

Wilson, P.H., 'Atrocities in the Thirty Years War', in M. O'Siochrú and J. Ohlmeyer (eds), *Plantation and Reaction: the 1641 Rebellion* (Manchester, 2013), pp. 153–75.

PART V
Experience and Praxis of War

The Peace of Prague – A Failed Settlement?

Martin Espenhorst (née Peters)

The Peace – Text and Context

On 20th/30th May 1635 – that is, 17 years after intensive fighting – the more than 80-page long Treaty of Prague was signed. The signatories were Ferdinand II (1578–1637) and Johann Georg I of Saxony (1585–1656). The two German signatories represented diverging confessional and political concepts and networks. The king was an integral part of the monarchy to the extent of personifying it, while the imperial prince felt indebted towards 'German Libertät' (the term will be explained in detail later in the text). The Prague peace treaty was written in German, which was common practice in the case of peace treaties between the emperor and German princes. Only contracts between the emperor and non-German powers were written in Latin. With the Treaty of Prague, two former rivals made peace. The Catholic emperor was the supreme feudal lord and source of all law, while the other, the emperor's arch marshal, a Protestant and prince-elector, was responsible for electing the kings of the Holy Roman Empire, and thus one of the empire's 'greats'. It is true that Ferdinand was seven years older than Georg, yet both were part of a generation that had been born before the Bohemian uprising of 1618/1619. Moreover, Johann Georg was the ruler of a territory with many links to the so-called Thirty Years' War[1] and the Reformation[2] – for example as a war theatre and as an intellectual centre of the Protestant movement. Despite the fact that Saxony had previously formed an alliance with Gustav Adolph of Sweden, one can assume that the signatories did not represent irreconcilable parties and attitudes. In contrast to Friedrich V of the Palatinate, the Saxon Johann Georg I behaved more moderately with the emperor. Both were determined, against objections from the French, for example, to restore peace in the German Empire and to bolster their reputations as 'Princes of Peace'.[3]

It was their intention, with the Peace Treaty of Prague, to create a viable political and constitutional foundation that would take account of the existing political and religious

---

[1] Cf. J. Burkhardt, *Vollendung und Neuorientierung des frühmodernen Reiches 1648–1763* (Stuttgart, 2006); R.G. Asch, *Thirty Years War: The Holy Roman Empire and Europe, 1618–1648* (London, 1997); J. Burkhardt, *Der Dreißigjährige Krieg 1618–1648* (Frankfurt am Main, 1992); G. Parker (ed.), *The Thirty Years' War* (London, 1984).

[2] C.f. T. Kaufmann, *Geschichte der Reformation* (Frankfurt am Main, 2009); M. Heckel, *Deutschland im konfessionellen Zeitalter* (Göttingen, 1983); H. Klueting, *Das Konfessionelle Zeitalter: 1525–1648* (Stuttgart, 1989); A. Schindling and W. Ziegler (eds), *Die Territorien des Reiches im Zeitalter der Reformation und Konfessionalisierung* (7 vols, Münster, 1989–1997).

[3] R.-P. Fuchs, *Ein 'Medium zum Frieden'. Die Normaljahrsregel und die Beendigung des Dreißigjährigen Krieges* (Munich, 2010).

differences and pluralities, thus leading to a common peace policy. The 'old order' of the empire was not to be reformed but rather restored.

Views and Interpretations

The Peace of Prague was certainly more than a failed dress rehearsal for the peace treaty of 1648, as Michael Kaiser rightly points out. After all, it can boast enduring accomplishments that retrospectively make it into a link.[4] Indeed, the emperor managed the 'Rekonjunktion mit fast allen seit 1630 von ihm abgefallenen Reichsständen' (Repgen).[5] Five years before, at the 1630 Diet of Regensburg, Protestant and Catholic estates of the empire had been openly rebelling against the emperor, which led to the dismissal of Wallenstein as well as the refusal to elect Ferdinand's son as king. However, Prague did not see the birth of a new system.

Researchers are particularly interested in two aspects of the Peace of Prague: first, the diplomatic deftness of the emperor – 'the emperor managed an enormous diplomatic triumph', according to Tryntje Helfferich[6] – strengthening his own political position within the empire by managing to regain his leadership over the German estates. Second, the renewed influence of the Catholic creed, as Hajo Holborn writes: 'The Peace of Prague was a great victory for the emperor. It increased his monarchical powers considerably and gave German Catholics the dominant position in the Empire'.[7]

Many researchers recognise the Peace of Prague as a turning point for an era. Eberhard Straub had his 1980 study *Pax et imperium – Spaniens Kampf um seine Friedensordnung in Europa* end in the year 1635.[8] And Dieter Albrecht, as early as 1962, chose the year 1635 as a reference point for his study on the foreign policy of Maximilian of Bavaria.[9] In the first volume of his work *Die Römische Kurie und der Westfälische Friede*, published in 1962, Konrad Repgen dedicates a separate chapter to the Peace of Prague, titled 'Papst, Kaiser und Reich 1521–1644'.[10] Repgen sees the year 1635 as a mere transition point on the long road from the Diet of Worms to the Peace of Westphalia in 1648. As a general rule, the Peace of Prague receives more attention from European historians. In his overview *Europa und das Reich im Dreißigjährigen Krieg*, published in 2008, Christoph Kampmann writes a separate chapter titled: 'Kein Friede ohne Europa: Der Prager Friede und sein Scheitern (1634–1638)'.[11] In this, Kampmann looks more closely at the concept of an imperial army, as it was proposed by the peace treaty, an idea that was much reviled by its contemporaries, leaving the Peace of Prague stuck with the label of a 'Monstrum pacis'.[12]

---

[4] M. Kaiser, 'Der Prager Frieden von 1635. Anmerkungen zu einer Aktenedition', *Zeitschrift für historische Forschung*, 28 (2001): pp. 277–97.

[5] K. Repgen, *Die römische Kurie und der westfälische Friede: Papst, Kaiser und Reich, 1521–1644* (2 vols, Tübingen, 1962), vol. 1, p. 295.

[6] T. Helfferich, *The Thirty Years War: A Documentary History* (Indianapolis, 2009), p. 165.

[7] H. Holborn, *A History of Modern Germany: The Reformation* (New Jersey, 1982), p. 354.

[8] E. Straub, *Pax et Imperium. Spaniens Kampf um seine Friedensordnung in Europa zwischen 1617 und 1635* (Paderborn, 1980).

[9] D. Albrecht, *Die auswärtige Politik Maximilians von Bayern: 1618–1635* (Göttingen, 1962).

[10] Repgen, *Kurie*, vol. 1, p. 295.

[11] C. Kampmann, *Europa und das Reich im Dreißigjährigen Krieg: Geschichte eines Konflikts* (Stuttgart, 2008).

[12] Burkhardt, *Der dreißigjährige Krieg*, p. 97.

All authors agree that the Peace of Prague had contributed to a secularisation of the conflict. Konrad Repgen pointedly interprets the peace with his well-known three-step plan, according to which the emperor followed three main goals: first, to unite all the estates behind him, second to secure his military sovereignty, and third to oust foreign powers from the empire.[13]

Georg Schmidt, in his 1999 study on the *Geschichte des Alten Reiches – Staat und Nation in der Frühen Neuzeit 1495–1806*, even identifies a glorification of the nation in the text and concludes: 'Wäre die vereinigte Reichsarmada erfolgreich gewesen, stünde der Prager Friede weit oben in der Vorgeschichte des deutschen Nationalstaats'.[14] Peter H. Wilson, on the other hand, focuses more on the privileges of the princes and territorial lords. In his epic work *Europe's Tragedy*, published in 2009, he calls it an important element in the development of the political and legal formula of 'German Libertät'.[15]

Ronald G. Asch looks at the breakup of princely alliances, such as the Catholic League or the Heilbronn League, in the Peace of Prague and the draft of Pirna. Asch interprets the introduction of federal law as a blueprint for a 'new model for the Empire's constitution', creating a new – albeit short-lived – balance between imperial authority and the German prince-electors.[16]

In the end, 1635 was no longer a contest between the alternatives of 'imperial absolutism' or 'federalism/Libertät', since the die had been cast for the political development in the old empire. For Johannes Burkhardt, the Peace of Prague was a turning point in that an alternative way of nation building had become impossible after 1635: Prague 'marked the turning point for both sides from concessions to consensus and compromise between universal and regional violence'.[17]

Properties and Participants

The negotiations took place in the Prague Castle and took eight days to complete. Both the location and the date of the peace settlement were reminiscent of the famous Defenestration of Prague on 23 May 1618. The city could look back on a certain tradition as a location for peace. As early as the second half of the sixteenth century, in 1589, 1595 and 1597, the then emperor signed peace treaties with Poland and Transylvania here. Choosing the imperial residence and centre of power as a place for peace was a clear signal, given that the emperor had to not only settle a variety of territorial disputes but also reaffirm his imperial authority in a Europe that was increasingly pluralised, both confessionally and politically. It is therefore not surprising that the Swedes did not agree on choosing Prague as a location, but suggested Breslau as a compromise. The emperor's goal was to demonstrate his authority. In the treaty it says (article 84):

---

[13] K. Repgen, *Dreißigjähriger Krieg und Westfälischer Friede. Studien und Quellen*, ed. by F. Bosbach and C. Kampmann (Paderborn and Munich, 1998), p. 331.

[14] G. Schmidt, *Geschichte des Alten Reiches. Staat und Nation in der Frühen Neuzeit 1495–1806* (Munich, 1999), p. 170.

[15] P. Wilson, *Europe's Tragedy. A History of the Thirty Years War* (London, 2009).

[16] R.G. Asch, 'The *ius foederis* re-examined: the Peace of Westphalia and the Constitution of the Holy Roman Empire', in R. Lesaffer (ed.), *Peace Treaties and International Law in European History. From the Late Middle Ages to World War One* (Cambridge, 2004), pp. 319–37, p. 331.

[17] Burkhardt, *Der dreißigjährige Krieg*, p. 99.

> *The electors, princes and estates of the Empire should show his Imperial Majesty all due and humble respect, honour, obedience, love and loyalty, and behave as befits all loyal and obedient electors, princes and estates.*[18]

On the one hand the Peace Treaty of Prague was a bilateral contract without the involvement of foreign powers. On the other hand, it did have a multilateral dimension in that a number of (imperial) estates, cities and alliances ended up joining it. The condition was that those princes who had been in Swedish service quit. The duke of Braunschweig-Calenberg, for instance, was a Swedish general and general of the County of Lower-Saxony. Without offering a comprehensive list of the estates that joined the Peace of Prague, I would still like to name a few: The prince-elector as well as the margrave of Brandenburg, the archbishop of Mainz, the archbishop of Cologne, the bishop of Paderborn and Münster, the Chapter of Münster, the bishop of Bamberg, the dukes of Braunschweig-Lüneburg, the landgrave of Hessen-Darmstadt, the duke of Saxony-Weimar, the duke of Saxony-Gotha, the duke of Mecklenburg-Schwerin, the princes of Anhalt, the countess of Lippe, the count of Zweibrücken-Hanau, the Hanseatic cities (inter alia Hamburg, Bremen) as well as a number of imperial cities (Ulm, Nürnberg, Erfurt, Memmingen, Frankfurt/M.). The Calvinist landgrave Wilhelm V of Hessen-Kassel joined the Peace of Prague at first, yet in 1636 he formed an alliance with France, a move that triggered a ban of the empire against him. The free imperial city of Strasbourg did not join the treaty, and the duke of Württemberg was explicitly excluded. Baden-Durlach and Nassau were also on the outside. Alliances between the estates, such as the 1633 Heilbronn League between Sweden and the Protestant estates, were dissolved.

The one thing that did not happen was a marriage between the peace-making dynasties. It would have sealed the peace treaty and was common practice in early modern peace-building.[19] Yet in view of the different confessional affiliations it would have been next to impossible to realise. However, on 15 July 1635, Archduchess Maria Anna of Austria, daughter of Ferdinand II, married Prince-Elector Maximilian of Bavaria, thus indirectly celebrating the intended political goals of the Peace of Prague.

The negotiator copy of the Peace of Prague was signed by three imperial and three Saxon diplomats: the influential imperial Privy Councillor and Count Maximilian zu Trauttmansdorff (1584–1650), the imperial envoy Count Ferdinand Sig(is)mund Kur(t) z von Senftenau (1592–1659), the imperial Aulic Councillor and scholar Dr. Justus von Gebhardt (1588–1656), the Saxon Privy Councillor David von Döring (1577–1638), the Saxon Councillor of Court and Justice Abraham von Sebottendorf (1584–1664) and the Saxon Councillor of Court and Justice Dr. Johann Georg von Oppel (1594–1661). The oldest delegate was Döring (58) and the youngest Oppel (41). All of the negotiators were part of the 'cream' of the diplomatic circles of the two signatories and its princes. The assigned Saxon diplomats purportedly felt a certain sympathy towards the emperor and Habsburg-Austria, while remaining sceptical towards the Swedes; Sebottendorf was even rumoured to have secretly converted to Catholicism.[20] With the exception of Trauttmansdorff, however, none

---

[18] K. Bierther, 'Der Prager Frieden von 1635', in *Die Politik Maximilians I. von Bayern und seiner Verbündeten 1618–1651*, Part II/10 (4 vols, Munich and Vienna, 1997), vol. 4, p. 1627; www.ieg-friedensvertraege.de, ed. by H. Duchhardt and M. Peters.

[19] M. Peters, 'Können Ehen Frieden stiften? Europäische Friedens- und Heiratsverträge der Vormoderne, *Jahrbuch für Europäische Geschichte*, 8 (2007): pp. 121–33.

[20] A. Schunka, 'Konfessionelle Liminalität. Kryptokatholiken im lutherischen Territorialstaat des 17. Jahrhunderts', in J. Bahlcke and R. Bendel (eds), *Migration und kirchliche Praxis: das religiöse Leben frühneuzeitlicher Glaubensflüchtlinge in alltagsgeschichtlicher Perspektive* (Köln, 2008), pp. 113–31, here p. 117.

of the diplomats of this circle would be present at the peace treaty negotiations in Münster and Osnabrück in 1648.

Almost all of the diplomats were able to enjoy personal benefits because of their participation in the peace settlement, experiencing a significant boost to their careers in its wake. Trauttmannsdorff was appointed imperial count in 1635 and Senftenau in 1636. A year later the latter became vice chancellor of the empire. Gebhardt was nominated knight of the empire in 1636, and finally, in 1656, baron of the empire. Sebottendorf, too, was awarded the title of baron. Oppel was given the imperial peerage on 1 December 1635, and in 1637 he became privy councillor and Comes palatinus caesareus. Yet for Döring the Peace of Prague was the beginning of the end of his influence within the Saxon court. He had been given a peerage in 1630, five years before the negotiations. In 1638, having been a rather controversial figure, the confidant of Johann Georg I of Saxony was dismissed from his service to the prince-elector at the age of 61. He died that same year.

Döring, the head of the Saxon delegation, had enjoyed a scientific education; he had studied law in Leipzig, earned his doctorate in Jena and worked at the Leipzig Court of Appeals. Among the Saxons, Johann Georg Oppel was also a Doctor of Law, having studied in Jena, Leipzig and Wittenberg, travelled to the Netherlands, England and France, and completed his doctorate in Basel in 1621. Oppel was part of Döring's family, having married one of his daughters. Gebhardt was in particularly high esteem at the time, being a member of the 'Doktorenbank' ('subsellium doctorum') and one of the most influential imperial aulic councillors of his time (Kampmann).[21] No theologian was part of the diplomatic corps.

Three copies of the Peace of Prague were produced – in vellum – for the emperor, the prince-elector of Mainz or rather the imperial chancellery as well as the prince-elector of Saxony. The imperial envoy Baron Ferdinand Kur(t)z, the elector's chamber secretary Baron Friedrich Lebzelter as well as the chancellor of Hessen-Darmstadt, Baron Dr. Anton von Wolff (1592–1641), transferred the documents.

Soon after its signature the Peace Treaty of Prague was published and commented on,[22] for example in the English-language pamphlet by Johannes Stella. It was also included

---

[21] Scientific works by D. v. Döring, *Theses De Iure Accrescendi* (1603) and *Bibliotheca iure consultorum theorico-practica exihens assertiones siue Conclusiones ciuiles, criminales & feudales: partim exipsis iuris uniuersi, diuini & humani fontibus limpidissimis delibatas, partim ex celeberrimorum probatissimorumque interpp. sententiis in foro* (1631); by J. v. Gebhardt, *Disp. inaug. de S. R. nationis Germanorum imperio* (1614); by J. G. v. Oppel, *Disputatio ordinaria de monetis ex jure tam publico quam privato deducta, ad Recessus praesertim Imperij Romano-Germanici, [et] electorales aliasve constitutiones directa* (1618) and *Synoptica totius iuris feudalis tractatio, quibusdam iuris publici et feudalis Saxonici differentiis illustrate* (1621); by F. S. K. v. Senftenau, *Selectiores aliquot quaestiones ex universo iure* (1623).

[22] *Tractatus Pragensis, siue Conditiones pacis initae, ac confirmatae, anno M. DC. XXXV. Maij XXX. inter Ferdinandum II. Imperatorem Roman. semper augustum. & Iohannem Georgium Electorem Ducem Saxoniæ: Ex autographo transmisso ad archiepiscopum Electorem Moguntinum. Additis quibusdam aliis ad eundem tractatum, eiusq[ue] promulgationem spectantibus. Abdruck des FriedensSchlusses von der Röm. Kays. Mayst. Unnd Churfürstl. Durchl. zu Sachsen zu Praag angerichtet/ Den 2/30. Maij Anno 1635. Mit Churfürstl: Durchl: zu Sachsen Freyheit. Gedruckt zu Dreßden durch Gimel Bergen/ Churf. Sächs. HoffBuchdruckern. Anno ut supra. Vindiciae secundum libertatem Germaniae contra Pacificationmem Pragensem das ist Rettung der alten teutschen Freybeit : gegen dem schädlichen und schändlichen pragerischen Friedens-Unfrieden … / [? by B.P. von Chemnitz]. 1635, [?1636]. FriedensPuncten, So zwischen der Röm: Keys: Majest. Und der Churf. Durchleucht. Zu Sachsen / unseren Allergnädigsten und Gnädigsten Herren / den 30 (20) May dieses 1635 Jahrs / in der königl. Hauptstadt Prag geschlossen und publicirt worden. Sampt Dem Keys: Patent / wie selbiges den 24 Junii / in deß H. Röm. ReichsStadt Nürnberg offentlich verruffen und angeschlagen worden. Gedruckt durch Jeremiam Dümlern. Deploratio Pacis Germanicae sive Dissertatio de Pace Pragensi, Tam infauste quam injuste inita Pragae Bohemorum 30/20 Maii: M.DC.XXXV. In qua artes & technae Austriacorum, vaecordia Saxonum, pericula Protestantium, & aeuitas belli à Francis & Suecis jure prolati evidentissime ostenditur, Authore Justo A. J. Cto. Lutetiae Parisiorum M.DC.XXXVI. J. Stella: Deploratio Pacis Germaniae sive dissertation de Pace Pragensi, 1636. N. Burgundi. I. C. Caesareae*

in the relevant early modern peace treaty collections.[23] Moreover, general treatises on peacekeeping and peace-making were published shortly before and throughout the year of the peace settlement.[24]

Events and Background

The 1635 Peace of Prague was the first ambitious attempt at achieving universal peace in the German Empire during the Thirty Years' War. Its goal, according to the preamble, was to restore a Christian, universal, honourable, cheap and firm peace within the Holy Roman Empire. The peace, the text continues further down, was conceived so that the

> *worthy German Nation would return to its previous integrity, tranquillity, liberty and security, and that the Holy Roman Emperor and his House, as well as electors, princes and estates of the Empire ... will receive restitution, whether adhering to the Catholic religion or the Augsburg confession.*[25]

The Peace of Prague pursued a high standard in that it was defined as an 'allgemeine Reichsbewilligung' (general authorisation of the empire), thus attaining equal level with fundamental imperial law, seeking to support and reinforce that very law:

> *His Imperial Majesty will govern electors, princes and estates of the Holy Roman Empire on the basis of law and justice, according to the fundamental laws, the Golden Bull and other laudable imperial constitutions as well as this treaty, and also with kindness and gentleness. He will bestow them with imperial friendship, grace, clemency and good, and guarantee them all equal rights, which are the foundation of the felicity of every empire.*[26]

The Peace of Prague was not conceived as a mere peace agreement ending a specific act of war, but it found itself in the midst of a multi-layered web of religious, diplomatic and military operations as well as political motives, many complicated events, processes and reciprocal effects: the death of the Swedish king Gustav Adolph (1631), the violent

---

Maiestatis, Electorisque Bavariae Consiliari et Historiographi, Comitis Palatini, Necnon Professoris Codicis in Academie Ingolstadiensi Vindiciae sive Refutatio Deplorationis Pacis Germanicae, sive Dissertationis de Pace Pragensi.

[23] M.C. Lundorp (ed.), *Der Römischen Kaiserlichen Majestät und des Heiligen Römischen Reichs Geist- und Weltlicher Stände, Chur-Fürsten, Graffen, Herren und Städte. Acta publica und schriftliche Handlungen* (1669), vol. 4; *Theatrum Europaeum* (1670), vol. 3; C. Gastelius, *De Statu Publico Europae Novissimo Tractatus* (1675); J. C. Lünig, *Das Teutsche Reichs-Archiv* (1713), vol. 3; F. C. Khevenhiller, *Annales Ferdinandei* (1726), vol. 12; J. Dumont, *Corps universel diplomatique du droit des gens: contenant un recueil des traitez d'alliance, de paix [...]* (1728), vol. 6/1.

[24] M.G. Vida, *Christopherus Colerus, Hymnus pacis* (1634); C. Bitschius and C. Friederich, *De pactionibus pacis: occasione sumpta ex l. Conventionum 5. 1 ff de Pact. quam*; Diss. jurid. politica Praeto Reppiniano (1635); C. Bitschius and C. Friederich, *Dissertatio iuridico-politica: De pactionibus pacis: occasione sumptâ ex l. conventionum. 5.* [Para]. 1. ff. de (1635); F. Henneken, *Pacis pact restituendae in Europa, partes* (1637).

[25] Bierther, 'Prager Frieden', p. 1623; Duchhardt and Peters (eds), www.ieg-friedensvertraege.de (see note 18).

[26] Bierther, 'Prager Frieden', p. 1626; Duchhardt and Peters (eds), www.ieg-friedensvertraege.de.

death of Wallenstein (1634), the Battles of Breitenfeld (1631) and Nördlingen (1634), and the discussion on the Edict of Restitution, to name just a few.

At the end of the year 1631, King Gustav Adolph and his army as well as that of Saxony, Sweden's ally, had taken Prague, Erfurt, Würzburg and Mainz. At the end of June 1632, Wallenstein, with the support of Maximilian of Bavaria, organised a counter-offensive for the emperor and the Catholic League. Then, on 16 November 1632, Gustav Adolph was mortally wounded in the Battle of Lützen in Saxony, so that from then on the Chancellor Axel Oxenstierna took over the leadership of the Swedish army. With the founding of the Heilbronn League in April 1633,[27] which was dissolved two years later in the Peace of Prague, Oxenstierna managed to secure the support of the Protestant estates in four imperial circles. Even France could be won over as an ally in the alliance agreement of Frankfurt am Main (1633 IX 5).[28] On 1 November 1634, the confederate estates, Sweden and France signed another alliance, this time in Paris.[29] Yet Sweden's policy of alliances did not deliver the desired results, the Protestant estates put strong limits on Swedish demands by insisting on the 'German Libertät'. This phase between 1632 and 1635 was marked by an extremely charged cooperation between Wallenstein and the emperor, which was prone to all sorts of suspicions and misunderstandings, leading to Wallenstein's ostracism in January 1634 and possibly also to his death in February. Meanwhile Spanish military units had landed in the empire, which, together with the imperial army of King Ferdinand of Hungary, besieged Nördlingen in August and managed to overwhelm the army of the Heilbronn League. The emperor was right in his assumption that he would now be able to renew the bonds with the renegade imperial estates that had previously cooperated with Sweden and France.[30]

Two months before the signing of the Peace of Prague, on 28 February 1635, the emperor and the prince-elector of Saxony had agreed on an armistice, a peace-making standard in those times. This meant more than just the end of a specific battle, a skirmish or the declaration of a military agreement; rather, it was seen as the beginning of universal peace or, as it was put then, the 'bessre[n] Verstellung der Friedens Tractaten'.[31]

When exactly did the negotiations in Prague begin? Kathrin Bierther has meticulously recapped the events that directly preceded the Peace of Prague. As early as the spring of 1633 – that is before the Battle of Nördlingen on 6 September 1634 – the emperor and Saxony held peace talks with the mediation of Denmark and Hessen-Darmstadt. Those talks would later lead to the 'Pirnaer Noteln' of 24 November 1634, a preliminary draft of the Peace of Prague. It was in June 1634 that the run-up to the Peace of Prague really began, when imperial and Saxon envoys met, with the mediation of Duke Franz Julius of Saxony-Lauenburg, in the Bohemian border town of Leitmeritz (today Czech Republic).[32]

The talks were continued in Pirna on 19 July 1634, watched by a suspicious Swedish queen. Yet the draft, which responded to a number of Saxon concerns, was not received very warmly, neither in Dresden nor in Vienna. The final text in Prague was swiftly written out in full, while many corrections and amendments had to be made to the initial draft of Pirna.[33]

---

[27] Duchhardt and Peters (eds), www.ieg-friedensvertraege.de.

[28] Ibid.

[29] Ibid.

[30] G. Schormann, *Dreißigjähriger Krieg 1618–1648* (Stuttgart, 2001); Christian Kunath, *Kursachsen im Dreißigjährigen Krieg* (Dresden, 2010).

[31] Duchhardt and Peters (eds), www.ieg-friedensvertraege.de.

[32] K. Bierther, 'Zur Vorgeschichte der Prager Friedensverhandlungen', in *Die Politik Maximilians I. von Bayern und seiner Verbündeten 1618–1651*, Part II/10 (4 vols, Munich and Vienna, 1997), vol. 1, pp. 25–236.

[33] *Pirnische und Pragische Friedens Pacten zusampt angestelter Collation und Anweisung der discrepantz und Unterscheids zwischen denenselben; Auf Maaß und Weise / wie davon in der hiernächstgesetzten Vorrede an*

Contents and Agreements

Many European peace treaties – 'big' as well as 'small' ones – were publicly presented, scientifically manipulated, translated and interpreted. Early modern scholars used peace treaties as evidence and sources for their analyses on history and international law. This was also true for the Peace of Prague. Among Protestants, the Peace of Prague did not enjoy a good press – at least not in the eighteenth century at the time of the 'Enlightenment'. The renowned law professor at the University of Göttingen, Johann Stephan Pütter, even called it 'luck' that France simultaneously started military actions against Spain, thus taking the previously negotiated peace immediately ad absurdum. The enlightened professor obviously distinguished between good peace and bad peace. The Peace of Prague, according to Pütter, did not fail because it failed to deliver peace. It failed, because it contained agreements that had to be prevented and annulled. For him, it was a biased peace. Pütter 'translated' the Peace of Prague therefore by fitting it into his historical world view that was shaped by religious schism. In 1786 he wrote:

> *Considering the predicament that the Peace of Prague had meant for the liberty of the German Empire and the Protestant religion, it was good luck for both of them that now even France intervened against the Spanish Netherlands, and that, after France had mediated an extension of the Swedish-Polish ceasefire by another 26 years (1635, September 12), the Swedish weapons gained the upper hand on the battlefield again.*[34]

What are the specific agreements in the Peace of Prague? Bierther groups them into four sections: 1) Ecclesiastics; 2) Judicial system and imperial Chamber Court; 3) Militia; and 4) Assecuratio pacis. This classification is justified. The peace agreement deals, first, with the practice of religion, church patrimony and property,[35] second, with the military[36] and third, with the constitution as well as the judiciary.[37] The treaty also intensively covers, fourth, the procedure of peace-making and contractual practice.[38] Another separate category contains the paragraphs on financing war and peace.[39]

The Peace of Prague was about the restoration of the 'old' nation, which, according to the text, had been based on integrity, tranquillity and 'Libertät'. The latter was a pivotal metaphor for justifying imperial international policies at the time,[40] which first showed up in

---

den Leser mit mehrem Bericht gethan wird (1636).

[34] J.S. Pütter, *Historische Entwickelung der heutigen Staatsverfassung des Teutschen Reichs, Zweiter Theil von 1558 bis 1740* (Göttingen, 1788), p. 41.

[35] For example ecclesiastical reservation, enfeoffment of the Protestant bishoprics, restitution of the Hildesheim bishopric to Braunschweig, religion and regiment forms in the imperial cities.

[36] I.e. imperial army, prisoners of war, billetings, burdens of war and contributions, as well as the laws of war.

[37] I.e. relationship between the Emperor and the estates, Imperial Chamber Court in Speyer, revisions, possibilities for appeals, coalitions, alliances.

[38] I.e. preliminary agreements, enforcement of the Peace of Lubeck, inclusion of foreign powers, involvement of (imperial) estates, publication and adoption, particularly by Saxony, accession arrangements, amnesty, peace objectives, accords of the estates, derogation, assistance, succour and compliance with the treaty.

[39] I.e. Palatinate and Count Palatinate Friedrich, costs of war, widow's claims, repayment claims by Tilly and the dukes of Mecklenburg, restitutions, war damage, assertions and claims by the interim owners, the occupation of the Empire as well as contributions.

[40] H. Duchhardt, '"Europa" als Begründungs- und Legitimationsformel in völkerrechtlichen Verträgen der Frühen Neuzeit', in H. Duchhardt, *Frieden im Europa der Vormoderne. Ausgewählte Aufsätze 1979–2011*, ed. by M. Espenhorst (Paderborn, 2012), pp. 111–20.

political and religious debates in the sixteenth century. 'Libertät' is a term that should not be translated as 'liberty' or 'privilege', even if many have done so. It mainly refers to the room for manoeuvre and effectiveness of policies by the imperial estates. Contrary to the term 'tranquillity', the 'teutsche Libertät' plays only a minor or no role at all in intergovernmental peace treaties. In the Prague peace treaty text the term shows up twice, in the 83rd paragraph, which talks about the 'wohlhergebrachten libertet, freiheit und hochheit',[41] aside from the quote above. In essence, by borrowing the term the emperor signalled his willingness to publicly respect the rights of the imperial estates. It is precisely the type of cooperative and consensus-oriented momentum that Johannes Burkhardt points out.[42]

The use of the term 'Libertät' identifies the signatories' goal to create a consensus between the emperor and the imperial princes and estates. However, one has to consider the fact that many of the princes' interests – in particular those of the Protestant princes – were discounted. This is not obvious at first glance, since the signatories also seemed to bridge opposing confessional positions. One of the crucial agreements of the peace, for example, was to adjourn the Edict of Restitution for 40 years. However, the emperor's demand to decide on all confessional questions himself, at minimum in all the Habsburg countries, sheds a somewhat different light on this agreement. Only Saxony was able to secure some of its own interests. The prince-elector received the Lower and Upper Lusatia as a Bohemian fiefdom as well as a number of cities separated from Magdeburg: Jüterborg, Dahme and Burg Querfurt (without the archdiocese). The archdiocese of Magdeburg and the principality of Halberstadt were awarded to the Saxons, as well.

Consequences and Results

The (imperial) estates had been important pillars of support for France and Sweden in the Old Empire. With the Peace of Prague, they turned towards the emperor, a move that laid the seeds for new conflicts, namely with France and Sweden. For them the alliance between the emperor and the imperial estates must have been a thorn in their sides. Sweden found itself on the defensive, not least because of the unpaid salaries for soldiers, while France decided to act and move from a covert to an open war against the Habsburgs. The charismatic Bernhard of Saxony-Weimar, a general of the Heilbronn League, went on to serve under the French. In the end, the Peace of Prague did not bring peace to Europe. On 19 May 1635, France declared war against Spain. Europe was not pacified: on the contrary, military conflicts even accelerated and amplified. The Peace of Prague had failed.

And yet: we can see the Peace of Prague as one step in the religious-political peace process that lasted for more than 100 years,[43] without calling it a flawless religious peace.[44] This peace process significantly started in 1555 in Augsburg. It then went via the Peace of Lübeck (1629 V 12/22) and the 1634 Peace Draft of Pirna to the Diet of Regensburg 1640, then to the Preliminary Treaty of Hamburg (1641 XII 25), finally reaching the Peace of Münster and Osnabrück in 1648. The peace execution day of Nuremberg 1650 and the Treaty of the

---

[41] Bierther, 'Prager Frieden', p. 1627 (see note 18).

[42] Burkhardt, *Dreißigjähriger Krieg*.

[43] M. Peters, 'Europäische Friedensprozesse der Vormoderne', *Jahrbuch für Europäische Geschichte*, 12 (2011): pp. 3–21.

[44] T. Brockmann, 'Die frühneuzeitlichen Religionsfrieden – Normhorizont, Instrumentarium und Probleme in vergleichender Perspektive', in C. Kampmann and M. Lanzinner (eds), *L'art de la paix. Kongresswesen und Friedensstiftung im Zeitalter des Westfälischen Friedens* (Münster, 2011), pp. 575–611.

Pyrenees (1659 XI 7) also need to be included. Looking at the Prague treaty text makes it quite obvious that there was an interconnection between all those different peace-making attempts, some, such as the Peace of Augsburg, Passau, Lübeck and Pirna, were explicitly mentioned in the text. The Treaty of Regensburg of 13 October 1630, between the emperor and France, was also mentioned (§ 22). Moreover, the convention of an imperial diet (§ 25) was announced.

The failure of early modern peace agreements was by no means an isolated case. Negotiations were based on a complex system of norms, habits, symbols, ideas and assessments. Heinz Duchhardt sees the chronically deficient and unimaginative structure of early modern peace treaty practice and theory as one reason for the 'Bellizität' (belligerence) of the era.[45] Certainly, early modern diplomats and politicians managed considerable achievements in peacekeeping and peace-building. They created peace-securing instruments and a common framework in international law.

Yet most of those early modern peace agreements were short-lived. More than 2,000 'intergovernmental' peace treaties were signed in Europe between 1450 and 1789.[46] None of these supra-regional agreements led to lasting peace. Not even the Peace of Westphalia created anything like a 'Westphalian System'[47] that would have lasted through modern times. This is why Michael Rohrschneider rightly calls even the Peace of Münster a failed peace settlement.[48]

Selected Bibliography

Albrecht, D., *Die auswärtige Politik Maximilians von Bayern: 1618–1635* (Göttingen, 1962).

Asch, R.G., *Thirty Years War: The Holy Roman Empire and Europe, 1618–1648* (New York, 1997).

Bierther, K., 'Zur Vorgeschichte der Prager Friedensverhandlungen', in *Die Politik Maximilians I. von Bayern und seiner Verbündeten 1618–1651*, Part II/10 (4 vols, Munich and Vienna, 1997), vol. 1, pp. 25–236.

Bierther, K., 'Der Prager Frieden von 1635', in *Die Politik Maximilians I. von Bayern und seiner Verbündeten 1618–1651*, Part II/10 (4 vols, Munich and Vienna, 1997), vol. 4.

Burkhardt, J., *Vollendung und Neuorientierung des frühmodernen Reiches 1648–1763* (Stuttgart, 2006).

Fuchs, R.-P., *Ein 'Medium zum Frieden'. Die Normaljahrsregel und die Beendigung des Dreißigjährigen Krieges* (Munich, 2010).

Helfferich, T., *The Thirty Years War: A Documentary History* (Indianapolis, 2009).

Holborn, H., *A History of Modern Germany: The Reformation* (New Jersey, 1982).

Kaiser, M., 'Der Prager Frieden von 1635. Anmerkungen zu einer Aktenedition', *Zeitschrift für historische Forschung*, 28 (2001): pp. 277–97.

Kampmann, C., *Europa und das Reich im Dreißigjährigen Krieg: Geschichte eines Konflikts* (Stuttgart, 2008).

Parker, G. (ed.), *The Thirty Years' War* (London, 1984).

---

[45] H. Duchhardt, 'Zwischenstaatliche Friedens- und Ordnungskonzepte im Ancien Régime: Idee und Realität', in R.G. Asch, W. Voß and M. Wrede (eds), *Frieden und Krieg in der Frühen Neuzeit. Die europäische Staatenordnung und die außereuropäische Welt* (Munich, 2001), pp. 37–45, here p. 43.

[46] Duchhardt and Peters (eds), www.ieg-friedensverträge.de.

[47] H. Duchhardt, 'Das "Westfälische System": Realität und Mythos', in *Frieden im Europa*, pp. 151–9.

[48] M. Rohrschneider, *Der gescheiterte Frieden von Münster. Spaniens Ringen mit Frankreich auf dem Westfälischen Friedenskongress (1643–1649)* (Münster, 2007).

Repgen, K., *Die römische Kurie und der westfälische Friede: Papst, Kaiser und Reich, 1521–1644* (2 vols, Tübingen, 1962).

Repgen, K., *Dreißigjähriger Krieg und Westfälischer Friede. Studien und Quellen*, ed. F. Bosbach and C. Kampmann (Paderborn and Munich, 1998).

Wilson, P., *Europe's Tragedy. A History of the Thirty Years War* (London, 2009).

23

The Settlement of 1648 for the German Empire

Axel Gotthard

'This was the low point'? – The Traditional Negative Judgements

When in the 1860s and 1870s the pro-Prussian mainstream of the German *Bildungsbürgertum* set about creating the narrative of a German nation state, the Peace of Westphalia stood for everything negative in German history that had to be overcome: the impotence of the nation and its fragmentation. The peace treaties of 1648 occupied a central and negative place in the national master narratives that highlighted 'France the perpetual enemy'[1] and 'Prussia's German mission'.[2]

Indignant following the Rhine crisis when nascent nationalism had lost its naïve aspiration to make all nations happy, and then disenchanted after 1848, relying now on *Realpolitik* and the Prussian spiked helmet, the newly emerging discipline of history persistently and passionately invoked tradition to bestow a venerable gloss on 'Prussia's German mission'. Since myths operate according to a binary code, a contrasting image was needed. The empire had to fall apart after 1648 so that the Prussian phoenix could rise from its ashes.

Numerous textbooks fixed this pro-Prussian legend very firmly in the nation's mind. Works from the decades around 1900 consistently asserted two incompatible consequences of the Peace of Westphalia: on the one hand it led to the petrification of the empire, as can be seen from the constant use of similes from the semantic field of geriatrics and the art of embalming. On the other hand the peace treaty led to the disintegration of the empire into a collection of individual sovereign states; it 'crumbled', 'melted away', 'dissolved' (terms which were often used in conjunction with the metaphors of petrification and rigor mortis).[3]

---

[1] The recurrent elements of the narrative are as follows: the victorious power of 1648 had ruined its eastern neighbour by disintegrating it into a confederation of states and by gaining the potential to intervene in German affairs at will as a guarantor of the peace; furthermore the Alsace had been given away in 1648. The only part of this that is true is that the vagueness of the territorial regulations regarding Alsace later encouraged Louis XIV's reunion policy. The question whether the guarantee of the treaty by external powers established a notion of collective European security will be discussed later in this book. It is not possible to deduce an exclusive French right of intervention from the obligation of the *transactionis consortes* to observe and protect the regulations of the treaty (IPO art. XVII §§ 4–7).

[2] For the twin myths in German historiography of 'decay of the empire since 1648' and 'Prussia's German mission', see A. Gotthard, 'Preußens deutsche Sendung', in H. Altrichter, K. Herbers and H. Neuhaus (eds), *Mythen in der Geschichte* (Freiburg, 2004), pp. 321–69.

[3] See Gotthard, *Sendung*.

The ideas that were once designed to make the foundation of the Prussian-dominated German Empire of 1871 appear inevitable and place it in a certain historical perspective, survived this empire for more than half a century. The leading historians of the Weimar Republic invariably insisted that the Peace of Westphalia marked the nadir of German history: 'This was the low point, the lowest point in our history'.[4] Another schoolbook asserted categorically: 'The clauses of the treaty will weigh Germany down in perpetuity like a lead weight'.[5] This was no doubt rather depressing for the students, though they could at least consider themselves fortunate for not having to memorise the history of the empire:

> 'the empire existed in name only: in reality from 1648 on there was simply a multitude of autonomous states ... Thus after 1648 one cannot speak of a history of the German empire, but merely of the history of these individual states.[6]

The Peace of Westphalia was frequently compared with that other *Schandfrieden* (ignoble peace), the Peace of Versailles.

'The Führer speaks. About the future liquidation of the Peace of Westphalia', Joseph Goebbels wrote on 3 May 1937. And on 29 February 1940, he noted: 'A grand formal reception in Münster. In the Friedenssaal. This is where the Peace of Westphalia was signed. We are going to rescind it.'[7]

When Hitler claimed on 30 January 1940 in the Berlin *Sportpalast* of the Western powers that 'their war aim is [to re-create] the Germany of 1648',[8] he could count on the mobilising effect of the term '1648': after all, condemnation of 1648 had been implanted into the minds of his audience long ago during their school days.

'We are going to rescind it', Hitler had promised.[9] Instead Prussia was obliterated after the end of World War II and the *Wirtschaftswunderland* (the Federal Republic, the country of the economic miracle) equated patriotism, which is natural in other civilised countries, with chauvinism. The myth of 'Prussia's German mission' lost its motivating and legitimating power and began to fade.

Surprisingly, however, the corollary of the alleged 'collapse of the empire' lived on. Under the influence of the Franco-German alliance, the idea of being 'at the mercy of the hereditary enemy', which people had believed fervently before 1945, was now set aside. The allegedly destructive impact of the Peace of Westphalia was no longer attributed to perfidious French manipulation. Yet the rest remained. The myth of the alleged collapse of the empire survived the hereditary enmity between Germany and France and developed a momentum of its own. Historians did not think it was worth bothering to re-examine the treaty; they were quite simply convinced that the traditional view of 1648 was accurate.

It is surprising how late the Bonn Republic – itself a federative structure that did not want to be a nation state and that dreamed about merging into Europe – discovered that emphatically federative early modern empire as a predecessor, an empire which also

---

[4] E. Marcks, 'Tiefpunkte des deutschen Schicksals in der Neuzeit', in E. Marcks, *Geschichte und Gegenwart* (Stuttgart, Berlin and Leipzig, 1925), p. 91. Ibid., p. 89: 'the predecessor of the bondage of Versailles'. Erich Marcks was at that time regarded as one of Germany's leading historians.

[5] M. Stoll, *Deutsches Werden*, Mittelstufe, vol. 3, 2nd edn (Bamberg, 1931), p. 99.

[6] J. Habisreutinger, *Ebners Geschichte der Neuzeit*, 22nd edn (Bamberg, 1930), p. 49.

[7] E. Fröhlich (ed.), *Die Tagebücher von Joseph Goebbels*, vol.1/4 (Munich, 1998), s. v. 3 May 1937; vol. 1/7, s. v. 29 February 1940.

[8] Quoted after F.A. Six (ed.), *Der Westfälische Friede von 1648. Deutsche Textausgabe der Friedensverträge von Münster und Osnabrück* (Berlin, 1940), p. VI.

[9] See note 7 above.

had not been a national state. The old negative views were still heard, particularly those concerning the Peace of Westphalia. Even legal and constitutional historians did not know any better, even Fritz Hartung in his constitutional history of Germany. For Hartung, too, the empire as a whole had been dead since 1648 (because it was, of course, simultaneously petrified and disintegrating); it only survived as a collection of individual parts (above all Prussia!). The historian of the empire after 1648, says Hartung, thus has 'to confine himself to recounting the more or less detailed story of the comic traits of the petrification process'.[10] In the *Deutsche Rechtsgeschichte* by Panitz and Eckhardt the chapter on 'the dissolution of the empire' does not begin with the year 1803 or 1806 as might be logical, but with a synopsis of the terms of the 1648 treaty![11] Otto Kimminich's *Deutsche Verfassungsgeschichte* went even further and in a preposterous inflation of the term sovereignty, which normally does not have a superlative, he talks about 'absolute and untrammelled sovereignty of the territorial rulers' after 1648.[12] Who could blame foreign writers, including English scholars,[13] for such publications, if they retailed that persistent legend!

Alongside the notion of 'disintegration' the related notion of the gradual 'petrification' of the empire also continued to run through historical writing. In 1991 a group of constitutional historians employed the even stronger notion that the imperial constitution had been 'set in stone': Central Europe had been shackled by a 'petrified' constitution since 1648. The development of the empire had been so utterly blocked that nothing moved at all; the settlement of 1648 left no possibility for development.[14]

If we turn to Fritz Dickmann's monograph on the Peace of Westphalia, first published in 1959 and still regarded as the standard work, we find the following conclusion at the end of 500 pages: 'This peace was national disaster for our nation and for the Holy Roman Empire ... it marked the beginning of a deadly disease to which it ultimately succumbed ... The year 1648 is one of the most catastrophic years of our history'.[15]

It is therefore hardly surprising that compendia and school textbooks still repeat the same old story. Almost all the textbooks published in the Federal Republic since 1949 mention the year 1648 as the beginning of the sovereignty of the imperial estates (*Reichsstände*) and even a printed proposal for a panel painting in 2006 summarised the situation under the following headings: 'Sovereignty of the Imperial Princes', 'the Emperor's loss of power', 'fragmentation of the Empire'.[16] A year later the *dtv-Atlas Weltgeschichte* listed the following under the heading 'results of the Peace of Westphalia': 'absolute sovereignty of the Imperial Estates, the Empire disintegrates into an association of states'.[17] The Peace of Westphalia remained the 'death certificate of the Holy Roman Empire'[18] for 'after the Peace of Westphalia

---

[10] F. Hartung, *Deutsche Verfassungsgeschichte vom 15. Jahrhundert bis zur Gegenwart*, 9th edn (Stuttgart, 1969), p. 152.

[11] H. Planitz and K.A. Eckhardt, *Deutsche Rechtsgeschichte*, 4th edn (Cologne and Vienna, 1981), pp. 272–3.

[12] O. Kimminich, *Deutsche Verfassungsgeschichte* (Frankfurt/M., 1970), p. 215.

[13] See B. Straumann, 'The Peace of Westphalia as a Secular Constitution', *Constellations*, xv (2008): pp. 173–88. The author mentions some doubts, does not recognise that the concept of 'sovereignty' simply does not fit into the history of the early modern German empire.

[14] Documentation and discussion of a presentation by Georg Schmidt in R. Mußgnug (ed.), *Wendemarken in der deutschen Verfassungsgeschichte* (Berlin, 1993), pp. 45–83.

[15] F. Dickmann, *Der Westfälische Frieden* (Münster, 1959), p. 494.

[16] J. Cornelissen et al. (eds), *Mosaik. Der Geschichte auf der Spur, B7. Lehrmaterialien* (Munich, Düsseldorf and Stuttgart, 2006), p. 67.

[17] H. Kinder and W. Hilgemann, *dtv-Atlas Weltgeschichte*, vol. 1, 39th edn (Munich, 2007), p. 255.

[18] J. Haller, *Die Epochen der deutschen Geschichte. Neue, durchgesehene Ausgabe* (Esslingen, 1959), p. 193.

one can no longer speak of the history of the German Empire, but only of the history of the individual sovereign states in Germany'.[19]

Can it be said that the Peace of Westphalia created territories? 'Germany is divided into 361 sovereign states', a 1993 handbook states, 'there were eight prince-electors, 69 ecclesiastic Imperial Estates and 96 secular imperial estates, 61 imperial cities and about 1,500 principalities, all in all 1,789 autonomous territories, a scatter of principalities and free cities.'[20] 'In addition to the larger secular and ecclesiastical territories in Germany, there were now numerous free imperial cities and a multitude of small and miniscule territories.'[21]

It might have strengthened the credibility of such nonsense outside the academic field that political scientists traditionally claim that the Peace of Westphalia had a similar impact on the rest of Europe's states: 'Ever since then, Europe remained diverse and inconsistent.'[22]

Historians of the modern period, as well as political scientists, social scientists and experts in international law, are fond of organising the past by declaring 1648 to be a universally suitable terminus for the beginning of the modern period. In such anachronistic present-centred accounts, the 'modern state system' originates in 1648; indeed, the 'peace treaty of superlatives' not only marks the 'effective beginning of our international system', but of all civilised history: for example every 'central government' now 'had a fixed location, a capital!'[23] The Peace of Westphalia is 'the starting point if we want to talk about either inter-governmental and domestic conditions, relationships or hegemonies'.[24]

For some years now political scientists and politicians have held that the state system which fell apart in 1989, or might yet fall apart in our own time,[25] was created in exactly 1648, and that we are currently living 'beyond Westphalia'.[26] Leading politicians also disseminate the clichés which their speech writers compose for them: the long-serving former German foreign minister Joseph ('Joschka') Fischer, for example, was fond of grandly reflecting that 'in 1989 the political system which had been established as a result of the Peace of Westphalia collapsed'.[27] Anyone who has become accustomed to allowing the prelude to modernity to begin with the year 1648, might also believe that this same year marked a profound rupture in the development of the empire which had clear negative implications.

At the same time there have been attempts to re-evaluate the peace treaties in recent years. In the first instance this happened because in the war-weary years after 1945 people

---

[19] K.-H. Neubig and E. Riechert (eds), *Geschichtliches Werden. Mittelstufe*, vol. 2, 3rd edn (Bamberg, 1974), p. 154. 'A noteworthy Imperial history … no longer exists after 1648': A. Sellen, *Geschichte kurz & klar* (Donauwörth, 1994), p. 142.

[20] P. Beyersdorf, *Geschichts-Gerüst von den Anfängen bis zur Gegenwart* (Hollfeld, 1993), p. 61.

[21] G. Frank, W. Höfft and W. Wulf (eds), *Grundzüge der Geschichte von der Frühgeschichte Europas bis zur Weltpolitik der Gegenwart* (Frankfurt/M., Berlin and Munich, 1971), p. 143.

[22] E. Krippendorff, *Staat und Krieg. Die historische Logik politischer Unvernunft* (Frankfurt/M., 1985), p. 272.

[23] E. Wolfrum, *Krieg und Frieden in der Neuzeit. Vom Westfälischen Frieden bis zum Zweiten Weltkrieg* (Darmstadt, 2003), pp. 3 and 33; Krippendorff, *Staat und Krieg*, p. 272; Wolfrum, *Krieg und Frieden*, p. 38.

[24] D. Kinkelbur, 'Den Krieg kaputtdenken – Zur Not-wendigkeit [sic] der Ergänzung politikwissenschaftlicher Fragestellungen durch polito-logische [sic] Vorgehensweisen', *Ethik und Sozialwissenschaften*, viii (1997), p. 280.

[25] To recall the main points: because of the transfer of 'national' sovereignty rights to supra-national institutions und because of the impotence of 'the state' in the face of international economic enterprises.

[26] G.M. Lyons and M. Mastanduno (eds), *Beyond Westphalia?* (Baltimore, 1995). Or do we still have to exorcise the fatal remnants of the Westphalian heritage out of the current political system? C.W. Kegley Jr. and G.A. Raymond (eds), *Exorcising the Ghost of Westphalia* (New Jersey, 2002).

[27] *Frankfurter Allgemeine Zeitung*, 7 October 2004, p. 42.

discovered that they were – quite simply – instruments designed to serve peace. This was not, however, accompanied by a turn in diplomatic history[28] towards the history of ideas and mentalities. What did pre-modern decision-makers think about peace or about war? On what conceptual premises was the intensive belligerence (*Bellizität*) of the early modern era based and which communicative purposes did the grandiloquent peace rhetoric in Westphalia have to fulfil? These kinds of questions about the conceptual background of the minutiae of diplomatic negotiations still need to be answered. The post-war era took the tercentenary of 1648 as a welcome opportunity to praise peace, 'Pax optima rerum'.[29] The evaluation of the constitutional regulations of '1648' did not, however, change in the slightest.[30] The advertisements for the jubilee-exhibition of 1998 again used the legend 'Pax optima rerum', together with three peace doves for good measure. Once again there was no re-assessment of the meaning of the peace instruments for the political system of the empire. Indeed the organisers of the exhibition were not interested in the empire: we were after all not provincials anymore, we were good Europeans. 'The peace of Münster and Osnabrück', they declared, 'was a European event. The ratification of the Peace of Westphalia marked the beginning of modern Europe', and so 'Europe celebrates the Peace of Westphalia'.[31] This kind of view has also shaped much of the research into the peace treaties over the last decade.[32] Westphalia became a European *lieu de mémoire*.

Over the last 50 years the 42 volumes of the *Acta Pacis Westphalicae*, published by the *Vereinigung zur Erforschung der Neueren Geschichte*,[33] have helped us to analyse the treaties more closely. This editorial enterprise was also initially shaped by European thinking. Thus we are presented with the French and Swedish instructions, but not those of any imperial estate. It was never even envisaged that the imperial estates would be included in the volumes devoted to 'correspondence'. Even so, the *Acta Pacis Westphalicae* do contain

---

[28] A. Gotthard, 'Krieg und Frieden in der Vormoderne', *Historische Zeitschrift*, Beiheft 44 (2007): pp. 67–94.

[29] This inscription on a commemorative coin of 1648 became the motto of the commemoration year 1948. See E. Ortlieb and M. Schnettger (eds), *Bibliographie zum Westfälischen Frieden* (Münster, 1996), section V (1948: pp. 186–9).

[30] Even if someone tried to re-evaluate and argued that the Peace of Westphalia turned the Empire into a small-scale Europe, they nonetheless carried forward the old prejudices: what qualified the 'already disintegrated German Empire', this alleged 'union of sovereign states', to become the 'model case of an international organisation', was its supposed 'federal orientation': K. von Raumer, ' Das Erbe des Westfälischen Friedens. Betrachtungen zu seiner 300. Wiederkehr', in E. Hövel (ed.), *Pax optima rerum. Beiträge zur Geschichte des Westfälischen Friedens 1648* (Münster, 1948), p. 48.

[31] These are the first sentences of the prefaces to the exhibition catalogue: K. Bußmann and H. Schilling (eds), *1648. Krieg und Frieden in Europa* (Munich, 1998).

[32] Apart from the significance of '1648' for the formation of the modern European powers, the new scholarly preoccupation with communication and media stimulated interest in the internal communications within the peace conference and the public commentaries on events at Münster and Osnabrück. 'Westphalia' was naturally also recognised as a venue for intercultural encounters and the nodal point of transnational networks. That did not, however, translate into an interest in the political system of the empire.

[33] This is an extraordinarily successful editorial enterprise with three different series: *Instruktionen* [instructions], *Korrespondenzen* [correspondence], and *Protokolle* [protocols]. For further information see M. Lanzinner, 'Die Acta pacis Westphalicae und die Geschichtswissenschaft', in G. Braun, C. Kampmann, M. Lanzinner and M. Rohrschneider (eds), *L'art de la paix. Kongresswesen und Friedensstiftung im Zeitalter des Westfälischen Friedens* (Münster, 2011), pp. 31–71. There also is a monograph series to accompany the edition which currently comprises 34 volumes, all dealing in one way or another with the peace conferences. The volumes on the politics of the emperor, of some of the imperial estates, of the electors, of the council of cities and of the confessional corpora are of particular relevance to the subject of this chapter.

some material on the role of the members of the empire: they document the work of the council of imperial cities in Osnabrück, much of the work of the college of electors and of the council of the princes in Osnabrück, and some of the work of the Corpus Catholicorum. Since negotiations with the council of princes in Münster and the Corpus Evangelicorum are missing altogether, it is difficult to reconstruct the struggle to negotiate the future shape of the imperial constitution.[34] Moreover, editions of printed sources do not directly influence the popular conception of history or the collective memory.

Even scholarly studies only do that after a considerable delay. The political system of the early modern empire only came to be a popular subject of research in the autumn of the Bonn Republic; this research flourished roughly between 1970 and 1990. There were numerous authorities on the early modern empire in this generation of (largely emeritus) professors and they knew of course that the empire remained alive beyond the year 1648, that it neither fell apart nor became petrified. When they wrote about interesting new developments in the late seventeenth and eighteenth centuries, they implicitly denied the clichés of petrification and decay – but they rarely did so explicitly. Scholarly insinuations and learned footnotes[35] did not make much impact on the established popular perception of the past. Axel Gotthard and Johannes Burkhardt both tried explicitly to deconstruct the myth of the decay of the empire.[36] The history of the critical reception of these two attempts to correct the popular myth remains to be written.

If we contrast what historians on the one hand and political scientists and experts in international law, as well as politicians, on the other hand usually claim about the Peace of Westphalia we find an interesting black and white contrast. The historians claim that the empire had no real history after 1648. The others argue that the Peace of Westphalia is the starting point for any consideration of modern European history. The individual evaluations differ, but on one point they all agree: the Peace of Westphalia marked a profound rupture. Is that in fact the case?[37]

The Second Religious Peace

The same pro-Prussian authors who claimed that the empire perished with the Peace of Westphalia appreciated as Protestants that it afforded protection to Lutherans and Calvinists. 'The Peace of Westphalia was purely destructive', declared Fritz Hartung, 'the peace treaty solved only one problem, the religious one'.[38] Solving the confessional problem but destroying the empire – can these two positions be maintained in the light of the current state of research? In fact it was the other way round.

---

[34] Lanzinner, *Acta pacis Westphalicae*, p. 60 emphasises: 'in the volumes so far the imperial level has been less strongly illuminated than the European level'.

[35] See D. Croxton and A. Tischer (eds), *The Peace of Westphalia. A Historical Dictionary* (Westport/London, 2002), s. v. Landeshoheit: 'German estates did not gain sovereignty'. According to the acknowledgements, this entry was written by Guido Braun.

[36] See A. Gotthard, *Das Alte Reich 1495–1806* (originally 2003; 4th edn, Darmstadt, 2009), pp. 96–107; A. Gotthard, *Preußens deutsche Sendung*; J. Burkhardt, 'Der Westfälische Friede und die Legende von der landesherrlichen Souveränität', in J. Engelbrecht and S. Laux (eds), *Landes- und Reichsgeschichte. Festschrift für Hansgeorg Molitor zum 65. Geburtstag* (Bielefeld, 2004), pp. 199–220.

[37] Actually it is not, not regarding the European political system, international law, or the history of the empire: only the latter can be discussed here.

[38] Hartung, *Verfassungsgeschichte*, p. 148 and p. 33.

The fifth article of the *Instrumentum Pacis Osnabrugense* (IPO) opens with a brief preamble which makes clear that the 'complaints made by electors, princes and estates of both confessions were the real cause and occasion for the present war' ['praesenti bello magnam partem gravamina, quae inter utriusque religionis electores, principes et status imperii vertebantur, causam et occasionem dederunt'.] The Thirty Years' War had for the most part been triggered by the confessional *gravamina* (complaints). Contemporaries associated such *gravamina* with quite specific ideas: around 1600, for example, the confessional parties had confronted each other with lists of *gravamina* and insisted that their opponents first of all had to deal with the issues that were disputed before normal political business in the empire could resume. These *gravamina* argued from the basis of the Peace of Augsburg and their authors denounced the way that their opponents had allegedly twisted and abused its provisions. The diplomats at Osnabrück wanted to construct their attempt to remedy the problems of the empire on a convincing diagnosis of its problems and their analysis of the origins of the Thirty Years' War told them that it had started as a religious war. They believed that for a long time the war had been about the 'proper' interpretation and application of the Peace of Augsburg.

The Peace of Westphalia thus can be seen as a second religious peace. It is much more elaborate and complex than the first religious peace in 1555, and for that reason this chapter cannot give a complete account of all of the numerous regulations it contained.[39] The first religious peace had sought to shroud many disputed points in rather vague words designed to promote compromise instead of clearly resolving them. The second peace treaty aimed to resolve all the issues, to allow no room for interpretation and to be as detailed as possible. The fundamental principle of the first religious peace, that the religious faith of the prince of an imperial estate should determine the faith of the population of his territory, was now relativised by the introduction of a base date, 1 January 1624.[40] The confessional status quo that prevailed in a territory on this date could not henceforth be altered by the ruler. No prince could promote the degree of confessionalisation in his territory beyond the status quo of 1624.

The first religious peace declared the two confessions that it recognised – Catholicism and the Augsburg Confession – to be equal, but it did not establish their legal equality.[41] The claim that it did so, which is frequently found in the scholarly literature, simply misses the flexible character of the first peace treaty. The Peace of Westphalia laid down that parity was a fundamental principle. For some institutions of the empire a strict parity of numbers was envisaged; for the imperial diet a procedural parity sufficed. The treaty even tried to provide for the eventuality that, despite its extraordinary detail, it had failed to provide a solution to some future problem: in such cases the resolution was to be reached in the spirit of 'aequalitas exacta' ['exact equality'] between the three confessions that were now recognised (Catholic, Lutheran and Reformed or Calvinist).

Was the second peace treaty, in particular the fifth article of the IPO, really as successful as most historians nowadays claim? Because the last one and a half centuries of the early modern empire were not well explored until recently, we have only known since the 1990s[42] that imperial politics was not 'de-confessionalised'. Just as after the first religious peace, there

---

[39] Further information and a bibliography: A. Gotthard, *Der Augsburger Religionsfrieden* (Münster, 2004), pp. 479–94.

[40] The contemporary term was 'Normaljahr' (normal year).

[41] Legal profession speaks of 'Parität' (parity). On the first religious peace and the principle of parity, see Gotthard, *Religionsfrieden*, pp. 162–70 and the index.

[42] See G. Haug-Moritz, 'Kaisertum und Parität. Reichspolitik und Konfessionen nach dem Westfälischen Frieden', *Zeitschrift für historische Forschung*, xix (1992): pp. 445–82; J. Luh, *Unheiliges*

were now soon new complaints. Religious processions remained literally life-threatening experiences. Stone-throwing was not uncommon, sometimes there was even gunfire: in Siegen, for example, four people were killed on Corpus Christi 1712.

We should, however, keep things in perspective. There was no religious persecution comparable to what occurred in France under Louis XIV; there was no equivalent of the Anglo-Irish religious controversies (which still endure today). After 1648 the confessional question never again threatened the very existence of the empire in the way that it had done in 1619. Can this be attributed to the quality of the IPO? The experience of those 30 years of conflict no doubt taught contemporaries that engaging in military conflict for the sake of the highest principles or ultimate truth could at best lead to pyrrhic victories but was certain to cost immeasurable human suffering. On the European continent armed conflict in pursuit of religious truth was no longer politically correct. And then in the last decades of the century the Enlightenment began to develop. The second religious peace had to prove itself in an entirely different mental and intellectual environment to the Peace of Augsburg.

The Balance of Power in the Imperial Constitution is Re-Adjusted

Was the confessional problem solved? Imperial politics were only gradually de-confessionalised after 1648. Having discussed the rather overrated passages of the peace treaties, let us now turn to the allegedly harmful ones! They are purportedly to be found in the eighth article of the IPO.[43]

If we examine this infamous article, it becomes immediately apparent that it represents a very small part of the Treaty of Osnabrück. Could so few words really have had such far-reaching consequences? Each single statement must be extraordinarily significant, one might think. So what do we find in this article? First of all the imperial estates get 'confirmation of their old rights and prerogatives, their liberty, free exercise of the *ius territoriale* in ecclesiastical and political affairs, their traditional rights as rulers, their regalian rights and their property' ['in antiquis suis iuribus, praerogativis, libertate, privilegiis, libero iuris territorialis tam in ecclesiasticis quam politicis exercitio, ditionibus, regalibus horumque omnium possessione, stabiliti firmatique sunto']. In other words, at the beginning of this allegedly revolutionary clause we find the confirmation of the old law.

There is one element in what is confirmed that has always stimulated the imaginations of readers: the ominous *ius territoriale* – a rather unfamiliar but by no means uncommon term. It is in this term that legions of harsh critics claimed to find the principle of sovereignty. Is this plausible? Even the context argues against this: the words *ius territoriale* are preceded by the archaic term 'prerogatives' and followed by not exactly modern 'regalian rights'. The meaning of this enumeration has to be considered as a whole. The 'teutsche Libertät' (German liberty) is made concrete, and its individual features are articulated; the conventional *Landesherrschaft*[44] (territorial regimen) of the imperial estates is confirmed.

Römisches Reich. Der konfessionelle Gegensatz 1648 bis 1806 (Potsdam, 1995); J. Whaley, *Germany and the Holy Roman Empire, 1493–1806*, 2 vols (Cambridge, 2012), vol. 2, pp. 150–57, 383–6.

[43] A. Oschmann (ed.), *Acta Pacis Westfalicae Serie III Abt. B. vol. 1,1* (Münster, 1998), here p. 130. This volume contains the critical edition of the IPO.

[44] In the course of the eighteenth century the term 'Landeshoheit' gained currency. Contemporary translations of the IPO use the term 'LandsObrigkeit', as does the translation in the critical edition: G. Braun, A. Oschmann and K. Repgen (eds), *Acta Pacis Westphalicae Serie III Abt. B, vol. 1,2* (Münster, 2007), pp. 368–76.

There is no mention of sovereignty. Indeed the French word *souveraineté* would never have been translated as *ius territoriale*: the most common Latin term would have been *maiestas*.

Those who later wrote about the treaty were unrestrained in their fury and indignation at its implications for Germany, but without cause: the first paragraph of the eighth article does not contain anything exciting or novel; it simply reinforces the old law, the conventional privileges, and gives the imperial estates nothing new. Elsewhere – particularly in respect of the confessional regulations – something was taken away, namely the absolute authority of rulers to dispose of the religious faith of their subjects. The base year specified in the fifth article of the IPO article in reality relativised the *ius reformandi* which the treaty still formally proclaimed.

What were the nefarious innovations in the second paragraph of the eighth article which allegedly destroyed the empire? The imperial estates were allowed to forge alliances with each other and with foreign countries, as long as those alliances served their own protection and were not aimed against the emperor and empire. The right to participate 'in omnibus deliberationibus super negotiis Imperii' is confirmed: imperial policy needed their approval. Some of these *negotiis* are mentioned explicitly and are highlighted (*praesertim*), for example, decisions on war and peace or alliances, imperial taxes and the promulgation or interpretation of imperial laws: hence the myth that in 1648 the emperor had been disempowered at the expense of the imperial diet. It is still often asserted that the competences of the imperial diet were vastly extended in the Peace of Westphalia,[45] especially regarding the foreign policy of the empire. In reality, no early modern emperor could conduct foreign policy unilaterally. The first imperial electoral capitulation (*Wahlkapitulation*) of 1519 envisaged, for example, that the emperor needed the agreement of the college of electors to form alliances with foreign countries or within the empire. In serious foreign policy issues, of course, the electors tended to defer to the greater competence of the imperial diet, and raising money at meetings of the electors was naturally out of the question.[46] There was an exception to this rule, though, in the 1620s and 1630s: the imperial diet ceased to meet, the pressure of war began to tell, no end of decisions needed to be made. The emperors acted autocratically[47] or after discussion with the electors, whose meetings took on the character of European peace congresses and who 'granted' the emperor an imperial tax at their meeting in 1636.[48] The Peace of Westphalia put a stop to such a centralised mode of rule without the imperial diet. It did not create anything new in fiscal terms or in matters of foreign policy, but it criticised the excesses of the most recent past. In Westphalia one tried to cope with the consequences of war, cleared away war damage, which included constitutional anomalies created by wartime circumstances. There was nothing innovative about that.

In reality the imperial estates had been practising the much-cited right to form alliances granted in 1648 for a long time. The Thirty Years' War had been fought out between the Protestant Union and the Catholic League, two German alliances. Such alliances, leagues and unions had existed in profusion in previous centuries and some of them had even included foreign countries. Thus the Protestant Union had contracts with England, France

---

[45] But see now J. Burkhardt, *Vollendung und Neuorientierung des frühmodernen Reichs 1648–1763* (Stuttgart, 2006), p. 47: 'The competences of the Imperial Diet were described and expanded'. See also Whaley, *Germany and the Holy Roman Empire*, vol. 2, pp. 53–65.

[46] See A. Gotthard, *Säulen des Reiches. Die Kurfürsten im frühneuzeitlichen Reichsverband*, vol. 1 (Husum, 1999), pp. 199–475.

[47] This had been the perception of many, even Catholic contemporaries. The extent to which the two Ferdinands personally saw it the same way and to which this was intended remains an open question. The latest studies (Lothar Höbelt 2008, Thomas Brockmann 2011) show the two emperors of the Thirty Years' War as driven by threatening surroundings.

[48] See Gotthard, *Säulen des Reiches*, pp. 378–83.

and the Netherlands. One remembered this venerable tradition[49] when one embedded the right to form alliances in the peace treaty. They also thought about the distribution of power within empire: 'for preservation and security' ['pro conservatione et securitate'] the imperial estates were allowed to form alliances for the purpose of self-protection. This was far from new, but still it was relevant in 1648. The Peace of Prague in 1635 had dissolved 'all unions, leagues and federations' ['alle und jede uniones, ligae, foedera']. The two emperors during the Thirty Years' War had repeatedly denounced all alliances formed without their permission as treason and 'secession'. Even in this respect the 1648 treaty restored normality and eradicated consequences of the war. The IPO's eighth article thus reads like a counterpoint to the Peace of Prague.

Of course, the European context would also change in time. The emerging system of international law would take the sovereignty of the individual states as its foundation. Does that mean that the right to form alliances established in 1648 had consequences that had not been foreseen at the peace negotiations? This cannot be denied entirely. The imperial estates were not, however, accepted as sovereign by the other European powers after 1648. The electors in particular felt insulted because their 'pre-eminence' was not recognised in ceremonial terms. In their electoral association (*Kurverein*) they might like to stylise themselves eloquently as guardians of the Christian West – yet the traditional leadership role of the empire was not recognised in the emerging system of international law and these pillars of the empire ('Säulen des Reiches') were not simply somehow less sovereign than other European rulers: they were not sovereign at all.[50] Even in the minds of contemporaries, the right to form alliances that was established in 1648 did not create sovereignty.[51]

The third paragraph, finally, lists the *negotia remissa*, the points to be discussed, that were not dealt with in the peace negotiations and that were left to future sessions of the imperial diet: imperial elections, the imperial electoral capitulation (*Kapitulation*), the right of the emperor to outlaw estates (*Reichsacht*), the three claims of the pre-eminence of the electors that had been under attack for a considerable time, then the constitution of the imperial circles and a number of fiscal problems, with which the imperial diet had already grappled fruitlessly in the sixteenth century. These and similar matters ('et similibus negotiis') were to be discussed at some later point. That could be interpreted as a mandate for reform. A small number of the Westphalian diplomats indeed did so; the princes aligned with Hessen-Kassel, Württemberg, Neuburg, and the Guelfs would interpret it this way after 1648. They would attack the traditional bulwarks of the pre-eminence of the electors (such as the right of the electors to elect a king or their exclusive right to produce the electoral capitulation for each new emperor). There was, however, nothing in the text of the peace treaty to justify this pressure to amend the empire's constitution; and even if it could be interpreted as a mandate for reform, little was gained since the nature and extent of such a reform was not specified. The first college of the imperial diet could not be won over. The electors always argued against the mandate for reform supposedly contained in the third paragraph by invoking the unambiguous confirmation of their privileges in the first paragraph. Did the

---

[49] And did not turn the territories of the empire into subjects of international law (in any case still embryonic in 1648)! 'This was ... simply old custom' is also the conclusion reached by Joachim Whaley in his comprehensive two-volume work: *Germany and the Holy Roman Empire*, vol. 1, p. 627. On p. 630 Whaley writes pointedly of the 'essentially conservative approach of the estates' at Westphalia.

[50] See Gotthard, *Säulen des Reiches*, vol. 2, pp. 799–824, 850. For information on the 1558 constitution of the association of electors that remained valid until 1806: ibid., vol. 1, pp. 35–197.

[51] One could argue that very few actually wanted to translate the competences of the imperial estates into sovereignty. For information on the contemporary discussion see B.M. Kremer, *Der Westfälische Friede in der Deutung der Aufklärung* (Tübingen, 1989).

eighth article of the IPO leave everything unchanged (§ 1) or did it encourage reform (§ 3)? One could argue about it endlessly and so it remained an open question.

It is therefore inaccurate to argue that the empire became petrified. Equally one cannot say that the empire only then received a constitution for the first time.[52] Certainly, in article 17, the Peace of Westphalia declared itself to be the perpetually valid fundamental law of the empire. The next *Reichsabschied*, or promulgation of laws at the end of an imperial diet, confirmed that in 1654. Yet, traditionally, the imperial constitution comprised all manner of 'leges fundamentales' (basic laws). In 1648, they simply added another one. Naturally the imperial electoral capitulation (*Wahlkapitulation*) valid at any given time was also considered to be part of the imperial constitution, and in that document the rules of the political system were elaborated in a much more extensive way than in the terse text of the eighth article of the IPO.

The great majority of the Westphalian diplomats did not want to create a new constitutional law but to re-establish a complex system of balanced powers that had existed since the Middle Ages: between emperor and imperial estates, between the electors and the other imperial estates. That balance periodically threatened to break down permanently in favour of the monarchical or oligarchical features of the empire, most recently in 1629 and in 1635, and before then, for example, in 1547–48 after the Schmalkaldic War. In Westphalia, they reset the balance, once again. They adjusted a screw here and there, but not too firmly of course, for that would have contradicted the open character of the imperial constitution.

A glance at the decades after 1648 shows clearly that the political system remained in flux. Between the 1630s and the 1680s the relative political significance of the various groups within the empire changed, notably to the detriment of the electors.[53] Even the question of who should represent the empire abroad had been left undecided in 1648. The famous 'admission controversy'[54] over who should be admitted to the Westphalian peace conferences was followed by another one at the *Exekutionstag* (the conference to decide on the manner in which the treaty should be implemented) in Nuremberg in 1649.[55] During the major peace conventions of the reign of Louis XIV the empire would only play a minor role. The organisational arrangements of the imperial circles continued to evolve after 1648, as can be seen in the attempt to introduce an imperial defence organisation in the years 1681–82 or in the formation of associations of imperial circles in the late seventeenth and early eighteenth centuries, which stood alongside the traditional leagues or associations of princes and other imperial estates. Sometimes these associations of imperial circles even played a part in the concert of the great European powers, even though that had not been envisaged in 1648.

The emperor too was able to live rather well with the adjustments made in 1648. Until recently this fact had mostly escaped scholars, largely because they resolutely ignored the one emperor who reigned longer than any other early modern emperor: Leopold I (1658–1705). An adequate biography of this monarch still remains to be written. On the basis of the disparate specialised studies of the last 25 years, however, it seems safe to conclude that under Leopold's reign both the imperial crown and the empire recovered from the

---

[52] Thus J. Burkhardt, 'Das größte Friedenswerk der Neuzeit. Der Westfälische Frieden in neuer Perspektive', *Geschichte in Wissenschaft und Unterricht*, xlix (1998). pp. 592–618: the empire finally had 'a formally drawn up and written constitution', and the term 'constitution' is to be understood in its modern sense (p. 597).

[53] See Gotthard, *Säulen des Reiches*, vol. 2, pp. 724–840.

[54] Latin *admittere* = admit (*zulassen*), that is who was allowed to speak on behalf of the Empire in Westphalia? Was it the emperor, or the emperor and the electors? Or was it all the imperial estates? Notably the latter suggestion prevailed, which was crucial for setting the direction of the negotiations.

[55] See Gotthard, *Säulen des Reiches*, vol. 2, pp. 755–6.

loss of reputation they had suffered in the 1630s and 1640s.[56] In short, the empire had neither been petrified nor fallen prey to 'crumbling'. The minority of imperial estates which actually wanted to loosen the ties of the empire never became a majority and those writers on imperial constitutional law who wanted to declare the empire a random association of states remained outsiders and were criticised by the mainstream. To put it in stock exchange parlance: the imperial growth curve began to soar steeply from the 1660s only to decline again slowly after 1700. The crash followed in 1740 but this is a whole new story which cannot be attributed to the Peace of Westphalia.

Selected Bibliography

Burkhardt, J., *Vollendung und Neuorientierung des frühmodernen Reichs 1648–1763* (Stuttgart, 2006).
Croxton, D., and A. Tischer (eds), *The Peace of Westphalia. A Historical Dictionary* (Westport and London, 2002).
Dickmann, F., *Der Westfälische Frieden* (Münster, 1959).
Gotthard, A., *Der Augsburger Religionsfrieden* (Münster, 2004).
Gotthard, A., 'Preußens deutsche Sendung', in H. Altrichter, K. Herber and H. Neuhaus (eds), *Mythen in der Geschichte* (Freiburg, 2004), pp. 321–69.
Gotthard, A., *Das Alte Reich 1495–1806*, 5th edn (Darmstadt, 2013).
Lanzinner, M., 'Die Acta pacis Westphalicae und die Geschichtswissenschaft', in G. Braun, C. Kampmann, M. Lanzinner, M. Rohrschneider (eds), *L'art de la paix. Kongresswesen und Friedensstiftung im Zeitalter des Westfälischen Friedens* (Münster, 2011), pp. 31–71.
Press, V., 'Die kaiserliche Stellung im Reich zwischen 1648 und 1740 – Versuch einer Neubewertung', in G. Schmidt (ed.), *Stände und Gesellschaft im Alten Reich* (Stuttgart, 1989), pp. 51–88.
Straumann, B., 'The Peace of Westphalia as a Secular Constitution', *Constellations*, xv (2008): pp. 173–88.
Whaley, J., *Germany and the Holy Roman Empire, 1493–1806*, 2 vols. (Cambridge, 2012).
Wolfrum, E., *Krieg und Frieden in der Neuzeit. Vom Westfälischen Frieden bis zum Zweiten Weltkrieg* (Darmstadt, 2003).

---

[56] A pioneer study: V. Press, 'Die kaiserliche Stellung im Reich zwischen 1648 und 1740 – Versuch einer Neubewertung', in G. Schmidt (ed.), *Stände und Gesellschaft im Alten Reich* (Stuttgart, 1989), pp. 51–88. The essentials of this reign: Gotthard, *Altes Reich*, pp. 108–18 with an annotated selected bibliography. The central problems of imperial policy in the century after the Peace of Westphalia seen through the archchancellery: A. Gotthard, 'Johann Philipp, Lothar Franz und das Reich', in P.C. Hartmann (ed.), *Die Mainzer Kurfürsten des Hauses Schönborn als Reichskanzler und Landesherren* (Mainz, 2002), pp. 17–63. See also Whaley, *Germany and the Holy Roman Empire*, vol. 2, pp. 18–102.

24

The Peace of Westphalia: A European Peace

Heinz Duchhardt

The Peace of Westphalia is undoubtedly a key document for historiography, the culture of remembrance, and public awareness in a number of nation-states, including the Netherlands, Germany, and Switzerland. Its European nature, its 'Europeanness', on the other hand, is not quite so obvious. This chapter will ask whether the Peace of Westphalia was a truly European peace by examining two aspects: the text itself, and the history of its reception.

The penultimate paragraph (§ 119) of the *Instrumentum Pacis Monasteriense* (IPM) extends an invitation to all European sovereigns to be included in the Peace on the suggestion of one of the parties to the treaty. At the time, that is, in October 1648, only the Republic of Venice, which was one of the two mediators, took up this invitation, but the intention of opening up the Peace to all (European) polities in this way was to create a sort of potential security partnership. To some extent, this could be seen as a substitute for a European security system based on recognition of existing borders, in other words, the status quo, which Richelieu had apparently been thinking about for some time. The *Instrumentum Pacis Osnabrugense* (IPO), dated on the same day (24 October 1648) and in many respects identical in wording and meaning to the Münster document, which was negotiated in parallel, is much more specific in this respect. In addition to the princes and free cities of the empire, the Emperor included (article XVII, § 10) the king of Spain, the duke of Savoy, the king of England, the king of Denmark and all of his large empire, the king of Poland, the duke of Lorraine, all the princes and city-republics of Italy, the States General, the Swiss cantons along with Graubünden, and the prince of Transylvania. The other party to the treaty, the Swedish Crown, included in it (article XVII, § 11) most of the states named above, as well as the French king, the king of Portugal and his empire (which was, due to the still fragile status of the new Bragança dynasty, vehemently disputed), and the grand duke of Moscow.

The 'Europeanness' of the Peace of Westphalia,[1] which did not exclude any of the Christian states of Europe, is reflected at the beginning of both *Instrumenta*, where the state of peace is extended beyond the two parties to the treaty to include all their allies and supporters, at least in the conventional form of the optative: 'pax sit christiana, universalis, perpetua.' As all the polities involved in the war had been connected with one of the two camps, the validity of the Peace was, in fact, intended to include the whole continent, with the exception, of course, of the Ottoman Empire.

---

[1] For Johann Stephan Pütter the inclusion of the European states alone was reason enough to claim that the Peace of Westphalia was European. It could be said, he suggested, 'that the whole of Europe is interested in this instrument of peace'. J.S. Pütter, *Geist des Westphälischen Friedens nach dem inneren Gehalte und wahren Zusammenhange der darin verhandelten Gegenstände* (Göttingen, 1795), p. 34.

On the 350th anniversary of the Peace of Westphalia in October 1998, no fewer that 19 heads of state – monarchs and presidents – of the states involved in the war or their successor states,[2] gathered in the Westphalian congress city of Münster to remember a peace that, in contemporary speeches, was held up as a sort of birth certificate for modern Europe. These dignitaries were the first to visit the major exhibition,[3] distributed over a number of sites, which was organised to mark the anniversary. Not by chance was it held under the patronage of the Council of Europe. The visitors noted, with some satisfaction, that in their respective home countries many commemorations of an academic and public nature were held: in Switzerland as in Poland, in Spain as in the Netherlands, in Sweden as in France. There will be no further mention here of Germany and the many events held there, and not only in the two cities associated with the congresses: the conferences, special exhibitions, publications, or the special commemorative stamps and coins issued to accompany them.[4]

We will leave these two observations without comment for the moment, and concentrate on what preceded the Peace, and what it was intended to end, namely, the Thirty Years' War. This was not a continental war in the same sense as the First World War because it always displayed various 'theatres of war', even at different times, which often had only an indirect connection with the military events happening in Central and Western Europe. The present volume gives an impression of the various European theatres of war, without even including the Smolensk War of the early 1630s, that is, Russia's quarrel with the Polish Commonwealth, and Russia's relations with Sweden which the Russian historian Boris F. Porshnev interprets as an integral part of the Thirty Years' War,[5] although others disagree. But contemporaries already saw this war as a whole, as a complex of disputes that were all somehow connected because, in one way or another, they touched on the interests of the leading powers of the time. From this point of view, the discussion that was conducted some time ago about the designation 'Thirty Years' War', asking whether it was contemporary or not, was not merely playful. Academically it was useful because it provided an insight into the mentality of contemporaries.[6] All of these regional conflicts of limited, not European, scope, may have been concluded by separate peace treaties such as Cherasco, Brömsebro, etc., which were not explicitly inserted into the Peace of Westphalia. Nonetheless, they formed part of a struggle for power and a pacification process which reshaped the contours of Europe and, in the long term, determined the place of the powers in the family of states.

Although it started as a German religious and constitutional conflict, the Thirty Years' War must be classified as a European war despite its multipartite nature. It was a war of state-building that was, at the same time, a war of state-formation and system-building. And this must also apply to the Peace in which it ended. Or was this not so?

Regardless of the observation made at the beginning of this essay that the two documents of 24 October 1648, which together are known as the Peace of Westphalia, contained an

---

[2] Belgium, Denmark, Germany, Estonia, Finland, France, Italy, Latvia, Liechtenstein, Lithuania, Luxemburg, the Netherlands, Norway, Austria, Poland, Sweden, Switzerland, Spain, and the Czech Republic. Britain, which had been actively involved in the opening phase of the war because of its dynastic relations with the Electoral Palatinate, was missing, as was, for example, Portugal, which owed the regaining of its independence to the war.

[3] K. Bussmann and H. Schilling (eds), *1648: Krieg und Frieden in Europa*, 3 vols (n. p., 1998).

[4] J. Arndt summed up the academic aspects of the year's commemorations in 'Ein europäisches Jubiläum: 350 Jahre Westfälischer Friede', *Jahrbuch für Europäische Geschichte*, 1 (2000): pp. 133–58.

[5] B.F. Porshnev, *Muscovy and Sweden in the Thirty Years' War 1630–1635* (Cambridge, 1995) is a compilation, designed for the 'Western' reader, of his relevant research.

[6] See, with a critical summary of the older research literature, K. Repgen, 'Zum Begriff "Dreißigjähriger Krieg"', in idem, *Von der Reformation zur Gegenwart: Beiträge zu Grundfragen der neuzeitlichen Geschichte* (Paderborn, 1988), pp. 25–9.

invitation to all partners of those concluding the treaty to allow themselves to be included in the Peace, it should first be noted that by no means did all the powers involved in the war make their peace with everyone, as was the case later, when all parties to war concluded bilateral peace treaties in Nijmegen (1678–79) and Utrecht (1713). One of the main warring parties, the Spanish Crown, brought itself to sign a separate peace only with the rebellious Netherlands, the *Vrede van Munster* of 30 January 1648. This formally recognised the Netherlands' independence and constituted them as a subject of international law (something which they had long been in reality). The Spanish Crown, however, for whatever reason, declined to put an end to its no less central war with France,[7] and a further 11 years were to pass before this was achieved in the Treaty of the Pyrenees.[8] But no peace was concluded between Sweden and Spain, for example, or between the Netherlands and the imperial forces, although in both cases there had been acts of war, without, of course, any explicit declaration of war having been made beforehand. Where a state of war existed in reality but not in law, and where there were no controversial claims, the times, and those involved, obviously recognised no need for regulation.

If we leave the *Vrede van Munster* aside for now, it was only some of the European powers who, after interminably protracted negotiations, declared themselves prepared to sign the peace treaties in October 1648: France, Sweden, the Emperor, and all the princes and free cities of the empire. The estates' participation in the two *Instrumenta Pacis* had not been foreseeable at the beginning of the negotiations. It was politically important, however, as the signatures of representative members of the Princes and Cities on the two documents of October 1648 allowed the pacification of Central Europe, which was seen as indispensable for the stability of the European system as a whole. Right up to Bismarck's time, it was an unwritten law of European politics that the centre of Europe had to be pacified but not power-politically overcharged. The solutions found in 1648 seemed to fulfil these basic criteria. At the same time, the provisions of 1648 gave individual princes a chance to Europeanise their policies. In individual cases, this might already have happened, but now the practice was legally guaranteed. The *jus foederis* gave them the opportunity to seek European alliance partners and thus to become actors beyond the borders of the Reich. The small proviso that such alliances were not to be directed against the Emperor and the Reich no longer amounted to much. Against the provisions of the general clause, which specified that the members of the Reich were not permitted to support either of the two parties in the continuing conflict between France and Spain, article 3 of the IPM allowed them to support one side or the other 'beyond the frontiers of the Holy Roman Empire' in future conflicts between the two Crowns. The fact that most of the princes – not to speak of the Free Cities – were not really able to make use of, or instrumentalise, this *jus foederis*, and were hardly capable of positioning themselves on the European stage, does not change the general point. At least the largest estates, especially those that acquired foreign Crowns (Saxony, Brandenburg, Hanover) were to become active participants in the European interplay of forces on the basis of the Peace of Westphalia. But it was also quite possible that a 'middling' princedom such as Electoral Mainz might conclude a treaty with the English Crown, or that the restless and ambitious Bishop of Münster could collect a number of European powers as allies in order to vent his anger on the neighbouring Netherlands. The Europeanising of the Reich was a direct consequence of the Peace of Westphalia.

---

[7] On this see now M. Rohrschneider, *Der gescheiterte Frieden von Münster: Spaniens Ringen mit Frankreich auf dem Westfälischen Friedenskongress (1643–1649)* (Münster, 2007).

[8] On the Treaty of the Pyrenees see now (with the older and more recent literature) H. Duchhardt (ed.), *Der Pyrenäenfriede (1659)* (Göttingen, 2010).

None of the European states made use of the opportunity, mentioned at the beginning of this essay, to be included in the 'universal' Peace of Westphalia (and thus to gain a higher degree of legal security for their polity). Nonetheless the peace treaty of 24 October 1648 counts as a 'European document', the 'mother' of all European peace treaties, one that many subsequent peace treaties of greater than regional relevance referred to regularly until the end of the *ancien régime*. These references to the Peace of Westphalia were not hidden away in the follow-up documents, but occurred in a prominent place, mostly in the first article. A small selection of examples may illustrate this. Naturally the many 'national' treaties in which the imperial estates were involved, such as, for example, the Confederation of the Rhine of 1658,[9] will not be included.

Thus the treaty of alliance between Sweden and the Netherlands of 30 September / 10 October 1681, for example, refers to the *fundamentum* of the treaties of 1648.[10] This is, however, a relatively isolated case, because treaties without the participation of a partner from the Reich found it difficult to take recourse to 1648. Shortly before this, the Imperial–Swedish and the Imperial–French peace treaties of Nijmegen had referred to the treaties of Münster and Osnabrück as the *fundamentum* and *norma* of the new peace. But they referred 'only' to the 'relevant parts' of the treaty, not to the 'total package'.[11] The same happened in the 1697 treaty of Rijswijk between the Emperor and the French Crown. This bilateral peace treaty was the first to speak of the *Pax Westphalica* as something to be re-imposed.[12] The same basic pattern of taking recourse to the Peace of Westphalia is found in the French–Imperial and French–*Prussian peace treaties which marked the end of the War of the Spanish Succession*.[13]

The convention that only peace treaties involving members of the Reich, or ones that had some sort of connection with the Reich's concerns, referred to the *Instrumenta Pacis* of 1648 changed fundamentally in the eighteenth century. As examples we may cite the peace treaties with which Britain settled its conflicts with the two Bourbon states in 1763 and 1783, the Paris Peace Agreements which Whitehall concluded with the French and Spanish Crowns, that is, without any participation by the imperial estates, and the Versailles Treaties of 1783. All of these documents name the Peace of Westphalia first in a long list of treaties which, as a whole, served as *base et fondement à la paix et au présent Traité*, and which were therefore confirmed and renewed in 1763 and 1783.[14] The partners to the treaty promised each other that they would observe them to the letter, as if they, that is, the two *Instrumenta* of 1648, were also included verbatim in the text. This development is so exciting because, as is well known, the peace treaties of 1763 and 1783 concerned problems outside Europe, which the documents of 1648 did not mention at all, and because only one of the partners to the treaty had been directly involved in the agreements of 1648. From the point of view of international law, this process has been described as follows:

> *In the course of the eighteenth century, the Peace of Westphalia and many other peace treaties [were] repeatedly incorporated into sets of agreements ... even when the*

---

[9] C. Parry (ed.), *Consolidated Treaty Series* (hereafter CTS), vol. 5, p. 164 (article 1).

[10] See H. Steiger, 'Der Westfälische Frieden: Grundgesetz für Europa?', in H. Duchhardt (ed.), *Der Westfälische Friede* (Munich, 1998), pp. 33–80, at 57. The text itself says that the contracting parties agree that 'ut dicti Tractatus Pacis Osnabrugensis in pleno vigore secundum eorum genuinum sensum maneant & rite observentur' (CTS, vol. 16, p. 136).

[11] See Steiger, 'Der Westfälische Frieden', pp. 59–60.

[12] Ibid., p. 61.

[13] Ibid., pp. 61–2.

[14] Ibid., p. 64. The passages of text can be found in CTS, vol. 42, pp. 284–5 and in CTS, vol. 48, pp. 441 and 483.

> *respective partners had not been involved in these treaties. This changed the status of the treaties of Westphalia. They became ... part of Europe's general legal and peace order, and they were obviously regarded as marking its beginning. But at the same time they lost their specific character. The terms fundamentum/base and norma/ norme were no longer used at this level. Thus despite its position as the starting point, the treaty of 1648 was not, in these agreements, recognized as the basis and norm of the European order, but was seen in association with all the other treaties that were incorporated in a similarly unspecific way. In the shaping of positive law, the idea seems to have come up that all these treaties together form the European order, the droit public de l'Europe – regardless of their specific provisions.*[15]

The idea that all these peace treaties of supra-regional significance, with the Peace of Westphalia at their head, constitute the European order can be found 15 years before 1763, in the Aachen Definitive Peace of 18 October 1748 between France, Britain, and the Netherlands. Article III of this document reads:

> *Les Traités de Westphalie; ceux de Madrid, entre les couronnes d'Espagne & d'Angleterre, de 1667 & de 1670; les Traités de Paix de Nimègue de 1678 & de 1679; de Ryswick de 1697; d'Utrecht de 1713; de Bade de 1714; le Traité de la triple alliance de la Haye de 1717; celui de la quadruple alliance de Londres de 1718; & le Traité de Paix de Vienne de 1738 , servent de base & de fondement à la Paix générale, & au présent Traitè; & pour cet effet ils sont renouvellés et confirmés dans la meilleure forme, & comme s'ils étoient insérés ici mot à mot.*[16]

This evidence leaves little room for doubt that in the eyes of both the general public and lawyers in pre-modern times, the Peace of Westphalia, along with other documents, had the status of a basic law for Europe. It was repeatedly invoked even when, in material terms, people had distanced themselves from it more or less clearly. We should not fail to mention that although they concentrated on the Holy Roman Empire, its pacification, and making it secure, the two *Instrumenta* of October 1648 contained a number of sections which applied to non-German concerns, that is, European matters. It is well known that the two *Instrumenta* are not logically and systematically structured, however, so that finding these non-German regulations is a tedious task.

A large proportion of them concerns the Apennine peninsula. These include Pinerolo passing into the sovereign ownership of France (IPM § 72), partially cancelling the Treaty of Cherasco, dated 6 April 1631, which had otherwise been ratified (IPM § 92); the financial compensation which France agreed to pay to the duke of Mantua on behalf of Savoy (IPM § 94); and the passing of Monferrato and other upper Italian places into the feudal ownership of the duke of Savoy in line with a title of acquisition dated 1634 (IPM § 95). Further, possessions in upper Italy (Rocheverana, Olmi, Caesola) were transferred to the ownership of the duke of Savoy while the previous feudal relationship of vassalage with the Reich was abolished (IPM § 96); the castles of Reggioli and Luzzara, plus the territories that belonged to them, were given back to the duke of Mantua, but the duke of Guastalla was able to institute legal proceedings (IPM § 97). Finally, the descendants of Count Cacherano were restored to the feudal tenure of Rocha and Arrazio (IPM § 97).

---

[15] Steiger, 'Der Westfälische Frieden', p. 65.
[16] CTS, vol. 38, pp. 305–6.

The expansion of the territories of the French Crown was important: this included the (final) reversion of the bishoprics of Metz, Toul, and Verdun on the western border (IPM § 70); the transition of Breisach, the Landgraviate of upper and lower Alsace, and the bailiwick (Landvogtei) via the Decapolis, the 10 imperial towns in Alsace (IPM § 73) – *with their self-governing status intact (IPM § 87); and the imposition of occupation law in the fortress of Philippsburg* (IPM § 76). Other measures that were important for France's geostrategic position were the razing of fortifications in Alsace and the strict neutralisation of the town of Zabern (IPM § 82).

Different arrangements applied to the border region between the German states and the Netherlands. The restitution of the duke of Croy, a supporter of France, was to include rule over Fénétrange, with the rights of the Holy Roman Empire remaining untouched (IPO § 28).

Other dispositions again applied to the imperial hereditary lands that were not part of the empire, that is, mainly Bohemia, whose inhabitants enjoyed the same amnesty as those who lived in the Reich (IPO § 52), and whose Protestant part was to have the same legal status, in principle, as the Catholic part (IPO § 55). In Silesia, which was treated as a territory annexed to the Bohemian Crown (and, as we know, was not covered by the constitution governing the imperial circles), the Protestants were granted special protection. The obligation of those of a different denomination to emigrate was lifted in their case, and in Schweidnitz, Jauer, and Glogau they were promised, or permitted to erect, three 'freedom churches' (IPO §§ 38–40).

Of course, the cession of imperial territories (Western Pomerania, Wismar, Bremen, and Verden) to the Swedish Crown as compensation also acquired a European significance because it meant that a foreign Crown had clearly shifted its borders southwards. This not only allowed it to improve its strategic position and gave it control of important river mouths, but also turned it into an actor on the Central European stage (IPO Art. X). Unlike the French Crown, it was permitted, via its diplomats, to get officially involved in the imperial diet in matters pertaining to the Reich.

Finally, perhaps the most important of the European concerns in the two *Instrumenta* was the famous IPM article VI, which laid down Basel's and Switzerland's exemption from the jurisdiction of the imperial Chamber Court, establishing the Swiss Confederation's legal independence. Thus the status in international law of the association of cantons, one which had existed for 150 years and longer, was indirectly sanctioned.

The European potential of the two *Instrumenta Pacis* was rounded off by the inclusion of other states in the Peace, or, in the case of the *Instrumentum Pacis Monasteriense*, by inviting them to join, as described at the beginning of this chapter. Of course, as already mentioned, there was not a single instance of this happening. Probably for this reason, the architects of later peace treaties refrained from turning this inclusion or invitation to third parties into a rule of thumb in international law. To this extent, the Peace of Westphalia was unique.

We shall now return to the point from which this essay started, that is, to the question of the 'Europeanness' of the Peace of Westphalia. Both parts of this Peace, in principle, regulated mainly the affairs of the Reich, and did this with great success for a considerable length of time. But individual provisions of the Peace clearly reached beyond the borders of the Holy Roman Empire of the German Nation. This applied especially to the rather fluid legal conditions in imperial Italy, but also to the western and northern borders of the Reich, to Switzerland, and to the imperial hereditary lands of the Crown of Bohemia along with Silesia.

A second factor, however, was even more crucial. The constitution and the newly adjusted system of checks and balances in the Reich were submitted to European supervision and control. The Reich was thus classified as a key European region, which could not endure one thing: a dynamic charge. The emerging European system was totally dependent on the centre of the continent being pacified. Its 'powerlessness' was intended to balance out the ambitions of its neighbours. The diplomats in Münster and Osnabrück thought in these or in similar terms and were fully capable of dealing with the category of 'Europe', as the indexes to the many volumes of the *Acta Pacis Westphalicae* show. There is much to suggest that the diplomats in Münster and Osnabrück were quite familiar with the metaphor of the 'European balance', that is, thinking in a systematic context, as was discussed controversially a number of years ago.[17]

The fact that the diplomats were at ease with the category of 'Europe' is reflected in the history of its immediate reception, as collections of documents on the history of the origins and consequences of the Peace of Westphalia were published all over Europe, in the Netherlands, the Reich, France, Sweden, Spain, Italy, and Switzerland.[18] And the Peace of Westphalia has remained on the agenda of European historiography since, regardless of all fluctuations. Yet despite the claims of various national histories, it was not acknowledged as a European event until its anniversary in 1948 (also an important date for the process of European unification). As an example, I cite a Dutch publication, an essay by J.A. van Hamel, illuminatingly entitled: 'De vrede van Munster. Fundament voor Nederland, fundament voor Europa.'[19] The fact that the publication of *Acta Pacis Westphalicae* was initiated in the late 1950s was certainly connected not only with a growing awareness, after the Second World War, of law in history and the theme of peace as such, which had already shaped Fritz Dickmann's magisterial synthesis of 1959,[20] but also with the process of Europeanisation, which was bearing its first fruits at that time. The Peace of Westphalia, to some extent, could be seen as the prototype of a European order.

Finally, we shall take a brief look at visual images in publications on the Peace of Westphalia which acknowledge it as a European event, beginning with what is probably the best known, the coloured woodcut of *Der Freudenreiche Postillon von Münster*. In many reprints, the trio of Vienna/Paris/Stockholm in the background exemplifies the European dimension of the peace.[21] The second line of text in a Dutch etching of 1648–49, *Soo slot het Hemel huys syn vreudge poorten open*, expresses what it is all about: 'Wanner de vrede wiert geslosten von Europen.'[22] An etching from Nuremberg, *Abbildung des hocherwünschten Teutschen Friedens*, at least provides a hint of the European dimension in the numerous diplomats surrounding the throne (with the Emperor, the Swedish queen, and the French king), although the title speaks of the 'German peace'.[23] A silver medal of the Peace of Westphalia designed with a strongly allegorical emphasis and struck by Sebastian Dadler in 1648, addresses the Europe motif directly in the inscription on its face: *Ambiguo pax et bellum luctamine certant, Pax, Europa vovet, laeta Trophaea ferat*.[24] And finally, the title of the most complete edition (1697)

---

[17] See K. Repgen, 'Der Westfälische Friede und die Ursprünge des europäischen Gleichgewichts', in idem, *Von der Reformation zur Gegenwart: Beiträge zu Grundfragen der neuzeitlichen Geschichte* (Paderborn, 1988), pp. 53–66.

[18] See H. Duchhardt with the assistance of E. Ortlieb and M. Schnettger (eds), *Bibliographie zum Westfälischen Frieden* (Münster, 1996), section III.1.

[19] Ibid., no. 1720, p. 187.

[20] F. Dickmann, *Der Westfälische Frieden* (Münster, 1959). Many updated editions have been published since.

[21] Reproduced in, among other, K.G. Kaster and G. Steinwascher (eds), '… *zu einem stets währenden Gedächtnis'*: *Die Friedenssäle in Münster und Osnabrück und ihre Gesandtenporträts* (Bramsche, 1996), p. 21.

[22] Kat. 1998, vol. 1, no. 650, p. 222.

[23] Reproduced in *1648 Krieg und Frieden in Europa*, catalogue, no. 721, p. 246.

[24] *Um Glauben und Reich: Kurfürst Maximilian I.*, exhibition catalogue (Munich, 1980), p. 489, no. 788.

of van Hulle's portraits of the Peace envoys in Münster and Osnabrück refers directly to the 'Europeanness' of the Peace of 1648: *Pacificatores orbis christiani sive icones principum ducum et legatorum qui Monasterii atque Osnabrugae pacem Europae reconcilarunt*.[25] All this is not to deny that in many places the Peace of Westphalia was linked with a national epithet, or seen in positively biblical terms, for example, *Teutscher Friede*, the return of the Golden Age, etc. But there is no doubt that for those producing the images, the European nature of the proceedings was frequently at least a factor.

There is much to suggest, therefore, that the Peace of Westphalia should be regarded not only as a Reich basic law that created a peace order of considerable longevity, but also as a European document. It was seen by contemporaries – *artists, designers of medals – as a European event, while subsequent generations classified it as a turning point in international law which gave rise to a European legal order*, quite apart from the fact that the two Instrumenta Pacis also contained much of substance that was European, while individual provisions looked far beyond the borders of the Reich.

What the Peace of Westphalia, seen in a European perspective, failed to achieve was to give the continent a comprehensive and, above all, a lasting, peace. As we know, it was the two guaranteeing powers (Sweden, France) who, just a few years after the Peace was signed, set it aside; and one of the central conflicts, that between France and Spain, was not resolved at all in 1648. The Treaty of the Pyrenees of 1659, which is seen as a complementary agreement, did not receive anything like as much publicity in its anniversary year of 2009 as the Peace of Westphalia did in 1998. The public echo was largely restricted to a specialist academic audience, and did not go much beyond a few conferences (Mainz, Luxemburg,[26] Paris, and Barcelona/Perpignan). The same is true of the Peace of Oliva of 1660, which re-ordered relations in north-eastern Europe, ultimately to the benefit of Sweden, which was able to assert its presence in the Baltic.[27] The Peace of Oliva must also be seen in connection with the Perpetual Peace of Cardis, concluded one year later, which stipulated that Russia had to restore its captured Livonian territories to Sweden. It could be said that Sweden only achieved the height of its significance in the Baltic in 1660–61, *without this necessarily being assumed to be a permanent state. Sweden's position as a great power was fragile from the start, given the country's limited resources*.

Even if these peace treaties – concluded on the Fasaneninsel, in Oliva near Danzig, and in Cardis – were of regional significance, unlike the congresses at which other European states participated, there are just as many publications on them, including English ones,[28] also bearing in mind the domestic caesura of the restoration of the monarchy, which see the peace treaties of 1659, 1660, and 1661 as turning points defining an era. Written from

---

[25] Reproduced in *Der Westfälische Frieden: Krieg und Frieden*, exhibition catalogue (Münster, 1988), p. 127, und in Kaster and Steinwascher, '… zu einem stets währenden Gedächtnis', p. 21. On this see now my essay: 'Eine verlegerische "Übersetzungsleistung": Zu van Hulles Porträtwerk der Gesandten des westfälischen Friedenskongresses von 1696/97', in H. Duchhardt and Martin Espenhorst (eds), *Frieden übersetzen in der Vormoderne. Translationsleistungen in Diplomatie, Medien und Wissenschaft* (Göttingen, 2012), pp. 274–7.

[26] M. Gantelet et al. (eds), *Dokumentation: La paix des Pyrénées et son impact en Lorraine et au Luxembourg/Der Pyrenäenfriede und seine Auswirkungen auf Lothringen und Luxemburg* (Luxembourg, 2010) (= Hémecht, vol. 62, issue 3/4).

[27] See also R. Frost, *After the Deluge: Poland–Lithuania and the Second Northern War, 1655–1660* (Cambridge, 2003).

[28] E.g. *The Cambridge Modern History*, vol. 5: *The Age of Louis XIV* (Cambridge, 1908); M. Beloff, *The Age of Absolutism 1660–1815* (London, 1954); and also up to T.C.W. Blanning, *The Culture of Power and the Power of Culture: Old Regime Europe 1660–1789* (Oxford, 2002). Of course, this is no longer the rule in more recent British historiography; see e.g. G. Treasure, *The Making of Modern Europe 1648–1780* (London, 1985).

a European perspective, they begin their accounts with these treaties rather than with the Peace of Westphalia, which is seen as more of a Central European matter. Of course, this cannot detract from the significance of the Peace of Westphalia as a political model and starting point in international law. The forms of negotiation that were developed at the Peace have not provided a lasting model, although the diplomatic ceremonial of Münster and Osnabrück had a considerable long-term impact, and some of the general conditions, such as holding congresses in neutral cities, became established as the norm. In terms of negotiations, however, every subsequent multilateral congress had to find its own 'style'. Nonetheless, until the end of the *ancien régime*, sources on the Peace of Westphalia formed an essential addition to the luggage of every diplomat despatched to take part in a peace congress.

We can be fairly sure that the heads of state of the many European countries that met at the scene of the events in 1998 were not all familiar with the central provisions of the two *Instrumenta Pacis*, especially as their various states were affected by them to very different degrees. But their advisers had successfully conveyed to them that this event concerned a European matter, and that by taking part in the festivities, they could present themselves as convinced Europeans after the Iron Curtain had come down and 'Europe', despite the Balkan wars, seemed to be moving towards a 'golden age'. They might also have heard of the intellectual construct of the 'Westphalian system', highly rated by Anglo-American social scientists in particular. This, it seems, attributes the system of internally and externally sovereign states back to the documents of 1648, and sees it as coming to an end only very recently, in the growing significance of non-governmental forces in politics. European historians, it must be said, are rather doubtful about this proposition.[29] Whatever the case, the Peace of Westphalia, highly valued, even venerated, during the *ancien régime*, was relegated to the background of public awareness in the nineteenth century, which was one reason why in 1898 there was hardly a culture of remembrance.[30] But after the Second World War it (once again) became a topos among the wider public, standing for peace orders in general, as it had already done in the pre-modern period. In the eighteenth-century peace treaties quoted above which referred to the Peace of Westphalia, no date, as a rule, was mentioned, in contrast, for example, to the peace accords of Nijmegen, Rijswijk, and Utrecht. Everyone with a certain level of education, who knew the (more or less popular) mnemonics about the Peace of Westphalia,[31] was able to define it and classify it historically. The date was no longer required.

Translated by Angela Davies

Selected Bibliography

Asbach, O., and Schröder, P. (eds), *War, the State and International Law in Seventeenth Century Europe* (Farnham, 2010).

---

[29] H. Duchhardt, '"Westphalian System": Zur Problematik einer Denkfigur', *Historische Zeitschrift*, 269 (1999): pp. 305–15.

[30] On this, taking a local example, H. Duchhardt, *Das Feiern des Friedens: Der Westfälische Friede im kollektiven Gedächtnis der Friedensstadt Münster* (Münster, 1997), ch. 3.

[31] Id., 'Der Westfälische Friede im "öffentlichen Bewusstsein" der Vormoderne: Lateinische metrische Merkverse', in *Menschen und Strukturen in der Geschichte Alteuropas: Festschrift für Johannes Kunisch zur Vollendung seines 65. Lebensjahres* (Berlin, 2002), pp. 243–9.

Asch, R.G., E.V. Wulf and M. Wrede (eds), *Frieden und Krieg in der Frühen Neuzeit: Die europäische Staatenordnung und die außereuropäische Welt* (Munich, 2001).
Bély, L. (ed.), *L'Europe des traités de Westphalie: Esprit de la diplomatie et diplomatie de l'esprit* (Paris, 2000).
Bussmann, K., and H. Schilling (eds), *1648: Krieg und Frieden in Europa*, 3 vols. (n.p., 1998).
Croxton, D., *Peacemaking in Early Modern Europe: Cardinal Mazarin and the Congress of Westphalia, 1643–1648* (Selinsgrove, NJ, 1999).
Croxton, D., and A. Tischer (eds), *The Peace of Westphalia: A Historical Dictionary* (Westport, Conn., 2002).
Dickmann, F., *Der Westfälische Frieden* (Münster, 1959).
Duchhardt, H., with the assistance of E. Ortlieb and M. Schnettger (eds), *Bibliographie zum Westfälischen Frieden* (Münster, 1996).
Duchhardt, H., *Das Feiern des Friedens: Der Westfälische Friede im kollektiven Gedächtnis der Friedensstadt Münster* (Münster, 1997).
Duchhardt, H. (ed.), *Der Westfälische Friede: Diplomatie, politische Zäsur, kulturelles Umfeld, Rezeptionsgeschichte* (Munich, 1998).
Kampmann, C. et al. (eds), *L'art de la paix: Kongresswesen und Friedensstiftung im Zeitalter des Westfälischen Friedens* (Münster, 2011).
Repgen, K., 'Der Westfälische Friede und die Ursprünge des europäischen Gleichgewichts', in id., *Von der Reformation zur Gegenwart: Beiträge zu Grundfragen der neuzeitlichen Geschichte* (Paderborn, 1988), pp. 53–66.
Teschke, B., *The Myth of 1648: Class, Geopolitics and the Making of Modern International Relations* (London, 2003).
Villaverde, F. (ed.), *350 años de la Paz de Westfalia: Del antagonismo a la integració en Europa* (Madrid, 1999).

A Peace for the Whole World? Perceptions and Effects of the Peace Treaty of Münster (1648) on the World Outside Europe[*]

Susan Richter

The Peace Treaty of Münster, as a separate agreement within the framework of the Treaty of Westphalia, ended the Eighty Years' War (1568–1648) between Spain and the United Provinces and achieved recognition of sovereignty for the States General as well as the consolidation of their territory.[1] The treaty thus represented a great success for the States General. At the same time, however, it represented a break with France.[2]

The Master of the Mint, Engelbert Ketteler, minted a medallion on the occasion of the Peace Treaty of Münster with the following text:

> PACIS. FELICITAS / ORBI: CHRISTIANO: QVA. RESTITVTA / QVA. AD. INCITAMENTUM. DEMONSTRATA /TOT. REGNIS. ET. PROVINCIIS / AD. VTRVMQVE. SOLEM. VTRVMQV3(ue) OCEANUM / TERRA. MARIQVE. PARTA SECURITAS /TRANQVILLITATIS: PVBLICAE / SPE. ET. VOTO /MONASTERY: WESTPHA / ANNO MDCXLVIII.[3]

---

[*] I wish to thank my student assistants Steve Bahn and Michael Roth for research on literature. I thank Prof. Wolfgang Michel, Faculty of Languages and Cultures, Kyushu University/Japan, for important information.

[1] On the course of the war and the interrupting ceasefire agreement, cf. H. Schilling, *Konfessionalisierung und Staatsinteressen. Internationale Beziehungen*, p. 540. I.A.A. Thompson, 'The Impact of War and Peace on Government and Society in Seventeenth-Century Spain', in R.G. Asch, W.E. Voß and M. Wrede (eds), *Frieden und Krieg in der Frühen Neuzeit. Die europäische Staatenordnung und die außereuropäische Welt* (Munich, 2001), pp. 161–80. Literature on the Spanish view of the peace treaty can be found in F. Marcos-Sánchez, 'The Future of Catalonia. A sujet brûlant at the Münster-Negotiations', in H. Duchhardt (ed.), *Der Westfälische Friede* (Munich, 1998), pp. 273–92.

[2] F. Wielenga, *Geschichte der Niederlande* (Stuttgart, 2012), p. 105. On the Treaty of Westphalia in general, cf. A. Osiander, *The States System of Europe, 1640–1990. Peacemaking and the Conditions of International Stability* (Oxford, 1994), pp. 19–89. L. Manzano Baena, *Conflicting Words: The Peace Treaty of Münster (1648) and the Political Culture of the Dutch Republic and the Spanish Monarchy* (Leuven, 2011), pp. 192 et seq.

[3] H. Galen, *Der Westfälische Frieden. Die Friedensfreude auf Münzen und Medaillen*. Katalog zur Ausstellung im Stadtmuseum Münster 11.3.–30.10.1988 (Münster, 1988), p. 45.

[*The fortune of peace has been restored in the Christian world and shown as an incitement; security has been achieved for so many states and provinces, on both sides of the sun and the sea, on water and on land. In the hope of general quietude, Münster in Westphalia in the year 1648.*]

This medallion presented the Treaty of Münster as peace among Christians, as did many other contemporary ceremonial coins and medallions, extending not only over Europe, but also over the entire globe and thus referring to communities outside Europe as well.[4]

The peace treaties of Münster and Osnabruck did not bring a global or world war to an end in 1648, according to research to date. This was not the Seven Years' War with its numerous battlefields outside Europe, the involvement of so many non-European figures in the acts of war, or the effect of these on native populations, and the displacement or partial loss of the power and influence of European countries on other continents;[5] rather, it was a war primarily of disunited Christianity, of regional military skirmishes and linking diverse conflicts of varying political and economic interests between individual European powers. The centre of military action lay in Europe, which, in retrospect, had been destroyed or weakened over 30 years on various battlefields and by skirmishes that flared up repeatedly, but now had been stabilised and newly ordered both structurally and legally by the treaties of Münster and Osnabruck.[6]

Jürgen Osterhammel therefore assumes that the peace concept of 1648 was not transferred to relations with states outside Europe, and that placing the internal relations in Europe on a legal basis had no influence on non-Christian cultures outside Europe, or at least was not adapted by these.[7]

Osterhammel's assumption that the peace treaties of 1648 had no influence on peoples and areas outside Europe is questioned in this chapter. Starting with the above-mentioned medallion and its message of peace directed overseas, the obligation of communicating and publishing the peace treaties of 1648 will be examined, using the Treaty of Münster as an example. The further focus of the chapter will be on the routes of communication, the contents, and the time limits, as well as on those to whom the communications were addressed. With regard to the latter, my task will be to show when, and for what reasons, trade partners and allies outside Europe were informed of the peace, but also what consequences this had for the politics of communities outside Europe. What did the peace treaties mean for powers outside Europe, and how did the States General communicate these to the trading partners and allies outside Europe? Did the treaties of 1648 have consequences for third parties, for

---

[4] B. Peus mentions a *taler* whose message on the obverse is PAX OMNIA RERUM and on the reverse HINC TOTI PAX INSONAT ORBI ('Peace echoes over the entire globe from here'). B. Peus, 'Die Medaillen auf den Westfälischen Frieden', in E. Hövel (ed.), *Pax optima rerum* (Münster, 1948), pp. 183 et seq. and 193.

[5] Stig Förster defines a world war as follows: 'In a world war, local and regional conflicts of all kind merge into a comprehensive struggle between coalitions and other parties. Peoples on all continents are drawn in. Fighting for their own interests, non-European powers play major roles. Without them, there is no world war.' S. Förster, 'The First World War. Global Dimensions of Warfare in the Age of Revolutions', in R. Chickering and S. Förster (eds), *War in an Age of Revolution, 1775–1815* (Cambridge, 2010), p. 102.

[6] J. Osterhammel, 'Einleitung: Krieg und Frieden an den Grenzen Europas und darüber hinaus', in R.G. Asch (ed.), *Frieden und Krieg in der Frühen Neuzeit: Die europäische Staatenordnung und die außereuropäische Welt*, p. 446. On the Peace Treaty of Münster, cf. W. Preiser, 'History of the Law of Nations. Ancient Times to 1648', in *Encyclopedia of Public International Law*, published under the auspices of the Max Planck Institute for comparative public law and international law, vol. 7 (Amsterdam, New York and Oxford, 1984), pp. 132–60.

[7] Osterhammel, *Einleitung: Krieg und Frieden*, pp. 462 et seq.

powers outside Europe who had some kind of legal relationship with, or were in some way obliged to, the former warring parties? The question of possible consequences of the peace for Europeans living outside Europe and in the service of former opponents will also be examined. This view provokes the question of whether Spain, for its part, communicated the peace to the outside world, and if so, how. A comprehensive investigation of these questions cannot be presented here, however; the examination of these questions must be presented in the form of samples. This chapter will therefore concentrate on the following: the post of Nieuw Nederland (New Netherland) with the city of Nieuw Amsterdam (New Amsterdam) in the West Indies, controlled by the Dutch West India Company (WIC); the post of Batavia in Indonesia, controlled by the Dutch East India Company (VOC);[8] and the post of the island of Dejima in Japan, also controlled by the Dutch East India Company.

Using this approach of examining the receipt and the effect of the news of peace in 1648, it seems possible to me to find evidence of the perceptions of the Thirty Years' War, or the Eighty Years' War, of peoples outside Europe, and thus an external perspective of these events. On the basis of research on the Seven Years' War the question of the use of native populations as auxiliary troops for the warring parties forces itself on one, as does the question of the perception or knowledge of peoples outside Europe who were involved in a conflict between European powers that was actually much larger. The difficulties for the protagonists in comprehending that their own actions showed global effects were pointed out by Egon Friedell in his *Kulturgeschichte der Neuzeit* in 1928: 'Canada was conquered at Rossbach – a context that was, however, completely understood only by English statesmen.'[9] Owing to a lack of sources, it is difficult to understand the involvement of the native populations in America or Asia in the military actions of the Dutch against the Spanish. The little material available offers primarily European perspectives. These did not take the effect of war on these peoples much into account, nor do they yield any considerations going beyond local skirmishes to include the larger political background. It would appear more profitable, then, to look at the external perspective on the war with the help of the significance of the peace treaties, directing our gaze towards a state which, along with its own contacts with the politically opposed Netherlands and Spain, as well as Portugal, which was conjoined to Spain in a personal union, possessed its own political interests with regard to these powers, and which offers sources with its own perspective, owing to its own written culture: the Edo Shōgunate of Japan.

The Obligation to Inform and Publish the Peace Treaty of Münster

The peace treaty[10] concluded between Spain and the States General (United Provinces) on 30 January 1648 in Münster, and ratified on 15 May of that year, established, in Article 79, the

---

[8] F.S. Gaastra, 'Die Vereinigte Ostindische Compagnie der Niederlande – Ein Abriss ihrer Geschichte', in E. Schmitt, T. Schleich and T. Beck (eds), *Kaufleute als Kolonialherren: Die Handelswelt der Niederländer vom Kap der Guten Hoffnung bis Nagasaki 1600–1800* (Bamberg, 1988), pp. 1–90. Ibid., *The Dutch East India Company. Expansion and Decline*, (Leiden, 2003).

[9] E. Friedell, *Kulturgeschichte der Neuzeit. Die Krisis der europäischen Seele von der Schwarzen Pest bis zum Ersten Weltkrieg* (Munich, 2007), p. 654.

[10] The ratification was not at all easy to attain on the Dutch side, because the delegate from Utrecht, Nederhorst, did not want to agree to the Spanish–Dutch peace treaty, as he was against an alliance with France. This is clear from the missive In dato den Eersten Februarij 1648. Gesondenuyt Munster, […] addressed to the States General.

obligation for both treaty partners to publish the treaty. This meant that the content of the treaty was to be made public in all spheres of influence of the treaty parties, and, after it had been taken note of, the parties were to cease all military action: 'Dictus tractatus ubique & ubi decet, statim à permutatis & extraditis hinc inde Ratihabitionibus publicetur: & tum omnes hostilitatum actus cessent.'[11]

For the publication of the peace treaty by the States General, Cornelis Musch (1593–1650), the Secretary of the States General, who dealt with the regular minutes of the sessions and other official documents, drafted a special mandate which was published in *Theatrum Europaeum*.[12] The mandate announced that, as of 15 May 1648, the day of the ratification of the peace treaty between the Netherlands and Spain, peace was declared, and all military actions had *aufhören und Endschafft* [zu] *nehmen* (to cease and be abolished).

The exceptions to this time limit were the Spanish and Dutch overseas territories, as well as the zones of influence of the Dutch East and West India Companies. In the Asian territories of the VOC, peace, according to the mandate, was not to be declared until 30 January 1649; in the West Indies, this was from 15 November 1648, a full half-year after the ratification. In addition, the peace declaration was to be made known in these areas as quickly as possible:

> *was anbelangt die Limites der Ost-Indianischen Compagny, so soll besagter Fried in denenselben nicht eher als auff den dreyssigsten Januarii deß 1649. Jahrs; (ist ein Jahr nach Schließung deß Friedens:) In West-Indien aber auf den funffzehenden November dieses jetzigen 1648. Jahrs (seynde ein halb Jahr nach Auswechslung der Ratificationen) seinen Anfang nehmen. Dabey gleichwol in Acht zu haben, dafern beyder Theile Publicationes vor ernennter Zeit zur Stelle kämen, daß alsdann alsobald alle Feindseligkeit auffhören, und der Fried seinen Anfang und vollkommenen Effect haben; auch aller Schade, so nach ernennten Terminen daselbst durch Hostilität geschehen möchte, unverzüglich restituiret werden solle. Inmittelst aber will man, so nach Ost- als Westindien, und an andere der Compagny privilegirte Plätze so bald immer müglich [sic!], die Publication deß gedachten Friedens befördern.*[13]

The deadlines for publication fixed by Musch, which were made known in Europe, do not match the dates in the minutes or the descriptions of the Peace Treaty of Münster written by the delegate and observer from the Republic of Venice, Alvise Contarini (1597–1651),

---

[11] Apud, *Tractatus Pacis Trigesimo Januarii* [...], § 79, pp. 39–40. http://www.lwl.org/westfaelische-geschichte/que/normal/que2603.pdf (accessed on 17/06/13).

[12] This mandate is also mentioned by J.C. Lünig, *Theatrum Ceremoniale Historico Politicum* [...], (Leipzig, 1719), p. 811.

[13] To paraphrase this quote: The mentioned Peace treaty should not be declared before the 30th of January 1649 (one year after the conclusion of peace). But in West-India, it should be announced on the 15th of November 1648 (half a year after the peace agreement). The Peace treaty should be declared as soon as possible in the spheres of influence by the trading company in East- and West-India. – *Theatrum Europaeum, oder außführliche und warhafftige Beschreibung aller und jeder denckwürdiger Geschichten, so sich hin und wieder in der Welt, fürnemblich aber in Europa und Teutschlanden [...] sich zugetragen*, vol. 6: 1647–1651 (Frankfurt am Main, 1663), p. 474. The reproduction of the content of the mandate in the Theatrum Europaeum – e.g. the instruction to publish the treaty – agrees with the Dutch text. Aitzema, *Verhael van de Nederlantsche vreeden Handeling* (S'Gravens-Hage, 1650), p. 557. The *Theatrum Europaeum* is a chronicle collecting events and chronology which gave a detailed report on the Thirty Years' War in text and illustrations every year; but it reported on other political events, and indeed other events generally. There is still no comprehensive investigation available. At the conference of the DFG project 'Welt und Wissen' with the TU Darmstadt and the Wolfenbüttel Library in 2011, a workshop was dedicated to this work. See H. Bingel, *Das Theatrum Europaeum. Ein Beitrag zur Publizistik des 17. und 18. Jahrhunderts* (Munich, 1909).

according to Konrad Repgen. Contarini apparently noted 15 December 1648 for the West Indies (a month later than Musch) and 15 June 1649 for Asia, which is some five months later than the date given by the Secretary of the States General.[14] But the mandate by Musch had legal validity. By this means, the same information was to be given in all Dutch zones of influence and along all their trade routes, so that nobody could act against the treaty's requirements in ignorance from this point onward.

The publication deadlines given for the territories outside Europe also show that sailing times, which depended on the monsoon winds, had been taken into account. Thus, the journey from the Dutch harbours to Java, or at least to the VOC headquarters in Batavia, took some six to eight months in the seventeenth century. The ships always left the Dutch harbours in December, in January, in April/May, and in September.

According to Musch's mandate, those who were to be informed of the peace treaty were the following persons occupying key positions within the Dutch West India and Dutch East India Companies:

> *Item aen den Gouverneur Generael in Ost-Indien, item an den President ende Hooge Raden, als oock den Lieutnant General over de Militie in Brasil, item aen den Admiral de Witte, item aen den Commandeur op de Cust van Guinea, item aen de Directeurs in Loande*[15] *de St. Paulo, ende St. Thome, item aen de Directeur in Nieuw Nederlandt.*[16]

> [One piece to the Governor General in East India, one to the President of the High Council, one to the Lieutenant General of Brasil, one to Admiral de Witte, one to the Commander of the Coast of Guinea, one to the Director of Loande de St. Paulo and St. Thome, and one of the Director of New Netherland.]

Non-European monarchs and chieftains were not taken into consideration by Musch's mandate.

Communication Routes

The information was transmitted in writing by the directors of the WIC or the VOC to the aforementioned local agents of the trading companies. It was then sent out to the individual factories[17] and traders, but especially to ships' captains, in writing.[18]

We can see how the process of communication was carried out, and what effect this had on the trading location, by examining the case of the WIC trading posts in New Netherland on the eastern coast of North America.

---

[14] Repgen refers to the dates given in the notes and descriptions made by the delegate from the Republic of Venice, Alvise Contarini (1597–1651). K. Repgen, 'Der Westfälische Friede: Ereignis und Erinnerung', *Historische Zeitschrift*, 267 (1998): p. 634. In Contarini's Relazies the dates for the ratification are given. Cf. on Contarini N. Papadopoli (ed.), *Relazione del Congresso di Münster del Cavaliere Alvise Contarini* (Venice, 1864).

[15] Luanda in Angola.

[16] L. v. Aitzema, *Verhael van de Nederlantsche vreeden Handeling* (S'Gravens-Hage, 1650), p. 558.

[17] The factories facilitated the purchase and sale of wares. Cf. D. Rothermund, *Europa und Asien im Zeitalter des Merkantilismus* (Darmstadt, 1978), pp. 94 et seq.

[18] The Dutch–Portuguese peace treaty, for instance, had been officially announced on 18 April 1645 in Batavia.

On 7 April 1648, the 19 gentlemen of the WIC sent a letter from Amsterdam to Petrus Stuyvesant (1612–1672), the *Directeur in Nieuw Nederlandt*, former governer of Curaçao and the new Director General of the possessions administered by the WIC in New Netherland, on the east coast of North America, with his headquarter in Nieuw Amsterdam. This letter informed Stuyvesant of the peace with Spain and the expected ratification of the treaty. It also told him that the Vice-Director of the WIC, Lucas Rodenbergh in Curaçao, had been informed of the Treaty of Münster and had been instructed on how to behave towards Spanish maritime traffic in consequence.[19] Stuyvesant was given the task of officially celebrating the conclusion of peace in Nieuw Amsterdam.[20] However, an exact date was not made known to him. At any rate, on his command, a celebration of the publication and of the newly acquired sovereignty of the States General took place in Nieuw Amsterdam on 1 February 1649, one year and one day after the Treaty of Münster was signed, accompanied by prayers of thanks and sermons.[21] It may be assumed that he had announced the peace treaty weeks beforehand and thus had communicated this to the captains prior to the celebration, as was intended, so that the treaty came into effect and was legally valid. No letters or documents pertaining to this from Stuyvesant could be found, however. Why Stuyvesant failed to do so cannot be resolved. There are different possible reasons, which will be discussed consecutively in more detail. As a first clue, Stuyvesant received an admonishment on the 12th of April 1650 by the general state.

> *Honorable. Whereas we are informed that the peace has not yet been published in New Netherland, and that, therefore, some prizes are still detained there notwithstanding we sent you already, on the 19th May, 1648, some copies of the Treaty. We, therefore, have resolved hereby again to direct and command you, that you cause on sight hereof, the Peace aforesaid to be proclaimed every where in that district, under the jurisdiction of this state, without remaining any longer in default herein; and accordingly some proclamations with divers copies of the aforesaid Treaty of peace in both languages, go herewith.*[22]

Apparently Spain didn't communicate the peace negotiations of Münster clearly enough, as the general states received several messages about hostile incidents with ships in the Caribbean. They referred as well to the Spanish and Dutch ships' complement and their passengers, who weren't aware of these peace negotiations. The Peace of Münster on behalf of the general states was not published for general knowledge in Nieuw Nederland (New Netherland) until 1650. Apparently only the city of Nieuw Amsterdam (New Amsterdam) knew about the conclusion of peace.

But the celebrations were rather one-sided. The very heterogeneous inhabitants of Nieuw Amsterdam, consisting of religious refugees from territories of varying denomination in the Holy Roman Empire prior to the effects of the Thirty Years' War, protestant Walloons from

---

[19] C.T. Gehring, *Peter Stuyvesant. Correspondence, 1647–1653* (Syracuse/NY, 2000), pp. 56, 79 et seq.

[20] The contemporary summary by Donck of the Dutch possessions does not, unfortunately, contain any hint as to how these celebrations were carried out. Donck, *Beschryvinge van Nieuw-Nederlant* (The Hague, 1656).

[21] I.N.P. Stokes, *The Iconography of Manhattan Island 1498–1909* (New York, 1915), vol 1, p. 32. On the composition of the population of New Netherland, cf. J. Jacobs, *New Netherland. A Dutch Colony in Seventeenth-Century America* (Leiden and Boston, 2005), pp. 52 et seq. Around 1664, New Netherland had somewhere between 7,000 and 8,000 people (ibid., p. 93). On the various creeds, cf. ibid, pp. 263 et seq.

[22] E.B. O'Callaghan, *Documents Relative to the Colonial History of the State of New York* (Albany, 1856), p. 399.

the Spanish Netherlands, British settlers, merchants and soldiers[23] from other European states who were in the service of the WIC, all of these did not receive the celebrations well. Thereby one gets an important point of view on the impact of the conclusion of peace on the Dutch people and it shows the reserved handling of Stuyvesant's obligation to spread the message of peace negotiations. The peace treaty, in the end, meant a break with the original purpose of the New Netherland colonies as a headquarters of the WIC. New Netherland had been founded in 1626; it and Manhattan had been not only trading posts, but important starting points for operations against Spanish shipping[24] and some Spanish territories; they were, in effect, strategic military bases for the WIC troops. The founding of the WIC was primarily a matter of political interest on the part of the States General, and only secondarily of economic interest. According to Hermann Wätjen, the constant military expeditions on the part of the WIC to Central and South America served mainly to force the Spanish king, Philip IV, to wage war at places far distant from one another, and thus to divide his forces. In this manner, a part of the feared Spanish Armada was to be kept tied down in the Atlantic by constant skirmishing.[25]

In the previous years of war these goals had been attained. The Portuguese had lost some of the trade in sugar, and Brazilian areas[26] where sugar cane was planted, such as Pernambuco, had been conquered (1630); the Dutch governorate in the Brazilian areas of Recife and Fortaleza (1637–1644), led by Maurits von Nassau-Siegen, had been preserved.[27] Nieuw Amsterdam had taken on a strategically important position for the sea and trade war[28] desired by the States General, and for the trading company WIC. If the main task of the WIC was to wage war, then peace endangered the purpose of the posts and the significance of the trading company in North America. This is why the 19 gentlemen of the WIC still opposed the Portuguese suit for a ceasefire in 1640 and the subsequent 10-year peace, following Portugal's independence from Spain under the leadership of the duke of

---

[23] The VOC, in the years following the Thirty Years' War, employed many former participants in that war. Thousands of these were demobilised soldiers. Owing to the lengthy war, many of them were no longer familiar with any sort of civilian life, and in many areas there was hardly any infrastructure left worth mentioning. Often these former soldiers and officers hired on with the VOC as seamen, military protection for traders and ships, or as traders in their own right. On the employees of the VOC, cf. J.G. Nagel, *Abenteuer Fernhandel. Die Ostindienkompanien* (Darmstadt, 2007), pp. 55 et seq. F. Ibold, J. Jäger and D. Kraack (eds), *Die Niederländer in Brasilien*, in *Das Memorial und Jurenal des Peter Hansen Hajstrup (1624–1672)* (Neumünster, 1995).

[24] Of significance was the capture of the Spanish Silver Fleet at Cuba by Piet Hein in 1628. The WIC had sufficient capital after this to send 67 ships into battle with the Portuguese to gain influence in Brazilian territory. G. Kahle, *Lateinamerika in der Politik der europäischen Mächte: 1492–1810* (Cologne, Weimar and Vienna, 1993), pp. 33 et seq.

[25] H. Wätjen, *Das holländische Kolonialreich in Brasilien. Ein Kapitel aus der Kolonialgeschichte des 17. Jahrhunderts* (Gotha, 1921), p. 35. Heinz Schilling, too, assumes that the conflicts in the Old World corresponded to skirmishes in the New. Apart from the battles in the Atlantic, Spanish–Dutch sea battles took place in Asia as well, such as those in 1636/37 near the Philippines. H. Schilling, 'Der Westfälische Friede und das neuzeitliche Profil Europas', in H. Duchhardt (ed.), *Der Westfälische Friede* (Munich, 1998), p. 8. For the view that the war with Spain on the seven seas was advantageous to the Dutch, cf. A. Weindl, *Wer kleidet die Welt? Globale Märkte und merkantile Kräfte in der europäischen Politik der Frühen Neuzeit* (Mainz, 2007), pp. 104 et seq. and 141 et seq.

[26] Brazil belonged to the Spanish crown by virtue of the union with Portugal.

[27] A revolt by the Portuguese sugar plantation owners marked the beginning of the decline of the Dutch in the year 1654. Against this background, Portuguese troops reconquered the last areas of Brazil under Dutch rule (Recife and Paraiba). C.R. Boxer, *The Dutch in Brazil, 1624–1654* (Oxford, 1957). F.L. Schlakwijlk, *Igreja e Estado no Brasil Holandês. 1630–1654* (Sao Paulo, 1982).

[28] On the definition of a sea war, cf. J. Warburg, *Das Militär und seine Subjekte. Zur Soziologie des Krieges* (Bielefeld, 2008), pp. 123 et seq.

Bragança.[29] Now, in 1648, peace had been concluded in Münster with the arch-enemy Spain. With this definitive end to the war, the WIC had to reconsider the future function of Nieuw Amsterdam. The main concern now was to transmute the military and trading post into a colony of settlers with agricultural interests, and thus to modify the existing structures of rule and administration.[30] For the inhabitants of Nieuw Amsterdam, their whole *raison d'être* was changed with the Treaty of Münster: to serve the interests of the States General and their war against Spain with a military presence in the Atlantic, or to profit from trade. For in the course of concluding the treaty, the reduction of troops on the part of the States General was a matter of discussion.[31] It is possible that Stuyvesant not only wanted to finish those naval raids which were already approved, but also tried to prevent his areas of influence from having a change of meaning and being reorganised for as long as possible.

The question of the future status and the old, and possibly new, relations of the inhabitants of Nieuw Amsterdam to the WIC and to each other – and these were people from different European countries, which, until recently, had been hostile to one another, but were now brought closer together through the Spanish–Dutch peace – was reflected in the *Breeden-Raedt* (detailed report) of 1649, a fictional dialogue between nine people on the rule of the WIC in New Netherland and Brazil. The characters are, among others, a Dutch skipper, a Spanish barber, a French merchant, a Portuguese soldier who had served earlier in Brazil,[32] and an impoverished English gentleman.[33] By discussing the role of each individual in the past years of war, in which they acted as friend or foe, serving the interests of the WIC, the publication opens up a spectrum of varying European viewpoints from outside Europe on the war and the recently concluded peace with Spain.

---

[29] C.R. Boxer, *The Dutch Seaborne Empire 1600–1800* (London, 1965), p. 86. Despite the ceasefire between the Dutch and the Portuguese, there was constant conflict in Brazil. Ibold, Jäger and Kraack, *Die Niederländer in Brasilien*, pp. 30 et seq. A. Weindl, 'Das universale Vermächtnis des Westfälischen Friedens – Europäischer Frieden und außereuropäische Welt', in *Publikationsportal Europäische Friedensverträge*, Institut für Europäische Geschichte (ed.), Mainz 2009-07-27, part 5. Waffenstillstandsvertrag der Generalstaaten mit Portugal von 1641 VI. In: H Duchhardt and M. Peters (eds), www.ieg-friedensvertraege.de/friedensvertraege.

[30] A settlers' committee was founded for negotiating with the WIC. On the new structures, which were modelled on the English colonies on Long Island, and greater freedom of trade, cf. R. Shorto, *New York – Insel in der Mitte der Welt. Wie die Stadt der Städte entstand* (Hamburg, 2004), pp. 228–9. Jacobs, *New Netherland*, pp. 133 et seq. M.G. Schuyler van Rensselaer, *History of the City of New York* (New York, 1909), pp. 286–7. Bein-Partenheimer, 'Der Ruf nach Mitbestimmung: Bürgerproteste in Neu-Niederland', in T. Beck, A. Menninger and T. Schleich (eds), *Kolumbus' Erben. Europäische Expansion und überseeische Ethnien im ersten Kolonialzeitalter* (Darmstadt, 1992), pp. 174 et seq. and 182. On the location and contemporary descriptions of New Netherland, cf. F.R.E. Blom, 'Picturing New Netherland and New York. Dutch-Anglo Transfer of the New World Information', in S. Huigen, J.L. de Jong and E. Kolfin (eds), *The Dutch Trading Companies as Knowledge Networks* (Leiden, 2010), pp. 103–28.

[31] The Venetian ambassador and observer of the peace negotiations, Contarini, had noted in the course of the ratification of the agreement that there was the intention to reduce soldiers in Europe. But this observer does not say to what extent this was also true of overseas territories.

[32] In April 1624, the WIC sent 1,250 soldiers to Salvador da Bahia in Brazil. P. Klemm, 'Die Holländer in Brasilien', *Staden-Jahrbuch* 43 (1995): p. 33. M. Van Groesen, 'Officers of the West-India Company, their Networks, and their Personal Memories of Dutch Brasil', in S. Huigen, J.L. de Jong and E. Kolfin (eds), *The Dutch Trading Companies as Knowledge Networks* (Leiden, 2010), pp. 40 et seq. D. Marley, *Wars of the Americas: A Chronology of Armed Conflict in the New World. 1492 to the present* (Santa Barbara, 1998), pp. 108 et seq.

[33] H.C. Murphy, *Vertoogh van Nieu Nederland, and Breeden Raedt in de Vereinichde Nederlandsche Provintien. Two rare Tracts printed 1649–1650* (New York, 1854), pp. 130 et seq. On the literary form of the Breeden-Raedt and the significance of this publication in the Netherlands, cf. D. Merwick, *The Shame and the Sorrow: Dutch-Amerindian Encounters in New Netherland* (Pennsylvania, 2006), pp. 151 et seq.

Yet it remains unclear whether Stuyvesant communicated the peace treaty to the native population. The WIC had contact with various tribes, such as the Mohawk and the Mohican, through the fur trade,[34] and also had had treaties of friendship with them since 1643 and 1645, respectively.[35] These tribes, as contractual partners of the Dutch, were integrated into the zone of protection of the Treaty of Münster according to § 5, as will be explained in more detail below. However, as these indigenous peoples had no contact with Spain at this time, and had not been used as auxiliary troops in any military action against Spain (in contrast to the native tribes in Brazil in the course of the Dutch-Portuguese struggles in the hinterland of Pernambuco),[36] and as the Spanish-occupied territories were far distant in the south and west of North America, the content and knowledge of the Treaty of Münster could have no consequences for them. The announcement of the peace in Asia had rather clearer consequences.

The Peace of Münster as the Trigger of a Trade Crisis Between the Dutch VOC and Japan

The peace treaty concluded between Spain and the States General on 30 January 1648 in Münster, and ratified on 15 May of the same year, stipulated in § 5 that the status quo of the mutually accorded privileges at the time of the treaty[37] was to remain; that this was also the case with the current territorial possessions of the parties[38] or the spheres of influence and the shipping traffic; or that the treatment of any territories possibly yet to be acquired in future was to be as set forth in the existing agreement:

> *Die Schifffahrt und Handlungen auf Ost und Westindien / sollen nach Ausweis und den Privilegien / so allezeit darüber gegeben oder noch gegeben werden möchten/ gemeß / gehandhabet werden / und zu mehrer Versicherung dessen / soll sich*

---

[34] The Dutch had given up their original monopoly on the fur trade in 1639. Bein-Partenheimer, 'Der Ruf nach Mitbestimmung', p. 172.

[35] E.B. O'Callaghan, *History of New Netherland* (New York, 1846), pp. 354 et seq.

[36] There is but little in the way of testimony, written or otherwise, on the use of native peoples as auxiliary troops. A painting by the Dutch painter Frans Post (1614–1680) shows the use of the native tribes in the Dutch–Portuguese guerilla war between 1644 and 1654, which, despite the ceasefire of 1641, flared up repeatedly. The picture was taken up in Kaspar van Baerle's *Res Brasiliae sub Comite Mauritio Nassoviae* (Leiden, 1647). Table IV. Maurits von Nassau had made alliances with numerous chiefs. Around 2000 Tapuy and members of other tribes, trained by the Dutch, served in the Dutch military until 1647. They then went over to the Portuguese side. G. Kahle, *Lateinamerika in der Politik der europäischen Mächte 1492–1810* (Cologne, Weimar and Vienna, 1993), pp. 36 and 39. Whether, and if so, how, the Treaty of Münster was ever made known to the Tapuy or any other Brazilian tribe, remains unclear owing to the poor state of the sources.

[37] This refers to the signing of the 12-year ceasefire between the Seven Provinces and Spain. J. Israel, *The Dutch Republic. Its Rise, Greatness and Fall 1477–1806* (Oxford, 1995), pp. 399–420. M.J. Van Ittersum, *Profit and Principle. Hugo Grotius, Natural Rights Theories and the Rise of Dutch Power in the East Indies 1595–1615* (Leiden and Boston, 2006), p. 286.

[38] The directors of the VOC gave Hugo Grotius the task, in the autumn of 1607, of composing a memorandum showing and discussing the position and goals of, and options open to, the VOC in the negotiations with Spain. In this memorandum, Grotius defined 'current territorial possessions' as regions in which military alliances had been made with South-East Asian rulers, or regions in which a European power had a military presence, secured with fortresses and garrisons. The memorandum is a part of Grotius's papers in the Dutch National Archives, *Grotius Papers*, Supplement I, fol. 295–299 and fol. 405–413. Cf. Van Ittersum, *Profit and Principle*, pp. 227, 279, and 281.

gegenwärtige Handlung und Ratification, so beederseits darüber auszubringen / erstrecken; und sollen unter jetztbemeltem Tractat und Handlung / begriffen werden / alle Potentaten / Nationen und Völcker / mit welchen die vorbenannte Herren Staten / oder die von der Oost und West Indianischen Compagnie von ihrentwegen in den Schrancken ihrer Privilegien / in Freundschafft und Verbündniß stehen.

[Navigatio & commercia in Orientali & Occidentali Indiis conserventur conformiter & juxta Privilegia in eum finem jam data vel deinceps danda; & ac majorem ejus securitatem serviat praesens tractatus & ratificatio hinc inde super eo producenda: comprehendanturque sub eodem tractatu omnes potestates, nationes, & gentes, cum quibus praedicti Domini Ordines aut Indiarum Orientalis ac Occidentalis Societates, eorum nomine, intra limites privilegiorum suorum sunt in amicitia & foedere.'][39]

[Shipping and trade in the East and West Indies shall be carried out in accordance to the disclosure and to the privileges granted now or later; in assurance whereto the present act and ratification shall be enacted by both sides; this Treaty and act do apply to all potentates, nations, and peoples with whom the above-named States or the East and West India Companies, within the bounds of their privileges, are befriended and allied.]

The agreement set forth in § 5 also implied all contracts on the part of the States General or the trading companies with foreign rulers and peoples, and gave a guarantee for such contracts. This meant that the Peace Treaty of Münster extended to all *potestates, nationes et gentes* with whom the States General and their two trading companies as partners, the VOC and the WIC, had entered into contractual relations over the years.[40] In other words, all non-European powers with whom the United Provinces had any legal relations were de facto under the remit of the Spanish–Dutch peace treaty; Spain was called upon to behave towards these powers in accordance with the treaty. At the same time, they were recognised by Spain as contractual partners of the Netherlands, and the content of the existing treaties was also recognised. Thus, the peace treaty did indeed extend across the globe, as the medallion mentioned at the beginning of this chapter maintained. The treaty integrated non-European powers in the sense that the two European powers directly involved in the treaty pledged themselves not to attack any of these non-European entities and to respect any existing trade monopolies in the sense of valid economic treaties, as well as any military alliances. Section 5 of the Peace Treaty of Münster was primarily of advantage to the Dutch, as Spain did not have any non-European treaty partners, and was not bound in *friendship or alliance*, but had conquered the indigenous peoples and robbed them of their sovereignty. As part of the Peace of Westphalia, the treaty of Münster was a treaty in which non-European powers

---

[39] The Spanish–Dutch treaty was composed in Dutch and French, in contrast to the treaty of the estates of the Holy Roman Empire, which was in Latin. Only later was the former translated into Latin. H. Dollinger, 'Alvise Contarini und seine Briefe an Giovanni Batista Felice Gasparo Nani', in H. Bertram (ed.), *Alvise Contarini und der Westfälische Friedenskongress in Münster: Ausstellung vom 4. bis 30. Oktober 1982* (Münster, 1982), p. 11. The Dutch text of the treaty of 30 January 1648 with the ratifications of the Spanish king and the States General can be found in: L. v. Aitzema, *Verhael van de Nederlantsche vreeden Handeling* (S'Gravens-Hage, 1650), pp. 565–96.

[40] Quoted according to the Tractatus Pacis Trigesimo Januarii..., http://www.lwl.org/westfaelische-geschichte/que/normal/que2603.pdf (accessed on 17/06/2013). On this, cf. A. Weindl, 'Das universale Vermächtnis des Westfälischen Friedens. Europäischer Frieden und außereuropäische Welt', in *Publikationsportal Europäische Friedensverträge*, Institut für Europäische Geschichte (ed.), Mainz 2009, part 3.

were mentioned as subjects of international law,⁴¹ but only so long as they were sovereign entities. The non-European powers as treaty partners of the VOC were not automatically treaty partners in the peace treaty of 1648, however. They were not automatically bound to peace with Spain, but were able to wage war against the Spanish crown, if they chose to do so.

Their sovereignty under international law accorded to them by Hugo Grotius was, then, not limited. Grotius viewed non-European peoples as sovereign equals, subject to international law. He basically applied Jean Bodin's (1529/30–1596) characteristics to define sovereignty. Sovereignty was shown in the *summa potestas* of the right to give laws, the ability of the highest legal instance, the right to name officials, fiscal rights, and the right to impose taxes. Grotius thus allowed that non-European peoples as active protagonists also had the sovereign right to wage war and to conclude alliances or treaties among themselves or with European powers.⁴² According to Grotius, this implied diplomatic relations between non-Europeans and Europeans, e.g. in the form of letters and embassies.⁴³ In the CIT, Grotius connected the right to wage war with the authority of the highest jurisprudence: 'Ius bellum indicendi sequitur potestatem iudicandi … Et consequenter is qui habet alios actus cum hunc non habet bellum quoque gerere non poterit'.⁴⁴

In contrast to Jean Bodin, Grotius regarded sovereignty as divisible. The VOC used this, in particular, in its dealings with various South-East Asian sultans and princes, in that the trading company had sovereign rights transferred to it to some extent in the trade agreements, and made use of these rights. In reality, many peoples of South and South-East Asia, in India, Malaya, and the Indonesian archipelago, were deprived of the right to a sovereign foreign policy by means of the contracts and treaties with the VOC. Alliances with other communities were expressly forbidden or only permitted after prior consultation with the trading company: 'niet en zullen vermogen eenige alliantien, ofte verbonden te maken met Spanjaards, Tidoresen, Macassaren, Bandanesen, Engelschen, Deenen, Franschen ofte andere natien, buiten expres consent, en voorweten van gemelde Gouverneur, ofte zyne successeurs.'⁴⁵

---

⁴¹ Weindl emphasises that this was the last European treaty to mention non-European powers as subjects of international law. That is correct, but only chosen powers were involved whose sovereignty had not been annulled in the course of colonisation. A. Weindl, 'Das universale Vermächtnis', part 11. Richter, 'Das Völkerrecht – Ein europäisches Phänomen?', ZRG (German. Abt.), 127 (2010): pp. 293–300.

⁴² 'Actus summae potestatis sunt omnes quos nemo iure superioritatis potest rescindere, puta, suprema legislatio et abrogatio, iurisdictio, veniae datio, magistratuum creatio et destitutio, publicorum onerum impositio et si qua sunt similia.' H. Grotius, 'Comentarius in Theses XI', in P. Borschberg (ed.), *Commentarius in Theses XI. An Early Treatise on Sovereignty, the Just War, and the Legitimacy of the Dutch Revolt* (Bern et al., 1994), here § 23. Abbreviated hereafter as CIT.

⁴³ Cf. H. Grotius, *De Jure Praedae Commentarius. Texte Latin, publié pour la première fois d'après le manuscrit autographe par Ger. Hamaker* (Paris and The Hague, 1869), p. 324. Grotius had studied matters concerning current laws of war, publishing this in 1627 in his *De iure pacis ac belli*, but had not dealt concretely with the war then going on. He intended to travel to the peace negotiations in Münster, but he died in 1645. Nevertheless, he is seen as one of the spiritual fathers of the peace treaty, which is emphasised by an allegory. H. Lahrkamp, *Dreißigjähriger Krieg und Westfälischer Frieden* (Münster, 1997), p. 305. Application of the allegory to Grotius and the Peace of Westphalia, 306. A.T. Serra, 'Die Lehre vom gerechten Krieg bei Grotius und Leibniz und ihre Bedeutung für die Gegenwart', *Studia Leibnitiana*, 16 (1984): pp. 60–72.

⁴⁴ CIT, § 41. Cf. Borschberg, *Hugo Grotius 'Commentarius in Theses XI'*, p. 150. J. Fisch, *Die europäische Expansion und das Völkerrecht. Die Auseinandersetzungen um den Status der überseeischen Gebiete vom 15. Jahrhundert bis zur Gegenwart* (Stuttgart, 1984), pp. 38–43.

⁴⁵ *Corpus Diplomaticum Neerlando-Indicum. Verzameling van Politieke contracten en verde verdragen door de Nederlanders in het Oosten gesloten, van Privilegebrieven, aan hen verleend, enz.*, ed. by J.E. Heeres (Gravenhage, 1907), p. 201, treaty with Banda 1624; similarly, N° LIV, 128, treaty with Banda 1617; N°

The Edo Shōgunate in Japan was, however, not among the states in which the Dutch were able to acquire sovereign rights. Their trading privilege was based solely on the sufferance of the Japanese and the obligation imposed on the VOC of not interfering in any way with politics or religion. From the end of the sixteenth century, the mood in Japan had turned against Christians and their missionaries. With the increasing unification and centralisation of the country, the connections with the Jesuits and Spanish (1624) or Portuguese traders became ever more tenuous. In 1637/38 a revolt of Christians on the peninsula of Shimabara near Nagasaki was triggered and was bloodily suppressed. The year 1639 then saw the prohibition of Christianity, with political measures such as deportation which ended the role of Christianity in Japan for the time being. From the Japanese point of view, Christianity represented a threat to their religious and political order, two things they saw as one. Reports from those parts of Asia that had been colonised by the Spanish and Portuguese strengthened this view, as did the missionary strategy of the Jesuits and other Spanish or Portuguese orders, which concentrated on the elite of the state. The mission, according to the official explanation for the deportation of Christians in 1639, was preparing the conquest of Japan by the Spanish and Portuguese.[46] Spain and Portugal thus represented an immense threat to the internal stability of the Japanese state. Foreigners, in particular Spaniards and Portuguese, the so-called 'southern barbarians', were forbidden to remain on land from now on. This was valid for all ships, too, for anchoring off the Japanese coast was also strictly forbidden and would have been answered without delay by military action.[47] As an alternative European trading power, only the representatives of the Dutch VOC were able to establish themselves in Japan, and took over the small trading post on the artificial island of Dejima[48] from the Portuguese. In Japanese eyes, they were not interested in missionary activity and thus represented no danger.[49] Furthermore, the war between Spain and the

---

XC, 220, treaty with Ambon 1628; N° XCI, 226, treaty with the Moluccas 1629; N° CXXV, 307, treaty with Banda 1637; N° CXXXVIII, 350, treaty with Malacca 1641; N° CXLVII, 381, treaty with Palembang 1642; N° CLII, 397, treaty with Coromandel 1643. Cf. J.A. Somers, *De VOC als volkenrechtelijke actor* (Gouda, 2001).

[46] Ludwig Riess translated the edicts directing the deportation of foreigners, from the *Nihon no ayumi*: 'Die Christenbande ist nach Japan gekommen, indem sie nicht nur ihre Handelsschiffe sandte, sondern auch danach trachtete, ein böses Gesetz zu verbreiten, die rechte Lehre umzustoßen, so daß sie die Regierung des Staates und den Land Besitz ergreifen konnte.' ('The Christian gang has come to Japan by not only sending their trading ships, but also to spread an evil law, to overthrow the proper teaching, so that they could take control of the state and the country.') Quoted from: L. Riess, 'Die Ursachen der Vertreibung der Portugiesen aus Japan (1614–1639)', *MOAG* VII (1898): p. 28. Cf. also M. Schrimpf, *Zur Begegnung des japanischen Buddhismus mit dem Christentum in der Meiji-Zeit (1868–1912)* (Wiesbaden, 2000), pp. 15 et seq, 32. On the Shimabara revolt, cf. in summary H. Pöcher, *Kriege und Schlachten in Japan, die Geschichte schrieben. Von den Anfängen bis 1853* (Vienna, 2009), pp. 137 et seq.

[47] F. Reichert, 'Reise- und entdeckungsgeschichtliche Grundlagen. Descriptio Regni Iaponico', in M. Schuchard (ed.), *Bernhard Varenius (1622–1650)* (Leiden, 2007), pp. 137 et seq.

[48] An *Opperhoofden* (head factor) represented the VOC's interests to the Japanese officials in Dejima and had to undertake a journey to the Shōgun's court in Edo (Tokyo) once a year. An *Opperhoofden* held his position as a rule for one year only. In 1648 and 1649, the following occupied this position: Frederick Coijet (3/11/1647–9/12/1648) and Dircq Snoecq (9/12/1648–5/11/1649). K. Vos, 'Dejima und die Handelsbeziehungen zwischen den Niederlanden und dem vormodernen Japan', in D. Croissant and L. Ledderose (eds), *Japan und Europa 1543–1929. Eine Ausstellung der '43. Berliner Festwochen' im Martin-Gropius-Bau Berlin* (Berlin, 1993), pp. 72–82. O. Nachod, *Die Beziehungen der Niederländischen Ost-Indischen Kompagnie in Japan im siebzehnten Jahrhundert* (Leipzig, 1897), pp. 297 et seq.

[49] In a letter from the Governor General there is a recommendation for the behaviour of the VOC towards the Japanese, namely that no missionary activity should be undertaken: '… mit Fleiß auf den Inhalt zu merken: Es scheint, wann wir uns mit der Beförderung des Christentums nicht einlassen/ und in Jappan [sic], was dieses anbelangt, Still halten werden/man sollte uns viel Freyheiten vergünstigen und eine verträgliche Handlung daselbst zulassen'. J.J. Merklein, *Zugabe zu H. Carons Jappan …* (Nürnberg, 1663), p. 238.

States General guaranteed the Japanese additional protection from the Spanish in their own territory. But the behaviour of the VOC employees was constantly, strictly, and critically watched over by the Japanese, and their freedom of movement on the island of Dejima was limited.

The equality under international law that Grotius had attributed to non-Europeans as a matter of course was also transferred to the use of titles for non-European potentates. Thus, the physician and traveller Engelbert Kämpfer (1651–1716) of Lemgo, who had been in the Dutch service in Japan from 1690 to 1692, accorded the Shōgun (actually the imperial commander)[50] of Japan the title 'Emperor'. He placed Japan in the same category as China, whose 'Son of Heaven' also had the title of Emperor in the European terminology.[51]

The Shōgunate of Edo, as a treaty partner of the VOC, was now among those *potestates, nationes et gentes* who, according to § 5 of the Peace of Münster, were current contractual partners of the VOC and thus to be respected, and not attacked, by the Spanish. The question is, how was the peace treaty communicated to the Japanese by the representatives of the VOC, and how did they receive this?

The *Generale Missive* of 18 January 1649 confirms that the High Government in Batavia in the Indonesian archipelago had taken cognisance of the report of the *vrede van Munster* (Peace of Münster).[52] When exactly the report had reached Java remains uncertain. But it must have arrived sometime during the year 1648, for the yearly embassy of the VOC from the island of Dejima to the Japanese Shōgun at the court in Edo informed the ruler of the peace between the States General and Spain, concluded within the greater framework of the Peace of Westphalia. Whether, and when, celebrations took place on the occasion of the ratification or the publication of the peace is not possible to say, owing to a lack of source material. The *Missive* of 31 December 1649, at any rate, makes no mention of any such celebration in the city of Batavia in the course of the entire year. The *Dag Register* for 1649 in Batavia would very probably yield this information, but the omnibus volume for the years 1649 and 1650

---

[50] The title and office implied a political and legal authority over other noble families which could be enforced, as well as the right to arrange foreign relations and trade. R. Zöllner, *Geschichte Japans. Von 1800 bis zur Gegenwart* (Paderborn, Munich and Vienna, 2006), p. 21. M.B. Jansen, *Warrior rule in Japan* (Cambridge u.a., 1995), Introduction.

[51] E. Kaempfer, 'Von dem Uhrsprung der Einwohner' in W. Michel and B. J. Terwiel (eds), *Heutiges Japan* (Munich, 2001), pp. 67–78. Caron had spoken of the majesty and the imperial dignity of the Japanese ruler, since kings and princes obeyed him, and he had the power over Japan *eigentümlich* (that is, as property and possessions). F. Caron and J. Schouten, *Wahrhaftige Beschreibungen zweyer mächtigen Königreiche, Jappan und Siam. Benebenst noch vielen andern, zu beeden Königreichen gehörigen, Sachen; welche im Vorbericht zu finden. Alles aus dem Niederländischen übersetzt ...* (Nürnberg, 1663), pp. 29 et seq. This refers to fiefdoms which, however, were still internally autonomous to a great extent. D. Taranczewski, 'Japan, der Feudalismus, Westeuropa, Ostasien', in H.-M. Krämer and T. Schölz (eds), *Geschichtswissenschaft in Japan. Themen, Ansätze und Theorien* (Göttingen, 2006), p. 45. On the status of Japan under international law, cf. H. Kleinschmidt, *Das europäische Völkerrecht und die ungleichen Verträge um die Mitte des 19. Jahrhunderts* (Munich, 2007), p. 18. S. Richter, 'Die Bewertung des chinesischen Kaisers in europäischen Druckwerken des 17. und 18. Jahrhunderts als Spiegel seiner völkerrechtlichen Gleichrangigkeit', *Jahrbuch der Staatlichen Kunstsammlungen Dresden*, 34 (2008): pp. 27–39.

[52] *Generale missiven van Gouverneurs-Generaal en Raden aan Heren XVII der Verenigde Oostindische Compagnie* (The Hague, 1960-76), vol 2, p. 332. The *Generale Missiven* consist of a comprehensive letter of information from the High Government in Batavia on events on ships and to do with trade in all of Asia; it was addressed to the 17 gentlemen of the VOC (*Heeren XVII*), and was composed once or twice yearly. These letters represented the institutionalised contact between the highest authority in the colony and the leadership of the VOC. This structure was also taken over by the Vgl. Jacobs, *New Netherland*, pp. 100 et seq.

is missing.[53] Also the *Dag Register* of the factory on Dejima does not make any special note of receiving the report of the conclusion of peace. A formal celebration on this small island was, of course, not to be expected.[54]

The news of the Peace of Münster had reached the Shōgun of Japan in 1648 through the VOC chief factor, the *Opperhoofden* of the factory of Dejima,[55] and had contributed to the greatest disquiet among the Japanese. How exactly the matter was presented to the Japanese can no longer be reconstructed. Apart from the journeys to the court, the news from Europe, especially oral reports on Spain and Portugal and letters from the Dutch Governor General in Batavia, was brought by the Dutch ships to Dejima, where it was translated into Japanese, out of loyalty and in the hope of retaining trade concessions, and transmitted as so-called *Oranda fūsetsu gaki* (formal reports of matters heard from the Netherlands) to the magistrate of Nagasaki and the Shōgun in Edo.[56] The news, despite the Netherlands filtering it carefully, was of great strategic value to Japan, for otherwise none, save the Chinese reports,[57] entered the country any longer. Unfortunately, the *Oranda fūsetsu gaki* for the seventeenth century have not been edited and are only available as manuscripts in the Japanese State Archives in Tokyo. It must therefore remain unclear for the time being as to when, to what extent, and above all, what information on the conclusion of peace in 1648 did reach the magistrate of Nagasaki and the Shōgun in Edo by this route.

The disquiet of the Japanese was caused by the fact that in the previous year, 1648, two Portuguese ships with an embassy from the king had landed in Nagasaki without permission. The Japanese were informed of the ceasefire agreed in 1643 between Portugal and the States General, and were irritated by it. They assumed now that, in consequence of this agreement and of the new peace with Spain concluded in Münster, the Dutch would possibly bring missionaries to Japan on their ships.[58] The usual yearly embassy of the chief factor of Dejima to the court of the Shōgun was therefore turned away in 1648 for reasons of mistrust on the part of the Japanese; the gifts offered by the VOC were not accepted. The Japanese required a special embassy from the States General on the model of the unwanted embassy from the Portuguese king in 1647; this was to be led by a noble and was to explain the situation and dispel the unrest. The Japanese made this known through the agent and head of the religions office, Inoue Masashige (1585–1661).[59] This wish was communicated

---

[53] The Dagh registers have been published by the Departement van Koloniën, *Dagh-register gehouden int Casteel Batavia vant passerende daer ter plaetse als over geheel Nederlandts-India*. 31 vols (The Hague, 1887–1931).

[54] C. Viallé and L. Blussé, *The Deshima Dagregisters: Their original tables of contents*. Vol. XI: 1641–1650 (Leiden, 2001).

[55] On the yearly journeys to the court, the route, gifts, and aims of the *Opperhoofden* of the Dejima factory in the 19th century, cf. C. Blomhoff, *The Court Journey to the Shōgun of Japan* (Leiden, 2000).

[56] I. Seiichi, *Oranda fusetsu-gaki* (Tokyo, 1976/79). F. Matsukata, *Oranda Fusetsugaki to Kinsei Nihon* (Tokyo, 2007).

[57] R.P. Toby, *State and Diplomacy in Early Modern Japan: Asia in the Development of Tokugawa Bakufu* (Princeton, 1984), pp. 124 et seq.

[58] Nachod, *Die Beziehungen der Niederlandischen Ost-Indischen Kompagnie*, p. 319. Briefly also: W. Michel, *Von Leipzig nach Japan — Der Chirurg und Handelsmann Caspar Schamberger (1623–1706)* (Munich, 1999), pp. 53 et seq.

[59] The Shōgunate valued diplomatic relations very highly, in order to position Japan within Asia. Diplomatic relations with Western powers such as the Netherlands were also valued. Toby, *State and Diplomacy in Early Modern Japan*, pp. 142 et seq.

by Batavia to Amsterdam, but there were no official diplomatic relations between the States General and the Shōgunate at Edo, and the VOC had to act immediately.[60]

The goal of the trading company consisted in reviving relations with the Japanese as rapidly as possible. François Caron (approx. 1600–1673) of the High Government, also known as the Council of East India, therefore himself put together a special delegation in Batavia in 1649, led by the lawyer and former rector of a school for Latin, Pieter Blokhuys (also known as Petrus Blockhovius),[61] and his representative, Andries Frisius. The scholar, who had no express knowledge of Japan, was to give the special delegation more dignity, as he was an influential person in Batavia. The delegation was sent from Batavia to the court at Edo, equipped with suitable accoutrements and valuable gifts, and was to clarify the incidents mentioned, and to calm the disquiet of the Japanese, but also to clarify once more, in person and in a conclusive manner, other matters which had exacerbated the doubts, such as the landing of the Dutch ship *Breskens* in Nambu in 1643, and to thank the representatives of Shōgun Iemitsu (1604–1651) for the friendly reception accorded the stranded seamen.[62] An essential reason for this delegation was also to represent the new contractual relations between the European powers following the end of the Eighty Years' War, or Thirty Years' War, to the Shōgun in such a way as to calm the Japanese, and to persuade them that the conclusion of peace between the States General and Spain would result in no threat, and that they should not doubt the loyalty and trustworthiness of the Dutch. The VOC delegation, which set off in the direction of Edo on 10 November 1649 and landed there on 31 December of the same year, also aimed at announcing and representing the newly acquired sovereignty of the States General by means of putting up a much more magnificent appearance than hitherto.

The delegation was given instructions and exact rules on the content, extent, and type of announcement to be made to the Shōgun. The author of these instructions, dated 27 July 1649, was most likely Caron himself, for, having spent many years in Japan, he possessed an excellent knowledge of the political goals and had experience in dealing with the Japanese.[63]

---

[60] R.H. Hesselink, *Prisoners from Nambu: Reality and Make-Believe in Seventeenth-Century Japanese Diplomacy* (Honolulu, 2001), pp. 142 et seq. W. Michel, *Der Ost-Indischen und angrenzenden Königreiche vornehmste Seltenheiten betreffende kurze Erläuterung – Neue Funde zum Leben und Werk des Leipziger Chirurgen und Handelsmanns Caspar Schamberger (1623–1706)*. Online Paper of Kyushu University, The Faculty of Languages and Cultures Library, No 1. Fukuoka: Hana-Shoin, March 2010, pp. 12 et seq. (no source named). This is also referred to in the report by Johann Jacob Mercklein, *Ost-Indianische Reise, welche er im Jahr 1644 löblich angenommen, und im Jahr 1653 glücklich vollendet ...* (Nürnberg, 1663), p. 418.

[61] The *Generale Missive* of 31 December 1649 reported to Amsterdam: ... *zending van Petrus Blockhovius als gezant naar Japan*. Generale missiven, vol. 2, p. 388. Merklein reports that the death of Blockhovius, who was gravely ill, had been reckoned with for the period of the journey and was to be used deliberately in the diplomacy. The Japanese were to believe that the high-ranking ambassador had died on his way to them. The delegation had mourning crepe along for this very purpose. Mercklein, *Ost-Indianische Reise*, p. 419.

[62] The ship was actually on a voyage of exploration, aiming to find islands with rich gold deposits. The Dutch, however, claimed a lack of food on board as the reason for the unauthorised landing. A. Montanus, *Denckwürdige Gesandtschafften der Ost-Indischen Geselschaft in den Vereinigten Niederländern/ an unterschiedliche Keyser von Japan ...* (Amsterdam, 1670), pp. 281–91. On the delegation of 1649 to the Emperor, cf. ibid., p. 25. Nachod, *Die Beziehungen der Niederländischen Ost-Indischen Kompagnie*, pp. 311et seq. Hesselink, *Prisoners from Nambu*, pp. 105 et seq.

[63] Boxer, *Jan compagnie in Japan, 1600–1817. An essay on the cultural, artistic and scientific influence exercised by the Hollanders in Japan from the seventeenth to the nineteenth centuries* (The Hague, 1936), p. XCVII. In 1639 Caron had himself led a delegation as *Opperhoofden* of the former factory in Hirado during a journey to the court of the Shōgun. Caron reported personally on the delegation led by Blockhovius and Frisius. Caron and Schouten, *Wahrhaftige Beschreibungen*, pp. 417–20.

He instructed Blokhovius and Frisius as follows with regard to the communications strategy to announce the peace with Spain:

> *Wegens de getroffen vrede tusschen 't Vereenigde Nederland, Spanjen en Portugael, waer voor niet sonder reden beducht stonden, dat het de Japansche kaisar oevel soude opnemen, alsoo de Spanjaerden en Portugeesen des selfs dood vyanden blijven, kond berichten: hoe (volgens 't verhael voor eenige tijd in Japan verspreid) 't gantsche Christendom, door langwijlige oorlog afgeflooft, haer zaementlijk ten vrede neigde. Sulx Vrankrijk en Sweeden met de Duitsche kaisar een verbond gemaekt hadden: in welk verbond sich inlieten Denemerken, Poolen en Italien. Alleenlijk Vrankrijk en Portugael bleven gewaepened tegen Spanje: soo nochtans dat diesweegen gevolmagtigden gesteld waeren tot bemiddeling der onderlinge verschillen: welke buiten twijfel eerlang stonden bygeleid te worden: alsoo, by droevige ervaerenheid, verwoesting op verwoesting wederzijds gevoelden: terwijl sich de Turk algemeine vyand der Christenen, niet sonder algemeine schrik van de Christenheid, meester maekte van verscheide sterkten, steden en landschappen. De vreede, die de Christensen onderling befluisten, strekt enkelijk daer toe, om de vereelde krachten te vereenigen, en de vereenigde tegen 't Tursche rijk aen tevoeren.*[64]

> *[Because of the peace concluded between the United Netherlands, Spain, and Portugal, which, as we have good reason to fear, the Japanese Shōgun will not receive well, as the Spanish and Portuguese remain his deadly enemies, you could report that all of Christendom, tired of long years of war [just as the report circulated some time ago in Japan has it], now tends in general toward peace, so that France and Sweden have made an alliance with the German Emperor, into which Denmark, Poland, and Italy have also entered. France and Portugal alone remain at war with Spain, but in such a manner as to have representatives used to mediate the mutual differences, which doubtless will be laid aside very soon, since both sides have learned through sad experience that devastation and destruction were received, while the Turk, the general enemy of Christendom, and not without widespread terror among Christians, has conquered various and sundry fortresses, towns, and territories. The peace that the Christians conclude among themselves is only intended to unite the disparate powers and to lead them united against the Turkish Empire.]*

At the same time, the instruction required the delegates to reveal only this necessary information of the peace treaty, and subsequently to excuse themselves from speaking of any other details of Dutch matters of state. Rather, they were to emphasise to the Shōgun that they were merchants, and that they pursued purely economic interests. The Japanese

---

[64] Instruction of the Government of East India in Batavia for the delegate Peter Blokhovius on the occasion of his journey to Japan of 27 July 1649, in A. Montanus (ed.), *Gedenkwaerdige gesantschappen der Oost-Indische maatschappy in 't Vereenigde Nederland aen de Kaisaren van Japan …* (Amsterdam, 1669), pp. 365 et seq. Montanus used a text of this instruction, preserved today in the Nationaal Archief in The Hague (Nederlandse Factorij Japan NFJ, No. 282). A copy exists under Verenigde Oostindische Compagnie VOC 873, fol. 60–9. (This is the 'Uitgaand briefboeken' for Batavia, the copy book with copies of official correspondence of the Gouverneur-generaal between 5 February and 30 December 1649.) On the instruction, cf. briefly Kapitza, *Japan in Europa. Texte und Bilddokumente zur europäischen Japankenntnis von Marco Polo bis Wilhelm von Humboldt* (Munich, 1990), vol. 1, pp. 570–72. Michel, *Von Leipzig nach Japan*, p. 230. J. Murdoch, *A History of Japan. Vol 3. The Tokugawa epoch, 1652 – 1868* (New York, 1926), p. 271. There is also a German translation of the instruction in Nachod, *Die Beziehungen der Niederlandischen Ost-Indischen Kompagnie*, p. CLXXV.

would then see, so the author of the instruction hoped, that the delegates were not in a position to render an account of the government of the States General.[65]

The instruction from Batavia is to be understood as a diplomatic and, in particular, placatory reaction to the announcement the previous year of the end of the Eighty Years' War and the peace with Spain. Clearly the VOC had completely underestimated the effect of this news on the Japanese and the consequences for the VOC's trade with Japan. For this reason, the instruction opens up an interesting view of the evaluation and external representation of the war and the Treaty of Münster on the part of the East India Trading Company for the benefit of non-European powers or treaty partners. The instruction declares the peace to be a purely internal European, Christian necessity, to enable the Europeans to act more successfully against their common enemy, the Ottoman Empire. The argument in the VOC instruction shows that the portrayal of Dutch interests in the peace with Spain was consciously suppressed, but that a concomitant phenomenon of the peace, one wanted by third parties, was raised to the status of an essential reason for the conclusion of peace. Since January 1645, alarming indications had increased of an impending escalation of the quarrel with the Ottomans. In the summer, an incident in the Eastern Mediterranean had been used by the Sublime Porte to dispatch a fleet to conquer Crete. Venice, especially, was interested in attaining peace in Europe, so as to receive help against the Ottomans.[66] Bernhard Rottendorf (1594–1671), the town physician of Münster, had emphasised, in his 1646 appeal for peace directed at all delegates in Münster, that peace in Christendom was needed, not least because the Republic of Venice urgently required help against the Ottoman threat.[67] The VOC delegation emphasised in turn to the Japanese ruler the necessity of this Christian alliance against the common enemy.

At the same time, the delegates were instructed to guarantee to the Japanese Shōgun that his enmity towards Spain and Portugal would not affect Dutch–Japanese interests and relations, or at least that the Japanese need not fear that they would again be confronted with missionaries as a consequence of the peace treaty, this time with the aid of the VOC. The instruction implies the clear statement of the VOC that the Treaty of Münster would have no effect on allies, but represented a purely European matter, although this was certainly much desired and regarded as necessary by the Dutch, too. The delegation quite explicitly emphasised the value of the Treaty of Münster for the States General; in this, a certain complaint by the VOC about the length of the war can be discerned. Peace, finally, depended on the grace of God and was concluded in his honour by a Christendom that had seen the light, for peace corresponded with the divine order of things. Peace could not be attained without the grace of God. This aspect did not need to be understandable for the Japanese, as non-Christians, but was expressly emphasised to them, nevertheless, by the delegation. This external representation of the peace treaty, chosen by the VOC, shows that Christendom wished to be seen again as a unified area of law and peace, a *respublica christiana*, or *christianus orbis*, as it had been regarded before the Reformation, during the wars against the Ottoman Empire. This goal of unifying Christendom was emphasised to the Japanese.[68]

---

[65] Nachod, *Die Beziehungen der Niederlandischen Ost-Indischen Kompagnie*, p. CLXXVI.

[66] Cf. on this B. Roeck, 'Venedigs Rolle im Krieg und bei den Friedensverhandlungen', in *1648: Krieg und Frieden in Europa* (Münster, 1998), p. 165.

[67] H. Lahrkamp, *Dreißigjähriger Krieg und Westfälischer Frieden* (Münster, 1997), p. 246.

[68] On this, cf. Roeck, Venedigs Rolle, p. 165. Andretta, *La diplomazia veneziana e la pace di Vestfalia (1643–1648)* (Roma, 1978). B. Haller, *Alvise Contarini und der Westfälische Friedenskongress in Münster*. Ausstellung vom 4. bis 30. Oktober 1982 (Münster, 1982), p. 39.

This understanding of Christendom as an entity unified against foreign religious powers, represented to the Shōgun by the VOC envoys, was given legitimation, too, by Hugo Grotius in his version of international law, which regarded Christendom as a closed inner circle entering into relations with peoples in the outer, non-Christian circle, to take up trade or to conclude treaties or alliances. For Grotius, this was desirable not only according to natural law, but also even according to divine law. All non-Christian peoples were seen by Grotius as less than equal with regard to their moral values in comparison to those peoples who were bound to law by the divine will.[69] The solidarity of the Christians was therefore emphasised by him on the basis of common moral values, and placed above all other interests.

The reasons for the peace with Spain, as chosen by the special envoys of the VOC, namely the war weariness and the necessity of Christian unity against a common enemy, were intended to dispel the Japanese disquiet, at least as far as the Europeans were combining their strength against the Ottomans, and Japan was thus not in the limelight. But this interpretation of the peace did entail the danger that the common religion of the Europeans could unify and propel its followers to concerted action against a non-Christian power. This might indeed have a disquieting effect on the Japanese. The VOC strategy was not without risk.

Because of the peace with Spain, discussions with Japanese court officials repeatedly took place during the stay of the VOC special envoys. The head of the religious office, Inoue Masashige (1585–1661), functioned as the chief Japanese negotiator, since he knew the Europeans well, being a former Christian himself.[70] The Shōgun himself did not take part for health reasons. Clearly, it was not easy to persuade the Japanese that the Dutch peace with Spain would not have any negative effect on them. Not until 20 January 1650, three weeks after the arrival of the envoys, was it possible to achieve agreement over the Spanish and Portuguese matters and to restore good relations with the Japanese. The Dutch gifts were now accepted, and valuable gifts given to the Dutch in turn, as tokens of goodwill towards the trading company. Following this mission, the trade on Dejima flourished for about 20 years.[71]

We are informed about the negotiations with Inoue Masashige and the Japanese doubts, not only from the Dutch perspective, through the diary of Anthonio van Brouckhorst, the

---

[69] Cf. P. Borschberg, '"De Societate cum Infidelibus" (Una obra juvenil de Hugo Grocio)', *Revista de Estudios Politicos*, 83 (1994): pp. 127 et seq. K. Makoto, 'Agreements between Nations: Treaties and Good Faith with Enemies', in O. Yauaki (ed.), *A Normative Approach to War. Peace, War and Justice in Hugo Grotius* (Oxford, 1993), p. 312. H. Grotius, *De Iure Belli ac Pacis Libri Tres. In quibus ius naturae et gentium item iuris publici praecipua explicantur*, curavit, B.J.A. De Kanter-Van Hettinga Tromp, R. Feenstra and C.E. Persenaire (eds) (= revised printing of the edition of Leiden 1939) (Aalen, 1993), Book 2, Chap. 15, IX. The outer circle, according to Grotius, comprised all mankind, who, regardless of religion, were bound to each other by natural law. In contrast, only the Christian peoples belonged to the inner circle, because for these peoples not only natural law was valid, but also divine law, owing to their specific agreement with the divine. Cf. M. Wight, *Systems of States* (Leicester, 1977), pp. 125 et seq. C. A. Stumpf, 'Völkerrecht unter Kreuz und Halbmond: Muhammad al-Shaybani und Hugo Grotius als Exponenten religiöser Völkerrechtstraditionen', *Archiv des Völkerrechts* 41/1 (2003): p. 98.

[70] A diary of his on the details of the negotiations exists. W. Michel, 'Medizin, Heilmittel und Pflanzenkunde im euro-japanischen Kulturaustausch des 17. Jahrhunderts', *Hōrin – Vergleichende Studien zur japanischen Kultur* 16 (2010): 19 –34. Here reference 16. On his activity with the envoys in 1649, cf. L. Blussé, 'The Grand Inquisitor Inoue, Spin Doctor of the Tokugawa Bakufu', *BPJS*, 7 (2003): pp. 40 et seq. For biographical information, cf. Hesselink, *Prisoners from Nambu*, pp. 57 et seq.

[71] Nachod, *Die Beziehungen der Niederländischen Ost-Indischen Kompagnie*, p. 327.

opperhoofd of the post at Dejima, but also from the other side, through the diary of Inoue himself.[72] Apart from the personal notes by the two negotiators, minutes exist.[73]

Summary

This chapter has shown first that the Treaty of Münster, as announced on Engelbert Kettler's medallion, was indeed announced and adhered to, even if such announcement did not necessarily happen within the agreed time frame, on both sides of the ocean in the zones of influence of the two Dutch trading companies, although celebrations were certainly only muted. The claim formulated on the medallion, of having achieved more security for many states and provinces throughout the world by means of the treaty, was primarily true of the two European parties to the treaty. The conclusion of peace ended the military actions on the seas of the world, which had been carried out by the Netherlands especially in overseas regions as part of the struggle for independence from Spain, by way of tying down Spanish power and breaking through the Spanish monopolies on contact, settlement, and trade legitimised by the Papal bull *Inter caetera*. The States General had been able to establish themselves as a European economic and trading power in all parts of the world by means of the war,[74] and brought enormous losses to the Iberian powers. The peace treaty now guaranteed the status quo of the Spanish and Dutch spheres of influence.

But the Treaty of Münster also created new problems. For the Dutch WIC, the end of the war meant the loss of a major factor in its *raison d'être* and its area of activity. In Asia, however, the conclusion of peace caused a few new conflicts with non-European trading partners of the VOC. This chapter has shown, using the example of the contractual relations between the VOC and Japan, that Jürgen Osterhammel's assumption that the concept of the peace of 1648 could not be transferred to the relations between Europe and non-European countries, and consequently was not adapted by the latter, is quite correct with regard to the legal aspects. However, the peace treaty did protect non-European partners of the two powers, Spain and the Netherlands, from hostile actions on the part of one or the other. But the assumption that the legalisation of internal European relations had no influence on non-European, non-Christian cultures has been shown to be false. Japan felt itself threatened by the peace treaty between the States General and Spain, and the possibility of an alliance between the two powers, particularly in view of the fact that the years of war between the two European states had offered Japan the greatest possible security from Spain, indeed, even the protection of the Dutch. The enormous uncertainty of the Japanese with regard to the news of the conclusion of peace had, after all, disrupted relations between the VOC and the court for a year, to the point where the trading activities of 1648 ceased altogether in some cases, such as the trade in porcelain, owing to the Japanese issuing no permits.[75] Explaining the peace treaty to Japan required some diplomatic effort and careful negotiations

---

[72] Nationaal Archief Den Haag, Nederlandse Factorij Japan, NFJ 63, Diary of Anthonio van Brouckhorst, entry of 18 January 1650, pp.19 et seq.

[73] A report by Inoue on the results, or at least his evaluation of the situation, apparently exists as well. Currently, enquiries are being made on these sources at the State Archives in Tokyo.

[74] Weindl, *Wer kleidet die Welt?*, pp. 61 et seq.

[75] T. Volker, *Porcelain and the Dutch East India Company as Recorded in the Dagh-register of Batavia Castle, those of Hirado and Dejima and other Contemporary Papers. 1602–1682* (Leiden, 1971), p. 124.

on the part of the trading organisation.[76] This succeeded, in that the peace was declared to be an internal affair for the Christians and its lack of consequences for the Japanese was emphasised. Japan was treated as an equal subject under international law in Grotius's sense, whose right to wage war against Spain via the Dutch was not questioned. That § 5 of the Treaty of Münster actually offered Japan protection against the Spanish by reason of their being contractual partners of the VOC, in that the status quo, and therefore Japan as a zone of influence pertaining to the VOC, was fixed in the treaty, was not particularly emphasised by the envoys. Why this simple fact was not adduced by the envoys remains unclear. Perhaps they felt that this would have made existing relations between the VOC and the Shōgunate appear too much like a colonial relationship towards Japan; perhaps this would have made the European perspective of Japan as a Dutch zone of influence too obvious, thus creating a new and threatening situation.

Selected Bibliography

Blom, F.R.E., 'Picturing New Netherland and New York. Dutch-Anglo Transfer of the New World Information', in S. Huigen, J.L. de Jong and E. Kolfin (eds), *The Dutch Trading Companies as Knowledge Networks* (Leiden, 2010), pp. 103–28.

Blomhoff, C., *The Court Journey to the Shōgun of Japan* (Leiden, 2000).

Gaastra, F.S., *The Dutch East India Company. Expansion and Decline* (Leiden, 2003).

Hesselink, R.H., *Prisoners from Nambu: Reality and Make-Believe in Seventeenth-Century Japanese Diplomacy* (Honolulu, 2001).

Israel, J., *The Dutch Republic. Its Rise, Greatness and Fall 1477–1806* (Oxford, 1995).

Jacobs, J., *New Netherland. A Dutch Colony in Seventeenth-Century America* (Leiden and Boston, 2005).

Manzano Baena, L., *Conflicting Words: The Peace Treaty of Münster (1648) and the Political Culture of the Dutch Republic and the Spanish Monarchy* (Leuven, 2011).

Marley, D., *Wars of the Americas: A Chronology of Armed Conflict in the New World. 1492 to the present* (Santa Barbara, 1998).

Preiser, W., 'History of the Law of Nations. Ancient Times to 1648', in *Encyclopedia of Public International Law, published under the auspices of the Max Planck Institute for comparative public law and international law*. Vol. 7 (Amsterdam, New York and Oxford, 1984), pp. 132–60.

Schuyler van Rensselaer, M.G., *History of the City of New York* (New York, 1909).

Toby, R.P., *State and Diplomacy in Early Modern Japan: Asia in the Development of Tokugawa Bakufu* (Princeton, 1984).

Van Groesen, M., 'Officers of the West-India Company, their Networks, and their Personal Memories of Dutch Brasil', in S. Huigen, J.L. de Jong and E. Kolfin (eds), *The Dutch Trading Companies as Knowledge Networks* (Leiden, 2010), pp. 39–58.

Van Ittersum, M. J., *Profit and Principle. Hugo Grotius, Natural Rights Theories and the Rise of Dutch Power in the East Indies 1595–1615* (Leiden and Boston, 2006).

---

[76] In Asia, the VOC had, in contrast to the WIC in North America, regular and professional, above all written forms and channels of communication with its trading partners. This permits the reconstruction of how the information on the peace treaty of 1648 between Spain and the Netherlands was communicated, thanks to the media and company reports, whereas the conduct of the WIC towards friendly native tribes remains unclear, owing to the irregular contacts and the primarily oral nature of communications between the two sides.

Index

Aachen 199
Aachen Definitive Peace (1748) 313
Aldobrandini, Pietro 106
Alexander VII, Pope 104
Alsace 98, 148, 276
Alte Veste, Battle of (1632) 146
Anhalt, Christian, Prince 29–30, 31, 129
Anne of Austria, Queen
    French Regent 95
    Louis XIII, marriage 87
Antwerp 167, 168, 174
    siege 171–2, 173
Asti, Treaty of (1615) 178, 179
Augsburg, Diet of (1566) 15, 194
Augsburg, Peace of (1555) 1, 6–7, 13, 16, 23, 40, 41, 127, 131, 137, 165, 193–204, 217, 293
    context 193–4
    and Edict of Restitution 211–12
    erosion of 197
    limitations 196–7
    main effects 18, 194–5
    problems resulting from 197–200
    Protestantism, legal existence, establishment of 221
    provisions 194–7
    religious faith, territorial basis 303
    and the Thirty Years' War, scholarship 200–204
August I, Elector of Saxony 21
Austrian Habsburgs 1, 2, 40, 42, 56, 180
    assistance from Spanish Habsburgs 56

Banér, Johan, Gen 152, 154, 155
Barberini, Antonio 109
Barberini, Francesco 108
Bärwalde, Treaty of (1631) 84, 90
    renewal 146
Batavia 321, 323, 331, 332, 333, 335
Bavaria 35, 46, 130, 159, 220
    France, alliance 90
    see also Maximilian of Bavaria
Bergh, Hendrik van den, Count 164, 166, 167, 168
Bethlen, Gabor, Prince of Transylvania/King of Hungary 119–20, 122, 133, 274

Black, Jeremy 26
Bodin, Jean 329
Bohemia
    Charles Emmanuel, candidature for crown 180
    crisis 23, 35, 129
    defeat, at Battle of White Mountain (1620) 44, 57, 87
    Frederick V, King of 32, 36, 43, 131, 179
    Hussite revolt 128
    Protestant nobles, replacement of 45, 132
    rebellion (1618) 43, 56, 87, 121, 128, 179–80
        as catalyst for Thirty Years' War 200
    Renewed Constitution (1627) 45
    status in Holy Roman Empire 41
    and Westphalian Treaty 314
    see also White Mountain, Battle of
Brandenburg 82
    and the Thirty Years' War 219
Braunschweig-Lüneburg 83
Braunschweig-Wolfenbüttel 83
Brazil, capture by Dutch 95, 325
Breda
    siege 171
    Spanish conquest of 88, 164, 171, 181
Breitenfeld, Battle of (1631) 144, 145, 157, 223, 224, 255, 278, 279, 291
Brisach (Breisach) 92, 93, 98, 154, 155
Bullinger, Heinrich 232–3
    Decades 233
Burkhardt, Johannes 112, 202, 287

Callot, Jacques, engravings
    Great Miseries of War 90
    Small Miseries 90
Calvin, John, *Institution* 233
Calvinism 131, 217
    outlawing of, in Edict of Restitution (1629) 206, 218
Carafa, Carlo 106
Cardis, Perpetual Peace of (1661) 316
Casimir, Ernst, FM 166, 167
Casimir, John 233
Castile 54, 59
    unrest 57, 60–61

Castro, duchy of 102
   war 103, 187
Catalonia, rebellion 59, 60, 95, 96, 155, 174, 187
Cateau-Cambrésis, Peace of (1559) 177, 236
Catholic League (*Liga*) 2, 40, 44, 46, 105, 130, 305
   effectiveness 274
   formation 23, 199
   Protestant Union, neutrality treaty 131
   triumph of 131–3
   see also Protestant Union
Charles Emmanuel I, Duke of Savoy 178, 179, 183
   candidature for Bohemian crown 180
Charles I, King of England 139, 145
Charles IV, Duke of Lorraine 148, 275
Charles V, Holy Roman Emperor 2, 15, 16, 19, 239
   imperial universalism 193–4
Cherasco, Peace of (1631) 109, 168, 188, 313
Christian IV, King of Denmark and Norway 3, 35, 46, 65, 70–71, 157, 276
   armed neutrality 73
   character 67
   commander, Lower Saxon Circle 69
   defeat
      at Wolgast 71
      by Tilly 135
   foreign policies 67–8
   significance of 75
   and 'Ten Barrels of Gold' 72
   territory 134
   Wallenstein, Peace of Lübeck (1629) 71
Clement VIII, Pope 105
coinage, Thirty Years' War 248, 250
Cologne War 198
Compiègne, Treaty of (1635) 91, 92
confessional absolutism, Edict of Restitution as 210, 213
Congregatio de Propaganda Fide
   establishment 106–7
   objective 4
Contarini, Alvise 322–3
Corpus Evangelicorum 82, 302
Crown, William 152

Day of Dupes 90, 183–4
Dejima Island 321, 330, 331, 332, 336
d'Enghien, Duke 95, 157, 158
Denmark
   Baltic trade, control of 66
   decline 74
   foreign policies 66
   Germanies, ties 66
   governance 66
   Jutland, occupation of 47, 70, 135
   kingdom, extent 65–6
   Lutheranism 66
   Oldenburg dynasty 66
   Sweden, relations 67, 71, 74, 134
   and Thirty Years' War 65, 69, 71–2, 74–5
   wealth, sources of 66
   see also Christian IV
Deputations Diet, Frankfurt (1642) 156
Dickmann, Friedrich 228
Dordrecht, Synod (1574) 28
Downs, Naval Battle of (1639) 59
Droysen, Johann Gustav 13
Dunkirk 96, 165, 168, 170, 171, 174
Duplessis, Armand Jean 165
Dutch East India Company (VOC) 321, 322, 327, 328, 337
Dutch Republic
   army, size 165, 166, 169
   Brazil, capture of 95, 325
   France
      alliance 169
      invasion of Spanish Netherlands 169–75
   revolt (1566–1648) 6, 245
   Spain
      counter-offensive against 166–8
      Treaty of Münster (1648) 62
      victories over 57, 58
      war (1621-1648) 163–75
   see also Netherlands; United Provinces
Dutch West India Company (WIC) 321, 323–4, 325, 326

Edict of Restitution (1629) 1, 5, 7, 47–8, 80, 137, 140–41, 142, 152, 196, 205–14, 291
   Calvinism, outlawing of 206, 218
   and Catholic conflicts 207–9
   as confessional absolutism 210, 213
   and Ferdinand II 205, 213, 226
   implementation 206, 221
      difficulties 212–13
   and the Jesuits 207, 210, 213
   and Peace of Augsburg 211–12
   as political policy 213–14
   Protestant resistance 206–7
   purpose 205
   as religious policy 209–13
   utopianism 212
   withdrawal of 48, 149, 214
Eggenberg, Johann von, Count 43
Elector Palatine
   land holdings 27
   powers 26
Electoral Palatinate (*Kurpfalz*) 2
   Calvinism 30
   confessionalisation thesis 31

debt 30
governance 26, 29
Lutheranism 30
networks 32–6
parishes 31
Reformation in 30
religious tolerance 31, 33
scholarship 25fn1
and the Thirty Years' War 25
see also Lower Palatinate; Upper Palatinate
Elliott, John H. 181, 184
England, Spain
truce 140
war 134
Eppelmann, Peter (Melander) 271
Este, Francesco de', Duke of Modena 188
Evans, Robert J.W. 209–10

Farnese, Odoardo, Duke of Parma and Piacenza 102, 187, 188
Ferdinand of Austria, Cardinal-Infante 57, 58, 59, 61, 148, 170, 172
Ferdinand I, Holy Roman Emperor 16, 17, 19, 22
Erasmian views 17
Ferdinand II, Holy Roman Emperor 2–3, 7, 23, 39–40, 41, 43, 49, 105
and Edict of Restitution 205, 213, 226
election circumstances 130–31
Leipzig Manifesto, repudiation of 144
Peace of Prague signatory 285
support from Maximilian of Bavaria 130, 137, 249
Ferdinand III, Holy Roman Emperor 3, 4, 39, 97
religious tolerance 50
Ferrara 102
Fleischmann, Anselm Franz 115
Four Monasteries Dispute (1601) 198
France
army
recruitment 94
size 94, 165, 170
Bavaria, alliance 90
Dutch Republic
alliance 169
invasion of Spanish Netherlands 169–75
expansion, and the Rhine 93
Italy, failure in 186–7
maritime policy 88
Maximilian of Bavaria, treaty 143
Savoy, war 178
Spain
Treaty of Monzón 88
victories over 59, 61, 95, 157
war 4, 58–9, 61, 88, 91, 92, 110
strategic position 90
Sweden, alliance 92, 143, 225
tax revolts 91
and the Thirty Years' War 88, 91, 92, 96
entry 236, 237
gains 98
goals 239, 276
legitimation 237–9
and the United Provinces 88
and Westphalian Treaty 314
Francis III, Duke of Mantua 178
Frankenthal 27, 272
Frederick Henry of Orange-Nassau, Duke 164, 166, 169, 170, 171, 173
Frederick IV, Elector Palatine 28, 29, 30
Frederick V, Elector Palatine 2, 25, 28, 29, 30, 105, 119
Elizabeth Stuart, marriage 32–3
in exile 46, 165
King of Bohemia 32, 36, 43, 131, 274
Frederik II, King of Denmark 66, 67, 68
Freiburg, Battle of (1644) 158
Friedrich Wilhelm, Elector of Brandenburg 156
Fronde revolt 96, 98

Gábor, Bethlen 5
Galileo Galilei 104, 110
Gallas, Matthias, Gen 158
Georg I, Prince of Transylvania 50
Georg II, Landgrave of Hesse-Darmstadt 224
Georg Wilhelm, Elector of Brandenburg 142, 218–19, 220, 222 *see also* Brandenburg
Germany
confessional regimes 21
confessionalisation thesis 14, 15
circles 18
currency regulation 18
imperial estates, meetings 18
Ottoman threat 21
Peasant War (1525) 16
post-1555, historiography 13–15
Reichshofrat 18, 19
Reichskammergericht
establishment 15
operations 18–19
religious conflict 21
religious decisions, devolution of 18
Ginetti, Marzio 110
Gotthard, Axel 199
Götz, Johan von, Gen 154
Gregory XIII, Pope 105, 107
Gregory XV, Pope 104, 105
church reforms 106
Grotius, Hugo 329, 336
Grumbach, Wilhelm von 20
Guez de Balzac, Jean-Louis, *Le Prince* 237–8

Gustav Adolph (Gustav II Adolf), King of
      Sweden 7, 48, 71, 78, 89, 109, 183
   and Brandenburg 219–20
   death 91, 149, 290
   defeat
      by Wallenstein 146
      of Tilly 144, 145
   manifesto of grievances 80, 142
   motives 141–2, 224
   'Saviour' of Protestantism 220, 225

Haan, Heiner 247
Habsburg Empire, Ottoman Empire
   conflict 115–16
   peace 118, 121–2
Habsburgs see Austrian Habsburgs; Spanish
      Habsburgs
Hamburg 67, 73
   Peace of (1641) 110, 156, 293
Hanau 154
Hatzfeldt, Melchior von 158
Heckel, Martin 14, 196, 201
Heidelberg
   destruction of 255
   strategic position 272
   University 27–8
Heilbronn League 58, 148, 276, 288, 291
Henri II, King of France 87
Henri IV, King of France 19, 178
Hessen-Cassel 82, 83, 145, 255, 272, 273, 276
   see also Wilhelm V
Heyn, Piet, ADM 57, 166
Hitler, Adolf, and Westphalian Treaty 298
Hobsbawm, Eric J. 246
Höchst, Battle of (1622) 132
Hohenzollern, Johann Sigismund von,
      margrave-elector of Brandenburg 33–4
Holstein-Segeberg 66
Holy Roman Emperor
   election of 2, 47
   historiography 39–40, 47
   member of universal *Casa d'Austria* 41–2
   monarchical head of Holy Roman Empire
      40–41
   roles 40
   ruler of Habsburg hereditary lands 41
Holy Roman Empire, dissolution of 51
Huguenot Wars (1562–1629) 237
Huguenots, French 127, 140, 165, 181
   defeat (1628) 182, 236
   revolt 182

Ibrahim I, Sultan 122
Ignatius of Loyola, St, canonisation 106
Ingoli, Francesco 107

Innocent X, Pope 4, 104, 110, 111, 187
Italy
   Spanish hegemony 177–8
   and the Thirty Years' War 181–9
   and Treaty of Westphalia 188–9

James I, King of England 32–3, 134
Jankov, Battle of (1645) 50, 97, 158
Janssen, Johannes 13–14
Japan, Dutch VOC, and Münster Treaty 330–38
Jesuits 7, 14, 34, 68, 206, 211, 330
   and Edict of Restitution 207, 210, 213
   monasteries controversy 209
Johann Friedrich II, Duke of Saxony 20
Johann Georg I, Elector of Saxony 142, 143, 144,
      153, 213, 220, 221, 222, 224, 226
   Peace of Prague signatory 285
   religious toleration 218
   see also Saxony
John IV, King of Portugal 60
Jülich-Cleves Succession crisis (1609–14) 178,
      200, 218–19, 219
Jutland, invasion of 47, 70, 71, 72

Kalmar War (1611–13) 67
Kampmann, Christoph 224
Karl IX, King of Sweden 67
Klesl, Cardinal, Bishop of Vienna 42, 43
Kötzschenbroda, Truce of (1645) 158
Kronberg, Johann Schweikard von, archbishop-
      elector of Mainz 34

La Rochelle
   siege 88, 181, 182, 236
   surrender 89, 236, 237
Lamormaini, William 140, 205, 209
Lanzinner, Maximilian, and Dietmar Heil 201
Laymann, Paul, *The Way of Peace* 211
Leipzig Manifesto (1631) 143, 222
   repudiation by Ferdinand II 144
Leopold I, Holy Roman Emperor 307–8
Leopold Wilhelm, Archduke 159
Lerida, Battle of (1642) 95
Lerma, Duke of 55, 130
Leuchtenberg, Landgrave of 29
Libertät 47, 291, 304
   meaning 293
   and Peace of Prague 285, 287, 292, 293
Liechtenstein, Karl von 248
   Governor of Bohemia 45
Livonia question 19–20
Lombardy, economic productivity 177
Long Turkish War (1593–1606) 5, 122, 127, 199–200
   see also Ottoman Empire
Lorraine, duchy of 90, 96, 148, 153, 225, 275, 309

Louis XIII, King of France 35, 88, 90, 157, 165, 171, 178–9
    Anne of Austria, marriage 87
    death 172
Louis XIV, King of France 4, 51, 95, 173
Louvain, siege 170–71
Lower Palatinate 27–8
    invasion by Sweden 58
Lower Saxon Circle 46, 135, 272, 276
Lower Saxon War (1625–9) 65, 72, 73, 74
Lübeck, Peace of (1629) 48, 71–2, 136, 139, 166, 219, 227, 293
Luther, Martin 224
Lutheranism, Saxony 218
Lutherans 217
Lützen, Battle of (1632) 146, 225, 291
Lyon, Treaty of (1601) 178

Maastricht, siege 168
Machiavelli, Niccolò
    Il Principe 237
    and religious war 234
Magdeburg
    bishop's legal status 198
    capture by Tilly 143–4, 222, 275
    destruction of 151, 222, 277–8
Mansfeld, Ernst, Count 132, 133, 272
    defeat by Wallenstein 135
Mantua and Monferrato, duchy of 57
    Duke of Nevers claim 57, 88, 140, 182
    strategic importance 178, 182
    succession conflict 88–9, 108, 109, 136, 167, 178–9, 181–5
        winners and losers 184–5
    see also Cherasco, Peace of
Mariastein convent, narrative of war 260
Matthias, Holy Roman Emperor 23, 39, 43
    Rudolph II, conflict 42
Maximilian of Bavaria, Duke 44, 45, 46, 132, 133, 159, 160, 272
    Ferdinand II, support to 130, 137, 249
    France, treaty 143
Maximilian I, Holy Roman Emperor 15, 224
Maximilian II, Holy Roman Emperor 16–17
Mazarin, Jules (Giulio Mazzarino) Cardinal 4, 90, 95, 96, 97, 98, 109, 157, 174, 184, 186, 187–8
Mecklenburg 82, 271, 272
Meinecke, Friedrich, *The Idea of the Reason of State* 93
Melo, Francisco de 61, 172, 173
Mercy, Franz von, Gen 157, 158
Milan, French claims on 186
Móhacz, Battle of (1526) 120
Moncada, Francisco de, Count 169

Monferrato 57, 108, 313
Montecuccoli, Ernesto, Count 166, 167
Montecuccoli, Raimondo 166
Monzón, Treaty of (1626) 88, 108
Munich, Treaty of (1619) 44, 45, 46
Münster, Treaty of (1648) 62, 188, 293, 294, 319–38
    Dutch VOC, and Japan 330–38
    influence outside Europe 320–21
    medallion 319–20, 337
    and New Amsterdam 324–7
    privileges, maintenance of status quo 327–8
    publication of 322–3
        communication routes 323–7
Murad IV, Sultan 119, 122
Musch, Cornelis 322, 323

Naples, revolts 62, 96
Nassau-Siegen, Maurits von 325
Netherlands 337
    armaments production 251
    Spain, and Münster Treaty 311, 322
    Sweden, alliance 236, 312
    see also Dutch Republic; Spanish Netherlands; United Provinces
Nevers, Charles, Duke of
    death 187
    loss of territories 184
    Mantua crown, claimant 57, 88, 109, 140, 182
New Amsterdam
    and Münster Treaty 324–5
    change of purpose 326
    communication of 327
    strategic position 325
Nordic Seven Years' War (1563–70) 19
Nördlingen, Battle of (1634) 7, 48, 58, 83, 91, 148, 186, 227, 236, 275, 291
normative year
    concept 221, 223, 226, 227, 227–8
    and Peace of Prague 228, 229

Oldenburg dynasty, Denmark 66
Oliva, Peace of (1660) 316
Olivares, Duke of 55, 56, 57, 58, 59, 87, 140, 164
    resignation 60
Oñate Treaty 42
Osman II, Sultan 117, 119
Osnabrück, Treaty of (1648) 9, 96, 110, 115, 160, 289, 293, 301, 304
Osterhammel, Jürgen 320
Ottoman Empire
    Habsburg Empire
        conflict 115–16
        peace 118, 121–2
    Poland, war 121

Safavids, war with 4, 5, 118–19, 122
and the Thirty Years' War 4–5
    neutrality 115, 116–17, 119, 120–21, 123
    threat to Germany 21
    see also Long Turkish War
Oxenstierna, Axel 3, 8, 73, 74, 77, 78–9, 91, 92, 146, 147, 157, 225, 291
    Heilbronn Convent, proposal to 83

Palermo, bread riots 61
papacy
    arts patronage 103
    congregational system 102
    Curia, reforms 102
    decline 111–12
    diplomacy 4
    Gregorian Conclave, reform 102
    nepotism 103–4
    padre comune 112
    revenues, decrease 103
    and the Thirty Years' War 101, 102–3, 105–10
        subsidies to Catholic states 104–5
Papal States
    food shortages 103
    territorial extent 101–2
Pappenheim, Gottfried Heinrich, Count 168
Passau, Peace of (1552) 137, 194, 221
Paul V, Pope 104
    foreign policies 105
Philip III, King of Spain 42, 55
Philip IV, King of Spain 55, 60, 148, 164, 165, 174
Philipp, Ludwig, Count Palatine 29
Piccolomini, Ottavio, Gen 155, 160, 170, 171
Pinerolo fortress 109, 183, 185, 188, 313
Pirna, Peace Draft of (1634) 149, 287, 291, 293
Poland
    Ottoman Empire, war 121
    Sweden, truce 80, 140
Poland-Lithuania 20
Pomerania 82
Poncet, Olivier 112
Portugal, rebellion 60, 95, 96
potestas, and *violentia* 9, 273
Powder Barrel Convention (1635) 273
Prague, Defenestration (1618) 56, 104, 129, 287
Prague, Peace of (1635) 9, 48–9, 81, 83, 92, 149, 151, 156, 228, 255, 285–94
    Catholicism, renewed influence 286
    consequences 293–4
    failure 49, 292, 293
    imperial diplomacy 286
    and 'Libertät' 285, 287, 292, 293
    nature of 288
    and normative year 228, 229
    participants 288–9
    in peace process 293–4
    preliminaries 290–91
    provisions 228, 275, 292
    publication 289–90
    purpose 285–6, 290
        imperial 287, 290
    scholarship on 286–7
    and secularisation of conflict 287
    signatories 285
    as turning point 286, 287
Protestant Union 2, 23, 31, 32, 33, 34, 35, 40, 43, 44, 274
    alliances 305–6
    Catholic League, neutrality treaty 131
    dissolution 222
    formation 23, 199
    military action 32
    see also Catholic League
Prussia 140, 219, 253
    disappearance of 298
    and Westphalian Treaty 297–8
Pyrenees, Treaty of the (1659) 4, 53, 104, 186, 189, 293–4, 316

Rákóczi, György, Prince 5, 123, 158
Ranke, Leopold von 111
Regensburg, Diet of (1630) 46, 48, 80, 89, 141, 155, 156, 183, 220, 286, 293
    normative year, establishment of 221, 223
Regensburg, Treaty of (1630) 89–90, 183–4
Reinhard, Wolfgang 14
religious war
    examples 234
    historiography 231–2
    and Machiavelli 234
    normative notion 232–3
    in sixteenth century 234–5
    Thirty Years' War as 231, 237, 240, 241–3
Remonstrants 164
Repgen, Konrad 111, 323
Rhine
    Confederation of (1658) 312
    and French expansion 93
Richelieu, Cardinal 58, 59, 88, 89, 90, 109, 140, 225
    absolutism 94
    death 95, 157, 172
    and European collective security 93
    foreign policy 165, 237
    internal threats 180–81
        triumph over 185
    Maximes d'Etat 239
    Testament politique 239
Rijswijk, Treaty of (1697) 312

Ritter, Moriz, *German History in the Age of the Counter-Reformation and the Thirty Years War* 13
Rivoli, League of 186
Roberts, Michael 83
Rocroi, Battle of (1643) 61, 95, 157, 172
Roe, Thomas, Sir 122
Rohan, Henri, Duke 163, 186
Rudolf II, Holy Roman Emperor 21, 119, 127, 197
  Archduke Matthias, conflict 42
  religious tolerance 22
  Royal Privilege grant 42

Sas van Gent, siege 173
Savoy 140
  France, war 178
Saxe-Weimar, Bernard of, Prince 92, 92–3, 148, 153, 154, 293
  death 155
Saxony 82, 131, 276
  Lutheranism 218
Scheldt, River 171, 172, 174
Schilling, Heinz 14, 21, 112
Schmalkaldic War (1546–8) 16, 194, 234, 307
Schmid, Johann Rudolf 122
Schmidt, Georg 15
Schulze, Winfried 14, 201, 203
Seven Years' War (1756–63) 320
Sicily, revolts 61
Sigismond III, King of Poland 89
Silesia 41, 45
Sixtus V, Pope 102
Smolensk War (1632–4) 310
sovereignty
  characteristics 329
  divisibility 329
  and Westphalian Treaty 304–5, 306
Spain
  army
    burden sharing 59
    composition of 58
    size 165
  Baltic Design 141, 147
  Breda, conquest of 88, 164, 171, 181
  Dutch Republic
    counter offensive by 166–8
    defeats by 57, 58
    trade, blocking of 57
    Treaty of Münster (1648) 62
    war (1621–48) 163–75
  England
    truce 140
    war 134
  France
    defeats by 59, 61, 95, 157

Treaty of Monzón 88
  war 4, 58–9, 61, 88, 91, 92, 110
  Italy, hegemony over 177–8
  Netherlands, and Münster Treaty 311, 322
  revenues 54
  territorial possessions 53–4
  and the Thirty Years' War 56
    chronology 53
  Union of Arms Union 59, 60
  United Provinces
    confrontation 54, 56, 87
    Eighty Years' War (1568–1648) 319
    treaty 4, 62, 97, 319, 321–2
  see also Castile; Catalonia; Spanish Habsburgs
Spanish Habsburgs 55
  assistance to Austrian Habsburgs 56
  internal rebellions 59
Spanish Netherlands 54, 56, 59, 61, 140, 153, 292, 325
  Dutch-French invasion 169–75
  see also Dutch Republic; Netherlands; United Provinces
Speyer, Protestation at (1529) 197
Spinola, Ambrogio 164, 166
Stettin, Peace of (1570) 19
Stralsund 141, 142, 147
Strasbourg Bishops' War 198
Stumsdorf, Truce (1635) 84
Suleiman the Magnificent, Sultan 120
Sweden
  defeat at Nördlingen 48, 236
  Denmark, relations 67, 71, 74, 134
  France, alliance 92, 143, 225
  German Protestant princes, alliances with 82–3
  and the Imperial Constitution 82–3
  invasion of Lower Palatinate 58
  Netherlands, alliance 236, 312
  Poland, truce 80, 140
  and the Thirty Years' War 6, 77–8, 79–80
    military organisation 84
    plundering expeditions 273
    territorial demands 81
    war aims 80–81, 276
    war finance 84
  and Westphalian Treaty 314
  see also Gustav Adolph
Switzerland, and the Westphalian Treaty 314

Thirty Years' War (1618–48)
  armaments production 251
  armies
    atrocities 266, 278
    attrition strategies 278, 281

345

camp followers 252
composition 279–80
contributions raised for 251, 270–71
entrenchments 280
field commanders 277
flying columns 279–80
general staff, imperial 277
imperial resources 271–2
maintenance of 249, 270
mutinies 270
pay issues 271
plundering 261–2, 273
raising of 249
retreats 280
size 255–6, 279
beyond Europe 9–10
civilian-military relations 252, 254
coinage 248, 250
conduct of war, attempts to regulate 91
confessional complaints, as trigger point 303
deaths
civilian 151, 254, 255, 259
military 253–4
destructiveness 163, 253, 259
disease, spread of 151, 254, 255
economic factors 246–7
and Electoral Palatinate 25
and European 'General Crisis' 246
as European War 310
fear
coping strategies 261, 265–6
and troop movements 259–61
institutional frameworks 276–7
and Kipper and Wipper inflation (1620–23) 248, 250, 254
local populations
assets protection 252
burdens on 251–2
as media war 142
mercenaries 270
opportunities 267
personal narratives 257–62
phases 1, 269–70
populations, effects on 253, 254, 256
pre-war events 199–200, 246–7
and the public imagination 139
refugees 252
as religious war 231, 237, 240, 241–3, 303
scorched earth strategy 278
sieges 163–4, 186, 278–9
strategies 273–6
sustainability 245
unpredictability of life 264–5
vulnerability
city dwellers 262

monks and nuns 263, 264
pastors 263
psychological 265–6
women 263–4
war councils 276–7
wealth redistribution 254
see also individual countries, eg Spain, Sweden etc
Tienen, destruction of 170
Tilly, Johann Tserclaes, Count 44, 46, 47, 65, 69, 70, 71, 132, 134, 255
capture of Magdeburg 143–4, 222, 275
defeat
by Gustav Adolph 144, 145
of Christian IV 135
Torstenson, Lennart, Gen 153, 156–7, 157, 158
Torstenson War 74
Trauttmansdorff, Maximilian von, Count 43, 50, 159, 289
Treitschke, Heinrich von 13
Trent, Council of 17, 30, 87, 101, 107, 208
Tschernembl, Georg Erasmus von 22

Ulm 32, 151, 159
Treaty of (1620) 87, 131
United Provinces 33, 55, 70, 73, 91
and France 88
Spain
confrontation 54, 56, 87
Eighty Years' War (1568–1648) 319
treaty 4, 62, 97, 319, 321–2
see also Dutch Republic; Netherlands; Spanish Netherlands
Upper Palatinate 28–9, 30
Upper Rhine Knighthood 28
Urban VIII, Pope 4, 104, 107–8, 187, 208
imperial politics 109–10
Urbino, duchy of 102
Usedom island 71, 141, 183, 220
Uskoks War (1615–17) 179

Valtellina valley 107, 108, 186
settlement of conflict 181
strategic position 88, 94, 180
see also Monzón, Treaty of
Vaughan, Dorothy, *Europe and the Turk* 117
Venice, Peace Treaty of (1644) 102
Victor Amadeus I, Duke of Savoy 183, 184, 185, 186
death 187
Vincenzo II, Duke of Mantua 182
violentia, and *potestas* 9, 273

Wallenstein, Albrecht von 45, 71, 80, 272
assassination of 91, 147

Baltic navy, building of 78
Christian IV, Peace of Lübeck (1629) 71
death 291
emperor
    dismissal by 48, 136, 141, 213, 220, 255, 275
    recall by 146, 275
Gustav Adolph, defeat of 146
imperial army 46–7, 69, 70, 135, 249–50
    self-funded 254–5
Lord High Admiral 136
Mansfeld, defeat of 135
personal wealth 250, 251
war
    materiel 250
    revenues 250
Weimar, Bernhard von 272–3, 276, 278
Werth, Jan van 271
Westphalia, Congress of (1643–9) 4, 156, 158–9, 159–60
Westphalia, Treaty of (1648) 1, 3, 50, 51, 84, 98, 110–11, 160–61
    350th anniversary (1998) 310, 317
    and alliances, right to form 305–6, 311
    and balance of power 307, 315
    and Bohemia 314
    Europeanness of 309, 311–12, 313, 314–15, 316
    failure 316
    and France 314
    historiography 298–300
    and Hitler 298
    implementation 307
    and modern state system 300, 301
    non-signatories 311
    and Peace of Versailles (1919) 298
    and Prussia 297–8
    publication, multi-volume 301–2
    as religious peace 303, 304
    and secularisation 111
    signatories 311
    sovereignty issue 304–5, 306
    and subsequent treaties 312–13, 316–17
    and Sweden 314
    and Switzerland 314
    visual images of 315–16
    see also Münster, Treaty of; Osnabrück, Treaty of
White Mountain (Bílá Hora), Battle of (1620) 44, 57, 87, 105, 131, 180, 222, 271
    consequences 132, 250
Wilhelm V, Landgrave of Hessen-Kassel 224, 228
Willing, Johann
    Instruction what the prince's estate is 233
    Simple Reminder 233
Wilson, Peter, *Europe's Tragedy* 201
Wimpfen, Battle of (1622) 132
Wismar 78, 81
Witte, Hans de 248, 250, 255
Wittelsbach dynasty 26, 29
Wittstock, Battle of (1636) 154
Wolff, Anton 221
Wolgast, Battle of (1628) 71
Worms
    Diet (1495) 15
    Edict (1521) 16, 193
Württemberg, Edict of Restitution, resistance to 206–7

Xanten, Treaty of (1614) 219

Zápolya, John, King of Hungary 120
Zeeden, Ernst Walter 14
Zsitvatorok, Treaty (1606) 5, 118, 119, 127
    extensions 121
Zusmarshausen, Battle of (1648) 160